The Myth of Victory

Other Titles in This Series

Conflict Resolution, Paul Wehr

Bibliography on World Conflict and Peace: Second Edition, Elise Boulding, J. Robert Passmore, and Scott Gassler

Other Titles of Interest

Strategies Against Violence: Design for Nonviolent Change, edited by Israel W. Charny

Limited War Revisited, Robert E. Osgood

Westview Special Studies in Peace, Conflict, and Conflict Resolution

The Myth of Victory:
What Is Victory in War?
Richard Hobbs

Richard Hobbs examines one of society's greatest problems: the need for reconciliation between the democratic dislike of war and the appropriate use of the military instrument in world politics. He questions whether the results obtained in war are worth the expenditures made and contends that victory gained from total war--war pushed to its outer limits--is illusory and not commensurate with the terrible cost.

The first part of his book surveys victory in past wars, through World War I, and discusses total war, strategic bombing, and psychological warfare. Part 2 covers World War II, the policy of unconditional surrender, and the results and costs of the surrenders of Italy, Germany, and Japan. In parts 3 and 4, Dr. Hobbs focuses on Korea, the Cold War, and Vietnam, and looks at differing concepts of victory. Attempting a response to the question "Is war the solution?" he reaches some conclusions about victory in war.

Richard Hobbs has combined more than twenty years of active military service with careers as author and professor. He retired from the U.S. Army in 1977 and is now vice-president of Teledyne International Marketing.

To Diane and Deanna,
who have suffered through their "tours" in Viet-Nam--
with the hope that they will never know war

The Myth of Victory:
What Is Victory in War?

Richard Hobbs
with a Foreword by Arleigh Burke

Westview Press / Boulder, Colorado

*Westview Special Studies in Peace,
Conflict, and Conflict Resolution*

Copyright © 1979 by Westview Press, Inc.

Published in 1979 in the United States of America by
      Westview Press, Inc.
      5500 Central Avenue
      Boulder, Colorado 80301
      Frederick A. Praeger, Publisher

Library of Congress Catalog Card Number: 79-4703
ISBN: 0-89158-388-2

Composition for this book was provided by the author.
Printed and bound in the United States of America.

Contents

TABLES AND FIGURES

Foreword

In this important book, Colonel Hobbs discussed the age old problem that has been of great concern to military men throughout the ages: "How best to convince an enemy in war that he cannot impose his control over our nation or our allies and then to terminate hostilities by taking action to reduce the probabilities of future conflict."

War is a political decision. It is made by the Head of State acting on behalf of the established government by and with the consent of that government. The decision is made to go to war as a consequence of activities that threaten the goals or existence of the state to such a degree that the political authority determines that all elements of the national power of the state should be used to preserve the state or its goals.

War is a political decision but it is fought by the military, under political direction for political goals. To win a war requires military power, of course, but also a great deal more. It requires political power, economic power, psychological power, and all other elements of national power, especially the spiritual and emotional support of the people of the country.

Conducting war to a successful conclusion requires the wise use of various elements of national power and a good estimate of the national power available to the enemy as well as the ways in which he might use it. That is never easily done and, as Colonel Hobbs points out, the United States as well as other nations made many mistakes in the wars of this century. Hitler was amazed at how easily his early aggressions succeeded and became disdainful of the resolution of the Allies and also of the cautious advice of his military. The Japanese overestimated the effects of their first attacks and they also underestimated the resolution of their enemies. The United States relied too much on the

expected results of strategic bombing and we too
underestimated the resolution of our enemies. Our
gravest error was in not having a clear national
political objective--a clear goal--and because of
that we forgot that the object of war is to control
the enemy, to convince them that they cannot control
us.

Our political leaders became absorbed in details of military operations with two natural consequences. They sometimes ineptly directed military
operations costly in lives and resources that did
not achieve commensurate results. Their concentration on military matters caused them to neglect
their own political and diplomatic duties.

Because we had no clear-cut postwar objectives
to guide our political planners, we drifted into
ill-considered surrender terms. In the highly
charged emotional atmosphere of fighting a war
against skillful, dangerous enemies who were intent
on defeating us we demanded complete enemy submission. Even after it became apparent to both our
side and the enemy's that the enemy would surely be
defeated, our demands were so onerous that the enemy decided to continue their hopeless fight rather
than accept what appeared to them to be unknown
conditions of merciless conquerors. The results
could have been predictable. The price the world
has paid has been tremendous.

Colonel Hobbs describes the background of past
wars and the dangers of excessive demands by the
victors. He expresses the concern of many of his
brothers-in-arms about the apparent lack of realization among political leaders, even now, of the
importance of the prudent use of the many elements
of national power to attain practical national objectives.

National power is the instrument of national
policy. It is the means by which every nation in-
fluences the trend of future events in the direction it desires. The use of power is necessary to
influence the future, and power must be used when
needed for a nation to be influential. To do this
a sound national policy to achieve the national objectives is required along with the skillful assessment and combination of the elements of national
power. If we neglect to take national power into
consideration we forfeit our possible influence, for
it is certain that both our friends and our enemies
will use their power as best they can to achieve
their objectives.

The Communist leaders have not deviated from

their long-range strategic objective of gaining political control over the world, but they have revised their tactics from direct pressure to political and psychological actions to expand their power
and influence and weaken our will and means to resist them. They have learned well the lesson of
history and they use all types of power in their
struggle for world domination, skillfully blending
their political, economic, military, and especially
psychological means in trying to make advances towards their goals. They try for large advances
when they think that can be done without much risk,
but settle for small advances when the risk of failure increases. They make great efforts to maintain
enough control of situations in various parts of
the world to keep the initiative and regulate the
probable risk. The Communists have demonstrated
their adeptness in the use of psychological means,
and although they do not instigate all the tensions
and subversive actions in the world, they actively
seek to gain advantage from them.
    The political leaders of democratically gov-
erned nations face formidable problems in determining the best courses of action to counter the actions of aggressive totalitarian nations who say
they intend to dominate the world - and are working
hard to accomplish just that. It is significant
that in recent years the Communists have emphasized
and augmented their political and psychological
power while they were urgently increasing their
military and economic power for use when they think
the time is right to apply those powers. They are
more than ever busily engaged in supporting every
effort to reduce our resolution, to create dissension amongst us, and to destroy support for any of
our government's policies that will hinder fulfillment of their aggressive designs. At the same time
they are creating situations to test our will, to
test the resolution of our government and our people. Should any of these tests convince them that
the United States is unstable or that the United
States either does not have the power to resist or
the willingness or skill to use our national power,
then they will take more drastic steps and that
quickly.
    Political personages in a democracy, by virtue
of becoming successful in their political profession, usually have had very little time to study
the philosophy and techniques of past wars, and so
they necessarily rely on advisors they personally
select. They customarily view any recommended

course of action with a weather eye cocked to the
effect that action may have on their own position
of power as well as on the best interests of the
United States. Communists have and will take advantage of this characteristic to weaken the resolution and power of our government.

It is important that we have knowledge of what
has happened in past conflicts, of how past wars
have been conducted and how they were terminated
and especially of the consequences of the war-end
settlements. The Myth of Victory is a valuable
book, for Colonel Hobbs' study and his concern for
the future is an excellent exposition of the problems facing us.

ARLEIGH BURKE

Preface

This study on Victory in war was written for the most part in 1962, while I was studying at the University of Lyon, France, on an Olmsted Scholarship. Words are inadequate to thank Major General George Olmsted (United States Army, Retired) for the vision of his fine Foundation which annually sends abroad three officers each from the Army, the Navy, and the Air Force for two years of graduate study outside the English-speaking world. I am proud to have been one of the first Olmsted Scholars.

The inspiration for writing on the subject of Victory came from Raymond Aron, particularly his book, A Century of Total War. I wish to thank Professors Raymond Guillien, Jacques Lambert, and Jacques Cadart, who were the members of the jury for my thesis at the Faculty of Law, for their assistance and support.

The thesis was entitled La Grande Illusion - La Victoire Totale and became, basically, Parts One and Two of this book. In the early 1960s, the theme of the thesis had a somewhat novel approach, but it was an idea that soon came to be generally accepted. The atmosphere changed later in the decade, particularly as the Viet-Nam War dragged on. Intertwined with our domestic social upheaval was the quandary of the American military over their role in society. The concept of Victory is strongly associated with the military such as General Douglas MacArthur's famous "There is no substitute for victory." Yet, the bitter debate over the American role in Viet-Nam further clouded the determination of Victory and the proper use of military power in diplomacy.

The Myth of Victory pursues the dilemma of whether the results obtained in war are worth the expenditures. It is contended that the victory gained from pushing war to its upper limits is illusory and not commensurate with the terrible cost.

The pursuit of Victory - even if limited - in a
guerrilla or limited war can also be exorbitantly
expensive. Reviewing the conflicts of history, the
search is for some substantial value of that elusive phantom -- Victory.

The book is divided into four parts with the
first two parts examining the great delusion --
Total Victory. Part One, "Total War," surveys victory in past wars and the First World War and then
reviews total war, strategic bombing, and psychological warfare. Part Two, "Unconditional Surrender,"
deals with the Second World War starting with the
background and development of the policy, the policy
in action in the surrenders of Italy, Germany, and
Japan, and the unfortunate results and costs of this
inflexible policy.

The last two parts bring the study up to the
present. Part Three, "Victory in the Nuclear Age,"
starts with a review of the spectrum of conflict and
then studies Korea, the Cold War, and Viet-Nam, and
ends with a look at the differing concepts of Victory in the world. Part Four, "War and Victory,"
tries to answer the age-old question "Is War the
Solution?", reviews total victory, and reaches some
conclusions on victory in war.

The Myth of Victory tries to answer the question: What is victory in war? It uses some of the
principles espoused by Clausewitz in On War and
calls for a return to Clausewitz, with emphasis on
the military as only one of several instruments of
foreign policy. In a democracy, one of our major
problems is to reconcile the democratic dislike of
war and the appropriate use of the military instrument in world politics.

This study lay relatively dormant through the
remainder of the 1960s as I went off to Viet-Nam
twice, separated by a tour teaching International
Relations at West Point. In 1971, I was selected
as one of the first Army Research Associates and
permitted to spend a year at the Center for Strategic and International Studies, Georgetown University, in lieu of attending the United States Army
War College at Carlisle Barracks, Pennsylvania.
This year afforded me the time to rework and complete my earlier study, particularly the addition
of a chapter on Viet-Nam, which was only beginning
to break on to the world scene in 1962.

I am particularly grateful to Admiral Arleigh
Burke, who founded the Center, for his generous sup-
port. Thanks are also due to Ambassador John
Steeves, then Chairman of the Center, Dr. Alvin J.

Cottrell, the Director of Research, and M. Jon
Vondracek, the Director of Communications, for
their support and suggestions, as well as to all
the members of the staff of the Center.

The years 1972-1978 are interesting because of
the changes seen. The war in Viet-Nam ended and
Southeast Asia disappeared from American conscious-
ness despite the on-going tragedy there. With the
fading away of Southeast Asia, our attention was
seized by the Middle East. The American people
were only bemused bystanders during the first three
Arab-Israeli wars. The October War of 1973, however, shocked America because of the rise of the
power of oil. We were no longer spectators; American vital interests were at stake in the Middle
East, so much so that another Arab-Israeli war
would be intolerable to the United States. The
elements of power - military, political, economic,
and psychological - were becoming clear for all to
see. The world had grown no more peaceful and the
definition of Victory no more precise.

Special thanks are due to Marianne Hinckle for
typing this manuscript.

My wife, Diane, endured both years of working
on the book as well as her two "short tours" while
I was in Viet-Nam. Young Deanna suffered through
one of each.

RICHARD W. HOBBS

Introduction

> Many a victory has been
> and will be suicidal to
> the victors.[1]
>
> -- Plato
>
> Before the road to victory,
> and peace can be traversed,
> it must be discovered.[2]

Man's memory dims quickly and wounds heal over.
A new generation has come of age in the world that
did not witness that cataclysm of the twentieth century, World War II. In the western part of what was
once Germany, modern new buildings have grown from
the piles of rubble and life is prosperous again.
On the other side though, the scars are still visible in what is the frontier of the Communist paradise, but which is, in reality, the largest concentration camp yet to appear on the face of the earth.
Europe is back on its feet and again playing an important role in world affairs. Hiroshima, the city
that disappeared one morning in 1945, is completely
rebuilt and is a thriving, lively city in the new
Japan.
    The Allies pursued that war to Total Victory
insisting upon the Unconditional Surrender of the
Axis nations. When the results, the destruction,
the loss of lives, the setback in the progress of
man's culture, are reviewed, the inevitable question
that comes to mind is, Was it worth it? The excit-
ing phantom of Total Victory that lured us forward
throughout a terrible total war proved to be a great
delusion. As in 1919, we found no peace after having paid the price of a great holocaust. The tensions in the world are at a fever pitch and, with
the armament levels that now exist, war is always a

1

possibility that hangs heavily over our heads.

War has been with us for a long time. Since
the beginning of recorded history, man has come in
conflict with his fellow man and resorted to the
force of arms to resolve his disputes. It is,
therefore, in the realm of wistful thinking to expect the immediate removal of war as a part of
international relations regardless of how much we
might like to see it banished from the world scene.
Since we cannot expect to remove it, it would appear
to be wise to adapt to it in an effort to obtain the
maximum return for mankind with the minimum loss.

In this light then, we will continually return
to the question of whether the results obtained in
war are worth the expenditures made. My theme,
then, for the pages ahead will be that the victory
gained from pushing war to its upper limits is illusory and not commensurate with the terrible cost.
Even the pursuit of a limited victory in a guerrilla
or limited war can be costly.

As we travel through history and even take a
glimpse into the future, we will continually be
sorting out some of the myths and searching for some
substantial value of that mysterious and enticing
shadow - Victory.

During the twentieth century, we have seen two
world wars in which we supposedly won glorious victories; yet, after each of them, we were not so sure
we had really won, for the high-sounding phrases
that the politicians had expressed to urge us on
lost their luster in the light of reality. Cities
were smashed with the glee of a child demolishing a
sand castle and dead were left behind leaving real
gaps in national populations. But when it was all
over, we had not done away with war, or brought
lasting peace, or even removed the great antagonisms; if we removed one, there was always another
that quickly rose in its place. Our failure in
these two wars should, by themselves, make us reconsider our goals in war. But the advent of new
technology makes it imperative. We must reexamine
our policies to determine a rational objective for
war that can be considered as victory. The blind
quest for Unconditional Surrender and Total Victory
will not be to our advantage the next time. They
were not to our advantage the last time, but the
odds have increased a thousandfold since then.

Admiral Radford, testifying before Congress in
1949, said: "...future war will extend far beyond
the province of the military. In planning to wage
war...we must look to the peace to follow....A war

of annihilation might possibly bring a Pyrrhic military victory, but it would be politically and economically senseless....the results of two world wars have demonstrated the fact that victory in war is not an end in itself."[3] It is basic to recognize that war is a means to an end and not an end in itself. What is this "means" and what is this "end"? Clausewitz clearly called war the "continuation of policy by other means" and maintained that "the political design is the object, while war is the means, and the means can never be thought of apart from the object."[4]

Down through the years we have harbored many different ideas on the theory and the conduct of war. Napoleon's fifth maxim states: "War should be made methodically, for it should have a definite object." Conrad Lanza commented: "A war without object would have no sense. Generals would not know what to fight for, and the troops and country would lose interest."[6]

There are many reasons for wars, ranging from preserving a nation, to freeing a country from tyranny, to fighting for independence, to making the world safe for democracy, to conquest. Wars have been fought for power, for ideals, for material gains of land, colonies, or trade advantages, and even for psychological reasons as a function of power politics.

There are harder views such as "war is absolute and the methods of waging it should only be determined with regard to a single object - the defeat of the enemy."[7] Others leaned toward "annihilation" as the "chief object of war."[8] Quincy Wright felt that war had tended to be regarded as the "absolute war" of Clausewitz -- "a struggle for annihilation rather than a procedure of adjustment and thus to be more costly and less serviceable as an instrument of policy."[9] Clausewitz, who gave us so much on the vast subject of war, listed three main objectives: "(a) To conquer and destroy the armed power of the enemy; (b) To take possession of his material and other sources of strength, and (c) To gain public opinion."[10]

Sun Tzu stressed the vital importance of the art of war to the state, but wisely counselled "There is no instance of a country having been benefited from prolonged warfare." "In war, then, let your great object be victory, not lengthy campaigns."[11] Montesquieu showed a great human touch in his pronouncement as to how nations should treat each other.

3

The law of nations is naturally founded on
this principle, that different nations ought
in time of peace to do one another all the
good they can, and in time of war as little
injury as possible, without prejudicing their
real interests.

The object of war is victory; that of victory
is conquest; and that of conquest, preservation. From this and the preceding principle
all those rules are derived which constitute
the law of nations.[12]

War, then, is a relation between state and
state, not between man and man according to
Rousseau, who saw the object of war as the destruction of the hostile state and who felt that it was
possible sometimes to kill the state without killing any of its people.[13] This concept places
Rousseau in the ranks of the modern thinkers.
Georges Clemenceau supposedly said that war
was too important to be left to soldiers. The obvious corollary, seldom heard, is that peace is too
precious to be left to politicians. War is a political act. Politics cannot be separated from war,
or war from politics. Political considerations do
not cease abruptly at the onset of war, and military considerations can never be far from the politicians' minds, even in times of peace. Unfortunately though there are many who try to separate
war from politics, a state of mind that led to the
particularly unfortunate training of the officers
of the American military before World War II, who
had a completely sterile political outlook drilled
into them, with some unhappy results during the war.
This attitude developed as a rigid and strict separation of military matters from all political matters. This separation - extending from the avoidance of petty political influence to the almost
automatic separation of "purely military" issues
from national policy - created an atmosphere among
senior officers that made it normal to exclude any
and all political issues from military matters and
created a feeling that the military should rigidly
eschew any political considerations. This resulted
in a tendency to plan combat operations and to
fight the war to a successful military conclusion
regardless of the political consequences to vital
national interests.[14]
Liddell Hart, writing in 1941, outlines these
consequences in what now reads like a prophecy:

4

If you concentrate exclusively on victory, with
no thought for the after-effect, you may be too
exhausted to profit by the peace, while it is
almost certain that the peace will be a bad
one, containing the germs of another war. This
is a lesson supported by abundant experience.
The risks become greater still in any war that
is waged by a coalition, for in such a case a
too complete victory inevitably complicates the
problem of making a just and wise peace settlement. Where there is no longer the counter-
balance of an opposing force to control the ap-
petites of the victors, there is no check on
the conflict of views and interests between the
parties to the alliance. The divergence is
then apt to become so acute as to turn the comradeship of common danger into the hostility of
mutual dissatisfaction - so that the ally of
one war becomes the enemy in the next.[15]

The general idea that the purpose of victory
should be peace is rather widely accepted now, even
though this still leaves the question shrouded in a
fairly nebulous cloud. Lord Hankey presented it
rather clearly. "The first aim in war is to win,
the second is to prevent defeat, the third is to
shorten it, and the fourth and the most important,
which must never be lost to sight, is to make a just
and durable peace. Emotionalism of all kinds, hate,
revenge, punishment and anything than handicaps the
nation in achieving these four aims are out of
place. It must always be kept in mind that after a
war we have sooner or later to live with our enemies
in amity."[16] His last point is particularly important as so few people during a war look beyond the
immediate wartime problems to the life in the postwar world. "War is like the passion of love. At
the moment of its exaltation the victims surrender
themselves to its dictatorship over their intellects
and powers of rational thought. Afterwards - as in
war - comes the peace of comradeship or the mockery
of disillusionment."[17] Senator Arthur Vandenberg
put it rather succinctly when he said: "We should
wage war not to win a war, but to win a peace."[18]
The creation of a lasting peace in modern times
has been a task confronted with many obstacles.
Making war and making peace have all too little in
common. Military men, successful at the complex
business of winning battles, rarely have talents for
solving the problems of peace. This has been true
of civilian wartime leaders as well. Their objec-

tive was the rapid and total defeat of the enemy. In the heat of combat the purposes of that defeat, the political ends of the war, were neglected. Few followed Clausewitz's rule. Presidents, prime ministers, and generals all became victory minded and forgot the kind of peace for which they were fighting. Where campaigns were fought, which enemy areas were to be occupied and what enemy resources were to be destroyed were decisions usually made on the basis of military considerations. Yet these questions of strategy shaped the character of the peace. From this loss of direction have come some of the major weaknesses of twentieth century peacemaking.

Total war imposed obstacles to a sound peace. Traditionally, peace meant the restoration of the status quo ante bellum. But a return to prewar conditions was impossible after a total war. Old ruling classes went down with military defeat or with failure of collaboration; the political and economic chaos of defeat produced social ferment with results impossible to foresee. Old alignments of nations were destroyed creating a world order with little resemblance to the prewar international structure. To calculate the achievement of military victory became, therefore, almost impossible.

Yet planning for peace in itself seldom met the criteria of sound diplomacy - the art of achieving the achievable. Since war as an institution was generally decried, nations embarked on a war attempted to invest the conflict with nonexistent values. Grandiose peace objectives, valuable in bolstering wartime morale, diverted attention from limited, achievable war aims. The result was failure to achieve either.[19]

If the objective of war should be peace, what then should be the victory in war that would facilitate peace? One view is that the best way to win a war is to prevent it from occurring, but this does little to alleviate the international problems tending toward war. We can have peace anytime we want it in the world conflict with Communism if we would just surrender to the Communists. But then it would be their definition of "peace" and that is certainly not what we are looking forward to for our future. The best victory is the one where an opponent surrenders without a shot being fired; the worst victory is one with a maximum of unnecessary and expensive destruction. It is most unlikely that the great struggle presently in progress will be settled by a surrender without a shot. Therefore we are going to have to fight hard for our peace and take

6

certain risks along the long, arduous road to peace, something that the world has never really known. As Winston Churchill said, "Why should we wait till the worst has happened before being ready to run risks? May not risks be run for peace, as great as those which, if the worst happens, will assuredly be run for victory?"[20] Those words by Churchill just before Munich when he was trying to stir the free nations to confront Hitler with a solid front fell upon deaf ears. For the failure to act when the risk was small, the Allies were forced to act later on when the risk had greatly increased and they paid a high price for that lack of initiative and mental daring.

Some naive people are quick to claim that it is the warrior who is always urging nations on to war. Frederick the Great and General Douglas MacArthur are two examples here, among many, of great soldiers who saw much of war and expressed their recognition of the futility of wars. Frederick the Great "seems to have realized the futility of attempts to achieve permanent worth by their means. In his Military Instructions he wrote: 'With troops like these (his soldiers) the world itself might be subdued, if conquests were not as fatal to the victors as to the vanquished.'"[21] General MacArthur, upon reviewing the findings of the War Crimes trials in the Far East, spoke of his "realization of the utter futility of war - the most malignant scourge and greatest sin of mankind" and his desire for "its renunciation by all nations."[22] However, as long as international anarchy reigns, there is little prospect of the elimination of war as the ultimate form of international intercourse. It is the supreme goal for which we always strive, but which we cannot permit to blind us to reality and the cold hard facts of life as they must be faced. As long as there are men on earth who would make slaves of us and force us to shape our lives to their mold, then we must maintain our alert and be prepared to face all eventualities.

The Communists have been avid students of war. Marx and Lenin were both ardent readers of Clausewitz and the militant vein is quite pronounced throughout Communist literature. Stefan Possony wrote that "Lenin valued Clausewitz so highly that when he went into hiding after the July uprising of 1917, he took with him two books - Marx's The Civil War in France and Clausewitz's On War."[23]

War is definitely recognized as an integral part of their strategy. "'Great questions in the

7

life of nations,' Lenin wrote in 1906, 'are settled
only by force.'"[24] William R. Kintner pointed out
the military nature of Communism that is implicit in
the Communist theory of revolution. The Free World
must realize that the Communists have worldwide
military aims and are organized militarily. The
Communists seek an unlimited objective, in military
terms, which can be attained only through universal
conflict. Destruction of the enemy's will to resist
is the ultimate objective of all military operations; however, the consistent aim of Communist
operations was not to reform existing governments
but to smash them. "The smashing, the destruction
of the existing system of states, is a purely military objective."[25] Alexis de Tocqueville probably
would not be too surprised at the great power
struggle in the world today for he was almost alone
in seeing the rise of America and Russia, all the
more amazing because it was almost a century and a
half ago.

> There are at the present time two great nations
> in the world, which started from different
> points, but seem to tend towards the same end.
> I allude to the Russians and the Americans.
> Both of them have grown up unnoticed; and
> whilst the attention of mankind was directed
> elsewhere, they have suddenly placed themselves
> in the front rank among the nations, and the
> world learned their existence and their great-
> ness at almost the same time.

> All other nations seem to have nearly reached
> their natural limits, and they have only to
> maintain their power; but these are still in
> the act of growth. All the others have stopped,
> or continue to advance with extreme difficulty;
> these alone are proceeding with ease and celer-
> ity along a path to which no limit can be per-
> ceived. The American struggles against the
> obstacles which nature opposes to him; the
> adversaries of the Russian are men. The for-
> mer combats the wilderness and savage life;
> the latter, civilization with all its arms.
> The conquests of the American are therefore
> gained by the ploughshare; those of the Russian
> by the sword. The Anglo-American relies upon
> personal interest to accomplish his ends, and
> gives free scope to the unguided strength and
> common sense of the people; the Russian cen-
> tres all the authority of society in a single

8

arm. The principal instrument of the former is
freedom; of the latter, servitude. Their
starting-point is different, and their courses
are not the same; yet each of them seems marked
out by the will of Heaven to sway the destinies
of half the globe.[26]

The fact as to whether or not there is actually
a serious conflict in process between the Free and
Communist Worlds depends on how affected one is by
the recurrent flare-ups in international tensions
and the interest one shows in current world problems. There have been innumerable examples of tension and conflict in thirty years. Perhaps there
was some insight into our relations when, referring
to Khrushchev's press conference in Paris after the
U-2 incident, one witness said, "'I got the sudden
feeling that there just wasn't room enough on earth
for both mankind and Communism.'"[27]
    The Communists are not rigid proponents of
quick victory, although they prefer it, for they
feel that time is on their side. Therefore, they
do not hesitate to conduct what Mao Tse-tung prefers to call "protracted war" - "...we point out
that the only way to win ultimate victory lies in a
strategically protracted war and reject the completely groundless theory of a quick victory."[28]
Even de Tocqueville was quick to realize that "No
protracted war can fail to endanger the freedom of
a democratic country." De Tocqueville observed two
of the results of the inertia of Democracy. "There
are two things which a democratic people will always
find very difficult, - to begin a war and to end
it."[29] And from these two, a great number of our
problems flow. Being too slow to act when aggressive actions could be nipped in the bud and, then,
when the lethargic monster is finally stirred,
fighting with such a force and hate that it cannot
easily stop, it tends not to know exactly what it is
fighting for. It fights emotionally, in anger, demanding unconditional surrender and seeking the
other side of the same coin - total victory. But
the atomic age has made this goal appear less than
practical and the Free World must reassess its con-
ceptions of war and, more particularly, of victory
in war. We must search for a rational objective in
war that perhaps could still be considered victory,
but that would be more in the realm of the realiz-
able. An unconditional surrender in the future with
millions of people lying dead and the great areas
of our modern civilization reduced to rubble would

9

certainly be "victory at any price" - but would it
be worth it?

NOTES

1. Stephen King-Hall, Total Victory (New York:
Harcourt Brace & Co., 1942), p. 3.
2. W. F. Kernan, Defense Will Not Win the War
(New York: Pocket Books, Inc., 1942), p. 2.
3. Henry A. Kissinger, Nuclear Weapons and
Foreign Policy (New York: Harper & Brothers, 1957),
p. 35. Admiral Radford was later Chairman of the
U. S. Joint Chiefs of Staff.
4. Karl von Clausewitz, On War (New York: The
Modern Library, 1943, translated by O. J. Matthijs
Jolles), p. 16.
5. L. L. Bernard, War and Its Causes (New York:
Henry Holt & Co., 1943), pp. 13,28. L. L. Bernard
wrote "surprising as it may seem, there is no
generally accepted comprehensive definition of war."
He then discussed economic, naturalistic, political,
judicial, theological, emotional, ethical, and
sociological concepts or characterizations of war.
For historical concept, he gave "War is organized
continuous conflict of a transient character between or among collectivities of any sort capable
of arming and organizing themselves for violent
struggle carried on by armies in the field (or
naval units on water) and supported by civil or in-
completely militarized populations back of the
battle areas constituted for, the pursuit of some
fairly well-defined public or quasi-public objective."
6. Conrad H. Lanza, Napoleon and Modern War,
His Military Maxims (Harrisburg, Pa.: Military
Service Publishing Co., 1943), p. 8.
7. Kernan, Defense, p. 110.
8. General Waldemar Erfurth, Surprise (Harrisburg, Pa.: Military Service Publishing Company,
1943), p. 32.
9. Philip Quincy Wright, The Causes of War and
the Conditions of Peace (London: Longmans, Green &
Co., 1935), p. 68.
10. General Carl von Clausewitz, Principles of
War (Harrisburg, Pa.: Military Service Publishing
Co., 1943, translated and edited by Hans W. Gatzke),
p. 45.
11. Thomas R. Phillips, ed. Roots of Strategy
(Harrisburg, Pa.: Military Service Publishing Co.,
1940), pp. 24 and 26.

12. William Ebenstein, Great Political Thinkers (New York: Rinehart, 1951), p. 398.

13. Ibid., p. 421.

14. See Brigadier General William J. Thompson, "Muzzle on the Military Mind," Army (February 1962), p. 34.

15. Chester Wilmot, The Struggle for Europe (New York: Harper & Row, 1952; 1963), pp. 715-716.

16. Maurice Hankey, Politics, Trials and Errors (Oxford: Pen-in-hand, 1950), pp. 26-27.

17. King-Hall, Total Victory, p. 3.

18. Paul G. Hoffman, Peace Can Be Won (Garden City, N.Y.: Doubleday & Co., Inc., 1951), p. 15.

19. See Harold Strauss, The Division and Dismemberment of Germany from the Casablanca Conference (Jan. 1943) to the Establishment of the East German Republic (Oct. 1949)(Ambilly: Les Presses de Savoie, 1952), p. 9.

20. Winston S. Churchill, Step by Step, 1936-1939 (London: Macmillan, 1934), p. 276.

21. Major General J.F.C. Fuller, A Military History of the Western World (New York: Funk & Wagnalls, 1954-1956), Vol. II, p. 192; italics in Fuller.

22. Major General Courtney Whitney, MacArthur, His Rendezvous with History (New York: A. A. Knopf, 1956), p. 282.

23. Stefan T. Possony, A Century of Conflict. Communist Techniques of World Revolution (Chicago: Henry Regnery Company, 1953), p. 20. Possony has a section entitled "Clausewitz, Communist Mentor", pp. 20-23.

24. George H. Sabine, A History of Political Theory (London: Harrap & Co., Ltd., 3rd Ed., 1959), p. 707.

25. William R. Kintner, The Front is Everywhere; Militant Communism in Action (Norman: University of Oklahoma Press, 1950) pp. 3-5.

26. Alexis de Tocqueville, Democracy in America ed. Richard D. Heffner (New York: New American Library, 1956) abridged, p. 142.

27. Harry and Bonaro Overstreet, The War Called Peace. Khrushchev's Communism (New York: W. W. Norton & Co., 1958), p. 48.

28. Mao Tse-tung, Selected Works (New York: International Publishers, 1954), Vol. II, p. 180.

29. de Tocqueville, Democracy in America, p. 278.

Part 1
Total War

1
Victory in Past Wars

> The only thing sadder than
> a great victory is a great
> defeat.[1]
>
> -- Wellington

> Those few battles of which
> a contrary event would have
> essentially varied the
> drama of the world in all
> its subsequent scenes.[2]
>
> -- Hallam

War has been a part of the history of man for
as long as there is written record and, no doubt,
before. Man has resorted to force repeatedly to
settle the disputes that he was incapable of resolving or unwilling to end by less violent means. The
usual wars of the past would be considered small by
our present day standards of violence; however, one
should keep in mind the size of the population of
times past, and the means available. In this light,
many of the old wars take on a dimension of cruelty
and violence that resembles modern total war.

The list of wars that took place before the
twentieth century is long and incomplete. There
were wars in parts of the world that are still unknown to the Western mind. The tribal wars of
Africa, the wars of Asia, the Middle East, and South
America barely appear in our history books. We cannot begin to review this long list. The one thing
we can try to determine is the concept of victory
in these wars of the past. Most of this period was
the time of kings or of some form of supreme ruler
over a country, region, people, tribe, or area in
which he could impose his influence. Often, war

15

took on a noble air bringing to mind knights in
flashing armor. This tendency appeared, waned, reappeared and seems to be always present to some degree throughout history.

> Military glory! It was a dream that century
> after century had seized men's imagination and
> set their blood on fire. Trumpets, plumes,
> chargers, the pomp of war, the excitement of
> combat, the exultation of victory - the mix-
> ture was intoxicating indeed. To command great
> armies, to perform deeds of valour, to ride
> victorious through flower-strewn streets, to
> be heroic, magnificent, famous - such were the
> visions that danced before men's eyes as they
> turned eagerly to war.
>
> It was not a dream for the common man. War was
> an aristocratic trade, and military glory re-
> served for nobles and princes.
>
> It was a dream that died hard.[3]

What, then, was a victory in this great "sport"
of the past? There were wars fought for adventure,
almost for the same reason as a man climbs a mountain - because it is there. Old tribal customs required a youth to kill an enemy to prove his man-
hood; this may still exist in places such as New
Guinea.[4] There were wars fought for trade, or agricultural regions, or ports, or rivers, but most
of these would fit under a broad heading of imperial
wars, where one group was trying to extend its empire and came into conflict with the interests of
another group. Previous historical eras are studied
from empire to empire, and any country trying to
build an empire had to have an army to gain it and,
therefore, to maintain it. The history of the
Greek, Roman, and Persian Empires reads like military history in that it seems to be dominated by a
series of wars. The interesting thing in most of
these wars is that their goal was not total victory
in the sense of completely destroying the enemy.
These, more often than not, were frontier wars in
which one empire was trying to encroach on the land
of another rather than a fight to the finish. This
is not to imply that there was not great destruction
and annihilation. Genghis Khan in his far-roaming
campaigns would completely destroy a city and all
its inhabitants if he was irritated for some reason.
It was written that his youngest son, Tuli, never

had to leave garrisons behind in occupation, for where he passed there was nothing left but uninhabited ruins - in towns of from 70,000 to 1,000,000 inhabitants nothing remained alive, not even a cat or a dog.[5] That the powers had the capability to inflict total victory long ago is shown by the destruction of Carthage.

However, great ideological conflicts appeared, mainly in religious wars and, later, during the French Revolution, culminating in the total wars of the twentieth century. The religious wars were the best examples of a search for total victory. They distinctly had as goals the changing of the enemies' system of government, more particularly their religion, and were fought with a savagery that reflected the hatreds ignited when men dispute religious questions. The best example probably is the Thirty Years' War, the greatest European war before the time of the French Revolution. It was an extremely complicated war between the Catholics and the Protestants begun as a struggle of German princes against the Holy Roman Empire, but with many political questions intertwined plus a curious combination of mercenary soldiers and opportunist princes and generals. Allies changed from time to time as they became fearful of the power combinations that others were creating. Germany, where the war was largely fought, was physically wrecked and, as such, ceased for a long time to play any part in European affairs. The devastation (in parts of Germany as much as a third of the population may have perished) did not result in a total victory for either side, but after four years of negotiations ended in the Peace of Westphalia. There now appeared, during the period between the Peace of Westphalia and the Congress of Vienna, a certain moderation in the conduct of war.

In many ways, warfare was a much more gentlemanly affair than it had been. Of course, much remained to be done to improve the lot of the common soldier, but the wholesale destruction of towns and the civilian involvement in war's horrors that marked the Thirty Years' War had lessened. Indeed, civilians had relatively little difficulty in traveling in belligerent territory. Wars became more like private quarrels between princes, and were largely fought by mercenaries or by a country's shanghaied "rabble." The nation in arms, conscripted to defend or to enhance the glory of la patrie, did not appear until after the French Revolution when France mobilized its forces against Russia and

Austria. But by that time, the Rousseau-Portalis
doctrine that war is a contention between governments and armies had been enunciated and became
fundamental to continental thought on war after
Napoleon's defeat.[6]

   This was also the period of history when ideas
of international law were evolving. They were realistic, not utopian; neither Thomas Hobbes nor
Grotius nor any jurist of the seventeenth and eighteenth centuries contended that war should be outlawed. Though accepting war as a part of international intercourse, Emerich de Vattel early saw
the fallacy of total victory, rejecting the pursuit
of war to the utter ruin of one of the parties. The
moderation with which victors frequently dealt with
the vanquished reflected an appreciation that the
disappearance of neighbors might lead to upheavals
and their replacement by similar or worse neighbors.
This moderation was, of course, not something new
in history. Churchill credited Julius Caesar's conquests as being "due almost as much to his clemency
as to his prowess."[7] Wars between major powers were
limited also by resources, often due more to consideration of domestic policy than by conscious choice.
For example, in the seventeenth century Louis XIV
employed almost his entire army for a period of
close to twenty-five years. Yet his military forces
used only a small proportion of the national resources because the government prevented him from
conscripting his subjects, confiscating property, or
levying income taxes. Therefore, his military
forces were limited by the availability of resources
and so were the wars he fought.

   Though the period of Napoleon Bonaparte can
certainly be referred to as a "world war," as its
actions and effects reached all parts of the globe,
it was in fact a series of short wars culminating in
the Treaties of Paris and the Congress of Vienna.
The terms meted out to France are particularly important as moderate terms were offered to the defeated enemy - no indemnity, no allied occupation,
not even the return of the art treasures which had
been looted from the galleries of Europe.
Napoleon's foreign conquests were surrendered, but
the essential unity of France remained intact and
the territory over which Louis XVIII ruled was
slightly more extensive than that of Louis XVI. The
reason for this moderation is understandable. The
disruption of France would have added too much
weight to one or another of the Continental Powers,
and it would have kindled a flame of vengeance in

the hearts of all Frenchmen. Here, basically then, we see the balance of power at work. The second Treaty of Paris was somewhat stiffer after Napoleon's attempted comeback; however, there were no intolerable humiliations. Europe thereupon embarked on a period of 100 years of relative peace.

During this period however, the United States got itself embroiled in an ideological, civil war. It was a war the very nature of which led to extremes. Since the North refused to recognize that the South could set up the Confederacy as a separate country, it had to go on to complete victory for the North, for Lincoln's goal was the restoration of the Union. What then was the Southern aim in the war? Since the Confederates could not hope to conquer the Northern states, their task was to resist conquest, that is, to tire the Federals out so they would abandon the war. Given the industrial capability of the North, this was unlikely. Indeed, once the call to arms was made, the motive of winning, and winning completely, became dominant on both sides; and such was the American resolution North and South that the wretched struggle had to go on from slaughter to slaughter until one side or the other was down and out. To fight to the end and die in the last ditch might make even defeat honorable; but to quit while there remained a shaky line of ragged troops would seem a dishonor. Here complete victory was necessary if America was to become a great country. However, the excesses, particularly of the Reconstruction period, left wounds that have not yet completely healed. Probably the smartest thing for the South to have done would have been to exhaust every effort to prevent the war. The great mistake of political strategy was when the Confederate government ordered the bombardment of Fort Sumter. Northern sentiment had been divided and, sooner or later, even the people of the other states would have become accustomed to a Southern Confederacy. "Thus it came about, as Vattel had held, that 'If you once open a door for continual accusations of outrageous excess...the sword will never be sheathed till one of the parties is utterly destroyed.'"[8]

This 100 year period in Europe was not truly free of war, but it might be referred to as a period of "sane" wars. Between the Congress of Vienna in 1815 and the outbreak of World War I, wars were limited by the political objectives of the opponents. Since they were fought for specific goals which did not threaten the survival of any of the powers, there existed a rough balance between the force employed

19

and the changes sought. The Austro-Prussian and
Franco-Prussian Wars are two good examples. In the
first, Bismarck did not wish to humiliate Austria,
or to annex part of her homeland, because the continued existence of Austria as a great power was essential to Prussia's security. His aim was to drive
the Austrians out of Germany, and in this he was
successful. Bixmarck's policy was equally clear-cut
in the Franco-Prussian War. It was to unite all
Germany under the leadership of Prussia, and French
determination to prevent this union was the cause of
the war, not the dynastic question in Spain, which
was a pretext. Except for the cession by France of
Alsace and German Lorraine with Metz, which popular
clamor compelled Bismarck to demand, these were not
wars of conquest, even less wars of annihilation.
Once their limited goals were obtained, both were
terminated by moderate peace settlements. They were
totally different in character from the American
Civil War, mainly because they were much more political conflicts, less influenced by economics or
ideologies, which tend to awaken the beast in man.
This war that served as the basis of almost fifty
years of French desire for revenge was not exactly
what Napoleon III was looking for. In 1870,
Napoleon was shopping for a war that he needed to
revive the languishing credit and refurbish the tarnished glitter of his thinly gold-plated empire.
But that is not to say that he wanted a war. That
is, unless it was an easy war, amply insured against
loss and promising bargain-counter laurels.[9] Napoleon did not get his type of war. Bismarck displayed his leadership by separating policy and emotion in his remark about the considerate treatment
accorded the French emperor when his people were
clamoring for blood: "Punishment and revenge have
nothing to do with policy."[10] This was a far cry
from the Allied approach after World Wars I and II.
To sum up the limited warfare of this period then,
the objective of nineteenth-century warfare was the
creation of risks which made continued resistance
appear more costly than the peace terms offered. As
the peace terms were more moderate, the margin of
superiority required was smaller. These wars ended
when a sovereign government agreed to the victor's
terms thereby assuming responsibility for their execution.[11]

After the Sino-Japanese War of 1895, it was
evident that Japan had won the war, but had lost the
peace. The Allies could sympathize with them because this was to become their habit in the twentieth

century. In this case, Russia, Germany, and France intervened and "advised" Japan to renounce possession of the Liaotung Peninsula, which she was forced to do. The Russo-Japanese War of 1904-05 should be classified as a nineteenth-century war. Japan fought for a compromise and not a total victory, which was beyond her reach. Total victory, not yet widespread, was slated to become characteristic of the great wars of the twentieth century. We have seen, then, that though total victory did appear in past wars; its quest was the exception rather than the rule. As long as war avoided religious or ideological questions, it tended to be more sane. What was the cost to mankind of all this warfare of the past? We know that there were great conquests, empires rose and fell, usually under the weight of the sword. But also, there were great losses. It is impossible to determine the losses from war in the past. We can quote figures from sample wars to give an idea, but the records are nowhere near complete enough to try to add these up and arrive at any meaningful total. Every man or woman or child killed changes the potential figures of the world population forever due to lost offspring. To this must be added the losses of wealth, buildings, livestock, crops, commerce, shipping, art, history, and the diversion of effort and materials to war that might more profitably have been used in other ventures. The effect on health should be remembered because the peoples of the world have lived, until recent times, under the threat of plague or other great epidemics that at times seemed about to sweep man off the planet and make war look like child's play.

It is significant to look at a few of these figures because man himself, along with the heavy hand of nature, has managed to remove an enormous number of his fellow creatures from the face of the earth. The thoroughness of obliteration is also of importance to us as sometimes entire peoples or nations were removed. For example: Assyria.

> The disaster in which the Assyrian military power met its end in 614-610 B.C. was one of the completest yet known to history. It involved not only the destruction of the Assyrian war-machine but also the extinction of the Assyrian state and the extermination of the Assyrian people. A community which had been in existence for over two thousand years and had been playing an ever more dominant part in

South-Western Asia for a period of two-and-a-half centuries was blotted out almost completely.[12]

In 404 B.C. when the members of the Peloponnesian alliance were debating the fate of Athens, "Corinth and Thebes urged that the city should be utterly destroyed and the whole people sold into slavery."[13] This the Spartans rejected and advanced less harsh proposals which were accepted.

Deaths on the field of battle often involved large numbers, but it is sometimes interesting to study them in terms of percentages also to get an idea of the intensity of a conflict. At the famous Battle of Cannae in 216 B.C. between Hannibal and the Romans, the Romans were massacred. Approximately 60,000 of the original force of 72,000 died on the field of battle. Count Schlieffen chose it as the classic example of the battle of annihilation.

In the Jewish War 66-70 A.D., after a terrible long siege, the city of Jerusalem was razed to the ground except for a few towers and a section of wall.

> The loss of life among the Jews was unimaginably high. During the siege, according to Tacitus, there were 600,000 people in the city. Josephus gives the number of prisoners as 97,000 not counting those crucified or ripped open, and adds that within a period of three months 115,800 corpses were taken out of one of the city gates alone by the Jews.

> The greatest part of the population of the Promised Land that was not massacred in the bloody Jewish War of 66-70 and in the Bar-Kokhba rebellion of 132-135 was sold into slavery....

> Archaeologists have found no material evidence of Israel's existence in Palestine after the year 70, not even a tombstone with a Jewish inscription.[14]

Those ripped open were victims of a demon rumor that the Jews swallowed their jewels before attempting escape. Those caught thus had their stomachs cut open. Man can so treat his fellow man like a beast! An early example of propaganda.

The days of Rome were not all glorious. As the economic resources dried up in the third century A.D.,

22

"The propertied class was exterminated and the bour-
geoisie eliminated. As requisitioning increased,
prices rose and the population fell from seventy to
fifty millions."[15] Genghis Khan (1162-1227) is infamous for having pillaged cities, leveled them, and
killed all the people. After the inhabitants of
Herat had rebelled and installed their own governor,
Genghis Khan sent an army and, after a six-month
siege, took the city. "For a whole week the Mongols
ceased not to kill, burn and destroy, and 1,600,000
persons are said to have been massacred within the
walls."[16]

We have already mentioned the terrible effects
of the Thirty Years' War. But even World War II, in
sheer depopulation, was not as devastating for
Germany as was the Thirty Years' War. It was quite
possible for human beings to die like flies without
the benefit of scientific destruction. The horrors
of modern war are not wholly unlike the horrors that
people have experienced through the ages. It could
probably be conclusively proved that the great number of casualties from war never falls on the soldiers. "When, in 1648, the Peace of Westphalia put
an end to the anarchy, Central Europe lay in ruins;
8,000,000 people are said to have perished, not
counting some 350,000 killed in battle."[17]

Medical science being what it then was, the
soldier still bore a heavy burden of casualties in
war. Normally casualties were appalling. At
Malplaquet (1709) one authority estimated the losses
of the Allies at 33 percent and another at 22 percent, and that losses of 15 to 25 percent were common during the Seven Years' War (1755-1763). At
Torgau (1760) Frederick lost 30 percent, and at
Zorndorf (1758) the Russians lost 50 percent - perhaps a world's record for a field army during a
single day's fighting in which the defeated side was
neither crushed nor unresistingly massacred.[18]
Europe was appalled at the slaughter of Malplaquet -
probably the largest and bloodiest battle of the
eighteenth century. Napoleon, though at war for
many years, suffered his greatest losses during the
wintry retreat from Moscow 19 October to 11 December
1812. The terrible cold, shortages of supplies, and
the harassing action of the enemy completed the destruction of Napoleon's original force. Of 611,000
who entered Russia, 400,000 died of wounds, starvation, and exposure, and 100,000 were taken prisoner.

There are no complete figures for the American
Civil War. However, if the Confederate wounded were
no more than half the Federal, the grand total of

the military casualties would exceed a million.
"The complete cost of the war would include a variety of other factors: billions of treasure
(Federal, Confederate, state, local, and unofficial),
untold retardation of economic development, ruined
homes, roads, buildings and fields, billions of dol-
lar-value in slaves wiped out, a shattered merchant
marine, and a wretched intangible heritage of hate,
extravagance, corruption, truculence, partisan excess (lasting for decades), and intolerance."[19]
    Thus we can see even from these few examples
that the cost over the years has been enormous. Even
in recent history, a period during which we consider
that 100 years were "relatively peaceful," total
deaths in war from 1793 to 1914 have been estimated
at almost 6,000,000.[20]
    The scars of death and destruction from the
past always seem to heal; man is basically a very
resilient animal. Unfortunately, though, there is
one other legacy from past wars: they have provided
the foundation for the ever-increasing totality of
the wars of the twentieth century. "Primitive wars
were fought almost exclusively for immediate and
material ends, while modern wars frequently aim at
political or even ideological results and their material objectives refer more to the future advantages than to those of the immediate present."[21] We
find modern war in a trend toward ideological aims
that are supposedly the reason for and the impulse
behind them. Whatever the actual motives behind a
war, it is now regarded as essential to find some
justification of a social or ethical character, even
if it is only a rationalization. At least a basis
of the ideological wars stems from the religious
wars of the past. The most common ideological appeal in the recent world wars was to the concepts of
freedom and democracy. These slogans have constituted outstanding ideological sanctions since the
time of the French Revolution, and the exploitation
of such symbols makes powerful propaganda.
    The American Revolution and, more importantly,
the French Revolution, played key roles in founding
twentieth-century warfare. "By 1783 the principal
seeds had been sown from which were to spring the
modern 'socialization' of war and its development to
those heights of total effort and total savagery to
which we are now accustomed."[22] Conscriptions
played an important role, as from August 1793 onward,
war became more and more unlimited and, finally,
total. In the fourth decade of the twentieth century, life was held so cheaply that the wholesale

massacre of civilian populations became as accepted
a strategic aim as battles were in previous wars.
"In 150 years conscription had led the world back
to tribal barbarism." A conscripted nation - a nation in arms, a nation fed on violent propaganda -
sought great, crushing victories as the way to secure peace, whereas they really made it much more
difficult or even impossible to secure. Although
conscription existed, historically, in early Greek
and Roman times, this problem primarily arose out of
the French Revolution, and is the key to our present
distresses.[23]
    Also from the French Revolution came the mass
armies that were later to become a part of total
war. More important, the mass army became the symbol of the nation state. Fervent nationalism, and
the world anarchy often found in its wake, is the
basis of the conflict of man in total war. The
First World War, instead of alleviating this problem
actually aggravated it by the creation of new European states, resulting in a ferment of nationalism.
The American Secretary of State, Cordell Hull, said:

> One of the greatest of all obstacles which have
> in the past impeded human progress and afforded
> breeding grounds for dictators, has been ex-
> treme nationalism. All will agree that nation-
> alism and its spirit are essential to the
> healthy and normal political and economic life
> of a people, but when policies of nationalism...
> are carried to such extremes as to exclude and
> prevent necessary policies of international co-
> operation, they become dangerous and deadly.
> Nationalism, run riot between the last war and
> this war, defeated all attempts to carry out
> indispensable measures of international eco-
> nomics and political action; encouraged and
> facilitated the rise of dictators; and drove
> the world straight toward the present war.[24]

    One Englishman made a far-seeing remark in 1935.
"'The sovereignty of the national state has been the
main cause of the failure of the League and the
post-war peace movement, as it was the ultimate
cause of the World War and will be the dynamic cause
of the next war, unless we can mitigate it in
time.'"[25] Change the word League to United Nations
and his statement might be just as valid now as it
was in 1935.
    The more perfect the technical side of war
grew, the less possible did it become politically

25

to limit its scope, until the world became so explosive that a pistol shot in an obscure corner was sufficient to detonate a global war. In its turn, this foretold that national wars would give way to coalition wars, and that, in the future, unless a nation was a partner in a coalition, its resources would prove insufficient to conduct successfully a war alone. So the wars of the past with their great victories, their great conquests, and their sometimes appalling losses pointed the way to the holocausts of terrible conflict that would be war in the twentieth century.

NOTES

1. Quoted in W. F. Kernan, Defense Will Not Win the War, p. 10.
2. Sir Edward S. Creasy, Fifteen Decisive Battles of the World, ed. Robert Hammond Murray (Harrisburg, Pa.: Military Service, 1943), with additional material by Murray, p. v.
3. Cecil Woodham-Smith, The Reason Why (New York: McGraw-Hill Book Company, Inc., 1954), pp. 1-2.
4. See the National Geographic (May 1962), p. 595.
5. Michael Prawdin, The Mongol Empire, p. 191, quoted in Fuller, The Second World War (London: Eyre and Spottiswoode, 1948), p. 407.
6. Wesley L. Gould, An Introduction to International Law (New York: Harper & Brothers, 1957), p. 54.
7. Churchill, Triumph and Tragedy, Vol. VI of The Second World War, 6 vols. (Boston: Houghton Mifflin Co., 1948-1953), p. 631.
8. Major General J.F.C. Fuller, The Conduct of War, 1789-1961: A Study of the Impact of the French Industrial, and Russian Revolutions on War and Its Conduct (Brunswick, N.J.: Rutgers University Press, 1961), p. 99.
9. Creasy, Fifteen Decisive Battles of the World, p. 574.
10. Quoted in Fuller, A Military History of the Western World, Vol. III, p. 131.
11. Kissinger, Nuclear Weapons and Foreign Policy, p. 89.
12. Arnold J. Toynbee, A Study of History (New York: Oxford University Press, 1956-1957) Vol. I, p. 338.
13. Fuller, A Military History of the Western World, Vol. I, p. 80.

14. Werner Keller, The Bible as History. A Confirmation of the Book of Books, tr. William Neil (New York: William Morrow & Co., 1956), pp. 407-408.

15. Fuller, A Military History of the Western World, Vol. I, p. 259.

16. Encyclopaedia Britannica (1944), Vol. 12, p. 1001.

17. Fuller, The Conduct of War, p. 15. William L. Shirer, The Rise and Fall of the Third Reich, p. 135, said "perhaps one third of the German people perished in this barbarous war."

18. See Fuller, The Conduct of War, p. 22.

19. J. G. Randall, The Civil War and Reconstruction (Boston: D. C. Heath & Co., 1953), pp. 687-688.

20. Charles F. Horne, Editor-in-Chief, Source Records of the Great War (Indianapolis: The American Legion, 1930), Vol. VII, p. 133, in the rear.

21. L. L. Bernard, War and Its Causes (New York: Henry Holt & Co., 1943), p. 73.

22. Walter Millis, Arms and Men: A Study of American Military History (New York: A Mentor Book, 1958), 1. 35.

23. Fuller, The Conduct of War, pp. 33, 36-37.

24. Radio address 23 July 1942. See L. M. Goodrich, Documents on American Foreign Relations, Vol. V, 1942-43, p. 10; also, Norman D. Palmer and Howard C. Perkins, International Relations: The World Community in Transition (Boston: Houghton Mifflin Co., 1953), p. 38.

25. Pacifism is not Enough (nor Patriotism Either), by Lord Lothian (Oxford University Press, 1935), p. 26, quoted in William Beveridge, The Price of Peace (London: Pilot, 1945), p. 52.

2
The War To End Wars

> I hold the first World War
> to have been the great ca-
> tastrophe of Western civi-
> lization in the present
> century.[1]
>
>   -- George F. Kennan

> The mind of a nation in
> dispute is its mob-mind,
> credulous and savage....
> Whenever the mob-mind
> rules, mankind shudders.
> Its voice is the evil ban-
> shee of nations.[2]
>
>   -- Homer Lea

1. Why War?

War came in 1914 and when it ended in 1918, except for the United States, the whole enormous edifice had crashed to earth - an epoch had gone up in
flames.
Could soldiers and statesmen have forseen the
results of their bickerings and chicaneries, their
intrigues and alliances, would they have precipitated the conflict? Winston Churchill reminisced
about a conversation with a German before the war.
"'I remember,' he said 'old Bismarck telling me the
year before he died that one day the great European
War would come out of some damned foolish thing in
the Balkans.' These words, he said, might come
true. It all depended on the Tsar."[3] The relative
peace that Europe had known for almost a hundred
years was shattered by that pistol shot in Bosnia.
What were the causes of this terrible war that

poured forth in Europe like an unyielding wave before the astonished eyes of the world? That assassination in Sarajevo was not the cause of the war; it was only the spark that ignited the powder keg.

As usual, the causes were many and varied. The fundamental causes for the war were the excesses of nationalism, militarism, and economic imperialism. The conflicting systems of military alliances, the anarchy of international negotiations, and frequent international crises exacerbated the confrontations. The period before the war cannot really be called "peaceful." There were many incidents and crises and these were met by various combinations of alliances. The diplomatic shifting and maneuvering finally separated Europe into two hostile groups -- the necessary condition for a world war as distinguished from a war involving only some of the powers.

This was a period of rising importance of two nations - Russia and Germany. The Germans felt that they needed and deserved a "place in the sun," which vaguely meant some degree of acknowledged supremacy like that of the British. The Germans insisted that they had to have a navy to protect their colonies, to secure their foreign trade, and "for the general purposes of their greatness." This was bound to clash with British views, and the naval race did nothing to ease world tensions. President Woodrow Wilson said on 11 September 1919, "'...the seed of war in the modern world is industrial and commercial rivalry... This war, in its inception, was a commercial and industrial war. It was not a political war.' And at about the same time John Maynard Keynes wrote in his The Economic Consequences of the Peace: 'The politics of power are inevitable, and there is nothing very much new to learn about this war or the end it was fought for; England had destroyed, as in each preceding century, a trade rival.'"[4] Therefore, the failure of Europe to assimilate the consolidated industrial Germany that arose after 1870 was, in a broad sense, a distant and basic cause of the war. While Germany continued to grow, Russia loomed in the East as an awakening giant whose potential resources, if developed fully, would permit her to become the dominant force in Europe. Thus, German fear of Russia as much as anything else precipitated that conflict.

The influence of the military had greatly increased, particularly in the form of mobilization plans. In time of crisis, the soldiers were in-

clined to jump to the conclusion that war was
"inevitable" and, accordingly, would urge the fatal
step of mobilization, thus actually making war inevitable. "As General Boisdeffre, the assistant
Chief of the French General Staff explained to Tsar
Nicholas: 'The mobilization is the declaration of
war.'"[5] These mobilization plans tended to remove
flexibility from diplomatic relations. A notorious
instance was the German "Schlieffen Plan," which
made it virtually impossible for Germany to go to war
with Russia except by invading France through Belgium. Count Alfred von Schlieffen, who became Chief
of the German General Staff in 1891, believed correctly that France was the more dangerous antagonist
and prepared a strategic plan to crush France before
the "Russian steam roller" could get moving.

The loss of Alsace and Lorraine had filled
France with hatred of Germany, and thus the war of
revanche was regarded as inevitable. All this tension throughout Europe led to a great buildup of
armaments, not too unlike our world of today. The
basis of their faith was that if all were armed, all
would be safe. Yet in spite of all their aggressive words, almost no European really wanted a general war. Therefore, as Herman Kahn put it, since
neither side really wanted war, it was presumed that
one side or the other would withdraw before things
got out of hand.[6] It has been said that, had the
German government known as a positive fact that
England would fight, the war might have been averted.
Consequently, the evasiveness of British policy was
given as a contributing cause of the war. In reality, however, the probability that England would
fight was so great that to underestimate it, as the
Germans did, was an act of criminal folly, for
England probably would have fought, commitments or
no commitments, for purely stragegic reasons.

The First World War ushered in the Era of Total
War, brought a peace that represented a lost Victory, was extremely expensive in lives and in material values and, worst of all, brought on the Russian
Revolution. It was the "tragedy" of 1914 that the
more backward or politically bankrupt parts of
Europe, through the alliance system, dragged the
more advanced parts automatically into ruin. Perhaps there is some merit in the statement that "The
Great War could no more have been avoided than an
earthquake or any other cataclysm of Nature's unknown forces."[7] Nevertheless, it made its mark on
history, particularly on Europe.

31

2. The Beginning of the Era of Total War

Although we will look into the idea of total
war in more detail later on, it is important to consider here that with the coming of the First World
War, we entered into the Era of Total War. As we
have seen, the American Civil War, a half century
earlier, should be referred to as the first total
war. However, it was fought at a great distance
from most of the rest of the world and was a civil
war. The world had to await the twentieth century
to see a large total war fought among nations.
     One of the major requirements for total war
was scientific progress which came specifically
from the Industrial Revolution. Modern production
techniques brought to the battlefield destructive
forces previously unknown. The drive for victory
in modern warfare led to striking at the economic
capacity that supported a large army even more than
striking at the enemy army itself. When a nation
mobilized totally for war, it had to expect that its
every segment was subject to attack, whether manned
by the military or by civilians. The war became
total due to the enormous requirements for resources of all types in order to continue the war
and the moves against the enemy populations in efforts to drive the enemy out of the war.
     The blockade of Germany had devastating ef-
fects and was continued on into 1919. Perhaps
800,000 noncombatants died in Germany during the
last two years of the blockade, from starvation or
diseases attributable to undernourishment. This
was fifty times the losses from submarine attack on
British shipping.[8] Germany tried to break the
blockade with the submarine, an invention that had
appeared in the American Civil War but which had
really played no role in the nineteenth century.
The Anglo-American strategic concept was that wars
can best be won by crippling the enemy's economy,
and this required war against civilians as well as
against the military. A strong continental expression of disagreement with the Anglo-American concept was the German insistence that unrestricted
submarine warfare was only retaliation against
Britain's illegal naval warfare against civilians.
With the advent of total war in World War I, civilians had considerably less hope of benefiting from
Rousseau's position that war is a relation only

between states.

Propaganda reached a new height as a weapon for stirring up mass hate. Stories of atrocities, real and make-believe, were widely circulated and each government loudly "proved" that the enemy was the aggressor and that, therefore, the war was being fought in self-defense for noble ideals and, as a result, must be pursued to the bitter end to rid the world of such scoundrels who had brought this terrible war down on the heads of each innocent country. A group in Britain stated that the scientists in Germany were not in support of Prussian militarism. The answer came back in the form of a Declaration of the Professors of the Universities and Technical Colleges of the German Empire, 23 October 1914. "The same spirit that rules the German army pervades the whole German nation, for both are one and we form part of it."[9] In an effort to differentiate between the government and the people, Wilson, in his War Message to Congress, 2 April 1917, said: "We have no quarrel with the German people. We have no feeling toward them but one of sympathy and friendship."[10] The "nation in arms" had to have idealistic goals for which to fight instead of simple strategic or political reasons.

After three years of neutrality, the United States entered the war in 1917, not for simple mundane reasons but to push a crusade to win the war to end all wars. Wilson continued in his War Message:

> We are glad, now that we see the facts with no veil of false pretense about them, to fight thus for the ultimate peace of the world and for the liberation of its peoples, the German peoples included; for the rights of nations, great and small, and the privilege of men everywhere to choose their way of life and of obedience. The world must be made safe for democracy. Its peace must be planted upon the tested foundations of political liberty.
>
> We have no selfish ends to serve. We desire no conquest, no dominion. We seek no indemnities for ourselves, no material compensation for the sacrifices we shall freely make. We are but one of the champions of the rights of mankind. We shall be satisfied when those rights have been made as secure as the faith and the freedom of nations can make them.[11]

These were certainly worthy aspirations for a peaceful world, but they were very difficult points to settle at a conference table or even to dictate to a vanquished foe. Unfortunately, the Americans did not even know what they wanted or, worse yet, what would be, in their vital interest, a real victory in this great war.

> The verbal battle of the propagandists, of which so much was made in later years, was fought in this vacuum of the American mind. It was fought because the American nation lacked even the rudiments of a settled foreign policy which could make clear whose victory and what kind of victory could best serve the vital interests of the United States. Because of this vacuum, the United States went to war in April 1917 for reasons which were never willingly or accurately avowed. And so they were never clearly recognized.[12]

Walter Lippmann continued this line of reasoning in explaining Wilson's failure regarding the League of Nations:

> He failed because in leading the nation to war he had failed to give the durable and compelling reasons for the momentous decision. The reasons he did give were legalistic and moralistic and ideological reasons, rather than the substantial and vital reason that the security of the United States demanded that no aggressively expanding imperial power, like Germany, should be allowed to gain the mastery of the Atlantic Ocean.... the nation never understood clearly why it had entered the war.[13]

That Americans dreaded becoming involved in European affairs was evidenced by years of isolation. Therefore, it is easier to understand why they accepted American participation in World War I on the basis that it was intended to "make the world safe for democracy" rather than to redress the balance of power in Europe.

However, these feelings were not solely American. Sir Norman Angell, in 1938, wrote, "In 1914 we entered a war which was to vindicate the rights of small nations...; to remove the menace of Prussian militarism; to end war; to make the world safe for democracy; to make this and other free countries secure from aggression, and place their eco-

nomic life on safe foundations."14 Regardless of
whatever reservations there may have been in the
minds of the men who invented the slogans, "a war to
end war" and "a war to make the world safe for democracy," millions of men and women responded to
them with moral fervor and approval and many thousands died for those ideals on the field of battle.

Nations pursuing total war find it difficult
to end a war in any way except the total defeat of
the enemy. Anything less would appear to be a be-
trayal of the people and their monumental efforts
and sacrifices. So it evolved that "The Allies
came to be interested only in a total victory over
Germany; a victory of national humiliation, of annexations, of crushing reparations. They resented
suggestions for an end of hostilities on any other
basis."15 Wilson had called for a "peace without
victory," one in which neither side would be completely crushed.

> As late as January, 1917, Wilson was still ar-
> guing against total victory. A "peace forced
> upon the loser, a victor's terms imposed upon
> the vanquished," he said, "would be accepted
> in humiliation, under duress, at an intoler-
> able sacrifice, and would leave a sting, a re-
> sentment, a bitter memory upon which terms of
> peace would rest... as upon quicksand." But,
> once we were in the war, these ideas were
> swept away by the powerful currents of war
> psychology. We were then as strong as anybody
> else in our determination that the war should
> be fought to the finish of a total victory.16

The human mind caught up in the flame of total
war psychology does not see problems in the same
perspective as the relaxed mind of retrospect.
Considerations that the balance of power in Europe
might have some importance were ignored.

> Considerations of the power balance argued
> against total victory. Perhaps it was for
> this very reason that people in this country
> rejected them so emphatically and sought more
> sweeping and grandiose objectives, for the ac-
> complishment of which total victory could
> plausibly be represented as absolutely essen-
> tial.17

Once blinded by total victory, the results of
which he had so clearly foreseen, Wilson pursued it

to the end. Even after Prince Max took over the
German government and asked for peace, Wilson replied that the Allies wholly mistrusted Germany's
sudden repentance, and would agree to no armistice
which did not include a military surrender.18 And
so it came about, the war ended with an armistice,
in word only, for it was much more like an unconditional surrender in which the victors did not
elect to take over the government of the vanquished, and the time was at hand to reap the rewards of total victory.

3. The Peace - Lost Victory

There had been earlier attempts at peace negotiations such as the unsuccessful House Missions
and the German Peace Note of December 1916. Even
though there were some favorable replies to the
exchange of notes, before they came to anything,
Germany had resumed unrestricted submarine warfare
which eventually led to American entry into the
war. So all of the early tries for peace came to
nought as each side still thought it could win.
"Those who choose the moment for beginning wars do
not always fix the moment for ending them. To ask
for an armistice is one thing, to obtain it is another."19
That armistice, which Hindenburg and Ludendorff had sought, bore the appearance of an unconditional surrender. Accordingly, Ludendorff
wished to continue the fight, declaring realistic-
ally that nothing could worsen the terms for Germany. There was never an armistice like that before. In Churchill's words:

Parliament was disposed to be suspicious of
the Armistice terms until they heard them.
But when the document was read overwhelming
thankfulness filled all hearts. No one could
think of any further stipulation. Immediate
evacuation of invaded countries; repatriation
of all inhabitants; surrender in good condition of 5,000 guns, 30,000 machine guns, 3,000
minewerfers, 2,000 aeroplanes; evacuation of
the left bank of the Rhine; surrender of three
bridgeheads on the Rhine; surrender of 5,000
locomotives, 150,000 waggons, 5,000 motor
lorries in good working order (and with spare
parts); disclosure of all mines, of delay-

action fuses, and assistance in their discovery
and destruction; immediate repatriation without reciprocity of all prisoners of war; aban-
donment of the Treaties of Bucharest and Brest-
Litovsk; surrender of 6 battlecruisers, the
best 10 battleships, 8 light cruisers, 50 of
the best destroyers; surrender of all submarines; the right of the Allies on failure of
execution of any condition to denounce the
Armistice within 48 hours. Such were the cove-
nanted clauses. And thus did Germany hand
herself over powerless and defenceless to the
discretion of her long tortured and now victorious foes![20]

Churchill's repeated use of the word surrender
and, in particular, his last sentence show that
this was no armistice - the German leaders surrendered, virtually unconditionally, in a railway car-
riage in the Compiegne Forest. With the crumbling
of the German Empire, Churchill showed remorse.
"Such a spectacle appals mankind; and a knell rang
in the ear of the victors, even in their hour of
triumph."[21]
  One of the great problems of coalition warfare
is effecting unity among allies. Differences in
national background, concepts of government and
their approach to war have left this problem still
generally unsolved. The two closest allies, France
and England, could not even get together on policy.
There had been ample time in the years before the
war for them to arrive at a common policy governed
by a positive political aim - the nature of the
peace they sought. However, in August 1914, there
was no Anglo-French position, and the military
point of view quickly filled the vacuum to become
the sole view; that is, the means monopolized the
end.[22]
  Allied disunity reached its climax at Paris in
1919, but continued thereafter and is still with us,
plaguing every step of our international relations.
The Allies were generally in agreement in their
sincere desire for peace but they could not agree
on the means by which they might attain this security. The Americans, and the British to a degree,
tended to put their faith in the reasonableness of
democratic institutions, whereas the French saw as
the solution the prevention of any future German
aggression by concrete guarantees.[23]
  The postwar period opened on a sour note with
the French demanding that the Peace Conference be

held in Paris. This got the whole tragic series of
events off on the wrong foot. The French refused
all proposals that the conference be held in a neutral country. They would accept no other location.
It was an unhappy choice because the German invasion had only exacerbated earlier feelings making
the French capital a hotbed of anti-German sentiment. The mood of the city, and particularly of
the press, urged for a hard peace and supported the
official French view when the peace delegations
disagreed. Fuller described the scene: "Thus it
came about that the primeval code of enmity dominated the Peace Conference, and in Clemenceau the
war-crazed democracies found their Cato."[24] The
feelings between Wilson and Clemenceau had grown
quite cold even before the conference opened as
Wilson wasted a month sitting around Paris waiting
for the Allies to agree to start the conference.
The Allies had great difficulty in agreeing on the
most elementary matters as each country reverted
more and more to its restricted national outlook.

> Few men have such broad vision that they can
> see earth as a whole, can realize all the in-
> fluence of that which happens far in the East
> upon him who dwells perchance in the farthest
> West. In the months that followed on the Ar-
> mistice, the thoughts of each ordinary man
> centered more and more upon his own nation,
> his own neighborhood, his own family, his own
> comfort.... The Central Powers of Europe had
> surrendered. Some disposition of them must be
> made. They must not be allowed strength ever
> to disrupt the world again. But on the exact
> methods by which this was to be done, scarcely
> any two men agreed, and no two nations were
> anywhere near agreement. Each studied the
> future from the viewpoint of its own nation-
> ality.[25]

With the eyes of the world fixed on Paris, the
"three old men" stepped into the limelight as the
stars of the show. They were a combination as varied as the nations they represented. President
Wilson was clearly tabbed as the idealist; he had
always been more adept at forming generalities than
in dealing with specifics. He had a flair for the
well-turned phrase and he used it repeatedly, such
as in his Thanksgiving Proclamation in November
1918: "Complete victory has brought us, not peace
alone, but the confident promise of a new day as

38

well, in which justice shall replace force and
jealous intrigue among nations."26 For Wilson and
many liberals and idealists, the formation of the
League of Nations redeemed whatever mistakes and
extravagances were contained in the treaties and
gave promise for a new order in world affairs. But
Wilson was more firmly grounded in his liberal beliefs than in an understanding of the history of
peacemaking. The Fourteen Points were excellent
propaganda and also quite worthy aims, but they
were bound to run into trouble with the real war
aims of the Allies many of which had been agreed to
in secret treaties: France wanted Alsace and Lorraine back, Great Britain was anxious to curb Germany's sea power, Italy wanted Italia irredenta,
the Balkan states desired complete independence,
and Japan wanted to extend her power in the Pacific.

It was a foregone conclusion that Wilson's
ideals would become quite tarnished and he had to
compromise a great deal to get his league of nations.
Though the British like to consider themselves the
realists of 1919, Great Britain was the home of
Wilsonian idealism, the achievement of British Lib-
eralism. Wilson was described by a journalist as
"Gladstone with an American accent." The League,
according to some, was just as much an English as
an American idea. Lloyd George had been quite liberal in his approach to the Peace Conference until
the hate at home threatened his political position.
He was too much of a politician to ignore, thereafter, the pleas to "hang the Kaiser" and "make
Germany pay" and his position hardened. Wilson had
a rough time at Paris but tragedy really befell him
when he went home and found the Senate against him,
and he lost all he had worked so hard for. Wilson
and Lloyd George worked for a peace of conciliation,
while Clemenceau worked for a peace of victory.

The total victory bug had bitten everyone.
When Clemenceau came to power in November 1917, he
made it clear that France was bent on absolute victory and would brook no half measures. Clemenceau
was an old man and he had waited a long time for
this day. One almost constant theme recurred in
French journals from 1871 to 1914: revanche, revenge for the defeat suffered at the hands of Germany.

> When he heard that Germany had accepted the
> terms of the Armistice, he exultantly ex-
> claimed: "Enfin! Il est arrivé ce jour que
> j'attends depuis un demisiècle! Il est arriveé

(sic) le jour de la revanche!"... His policy
was to put back the clock and undo all that
Germany had accomplished since 1870. He
"stood throughout the Peace Conference," writes
C. Howard Ellis, "for nothing but hatred and
fear, and a cynically frank desire to cripple
and fetter (Germany) for ever." It was he and
not the President who dominated the Conference,
and to him the President's Charter was senti-
mental humbug: "Quatorze commandements!" he
contemptuously exclaimed, "C'est un peu raide!
Le bon Dieu n'en avait que dix!" And to the
misfortune of France, out of his slogan "La
guerre est finie, la guerre continue" emanated
the catastrophe of 1940.[27]

Clemenceau and Wilson "remained courteous, but
there was certainly no friendly feeling between
them. 'If you can persuade me that your plans are
better for the peace of the world, I am willing to
listen and to learn,' said Mr. Wilson. 'And if you
can persuade me, so much the better,' replied M.
Clemenceau. 'Only - you cannot!'" [28] That would
not normally be considered the diplomatic approach.
"'Great in criticism and destruction only' - that
was the stereotyped description."[29] Clemenceau delighted in referring to Lloyd George as the most
ignorant man he ever met. Lloyd George's ignorance
of European geography and of the racial and economic problems of Central and Eastern Europe was notorious. Of the Big Four, Sumner Welles felt that
Clemenceau was the most realistic and the most consistent in that he never wavered in his determination to obtain security and reparations for
France[30] - although both proved to be illusory.
It is interesting here to note the feelings of
two important British statesmen on American participation in the war.

... in August 1936 - Mr. Churchill in a statement to William Griffen, editor of the New
York Enquirer, is reported by the latter to
have said that "America should have minded her
own business and stayed out of the World War.
If you hadn't entered the war the Allies would
have made peace with Germany in the Spring of
1917. Had we made peace then there would have
been no collapse in Russia followed by Communism, no breakdown in Italy followed by Fascism, and Germany would not have signed the
Versailles Treaty, which has enthroned Nazism

40

in Germany. If America had stayed out of the war, all these 'isms' wouldn't to-day be sweeping the continent of Europe and breaking down parliamentary government, and if England had made peace early in 1917, it would have saved over one million British, French, American, and other lives."[31]

The ability to make America responsible for all the world's problems was already developed to a high degree even before World War II. The other view was by Ramsay MacDonald who, in August 1917, told Wilson that there were some who "regret" US entry

"...because (a) they do not think that American help was required in order to compel any of the Powers to make a reasonable peace; and (b) they think that America, out of the war, would have done more for peace and good feeling than in the war, and would also have had a better influence on the peace settlement." Further he wrote: "... whilst you can have peace without victory, history shows that as a rule nations have had victory without peace."[32]

This was an astute observation of history.

It seems clear that the combination of commitments and "hard facts" largely predetermined the Peace of Paris. It was a long document of over 200 pages that had been long fought over by the Allies before being presented to the Germans. They sent 443 pages of reply, but except for one small change, it was the treaty under threat of invasion if they failed to sign. The old ministry resigned rather than sign, but the new ministry reluctantly accepted the treaty unconditionally on 23 June 1919. As months passed, it gradually became apparent that those gathered at Paris who had the power to shape the future world were departing more and more from the crisp principles of the Fourteen Points, partly because of the greed of some of their governments, partly because of political expediency, and, finally, because of clamor at home for immediate demobilization and a speedy windup of the job of peacemaking. These arbiters of human destiny seemed less and less like prophets and more and more like harassed, tired, and irritable old men. The aura of emotional optimism evaporated in a wave of cold and cynical pessimism. General Smuts wrote his

41

wife on 20 May 1919, "It is a terrible document, not a peace treaty but a war treaty, and I am troubled in my conscience about putting my name to such a document." On 3 June, he wrote to Mrs. Gillet, "The last battle of the war is being fought out in Paris, and we look like losing that battle and with it the whole war."[33]

John of Salisbury wrote long ago: "Once a certain man of Privernum, when asked how the captives from his city would keep the peace if they were granted amnesty, replied to the Roman consul: 'If you grant them an advantageous peace, they will keep it forever; if a disadvantageous one, they will not keep it long.'"[34] Peace should not be dictated if it is to be genuine and lasting, but negotiated so as to bring into accord the interests of the warring nations. The Versailles peace was not a real peace; in fact one could almost say that it was not even an armistice because, although the military operations had ceased, the economic and political struggle went on. More has probably been written about the Treaty of Versailles than about any other treaty in history. We need only to look at a couple of points in it as it is still important as an indication of a basic problem - that of winning the war and then losing the peace.

> To demand from the vanquished the recognition of war guilt was one of the incredible mistakes committed at Paris. The intention of those who formulated the fateful paragraphs was probably not to humiliate Germany. It sprang from the French passion for logic. Germany was to be saddled with reparations.[35]

The theory was that reparations would use up all German foreign exchange and there would be nothing left for rearmament.

> In theory this system worked very well. In practice, however, reparations were paid not by Germany but by her foreign creditors. Germany regularly borrowed abroad the amounts paid in reparations, which meant that it was possible for her to make reparation payments without materially interfering with her capacity to import. Indeed, since the loans from abroad were in excess of the amounts paid in reparations during a number of years, Germany had a regular import surplus.[36]

42

These statements were probably somewhat biased since they were written during World War II; however, Germany, the great debtor, borrowed more money between 1924 and 1930 than she paid in reparations. Therefore, the payments actually made were merely bookkeeping manipulations. The Reparations Commission reported in April 1921 that Germany's bill should be fixed at about 32 billion dollars. By the summer of 1923, the German mark had sunk to 20,000,000 to the pound (245 in early 1921), and Germans were using their currency for wallpaper.[37]

Encouraged by irresponsible propaganda, the peoples of the victorious nations believed that they could replace all their war costs with German reparations.[38] The French finance minister, M. Klotz, justifying his extravagant expenditures on reconstruction, advertised the slogan: "Germany will pay for everything." Marshall Foch, though not a financial expert, was realistic enough to declare: "With this treaty, Germany will pay us in funny money." In Great Britain Mr. Lloyd George, on the advice of a committee of financial experts, went to the elections of 1918 with a program of collecting many billions of dollars from Germany.[39] One of the problems was that all the reparations claimants wanted cash instead of goods transfers, each hoping that someone else would take the goods that would make the payments possible.[40]

> Only by degrees did the stunning truth reach
> out to the mind of the common man, that Ger-
> many could not pay. Hence there was to be no
> satisfying restitution. Destruction is so
> much easier than creation.[41]

> There, then, lay the root difficulty. Germany
> could not pay! To an American, comparatively
> little injured by the War, the philosophic
> conclusion came easily enough. "In that case,
> let her pay what she can. Cancel the rest."
> This easy critic was scarce prepared for the
> fierce European response, "Then will you pay
> for her? Will you make good to us from your
> abundance?" To the American this seemed only
> another demand for charity, and he had been
> already largely charitable. The European
> looked upon the situation in another light.
> He had suffered to save civilization, which
> included saving the American. The latter, af-
> ter long prospering in trade from the War, had

only joined it just at the end, and hence had done but a small part of his fair share. It was only just that he should now contribute money where the others had paid so much more heavily in blood. Here came a widening breach between the European and the American. Whatever the latter might do to aid seemed to the former insufficient. [42]

This strange logic still exists and is a current Allied problem in the Cold War. As of 30 June 1971, twenty European countries still owe the US $22,695,277,117.84 as debts from World War I. [43] The Allies were unhappy with their treaty even before they finished it. "When Marshal Foch heard of the signing of the Peace Treaty of Versailles he observed with singular accuracy: 'This is not Peace. It is an Armistice for twenty years.'"[44] In the years after the war, there were continual problems with the implementation of the treaty, and the Germans quickly devoted themselves to negating the Versailles Treaty. A recurrent problem was German evasion of reparations payments which led to repeated Allied concessions, made usually upon British insistence and almost invariably at the expense of France. The impression was soon created that Great Britain was operating as arbiter, or at least as a mediator, between France and Germany, rather than as the ally of France in executing the provisions of the Versailles Treaty. This disunity between Britain and France was the last fatal weakness with the practical result that the Treaty was neither modified honorably as the British desired nor enforced as the French desired. And so it turned out that the treaty, for practical purposes, was either too severe or too lenient. It was too severe to conciliate, and too lenient to destroy. The victors should have dealt more moderately with the new German republic, which professed their own ideals, much as the monarchial victors over Napoleon in 1814 had dealt moderately with the French Bourbons, regarding them as a regime akin to their own. As it was, the Allies imposed upon the German Republic about the same terms that they might have imposed upon the German Empire. They naively played the game of Ludendorff and the German reactionaries, because it was the Social Democrats and liberals who bore the "shame" of Versailles.

There had been great optimism such as Sumner Welles reflected:

Most of us who came of age shortly before the
outbreak of the first World War passionately
believed when the last shot was fired on November 11, 1918, that we were headed toward a new
and better world. We were confident that the
errors of the past were to be valiantly correc-
ted; that human wrongs would all be righted;
that the self-determination of peoples would
end oppression; that human freedom and individual security would become realities; that war,
in this new dawn breaking over the earth, was
now a nightmare of the past.[45]

Unfortunately, though, this optimism faded
away. Some blamed America because she withdrew from
the bickerings in Europe, saying, "America refused
to lead;" but, even if she had led, Europe would not
have followed. As World War I receded into the past,
and as mankind welcomed the new years of peace,
thoughtful men could evaluate with greater perspective the popular slogans of the war years. It became clear that decisive victories on the battlefield were not followed by equally decisive victories at the conference table. There was the disillusionment that followed upon the recognition that
the world had not been made "safe for democracy."
Churchill summed it up eloquently on Armistice Day,
1937.

Armistice does not mean Peace.... The Peace had
still to be made, and Peace was never made, except on paper.... Then came a period which it
was easy to predict, when the victors forgot,
and the vanquished remembered.... We entered
upon that strange period in our history which
may be called "The Aftermath." This phrase
marks the state of national prostration, the
loss of theme, which will long excite the curi-
osity of historians. The disease of Defeat was
Bolshevism. But Bolshevism, in Foch's remarkable words, "never crossed the frontiers of
Victory." The disease of Victory was different. It was an incapacity to make Peace.[46]

4. The Cost

The most terrible war up until that time had
wrought havoc upon the belligerents and the toll in
lives and property was enormous. Who, then, won the

45

First World War? It is fairly safe to say, "that
though Germany undoubtedly lost the war, no one
really won it, and Germany finally persuaded herself
that she had not lost it."[47] France, though victorious, lost the friendship of England and of the neutral countries and, in spite of her punitive program, received no reparations.

The fever of total victory resulted in payment
of a high price. "The German military colossus was
broken, we may say with confident hope, forever.
The cost to Europe had been terrible, immeasurable;
but the victory was complete. The Great War had
achieved its purpose."[48] This faith in total victory is all the more interesting in that it was
written over a decade after the war. It was a Pyrrhic victory for France and England as the war had
"lasted too long." The holding out by the West "for
complete victory was ill-advised because it entailed
exhaustion."[49] The West failed to realize that prolonged warfare in the industrial age was certain to
be self-defeating.

A gap appeared during the war between military
and political planning. The military staffs developed plans for total victory because in such
plans no political limitations interfere with the
full employment of power, and all factors are under
the control of the military. However, the political leadership was unable to give these military objectives a political expression in terms of peace
aims. It was forgotten that the quick decision of
nineteenth-century warfare had been due, primarily,
to the willingness to acknowledge defeat. And defeat was acknowledged with relative ease because it
did not threaten the national survival. When total
victory became the war's aim, however, the result
was a conflict of ever increasing violence which
petrified its hatred in a peace treaty that stressed
more the redressing of sacrifices than the stability
of the international order.[50] The propaganda-fed
hate of total war had led people to forget the purpose of war. The peace and stability of the world
were given less importance than the punishment of
the conquered. To strive to reduce a modern industrial country to an agricultural and pacific level
was retrogression and not likely to succeed.

"The total defeat of Germany was due to three
cardinal mistakes: the decision to march through
Belgium regardless of bringing Britain into the war;
the decision to begin unrestricted U-boat war regardless of bringing the United States into the war;
and thirdly, the decision to use the German forces

liberated from Russia in 1918 for a final onslaught
in France. But for the first mistake they would
have beaten France and Russia easily in a year; but
for the second mistake they would have been able to
make a satisfactory peace in 1917; but for the third
mistake they would have been able to confront the
Allies with an unbreakable front on the Meuse or on
the Rhine, and to have made self-respecting terms as
a price for abridging the slaughter."[51] These three
errors were committed by the same group that had
provided the German Empire with such great power --
the German General Staff. The great error was that
these decisions were made by the military when, in
reality, they were political decisions of the highest order. And so it was that when, at the end,
"the throng of uniformed functionaries who in the
seclusion of their offices had complacently pre-
sided over this awful process, presented Victory to
their exhausted nations, it proved only less ruinous to the victor than to the vanquished."[52]
     When the fighting stopped on 11 November 1918,
1,564 days after it had started, the world had been
through its bloodiest and most costly war. The figures were staggering. Of 65,000,000 men mobilized,
over 8,000,000 were dead, and the loss in civilian
lives was similar. Over 21,000,000 were wounded and
there were nearly 8,000,000 prisoners and missing.
Nearly 61 percent of the total number of men killed
in the fighting forces belonged to the Allies. In
comparative figures, the deaths among military personnel alone amounted to twice those of the total
of the six bloodiest wars of the Western world in
the nineteenth and early twentieth centuries.[53] War
strikes not only the man in uniform, particularly
now in total war, some ten millions of civilians
died through privation, pestilence, and actual gun-
fire. There were 9,000,000 fatherless children,
5,000,000 widows, and 10,000,000 refugees. One estimate of the direct cost of World War I was 186
billion dollars, whereas estimates of the indirect
costs - "the capitalized value of lives lost and
property destroyed" - ranged from 150 billions to
almost 500 billions.[54] The figures vary with sources, but see Table 2.1 for a general idea of the
costs of the war. The determination of which costs
were actually war costs and which were not is extremely difficult; however, although the exact figures may be in doubt, their magnitude is what is
important and what gives a picture of the enormous
expense of the war. "For a period of 25 months,
from April, 1917, through April, 1919, the war cost

Table 2.1 COSTS OF THE WAR AT A GLANCE[57]

COST IN HUMAN LIFE

```
Army deaths.........................................8,000,000
Civilian deaths.....................................8,000,000
Permanent human wrecks from wounds, etc.............6,000,000

    Total human loss (chiefly of vigorous males)    22,000,000
```

COST IN PROPERTY DESTROYED

```
France (factories, farms, public works, etc.) $ 10,000,000,000
Belgium....................................... 5,000,000,000
Other surviving countries.....................13,000,000,000
Russia (losses really incalculable)...........20,000,000,000
Ships (chiefly British)....................... 3,500,000,000
Cargoes....................................... 4,500,000,000

    Total direct property loss.................$ 56,000,000,000
```

COST IN MONEY

```
Government expenditure by Allies..............$105,000,000,000
Government expenditure by Central Powers...... 65,000,000,000
Increased charitable expenditures............. 2,000,000,000
Loss by bankruptcy of Russia, Turkey, etc..... 30,000,000,000

    Total direct money loss....................$202,000,000,000
```

TOTAL FINANCIAL ESTIMATES OF COST

```
Human life (as based on life insurance
    figures)..................................$ 70,000,000,000
Direct property destruction................... 56,000,000,000
Money loss.................................... 202,000,000,000
Indirect property and money loss (through
    lack of usual peacetime products)......... 150,000,000,000

    Final total............................... $478,000,000,000
```

NOTE: As a basis for valuing this enormous sum of almost half
a trillion dollars, take the fact that the total wealth of the
United States, the richest country in the world, was valued at
$220,000,000,000 in 1916. In other words, if the United States
and another country, equally wealthy, had been engulfed in
some vast earthquake, without loss of human life, the financial
loss would have scarce equaled that of the War.

the United States considerably more than $1,000,000
an hour."[55] The Carnegie Endowment for International Peace stated in 1940 that the new war had already
cost the United States 57 billion dollars and gave
as their fiture for the cost of the first war,
$337,846,189,657.[56] Figures of this order are in-
comprehensible. One historian who arrived at the
total war cost of $400,000,000,000 in property ex-
plained it this way -- this amount of money would
build a $2,500 house with $1,000 furniture on five
acres of land worth $100 an acre for every family in
the United States, Canada, Australia, England, Wales,
Ireland, Scotland, France, Belgium, Germany, and
Russia. There would still be enough to provide each
country with a $5,000,000 library and a $10,000,000
university, endow salaries for 125,000 teachers and
125,000 nurses, and then buy up France and Belgium.
That should be enough to make one stop and wonder
about the sensibility of war. Whether this expenditure of blood and treasure was justified by the results is an unanswerable question because we do not
know the "or else."

One of the high costs of the war was the end of
the age of European supremacy. Europe, which had
always been the center of the Western world and had
influenced if not dominated the rest, had been sliding before the war, but this great debacle pushed
her under. Modern technology had opened up the rest
of the world and had brought trade to and from all
corners. World War I shattered the well-integrated,
nineteenth century system. It destroyed financial
stability in most countries and saddled the world
with huge reparation payments and war debts with
which the conventional trade-adjustment mechanism
could not cope. The United States had become a creditor nation requiring a more significant role in international relations even though the Americans temporarily tried to withdraw behind their oceans and
isolate themselves.

The disunity between the Allies and the general
lack of ability to make peace left the door wide
open for the Second World War.[58] However, as the
interwar years revealed, the most powerful victor
must possess a will to act if its power is to be
translated into influence. When a nation is declared to be criminal, there must be some means
available for that nation to resume its place in the
world community; we cannot pretend it no longer exists. For the Germans the Versailles Treaty was
simply a continuation of the war by other means,
whereas in the opinion of the Allies the resistance

of the German people was a sure sign of German war
guilt. Neither interpretation takes into account
the elementary psychology of nations. Germany was
condemned to disgrace as a criminal nation, and that
gave the Germans courage in their struggle. While
the winners returned to their normal complacency and
bickering, the losers studied the war to see what
had gone wrong.

> As is usual in war, it was the losing side
> which learnt most. Whereas the victors looked
> upon the war as an incident which had been
> liquidated, the vanquished saw in it the con-
> sequence of faulty action. To Russia and Ger-
> many the supreme lessons of the war were the
> increasing necessity for (1) political author-
> ity in war; (2) national discipline in war; (3)
> economic self-sufficiency in war; and (4) tech-
> nology in war. And the same factors affected
> peace also, in order to be prepared for war.[59]

The political authority and national discipline
were effected by strong dictatorships. Economic
self-sufficiency and modern technology required considerable work and the Germans lost little time in
getting started. In 1924, the German Government ordered a census of machine tools. From that time onward, the specifications of all machine tools had to
be submitted to the Reichswehr. The plan was that
newly manufactured machine tools should be easily
convertible to arms production. A strong and modern
machine tool industry is a prerequisite for sustained war. The miracle of German reconstruction
that in a few short years presented Germany on the
European scene with a new army was based on this capacity for the production of machine tools which
they had systematically rebuilt. Thereafter, Germany developed her production of synthetic oil and
rubber even though it was not economically profitable. In addition to the strategic value for war,
they reaped a bonus in that it created employment
which, thereby, increased the popularity of the Nazi
regime. German tank, poison gas, and airplane factories were secretly set up on Soviet territory and,
really planning ahead, Germany bought oil-boring
machinery even though there was not any obvious eco-
nomical use for it - they kept it until they got the
Polish and Rumanian oilfields.
The specter of Versailles always hung over the
head of the Weimar Republic in its struggle to come
of age. The political responsibility for the

50

Versailles Treaty was a cause of its demise and of the rise of National-Socialism. The "tyranny of Versailles" weighed heavily on German minds. Goering recounted how he searched for a revolutionary group and joined the Nazi Party because it was "the only one that had the guts to say, 'To hell with Versailles!'"[60] And so it went and Germany was soon on the march again.

The Great War showed that a radical change in international relations was needed to allow nations to be secure. No nation could be safe by its own arms or by alliances. Collective security was the answer, but acceptance of the obligations of collective security involved a break with deeply rooted traditions; the revolutionary period in the world's history heralded by the first total war called for radical measures.[61] But the nations were too smug in their exaggerated nationalism, too busy in their new rivalries, new intrigues, and new alliances, too busy building armies and navies. The nations of the world were once again sliding toward war. Will mankind ever learn its lesson? The war was a victory for democracy, though indeed a bitter one. It furthered a process as old as the French and American revolutions. But for the basic problems of modern civilization, industrialism, nationalism, insecurity, and competitive struggle, it gave no answer.

5. The Russian Revolution

There remains one result of the First World War that we must consider, not as a study in victory, but because of its influence on history and the key role it would play in future world affairs. That is, of course, the Russian Revolution of 1917. This was a direct product of World War I in that this unpopular war brought down the already tottering Czarist government. The roots of the revolution went back many years, but events finally burst forth in late 1916 and early 1917 to topple the Czar. This was not accomplished by the Communists (or Bolsheviks as they were then called), but by the Social Revolutionaries under Kerensky. Lenin failed once, in July, in an attempt to overthrow Kerensky and had to flee. However, in the Fall, he was back and this time he was successful. Lenin and the Bolsheviks did not bring about the Russian Revolution. They captured it and turned it to their advantage. Once in power, and having been repudiated at the polls

51

showing they did not have popular support, they proceeded to smash all opposition and establish their dictatorship. The newly elected Assembly was dispatched at gunpoint. "The dissolution of the Constituent Assembly by the Soviet Government," as Lenin observed to Trotsky, "means a complete and frank liquidation of the idea of democracy by the idea of dictatorship." The dictatorship of the proletariat was now established. Two months later, in March 1918, the Bolsheviks renamed themselves the Communist Party.[62]

The Soviet Council of People's Commissars met for six hours every day under Lenin's chairmanship, and a fantastic stream of decrees poured out of Smolny. The program that evolved, the likes of which had never been seen in the world before, uprooted every institution and tradition in Russian life. Private ownership in land was abolished followed by the nationalization of the banks, the merchant marine, and all industrial enterprises. The stock market was eliminated as were rights of inheritance.[63] Russia would never be the same again! Lenin had to consolidate his position and to do that he had to terminate the war with Germany. He was certainly in no strong bargaining position as the results of Brest-Litovsk clearly reflected. "Russia's losses were appalling: 26 percent of her population, 27 percent of her arable land, 73 percent of her iron industries, 75 percent of her coal fields. For this she had paid 2,500,000 in dead and wounded among her soldiers alone."[64] It could be expected that one day Russia would try to regain these lost lands. Russia plunged into a period of terror the likes of which had never before been seen, and into the throes of civil war.

The Allied governments still wanted Russia in the war against Germany, believing that Bolshevism was a temporary madness that, with a little effort, could be stopped. There followed a period of Allied intervention in Russia; but, as was so characteristic of many Allied ventures, it was so racked with disunity that the piecemeal efforts put forth yielded nothing but greater enmity.[65] This should probably be regarded as one of the greatest failures of the Western powers. The British and Americans were anxious to rid themselves of all military entanglements after the Armistice and were quick to drift into their old complacent ways. This continued failure to look ahead and lack of willingness to make the necessary sacrifices to solve the crucial problems of the moment before they eventually come

smashing down on us in the form of war will haunt
the free nations for years to come. Communist tactics should have been no surprise. All the Bolshevik plans were known in advance. Lenin had announced them even more clearly than Hitler had announced his plans in Mein Kampf. The Germans lived
to rue the day they secretly transported Lenin from
Switzerland to Russia to set the world in a turmoil
that persists to this day.

With various groups of anti-Communists fighting in the civil war and the halfhearted Allied
pressures on the east and west and the north and
south, Russia was treated as a leper and as an out-
cast nation. The Bolsheviks generally quelled the
civil war by 1920 although Poland, with significant
French support, obtained much additional Russian
territory by the Peace of Riga. Lenin had to have
peace in order to start building. The "Iron Curtain" had really already fallen. By the mid-
twentieth century the Soviet Union was still not
conducting as much foreign trade as was the Russian
Empire on the eve of the First World War. Except
for the lost lands in the West, the Communists had
under their power the old Czarist Empire which they
now reorganized and designated as the Union of Soviet Socialist Republics.

By the end of the civil war and intervention,
hundreds of thousands of people had starved to
death - out of Petrograd's 2,000,000 inhabitants
only 700,000 remained.[66] Then, famine struck. Here
the outside world made a humanitarian decision to
help the Russian people and much relief aid was provided. It should be very seriously reviewed to determine whether it was more humane to aid the people
and thereby assure the Communists of staying in
power or to have refused the aid in hopes of topp-
ling the Communist regime, which thereafter liquidated many more people than were saved from starvation.

The Red Terror was successful. Along with the
Red Army, it firmly established the Communist regime. The Jacobin Terror paled before the Bolshevik
Terror whose goal was to wipe out whole classes.
This goal was carried out with utter ruthlessness
and, probably, no accurate figures will ever appear
to show how many millions of people were liquidated
to bring this great, "classless" social system into
being. No bourgeois, as such, ever again presumed
to take part in the politics of Russia. But all was
not rosy for the Communists. In Lenin's last article in March 1923, he admitted what a mess things

53

were in. He was a disillusioned man. Fuller hit
him a parting blow: "'Qui veut faire l'ange, fait
la bête,' such is the uninscribed epitaph on Lenin's
tomb."[67]

The consequences of the October Revolution in
Russia were not to be felt in great measure until
Stalin consolidated his power and reaped the har-
vest of victory in World War II. But the products
of this revolution, the Soviet Union and the continued threat of world Communism, will be with us
as an undercurrent throughout the chapters ahead
and are of utmost importance in world politics today. This revolution, coming in the turmoil of the
First World War, was certainly one of the most significant events in modern history. In its name,
millions of human beings have been killed, millions
more exploited in slave-labor camps, and a billion
people have been brought under the control of a totalitarian dictatorship.

NOTES

1. Kennan, Russia and the West under Lenin and
Stalin (Boston: Little, Brown & Co., 1961), p. 47,
emphasis in original.
2. Homer Lea, The Valor of Ignorance (New York:
Harper & Brothers, 1942), p. 139.
3. W. S. Churchill, The World Crisis 1911-1918
(New York: Scribner's, 1923-31), 6 vols., p. 112,
in conversation with Herr Ballin over from Germany
just before World War I.
4. Fuller, A Military History of the Western
World, Vol. III, pp. 173-174.
5. Herman Kahn, On Thermonuclear War (Princeton
University Press, 1961), p. 359.
6. Ibid., p. 358.
7. Horne, Source Records of the Great War, Vol.
I, p. xvii.
8. See Fuller, The Conduct of War, p. 178.
9. Charles F. T. Brooke, ed., War Aims and
Peace Ideals (New Haven: Yale University Press,
1919), p. 6.
10. Ibid., p. 227. Also in Thomas P. Brockway,
Basic Documents in United States Foreign Policy
(Princeton: D. Van Nostrand Co., 1957), p. 87.
11. Ibid., p. 229, my italics.
12. Walter Lippmann, U. S. Foreign Policy:
Shield of the Republic (Boston: Little, Brown & Co.,
1943), pp. 32-33.
13. Ibid., p. 37.

14. Sir Norman Angell, The Great Illusion, Now (Harmondsworth: Penguin Books Ltd., 1938), p. 15.

15. George F. Kennan, American Diplomacy 1900-1950 (Chicago: University of Chicago Press, 1951), p. 63. Fuller, The Conduct of War, p. 177, said the war was ended, "not by fighting, but by famine and revolution." He saw as the two most important factors the British blockade and skillful British propaganda.

16. Kennan, American Diplomacy, pp. 66-67.

17. Ibid., p. 67.

18. Horne, Source Records of the Great War, Vol. VI, p. xxxviii. See also Fuller, The Conduct of War, p. 182.

19. Churchill, The World Crisis, p. 814.

20. Ibid., pp. 817-818.

21. Churchill, The World Crisis, p. 817.

22. Fuller, The Conduct of War, p. 152. General Fuller called Marshal Foch "one of the few outstanding generals of World War I. Nevertheless, he was so carried away by his theory that the offensive à outrance could alone lead to victory, that he was blind to its contradictions." p. 122, phrase in French and italics in original.

23. William Beveridge, The Price of Peace (London: Pilot, 1945), p. 21, including some quotes from Harold Nicolson's Peacemaking, 1919. France wanted a strong League of Nations, capable of watching over Germany, enforcing peace treaties, having for this purpose a military force, a true instrument of collective security. The Anglo-Saxons, on the other hand, were hostile to this "international militarism," estimating that a military force would threaten to limit national sovereignty. Pierre Gerbet, Les Organisations Internationales (Paris: Presses Universitaires de France, 1958), p. 18.

24. Fuller, The Conduct of War, p. 221.

25. Horne, Source Records of the Great War, Vol. Vii, p. xiv.

26. Ibid., Vol. VI, p. 431.

27. Fuller, The Conduct of War, p. 219, Clemenceau's quotes are in French and italicized in the book.

28. Horne, Source Records of the Great War, Vol. VII, pp. 49-50.

29. Ibid., Vol. VII, p. 61.

30. Sumner Welles, The Time for Decision (New York: Harper Brothers, 1944), pp. 13-14. Walter Lippmann, US War Aims (London: H. Hamilton, 1944), p. 99, felt (in 1944) that Clemenceau was right and Wilson wrong. In 1919, the world needed a lasting

settlement with Germany. Wilson, preferring peace
in general, forgot about Germany.

31. Fuller, A Military History of the Western
World, Vol. III, p. 271.
32. Ibid.
33. William K. Hancock, Four Studies of War
and Peace in this Century (Cambridge: University
Press, 1961), pp. 35-36.
34. From "The Statesman's Book", in Ebenstein,
Great Political Thinkers (New York: Rhinehart & Co.,
1951), p. 202.
35. Egon Ranshofen-Wertheimer, Victory Is Not
Enough: The Strategy for a Lasting Peace (New York:
W. W. Norton, 1942), p. 26.
36. Paul Einzig, Can We Win the Peace? (London:
Macmillan, 1942), p. 50. See also Fuller, The Conduct of War, p. 223. The Allies had quickly discovered, that if they were to revive their international trade, "it was more profitable for them to
restore Germany's economy than to shackle it."
37. See William L. Shirer, The Rise and Fall of
the Third Reich, A History of Nazi Germany (Greenwich, Conn.: Fawcett Publications, 1962), pp. 95-97.
The mark went on to trillions to the dollar (Fuller
gives the figure 4,200,000,000,000 in November).
Shirer says "the government deliberately let the
mark tumble in order to free the State of its public debts, to escape from paying reparations and to
sabotage the French in the Ruhr." p. 96.
38. Ferdinand O. Miksche, Unconditional Surrender, The Roots of World War III (London: Faber &
Faber, 1952), p. 146.
39. Einzig, Can We Win the Peace?, p. 136.
40. Ibid., p. 131.
41. Horne, Source Records of the Great War,
Vol. VII, p. xxvii, italics in original.
42. Ibid., Vol. VII, pp. xxviii-xxix.
43. The 1972 World Almanac and Book of Facts,
Lumay H. Long, ed. (New York: Newspaper Enterprise
Association, Inc.), p. 478.
44. Churchill, The Gathering Storm, Vol. I of
The Second World War (Boston: Houghton Mifflin Co.,
1948-53), p. 7.
45. Welles, Time for Decision, p. 3.
46. Churchill, Step by Step 1936-39 (London:
Macmillan, 1943), pp. 176-177. See also Fuller, The
Conduct of War, p. 217.
47. Beveridge, Price of Peace, pp. 25-26. Hin-
denberg's election as President in March 1925 manifested the victory of the myth of an 'undefeated'
Germany." Paul Kecskemeti, Strategic Surrender: The

<u>Politics of Victory and Defeat</u> (Stanford: Stanford
University Press, 1958), p. 124.
     48. Horne, <u>Source Records of the Great War</u>,
Vol. VI, p. xl.
     49. Kecskemeti, <u>Strategic Surrender</u>, p. 234.
     50. Kissinger, <u>Nuclear Weapons and Foreign
Policy</u>, p. 88.
     51. Churchill, <u>The World Crisis</u>, p. 671.
     52. Ibid., p. 534.
     53. Palmer and Perkins, <u>International Rela-
tions</u>, p. 455.
     54. Ibid., pp. 274-275.
     55. Horne, <u>Source Records of the Great War</u>,
Vol. VII, p. 147 (rear of book).
     56. <u>The Cost of War</u> (Washington, D.C.: Carnegie
Endowment for International Peace), pp. 2 and 4.
     57. Horne, <u>Source Records of the Great War</u>,
Vol. VII, this table is presented along with a
group of tables at the back of the book.
     58. Horne, <u>Source Records of the Great War</u>,
Vol. III, pp. xiii-xiv, said that in 1915 Germany
lowered its goal from world victory to European victory. "World victory was now quite frankly laid
aside as too large an attempt. It was to be the
goal of a later war, for which this one was to prepare the foundations." This statement is all the
more interesting as it was written in 1930.
     59. Fuller, <u>A Military History of the Western
World</u>, Vol. III, p. 379.
     60. G. M. Gilbert, <u>Nuremburg Diary</u> (New York:
Farrar, Strauss and Company, 1947), p. 67.
     61. Beveridge, <u>Price of Peace</u>, pp. 28-29.
     62. For a good, short review of the Russian
Revolution, see Possony, <u>A Century of Conflict</u>,
pp. 27-28.
     63. Alan Moorehead, <u>The Russian Revolution</u> (New
York: Harper & Row, 1958), p. 261.
     64. Palmer and Perkins, <u>International Relations</u>,
p. 452.
     65. Kennan, <u>Russia and the West under Lenin and
Stalin</u>, p. 117, called these interventions "serious
mistakes." They made a deplorable impression in
Russia and strengthened the Bolsheviks. They compromised the enemies of the Bolsheviks, and he is
not sure the Bolsheviks would have prevailed without
"this ill-conceived interference."
     66. Fuller, <u>The Conduct of War</u>, p. 199.
     67. Fuller, <u>The Conduct of War</u>, pp. 200-201,
sentence italicized and in French in original.

3
Total War

Theirs not to reason why,
Theirs but to do and die:
Into the valley of Death
Rode the six hundred.[1]

-- Tennyson

War, in short, was no
longer for the warriors.[2]

1.   The Growth of the Idea of Total War

There are often differences of opinion as to
the definition of total war; however, upon closer
scrutiny, they are usually differences over fine
points and not really of substance.   Total war is
conceived as the nation in arms,[3] unlike the warfare of the past with armies in the field and life
continuing almost normally back home.   In the days
of weapons with very restricted ranges and modes of
transportation that were limited, it was fairly
easy to maintain a difference between the military
front and the people back home.   However, with the
introduction of the airplane and now the missile,
the modern battlefield in total war knows no limits
and there is not much meaning in the expression
"home front."   Whereas, the enemy army was usually
the main target before, we find now that the industry and economy of a country and the morale of its
people are more often considered as targets in
total war.
Total war comes about when the object of war is
to remove completely the enemy government or even to
extinguish any trace of the enemy as a separate nation.   One good way to visualize this is to think
of a civil war in which one government or the other
has to be completely destroyed for the nation to

continue to exist. An example of this was in
America from 1861-1865. "The Civil War was the
first of the modern total wars, and the American
democracy was almost totally unready to fight it."[4]
Both sides were slow to grasp the fact that it
would be a long war. Once this was finally realized, then the industrial dominance of the North
assured its victory. The march through Georgia by
General William T. Sherman brought home to the
South the hard fact that the Union could overpower
them.

> By mid-November, Sherman, who more than any
> Civil War general grasped the concept of total
> war, was ready to flame across Georgia, bring-
> ing the destructiveness of modern war to the
> heart of the Confederacy and demonstrating to
> the Southern people that the Union possessed a
> power which could not be resisted. What he was
> going to do might not be war, Sherman explained
> to Grant, but it was certainly statesmanship.[5]

Six months later the war was over, the Confederacy dissolved and the United States reunited
as one country. However, total war is not synonymous with civil war. The actions of Hitler whereby
he had Germany on a war footing and intended to assimilate certain other countries, particularly in
the east, are examples of total war. Certainly the
living embodiment of total war is Communism.
The Communists are continually at war and, as
such, completely direct the lives of their people
in a more strict manner than we ever do even in the
darkest periods of war. This centralized control
of every facet of Communist life permits the leadership to maneuver or react quickly in world politics.
The Communists recognized that military action is
only a small, and often insignificant, part of warfare. Marx and Engels have been called "the
fathers of modern total war." Modern strategists
discovered the four aspects of warfare -- diplomatic, economic, psychological, and as a last resort,
military.[6] This was common knowledge to the Communists. Total war, as developed into a science by
the Communists, is a much more serious thing than
anything we encountered in World War II.
The British Chiefs of Staff noted during the
war in a paper to Churchill:

> Total war is not an affair of military forces
> alone, using the word "military" in the widest

sense of the term. There are political, economic, industrial, and domestic implications
in almost every big war problem.[7]

Many people think that Total War is so-called
because it involves all the resources of the nation.
This puts the cart before the horse. It is the unlimited issues at stake that make a war total in
character. The issues that arise between groups of
men and that can truly be described as unlimited
are spiritual and emotional in character. In such
conflicts, one encounters terms such as "our way of
life," "our national independence," "our liberty,"
and "our freedom." When these are at stake, everything is thrown into the fray.[8] As Marshal Foch
observed, the wars of kings were ended; the wars of
peoples were beginning.[9]
Total war is a special case rather than being
the "normal" form of conflict. It results from an
abdication of political leadership or when differences are so extreme between the contenders that
the total destruction of the enemy appears to be
the only worthwhile goal. War was based on "purely"
military considerations only during short periods
of history: during the religious wars of the six-
teenth and seventeenth centuries, during the ideological schism of the wars of the French Revolution,
and during the cycle of wars beginning with World
War I. Between these outbreaks of maximum violence,
war was considered an extension of policy. In 1914,
war suddenly seemed to become an end in itself.
After the first few months of the war, none of the
protagonists would have been able to name an objective other than the total defeat of the enemy, or
other such extreme objectives, which amounted to
unconditional surrender.[10]
World War II worsened the situation with the
participants lost in their quest for Total Victory.
Some idea of this fever of democracy at Total War
can be seen in these extracts from President Roosevelt's Budget Message to Congress, 11 January 1943.

I am transmitting herewith a war Budget exceeding 100 billion dollars for the fiscal
year beginning July 1, 1943.

We wage total war because our very existence
is threatened. Without that supreme effort we
cannot hope to retain the freedom and self-
respect which give life its value.

Total war is grim reality. It means the dedi-
cation of our lives and resources to a single
objective: Victory.

Total war in a democracy is a violent conflict
in which everyone must anticipate that both
lives and possessions will be assigned to their
most effective use in the common effort - the
effort for community survival - National survival.

In total war we are all soldiers, whether in
uniform, overalls, or shirt sleeves.[11]

Total war requires nothing less than organizing
all the human and material resources of the
Nation.[12]

Here we see both aspects mentioned above: the
use of all resources and the unlimited issue at
stake.
      The turn of the century saw the Hague Confer-
ences striving to control war. Even though regulations governing wars grew constantly in volume in
the twentieth century, total war was reestablished
by the totalitarian powers. A German description
of total war refers to the utter destruction of the
vanquished nation and its final and complete disappearance from the stage of history.[13] Both the
democratic and totalitarian approaches had as final
objectives the removal of the enemy government. The
first wished to "liberate" the people and then let
them establish a free government, retaining their
status as a nation. However, the second wished to
remove not only the government but also the bonds
of nationality and assimilate the people into the
conquering empire. This concept did not die in the
bunker with Hitler; it remains a basic Communist
concept, though it is now in much more skillful
hands.
      The war had not started out as a total war.
Hitler pushed ahead to see how far he could go;
when he found the Allies shivering in their boots,
he pushed harder. The war probably did not really
become "total" before 1943. It was not until then
that the countries on both sides had fully mobilized their resources and their populations.
Hitler's plans were unsure; he thought little of
the English except that he vaguely hoped to come to
some form of an agreement with them. He thought
even less of the Americans, who were so far away,

and generally omitted them from his plans. His
flexible plans gradually turned to inflexible pressure to continue the war to the end, particularly
as the tide turned against the Nazis. The Unconditional Surrender formula did not help matters any.
As one German wrote:

> The decision to pursue the struggle at all
> costs was certainly made easier by the demand
> for "unconditional surrender" by the Allies.
> Since the Casablanca Conference,...it was a
> bogey man that nipped in the bud all tenden-
> cies toward any settlement and gave the real
> impetus to "total war."[14]

Unconditional Surrender goes hand in hand with
Total War and Total Victory. If Total Victory is
the goal of Total War, then Unconditional Surrender
is the manifestation of this victory, the act by
which the defeated nation falls prostrate before
the victor yielding all, its army, its economy, its
very existence.

Total War is ideological warfare, because nations are fighting for ideas, or against ideas, the
fine line of difference being determined, perhaps,
by who initiated hostilities. It is not by mere
chance that the word "crusade" becomes fashionable
in such wars. This type of warfare is often illogical, emotional, ruthless, and oblivious to postwar consequences, particularly for the offended nation. Democracies fighting total wars have shown
that they tend to become so emotionally absorbed in
the war that they never grasp the political problems which, if not properly solved, deprive the war
of any reason. It appears that the Communists fight
a total war without becoming so emotionally involved. Therefore, they are able to keep their
eyes on their political aims. This is an extremely
important point and shows our great weakness in the
event of a total war against the Communists. This
weakness is repeatedly demonstrated in the world of
sports. An athlete who becomes angry forgets the
fine points of his training and is quite often defeated by an athlete of lesser ability but who
manages to keep a cool, calculating approach to the
contest.

With nations defending, or attacking in accordance with, ideas of the utmost importance to them,
it is very easy to slip into the grip of the axiom,
"the end justifies the means." We have seen this
folly in the religious wars where "pious" people

led the attack to slay the "infidels." The world is still full of pious people and anyone who does not believe like they do is potentially an infidel. The nation's divine mission, be it the democratic crusade of Woodrow Wilson's America, the Nazi drive for a new world order, or the Soviet liberation of oppressed workers and peasants, precludes moderation and makes treason out of compromise. Since national ends are moral ends, conflicting aims of other peoples are necessarily bad. Therefore any means promoting national ends, particularly when embodied in the single will of a leader, are moral.

The vast destruction of World War II is explained in this fashion as being necessary. People like to reassure their consciences by fighting a "just" war and by fighting for what is "right."

In an election speech (March 24, 1936) shortly after retaking the Rhineland, Hitler declared himself to be a moral crusader above the law:

"If the rest of the world clings to the letter of treaties, I cling to an eternal morality. If they raise objections about paragraphs, I hold by the vital eternal rights of my people, by the equality of rights and duties. If they try to read avowals of guilt into such letters and paragraphs, then I, as the representative of the German people, must assert the nation's right to live - its honour, freedom and vital interests."[15]

One authority observed that Total War has coincided with total democracy and total autocracy.[16]

Another aspect of total war is its brutality and lack of support for the so-called rules of war. When a war is conceived as a holy war in which the enemy, be they Fascists or infidels, are damned in the eyes of God, of prophet, and of the faithful, then no rules are needed. The atrocities, brutalities, and general destructiveness of World War II were certainly not a credit to the level of civilization that we thought we had attained in the twentieth century. Churchill wrote at the beginning of his monumental work on the war:

Now in the Second World War every bond between man and man was to perish. Crimes were comitted by the Germans, under the Hitlerite domination to which they allowed themselves to be subjected, which find no equal in scale and wickedness with any that have darkened the human record. The wholesale massacre by systematized processes of six or seven millions of men, women, and children in the German execution camps exceeds in horrow the rough-and-ready butcheries of Genghis Khan, and in scale reduces them to pigmy proportions. Deliberate extermination of whole populations was contemplated and pursued by both Germany and Russia in the Eastern war. The hideous process of bombarding open cities from the air, one started by the Germans, was repaid twenty-fold by the ever-mounting power of the Allies, and found its culmination in the use of the atomic bombs which obliterated Hiroshima and Nagasaki.[17]

We will see more about the destructiveness of bombing in the next chapter.

The Nuremberg Judgment stated:

War crimes were committed on a vast scale, never before seen in the history of war.... There can be no doubt that the majority of them arose from the Nazi conception of "total war", with which the aggressive wars were waged. For in this conception of "total war", the moral ideas underlying the conventions which seek to make war more humane are no longer regarded as having force or validity. Everything is made subordinate to the over-mastering dictates of war....War crimes were committed when and wherever the Fuhrer and his close associates thought them to be advantageous. They were for the most part the result of cold and criminal calculation.[18]

As General Roudenko of the Soviet Union said in his opening remarks at the War Crimes Trials on 8 February 1946:

The accused knew that cynical contempt of the rules and customs of war was a most serious crime. They knew it, but they hoped that total war, assuring them victory, would bring immunity.
     Victory did not follow the path of these crimes.[19]

These crimes certainly represented a low point

65

in man's treatment of his fellow man.

However, horror in war is not new. There are examples of it throughout the pages of history. In 55 B.C. there was a mass migration of German tribes across the lower Rhine in the areas of what is now Belgium and Holland. Caesar acted, forcing them into a confluence of two rivers. Here the entire nation of 430,000 people was slaughtered, while only a few Romans were wounded. Arnold Toynbee gave one example of a leader who could have been known for his deeds for his country against its enemies but instead is known for his barbarism.

> To the vast majority of those to whom the name of Timur Lenk or Tamerlane means anything at all, it commemorates a militarist who perpetrated as many horrors in the span of twenty-four years as the last five Assyrian kings perpetrated in a hundred and twenty. We think of the monster who razed Isfara' into the ground in A.D. 1381; built 2,000 prisoners into a living mound and then bricked them over at Sabzawar in 1383; piled 5,000 human heads into minarets at Zirih in the same year; cast his Luri prisoners alive over precipices in 1386; massacred 70,000 people and piled the heads of the slain into minarets at Isfahan in 1387; massacred 100,000 prisoners at Delhi in 1398; buried alive 4,000 Christian soldiers of the garrison of Sivas after their capitulation in 1400; and built twenty towers of skulls in Syria in 1400 and 1401.[20]

So the millions who have died in the Soviet Union since 1917, in the German attempt to liquidate the Jews and the other victims in German concentration camps, and the many more millions that have died in China since the war, place Stalin, Hitler, and Mao Tse-tung on the list of infamous tyrants of history.

There has always been destruction associated with war, but the advent of total war made a quantum jump in this field. A certain amount of this must be attributed to technological advances, but a great deal must also be blamed on the concept of war itself in its modern religious form. Much of the destruction of World War II was not necessary and when viewed in the stark light of reality, it was unwise because it was the victor who had to turn around and rebuild that which he had destroyed. It takes a real wizard to figure that one out militarily, economically, politically, diplomatically, psychologically, practically, or any other way. It is of interest to note that, "Between the Renaissance and 1940, there are no examples of a city razed or a population exterminated. The campaigns of Napoleon and the First World War did not destroy a single city - if you exclude Moscow which was burned by the Russians themselves, and even then well after the city had been taken."[21] But in the 1940s, we prided ourselves on our ability to smash cities and the hundreds of thousands of people therein, culminating in our modern scientific ability to obliterate a whole city in seconds and to turn thousands of square miles into a radioactive deathland in a few hours. The capability of man's mind to cope with the problems between men and nations has not matched his scientific ability. In modern war, man can only talk of destroying in minutes that which it has taken centuries to build. Thanks to the bomber, and its offspring the ballistic missile, the entire economy and the entire population of a country have become targets of war.

2.   Some Economic Aspects of Total War

Throughout a great part of history, war has been thought of as a conflict between armies, and even, sometimes, as a contest between two teams of belligerents. Of course, there are many examples in history where the cities and the civilian population became embroiled in the conflict. There were cities that were completely destroyed and their people slaughtered or sold into slavery. The ancient practice of plunder and looting did bring the civilians in the path of the enemy army and under their harsh treatment. But in the past, going from the level of the city to that of the nation, there are fewer and fewer examples of complete destruction and there is less of a tendency to aim at the annihilation of the people and the obliteration of their economy. Though their technological level was not high, nations at war were capable of great destruction as the end of Carthage testifies. Hate always managed to bring out the worst in man, and in modern times, hate was a principal ingredient in ideological, total war. Total war makes the adversaries think in terms of "smashing" the enemy even though the one may have no desire to take over the government of the other. This happened to the

Allies in World War II. The Western Allies had no
desire to take over Germany and Japan, but in their
blind hatred, they managed to wreak unimagined destruction on those two countries only to have to
turn around and rebuild them after the war.

Much of this power to decimate must be attributed to the advances in weaponry. The human mind in
anger is not capable, evidently, of rational restraint. The great destruction of World War I was
primarily caused by artillery and was therefore restricted to the battlefield. If the capability had
existed to fire farther, no doubt they would have,
as evidenced by the firings on Paris. It was in
this war that the airplane came into use and with
it a potential weapon of destruction that could
carry the war home to the enemy. The airplane
opened up new paths for the ever-fallible human
mind. Between the two wars, the Douhets and Sever-
skys got to thinking: if the airplane is used to
bomb the enemy army, then it is just modification
of artillery. But the enemy army has to have food,
weapons, ammunition, clothes, and thousands of
other supplies; if factories, transportation systems, and civilian populations were attacked, the
enemy army could be isolated and the people terrorized so they would quit the war. But the factories
are usually in cities, the key hubs of transportation are found in cities, and the greatest concentration of the people who run the factories and the
transportation are located in cities, so it was inevitable that the target should be the enemy cities.
Therefore, assumption of the enemy economy as a primary target automatically made the enemy population
a primary target. All of this thinking is absolutely logical from the military view of how to attack the enemy by the means available to destroy
the enemy and to end the war. But politically, this
is absolutely illogical and removes war from its
only explainable role, that as a continuation of
policy by other means.

The solution is to change the enemy form of
government or policies, not to remove the enemy nation. The desires of World War II were met when
the Germans, Italians, and Japanese were put under a
peaceful form of government. This did not necessarily require the destruction of many cities.

We were obsessed with winning the war as fast
as possible. Why should speed be the controlling
factor? If a war could be terminated in four years
for some price and could be ended in five years for
one half the price, which is the bargain? If any

68

enemy form of government could be overthrown by internal revolution with some outside support, but without the terrible destruction and high losses of war, would not this be a better solution? Certainly this is intervention in the affairs of other countries, but is not war also intervention? What could be a bigger intervention than atomizing an enemy city with all its culture, people, history, and economic life? There is no way of showing that the results of the war were economically plausible. The Americans pride themselves on being good businessmen, but how can they ever explain the astronomical cost of war? It is certainly time for a reevaluation of the role of total war. It is something that has been with us for quite some time now.

In the American Civil War, Grant saw the new form and Lee did not.

> The modernity of Grant's mind was most apparent in his grasp of the concept that war was becoming total and that the destruction of the enemy's economic resources was as effective and legitimate a form of warfare as the destruction of his armies. What was realism to Grant was barbarism to Lee. Lee thought of war in the old way as a conflict between armies and refused to view it for what it had become - a struggle between societies. To him, economic war was needless cruelty to civilians. Lee was the last of the great old-fashioned generals. Grant the first of the great moderns.[22]

Since the Industrial Revolution, economics have become more and more important (and probably less understood) on the world stage. Keynes, writing in his The End of Laissez Faire, mentioned the economic causes of war, particularly the pressure of population and the competitive struggle for markets which he felt played a predominant role in the nineteenth century.[23]

Economic warfare is not new. Tariffs, subsidies, dumping, preemptive buying, blacklists, and blockades are economic warfare weapons. The submarine is a military weapon that the Germans twice used to try to seal the British Isles economically. The Allied blockade of Germany in the first war was rather effective and continued after the armistice. But whether it be called economic warfare, all-out war, or total war, the enemy economy has become a prime target. This was quickly shown in the opening campaign of World War II in Poland. Industry,

69

transportation, and civilian activities which formerly functioned unmolested behind battle lines were now vulnerable to attack. The Germans continually cried that it was economic conditions that were forcing them to seek additional "living space."[24] The same excuse was picked up by others and was even reported to Washington. An acting military attaché in Berlin sent in a report:

> ...expressing the expectation that if Germany could not coerce Poland through negotiation she would attack within the next thirty days. He added: "The present situation when viewed in the light of an active war which Germany is now in the process of waging becomes clear. It is an economic war in which Germany is fighting for her very existence. Germany must have markets for her goods or die and Germany will not die." From which it is evident that the Military Attaché was not only attending to his job of observing the Wehrmacht and the Luftwaffe; he was also listening faithfully to Goebbels' propaganda and reflecting it in his official reports.[25]

Though Hitler's conflict with the world was really ideological due to his ideas of superiority that included the subordination or liquidation of certain peoples, he had gotten into economic tangles. Hitler changed the base of German currency from gold to a production base. This financial move was aimed particularly at the United States, which held the bulk of the world's supply of gold.[26]

Hitler's economic ideas were the cause of his fiasco in Russia. His eyes were on economic goals, so much so that he disregarded the military aspects of how to get them. He took his eyes off the Red Army which was the one thing that could keep him from taking the economic prizes that had hypnotized him.

> Germany's ultimate objectives in the attack on the Soviet Union were primarily of an economic nature. The campaign was intended to introduce the vast food resources of Russia into the European economy and make Russian raw materials available for the Four-Year Plan. With the USSR's 'boundless riches under her control,' as Hitler put it, Germany would be "unassailable" and would control the necessary potential for waging "future wars against continents."[27]

The idea of defeating Russia in a few short
summer months was a tremendous undertaking. Geography alone, the great distances involved, made this
a strategist's nightmare. There was disagreement
between Hitler and his military staff: he wanted to
go after the economic prizes; they wanted to cut
off the Russian Army so that it could not withdraw
to the East and thus remain intact to haunt them.
General Gunther Blumentritt wrote:

> Hitler's primary objectives were dictated on
> economic grounds. He wanted the rich grain
> lands of the Ukraine, the industrial area of
> the Donetz basin and, later, the Caucasian
> oilfields.
>
> Brauchitsch and Halder saw the campaign from
> another point of view. They wished to elimi-
> nate the Red Army first and go for the econom-
> ic prizes only when that had been achieved.[28]

The fears of the staff materialized and the
German Army was trapped in the icy grip of Russian
winter.

The Second World War was well under way and
the United States, though not yet into the shooting
part, was economically involved through her assistance to the Allies by lend-lease. We became quite
deeply involved in the war by this aid, and American entry into the war was considered by many as a
logical result of lend-lease. It should have been
clear to us that Europe, one of the world's main
industrial regions, was still vitally important to
the future, and that the key to Europe was Germany.
However, we proceeded, systematically, to destroy
Germany. Japan, the most advanced nation in the
Orient, dreamed of driving all foreigners out of
Asia. We proceeded to burn Japan out too, and ironically we fulfilled their dream for them as well;
World War II ended the old empires and enhanced the
Soviet empire. It is impossible to think of war
in purely military terms. War is politics, international politics, and the military aspect is only
one part. We must not forget that much of warfare
is economic in nature being an effort to destroy
the enemy's warmaking capacity. We overdid this in
blind hatred without weighing the vastly more important matters of postwar power relationships in the
world.

We won the war militarily, but we are not so
sure we won it politically and economically. The

real lesson of the war, perhaps, is to determine
which is really more important. The road to Total
Victory was long, hard, expensive, and disappointing. We listened too much to our hearts and propaganda and not enough to cold, hard logic. We listened to people who wanted to destroy and, like
little children, we gleefully agreed in our drive
to "smash" them and "teach them a lesson." We still
have such people around. We tend to fight wars for
wars' sake and disregard their effects - much like
a football game, as soon as it is over, everybody
wants to go home. But the important part is just
commencing when the war is over, for that is when
the purposes of the war are either fulfilled or
lost. Each time we went home and still did not
understand why we lost the peace.

NOTES

1. "The Charge of the Light Brigade," Alfred
Lord Tennyson.
2. William S. White, Majesty and Mischief. A
Mixed Tribute to FDR (New York: McGraw-Hill, 1961),
p. 51.
3. Brigadier General S.L.A. Marshall, Men
Against Fire (Washington, D.C.: Combat Forces Press,
1947), p. 28, called it a "state of war in which
all of the assets and aspects of the lives of nations are faced with attack, and in consequence, all
elements and resources of the engaging peoples must
be subject to use in the defense."
4. T. Harry Williams, Lincoln and His Generals
(New York: McGraw-Hill Book Co., Inc., 1954), p. 3.
5. Ibid., p. 340.
6. Possony, A Century of Conflict, p. 8. He
added that, "Actually, Engels even saw the fifth
element of modern war: technology." p. 9.
7. Churchill, Closing the Ring, Vol. V of The
Second World War, pp. 336-337.
8. King-Hall, Total Victory, pp. 22-23. He
gave examples: the assault of Persia on Greece, 480
B.C., Carthage, and the religious wars of the
seventeenth century.
9. See Fuller, The Conduct of War, p. 31.
10. Kissinger, Nuclear Weapons and Foreign
Policy, pp. 87-88.
11. L. M. Goodrich, ed., Documents on American
Foreign Relations (Boston: World Peace Foundation,
1942), Vol. V, 1942-1943, p. 70.

12. Ibid., p. 76. "Food is a primary weapon of war. An adequate supply is, therefore, a basic aspect of a total war program." Ibid., p. 73.

13. Bernard, War and Its Causes, p. 53. Joseph Goebbels, The Goebbels Diaries, ed. and tr. by Louis P. Lochner (Garden City, N.Y.: Doubleday, 1948), p. 367, on 10 May 1943 entered that the Führer was satisfied with the total war measures taken so far. He also made this observant remark. "During total war, however, war must not be conducted against women. Never yet has such a war been won by any government. Women, after all, constitute a tremendous power and as soon as you dare to touch their beauty parlors they are your enemies."

14. Walter Lüdde-Neurath, Les derniers jours du troisième Reich, Le gouvernement de Doenitz, tr. René Jovan (Paris: Berger-Levrault, 1950), pp. 16-17, my translation.

15. Quoted in Wesley L. Gould, An Introduction to International Law (New York: Harper & Brothers, 1954), p. 113.

16. King-Hall, Total Victory, p. 165.

17. Churchill, The Gathering Storm, p. 17.

18. L. C. Green, International Law Through the Cases (London: Stevens & Sons Limited, 1959), p.687, italics in original.

19. Le procès de Nuremberg (Paris: Office français, 1946), Vol. I, p. 97, my translation.

20. Toynbee, A Study of History, Vol. I, p. 347.

21. Gaston Bouthoul, Sauver la guerre (lettre aux futurs survivants) (Paris: Grasset, 1961), p. 11, my translation.

22. Williams, Lincoln and His Generals, pp.313-314.

23. Ebenstein, Great Political Thinkers, p. 649.

24. Professor E.H. Carr pointed out we lost the peace in the first war because of a disintegration policy. He says we should have aimed at integrating Europe if only to remove the economic causes of war. The 20 Years' Crisis (London: Macmillan & Co., Ltd., 1961), p. 230.

25. Robert E. Sherwood, Roosevelt and Hopkins (New York: Harper & Brothers, 1948), p. 116.

26. Fuller, A Military History of the Western World, Vol. III, p. 369. It is interesting to note that, "In Germany, the government actively encouraged the growth of cartels and other monopolistic forms of business. Eventually, these big business interests were instrumental in supporting Hitler's

73

rise to power. Monopoly in Germany led to fascism and ultimately to war." Clifford L. James, *Principles of Economics* (New York: Barnes and Noble, 1960), p. 269.

27. Edgar M. Howell, *The Soviet Partisan Movement 1941-1944* (Washington, D.C.: DA Pamphlet 20-244, August 1956), p. 20. The Four-Year Plan was set up in 1936 under Goering to make Germany self-sufficient in strategic war materials.

28. Seymour Freidin and William Richardson, Editors, *The Fatal Decisions* (New York: Berkley Publishing Corp., 1958) transl. by Constantine Fitzgibbon, p. 52. General Blumentritt was Chief of Staff of the German Fourth Army in Russia. Field Marshal von Brauchitsch was the Commander-in-Chief and General Halder was Chief of the General Staff.

4
Strategic Bombing

Victory through air power.

-- Alexander Seversky

The victory of a nation
through the total destruction of its rival inflicts
an incurable wound on
civilization itself.[1]

-- Raymond Aron

1. The Policy

The period between the two wars saw the development of the airplane from a contraption into a
modern instrument of commerce and of war. Its military development advanced in the Spanish Civil War
and the Japanese war in China. With the outbreak of
the Second World War in 1939, it was destined to
come into its own. On 1 September, President Roosevelt issued an appeal to Britain, France, Germany,
and Poland not to bomb unfortified cities and civilian populations. Hitler immediately endorsed
the President's plea, and on the 2nd, the British
and French governments declared they were in sympathy with the humanitarian sentiments expressed by
the President. That was about the extent of the restraint shown for the duration of the war. On 15
May 1940 attacks were authorized for the first time
east of the Rhine, and the Ruhr was hit that night,
mainly on oil and railway targets.[2] In the 16
December attack on Mannheim, the first wave of bombers dropped incendiaries. The following waves
were ordered to aim at the fires raised in the initial attack. The purpose of the attack was to concentrate the maximum amount of damage in the center

75

of the town.[3]
Certainly, an impulsion for this form of attack came from the German air strikes on England. Churchill observed in October 1940 while visiting a bombed area in London,

> ...a harsher mood swept over this haggard crowd. "Give it'em back", they cried, and "Let them have it too." I undertook forthwith to see that their wishes were carried out; and this promise was certainly kept. The debt was repaid tenfold, twentyfold in the frightful routine bombardment of German cities, which grew in intensity as our air power developed, as the bombs became far heavier and the explosives more powerful. Certainly the enemy got it all back in good measure, pressed down and running over. Alas for poor humanity![4]

Churchill's pity for humanity came a little too late.

Yet, the mainland of Europe was bombed before England was, and there is evidence to indicate that the air strategists adopted this policy many years before the war. It was apparently also accepted by the British Government and so was not merely a forced reaction to the German policy of destruction from the air.[5] The official British history stated that England had decided well before 1939 that the bomber objective was to terrorize the civilian population into making peace demands rather than hitting industry.[6] Both forms were to be used, striking both the enemy industry and the enemy population. General Arnold, head of US air forces, wrote, "These operations were called strategic bombing, and their aim was to reduce drastically the enemy's ability and will to wage war."[7]

Strategic bombing was thus not something that suddenly appeared in the war. It was a doctrine that had been building since the first war. After the terrible ordeal of trench warfare, there was much study of how to fight the next war without getting stalemated in the mud again. Most of this discussion centered on how to return mobility to the battlefield, perhaps using that other important innovation of the first war, the tank, so as to defeat the enemy military force. The protagonists of strategic bombing did not insist on the defeat of the enemy's land and sea forces as essential to victory, but contended that the enemy could be defeated faster and more cheaply by attacking,

instead, his centers of production and population.
This form of attack would not only deprive the
enemy of the weapons he needed for offense and defense, but would also dislocate the economic and
physical life of his country and finally would so
terrify the population that it would clamor for
peace.

The leading exponent of this doctrine was the
Italian, General Guilio Douhet, who put forth his
ideas in his book, The Command of the Air, in 1921.
He saw the war of the future once more involving
all nations and all their resources. He foresaw
continuous fronts and stalemate again. What then
was the answer? It was to transfer war into the
air and attack the civil population, because once
its will was broken by terror the whole machinery
of government and with it of military direction
would collapse. To him, this form of warfare was
to be more merciful because it was to be very short.
He did not think that there might be considerable
modernization in other forms of warfare also and
could only repeat his central theme that air power
alone could win a war.[9] Admiral Sir Gerald Dickens
called Douhet, "Another striking example of the
technical mind hypnotized by the machine itself and,
so, unable to grasp that this machine was but another means to the same end as existed before it
was invented."[10]

The ultra-enthusiasts proclaimed that no nation, including Britain, would put up with the
bombing of its towns for more than a few days even
on the comparatively small scale of attack visualized before the war. The British knew how utterly
wrong that opinion was both as regards themselves
and Germany. They knew, on the contrary, that their
morale was strengthened. Why should they have
thought it possible so easily to affect German morale?[11] Churchill, who became one of the great exponents of strategic bombing, was not so sure of
its value in 1938.

> It may, however, be said with some assurance
> that the whole course of the war in Spain has
> seemed to show the limitations rather than the
> strength of the air weapon. The extravagant
> claims of a certain school of air experts have
> not been fulfilled.[12]

Churchill continued,

> ...air attack upon the civil population and

77

upon the factories producing munitions and
upon the economic springs of the country....So
far from producing panic and a wish to surrender, they have aroused a spirit of furious and
unyielding resistance among all classes. They
have united whole communities, otherwise
deeply sundered, in a common hatred of such
base and barbarous methods. I, therefore, remain convinced that where the strength of the
air forces is equal, the side which consumes
its energy upon slaughter of the civil population is likely to encounter surprising disappointment.[13]

Even Seversky, who also was going to win the
war with air power, admitted that civilians can
"take it." However, he felt enemy morale could be
destroyed by precision bombing.[14]
The British Chiefs of Staff nevertheless put
their seal of approval on the doctrine on 31 July
1941 as the new weapon on which they would princi-
pally depend for the destruction of German economic
life and morale.[15] Seversky was in agreement feeling that it was a virtual guarantee of victory. He
closed his book with "There is no other road to
victory."[16] The justification, once the basic decision had been made, was easy. The moral argument
about strategic bombing then tended to degenerate
into the drawing of distinctions between necessary
and unnecessary destruction. This, however, merged
with and became indistinguishable from the strategic argument, for it was obviously against every
strategic precept to waste bombs, bombers, and
bomber crews on attacks that were not held to be
necessary.
The policy was endorsed at the highest level
with the directive to the American and British
bomber commands in the United Kingdom from the Unconditional Surrender Conference at Casablanca in
1943 which directed that their primary objective
be -- "the progressive destruction and dislocation
of the German military, industrial and economic
system, and the undermining of the morale of the
German people to a point where their capacity for
armed resistance is fatally weakened."[17] With this
order, precision bombing was abandoned for area or
"strategic" bombing to devastate Germany and terrorize the civilian population. The main target
became cities which are appealing targets in war
because they produce for war, they are the transportation and supply bottlenecks of a national

system, and because more people can be killed there. They are vulnerable targets because they must remain exposed; the masses of people, the factories, and the communications system cannot go underground.[18]

This "city-busting" policy was energetically pursued. A total of 2,770,540 tons of bombs was dropped on Europe by the air forces of Great Britain and the United States.[19] More than two and a half million bombs were dropped, not always on their targets. German civilian morale was shaken but not broken. German transportation was disrupted but not destroyed. The physical destruction was appalling although industry was not reduced as had been expected. An example of the effect on the civilians is the three night attacks on Hamburg. Approximately one-third of the dwellings were destroyed, and from sixty to one hundred thousand civilians were killed.[20] Attacks on 61 cities with a combined population of 25,000,000 destroyed or heavily damaged 3,600,000 dwelling units, or about 20 percent of Germany's total, leaving 7,500,000 people homeless, killing about 3,000,000 people and injuring some 780,000.[21] The physical destruction from the air attacks on Japan approximated that suffered by Germany, even though a far smaller tonnage of bombs was dropped. Some 40 percent of the built-up area of the 66 Japanese cities attacked was destroyed. About 30 percent of the entire urban population of Japan lost their homes and many of their possessions.[22] This bombing also resulted in 260,000 killed, 412,000 injured, 2,250,000 buildings levelled and 9,000,000 people made homeless. The atomic bombs added 110,000 killed and 60,000 injured.[23] But it did not require atomic bombs to make great destruction. General LeMay's low-level incendiary raid on Tokyo on 9 March 1945 is a good example. Some 15.8 square miles of the heart of Tokyo were burned out in the most destructive air attack in history prior to the use of the atomic bomb.[24] Of the 66 Japanese cities mentioned, almost 169 square miles were destroyed or damaged. The destruction, including that caused by the two atomic bombs, amounted to over 42 percent of the urban industrial areas involved. General Arnold proudly reported, "Never in the history of aerial warfare has such destruction been achieved at such moderate cost."[25]

In the heat of our self-consuming hate during the war, our leadership was proud of the destruction. "The havoc and devastation created by these British flyers, now joined by our own air forces,

79

are crippling war plants, munitions factories, ship-
yards and railways and gravely impairing the German
effort to maintain the earlier levels of war production," declared Sumner Welles.[26] Churchill told
the United States Congress, "Surveying the whole
aspect of the air war, we cannot doubt that it is a
major factor in the process of victory. That, I
think, is established as a solid fact." Further on,
he told them, "It is the duty of those charged with
the direction of the war to overcome at the earliest
moment the military, geographical, and political
difficulties and begin the process, so necessary
and desirable, of laying the cities and other munitions centers of Japan in ashes. For in ashes they
must surely lie before peace comes back to the
world."[27] Democracy at war!
     After the war, Churchill reviewed the contri-
bution of strategic bombing.

> In judging the contribution to victory of stra-
> tegic airpower it should be remembered that
> this was the first war in which it was fully
> used. We had to learn from hard-won exper-
> ience....We certainly underestimated the strong
> latent reserve in Germany's industry and the
> great resources she had gained from Occupied
> Europe. Thanks to well-organized relief mea-
> sures, strict police action, and innate dis-
> cipline and courage, the German people endured
> more than we had thought possible. But al-
> though the results of the early years fell
> short of our aims we forced on the enemy an
> elaborate, ever-growing but finally insuffi-
> cient air defence system which absorbed a
> large proportion of their total war effort.
> Before the end we and the United States had
> developed striking forces so powerful that
> they played a major part in the economic col-
> lapse of Germany.[28]

There is little doubt that strategic bombing
brought about the economic collapse of the enemy,
but there are those who do not think this was wise.

2. A Critique of Strategic Bombing

     The big decision was the change from precision
to area or strategic bombing. Critics claimed that
this decision was strategically unsound, that it

delayed victory almost to the point of inviting defeat, and that it was largely responsible for the
magnitude of the problems of the Cold War. Admiral
Dickens and General Fuller were two of the severest
critics of strategic bombing.
Here is a typical criticism from the Admiral.

And yet the military mind, or shall we say the
ordinary man - though that may be rating the
military man rather too high in Seversky's
opinion sees that with all this bombing, the
German armies were still fighting well up to
the final phase of the war against the might
of the armies, navies, and air forces of the
British Empire, the United States and Russia,
and that, despite the terrible air blows
against the German nerve centres and population, the war was lasting much longer than the
previous war, and that German centres of production somehow in the sixth year of the war
were turning out vast numbers of tanks (more
powerful than ours), were ahead of us in jet-
propelled aircraft, were manufacturing huge
quantities of such entirely new weapons as
flybombs and rocket bombs, had added devices
to their U-boats which gave them a new lease
of life, were turning out artillery, mortars,
machine guns and rifles as effectively and in
as great quantities as ever.[29]

General Fuller could always join in with one
of his own strong criticisms.

Since May 11, 1940, when Mr. Churchill inaugu-
rated the bombing of German cities, the policy
of obliterating the enemy's industrial and
residential areas had proved a failure; it had
not reduced production, which had advanced by
leaps and bounds, and it had fortified, not
lowered, German civil morale.[30]

Fuller, particularly unhappy with Churchill's
resorting to strategic bombing, felt Churchill was
so obsessed by hatred of the enemy "that he fell
back on methods of war long discarded by civilized
nations."[31]
Walter Millis also attacked the use of strategic bombing. Summing up the United States Strategic Bombing Survey, that was established late in
the war to evaluate our effort, he wrote, "that
strategic bombing, when armed only with TNT and

incendiary weapons, had cost much more in over-all effort, had involved much greater casualties and had produced much smaller military results than had been expected."[32] Millis agreed that all this "destruction helped to prepare the ultimate German collapse," but to him, "the traceable military results were uniformly disappointing."[33] General Gavin, an old paratrooper and an air enthusiast but no supporter of the go-it-alone school of strategic bombing, observed, "One of the most interesting aspects of our bombing effort was that German production increased in the same ratio as our bombing effort until late in 1944."[34] until, as Millis said, "well after the ground armies were ashore to make good the job at which the airplanes had been unsuccessful."[35] For an idea of these increases in German production, see Figure 4.1, German Aircraft Production and Figure 4.2, German Combat Munitions Output.

The production of the V-1 and V-2 rockets showed great skill by Germany, skill that provided the basis for the great postwar missile achievements of both the United States and the Soviet Union; and the fact that our massive air attacks did not stop them is significant. Fuller felt it was impossible to destroy German industry and that we should have concentrated on coal and oil. Had they been steadily reduced, then, eventually 90 percent of German industry would have come to a standstill.[36] The idea that Germany could have been defeated by air power if properly applied received much support from an interview with Speer, German Production Minister, after the war. In reply to the question, Do you believe strategic bombing alone could have brought about the surrender of Germany?, he answered "...yes. The attacks on the chemical industry would have sufficed, without the impact of purely military events to render Germany defenceless."[37] He also mentioned ball-bearing plants and power stations. This implied that if the enormous Allied effort had been concentrated on some logical goal, there would have been no need for the wanton killing and destruction resulting from throwing thousands of bombs at random at cities and expecting to win the war immediately because of this terror.

As Herman Kahn put it, "one of the big disappointments of World War II was the impact of strategic bombing."[38] As he noted, "We know now that the capability for strategic bombing as it existed then had been exaggerated, but it took three or

Figure 4.1   GERMAN AIRCRAFT PRODUCTION *

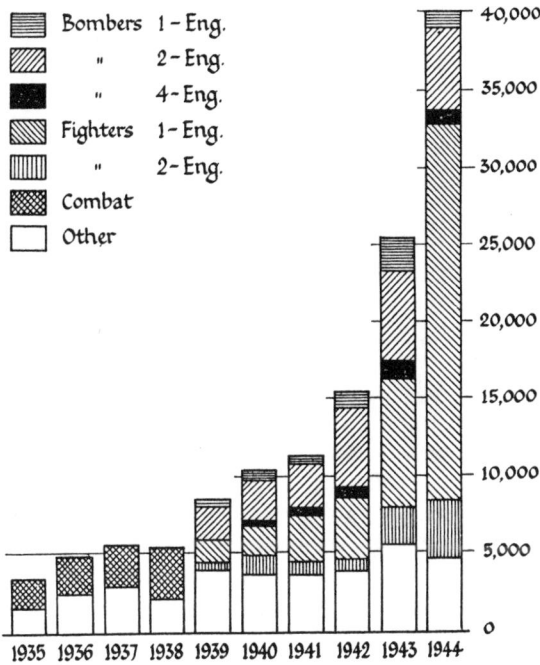

U.S. Strategic Bombing Survey.

* This is Chart No. 7, USSBS, Over-all Effort (European War), p. 92.   It may also be found in Fuller, The Second World War, p. 225, or The Conduct of War, p. 283.   The USSBS has many charts in it including Chart No. 12, p. 194, which shows the continued increase of German aircraft engine production; and Chart No. 14, p. 110, showing the continued increase of production of anti-friction bearings.

Figure 4.2   GERMAN COMBAT MUNITIONS OUTPUT *

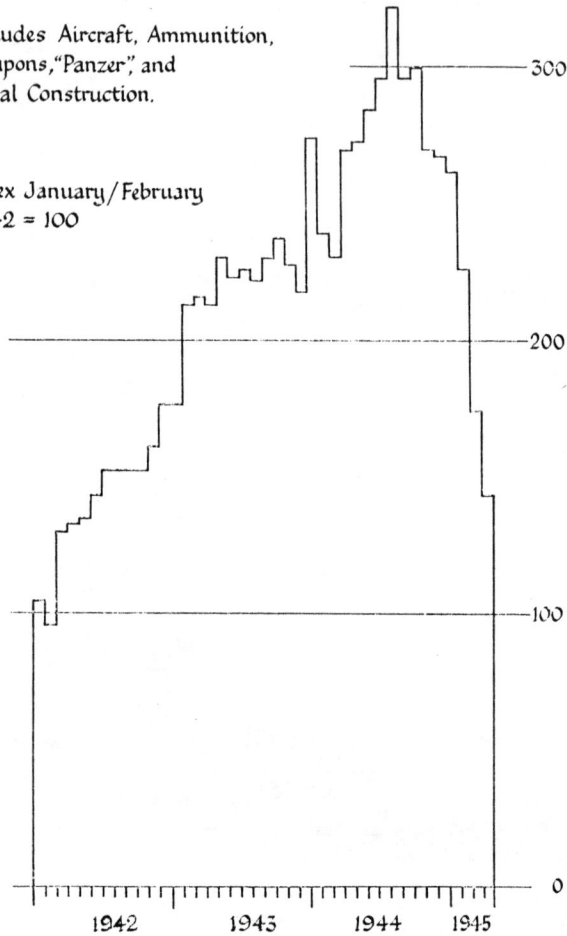

Includes Aircraft, Ammunition,
Weapons,"Panzer", and
Naval Construction.

Index January/February
1942 = 100

300

200

100

0

1942   1943   1944   1945

U.S. Strategic Bombing Survey.

* This is Chart No. 15, USSBS, Over-all Effort (European War),
p. 112. It may also be found in Fuller, The Second World War,
p. 227, or The Conduct of War, p. 284. Note that even in the
last month before surrender, German output was 150% of January
1942 output, and that was after the war had been in progress
for over two years. Other USSBS charts are Chart No. 20. p.
128, Powder and Explosives Production which continued to increase to the end of the war; Chart No. 25, p. 138, German Rail
Traffic, which also increased to the end; and Chart No. 26,
p. 140, Panzer Production, which increased until 1945.

84

four years of war to show this convincingly."[39] The
prewar claims by the Douhet supporters were fantastic. If one is interested in their claims of how
cheap they would make war and how they would win it
in 72 hours, those embarrassing statements are in
the historical record.[40] The sad part is that they
never learn, for we still have these wild enthusiasts who are going to win the next war in a matter
of hours.
     The official British history pointed up the
lack of significant results by strategic bombing
until the last year of the war. For the years 1940
and 1941, they reported "no great damage had been
done to Germany."[41] For 1942, "The damage, while
considerable, was in no case of significant extent."[42] Then for 1943, German armaments production was not only maintained but much increased during the first half of the year. It remained at that
level during the second half and then rose again in
the first half of 1944, reaching its peak in
midyear.[43]

> It is thus apparent that the area bombing was
> very far from inflicting any crippling or de-
> cisive loss on the enemy and had not prevented
> the great increase in armaments carried out in
> this period. Whatever reservations be made
> about the reliability of some of the statis-
> tics and computations there is no doubt about
> the main fact.[44]

     However, the great area offensive of March
1943 to March 1944 did not meet Allied hopes or indeed German fears. It was clear that "German war
production increased and increased again, that the
German people remained loyal and obedient and that
the German armed forces continued to fight with
great bravery and with no less efficiency than before."[45] It was not until late in the war that
strategic bombing could claim that its destruction
was doing something. "In the last year of the war
Bomber Command played a major part in the almost
complete destruction of whole vital segments of German oil production, in the virtual dislocation of
her communications system and in the elimination of
other important activities."[46] Similar admissions
can be found throughout the U.S. Strategic Bombing
Survey.
     Raymond Aron placed the results in perspective
when he evaluated this policy: "Strategic bombing
seems to have played a smaller part in the victory

than in the postwar difficulties."[47] The world political leadership should study and try to learn
from this phase of the war, for it would be perhaps
even more applicable in the event of modern total
war. Fuller expressed Aron's point in a little
more colorful manner. "And what was the final result of this Mongoloid destructiveness? That,
while the First and Second Fronts were advancing to
win the war, the Third Front was engaged upon blowing the bottom out of the peace which was to follow
its winning; for cities and not rubble heaps are
the foundations of civilization."[48] Another author
slashed out on logical economic grounds of self-
interest that the systematic destruction of German
industrial power was hurting ourselves in the long
run. The prosperity of the Continent in the past
had largely depended upon German industry, and the
continental market, including Germany, was the best
market for British exports.[49]
     The British could not see this however, even
though they are a people whose very existence is
based on trade and who have often compromised their
principles in the past to maintain their position.
An Englishman, Percy Corbet, prepared a study in
1941 called War Aims and Postwar Plans. He concluded that, despite the destruction that war would
bring, Germany would inevitably play a major role
in postwar European economic recovery and therefore
the maintenance of German productive capacity was
essential to European economic well-being. However,
destruction of Germany's war capability would also
destroy German potential to contribute to postwar
economic reconstruction in Europe and would weaken
European economic prosperity. Therefore, he concluded, "a policy of total repression would be both
dangerous and wasteful."[50] This was not an official document but solely the work of one man. It
does show, however, that at least this one was able
to look at war with a realistic eye and try to see
what the effect would be of the actions contemplated so that strategy could be in accordance with
the desired political goals.
     The effort put into air power was quite sig-
nificant, supposedly 40-50 percent of British war
production and 35 percent of American production.[51]
This was a fantastic amount compared to the return.
Fuller claimed that the total cost of the Super-
Fortress organization was $4,000,000,000, and he
felt that the money was not profitably spent. He
felt that the terrible destruction in Japan, really
meant not only the destruction of Japan's war po-

tential, but also of her peace potential which was "strategically uneconomic."[52]

Not that we consider the Russian state a model to copy, but we should remember that they conducted their part of the entire war without any strategic air force to speak of. The war was ended not because of the great carnage from the air but when the army on the ground took physical possession of the enemy territory. There is little doubt that a modern nation can be brought to its knees by intelligently applied air power in conjunction with intelligent employment of other military, economic, psychological, and political means. But this was not the strategic bombing of World War II. It was basically irrational and without objective, for it was trying to destroy all the enemy industry, transportation, raw materials and, at the same time, to terrorize the people into surrender. It was spread so thin, attacking whatever came to mind, that it never really achieved any of its objectives. Its supporters swamped us with propaganda as to how they were winning the war; their statistics were marvelous, often exceeding the physical forces of the enemy; and the fact that they had to keep redestroying some of their targets did not deter them. Dickens wrote, "During the war our people believed that we were achieving more by bombing than we were in fact achieving or were capable of achieving, and this was due to a reprehensible form of publicity."[53] These wild claims duped not only the people but also the governments. We are still living under the influence of "strategic bombing" thinking, only now the damage that they can do is really beyond comprehension. However, their strategy is still the same; they want to "destroy" the enemy into submission. The liklihood for success in this approach remains about as it was in 1940.

The conclusion is that, "as an experiment, the strategic bombing of Germany up to the spring of 1944 was an extravagant failure. Instead of shortening the war, its cost in raw materials and industrial manpower prolonged it."[54] Its great result was destruction, scars that lasted for many years, and billions spent by us in rebuilding what we had so haphazardly knocked down. Fuller felt that "the obliteration of cities by bombing was probably the most devastating blow ever struck at civilization "[55] and those bombs were like firecrackers in comparison with the toys that modern science has placed in the hands of our supporters of victory through air power. Anne Armstrong wrote that many

German officers viewed war professionally and desired to restrict destruction. In the democracies also there were professional soldiers who stressed limiting warfare against civilian targets. This was revealed in the debates among the Anglo-American generals concerning strategic air warfare. There was certainly no unanimity among Western strategists about the efficacy or morality of saturation bombing, for example, any more than there was on the policy of Unconditional Surrender; but, in each case, the advocates of the extreme position carried the day. The Allies pursued an unlimited objective with unlimited means.[56] The only result that could come from this was more and more destruction.

3. Destruction

There is only one way to describe strategic bombing and it is not "quick victory" due to fewer dead or enemy surrender because they have been terrorized into it; it is only the single word: destruction. It is truly fantastic the amount of destruction created in Europe and Asia during the war, and that was a war in which only two atomic bombs were used. The mass attack against the civilian population was not the answer as the Bombing Survey revealed -- "heavy, sustained and accurate attack against carefully selected targets is required to produce decisive results when attacking an enemy's sustaining resources."[57] The British found the same answer. In their interview with Speer he answered that the form of attack the most effective in weakening the German war effort was mass attacks by day because they were "based upon economic considerations and inflicted heavy damage on precise targets."[58] This should have made the British wonder about their night bombing. When asked to list the various targets in order of priority, Speer listed attacks on cities fifth of six with naval, shipping, and airfields being last, and key points in basic industries being first.[59] When asked whether the British or American bombers caused more concern, he replied, "The American attacks, which followed a definite system of assault on industrial targets, were by far the most dangerous. It was in fact these attacks which caused the breakdown of the German armaments industry."[60] The Americans were not really that successful in precision bombing, notably with the great defeat of the attacks against the Schweinfurt ball bearing factories in the summer of 1943.[61] The British themselves finally admitted that the "night bomber was more a bludgeon and less a rapier than had been supposed."[62]

Air power is of enormous importance in modern warfare, particularly if it can be made to work with the other military means rather than trying to win the war alone. It is not the great panacea and cannot do everything. There is no doubt of its great destructive power, but it also has many other capabilities that are often more important. Fuller criticized the air people for overemphasizing this one capability at the expense of the revolutionary advance in logistics.[63] Aerial reconnaissance has reached an importance of the highest level as evidenced by the U-2 and subsequent aircraft and satellites. But air power has its limitations as we discovered again in Korea and Viet-Nam. During the Pacific war, in the battle for Leyte, Japanese troops continued to pour ashore in the north of Leyte despite American air superiority. Major General Toshi Mishimura, of the Fourteenth Area Army claimed that more than 45,000 troops and 10,000 tons of materiel were landed, despite the fact that 80 percent of the Japanese vessels in this operation were sunk by American planes.[64] And those reinforcements made a lot of difference to the men fighting in the jungle. General Marshall, reporting on the invasion of France, spoke of German Generals Keitel and Jodl pointing to Allied air power as the decisive factor in the German defeat. But this was not air power employed in strategic bombing but in the interdiction role, to isolate the battlefield. This was not air power working alone but in conjunction with and in support of the rest of the armed forces. General Arnold made the amazing discovery that this damage could work against us as well as the enemy. "Curiously, the effectiveness of the air's part in facilitating the advance worked to our disadvantages, too. The bridges were destroyed, railroads battered. Chokepoints of highways were torn up by our bombs. Supply and transport were just as important to us as to the Germans."[65]

The real destruction was done farther away from the battlefield though. "In fact, the mass bombing of great centres of population means a speed-up of human slaughter, misery and material destruction superimposed on that of the military fighting front."[66] This same author quoted Fuller:

89

Writing in the Evening Standard for Jan. 4th,
1944, on man's unlimited propensity for destruction, Major-General J.F.C. Fuller said:

"In the last War it was the artillery
battle; in this war it is air bombardment. By
means of the one he obliterated entire battlefields, and by doing so denied to himself all
possibility of exploiting the initial success
gained by becoming bogged in the sloughs he
created. By means of the other he annihilated
great cities and vast industrial areas, and in
consequence had pulverised the very foundations
upon which eventual peace must one day be
built."[67]

"These appalling slaughterings, which would
have disgraced Attila,"[68] as Fuller put it, were
sometimes rationalized on the basis of military necessity; but we have seen that this was not so, in
that one of the aims was to terrorize the civilian
population into surrendering. If our aim was to
change the forms of government in Germany and Japan,
then we were obstructing our own path, for the
greater the destruction suffered by a society, the
more difficult it is to establish a democratic regime in it. This was something the air enthusiasts
could never understand. They looked at the problem
of how to win the war and ignored what was to happen
thereafter. Dickens lashed out at Seversky for this.

Those who drop a principle or two in the excite-
ment of handling a new weapon are not good
strategists. Let us then beware of the Seversky type as a reformer of strategy. He con-
fuses means and ends; the abstract, the psychological and the imponderables do not interest
him and the Art of War is a closed book....
How his brain 'revs up' when he sees the possibility of a bigger and brighter explosion than
ever before - never mind where the explosion,
so long as there is a good bang and the destruction is enormous![69]

Seversky tried to get to the bottom of the matter when he asked, "Does the attacker aim at the
possession of the enemy country or at its elimination as an economic and political factor?"[70] Unfortunately, however, he made the mistake of accepting
the second choice as his basis for the war and therefore turned his technical skill to the destruction
of the enemy. If he had reworded his first alterna-

90

tive to something like the temporary possession of
the enemy country for rehabilitation and the eventual establishment of a free, democratic country, he
might have seen that the destruction of strategic
bombing would have hindered our efforts. Seversky
certainly understood this for he wrote, "The war of
possession calls for ground forces, for aviation coordinated with those forces, for air power on a
tight leash in order to avoid unnecessary destruction."[71] It is perfectly clear from the record of
the war that we did not intend to destroy Germany
and Japan; therefore, this mistaken assumption of
alternatives by Seversky is the basic error committed by the proponents of strategic bombing.

Destruction is not in the interest of any party
in modern war. Many centuries ago, when an enemy
could be destroyed and the area either taken over or
left to rot, this was a feasible policy. But the
world is too small now, and international relationships are too closely interwoven. In those days,
one part of the world did not even know of the existence of the others. Now we keep informed hourly of
activities in the remotest parts of the world, actually watch events there by means of satellite re-
layed television, and men and materiel can reach any
part of the world in hours or they can send their
thermonuclear messengers in minutes. Any country
that can conduct modern war represents a significant
industrial base and, therefore, can be considered
important in world commerce and world affairs. Its
destruction, then, leaves a gap which must be filled.
Therefore, the logic of winning a war now should be
how to do it with no destruction or, at least, the
very minimum of destruction. We have not yet ma-
tured sufficiently to see this point. It would be
ridiculous for mankind to pay the price of another
World War; there are more efficient and more logical
ways to accomplish the desired ends. It is certainly incongruous that man, in his desire to atomize
the world, ignores and belittles the one form of
warfare that can reduce the slaughter of our fellow
man and has the added characteristic that it causes
NO DESTRUCTION. This is chemical and biological
warfare.

I would like to make a short digression here to
discuss this "inhumane" form of warfare, as it is so
often referred to in propaganda, not to advocate it
but to try to put it in perspective in the period of
megatonnage. Chemical warfare has been with us for
a long time. The use of fire as a chemical weapon
is older than recorded history itself. Chemical

warfare reached perhaps its greatest effectiveness
with the introduction of poison gas. This began on
a large scale in the First World War, but it was but
little used in the second, evidently because the
Axis powers realized that if they reintroduced it,
they would themselves be the chief sufferers.[72]
Therefore, the Axis, by refusing to use a weapon
that would probably hurt them more than the Allies,
actually managed to partially disarm the Allies from
using chemical warfare by their not using it. We
carried millions of tons of chemicals all around the
world, but they were never used. It is evident that
there is a major deterrent effect with chemical and
biological warfare as with nuclear warfare.

In the first war, when the Germans introduced
gas, the effect was panic, but the Germans failed to
realize that they had a battle winner and did not
exploit it. Out of the 258,338 American casualties
suffered in the war - 70,752 or 27.4 percent, were
gas casualties. Also, while 46,419 of the total
casualties were fatal, only 1,400, or 2 percent, of
gas casualties died compared with 24.85 percent.
"Contrary to common belief, gas was the most humane
weapon used in the war, and one of the most effective;" even when gas masks gave 100 percent immunity, when worn they reduced the soldier to half a
fighting man, and gave little protection against
mustard gas.[73] Liddell Hart wrote: "Even in World
War I the most effective chemical weapon was mustard
gas, which disabled more but killed fewer than any
other important weapon. Moreover it favoured, and
aided, defence by its obstructive and delaying effect."[74] Only one in fifty of the American gas casualties died compared with one in four of those
caused by bullets or high explosive shells. Thus, a
soldier disabled by gas had twelve times better
chances of recovery. It was clear from the death
ratios among casualties that poison gas, as used in
the First World War, was far more humane as a weapon
than shells, bombs, or even bullets. The relative
humaneness of chemical weapons was all the greater
because the military effect was achieved without the
destruction of towns and devastation of countries
inevitably produced by explosive weapons.[75]

Referring to the agreements to denounce the use
of gas, he wrote, "That denunciation was an emotional revulsion, particularly against a novelty in
weapons, rather than a reasoned conclusion from the
facts of war experience."[76] New gases have been developed which are far more effective in stopping
aggression. They can literally "make a cat fright-

ened of a mouse" or can kill almost instantaneously
even if masked. "Thus the main effect of the Washington and Geneva prohibition of gas was, ironically
and tragically, to preserve for the battlefields of
the future the more fatal effects of high explosive,
and also its shattering effects on the structure of
civilised society. For explosive weapons destroy
the economic foundations of a return from war to
peace."[77]

Kingston-McCloughry took a more realistic view
of why and when these weapons are used than is the
average view presented in official circles. He felt
that great powers only go to war when they believe
they have an advantage over their opponent, and once
having initiated war they are liable to use an ostensibly outlawed weapon if they think it will bring
them any great gain. To him, any suggestion that
the use of an internationally prohibited weapon such
as poison gas during the Second World War, was can-
celled by the moral censure of world opinion or the
fear of retaliation is an over-simplification. "The
reasons for its non-use were those of military expediency and not of moral proscription."[78] Peter
Fleming presented an interesting discussion of proposed British plans to use mustard gas if invaded by
the Germans. This was to have been regarded as a
"last resort," but he made his point that "the British would not, in a crisis, have foregone the use
of gas."[79] The threat to use gas was often mentioned in the Stalin-Churchill correspondence with
Great Britain threatening to retaliate on Germany if
the Nazis used gas on Russia.[80]

President Roosevelt made the American position
quite clear.

> From time to time since the present war began
> there have been reports that one or more of the
> Axis powers were seriously contemplating use of
> poisonous or noxious gases or other inhumane
> devices of warfare.
>
> I have been loath to believe that any nation,
> even our present enemies, could or would be
> willing to loose upon mankind such terrible and
> inhumane weapons....
>
> Use of such weapons has been outlawed by the
> general opinion of civilized mankind. This
> country has not used them, and I hope that we
> never will be compelled to use them. I state
> categorically that we shall under no circum-

93

stances resort to the use of such weapons unless they are first used by our enemies.[81]

This policy has not changed up to the present
and President Nixon extended that renunciation to
the first use of incapacitating chemicals and even
took the unilateral step of destroying biological
agent stockpiles.
In June 1944, General Eisenhower received an
urgent message from Churchill regarding a possible
indication that the Germans might use gas on Allied
troops. Ike thought it might be a "last-ditch effort of the Germans to stave off final defeat." But
as his aide recorded, "We have lots on hand for
counterattack if they start the bad business."[82]
Liddell Hart, a world-renowned military writer,
visualized limiting the effects of total war by the
use of chemical instead of nuclear weapons. He saw
chemical weapons as more effective in checking invasion and delaying advancing movement on land than
against stationary forces and cities. He felt it
absurd to forego the defensive use of mustard gas,
the most obstructive yet least lethal of weapons,
while planning the use of nuclear weapons - "Which
are weapons of mass-slaughter, and violate the law-
ful code of warfare on more counts than such a weapon as mustard gas, which is relatively humane. The
ban has become still more nonsensical since the development of non-lethal nerve gases which annul the
will to fight."[83]
Fuller wrote, while advocating the use of a
toothache gas, "Why do we not adopt such a common-
sense method? Because we lack imagination, and because we do not possess the courage to face public
opinion and do it."[84] It is truly an unusual world,
where we continue to accept as normal and humane for
people to have arms and legs blown off, holes shot
into their bodies, or otherwise be maimed for life.
The atomic weapons have extended this killing to
more people farther away and have added a new ingredient, radiation. Yet to be killed by gas, or
better yet, to be only attacked by gas but not
killed, is considered "inhumane." What is the difference between standing under an exploding artillery shell or bomb or being shot in the face, and
being quickly killed by gas, the newer forms of
which can kill in seconds? What is more important
is that there is the possibility of using a chemical
or biological agent[85] that only temporarily deranges
you or makes you sick. And many times more important is that none of these agents has any effect

94

on buildings, roads, railroads, etc. We use riot
control agents such as tear gas in handling mobs,
and that is not referred to as inhumane; yet, we
cannot legally use even non-lethal, incapacitating
chemicals in war; we must kill the enemy or maim him
instead! Although we all abhor the possible use of
such agents, it would appear that logic is not the
basis of our policy.

Vera Brittain let loose with a final broadside
against area bombing. "The tortures to which we
have subjected civilians including children, in our
'saturation raids' far exceed the sufferings caused
by poison gas between 1914 and 1917." She confi-
dently predicted that the "callous cruelty" with
which we destroyed innocent human life in Europe's
most crowded cities, and the vandalism which obliterated historic treasures in some of her loveliest,
"WILL APPEAR TO FUTURE CIVILISATION AS AN EXTREME
FORM OF CRIMINAL LUNACY WITH WHICH OUR POLITICAL AND
MILITARY LEADERS DELIBERATELY ALLOWED THEMSELVES TO
BECOME AFFLICTED."[86]

Strategic bombing is an extremely inflexible
weapon. It can only stand aloof as a deterrent or
if that fails, strike. It cannot occupy, supervise,
assist, support, or aid in any form of intermediate
action - it is either NO or GO. The concept is
still very much with us and has graduated from the
manned bomber now to the guided missile. But there
is little use for an intercontinental ballistic
missile with a 10 megaton H-bomb other than to rust
as a deterrent or smash a city in a war. It is too
big to hit most "military" targets except possibly
a heavily protected missile site, and besides the
people who created it will quickly tell you it is
too expensive to be used on anything less. The enthusiasts are still active. "Take up the broader
duty of understanding and preaching the role of air
power... The people who won't face the truth...must
be told repeatedly, earnestly, logically that air
power will save the world from destruction...".[87]

Fuller wrote that "The aim of strategy is to
clinch a political argument by force instead of
words." He then expanded on this point. Destruction as the end of battle is the common doctrine,
and in World War I it led not only to the defeat of
the object of war itself; for "the destruction
wrought during it so unhinged the nations mentally
and morally that the peace established on this neu-
rosis has proved itself no less destructive." The
main reason for this fatal doctrine was ignorance of
the true object of war, which is "to establish a

more perfect peace." Its popularity resulted from
mental lethargy; for to think like a wild beast is
easier than to think like a philosopher. For the
true object of war to be gained, then this destructive mania must be eliminated. This means that war
must be lifted from the cockpit of the physical
struggle into the realm of intellectual and moral
conflict.[88]

Dickens felt obliged to ask, "...did not so
much destruction often greatly incommode us?"[89]
The men who were responsible for the rebuilding of
Germany and Japan certainly must have wondered too.
The Admiral summed it all up: since there is so
much inevitable and unavoidable destruction, we must
prevent it getting completely out of hand. Much of
the damage caused by strategic bombing does not re-
coil on the victor until after the war is over.
Should that preoccupy the winning side while the war
is still raging? Not if "the bombing is really the
best way of helping to win the war;" but if we are
not sure that it is the best way, we must think much
as follows. The aggressor undertakes war as an instrument of policy. The non-aggressor, such as ourselves, does not - until he has been attacked. "His
war policy then is, first, to save his skin and,
then, to fight for a peace which he thinks is worth
having." Much of the rehabilitation of nations, including ex-enemy nations, has to be carried out at
our expense. Nations were starving, shipping and
transportation were inadequate, many essential materials were unobtainable - everywhere there was
disillusionment and bitterness. In fact the burden
of victory was crushing and the problems it has set
up fill us with deep anxiety. "Could victory have
been gained at a less terrible cost?"[90]

In sum, strategic bombing was an expensive
failure that welded the people together rather than
breaking them, contributed little to victory, complicated the peace, and may have prolonged the war
by as much as a year.[91]

NOTES

1. Raymond Aron, The Century of Total War (Garden City, N.Y.: Doubleday & Co., 1954), p. 171.
2. Sir Charles Webster and Noble Frankland, The
Strategic Air Offensive Against Germany 1939-1945
(London: H. M. Stationery Office, 1961), Vol. I,
p. 144.
3. Ibid., Vol. I, pp. 225-226, approved by the

War Cabinet 13 December 1940.

4. Churchill, Their Finest Hour, Vol. II of
The Second World War, p. 349.

5. Admiral Sir Gerald Dickens, Bombing and
Strategy; The Fallacy of Total War (London: S. Low,
Marston & Co., 1946), p. 3.

6. Webster and Frankland, Air Offensive Against
Germany, Vol. I, p. 86. With this strategy, they
saw little need for an army or navy. See Appendix
2, Vol. IV, pp. 71-76, for a May 1928 document about
striking production means. They saw this form of
war as inevitable.

7. War Reports of General of the Army George C.
Marshall, General of the Army H. H. Arnold, and
Fleet Admiral Ernest J. King (Philadelphia: J. P.
Lipincott, 1947), p. 359, italics in original.

8. See Fuller, A Military History of the Western World, Vol. III, p. 381.

9. See also Fuller, The Conduct of War, pp.
240-242, for Douhet's views. See pp. 279-287 for
Fuller's views on strategic bombing.

10. Dickens, The Fallacy of Total War, p. 18.

11. Ibid., p. 26.

12. Churchill, Step by Step 1936-39, p. 268, 1
September 1938, "Is Air-Power Decisive?"

13. Ibid., p. 271, my italics. Churchill also
noted "the undoubted obsolescence of the submarine
as a decisive war weapon..." p. 270; but then you
cannot always be right. See Comte Ciano, Archives
secrètes (Paris: Plon, 1948), p. 363, Hitler's comment to Mussolini in March 1940. "The technicians
tend to conclude - from the experience in Spain and
China - that the air arm does not have a decisive
value, but that the infantry remains, as in the
past, an essential factor." My translation.

14. Alexander Seversky, Victory Through Air
Power (London: Hutchinson, 1942), p. 93.

15. Webster and Frankland, Air Offensive
Against Germany, Vol. I, p. 133.

16. Seversky, Victory Through Air Power, pp.
157-158.

17. Webster and Frankland, Air Offensive
Against Germany, Vol. II, p. 12. See also U.S.
Strategic Bombing Survey (hereafter USSBS), The Effects of Strategic Bombing on the German War Economy (Washington, D.C.: Government Printing Office,
1945), p. 2, and Wilmot, The Struggle for Europe,
p. 155. Chester Wilmot pointed out that the effects
in 1943 were not proportional to the increased effort. Steel production was hardest hit with a reduction of only 6.4%.

The British comments on the Chief of their Bomber Command are interesting. "Sir Arthur Harris was fired with a burning conviction that the strategic air offensive was the only means by which the war could be won in reasonable time and at bearable cost." Webster and Frankland, Air Offensive, Vol. I, p. 341. "It is now possible to see how the Commander-in-Chief, Bomber Command, though theoretically only responsible for carrying out a policy decided by his superiors, was, in practice, in a very strong position to influence the making of that policy." He was a man of "strong convictions" and "unshakable determination." p. 345. Harris then took the part about the German people as his main objective. Vol. II, pp. 14-15.

18. S.L.A. Marshall, Men Against Fire, p. 31. He also wrote "Air power unsupported by the forces of the battlefield is a military means without an end." p. 35. General Marshall was the Chief Historian for the U.S. Army in the European Theatre.

19. USSBS, Over-all Effort (European War), p. 11. 20.6% or 560,493 tons were dropped on France; 25.3% on industrial areas, p. 5.

20. US Federal Civil Defense Administration, Impact of Air Attack in WWII, Division II, Vol. I, p. 16, late July and 1 August 1943.

21. USSBS, Over-all Effort (European War), p. 72; also in Fuller, The Conduct of War, p. 282.

22. USSBS, Summary Report (Pacific War) (Washington, D.C.: Government Printing Office, 30 September 1945), p. 17.

23. David H. James, The Rise and Fall of the Japanese Empire (London: Allen & Unwin, 1951), p. 287.

24. General Arnold in War Reports, p. 440.

25. Ibid.

26. Address by Acting Secretary of State Welles at National Foreign Trade Convention in Boston 8 October 1942, Goodrich, ed., Documents on American Foreign Relations, Vol. V, 1942-1943, p. 17. Unfortunately, his information was not too good, because, as we will see, German production was going up, not down.

27. Before a Joint Session of Congress 19 May 1943, ibid, pp. 259-260.

28. Churchill, Triumph and Tragedy, pp. 541-542.

29. Dickens, Fallacy of Total War, p. 16.

30. Fuller, A Military History of the Western World, Vol. III, p. 558.

31. Fuller, The Second World War, p. 402.

32. Millis, Arms and Men, p. 277. The findings of the USSBS were embodied in over 200 detailed reports.

33. Ibid., p. 255.

34. Lieutenant General James M. Gavin, War and Peace in the Space Age (New York: Harper & Brothers, 1958), p. 98. Chester Wilmot wrote, since there was "a substantial 'cushion' of reserve capacity to absorb the initial impact of the Allied offensive, Speer was able to maintain - and increase - the output of arms and munitions even in the heavily damaged cities. From Hitler's point of view the indiscriminate British bombing had certain advantages, because it awakened in the German people an urgent sense of national danger and a readiness to make sacrifices which hitherto he had been reluctant to demand." Wilmot, The Struggle for Europe, p. 155.

35. Millis, Arms and Men, p. 255.

36. Fuller, The Second World War, p. 223. See also The Conduct of War, pp. 285-286.

37. Webster and Frankland, Air Offensive Against Germany, Vol. IV, p. 284, italics in original.

38. Kahn, On Thermonuclear War, p. 379.

39. Ibid., p. 375. According to "...British expectations, the official government staff estimated on the basis of World War I and the Spanish Civil War that the Germans would achieve about 50 casualties per ton of bombs dropped, one-third of which would be fatal (actual World War II experience was less than a tenth of this) and that for every physical casualty there would be about three psychic ones roaming around the streets and countryside contributing to the chaos and disorganization." p. 376.

40. See for example Gavin, War and Peace in the Space Age, pp. 96, 97, and 102.

41. Webster and Frankland, Air Offensive Against Germany, Vol. I, p. 299. Fuller, The Second World War, p. 224, said the effort during 1940-1942 "was one of sheer waste of effort: it was one of 'uneconomic' and not of 'strategic' bombing.

42. Ibid., Vol. I, p. 488.

43. Ibid., Vol. II, p. 224.

44. Ibid., Vol. II, p. 268, my italics.

45. Ibid., Vol. III, p. 288.

46. Ibid. See General Dwight D. Eisenhower, Report by the Supreme Commander to the Combined Chiefs of Staff on the Operations in Europe of the Allied Expeditionary Force (Washington, D.C.: Government Printing Office, 1946), pp. 15-16 for his problems when considering bombing French cities, particularly

after the decision to destroy the French railway
system. Fuller, A Military History of the Western
World, Vol. III, p. 381 fn. stated that "The French
were opposed to 'strategic bombing.'"

47. Aron, Century of Total War, p. 40.

48. Fuller, The Second World War, p. 317.

49. Vera Brittain, Seed of Chaos, What Mass
Bombing Really Means (London: New Vision Publishing
Co., 1944), p. 10.

50. Quoted and discussed in Anne Armstrong, Unconditional Surrender. The Impact of the Casablanca
Policy upon World War II (New Brunswick, N.J.: Rutgers University Press, 1961), p. 53, discussion
pp. 52-55.

51. Fuller, The Second World War, p. 286, quoting from USSBS, Over-all Effort (European War).

52. Fuller, The Second World War, p. 387-388.

53. Dickens, The Fallacy of Total War, p. 41.
He pointed out that we claimed we never missed yet
we had to destroy some targets several times and we
bombed cities in Holland and Switzerland, pp. 41-42.

54. Fuller, The Second World War, p. 231. Fuller stated that the "air attack on Germany only became a true strategical operation when it was directed against the sources of energy and the means
of distribution." The Conduct of War, p. 286. This
was only in the last year of the war and mainly after
the Normandy invasion.

55. Ibid., p. 407.

56. Armstrong, Unconditional Surrender, p. 164.

57. USSBS, Summary Report (Pacific War), p. 28,
my italics. Air Vice-Marshal E. J. Kingston-
McCloughry, The Direction of War; A Critique of the
Political Direction and High Command in War (London:
Jonathan Cape, 1955), pp. 190-191, mused about this
target selection when he visited Heidelberg which
was unbombed. "Sometimes it is the government policy which decided what targets are to be attacked;
sometimes it is military policy; but most disturbing,
sometimes it can be the whim or mood of a single
man."

58. Webster and Frankland, Air Offensive Against
Germany, Vol. IV, pp. 381-382.

59. Ibid., p. 382.

60. Ibid., p. 383, italics in original.

61. See Millis, Arms and Men, p. 259. He said
the USSBS found no evidence that the attacks on the
ball bearing industry had any effect on war production. After the heavy American losses (62 of 228)
on the Schweinfurt raid, Germany relaxed and did
nothing about air defense. They failed to put

emphasis on building fighters, Wilmot, The Struggle for Europe, pp. 155-156. Hitler had put off the construction of a jet fighter in 1940 because he said the war was about over. They did not start on them until 1942 and then the Me 163 was given priority - it required special fuel and could fly only 7 minutes. It was finally given up; its chemical plant had been destroyed so there was no fuel for it. The Me 262 was finally started but much time had been lost, pp. 156-157.

62. Webster and Frankland, Air Offensive Against Germany, Vol. I, p. 233. On p. 245, they discuss the mistaken assumptions made as to the average error to be expected on a clear moonlit night. "Above all, the new estimates showed that nothing more than area bombing was operationally feasible on dark nights." p. 247. A Japanese woman, Sumie Seo Mishima, The Broader Way: A Woman's Life in the New Japan (London: Gollancz, 1954), p.24, wrote of the attacks on Tokyo, "We soon discovered that night attacks were mostly directed at residential sections."

See Sir Solly Zukerman, "Judgment and Control in Modern Warfare," Foreign Affairs, January 1962, p. 206, for some of our unrealistic estimates of the capacity of aircraft to find targets, power of their bombs, resilience of people under attack, economic consequences of our attacks, and "the functional significance of different target systems. We had to learn the hard way."

63. R.A.F. Command in England was so obsessed by strategic bombing that it almost entirely overlooked the importance of supply by air. Had it been truly air-minded, it would have appreciated that the revolution effected by the airplane was not that it enabled vertical bombardment to supplement or replace horizontal bombardment, but that it turned space into a road and thereby opened an entirely new sphere in logistics. Fuller, A Military History of the Western World, Vol. III, p. 502.

64. Whitney, MacArthur, p. 177.

65. General Arnold in War Reports, p. 371.

66. Brittain, Seed of Chaos, p. 9, italics in original.

67. Ibid., p. 100, italics added by Brittain.

68. Fuller, The Second World War, p. 228.

69. Dickens, Fallacy of Total War, p. 14.

70. Seversky, Air Power, p. 67, italics in original.

71. Ibid., p. 71, my italics.

72. Bernard, War and Its Causes, pp. 65-66.

There are numerous examples of its use in history. For instance, "smoking-out the defenders 'by the noxious fumes of a wood,'" in 1571, the fall of Famagusta, the Ottoman Turks under Mustafa against the Christians. Fuller, A Military History of the Western World, Vol. I, p. 564. "In 1812 Dundonald suggested the use of burning sulphur as an asphyxiant, and in 1855 he revived the idea, and urged its use against Sevastopol, but his proposal was rejected as too horrible to contemplate." The Conduct of War, p. 90.

73. Fuller, The Conduct of War, p. 174.

74. B.H. Liddell Hart, Deterrent or Defense, A Fresh Look at the West's Military Position (New York: Frederick A. Praeger, Publishers, 1960), p.83.

75. Ibid., p. 85.

76. Ibid., p. 84.

77. Ibid., p. 85.

78. Kingston-McCloughry, The Direction of War, pp. 223-224. He said we kept gas ready. After Hitler lost air supremacy, it was not to his advantage to use it. See also Webster and Frankland, Air Offensive Against Germany, Vol. III, p. 288, in support of this last point.

79. Peter Fleming, Operation Sea Lion, The Projected Invasion of England in 1940 - An Account of the German Preparations and the British Countermeasures (New York: Simon & Schuster, 1957), pp.293-294.

80. See Ministry of Foreign Affairs of the U.S.S.R., Stalin's Correspondence with Churchill, Attlee, Roosevelt and Truman 1941-1945 (Moscow: Foreign Language Publishing House, 1957; New York: Dutton & Co., 1958).

81. Goodrich, Documents on American Foreign Relations, Vol. V, p. 198, 8 June 1943.

82. Harry Butcher, My Three Years with Eisenhower (New York: Simon & Schuster, 1946), pp. 577-578.

83. Liddell Hart, Deterrent or Defense, p. 62.

84. Fuller, Armored Warfare (Harrisburg, Penn.: Military Service Publishing Co., 1943) p. 69.

85. There are many different biological agents causing diseases that are fatal to man or animals or only make them sick for a period of time. Biological warfare has one quite different characteristic from chemical warfare in that it can cause epidemics and thereby spread, while chemical attack is generally restricted to the area of attack and for most agents lasts only a few minutes.
Possony, A Century of Conflict, p. 364fn, wrote,

"Biological weapons are the fulfillment of the sabateur's dreams. Not unexpectedly, the soviets have shown exceptional interest in biological weapons - and in the water-supply system of American cities."

86. Brittain, Seed of Chaos, p. 116, capitalized part in the original.

87. Air Force Chief of Staff, General Hoyt S. Vandenberg to graduates at an Air Force base, Time magazine, 29 June 1953.

88. Fuller, Armored Warfare, p. 44, italics in original.

89. Dickens, The Fallacy of Total War, p. 39.

90. Ibid., p. 41.

91. See Hans Rumpf, The Bombing of Germany transl. by Edward Fitzgerald (New York: Holt, Rinehart and Winston, 1962), an interesting book from the German side, particularly, pp. 205-214.

5
Psychological Warfare

> This war will be settled
> in the rear, not in the
> trenches.
>
> -- Lenin

> The spoken word is the
> sole force capable of pro-
> ducing really great revo-
> lutions of sentiment.
>
> -- Adolf Hitler

1. The Conflict for the Minds of Men

Most of us think of war in the simple terms of
armed conflict between military forces. In reality,
that is only one part of warfare. We are not always
aware of the often unheralded behind-the-scenes activities in the economic, political, and psychological spheres. Psychological warfare, in one form
or another, is as old as history. The Pharaohs and
the Prophets were experts in the field. The leaders
of the French and American Revolutions and Napoleon,
thereafter, used it with visible success. It is a
form of warfare with which we have become more familiar in recent years, but which we still do not
seem to really appreciate or understand. It is a
major ingredient of total war because it lends
itself so well to the ideological struggle. We have
all been subjected to it repeatedly, particularly in
World War II, although most of us probably never
realized it, and we face it every minute of every
day during the Cold War.
Perhaps we should start by getting an expert's
definition:

"...psychological warfare may be defined as
the planned use of <u>propaganda</u> and <u>other actions</u>
designed to influence the opinions, emotions,
attitudes, and behavior of enemy, neutral, and
friendly foreign groups in such a way as to
support the accomplishment of national aims and
objectives."[1]

Since propaganda will be discussed in the next
section, perhaps we should define it now to show
that though the two are closely linked, they are not
synonymous. Propaganda "may be defined as the
planned dissemination of news, information, special
arguments, and appeals designed to influence the beliefs, thoughts, and actions of a specific group."[2]
Propaganda then is but a part of psychological warfare.
    Clausewitz, who recognized elements of war
besides physical force, observed that the object of
combat need not always be the destruction of the
enemy's forces. The objective can often be attained as well without combat taking place at all.[3]
The idea of a bloodless victory brought about "by
trickery, subversion and the sapping of his enemy's
morale" fascinated Hitler. "'Our strategy is to destroy the enemy from within to conquer him through
himself.'" He repeatedly returned to this theme.
"'What is the object of war? To make the enemy capitulate. If he does, I have the prospect of wip-
ing him out. Why should I demolish him by military
means if I can do so better and more cheaply in
other ways?'"[4] This idea of beating the enemy from
within brought a new term into our vocabulary that
was widely used in the second war: Fifth Column.
The term actually dates from the Spanish Civil War
when, in October 1936, the forces of General Franco
were closing on Madrid from four directions. In a
radio broadcast, they proclaimed that in addition
to the four columns in the field there was a fifth
in Madrid. Designed to trouble men's minds, the
expression has lived on. In times of violence and
double-dealing, the idea was, in effect, a new conception of treachery. It was widely used throughout the war and the countries of Western Europe are
a mute testimony to its effectiveness after the war
in the hands of the Communists, the grand practitioners of psychological warfare. "Coined for purposes of psychological warfare, the phrase had a
certain cogency, a technical bravura; it was intended to provide uneasiness and mutual distrust in
a situation of danger, and it went on promoting

106

them."[5]

Psychological warfare is a basic tool of Communist ideology.[6] Lenin, with almost no army, came to terms at Brest-Litovsk taking Russia out of the first war. For him, the all-important lesson of the negotiations was that, without the backing of adequate armed force, little can be expected from psychological warfare. Therefore, he directed Trotsky to build a Red Army. This points up once again that we are not speaking of an absolute weapon but of another means in the arsenal to be used in conjunction with the others. Marshal Bulganin wrote in a book, in 1948, that he favored replacing the ill-defined German concept of total war with that of the politico-military war. Modern war, to him, is both a national and a social conflict. Propaganda is as effective a weapon as conventional military measures. Political techniques can paralyze an army through destructive propaganda aiming at the neutralization (rather than the annihilation) of hostile forces. Psychological warfare can be the major factor in the overthrow of a defeated nation's government and its replacement by a regime socially and politically acceptable to the victor.[7]

In their struggle for the minds of men, the Communists have given us another new term: brainwashing. We particularly encountered this with our prisoners captured in the Korean War. However, it should have been apparent to us with the "confessions" recited in the Russian purge trials before World War II and a few others after the war. This is the peak of ideological warfare. As Susy, a character in Paul Gallico's novel, Trial by Terror, said upon the release of her friend from a Communist prison, "'They sent his body back. But there isn't anything in it. He's not there any more.... His mind is gone.'"[8]

A good example of the importance of psychological warfare is the German invasion of Russia. The Germans moved against the Soviet Union in June 1941 without a psychological warfare plan. The failure to forecast accurately the predisposition of Soviet subjects and to orient their propaganda and policy pronouncements in line with the real interests of both the German High Command and the Russian people led the Nazis to lose an opportunity to subjugate great parts of the Soviet Union.

Defecting Red Army officers, prisoners, and intelligence agents reported that German propaganda was poor and had completely failed to understand the Russian thought process. "The Russian people, and

107

probably a good portion of the Red Army, could have
been won over, they believed, if definite promises
had been made and a definite program outlined for
the political and economic future of the USSR."[9]
The German propaganda effort was not well thought
out. The important point to make was that the Wehrmacht was entering Russia to free the people from
Soviet tyranny and not as their enemy. After ten
horrible years of collectivization which had cost
the lives of some 10,000,000 people, Hitler had the
opportunity to disintegrate the colossus, by cross-
ing the Russian frontier as a liberator, and ending
collectivization.

It should never be forgotten that the Germans
were greeted as liberators at first and they lost
this position only through their own ruthless stupidity. Ukrainian volunteers were even used to help
supplement German security troops.[10] By the end of
the winter of 1941-1942, an unprecedented number of
prisoners -- nearly 5 million -- had passed through
German prisoner of war camps on the Eastern front.
Groups of division size or larger surrendered together. It was only after the Russians had been
subjected to brutal prisoner-of-war and occupation
policies, and they began to understand the Nazi war
aims of partition and colonization of Russia, that
their friendship or indifference turned into fear
and hate and they really began to defend themselves
against the invader.[11] By policy blunders and brutality, the Germans themselves aided Stalin in turning an unpopular war into an all-out, patriotic
struggle for Mother Russia.

As in the days of Napoleon, the farther the
German advance progressed the less friendly the
people became; but in the rural parts of the
Ukraine, the attitude of the people remained at
least neutral as late as December.[12] In the
Ukraine, where the Germans had found so much support, they confiscated all radios, both receivers
and transmitters, regardless of the loss of that invaluable propaganda medium.[13]

As partisan activity began to rise, German
propaganda remained negative and "even verged on
the hypocritical." It was aimed at keeping the
people from supporting the partisans, but "They were
to be promised nothing."[14] When the Russians became aware that the Germans were not there to lead
the Soviet people to a happier future or to help
them gain full freedom or political independence,
they slowly, and often reluctantly, turned away.[15]
German propaganda depicted the Russian people as

the embodiment of everything murderous, barbarian, and "oriental." This messianic ideological crusade was thus directed against the Russian people rather than against the Soviet regime. Typical of crusades, once the die was cast it was impossible for Germany to fight a war of limited objectives. Victory or defeat therefore had to be total.[16] High-level German hate had driven them into a total war.

It would be unfair to say no German leaders saw their problem. Many German leaders expressed concern over the possible negative reaction of the Russian natives to such obvious exploitation and the effect it might have on the entire war effort, but all these forebodings, as so often happens, were ignored.[17] Psychological warfare is an instrument of high-level policy, and though they chose to ignore the counsel of the leaders on the spot, the German leadership conducted it from the highest level. Hitler saw the war with Russia as a fight to the finish between "two opposite political systems," therefore the territory was to be "prepared" for the ensuing political occupation. This task was given to Heinrich Himmler, leader of the SS troops and chief of German Police to "carry out independently of all other agencies and on his own responsibility."[18] Planning papers of the Army High Command "actually disclose an effort to incite the German forces to atrocities against the Red Army, and the opening paragraph of the OKW Regulations states flatly that the Russian soldier is not to be honorably treated in accordance with the terms of the Geneva Convention."[19] The orders for the occupation were truly brutal. They called for the liquidation of guerrillas, commissars, Communists, anybody in the way. "Moscow and Leningrad were to be leveled and made uninhabitable so as to obviate the necessity for feeding the populations through the winter."[20]

Communist propaganda was able to capitalize on these many German bad points, but they also stressed the long arm of the Communist Party and that people had better stick with them or they would have to pay the consequences when they got back.[21] In sum, the failure of the German occupation was the failure to understand the Eastern peoples, to treat them as human beings, and admit them as equals into the New Order being created. The Germans failed to outline a definite program, including the basic desires of the people, to broadcast it with an effective propaganda line, and to carry it out; and they failed to provide a standard of living and set up a system of social justice at least equal to that formerly provided by the Soviet Government.[22] This summary points up the importance of psychological warfare policy and its close relationship with economic and political policy. Yes, there is more to war than just armies shooting at each other, and psychological warfare is not just some pet idea for eccentrics; it is an important aspect of overall strategy in the political policy of a nation.

Democracies, living in their idealistic cloud, do not like anything that smacks of subversion or underhandedness. The United States, then, has never been able to find itself in psychological warfare. It gave it the old college amateur try during the war and then promptly went back to sleep when "peace" came. Foreign propaganda activities were initially divided between the Office of Strategic Services (OSS) and the Office of War Information (OWI), with the latter limited to open, as contrasted to secret, activities. As this division of responsibility led to numerous controversies, the OWI was directed by an Executive Order of 9 March 1943 to conduct all activities related to United States propaganda abroad, with the exception of Latin America.[23]

Psychological warfare, to be effective, needs a voice in high circles. The effectiveness of OWI suffered because its top spokesmen were not included in high-policy discussions. It has been repeatedly recommended that any future war cabinet, or similar body, include a representative of United States propaganda agencies. The most important news during war is "produced" in battle and by statesmen or their ghost writers. American propagandists had virtually no influence on these productions during World War II; they functioned as wholesale and retail agents in the news business. Important propaganda policies depended upon general policies that were "oriented toward speedy military victory rather than toward a desirable distribution of political power after victory." President Roosevelt's announcement of the war aim of Unconditional Surrender was an example. Assuming the political need for this war aim, its psychological repercussions could have been foreseen to be considerable, to the extent that it would have been worthwhile to explore them in advance. The desireable effects on the Soviet leadership and on the resistance elements in occupied Europe could have been maximized and the undesirable effects on the

110

Germans could have been minimized without sacrifice of principle.[24]

The striking contrast between the bleak slogan of Unconditional Surrender and the propaganda appeal of Wilson's Fourteen Points in World War I illustrates the axiom that the upper limits of psychological warfare are set by broad national policy objectives. The formulation of the policy of Unconditional Surrender did not benefit from the advice of any psychological warfare men. Consequently, this policy greatly handicapped the Anglo-American psychological warfare effort against the Axis powers.[25]

A typical expression of contempt for psychological warfare is the comment by Thomas K. Finletter, former Secretary of the Air Force and Ambassador to NATO. "Psychological warfare had its extravagances a while, but they have been put to rest by the definitive report of a committee headed by William H. Jackson which recommended that the United States give up psychological warfare."[26] And it appears that we have given it up for the most part. Regardless, it is still an instrument that played a significant role in World War II and may well have played the dominant role in the Cold War. Even if one does not like any aspect of psychological warfare, it behooves one to understand it so that it can be effectively combatted.[27]

2. Propaganda

Propaganda is something we experience every day. Advertising in all its many forms to influence us to buy some product is propaganda. The attempt to influence our fellow man is as old as man himself; it is used by government, church, business, and almost all types of organizations. It can be aimed against kings and queens[28] or other heads of states or against an enemy people or against one's own people. The word "propaganda" gained its bad connotation in English from the vast quantities of official statements issued by the governments engaged in World War I. Each claimed their own cause was completely just, and their own conduct above reproach, but that the enemy was worse than savage, and backed up their accusations by the sometimes fictional details of sensational atrocity stories. The unification of opinion in support of the government was the first task for war propaganda in each country and the best solution was to convince the

populace of the war guilt of the enemy. So since
not everybody could be guilty of everything, not all
of the stories were always true. As people became
aware of this, propaganda picked up a new meaning as
being false or misleading information to incite people to support some cause.

As often as not, propaganda is directed at the
internal audience. Total war, with its ideological
flavor and requirement for wide support by the people to provide the tremendous industrial output as
well as their moral support in the righteous effort,
depends on propaganda to a great extent, particularly to generate the ideological fervor and hate
needed to conduct total war.29 The Fascists, Nazis,
and Communists (like the Crusaders) have all been
masters of the art. With strict censorship, so that
nothing may be refuted, official propagandists developed the technique of the "big lie" -- a false-
hood in itself so atrocious as to be incredible, but
which, by continuous repetition with infinite variations and additions is finally accepted as true
with the people believing the government's "story."

This is not some wild story from history; this
continues today. There are thousands of examples:
just look at any piece of Communist literature or
listen to a Communist broadcast, or even in other
states where the media are govenment controlled.
The hate-America campaigns, the distortion of facts
about Western life, and the lies about the actions
of Western governments are only some of the more obvious examples. This can happen any time that the
government controls the media of communication and
keeps the society closed.

A perfect example appeared in the Viet-Nam War.
Hanoi and the National Liberation Front decided "to
build up Nguyen Van Be as their number one hero of
the war." He had supposedly been killed in battle
doing glorious deeds. However, Nguyen Van Be was
captured in South Viet-Nam very much alive and he
clearly admitted that he had been overwhelmed in
that short "heroic" firefight and had not even fired
his weapon. The North Vietnamese did not change
their campaign. Anyone who said Be was alive was
threatened with being shot on the spot. Be and all
in contact with him were marked for execution. The
reward for "cancelling" Be was quoted at 2 million
piastres. As a captured senior North Vietnamese officer said, they will outlast you until there are no
witnesses left. This showed the importance of the
"cult of revolutionary heroism" in motivation indoctrination. "To admit that the brilliant ideal and

112

shining example does not really exist brings morale shattering disillusionment which simply cannot be tolerated."[30]

Man is not nearly the rational being that had been supposed; Hitler demonstrated that rather well. It has been said that there can be no propaganda without hate. While probably not always true, hate is certainly a basic ingredient in war propaganda. Go back to the days of World War II and review what was printed in the newspapers and magazines. It is almost embarrassing now to read some of the things we said about the Germans, Italians, and Japanese (also the Russians but in the opposite manner). But hate is a powerful force. As one man has said, give me something to hate, and within twenty-four hours I guarantee I can establish a strong propaganda campaign anywhere.[31]

Hitler well understood the value of propaganda. He told his generals on 22 August 1939, "'I shall give a propagandistic cause for starting the war -- never mind whether it be plausible or not. In starting and making a war, not the Right is what matters but Victory.'"[32] Hitler had long thought out his use of propaganda; he was like an actor on a stage, particularly when in front of a crowd. He had a definite psychology of leadership, even the title he took, Führer, which means "Leader," was a part of this. Hitler characterized the leader in propaganda terms. No trick was overlooked. He stressed the advantage of oratory over written argument, and the effects of lighting, atmosphere, symbols, and the crowd. He exploited the advantage of meetings held at night when the power to resist suggestion is low. He practiced leadership in terms of skillful use of suggestion, collective hypnosis, and every kind of subconscious motivation with the key to its success being "clever psychology" and the "ability to sense the thinking processes of the broad masses of the population."[33] For Hitler, the leader could manipulate the masses of people as an artist molds clay. He used hate adroitly, turning it on the Jews, certain types of art, certain books; he was almost able to turn it off and on at will.

As we will see, one of our mistakes of the war was in not differentiating between the Nazis and the German people. Chamberlain started out right, but the policy was changed when Churchill took over the government. Chamberlain declared in his first broadcast to the enemy: "We are not fighting against you, the German people, but against a tyrannous and foresworn regime." The propaganda instructions to the

113

new Ministry of Information were to attack the Nazis, but not the millions they dragooned.[34]

The Times of London reported Churchill's speech in the House of Commons in April 1940: "The Nazi Government, the German Government -- I do not know how you can distinguish them; they seem all to be mixed up together (Cheers) Nazis and Germans, Germans and Nazis."[35] Goebbels pointed up the mistake we made by his diary entry for 27 March 1942.

> A much more clever form of propaganda against the Reich has been proposed in the United States. The idea is not to go against the German people but against Nazism. I sense a certain danger. Fortunately the enemy propaganda is not so unified and consistent as to be able to stick to such a propaganda slogan for a period of years. If this were the case we would face great difficulties every time we were under a new, heavy strain.
>
> If I were on the enemy side, I should from the very first day on have adopted the slogan of fighting against Nazism, but not against the German people. That's how Chamberlain began on the first day of the war, but, thank God, the English didn't follow through. I gave orders that the German press is not to publish or discuss turns of speech such as are being used increasingly in the American press. One should simply not talk about these things. Even if you agree about them you nevertheless spread them.[36]

We never saw our mistake. The Atlantic Charter contributed almost nothing to rouse the populations of Germany and Italy against their masters and to allay their fears. Allied propaganda did not enlist the peoples of the totalitarian countries in the downfall of their masters, did not make them partners in the effort to oust them.[37] Even so, with the psychological war aims we finally settled on, we tried to secure them by military means. In spite of Mr. Chamberlain's pronouncement, once a psychological war aim had been fixed upon, the Allies tried to attain it solely by military means. "This was their greatest political blunder of the war."[38]

Good material for propaganda can come from almost anywhere, and often from the most unlikely places. The entries Goebbels made in his diary give a good insight into the thinking of someone "creating"

114

propaganda. For example, Goebbels was able to use the announcements by Sir Stafford Cripps to his own advantage in the German propaganda.

> Cripps continues to carry on agitation on be-
> half of the Bolsheviks. For us he is a propa-
> gandist whom we simply could not pay more money.
> I therefore ordered the press not to picture
> him as an outsider. On the contrary, we must
> represent him as a sort of mouthpiece for
> Churchill. Of course he isn't that actually,
> but he is most useful to us that way.[39]

This shows that not all propaganda is the product of people in a big office dreaming it up; much of it is shrewd adapatation or "twisting" of normal news items.

Admiral Leahy, while he was Ambassador to Vichy, recounted his first encounter with psychological warfare on 4 February 1942. The British dropped leaflets in France with the American flag printed on one side and a picture of the Statue of Liberty on the other. They were entitled "Message from America to the People of France." The message contained, "To the country that gave us the Statue of Liberty we will give liberty." and ended with "Keep up your courage. When our victory comes, when victory comes to all the Allies, you will be among the victors."[40] The Russians put leaflets and public address systems to good use in an impressive propaganda campaign supporting their counterstroke in the winter of 1941-1942. The German troops were reminded of "the French campaign of 1812, the deep snow and bitter cold to which they were unaccustomed, the immediate danger of death by freezing far away from the German homeland, the resurrection of Soviet strength, and the turn of the tide of battle, all of which made a strong emotional impression on the German command and, to an even higher degree, on the troops."[41] Kato wrote that "By all odds the greatest propaganda success of the war was the American practice of dropping leaflets from the air."[42] The same idea was employed on the small packages of cigarettes, matches, candy, pencils, sewing kits, etc., that were slipped into the Philippines by submarine. Each package displayed the crossed American and Philippine flags on one side, and on the other the quotation "I shall return" -- printed over MacArthur's signature.[43] The power of "hope" also can be very strong.

We have already seen how psychological warfare

works best with high-level support. Goebbels worked
at the highest level and with full access to the
most secret intelligence and to Hitler.[44] The British also were organized so that they had high access.[45] American propagandists, however, merely reported or interpreted events rather than formed policy.[46] President Roosevelt thought that the OWI had
something to do with censorship, and Cordell Hull
sometimes gave the impression of holding the same
belief. Elmer Davis, OWI's Director, received little
cooperation from other high officials, and often had
difficulty in finding out what United States policy
was.[47]

What is not said sometimes may be propaganda
just as much as a deliberate statement. As an example, OWI's request for a statement on Vichy and
Petain received no response for eight months, and
nothing was ever said about alleged American intentions to install a military government in liberated
France. Inaction or the absence of a policy may
have propaganda effects fully as great as those of
positive action or a clearly formulated policy.[48]
Lack of coordination between those conducting psychological warfare and others forming policy in the
government can create embarrassing moments. When
American authorities were attempting to persuade the
Italian government of Marshal Badoglio to proclaim
an armistice in 1943, OWI was not informed of these
negotiations. Consequently, it made the blunder of
bitterly attacking the Badoglio government in overseas broadcasts. When informed of the discussions
in progress, the OWI was forced to change its line
abruptly -- a procedure that discredited the propagandists and also reflected on the country they represented.[49] It should be clear that propaganda is
only an expression of policy and should not be left
to operate independently.

Anne Armstrong made a profound observation on
the effect of total war propaganda on democracies.
"In a democratic society it takes a long and moralistic propaganda campaign to arouse public opinion
to war fever; once this fever has been aroused, once
war has been proclaimed for absolute moral purposes,
it is difficult to stem the tide."[50] It is interesting to read an evaluation of American public opinion
before the war as seen by a foreigner, the Polish
Ambassador at Washington, Count Jerzy Potocki, in a
report to the Polish Foreign Office, 12 January 1939.

"Public opinion in America nowadays," he wrote,
"expresses itself in an increasing hatred of

everything...connected with National Socialism.
Above all, propaganda here is entirely in Jewish hands..." and "when bearing public ignorance in mind, their propaganda is so effective
that people here have no real knowledge of the
true state of affairs in Europe.... It is interesting to observe that in this carefully
thought-out campaign -- which is primarily conducted against National Socialism -- no reference at all is made to Soviet Russia. If that
country is mentioned, it is referred to in a
friendly manner and people are given the impression that Soviet Russia is part of the
democratic group of countries. Thanks to astute propaganda, public sympathy in the U.S.A.
is entirely on the side of Red Spain.... President Roosevelt was first in the field to give
expression to this hatred of Fascism. He had a
two-fold purpose in mind: firstly, he wanted to
divert American public opinion from difficult
and complicated problems.... Secondly, by creating a war-panic... he wanted to induce Americans to endorse his huge program of armaments....

"In this campaign of hatred, individual Jewish
intellectuals such as Bernard Baruch, Lehman,
Governor of New York State, Felix Frankfurter,
the newly appointed Supreme Court Judge, Morgenthau, the Financial Secretary, and other
well-known personal friends of Roosevelt have
taken a prominent part in this campaign of
hatred. All of them want the President to become the protagonist of human liberty, religious freedom and the right of free speech."[51]

Of course there are many exaggerated or misin-
terpreted ideas in his report, but he was not completely wrong. It would probably be giving the
government too much credit to say that they had
really done as much with propaganda as he reported.
The results in the war would seem to refute this
government ability.
In actual fact, the reaction of the Americans
was slow, but their hate burst forth after the attack on Pearl Harbor. This hate, and the resultant
drive for Total Victory, blinded us to many of the
more subtle aspects of the war and caused us to make
some mistakes and misjudgments. Hanson Baldwin observed that wartime propaganda added to the illusion;
all our enemies were knaves, all our Allies were

117

friends and comrades. Military victory was our only purpose. We fought Total War with all the zeal and energy and courage for which Americans are famous, but we fought to win; in the broader sense of an objective, we did not know what we were fighting for.[52] Propaganda was not truly the cause of this because it was just a reflection of the views of national leadership. Nevertheless, our propaganda, once carried away with itself, did become an obstacle to sensible policy and did manage to limit our flexibility. The trouble General Eisenhower had with Admiral Jean Darlan is one example. Darlan, who was placed in civilian command as High Commissioner in North Africa, had been billed by propaganda and publicity for two years as pro-Nazi, having replaced Laval as Vice-Premier of Vichy France. For the public suddenly to accept him as a patriotic and earnest Frenchman was doubtful.[53]

General MacArthur's headquarters received word of atrocities against prisoners-of-war in the Philippines and so a statement was prepared. It was never published; orders were received that same day from Washington forbidding the release of any of the details of those atrocities. "The Administration was committed to a maximum Europe-first effort and did not want the American people aroused to the point of demanding a greater effort against Japan until the war in the European theater had been concluded."[54] Freedom of speech and strong propaganda are usually incompatible.

One of the requests throughout had been for a definition of peace aims with the contention that it would help towards victory through its effect on public opinion at home and in the enemy camp as well as in conquered countries, and in neutral countries.[55] The Unconditional Surrender policy did little to define the peace aims, and the most powerful weapon that could have been given to overt strategic propagandists consequently remained unused in World War II.[56] After the death of President Roosevelt and the accession of Mr. Truman to the presidency in April 1945, it was decided to spell out in greater detail the meaning of Unconditional Surrender and to address the decision-making elite in the Japanese government by means of radio. The man chosen was Captain (later Admiral) Ellis M. Zacharias, who personally knew many of the Japanese leaders and was therefore able to direct his remarks directly to these men. His objective was to convince the High Command that there was an alternative to total annihilation and enslavement, and that, therefore, fur-

ther resistance was senseless.[57] The Zacharias
broadcasts were apparently rather effective in bringing about the Japanese surrender.[58] This was a case
of almost pure propaganda conducted by radio over
thousands of miles; nevertheless, the Unconditional
Surrender policy had to be altered before a surrender could be effected. We refused to alter it in
the Potsdam ultimatum to Japan on 26 July 1945.
"Not a word was said about the Emperor, because it
would be unacceptable to the propaganda-fed American
masses."[59] Propaganda is a two-edged sword; sometimes it can have a great effect on the enemy, and
sometimes if it has gotten carried away a bit it can
work against us. This was a case where we were
blinded by our own propaganda.
     Propaganda does not require it, but it operates
best with a basis of truth. Kato wrote that the
Japanese were "hopelessly beaten in psychological
warfare," not because of great Allied ability but
because the Allied propaganda was based on truth,
while the Japanese had been unwilling to deal with
truth almost from the beginning.[60] This points up
the importance of counter-propaganda. The French,
Dutch, Belgians, and others who were under enemy occupation looked to broadcasts from abroad to give
them the truth. The Philippines were in the same
situation after their fall. The Japanese controlled
all forms of internal propaganda concerning the progress of the war bearing down heavily on Filipinos,
but it was also hurting the morale of those Americans still at large. Time after time, in their radio
messages to our headquarters, guerrilla leaders
pleaded for Allied counter-propaganda.[61] A similar
situation continues throughout the world in the radio
competition between the Free World and the Communist
World.
     The Communists pour forth a mass of propaganda
unlike anything seen before in history. Their radio
broadcasts are measured by many hours per week in
many different languages; their written propaganda
is measured in tons each month. This mass of false
promises and untruths flows into Western Europe, the
Americas, Asia, and Africa. The magnitude of it is
unbelievable; here are a few figures of the effort
in West Germany.

     Propaganda in West Germany is directed by an of-
     fice of the East German central committee with
     16,000 agents in the Federal Republic, among
     them hundreds of instructors. The number of
     pamphlets coming across the frontier each month

119

has risen from 320,000 in 1957 to 12 million.
There are now 45 East German wireless transmitters, and its television programme reaches a
West German audience larger than the East German population. Numerous illegal communist papers are printed in West Germany, including 11
Land papers, more than 100 works papers, and 25
magazines.

Further, the Ministry states that 8,400,000
marks (about £700,000,000) /almost $2 billion/
are yearly spent on the propaganda campaign
against the West; that there are sixty-three
Communist Parties in Western and neutral countries, each an active fifth column, and that
there are hundreds of front groups directed by
fifteen pro-Communist world organizations, controlled by a central committee in Prague, which
may be regarded as a successor to the Comintern.
Such is the reverse of Khrushchev's "peaceful
coexistence".[62]

This is really propaganda mass-produced on a
professional level with the highest support and direction from the Communist high command.
The Russian people have been under this sort of
thing for over half a century and know little else,
and it has had its effect. Averell Harriman, who
spent many years in Russia in important positions,
wrote that "The massive Soviet propaganda machine
has, I believe, convinced most Soviet citizens that
the United States is the greatest threat to peace in
the world today."[63] He added that "If the Communist
leaders should find it to their convenience to warm
the cold war, they will have the Soviet people behind them. There will be no question in the Soviet
public's mind that the aggressor is the United
States."[64] This is a product of the controlled press,
which has served throughout the years to prevent the
impact upon the minds of the Soviet citizens of all
unwanted news and ideas from the outside world, and
to insure the impact upon those minds of the official line on every subject. Censorship and propaganda have been two sides of the same coin.[65] Truth
has no value to the Communists; the people are to
accept as the truth that which the Communists tell
them. Advancing education in the Communist World
has created problems, however. Harriman noted that
"Since knowledge is probably the greatest enemy of
false propaganda, the Communist Party's controllers
of though are finding that task more and more

difficult."66

The Communists have gone a long way toward
adopting the three slogans of the "Party" in George
Orwell's 1984: WAR IS PEACE, FREEDOM IS SLAVERY,
IGNORANCE IS STRENGTH.67 Where else would a country
build a wall to keep its people in rather than to
keep an enemy out? To us who treasure our freedom
of speech, this thought control of the Communists is
almost unbelievable, but it exists and it plays an
important role in Soviet internal politics and, because of its resultant support, an important role in
international relations. Though the Russian people
are basically friendly to the United States, they
know so little of the truth about America and the
West that in the event of war their conditioned
thinking would probably keep them in support of the
Communists. The Communists must control thought so
completely that they have a problem with history.
In Arthur Koestler's Darkness at Noon, "Rubashov remarked jokingly to Arlova that the only thing left
to be done was to publish a new and revised edition
of the back numbers of all newspapers."68 But this
is not as completely far-fetched as one might think,
for the New York Herald Tribune of 12-13 January
1963, reported that the Bulgarians were about to re-
write history in line with de-Stalinization.69 All
textbooks and school aids were to be rewritten to
reflect the "historic truth." The only trouble is
that under Communism, the historic truth may change
every few years!

It is evident that when propaganda moves into a
large scale, its first casualties are freedom of
speech and freedom of the press for they might tend
to refute the propaganda "line." We see these freedoms continually being weakened in the United States.
The Cuban crisis of 1962 brought a new use of controlled information to America and even more tight-
ening of the controls on the freedom of speech in
the military. The gagging of society is what General MacArthur called the "totalitarian way." As he
said, "The American people are entitled to know the
facts."70 If they do not know the facts, then they
are not capable of voting and deciding on important
issues; if they are not capable of voting, then
there is no basis for democracy. The control of all
information is the first step of dictatorship; there
is no dictatorship with freedom of speech, and there
is no free country where there is no freedom of expression! That is the real danger of the "muzzling"
of the military or any other part of a free society.71
Propaganda whether it is used for good or evil is a

121

weapon.

Total war, then, is the employment of potentially every available resource in support of a war that is fought for an ultimate objective, survival, and the continuation or expansion of a way of life. Being ideological in nature, it takes on the form of a crusade to smash the "infidels," only, in this modern age, we do not use the sword but modern bombers and missiles for blind destruction through strategic bombing. It represents the employment of every imaginable facet of conflict between nations: economic, political, psychological, and military. This struggle for the minds of men continues unabated in the Cold War (it is debatable as to whether it has ended), which may very well prove to be one of the most important wars in the history of man.

In World War II, the concept of Total War led us down a false path blindly chasing the illusion of Total Victory. The great manifestation of this chase was the Casablanca formula demanding of the Axis their Unconditional Surrender.

NOTES

1. William E. Daugherty and Morris Janowitz, A Psychological Warfare Casebook (Baltimore: Johns Hopkins Press, 1958), p. 2, italics in original.
2. Ibid. As the authors point out, there is much disagreement over what name to use for this type of "political activity." Palmer and Perkins, International Relations, p. 206, point out that, "Propaganda is psychological warfare when it is used to weaken enemies rather than to influence friends."
3. Clausewitz, On War, p. 26.
4. Peter Fleming, Operation Sea Lion, pp. 113-114.
5. Ibid., pp. 57-58.
6. "'Propaganda,' wrote Lenin in 1905, 'is of crucial importance for the triumph of the party.'" Palmer and Perkins, International Relations, p. 207. See also "Communist Psychological Warfare" by Stephan T. Possony in Walter F. Hahn and John C. Neff, eds., American Strategy for the Nuclear Age (Garden City, N.Y.: Doubleday Anchor Books, 1960) p. 129.
7. Possony, A Century of Conflict, p. 353.
8. Paul Gallico, Trial by Terror (New York: A Dell Book, paperback, 1951), p. 353.
9. Howell, The Soviet Partisan Movement, pp. 111-112.
10. Ibid., p. 53.

11. Daugherty and Janowitz, Psychological Warfare, p. 269, from the section on "German Psychological Warfare - Soviet Union," by Paul Blackstock.
No use was made of Russian Lieutenant General Vlas-
sov.
  12. Howell, The Soviet Partisan Movement, p. 61.
  13. Ibid., p. 57.
  14. Ibid., p. 60.
  15. Ibid., p. 97.
  16. Paul Blackstock in Daugherty and Janowitz,
Psychological Warefare, pp. 266-267.
  17. Howell, The Soviet Partisan Movement, p. 22.
  18. Ibid., p. 16.
  19. Paul Blackstock in Daugherty and Janowitz,
Psychological Warfare, p. 267; he then quoted the
paragraph.
  20. Howell, The Soviet Partisan Movement, p. 19.
  21. Ibid., pp. 63-65.
  22. Ibid., p. 98.
  23. United States. National Archives, Federal
Records of World War II, Vol. I. p. 548.
  24. Hans Speier, "The Future of Psychological
Warfare," Public Opinion Quarterly, 12:7-8 (1948)
(quoted in Daugherty and Janowitz, Psychological Warfare, p. 305), my italics.
  25. Daugherty and Janowitz, Psychological Warfare, p. 260. Even though it was almost impossible
to make Unconditional Surrender attractive to the
enemy, there was still some room for maneuver left.
The propagandists were forced to rely on more basic
appeals that were possibly even more effective. Examples: Allied victory is inevitable so why prolong
a losing struggle, and the free world, in contrast
with the Axis, can be trusted even by a vanquished
foe.
  26. Thomas K. Finletter, Power and Policy, U.S.
Foreign Policy and Military Power in the Hydrogen
Age (New York: Harcourt, Brace and Co., 1954), p.
126. The Psychological Warfare Board was abolished
and replaced by the Operations Coordinating Board
under the National Security Council.
  27. For further reading, see Robert Strausz-
Hupé, William R. Kintner, and Stefan T. Possony, A
Forward Strategy for America (New York: Harper &
Brothers, 1961), Chapter 8, "Psychological Operations," p. 253.
  28. See for example Fuller, A Military History
of the Western World, Vol. I, p. 219, for the Roman
propaganda campaign against Cleopatra in 33-32 B.C.
in the power struggle between Mark Antony and
Octavian.

29. Referring to World War I, "'One of the most appalling revelations of the entire war,' wrote Morison and Commager, 'was the ease with which modern technique and mass-suggestion enables a government to make even a reasonably intelligent people, with an individualistic, democratic background, believe anything it likes.'" Fuller, The Conduct of War, p. 180.

30. Message No. 10 from JUSPAO-Saigon to USIA Washington, Subject: "Nguyen Van Be Campaign Report," 7 August 1967.

31. See Fuller, The Conduct of War, p. 35.

32. Gould, An Introduction to International Law, p. 131.

33. George H. Sabine, A History of Political Theory (London: Harrap & Co., Ltd., 3 Ed., 1959), p. 734.

34. B. G. Ivanyi, Route to Potsdam. The Story of the Peace Aims 1939-1945 (London: A. Wingate, 1945), p. 8.

35. From The Times, 12 April 1940, quoted in King-Hall, Total Victory, pp. 127-128.

36. Goebbels, Diaries, p. 147.

37. Ranshofen-Wertheimer, Victory Is Not Enough, pp. 128 and 130.

38. Fuller, A Military History of the Western World, Vol. III, p. 379. He added, "Almost equally monstrous was their military blunder, which was to build their military forces on the experiences of the first half of the First World War -- the period of stalemate -- instead of on the second half -- the period of mobility -- whereas, Hitler, in opposition to the majority of his generals, did exactly the reverse."

39. Goebbels, Diaries, p. 81, 13 February 1942. Cripps was a leftist and was sent as the British Ambassador to Moscow.

40. Admiral William D. Leahy, I Was There (New York: Whittlesey House, 1950), p. 72.

41. Howell, The Soviet Partisan Movement, p. 34.

42. Masuo Kato, The Lost War (New York: A. A. Knopf, 1946), p. 152, in spite of discrepancies in drawings and poor translations.

43. Whitney, MacArthur, p. 133.

44. See Daugherty and Janowitz, Psychological Warfare, pp. 234 and 307. This of course does not prevent mistakes. Peter Fleming, Operation Sea Lion, p. 306, called the German propaganda against the British in 1940 "idiotic." He said that even before Hitler actually decided on invasion, "his propaganda machine was working for the British Government."

45. See Ibid., p. 307.
46. See Ibid., pp. 276 and 304.
47. Ibid., p. 304.
48. Ibid., p. 305.
49. Ibid., p. 306.
50. Armstrong, Unconditional Surrender, p. 165.
51. Quoted in Fuller, A Military History of the Western World, Vol. III, p. 373. On pp. 369-370, Fuller called Roosevelt's notorious "Quarantine Speech" (against all aggressors) of October 1937 a move to divert public attention from the desperate internal situation (high unemployment due to the depression of September of 1937) and because of the impending elections.
52. Hanson Baldwin, Great Mistakes of the War (New York: Harper & Brothers, 1950), p. 3.
53. Butcher, My Three Years With Eisenhower, p. 202, 26 November 1942. Darlan was assissinated by the Free French on 24 December 1942.
54. Whitney, MacArthur, p. 148.
55. Paul Einzig, Can We Win the Peace? (London: Macmillan, 1942), p. 16.
56. Daugherty and Janowitz, Psychological Warfare, p. 306.
57. Ibid., p. 261.
58. See Ibid., p. 286. Quoting from Zacharias' book, he stated that Japanese newspapermen were unanimous in agreeing that our propaganda shortened the war and made possible a bloodless occupation.
59. Fuller, A Military History of the Western World, Vol. III, p. 625.
60. Kato, The Lost War, p. 135. See also pp. 139 and 150. See pp. 143-144 for how effective atrocity propaganda can be conducted by a whispering campaign. The Japanese were convinced that all their male population would be destroyed and the women made mistresses or at least raped. This idea was destroyed only by truth. After the Americans had been in Japan for some days, the women began to reappear (from the hills) when it became obvious that they were not being mistreated.
61. Whitney, MacArthur, p. 133.
62. Fuller, The Conduct of War, p. 326, quoting from the Defense Ministry of the Federal Republic of West Germany. In his Appendix VI, p. 343, he listed some of the main propaganda organs with a description of each.
63. Averell Harriman, Peace with Russia? (New York: Simon and Schuster, Inc., 1951), p. 162.
64. Ibid., p. 163.
65. The Overstreets, The War Called Peace.

Kruschchev's Communism, p. 146. The "controlled press" is internal; the "conspiratorial press" is external - against non-Communist countries.

66. Harriman, Peace With Russia?, p. 148.

67. George Orwell, 1984 (New York: A Signet Book, 1949), p. 7.

68. Koestler, Darkness at Noon (New York: The Modern Library, 1941) tr. Daphne Hardy, p. 117.

69. European Edition, p. 3.

70. "ABC's of the big debate; Marshall vs. MacArthur." U.S. News, 18 May 1951, p. 20. See also Whitney, MacArthur, p. 495.

71. 1962 was the year of "muzzling" hearings in the US Congress. There are innumerable examples of it. General Gavin mentioned how, in 1948, one of his articles was muzzled because of Air Force objections. War and Peace in the Space Age, p. 103. The parts objected to by the Air Force have since been shown to be quite valid suggestions for the improvement of our military posture. If the military voice is muzzled, then there is no one who can speak with any authority on the future path our military should take. The civilian members certainly cannot provide this information to the people and besides most of them are political appointees with a vested interest in the Administration.

These officers are not usually attacking the government as such, but are usually only trying to keep the public informed on what are often critical problems upon which our very freedom can rest.

Part 2
Unconditional Surrender

Chronology
of World War II

- 1939 -

1 September	Germany invaded Poland
3 September	Britain and France declared war on Germany
17 September	Russia invaded Eastern Poland
30 November	Russia attacked Finland

- 1940 -

13 March	Peace between Finland and the USSR
9 April	Germans landed in Denmark and Norway
10 May	Start of German campaign in the West. Churchill became British Prime Minister
14 May	Holland capitulated
17 May	Pétain became head of French Vichy government
27 May	Belgium capitulated
28 May - 4 June	Evacuation at Dunkirk
10 June	Italy declared war on Britain and France
16 June	Red Army occupied Baltic states
25 June	French armistice with Germans
13 September	Italy attacked Egypt

129

12 February	General Rommel assumed command in North Africa
11 March	United States Lend-Lease Bill
6 April	German offensive against Yugo-slavia and Greece
22 June	German invasion of the USSR
14 August	Atlantic Charter
8 September	Germans reached Leningrad
12 November	Germans reached Moscow
6 December	Failure of German offensive against Moscow; start of Russian counteroffensive
7 December	Pearl Harbor attacked by Japanese. US entered the war
19 December	Hitler assumed personal command of the Wehrmacht

- 1942 -

1 January	United Nations Declaration
21 January	German offensive in North Africa
9 March	Fall of the Netherlands East Indies
18 April	Doolittle Tokyo raid
6 May	Fall of Corregidor
28 May	Battle of the Coral Sea
4 June	Battle of Midway
7 August	Invasion of Guadalcanal
25 August	Germans reached Stalingrad
3 November	English breakthrough at El Alamein
8 November	Allied landings in North Africa

- 1943 -

14-28 January	Casablanca Conference: Unconditional Surrender
22 January	End of Papuan Campaign
30 January	Capitulation of German Sixth Army at Stalingrad
12 May	Capitulation of Afrika Korps
10 July	Allied landing in Sicily
25 July	Fall of Mussolini
3 August	Russian offensive
17-24 August	First Quebec Conference
3 September	Secret armistice between Allies and Italy
9 September	American landing at Salerno
19 October- 1 November	Moscow Conference
6 November	Russians took Kiev
23-26 November	Cairo Conference
28 November- 1 December	Teheran Conference

- 1944 -

22 January	Anzio landing
6 June	Normandy landings
15 June	Landings on Saipan in the Marianas
19-20 June	Battle of the Philippine Sea
25 July	American breakout at Avranches
27 July	Battle south of Warsaw
4 August	Americans took Florence

131

15 August	Landings in Southern France
11 September	Americans reached German border
11-16 September	Second Quebec Conference: Morgenthau Plan
10 October	Russian breakthrough to Baltic Sea
16 October	Red Army in East Prussia
19 October	Russians took Belgrade
23-26 October	Battle of Leyte Gulf. Invasion of the Philippines
16 December	German counteroffensive in Ardennes

- 1945 -

18 January	Germans left Warsaw
4-12 February	Yalta Conference
19 February	Invasion of Iwo Jima
4 March	Manila cleared
30 March	Russians occupied Danzig; moved against Vienna
1 April	Invasion of Okinawa
13 April	Russians took Vienna; Americans reached the Elbe
24 April	Berlin encircled by Russians
25 April	American and Russian troops met at Torgau on the Elbe
2 May	Berlin fell
4 May	American troops from Italy and South Germany met at Brenner Pass
7-8 May	Unconditional Surrender of Germany
6 July-7 August	Potsdam Conference

6 August	Atomic bomb on Hiroshima
8 August	Soviet Union declared war on Japan and invaded Manchuria the next day
9 August	A-bomb on Nagasaki
14 August	Japan surrendered
2 September	Japanese surrender signed on the battleship _Missouri_ in Tokyo Bay

6
The Policy
of Unconditional Surrender

> This was perhaps the big-
> gest political mistake of
> the war.[1]
>
> -- Hanson Baldwin
>
> Henceforth these two words
> were to hang like a
> putrifying albatross around
> the necks of America and
> Britain.[2]
>
> -- J. F. C. Fuller

1.   Versailles to Pearl Harbor

The First World War, which ended with the boom-
ing cannon at Versailles and should have ended before the Russian Revolution, was not necessarily inevitable.   The slide from the First into the Second
World War required an almost incredible combination
of stupidity and bad luck.[3]   The stupidity was in
great abundance in the Allied capitals and as for
luck, it could be said that the dictators had a good
run until the early 1940s.   We have already reviewed
the German problems that arose after Versailles.
After the collapse of the Weimar Government, Germany
was already once again on the rise.   Mussolini had
come to power very shortly after the end of the war,
and the Japanese military faction pressed its influence from the early 1930s on.

The Allies, particularly those who had been
bled white in the first war, did not want another
war and did everything to try to prevent it.   However, as is so often the case with good intentions,
their actions only served to bring on the very catastrophe that they were trying so desperately to
avert.   In 1934, "Ramsey MacDonald still continued
to urge the French that they disarm themselves by

reducing their army by 50 percent, and their air
force by 75 percent.... Probably as much as any
other single group I think that these men of good
will can be charged with causing World War II."[4]
Herman Kahn continued, "In May of 1935 the British,
anxious to allay their anxieties cheaply, signed a
naval agreement with the Germans, an act which probably ranks as the height of idiocy."[5] The French
did not exactly follow the advice of their English
friend, but they were not overly stalwart in their
own right. This was a period of French political
unrest and the development of the Maginot Line. In
spite of increasing French suspicions, France allowed Germany to rearm at a time when the French
Army was strong enough to handle Germany alone.
The Maginot Line mentality must have been a contributing factor.[6] Seversky was a little harsh
when he wrote "France was living in a fool's paradise of false safety behind its 'impregnable' forti-
fication. It was a paradise in which nearly everybody made fat commissions and complicated 'deals,'
flaunting the kind of patriotism that paid dividends."[7]

Hitler had figured the French political tem-
perature correctly when he ordered his generals to
move into the Rhineland. They all objected that
the French would not tolerate it. Hitler went
ahead with three battalions (barely 2000 men). German anxieties lasted one week. After that, Hitler
could turn to his generals and say, "Who was
right?"[8] Later Hitler told Austrian Chancellor von
Schuschnigg, while taking over Austria:

> ...England will not lift a finger for Aus-
> tria.... and France? Well, two years ago when
> we marched into the Rhineland with a handful
> of battalions - at that moment I risked a
> great deal. If France had marched then, we
> should have been forced to withdraw.... But
> for France it is now too late![9]

French hesitancy continued right into the period of the "phony war." Hitler calculated that
France and Britain, despite their solemn pledges to
Poland, would not intervene in the war. One German
general reported that

> ...to the astonishment of many German officers,
> the French, who must have been well aware of
> our temporary weakness, did nothing. ...Once
> again Hitler had been proved right in his

136

assertion that the French would throw away
their golden opportunity; failing to exploit
Germany's delicate position by means of an immediate attack. They lost their chance of inflicting a severe defeat on Hitler's Germany.[10]

Although the French and English were not successful in their handling of the worsening world
situation, the Americans tried only to bury their
ostrich heads deeper into their isolationist sand.
"Don't let us get tied up in Europe" had always been
a formidable argument. According to Churchill, it
"had undoubtedly led to the Second World War through
the ruin of the League of Nations by the withdrawal
of the United States."[11] Robert B. Lockhart, later
the Director General of the British Political Warfare Executive, visited the United States early in
1939. "Lockhart summarized the average American's
attitude toward Britain's problems in these words:
'We Americans went into the last war to save democracy. We pulled you out of a hole and we received
very grudging thanks. At Versailles and after Versailles you trampled on democratic ideals. Now,
largely through your own fault, you are in trouble
again and you want our help. Well, we've learnt our
lesson.'"[12] No doubt these were oversimplifications
of the American view, but there was certainly very
little American interest in the events leading to
the war. American sympathies for the Allies rose in
1939 and 1940, but most Americans did not really
consider it an American war until after the Pearl
Harbor attack on 7 December 1941.
      The tensions between the United States and
Japan had been mounting for some years. The Japanese had been on the march for a long time. Ambassador Joseph Grew in Tokyo had reported to Washington, in September 1932, that "the Japanese Government intends to proceed with its program in Manchuria unless prevented by superior physical
force."[13] On 27 January 1941, almost a year before
Pearl Harbor, Ambassador Grew reported:

> There is a lot of talk around town to the ef-
> fect that the Japanese, in case of a break with
> the United States, are planning to go all out
> in a surprise mass attack on Pearl Harbor.[14]

Hull mentioned the cable from Grew in his book
and said the information was sent on to the War and
Navy Departments.[15] It is most amazing that, considering the way relations had deteriorated between

137

the two countries and the way negotiations had bro-
ken down, we still suffered such a surprise attack.
Some authors have tried to establish that since
America was already quite committed in the war, particularly through our lend-lease aid, President
Roosevelt wanted the enemy to attack us to move the
American people and the Congress, who were still not
behind the war, to enter the war. "But the President's problem remained: how was he to bring the
United States into the war? The answer was, since
Hitler refused to be provoked into a declaration of
war on the United States, Japan must be provoked
into war."[16] Fuller called the ten-point proposal
to Japan (based on a memorandum to Morgenthau from
Harry Dexter White, whom we will meet again) an ultimatum. However, we had broken their code and followed each step right up to the point where Roosevelt, reading the decoded answer to the ten points
on 6 December said "This means war." - still no word
to Hawaii. The last part of the fourteen-part Japanese answer even gave the hour when it was to be
presented to the American Government - 1 P.M. (7:30
A.M. - Hawaii time) - still nothing to Hawaii. General Marshall finally sent an alert, but it did not
get there until six hours after the attack. Fuller
called this the "astonishing story of how the Japanese were maneuvered into war by President Roosevelt...".[17] Duped or not, the American people now
burst into the war with the fanatacism of democracy
in anger. Sir John Dill summed up the American situation quite succinctly to Lord Alanbrooke on 3
January 1942: "'At present this country has not -
repeat not - the slightest conception of what the
war means, and their armed forces are more unready
for war than it is possible to imagine. Eventually
they will do great things...'".[18] Some of the Allies were never to realize what the war meant, and
so it came about that the conflict drifted into
Total War.

2. War Aims

The Axis powers, having started the war, operated under some definite, clear-cut war aims; but
the Allies, having been forced into the war to defend themselves, had great difficulty in determining firm war goals. The first problem, naturally,
was the ever inherent weakness of allies; they may
well agree upon common defense measures, provided

the danger is great enough, but they have a very difficult time arriving at common goals in the offensive. When two allies as potentially close as the Americans and the British could not agree, then it was really a pipe dream to expect great things from an alliance with an opposing ideology, Communism. The Allied problem then, and this is still a contemporary problem of alliances, was to determine what could be said that would still assure their people that the government had matters well in hand and yet would not cause dissension within the ranks of the Allies. The simplest solution to this was always to speak in generalities, announce high-sounding moral goals and use good propaganda phrases such as Unconditional Surrender and Total Victory.

Unfortunately, this was the path chosen in World War II; the ideological war was on to wipe out "evil." Blind hatred, whipped up by propaganda, set the pace for a twentieth-century crusade. Roosevelt stated on 6 January 1942,

> Our own objectives are clear; the objective of smashing the militarism imposed by warlords upon their enslaved peoples - the objective of establishing and securing freedom of speech, freedom of religion, freedom from want, and freedom from fear everywhere in the world.[19]

Who could refuse to agree with that? These are all worthy goals but they do not fit exactly as the political aims of war. The use of the word "victory" can always be called upon as a non-controversial aim. Roosevelt proclaimed: "'Victory in this war is the first and greatest goal before us. Victory in the peace is the next.'"[20] The order of priority is probably correct, as one can argue that it does no good to talk about winning the peace if you lose the war. The real error comes in making such a clear-cut differentiation between war and peace. They both still represent periods of international relations, one being only somewhat more unfriendly than the other.

Under the emotional guidance of Roosevelt and Churchill, the Great Crusade progressed. By the time of the Casablanca Conference, the United States had committed itself to an all-out war effort aimed at the complete defeat of the enemy and the overthrow of the Nazi and Japanese governments. Beyond that the war aims of the United States and its allies were unclear.[21] Walter Lippmann wrote in 1944, "Our primary war aim must be unalterable: it must be

139

to make it as impossible for Germany to hold the balance of power in Europe as for Japan to hold it in Eastern Asia."[22] At least someone was talking in political terms rather than straight propaganda and hot emotion. It is interesting to contrast the British and American approaches. The British used all of their energies to safeguard those things considered necessary for the preservation of the British Empire. The Americans devoted their efforts exclusively to destroying the Germans, with not too much thought about the future.[23] The Americans looked at the war militarily and the British politically. The American aim was to defeat the German Army in the field; the British aim was to achieve political objectives.[24] Herein rests the basis of most Anglo-American differences during the war. The Americans refused to recognize that military victory is only the first step in achieving a political solution to whatever problem had led to war, and saw military victory as the end itself.

The Allies were continually haunted by the specter of the failure to gain lasting peace from the First World War, so they were determined not to repeat the mistakes of their predecessors. From this an illusion grew: "Steer clear of the mistakes that marred Number One and you have the recipe for winning Number Two."[25] Many Germans had convinced themselves that they had not lost the first war, so the Allied resolve was to teach them a lesson this time and thoroughly trounce them. The policy of Unconditional Surrender was also meant to stop a legend being fostered for the second time that Germany was invincible and had been "cheated" of victory through no fault of her "supermen" warriors - who were capable of taming the world - but through the treachery or cowardice of others. To compel the Germans to understand that they had been squarely beaten at their own chosen game of waging war would, it was hoped, end one Teutonic myth, kill one bug in the German brain, and cleanse the postwar atmosphere of an obdurate fever.[26] President Harry Truman described this same point:

> ... at Yalta, the Allies knew that the complete defeat of Germany was only a matter of time, and they wanted the German people to know that the German armies had been totally defeated in the field as well as in all other respects. Germany at that time had already suffered enormous destruction, but destruction even on such a scale does not necessarily mean military defeat. There

140

must be a collapse of all military effort, and this collapse was what the Allies wanted to impress clearly on the German people. The Allies had not forgotten what had happened after World War I. [27]

Even though Great Britain and America had renounced any desire for territorial gain, they wanted freedom of action to "remodel" the enemy states. [28] In refusing to negotiate with the enemy, they placed their faith instead in Unconditional Surrender - going to the limit in dismantling the German and Japanese power structure. They reduced the problem of forestalling future wars to that of administering to the disturbers of the peace a lesson they would never forget. This was perhaps the most salient feature of the Western approach to the problem of war and peace. [29] Kecskemeti concluded that "Permanent peace rests on a weak foundation indeed if it depends on the undying memory of a just chastisement." [30] However, this was the foundation prepared by adopting the policy of Unconditional Surrender.

Total Victory was a prerequisite to implementing the sweeping changes in the enemy societies envisioned by Allied policy. Another factor was the difficulty of the major Allies, Great Britain, the Soviet Union, and the United States, in agreeing in advance on any concrete peace plans. Without specific agreements, the general commitment to the all-inclusive phrase Total Victory, the result of Unconditional Surrender, served as a substitute for war aims. [31]

Roosevelt joined the Total Victory chorus as soon as the United States entered the war. In his radio address to the nation following the declaration of war with the Japanese Empire, 9 December 1941, he stated:

I repeat that the United States can accept no result save victory, final and complete. Not only must the shame of Japanese treachery be wiped out, but the sources of international brutality, wherever they exist, must be absolutely and finally broken. [32]

Vice President Henry Wallace supported this position on 8 May 1942 with his statement that "the will of the American people is for complete victory. No compromise with Satan is possible. We shall not rest until all the victims under the Nazi yoke are freed. We shall fight for a complete peace as well

as a complete victory."[33]
　　Roosevelt, in his Annual Message to Congress,
6 January 1942, mentioned above, continued:

> No compromise can end that conflict. There
> never has been - there never can be - success-
> ful compromise between good and evil. Only
> total victory can reward the champions of tol-
> erance, and decency, and faith.[34]

Roosevelt thus clearly stated his policy of no
compromise from the very beginning and over a year
before the Casablanca Conference. The theme of Total Victory recurred in the President's statements
from then on. On 3 September 1942, FDR, in a radio
address, said:

> We have profited by our past mistakes. This
> time we shall know how to make full use of vic-
> tory. This time the achievements of our fight-
> ing forces will not be thrown away by political
> cynicism and timidity and incompetence.

Then referring to the Four Freedoms, he added,
"Only on those bold terms can this war result in
total victory.[35] The idea of Total Victory found
support not only among those on the highest level.
It had a magnetic propaganda appeal and attracted
wide support. The following is a sample:

> The only reasonable safeguard against a revival
> of militarism in Germany is the defeat and an-
> nihilation of Hitler's armed forces, and the
> adoption of adequate measures to prevent their
> reconstitution. If for the sake of early peace
> the Allies should decide to forgo this safe-
> guard, and concluded peace with an undefeated
> Germany, another war would be a mere question of
> years, or perhaps months. To conclude peace
> before winning total victory is a sure way of
> losing the peace - and also of losing the next
> war.[36]

The seal of approval, however, was put on it at
the highest levels. The United States Senate was
committed to the policy of Total Victory by the Con-
nally Resolution.[37]
　　George F. Kennan pointed out that, "At the bottom of this whole subject lay the commitment of the
Western Allies to the principle of unconditional
surrender. It is idle, I think, to try to assign to

either Churchill or Roosevelt the exclusive responsibility for this commitment. I cannot see that it was ever absent from the calculations of either government."[38] As it evolved, the most important political questions of the century were determined emotionally and under the influence of our own propaganda. It seems dangerous to national interests as well as unreasonable to have permitted policy to be directed by a propaganda slogan. The Anglo-American propaganda offensive proclaimed Prussia-Germany, not just the Nazi Government, a warmongering, outlaw society; therefore, Allied policy had to be directed toward the total defeat, punishment, and reconstruction of German society rather than toward the simple goal of the overthrow of the Nazi regime. Such far-reaching war aims were a basic factor underlying the policies of Total Victory and Unconditional Surrender.[39] Seeing the importance of the policy of Unconditional Surrender in World War II, we should now review the background of the formation of this policy that set the pace for the war and the years to follow.

3. Formulation of the Policy of Unconditional Surrender

Prime Minister Churchill and President Roosevelt met at Casablanca, in January 1942, along with their military advisers. On 24 January the two wartime leaders held a press conference that closed the meeting. It was at this time that Roosevelt, in what Arthur Bryant called "an unexpected postscript,"[40] proclaimed the demand for the Unconditional Surrender of the Axis countries. Chester Wilmot described it as "an announcement which, for good or ill, was to have a profound influence on the war and, therefore, on the character of the post-war world. Roosevelt told the correspondents that the Allies were determined to demand the 'Unconditional Surrender' of Germany, Italy and Japan."[41] His remarks are recorded to this effect:

> Peace is to come, Mr. Roosevelt said, by total elimination of German, Italian, and Japanese war power. This doesn't mean destruction of the people in those unhappy countries, but total and merciless destruction of the machinery they have built up for imposing totalitarian doctrine on the world.

143

In this connection the President reminded his listeners of the famous American General Ulysses Simpson Grant, whose initials U.S. were adapted to express his resoluteness in the nickname "Unconditional Surrender" Grant. The democracies' war plans were to compel the "unconditional surrender" of the Axis.[42]

FDR implied that his announcement was unpremeditated.

He said, "We had so much trouble getting those two French generals together that I thought to myself this was as difficult as arranging the meeting of Grant and Lee - and then suddenly the press conference was on, and Winston and I had no time to prepare for it, and the thought popped into my mind that they had called Grant 'Old Unconditional Surrender' and the next thing I knew, I had said it."[43]

Even though Roosevelt implied that he was unprepared at the press conference, Sherwood wrote that Harry Hopkins recorded in his description of the conference that Roosevelt spoke from notes. Also, the photographs of the conference show him holding several pages.

Those pages contained the following paragraph:

The President and the Prime Minister, after a complete survey of the world war situation, are more than ever determined that peace can come to the world only by a total elimination of German and Japanese war power. This involves the simple formula of placing the objective of this war in terms of an unconditional surrender by Germany, Italy and Japan. Unconditional surrender by them means a reasonable assurance of world peace, for generations. Unconditional surrender means not the destruction of the German populace, nor of the Italian or Japanese populace, but does mean the destruction of a philosophy in Germany, Italy, and Japan which is based on the conquest and subjugation of other people.[44]

The President's son Elliott recorded, on 23 January (the day before the press conference), that "it can be recorded that it was Father's phrase, that Harry took an immediate and strong liking to it, and that Churchill, while he slowly munched a

mouthful of food, thought, frowned, thought, finally
grinned, and at length announced, 'Perfect! And I
can just see how Goebbels and the rest of 'em 'll
squeal!'"[45]
Elliott continued with:

Father, once his phrase had been approved by
the others, speculated about its effect in another direction.

"Of course, it's just the thing for the Russians. They couldn't want anything better.
Unconditional surrender," he repeated, thought-
fully sucking a tooth. "Uncle Joe might have
made it up himself."[46]

Elliott conveyed his father's strong feelings
on the subject: "'Unconditional surrender.' He put
no exclamation point after it; there was only determination."[47]
Sherwood wrote to Churchill inquiring about his
role in the determination of the policy of Unconditional Surrender. His reply was:

I heard the words "Unconditional Surrender" for
the first time from the President's lips at the
Conference. It must be remembered that at that
moment no one had a right to proclaim that Victory was assured. Therefore, Defiance was the
note. I would not myself have used these words,
but I immediately stood by the President and
have frequently defended the decision. It is
false to suggest that it prolonged the war.
Negotiation with Hitler was impossible. He was
a maniac with supreme power to play his hand
out to the end, which he did; and so did we.[48]

Churchill's memory was not too accurate on this
point as he had discussed it at Casablanca and even
sent a cable back to the War Cabinet in London.

I should be glad to know what the War Cabinet
would think of our including in this statement
a declaration of the firm intention of the
United States and the British Empire to continue the war relentlessly until we have
brought about the "unconditional surrender" of
Germany and Japan. The omission of Italy would
be to encourage a break-up there.[49]

The War Cabinet answered that they were in

145

agreement except that they advised that Italy be included.[50] Churchill, after rechecking his wartime records, admitted his mistake and so acknowledged it in the House of Commons. Churchill defended his support for the policy saying that if the real conditions the Allies intended to impose on Germany were released, the Germans would really have fought with the vigor of cornered rats. If one used the infamous Morgenthau Plan as an example, one would have a good case.

> My principal reason for opposing, as I always did, an alternative statement on peace terms, which was so often urged, was that a statement of the actual conditions on which the three great Allies would have insisted and would have been forced by public opinion to insist, would have been far more repulsive to any German peace movement than the general expression "unconditional surrender."[51]

Thus the policy of Unconditional Surrender, with at least the approval of the British War Cabinet, came into the open. It was to be reiterated continually to the end of the war and, no doubt, played a significant role in the conduct of the war, or, more importantly, the termination of the war and the many problems of the postwar period. What, then, were some of the reasons behind this policy?
John Gunther, in his book on Roosevelt, wrote:

> ... the President had several motives in making the initial declaration. (1) To encourage Russia.... (2) Some silly people had been whispering about negotiations between the western allies and Hitler, and Roosevelt wanted to shut them up. (3) FDR hoped that the statement would tighten things up on the home front, and tell anybody still lukewarm about the war that it was going to last a long, long time. (4) For the sake of the future peace, he felt that it was necessary for Germany to be beaten actually in the field, so that the German people would never again be able to say as they had said after World War I, that their armies had not been legitimately defeated. (5) He wanted to encourage the submerged peoples in France, the Balkans, and elsewhere, who had suffered most from Hitler, by telling them that they would be avenged.[52]

Probably the consideration weighing most heavily on his mind was the Russian problem. Stalin had refused to meet with them at Casablanca because he said it was unnecessary for him to travel to discuss strategy when all that was needed was for the Western Allies to open the Second Front.[53] There was a mutual distrust that either Russia or the Western Allies might come to terms with Hitler and terminate the war. Unable to satisfy Stalin by opening a second front, they at least wanted to calm Soviet suspicion that the West might make a compromise peace at Soviet expense. Mutual suspicion and constant recrimination thus were basic to the demand for Unconditional Surrender in the desire to reassure Soviet leaders that there would be no compromise with Hitler and that the Allies would fight on to Total Victory.[54] Since the Soviets had already made one deal with the Nazis, there was the fear among the Western Allies that it might happen again. They also worried that Russia would be beaten, and so they bent over backwards to give them everything they wanted and demanded nothing in return. We could have acted a little more wisely if we had only believed our own Ambassador there. On 6 June 1938, he reported that "it would be very difficult and possibly impossible for Japan, or Germany, or both, to 'conquer' the U.S.S.R."[55] He continued, "It is probable that the Soviet Union could defensively maintain its entity against any combination of two hostile powers." Against more than two powers, some area would be occupied but "present military forces would prevent decisive defeat and it is unlikely that permanent gains would accrue to the invading armies."[56] This evaluation proved quite accurate and deserved more respect in Washington.

Unconditional Surrender provided a catch-phrase around which the Allies could rally, a simple slogan on which the major Allies could agree even with their different political aims in Europe. The policy was diplomatically ambiguous avoiding open disagreements among them. It was a policy of the lowest common denominator. Unconditional Surrender was essentially a policy of Total Victory. The United States Senate was not agreed on the nature of the peace, which ought to have been the American war aims, as revealed in the divergent views debated in the Foreign Relations Committee. Unconditional Surrender, again, was the lowest common denominator; all factions could agree upon pursuing Total Victory to win the war.[57] Rallying around Unconditional Surrender helped the Allies to affirm both their confidence in their own strength and their desire to obtain a total victory over an enemy that waged total war.[58] A certain unity was gained by strengthening Allied determination to pursue the war to Total Victory, and it served to forestall German attempts to split the United Nations coalition.[59] Unfortunately, the inherent weakness of a coalition caused a great loss of effort to be expended just in maintaining the coalition.

The call for defiance as explained by Churchill does not seem to have been completely justified. Certainly the war was not over, but the long-range outlook was highly favorable to the Allies and did not demand a political commitment that was so expensive as to endanger the net gains to be achieved from the war. Churchill himself saw no more doubt about the final outcome after Pearl Harbor and the American entry into the war. "Many disasters, immeasurable cost and tribulation lay ahead, but there was no more doubt about the end."[60] The Russian offensive at Stalingrad had started on 10 January 1943; the German Sixth Army was already in trouble and surrendered only a few days after the Casablanca Conference was over. From the viewpoint of the Allied planners, the strategic picture had begun to improve, and there was little question at Casablanca that the long-range prognosis was good. Eisenhower recorded that "at the Casablanca Conference, in January 1943, the combined Chiefs of Staff felt that the time had come at least to evolve the outline tactical plan for cross-Channel operations."[61] Rommel had been defeated in Egypt and Churchill could report that, "We have victory - a remarkable and definite victory."[62] It was upon this same occasion that he made his famous remark: "Now this is not the end. It is not even the beginning of the end. But it is, perhaps, the end of the beginning."[63] The Allies were visibly on the offensive and, with the benefit of hindsight, it appears that they greatly underestimated their own position in committing themselves to the policy of Unconditional Surrender. One of the real traits of leadership is, first of all, to know one's self and then to know one's opponent. The Allied leadership appears to have been deficient on both counts.

The quest for Total Victory by the means of Unconditional Surrender thus became the basis of Allied policy. Certain themes appeared throughout the President's speeches no doubt for their propaganda effect to stir up enthusiasm, but these same themes often appeared in policy statements as well. Thus,

what began as propagands slogans became aims of policy, and contributed to the President's insistence
throughout the war on achieving nothing less than
Total Victory through the total destruction of enemy power by Unconditional Surrender. Under this
type of policy, the clear, calculating mental processes gave way to the whims, hates, and desires of
the emotions.

4. Emotional War

Democracies, which are so slow to get their ire
up when some other country imposes on them, fight
with an emotional ferocity, once stirred, that is
unbelievable and seemingly inconsistent with their
principles. The two leaders of the Western Allies
are perfect examples, and they set the pace in World
War II. Churchill made his vow for victory at all
costs on his first day in power.

> What is our aim? I can answer in one word:
> Victory - victory at all costs, victory in
> spite of all terror; victory, however long and
> hard the road may be; for without victory,
> there is no survival.[64]

It should be remembered that this vow was made
in dark days and was important in strengthening the
will of the people to resist.

When Churchill quickly came to the aid of Communist Russia when it was invaded by Germany, he was
asked if he, arch anti-Communist, was not changing
his theme about Communism. His answer showed his
whole emotional tenor toward the war.

> "I have only one purpose, the destruction of
> Hitler, and my life is much simplified thereby.
> If Hitler invaded Hell I would make at least a
> favourable reference to the Devil in the House
> of Commons."[65]

In his radio broadcast after Germany invaded
Russia, Churchill said:

> We have but one aim and one single, irrevocable
> purpose. We are resolved to destroy Hitler and
> every vestige of the Nazi regime. From this
> nothing will turn us - nothing. We will never
> parley, we will never negotiate with Hitler or

any of his gang.... Any man or state who fights
on against Nazidom will have our aid. Any man
or state who marches with Hitler is our foe.[66]

Life is not yet that simple so that everything
falls so neatly into categories of black and white.
Fuller lashed out hard at Churchill:

> From this and similar utterances it is clear
> that Mr. Churchill had no conception of the
> task demanded of him in his capacity of Prime
> Minister and Minister of Defence. Firstly, it
> should have been to win a peace which would be
> profitable to his country, and there could be
> neither moral nor political advantage in sub-
> stituting Stalin for Hitler. Secondly, because
> he had postulated the extirpation of Hitler and
> Hitlerism as his aim, he should have differen-
> tiated between the Nazi regime and the mass of
> the German people. Had he done so, he would
> have seen that his most profitable ally was the
> extensive anti-Hitler faction in Germany, and
> in accordance with his declaration he would
> have given it his aid. But, overmastered by
> his emotions, he committed the selfsame blunder
> that Hitler had made when he failed to disting-
> uish between the pro- and anti-Stalinist peo-
> ples of the U.S.S.R. This blunder prolonged
> the war by years, and in spite of the ultimate
> victory, it lost the peace and made the war an
> absurdity.[67]

Commenting on Churchill's statement that he had
not become Prime Minister to preside over the liquidation of the British Empire, Fuller remarked: "Yet
his hatred for Hitlerism had so blinded him politically and strategically that this is exactly what he
potentially did. By destroying the balance of power
in Europe, he wrecked the foundation upon which the
British Empire had been built, and without which it
is unlikely for long to endure."[68] An aide to Admiral Doenitz observed shortly after the war that
England would not slow down and realize that she
was playing the game of the strongest adversary, and
that by winning a total victory over Germany she
would really lose the war. Doenitz summarized these
ideas: "Churchill will probably go down in history
as the conqueror of the Second World War, but also
as the grave digger of the British Empire."[69]
The American President joined Churchill in being overly emotional and sometimes losing sight of

150

the real purpose of the war. His hatred was also
focused on Hitler. Hopkins recounted that there was
absolutely nothing more important in the world to
Roosevelt than to beat Hitler.[70] One of Roosevelt's
favorite claims was that the Axis countries all
worked together closely, and that they were executing
their joint plan to take over the world, whereas
they were, in fact, not at all close in their coordination, probably much less so than the Allies. It
was revealed in later years, through top-secret diplomatic papers captured from Nazi Germany, that German authorities knew more than seven months before
Pearl Harbor that the State Department had cracked
Japan's vital coding system. There was nothing to
indicate that Nazi authorities warned Japan that
their secret code system had been cracked wide open
by American intelligence.[71] That is not close cooperation!

The combination of rampant emotionalism and
ideological aims forced upon the war the air of a
crusade. Britain and France announced an ideological crusade against Hitler and Hitlerism. Churchill
explained the war aim in no uncertain terms: "This
is not a question of fighting for Danzig or fighting
for Poland, we are fighting to save the whole world
from the pestilence of Nazi tyranny and in defence
of all that is most sacred to man." Therefore, the
war was considered "a Manichean contest" between
Good and Evil.[72] This form of moral war implied,
for Roosevelt, not only a total victory including
total disarmament of the enemy and then punishment
for the war criminals, he also wanted to teach the
Germans a lesson. This involved the reeducation of
the enemy population. Roosevelt felt that all Germans were guilty. He complained that many Americans
held the view that the German people as a whole were
not responsible for the war, that only a few Nazi
leaders were responsible.[73] FDR said, in a message
to Congress, in February 1945, that the German people had to be absolutely convinced that Unconditional Surrender was the only way for them to start
again to be a people who can be decent neighbors in
the world.[74]

The search for Total Victory is inherent in an
American approach to wars against aggressors. Such
wars have but one political objective, eliminating
all political forces responsible for aggression, and
this must be completed before peace is restored.
This approach to conflict as Good pitted against Evil
is essentially a crusade. The enemy is the personi-
fication of violence and strife, whereas the friendly

side fights for universal peace and harmony. This crusading concept of war has been vigorously criticized in recent years as unrealistic. Yet democratic cultures are profoundly unwarlike; war can be justified to them only if it is waged to eliminate war. It is this crusading ideology which is reflected in the conviction that hostilities cannot be ended until the evil enemy system has been eradicated.[75]

General Eisenhower considered the war to be a crusade. Referring to not speaking to captured German generals and rejecting the premise that all professional soldiers are comrades-in-arms, he said:

> For me World War II was far too personal a thing to entertain such feelings. Daily as it progressed there grew within me the conviction that as never before in war between nations the forces that stood for human good and men's rights were this time confronted by a completely evil conspiracy with which no compromise could be tolerated. Because only by the utter destruction of the Axis was a decent world possible, the war became for me a crusade in the traditional sense of that often misused word.[76]

The crusade fever breeds intense hate. Lord Hankey wrote that "we must not forget that Unconditional Surrender and War Crimes Trials are themselves part of a philosophy of hate that grew up without noticing it during the war."[77] This hate stirs the people to a great effort but it has the bad influence of leading those in influential positions to make irrational estimates and decisions. Hitler said, "I cannot feel insulted by Roosevelt because, just as with President Wilson, I consider Roosevelt to be insane."[78] What is interesting is that both Churchill and Roosevelt felt that Hitler was insane. The truth is much more likely to be that they were all wrong. But this feeling among three heads of state made rational international relations difficult if not impossible; so each side was intent on eliminating the other completely. This gave Unconditional Surrender essentially an emotional basis. The ability to shift attitudes overnight is amazing. Issues at stake between ourselves and another power yesterday were not worth the life of a single American boy. Today, nothing else counts; our cause is holy; cost is no consideration; violence must have no limitation short of Unconditional Surrender. Democracy fights in anger.[79]

152

5. Explanations and Attempts To Modify
    the Policy of Unconditional Surrender

The idea of pursuing the war to the Unconditional Surrender of the enemy seemed like a policy
that could be easily agreed to by the Allies even
though they could not agree on specific points.
However, there were many people in the Allied governments who were strongly opposed to the policy and
tried to get it changed. These opponents presented
many valid reasons for modification; but, when they
departed from the magic words, they discovered the
astonishing fact that to the wartime leaders of the
Allies the substance was not clear at all.[80]
FDR returned to Washington on 31 January 1943
from Casablanca. Stalingrad was already established
as a great triumph and, to many people, the road to
victory now appeared to be a broad, smooth highway
with the traffic signs all one-way. Robert Sherwood
noted that the arguments about Unconditional Surrender "were already beginning and were to continue
throughout the war and perhaps far into history."[81]
On 12 February Roosevelt made another pronouncement:

> ... the only terms on which we shall deal with
> any Axis government or any Axis factions are
> the terms proclaimed at Casablanca: "Uncondi-
> tional Surrender." In our uncompromising poli-
> cy we mean no harm to the common people of the
> Axis nations. But we do mean to impose punish-
> ment and retribution in full upon their guilty,
> barbaric leaders.... it is a policy of fighting
> hard on all fronts and ending the war as quick-
> ly as we can on the uncompromising terms of un-
> conditional surrender.[82]

The President softened his position somewhat
some months later when, in his message to Congress
on 25 August 1943, he said:

> "Except for the responsible fascist leaders,
> the people of the Axis need not fear uncondi-
> tional surrender to the United Nations. ... The
> people of Axis-controlled areas may be assured
> that when they agree to unconditional surrender
> they will not be trading Axis despotism for
> ruin under the United Nations. The goal of the
> United Nations is to permit the liberated peo-
> ples to create a free political life of their
> own choosing and to attain economic security."[83]

One group whose work was handicapped by this policy was the one handling Allied propaganda. Many attempts were made to get a clarification of the policy or a softening of it, but all to no avail.[84] Sherwood, who spent a long time studying Roosevelt and Hopkins and should be considered an expert, stated categorically that this policy was no light statement made to fill up a press conference, but that Roosevelt's eyes were wide open when he made it. The announcement of the policy was deeply deliberated. It was "a true statement of Roosevelt's considered policy and he refused all suggestions that he retract the statement or soften it and continued refusal to the day of his death."[85] In fact, he restated it many times.

At Teheran, Stalin expressed his dissatisfaction with the policy and pressed for its definition. He questioned the advisability of a policy with no definition of what terms would be imposed upon Germany. Stalin felt that to leave Unconditional Surrender unclarified merely served to unite the German people, whereas to outline specific terms, no matter how harsh, and tell the German people that this was what they would have to accept, would hasten German capitulation.[86] This assessment of Unconditional Surrender showed Stalin to be a hard political realist. He preferred concrete political programs to high-sounding phrases. Stalin suggested that the Allies write a common statement listing their demands. Roosevelt and Churchill were against it. Anthony Eden proposed the use of a different term - "prompt surrender."[87] No change was made but the Russians and British continued to press the Americans to modify this policy.

Molotov asked Ambassador Harriman for a definition of the term on 31 December 1943, because he said it played into Goebbel's hands.[88] In this regard, Secretary of State Cordell Hull wrote a memo to FDR on 14 January.

> "It is my understanding," I said, "that the Soviet interest in this matter is not based on any desire to weaken the principle of unconditional surrender or to offer milder terms to enemy countries but rather on the belief that the present undefined "unconditional surrender" affords enemy propaganda an opportunity to play on the natural fear of the unknown in the minds of their people and consequently stiffens their will to fight....

In view of the Soviet interest in this matter, do you approve of discussion with the Soviet and British Governments to explore the desirability of some public definition for propaganda exploitation of the terms of unconditional surrender to be imposed on the respective enemy countries?" FDR answered on 17 January, "Frankly, I do not like the idea of conversation to define the term 'unconditional surrender.'"[89]

The Soviet Union modified the principle in their peace treaty with Finland negotiating specific subjects. Great Britain and Russia then asked the United States to modify the policy relative to the satellites in March 1944. FDR replied 1 April, "it would be a mistake, in my judgment, to abandon or make an exception in the case of the words 'unconditional surrener.'"[90] Hull wrote the President again on 4 April and received the answer 5 April:

"I understand the problem thoroughly," he said, "but I want at all costs to prevent it from being said that the unconditional surrender principle has been abandoned. There is real danger if we start making exceptions to the general principle before a specific case arises."

"I understand perfectly well that from time to time there will have to be exceptions not to the surrender principle but to the application of it in specific cases. That is a very different thing from changing the principle."[91]

The pressure continued, as Hull noted in April 1944, "The British and Russian Governments continued strongly to press the point that some modification of unconditional surrender, at least in the case of the Axis satellites, should be made."[92] The Germans tried to get an interpretation of the policy and ran into the same stone wall. At the end of 1943, the United States received an aide-memoire from the British Embassy informing them that peace feelers had been received by Britain through Sweden from Heinrich Himmler and a prominent member of the German Foreign Office. Himmler was ready to send a Nazi party official and an army officer to meet with British officials to get a definition of "unconditional surrender." The British plan, to which the United States assented, was to reply that the United Nations demanded unconditional surrender, and that no further interpretation was required.[93]

Churchill had an interesting explanation. He
said that the real conditions were so terrible that
even Unconditional Surrender sounded better. On 14
January 1944, Churchill outlined to the War Cabinet
those conditions that would have to be imposed on
Germany to satisfy both Western public opinion and
Soviet demands: partition of Germany, which would
lose all territory east of the Oder, reparations,
occupation, long-term imprisonment for all of the
General Staff, execution of war criminals, maintenance in Russia and elsewhere of several million
Germans to rebuild the ruins, total disarmament
without hope of rearming, and prohibition of all
aviation. The Prime Minister thought that the German people would prefer the "imprecise terrors" of
Unconditional Surrender. The conditions for peace
that would satisfy the wrath of the conquerors towards Germany seemed so appalling, once on paper,
that their publication would only have encouraged
German resistance.[94] On 22 February, in the House
of Commons, Churchill explained that Unconditional
Surrender did not mean that the German people would
be enslaved or destroyed. It meant however that the
Allies would not be bound to them at the moment of
surrender by any pact or obligation. Unconditional
Surrender meant that the victors had a free hand.[95]
The only obligations that they would be accountable
for were moral obligations to civilization.

In April 1944, Under Secretary of State Stettinius was in England. General Eisenhower's aide
recorded the visit.

There have been discussions with him as to the
meaning of "unconditional surrender" as applied
to Germany. Any military person knows that
there are conditions to every surrender. There
is a feeling that, at Casablanca, the President
and the Prime Minister, more likely the former,
seized on Grant's famous term without realizing
the full implications to the enemy. Goebbels
has made great capital with it to strengthen
the morale of the German Army and people. Our
psychological experts believe we would be wiser
if we created a mood of acceptance of surrender
in the German Army which would make possible a
collapse of resistance similar to that which
took place in Tunisia. They think if a proper
mood is created in the German General Staff,
there might even be a German Badoglio. To accomplish the proper mood, there would need to
be a new American-Anglo-Russian statement to

156

define "unconditional surrender." Then we
could tell the German people, by radio and pamphlet, the methods of demilitarization we pro-
pose; that we maintain the right to seize and
try war criminals; that there will be orderly
transfers of population, and that there will be
restoration of freedom of religion and for
trade unions. After the three governments had
agreed and announced such definitions, our
staff feels that the Supreme Commander should
make a declaration after the landing to the
German commander in the west, reciting, in sol-
dierly language, the principal points of surrender terms. It is believed this would short-
en the war. General Ike strongly advocates
this view and asked Ed Stettinius to transmit
it to the President, which he did by cable.[96]

Hull mentioned this cable[97] and the reaction,
according to Strauss, was that FDR got angry because
of the constant bickering over his principle.[98]
Admiral Leahy, the most senior military officer,
wrote that Unconditional Surrender was never discussed with the Combined Chiefs of Staff and caused additional problems. Before the end of the war, there
were occasions when it might have been advantageous
to accept conditional surrender in some areas, but
it was not permitted.[99] Along with many others, the
military men were not in favor of the policy of Unconditional Surrender either.
Upon the death of Roosevelt, the mantle of the
sacred principle of Unconditional Surrender was
picked up by President Truman. On 8 May 1945, when
announcing the surrender of Germany, he tried to explain the policy without changing it.

Our blows will not cease until the Japanese
military and naval forces lay down their arms
in unconditional surrender.

Just what does the unconditional surrender of
the armed forces of Japan mean for the Japanese
people?

It means the end of the war.

It means the termination of the influence of
the military leaders who brought Japan to the
present brink of disaster.

It means provision for the return of soldiers

157

and sailors to their families, their farms and
their jobs.

And it means not prolonging the present agony
and suffering of the Japanese in the vain hope
of victory.

Unconditional surrender does not mean the extermination or enslavement of the Japanese
people.[100]

In retrospect, it would seem to have been so
easy to have dropped the phrase altogether, particularly for a new president. Though the point of the
policy all along had been to keep from making promises or concessions, near the end of the war, however, it became Allied policy to announce some postwar intentions. Toward the Japanese this policy assumed important proportions and, moreover, it was
stated that the carrying out of these intentions was
contingent on Japanese surrender before invasion.
The broadcasts by Admiral Zacharias became the main
vehicle for the elaboration of these intentions.[101]
Harry Hopkins made a trip to Moscow for President Truman in May 1945.

As to Japan, Hopkins reported that Stalin preferred to go through with unconditional surrender in order to destroy the military might and
forces of Japan once and for all. He felt, however, that if we stuck to unconditional surrender the Japanese would not give up and we would
have to destroy them as we did Germany. If
they offered to surrender, however, in an effort
to seek softer terms, the Allies should depart
from the announced policy of unconditional surrender and be prepared to accept a modified
surrender. He visualized imposing our will
through occupation forces, thereby gaining substantially the same results unconditional surrender would be expected to bring.[102]

Stalin sought a total victory, if it were possible, but he desired it at the lowest possible
cost.[103] At Potsdam in July 1945, Stalin received
messages from the Japanese trying to get around the
policy of Unconditional Surrender. Stalin showed
one of these to Churchill, who shortly thereafter
had a conversation with Truman. Churchill wrote:

158

... I dwelt upon the tremendous cost to American
and to a smaller extent in British life if we
enforced "unconditional surrender" upon the
Japanese. It was for him to consider whether
this might not be expressed in some other way,
so that we got all the essentials for future
peace and security and yet left them some show
of saving their military honour and some assurance of their national existence, after they
had complied with all safeguards necessary for
the conqueror. The President replied bluntly
that he did not think the Japanese had any military honour after Pearl Harbor. I contented
myself with saying that at any rate they had
something for which they were ready to face
certain death in very large numbers, and this
might not be so important to us as it was to
them.[104]

Hull admitted that the various public statements by the Allied leaders to soften the interpretation of Unconditional Surrender did not hasten the
surrender of Germany. The Nazi propaganda machine
stressed its drastic interpretation of Unconditional
Surrender until the end.[105] Roosevelt's determined
protection of "his" principle persisted. In Fuller's
biting words:

... what unconditional surrender implied was
that war was no longer to be accepted as an instrument of creative policy - the establishment
of a profitable and stable peace - but that it
was to be an instrument of pure destruction.
From Casablanca a vulture was unleashed to bat-
ten on the entrails of Europe.

Like the Bourbons, Roosevelt and Churchill had
learnt nothing and forgotten nothing. Both had
before them the example of the abortive peacemaking of 1919, from which Hitler had sprung,
and although both the American and British psychological warfare experts pressed for a definition of what "unconditional surrender" meant,
all of their efforts foundered on the rock of
Roosevelt's opposition.[106]

Because the Allies insisted on keeping their
hands free, the war had to go on pursuing Total Victory in the sterile vacuum of no negotiations.

6. No Negotiations

International affairs of the past had usually
involved the give and take of diplomatic talks.
This also applied to the termination of wars. The
normal course of events for many centuries had been
an armistice, a peace conference, and a peace treaty;
with the policy of Unconditional Surrender, however,
there would be no talking with the enemy, and their
guilty, barbarian leaders would be punished. Since
the enemy leaders were prejudged "guilty" and since
it was a war of Good versus Evil, the Allies could
not compromise themselves by even talking to those
enemy leaders, much less coming to any terms with
them. Regardless of how history eventually treats
Roosevelt's wisdom or lack of wisdom in announcing
the Unconditional Surrender policy at Casablanca, it
is clear that what he in effect said was: there will
be no negotiated peace or compromises with our enemies who initiated this war against us. There would
be no "escape clause" provided by another Fourteen
Points. Roosevelt's fear of a negotiated peace, another Munich, was a major factor in his thinking
throughout the war.[107]
This feeling that the Allies could not negotiate with the enemy was widely held and was not
just a quirk of Roosevelt's. A general feeling was,
what would become of the United Nations Charter if
this war of aggression ended with a bargain with the
aggressor? Would not Goebbels then be right in his
appeal to the Germans to fight until the adversary
renounced his demands?[108] Anthony Eden, speaking on
29 July 1941, said: "A peace with Hitler is a contradiction in terms. There can be no peace with
such a man, there can only be a truce, an uneasy
truce which will give him time to overhaul and oil
his war machine, a truce which will give the German
people a breathing-space before he and they resume
the war."[109] Some who tried to determine with whom
the Allies could negotiate in Germany came to the
conclusion that the case against concluding an armistice with any civilian power whatever its character was nearly as strong as the case against negotiating with Hitler or the generals. There was nobody with whom an armistice could or should be concluded. The Allies had no other choice but to battle
their way through all resistance and proceed to the
center of the fallen power.[110] There was the fear
that a negotiated peace would be dangerous if Germany
were permitted to retain her control over the Conti-

160

nent; also the problem of a political party that
concluded peace without victory, which might very
easily be removed from power at the next election.[111]
Even Stalin, who followed a quite different
policy toward Germany than did the Western Allies in
that he tried to divide the Nazis from the German
people and at least spoke of negotiations, could
make propaganda about talking with the German leaders. In his Order of the Day, 1 May 1943, he said:

> But of what kind of peace can one talk with the
> imperialist bandits from the German-Fascist
> camp who have flooded Europe with blood and
> studded it with gallows? Is it not clear that
> only the utter routing of the Hitlerite armies
> and the unconditional surrender of Hitlerite
> Germany can bring peace to Europe? Is it not
> because the German Fascists sense the coming
> catastrophe that they babble about peace?[112]

The Allies faced the basic dilemma that a compromise peace was impracticable and unthinkable with
Hitler. While it was probably not wise to talk a
lot about Unconditional Surrender and make it into a
wartime slogan, there was, in reality, no promising
alternative but to continue this unhappy struggle to
its bitter end.[113] Churchill wrote while he was at
Yalta:

> I then speculated on the future. If Hitler or
> Himmler were to come forward and offer uncondi-
> tional surrender it was clear that our answer
> should be that we would not negotiate with any
> of the war criminals. If they were the only
> people the Germans could produce we should have
> to go on with the war. It was more probable
> that Hitler and his associates would be killed
> or would disappear, and that another set of
> people would offer unconditional surrender. If
> this happened the Great Powers must immediately
> consult and decide whether they were worth
> dealing with or not. If they were, the terms
> of surrender which had been worked out would be
> laid before them; if not, the war would be con-
> tinued and the whole country put under military
> government.[114]

Churchill seemed to have had an unusual idea of
just what Unconditional Surrender would mean when he
refused to accept it from some leader. There is almost no negotiation involved in such a surrender;

161

just agreement for someone to come sign it. Then
the victor takes over the loser's country to do as
he desires. This is basically what took place in
Germany. Hitler chose Doenitz as head of state because he had never been in politics and therefore
hoped Doenitz could negotiate with the Allies.[115]
Even though the Allies found him "acceptable" by the
Churchill approach, he was shortly afterwards put in
prison.

Just as the Allies did not intend to negotiate
with Hitler, he had no intention of negotiating with
the Allies. On 23 November 1939, in the flush of
early victories, Hitler said: "I will end the war
only with the destruction of the enemy. I will accept no compromise. I will fight and never surrender. The destiny of the Reich depends on me and me
alone."[116] Raymond Cartier noted that Hitler "was
quite sensitive about his horoscope. The stars and
the lines in his hand indicated that he would know
a striking success, a dizzying rise, but that his
career would be suddenly and prematurely interrupted.
He concluded that he would die young; that obsessed
him."[117] This fear perhaps drove him to act hastily; at least, it drove him to ban the profession
and put all astrologers in concentration camps.
When Hitler and Mussolini met at Brenner Pass on 18
March 1940, Hitler said that he was going to continue the fight to victory.[118] Field Marshal Rommel,
who in late 1943 saw no chance of German victory,
felt that Hitler lived in a world of illusion and
that he would not consider making peace. Rommel
said "He will fight, without the least regard for
the German people, until there isn't a house left
standing in Germany."[119] Goering said at Nuremburg
that "'Hitler would have been able to negotiate if
he could have visualized the results, but he was absolutely against desperate and hopeless negotiations.'"[120] It seemed that Hitler, assured of not
being able to survive defeat, played for all or
nothing.

We will see in later sections the difficulties
encountered when negotiations to surrender were actually initiated. We have already seen how the German peace feelers of late 1943 were quickly refused
on the basis of Unconditional Surrender with no further explanation. In February-March 1945, talks
were conducted in Bern in an effort to arrange the
surrender of the German army in northern Italy.
Upon hearing of the talks, the Russians became absolutely obnoxious and raged vehemently, until the
Western Allies broke off the talks. Roosevelt was

deeply upset by the Russian attitude and Churchill
was convinced that this bitterness accelerated the
President's death. The problems with the Russian
ally were beginning to grow worse and would not a-
bate thereafter. The Casablanca demand was the root
cause of this failure of the Bern talks.[121]

The antagonists in the worst war in history had
maneuvered themselves into a terrible position where
the winners could offer no terms, however severe,
and the losers could not ask for any, however sub-
missive. The Battle of the Ardennes, or the Battle
of the Bulge as it is popularly known, was the last
offensive effort of the German army; with Von Run-
stedt's defeat, there was absolutely no reason for
additional fighting and, in a sane war, hostilities
would have immediately ended. But "because of unconditional surrender the war was far from being
sane." The Western Allies were "gagged by this idiotic slogan." Thus, Hitler, like Samson, pulled
the edifice of Central Europe down upon himself, his
people, and their enemies. With the war already ir-
retrievably lost, his political aim was chaos, and
"thanks to unconditional surrender he was in a position to achieve it."[122]

It was a basic assumption by the Allies that
the war had to be fought to Total Victory. Since an
attrition strategy was employed, fighting would continue until the enemy surrendered without negotiations, as the peace terms were to be unilaterally
imposed.[123] It is a political fact of life: "A
surrender agreement is essentially a political bargain. To aim at obtaining surrender while ruling
out all bargaining on principle is a contradiction
in terms."[124] The delay in arriving at each surrender enabled third parties, particularly Russia, to
make gains at Allied expense. The Allies neglected
the fact that a speedy qualified surrender would
have served their interests better than either a
rigid unconditional surrender or a delayed qualified
surrender. What would have best served Allied interests was a negotiated surrender without a political vacuum; however, that was precluded by the no-
negotiation and no-recognition restrictions.[125]
This inflexible policy of no negotiations prolonged
the war, thereby causing more unnecessary loss of
life and additional destruction.

NOTES

1. Hanson W. Baldwin, Great Mistakes of the

<u>War</u> (New York: Harper & Brothers, 1950), p. 14.
2. Fuller, <u>The Second World War</u>, p. 258.
3. Aron, <u>The Century of Total War</u>, p. 96. Fuller recognized that Hitler started the war, but he
also saw no doubt that "Clemenceau, the uncontrolled
and all-controlling chairman of the Peace Conference,
and his masterpiece the Treaty of Versailles" precipitated Hitler. <u>The Second World War</u>, p. 23.
On pp. 17-18, Fuller called this treaty the
"immediate cause" of World War II, because it violated the Armistice of 11 November 1918. This "dishonourable action" permitted Hitler to marshal the
whole of Germany behind him and to justify in the
eyes of the German people each infringement of the
treaty he made." See also Ferdinand O. Miksche, <u>Un-</u>
<u>conditional Surrender: the Roots of World War III</u>
(London: Faber & Faber, 1952), p. 154.
Kennan, <u>Russia and the West</u>, p. 164, said
that events leading to 1939 were based on Allied
government actions in 1918 and 1919, and that the
relationships between the major nations followed a
logic that resembled a Greek tragedy.
4. Kahn, <u>On Thermonuclear War</u>, pp. 390-391,
italics in original. See also Miksche, <u>Uncondition-</u>
<u>al Surrender</u>, pp. 161-162. He called France's poli-
tical instability one of the major causes of the war
and stated that it was the "indecision of the West"
that allowed Hitler to carry his plans into effect.
5. Ibid., p. 393, italics in original.
6. Einzig, <u>Can We Win the Peace?</u>, p. 47-48. See
Fuller, <u>A Military History of the Western World</u>,
Vol. III, p. 386, for his appraisal of the state of
the French Army. He felt it was out-of-date and
corrupted by the leftist ideas of Blum's <u>Front Popu-</u>
<u>laire</u> government; also that the people were defeat-
ist, preferring occupation by Hitler to war. See
Possony, <u>The Century of Conflict</u>, pp. 249-251, for
Communist activity in the French Army and among the
French people in 1939-40, regarding sabotage, slow-
downs, etc. See Admiral Leahy, <u>I Was There</u>, p. 40,
for his statement "Many French officials seemed to
prefer Nazism to the danger of Communist domination."
when the Germans invaded Russia.
7. Seversky, <u>Victory Through Air Power</u>, p. 115.
8. Raymond Cartier, <u>Les secrets de la guerre</u>
<u>dévoilés par Nuremberg</u> (Paris: Arthème Fayard, 1946),
p. 62. See also Alfred Vagts, <u>Defense and Diplomacy.</u>
<u>The Soldier and the Conduct of Foreign Relations</u>
(New York: Kings' Crown Press, 1958), p. 367. He
said Hitler's pseudo-victories "could never have
been successful if France had interposed, as the

protesting Wehrmacht generals were only too well aware."

9. Churchill, The Gathering Storm, p. 263. See Churchill, Step by Step, p. 264, referring to the German maneuvers of August 1938, the "optimists" or appeasers could rationalize anything. See also Cartier, Les secrets, p. 97, about Munich.

10. Lieutenant General Siegfried Westphal in The Fatal Decisions edited by Seymour Freidin and William Richardson, pp. 14-15.

11. Churchill, Triumph and Tragedy, p. 556.

12. Robert Sherwood, Roosevelt and Hopkins (New York: Harper & Brothers, 1948), pp. 130-131. This passage was omitted from the French translation.

13. Joseph C. Grew, Ten Years in Japan (New York: Simon & Schuster, 1944), p. 39.

14. Ibid., p. 368. See also Grew, Turbulent Era, A Diplomatic Record of Forty Years 1904-1945 (Boston: Houghton Mifflin, 1952), Vol. II, pp. 1282-1289, for warnings from the United States Embassy in Tokyo.

15. Cordell Hull, The Memoirs of Cordell Hull (New York: The Macmillan Company, 1948), Vol. II., p. 984.

16. Fuller, A Military History of the Western World, Vol. III, p. 450. See also Vagts, Defense and Diplomacy, pp. 370-371

17. Ibid., pp. 450-456. Vagts, Defense and Diplomacy, p. 325, presented the same idea that FDR knew war was coming, but gave no warning so that the Japanese would attack first, then Congress would declare war.

See also Grew, Turbulent Era. He did not consider the ten points to be an ultimatum. He tried to explain to the Japanese that they embodied all their desires and could be referred to their people as a diplomatic victory without war, Vol. II, pp. 1247-1249. Yet Grew did say that the American position in Washington was "almost completely inflexible," Vol. II, p. 1334; see also pp. 1335-1340; and that Washington, because of having broken the Japanese code, was able "to learn that the Japanese Government was rapidly going ahead with its plans of conquest even while talking peace with us." Vol. II, p. 1244.

See also William L. Shirer, The Rise and Fall of the Third Reich. A History of Nazi Germany (Greenwich, Conn.: Fawcett Publications, Inc. 1962), pp. 1157-1167; on the Saturday night before the attack "the Navy Department informed the President and Mr. Hull that the Japanese Embassy was destroying its codes." p. 1167.

18. Arthur Bryant, The Turn of the Tide, A History of the War Years Based on the Diaries of Field Marshal Lord Alanbrooke, Chief of the Imperial General Staff (Garden City, N.Y.: Doubleday and Co., 1957), p. 234.

19. Annual Message to Congress, see Goodrich, Documents on American Foreign Relations, Vol. IV, 1941-1942, p. 48.

20. State of the Union Speech, 7 January 1943, Sherwood, Roosevelt and Hopkins, p. 667, also not included in the French translation. Also in Goodrich, Documents on American Foreign Relations, Vol. V, p. 40.

21. Armstrong, Unconditional Surrender, p. 61. B. G. Ivanyi, Route to Potsdam. The Story of the Peace Aims 1939-1945 (London: A. Wingate, 1945), p. 7, wrote, "Had Britain entered the Hitler war with as many guns as peace aims, as many 'planes as plans, an army as numerous as the arguments about what the struggle portended, victory would have been swift."

The American approach was to win the war as fast as possible without adventures. See Elliott Roosevelt, As He Saw It (New York: Duell, Sloan & Pearce, 1946), p. 186, for FDR's view at Teheran; Goodrich, Documents on American Foreign Relations, Vol. V, p. 12, for a radio address by Hull 23 July 1942; and Chester Wilmot, The Struggle for Europe, p. 715, about General Marshall.

The desired peace was often mentioned but never in precise terms. See speeches in Goodrich, Vol. V; FDR, p. 201; Under Secretary of State Welles, pp. 48-49 and p. 609; and Assistant Secretary of State Acheson, p. 109.

It is interesting to note that Chamberlain made a distinction between war and peace aims. He called for the defeat of the enemy as the war aim and the formation of a "new Europe" as the peace aim, radio speech 26 November 1939, "Post-war peace objectives" International Conciliation, February 1940, no. 357, pp. 40-41. Lord Halifax, on p. 43, listed his war aims to the House of Lords: liberation of those peoples who had lost their liberties, freedom from constant fear of aggression in Europe, and safeguard of freedom and security.

22. Lippmann, U.S. War Aims, p. 71, fully italicized. See pp. 96-97 for other political goals including Russian influence to be recognized in Eastern Europe, by necessity.

23. Leahy, I Was There, p. 238.

24. Armstrong, Unconditional Surrender, p. 45.

25. Ivanyi, Route to Potsdam, p. 10. He said there was more wailing in Britain about Versailles than about what the Germans were doing in 1939 and 1940.

26. Ibid., p. 67.

27. Harry S. Truman, Year of Decisions, Vol. I of Memoirs (Garden City, N.Y.: Doubleday & Co., 1955), p. 208.

28. Dr. K. F. Zemanek, University of the Saar, "Unconditional Surrender and International Law," Association des auditeurs et anciens auditeurs de l'Academie de droit internationale de la Haye, Annuaire 26, 1956, p. 34. There was strong pressure for dismemberment of Germany even though both the Foreign Office and the State Department saw that it would not be to our advantage. See Sir E. Llewellyn Woodward, British Foreign Policy in the Second World War (London: H. M. Stationery Office, 1962), p. 469, and Strauss, The Division and Dismemberment of Germany, p. 35.

29. Paul Kecskemeti, Strategic Surrender: The Politics of Victory and Defeat (Stanford: Stanford University Press, 1958), p. 239.

30. Ibid., p. 240.

31. Armstrong, Unconditional Surrender, p. 34.

32. Goodrich, Documents on American Foreign Relations, Vol. IV, 1941-1942, p. 41. See Einzig, Can We Win the Peace?, p. 103, about not letting Germany off easy again for they would try once more in a few years.

33. Speech, "The Price of Free World Victory" presented in New York City to the Free World Association, Goodrich, Documents on American Foreign Relations, Vol. IV, 1941-1942, p. 69. See King-Hall, Total Victory, p. 56, for at least one person who was looking toward an armistice rather than Total Victory.

34. Armstrong, Unconditional Surrender, p. 17.

35. Goodrich, Documents on American Foreign Relations, Vol. V, p. 15.

36. Einzig, Can We Win the Peace?, p. 34, written in 1942 under the pressure of events and not as hindsight. See also p. 35.

37. Armstrong, Unconditional Surrender, p. 63. Senate Resolution 192, 5 November 1943. "Resolved, that the war against all our enemies be waged until victory is achieved.

"That the United States cooperate with its comrades-in-arms in securing a just and honorable peace." U.S. Department of State, A Decade of

American Foreign Policy 1941-49 (Washington, D.C.:
U.S. Government Printing Office, 1950), p. 14.
   38. Kennan, Russia and the West under Lenin and
Stalin, p. 366.
   39. See Armstrong, Unconditional Surrender,
p. 30.
   40. Bryant, Turn of the Tide, p. 458.
   41. Wilmot, The Struggle for Europe, p. 121.
   42. Goodrich, Documents on American Foreign Relations, Vol. V, 1942-1943, p. 255.
   43. Sherwood, Roosevelt and Hopkins, p. 696.
John Gunther wrote how FDR "loved to 'pull' surpris-
es and put on a show." Roosevelt in Retrospect. A
Profile in History (New York: Harper & Brothers,
1950), p. 57.
   44. Ibid.
   45. Roosevelt, As He Saw It, p. 117.
   46. Ibid.
   47. Ibid., p. 119.
   48. Sherwood, Roosevelt and Hopkins, p. 696.
   49. Churchill, The Hinge of Fate, Vol. IV of
The Second World War, p. 684.
   50. Ibid., p. 686.
   51. Ibid., p. 689.
   52. Gunther, Roosevelt in Retrospect, pp. 361-
362, italics in the original.
   53. Possony, A Century of Conflict, p. 269,
stated that Soviet calls for Allied landings in
France in 1942 and 1942 were not so much to aid them
as in hopes of an Allied defeat that would result in
a relative increase of Soviet power. If this had
happened, the Soviets might have occupied all of
Germany and possibly France.
   54. William L. Langer, "Political Problems of a
Coalition," Foreign Affairs, October 1947, p. 85.
He concluded that it "was an unfortunate and costly
move, and that it was too high a price to pay for
Stalin's peace of mind."
      See also Pierre Renouvin, Histoire des Re-
lations Internationales (Paris: Librairie Hachette,
1958), Vol. VIII, p. 321. He felt Stalin was convinced that a compromise peace was excluded. The
pledge not to make a separate peace had been included in paragraph (2) of the United Nations Declaration at Washington, 1 January 1942 (the name, United
Nations, which at first applied to the powers fighting the Axis, was later the name of the organization); see William L. Neumann, Making the Peace 1941-
45. The Diplomacy of the Wartime Conferences (Washington, D.C.: Foundation for Foreign Affairs, 1950)
p. 24.

55. Joseph E. Davies, Mission to Moscow (New York: Simon & Schuster, 1941) p. 408.

56. Ibid., p. 410.

57. Armstrong, Unconditional Surrender, p. 39.

58. Maxime Mourin, Le drame des États satellites de l'Axe de 1939 à 1945. Reddition sans conditions (Paris: Berger-Levrault, 1957), p. 14. See also Armstrong, Unconditional Surrender, p. 9.

59. Kecskemeti, Strategic Surrender, p. 218.

60. Churchill, The Grand Alliance, Vol. III of The Second World War, p. 607.

61. Eisenhower, Operations in Europe, p. 1.

62. Speech at Lord Mayor's Day Luncheon, Mansion House, London, 10 November 1942 (Anglo-American invasion of North Africa had started on 8 November), Churchill, War Speeches, 1942, compiled by Charles Eade (London: Cassel and Co., 1943), p. 213.

63. Ibid., p. 214; see also Goodrich, Documents on American Foreign Relations, Vol. V, p. 204.

64. Churchill, Their Finest Hour, p. 26.

65. Churchill, The Grand Alliance, p. 370.

66. Ibid., p. 372.

67. Fuller, A Military History of the Western World, Vol. III, p. 449; he made a third point that Churchill should not have been so quick to aid Russia but have gotten concrete concessions. (pp. 449-450).

68. Fuller, The Second World War, p. 400; see also p. 27.

69. Walter Lüdde-Neurath, Les derniers jours du troisième Reich, Le gouvernement de Doenitz, pp. 19-20.

70. Fuller, The Conduct of War, p. 269. It is interesting that in Japan, the death of FDR "was reported sympathetically in the press." They thought it might lead to less Allied antagonism toward Japan. David H. James, The Rise and Fall of the Japanese Empire (London: Allen & Unwin, 1951), p. 301

71. New York Herald Tribune, European edition (Paris: 27-28 October 1962). See also General George C. Marshall, The Winning of the War in Europe and the Pacific, p. 3 about the lack of a master plan.

Fuller called the "second American crusade" more disastrous than the first, and blamed it on Roosevelt. Also "From the captured German archives there is no evidence to support the President's claims that Hitler contemplated an offensive against the western hemisphere, and until America entered the war there is abundant evidence that this was the one thing he wanted to avert." A Military History of the Western World, Vol. III, p. 629

72. Fuller, The Conduct of War, pp. 250-251; for the crusade nature of World War II, see Fuller, The Second World War, pp. 398-400.

73. Armstrong, Unconditional Surrender, p. 71.

74. Jean Cuny, La capitulation sans conditions de l'Allemagne et ses précédents historiques (Berlin: Imprimerie Nationale, 1947; Law thesis, Paris: 1946), p. 36.

75. Kecskemeti, Strategic Surrender, pp. 25-26.

76. Dwight D. Eisenhower, Crusade in Europe (Garden City, N.Y.: Doubleday & Co., Inc., 1948), p. 157, his title also reflected this.

77. Hankey, Politics, Trials and Errors, p. 49.

78. Before Reichstag, 11 December 1941, issuing Declaration of War, Goodrich, Documents on American Foreign Relations, Vol. IV, 1941-1942, p. 622. See also Shirer, Rise and Fall of the Third Reich, pp. 1173-1174. See Cartier, Les secrets de la guerre, p. 35, for his comments about Hitler as a Great Captain and a fool.

79. George F. Kennan, American Diplomacy 1900-1950 (Chicago: University of Chicago Press, 1951), p. 65, a good discussion of democracy going to war; the fact of provocation becomes the main issue.

80. Zemanek, "Unconditional Surrender and International Law,", p. 31.

81. Sherwood, Roosevelt and Hopkins, p. 695.

82. Goodrich, Documents on American Foreign Relations, Vol. V, 1942-1943, p. 44.

83. Cordell Hull, Memoirs, Vol. II, p. 1571. Secretary of State Hull was for a more "flexible" surrender policy. He saw, perhaps, severe terms for Germany and Japan and "substantial adjustments away from the terms of unconditional surrender" for Italy and the Axis satellite states; see p. 1570.

84. Daugherty and Janowitz, A Psychological Warfare Casebook, p. 275.

85. Sherwood, Roosevelt and Hopkins, pp. 296-297, not in French translation.

86. Teheran Conference was 28 November-1 December 1943, ibid., pp. 782-783. See also Neumann, Making the Peace, p. 67.

87. Mourin, Le drame des états satellites de l'Axe, p. 21.

88. Strauss, Division and Dismemberment of Germany, p. 53.

89. Hull, Memoirs, Vol. II, p. 1573; see also Strauss, p. 61.

90. Ibid., pp. 1574 and 1576.

91. Ibid., p. 1577.

92. Ibid., p. 1579.

93. Strauss, Division and Dismemberment of Germany, pp. 52-53; Hull, Memoirs, p. 1573.

94. Mourin, Le drame des états satellites de l'Axe, p. 22.

95. Churchill, The Hinge of Fate, p. 690.

96. Harry Butcher, My Three Years with Eisenhower, p. 518. Butcher was the naval aide to General Eisenhower. It is interesting that the preceding sentence is, "Ed Stettinius told me the President was far from well and that he is becoming increasingly difficult to deal with because he changed his mind so often." This was before his election to his fourth term, before Yalta, and one year before his death.

97. Hull, Memoirs, p. 1578.

98. Strauss, Division and Dismemberment of Germany, pp. 53-54.

99. Leahy, I Was There, p. 145.

100. Truman, Year of Decisions, p. 207, italics in original. This speech was broadcast to the Japanese by Zacharias; see Daugherty and Janowitz, Psychological Warfare, p. 288. All fourteen broadcasts are reprinted in his book, Secret Missions, pp. 399-424.

101. Daugherty and Janowitz, Psychological Warfare, p. 282.

102. Truman, Year of Decisions, p. 265. Possony, A Century of Conflict, pp. 312-313, called Hopkins the "éminence grise of American dealings with Communism." Possony felt the Communists were strongly against modification of the Unconditional Surrender of Japan because they wanted to get into that area and they were afraid we would make peace before they could make their move.

103. Armstrong, Unconditional Surrender, p. 58.

104. Churchill, Triumph and Tragedy, p. 642.

105. Hull, Memoirs, p. 1582.

106. Fuller, A Military History of the Western World, Vol. III, p. 508.

107. Sherwood, Roosevelt and Hopkins, p. 126.

108. Mourin, Le drame des états satellites de l'Axe, p. 27.

109. Goodrich, Documents on American Foreign Relations, Vol. IV, 1941-1942, p. 588, to Foreign Press Association, London.

110. Ranshofen-Wertheimer, Victory is Not Enough, pp. 217-218, written in 1942.

111. See Einzig, Can We Win the Peace?, pp. 27 and 30.

112. Goodrich, Documents on American Foreign

171

Relations, Vol.. V, 1942-1943, p. 210. He probably
did this "to allay Allied uneasiness about his se-
ductive propaganda to the Germans," but on 6 November 1943, he was back to his appealing approach, see
Kecskemeti, Strategic Surrender, p. 226.
    113. Kennan, American Diplomacy, pp. 87-88.
    114. Churchill, Triumph and Tragedy, p. 352.
    115. See Lüdde-Neurath, Les derniers jours du
troisième Reich, pp. 67-68.
    116. Cartier, Les secrets de la guerre, p. 38,
my translation. This resolve not to negotiate was
probably propaganda at first and from 1943 on real
policy. There appears to be no other explanation of
Hitler's policy toward England, particularly since
he never was very serious about invasion, than that
he hoped to negotiate a settlement. See Shirer,
Rise and Fall of the Third Reich, pp. 982-995. See
also Fleming, Operation Sea Lion, pp. 17 and 72;
Heinz Guderian, Souvenirs d'un soldat, transl. by
François Courtet (Paris: Plon, 1954), pp. 122-123;
and Comte Ciano, Archives secrètes, p. 376.
    117. Ibid., p. 39, my translation.
    118. Ciano, Archives secrètes, p. 365.
    119. Armstrong, Unconditional Surrender, pp.
123-124, Rommel was forced to commit suicide for his
part in the abortive July 1944 attempt on Hitler.
See also pp. 128-129. See also Guderian, Souvenirs
d'un soldat, p. 417 about Speer telling Hitler it
was not right to blow up the factories, bridges, etc.
It would bring misery to the German people.
    120. Mourin, Le drame des états satellites de
l'Axe, p. 33, my translation. Goering said if Hitler had been assassinated, he would have fought to
the end, too, against Unconditional Surrender.
    121. See ibid., pp. 29-32, for the terrible
exchanges between "Allies."
    122. Fuller, The Second World War, p. 355, see
also Kecskemeti, Strategic Surrender, p. 227.
    123. Kecskemeti, Strategic Surrender, p. 215.
    124. Ibid., p. 236.
    125. Ibid., p. 229.

7
Unconditional Surrender
in Action

> What then is unconditional
> surrender by a state? It
> is the surrender of every
> last bargaining right by
> the people and their repre-
> sentatives.[1]
>
> -- S.L.A. Marshall

1. Prolonged the War

The quest for Total Victory by refusing to negotiate with the enemy and demanding Unconditional
Surrender would appear to have prolonged the war.
The absolute refusal to consider backstage contacts
with the enemy to see if any mutually acceptable basis for terminating the war existed, feeling that it
would detract from complete victory and jeopardize
the peace, interfered with the rapid termination of
the war. As Lord Hankey put it, no German leader
"was willing to sign such humiliating terms as unconditional surrender... this unfortunate phrase
prolonged the war for the German people to the last
extremity of human endurance."[2] We will examine the
effect on the anti-Nazi opposition later; Fuller
felt that Unconditional Surrender "crippled opposition to Hitler within Germany" and added two years to
the war.[3] Kecskemeti conservatively felt the policy
may have needlessly prolonged the war, "not because
of the effect of the slogan," but because it "prevented the Allies from handling surrender situations
in the most efficient and expeditious manner."[4]
Anne Armstrong, whose Unconditional Surrender
will long remain a primary reference on the subject,
concluded that if Unconditional Surrender is interpreted as a policy of refusing to compromise and

173

rejecting a negotiated solution, "then it seems quite clear that it did lengthen the war."[5] General Albert C. Wedemeyer concluded that, in addition to certain errors in strategic planning, Unconditional Surrender lengthened the war by a full year.[6]

A negotiated settlement any time after January 1945 would not have reduced the value of the lesson of complete and utter defeat which had been inflicted on the Germans, and it would have saved thousands of lives on both sides. More important, the continuity of a government by those responsible German elements already in covert opposition to Hitler might have precluded the opportunity for the Russians to establish a separate East German government.[7] Had the Allies been willing to accept more conventional peace terms than those anticipated by Big Three wartime conferences, peace might have been obtained in January or July 1943, in January or July 1944, or in January 1945. To illustrate the saving in lives alone, the United States Army (and Army Air Corps) battle casualties in the Atlantic Theater were as follows:

> January to June 1943....20,671 dead and wounded
> July to December 1943...30,546 dead and wounded
> January to June 1944...117,903 dead and wounded
> July to December 1944..360,486 dead and wounded
> January to May 1945....222,360 dead and wounded.[8]

This amounts to over 760,000 if the war had stopped after Stalingrad. These figures do not include the casualties of the other Allies or the Axis. The casualties, particularly among civilians, were highest during the last years of the war.

Those last years were trying ones for many of the German generals. They knew the war was lost and many spent much time discussing ways and means of arranging a surrender. A major cause for the refusal of these generals to act appears to have been the Allied insistence on Unconditional Surrender. The policy was an insurmountable barrier of conscience for many field and staff commanders who continued to fight from what they considered sheer lack of alternative.[9] Liddel Hart, who interviewed many of the German generals after the war, reported: "All to whom I talked dwelt on the effect of the Allies 'unconditional surrender' policy in prolonging the war."[10]

This policy was so strictly adhered to in propaganda dissemination that the Supreme Commander could not even make an announcement to the miners in

the Saar of the good treatment they would get if
they "stayed put" when the Germans withdrew. The
State Department and Foreign Office representatives
were so afraid of violating high policy that it was
referred to Washington, and their fears proved well
founded. Refusing "'to permit the Supreme Commander
to state the terms and methods of military surrender
certainly decreased the readiness of German commanders in the field to surrender, and so quite needlessly prolonged the war.'"[11] Unconditional Surrender
was an expensive phrase and policy in that it prolonged the war, greatly increased the cost, and destroyed the European balance of power by prolonged
and intensified devastation thereby enhancing Russian influence on the Continent.

Though mention is most often made of Germany,
the same problem existed in regard to Japan. Even
though it was clear that the longer the war continued the more hopeless Japan's situation would become, Japanese police-state methods and Allied unwillingness to clarify the future status of the
throne inevitably lengthened the war.[12] The British
Foreign Office was able to see "that unqualified insistence on unconditional surrender was helping to
prolong Japanese resistance.[13] Had the war ended in
May 1945, and "but for the political and strategical
lunacy induced by the policy of unconditional surrender it might well have done so," Russia would not
have been invited in with a free hand to expand her
influence over the Far East.[14]

The consensus of German writers was that the
demand for Unconditional Surrender was psychologically unwise because it stiffened the troops' will
to resist and, therefore, increased the cost of Allied victory. The strength of the anti-Nazi resistance forces was undermined and also seems to have
contributed to the lengthening of the war. The
claim that Unconditional Surrender prolonged the war
is a criticism of a policy of no compromise, refusing to negotiate, and pursuing the war to the final
destruction of the enemy. A more flexible general
policy and a more moderate war aim would have better
served the interests of the Western Allies. The
claim that the Casablanca policy stiffened resistance is basically a criticism of Unconditional Surrender as propaganda. Even with the same war aim,
the phrase Unconditional Surrender could have been
avoided since it played into Goebbels' hands.[15]

While the war was still in progress, the Allies
announced that those German officers and men and
members of the Nazi Party who had committed atroci-

175

ties and war crimes would be tried for their offenses after they were captured.[16] This was not likely to make them come rushing up to surrender. As Eisenhower himself put it in a press conference: "If you were given two choices -- one to mount the scaffold and the other to charge twenty bayonets, you might as well charge twenty bayonets."[17] Fuller felt that Unconditional Surrender offered nothing but "total incineration." Also, at this critical time in the war, "instead of the Allied Powers attempting to bring the conflict to a sane political end by astute psychological attack, no effect was missed to stimulate German resistance. Lists of so-called war criminals were issued, whole organizations, such as the German General Staff and the Nazi Party, were proscribed, and at this crucial moment the Morgenthau Scheme was published, which demanded that Germany should be partitioned, devastated, pillaged and pastoralized!"[18] The Allies offered no incentive to the Axis; they only repeated continually that they were going to impose Uncondition Surrender. The German will to resist was strengthened by each statement of the Allied leaders. Liddell Hart wrote in mid-1943:

> A good slogan... is not necessarily identical
> with good strategy and policy.... When, in war,
> the opponents are beginning to wilt, a rigid
> demand for unconditional surrender has a natur-
> al tendency to stiffen their resistance, and
> may even cement an incipient crack. This ele-
> mentary truth was pointed out in the first
> classic work on the art of war, that of the
> Chinese master-strategist Sun Tzu, in 500 B.C.
> "Honorable capitulation" is a more reassuring
> and, therefore, more inviting formula, while
> just as flexible.[19]

Regardless of the real intentions of any antagonist, the proclamation of a policy of Unconditional Surrender is a pill hard to swallow for any country; it is a policy of despair. As a German proverb says: "Despair gives courage to a coward," or as a French proverb puts it: "Le désespoir redouble nos forces."
It must be recognized that there are some who do not feel that the Casablanca policy prolonged the war. Woodward stated that "nothing in the course of events suggests that the Nazi control of Germany lasted longer owing to the Allied demand for unconditional surrender."[20] Gunther apologized for

176

Roosevelt with "In any case the formula did little if any harm. It had small effect on the major course of events.... Unconditional surrender did not prolong the war; Hitler, we know now, would have fought to the last gasp anyway, and so did the Japanese."[21] This is rather weak and completely overlooks the effect on any internal opposition to Hitler. Kecskemeti somewhat tempered his other statements on the effect of the formula by saying

> ...the generally assumed causal relationship between the formula of unconditional surrender and the length of the war is illusory. The length of the war was determined largely by other factors, including the Allies' objective of total victory and Hitler's (and the Japanese war extremists') refusal to admit the possibility of any kind of surrender.[22]

This would appear to be getting down to fine points as it appears there is more than a casual relationship between Unconditional Surrender and Total Victory.

Nevertheless, the consensus of opinion is that the policy of Unconditional Surrender, or, if you prefer, the uncompromising mental outlook behind it, delayed the agreement between the antagonists to terminate the war. We should now look at the effect of this policy on the surrenders of the three principal members of the Axis.

2. Italy - the First Test of Unconditional Surrender

In the summer of 1943, after more than twenty years in power, Mussolini's world came tumbling down on him and he was forced to resign. The man who replaced him was Marshal Badoglio and there followed a period that could have been written for high comedy if it had not been so serious to the players. Badoglio wanted to quit the Axis and join the Allies against Germany, but he had to be very careful of his moves to prevent German discovery of his plans. His first problem was to find someone among the Allies with whom he could talk. Marshal Badoglio made it known to British and Swiss representatives that he "had tried everything to make contact with the British government." But the latter, convinced that Italy would fall like a ripe fruit, considered such

177

a contact useless.[23]

The Marshal wrote that he was unable to contact London or Washington through the representatives at the Vatican because the Germans would find out; also, the American personnel had no codes. Badoglio had sent a functionary to Lisbon in June to try to make contact with the Allies[24] and it was through the contacts in that city that the negotiations eventually were made. However forty days were lost and, in the meantime, many German divisions were rushed into Italy and even though Italy left the war, German-occupied Italy remained.

Whereas Badoglio's emissaries wanted to talk about Italy joining the Allies, all the Allied representatives could discuss was Unconditional Surrender. This was a good example of the inflexibility of Roosevelt's Casablanca formula. Even though an internal revolution had taken place, the Italians were still considered allies of Germany.[25]

The uncompromising formula had placed the Allies in the unfortunate position that when Badoglio was named to replace Mussolini, they had no plan of action. The Allies had an emotional block concerning any rapprochement with Badoglio. Unconditional Surrender, as applied to Italy, was based on the premise that it would enable the Allies to preserve their moral integrity without sacrificing military expediency. In fact, it lost both. When Mussolini resigned FDR said:

> Our terms to Italy are still the same as our terms to Germany and Japan - Unconditional Surrender.
>
> We will have no truck with Fascism in any way, shape or manner. We will permit no vestige of Fascism to remain.[26]

One author coldly described the slow Allied reaction. "They went on talking woodenly of unconditional surrender, and bombed Rome again."[27]

Though the term Unconditional Surrender was often loosely used, the surrender of Italy was not unconditional, but, as Hull clearly stated; "a negotiated surrender, and the terms of the armistice were agreed to in duscussions in Lisbon, Portugal, between representatives of the Anglo-American Combined Chiefs of Staff and Marshal Badoglio."[28]

General Eisenhower wrote that "the Italians wanted frantically to surrender"[29], but they wanted protection from the Germans. He noted that the "negotiations for the Italian surrender had been dragging along. They were very intricate."[30] Harry Butcher noted, on 27 July 1943, that General Eisenhower wanted to give the Italians a chance to send an emissary from King Victor Emmanuel to negotiate quickly for peace with honor.[31] Churchill still wanted them to surrender but he did relent a little on 9 August when he wrote to the Foreign Secretary:

> ...while they have to make a formal act of submission, our desire is to treat them with consideration, so far as military exigencies allow. Merely harping on "unconditional surrender," with no prospect of mercy held out even as an act of grace, may well lead to no surrender at all. The expression "honourable capitulation" has also been officially used by the President, and I do not think it should be omitted from the language we are now to use.[32]

What had appeared to be a quick collapse of Italy vanished in early August. Butcher observed that around the headquarters, they attributed this to the hard-boiled attitude of the Prime Minister and the President and their public insistence upon Unconditional Surrender after Mussolini was ousted.[33] On 17 August he got a sample of British feeling. MacMillan was dejected -- the British public, he reported, seemed tired of the war but, oddly, was insistent on Unconditional Surrender. The two simply did not fit. The war could have been shortened by giving Italy honorable terms, not to mention the saving of lives.[34] The big problem was that we were trying to conduct one-sided negotiations in Lisbon. The Italian envoy general in Lisbon was in a hopeless position. His purpose was to discuss how Italy could assist against Germany. General Bedell Smith could only discuss Unconditional Surrender.[35] This inflexibility was no credit to the political awareness of the Allies.

Marshal Badoglio's problems continued right up to the signing of the armistice on 3 September and then even worsened afterward. He considered the armistice to have been honorable, then, later in the month, he was given a new text entitled "Unconditional Surrender of Italy."[36] Ike had felt that the terms of even the first agreement were unduly harsh. "He suspects that our home governments want to make a propaganda Roman holiday by publicizing to the entire world the stern restrictions

of the surrender."[37]   However, to get Badoglio to
sign the second document required Ike's word that he
would try to get it changed. The document had been
drawn up by the governments and not by the military
commanders on the spot. Badoglio signed it only because he was convinced of Ike's good faith.[38] Badoglio wrote of Ike:

> "I give you my word as a soldier that I am going
> to do all in my power to have the phrases of
> the actual armistice changed in the sense indi-
> cated by General Smith. In the meantime, the
> document will be kept absolutely secret. Have
> faith in me and please sign."... I signed.
> Eisenhower kept his word.[39]

After the toning down of the second armistice,
Badoglio wrote FDR: "The armistice that was signed
on my orders on 3 September by General Castellano
contained no clause alluding to the surrender of
Italy." He was most unhappy with the additional
clauses that he had been forced to sign particularly
since they were entitled "Unconditional Surrender of
Italy."[40] All the delay had greatly reduced the control of the Badoglio government and it was never
used to any significant extent against the Nazis.[41]
     The first test of Unconditional Surrender had
not shown it to be too useful. Instead of harping on
Unconditional Surrender, the Allies should have
called on Italy to join the United Nations in driving
out the Germans. This would have led Badoglio to
call for open revolt, confident that the Allies would
help him. But no! Unconditional Surrender was still
the Allied cry, meaningless to Italian ears, unless
it meant that the Allies were more intent on humiliating Italy than on defeating Germany. The armistice could have been signed much earlier, then the
Germans would not have had time to solidly occupy
Rome and northern Italy, to replace the Italians in
southern France and the islands, to liberate Mussolini, and to send tens of thousands of Italian laborers to Germany. The morale effect would have been
much greater, and immediate Anglo-American military
action could have transformed the face of the war in
southern Europe.
     And so it was that the strategic reason for be-
ing there was lost. Unconditional Surrender transformed the "soft underbelly" of Europe into a croco-
dile's back, prolonged the war, devastated Italy, and
wasted thousands of lives. Unconditional Surrender
had not proved effective, yet it was not to be aban-

180

doned. Those Americans most directly concerned with
the cost of maintaining the demand for the Unconditional Surrender of Italy, the generals at the front,
became the severest critics of the policy of continuing to insist on the Unconditional Surrender of
Germany.[42] The demand for Unconditional Surrender
as such did not prolong Italian belligerency. However, as a method of terminating a phase of the war,
it was inept. The refusal to pay any political
price for surrender made the job of separating Italy
from Germany more expensive. Italy was out, next
stop, Germany.

3. The Fight to the End in Germany

Even though it was Japan that had attacked the
United States and brought it into the war, the American leadership managed to keep its eyes and hate
oriented on Germany throughout the war. The Americans and their Allies relentlessly pursued the Germans until that day in May, when Jodl, after having
signed the Unconditional Surrender of Germany said:

"Sir, by this signature, the German people and
the German army are delivered completely to the
mercy of the conqueror. In this war which has
lasted over five years, both have supplied more
effort and withstood more suffering than perhaps any other people of the world. At this
hour, nothing remains for me but to hope for
the clemency of the conqueror." He received no
answer and withdrew.[43]

With that signature, the "Thousand Year Reich"
of Adolf Hitler disappeared from the face of the
earth.
The surrender was almost an anticlimax, the
country having been almost completely overrun by the
Allied armies. The war had really been lost years
before; but, between the fanatical drive of Hitler
and the stiffness of the Allies, there was little
effort to end it. We have seen how Hitler had no
intention of surrendering, but several of his followers made secret approaches to the Allies. Churchill
wrote: "All these proposals were of course rejected.
Our terms were unconditional surrender on all
fronts."[44] All approaches were met either with complete silence, or "in the case of neutral governments, with the reply that there could be no

181

negotiations until the Nazi Government has been destroyed."[45]

The German's great fear was not so much of the Allies in the west but of the Russian armies that were descending on them from the east. Because of this, the Germans repeatedly tried to surrender or come to some terms in the west while continuing the war in the east.[46] To have come to terms unilaterally with the Germans would, most likely, have been in the best interests of the Western Allies but they stuck by their ties with the Russians, much to their regret in later years. Admiral Doenitz, in the few days he had, was faced with these two different attitudes: "Make peace at last" came the cries from the west. "Save us from the Russians" implored those in the east.[47] German civilians begged their military defenders in the west to let the Allies advance without resistance. They fled en masse in the east before the approaching Russians. Entire armies that were fighting on the Russian front tried to surrender to the Western Allies.[48] The Germans tried to stall right to the last to let as many as possible reach the Western lines to surrender. Eisenhower finally threatened to close the lines altogether if they did not surrender completely.[49] The Admiral was fairly successful though -- two and a half to three million German soldiers and civilians escaped from the path of the Russians during his brief tenure.[50]

One German general was told that he would have to let his troops be captured by the Russians and that they would be treated according to the laws of war and would soon be back at their homes. "With the Russians, answered the German general, you can negotiate only when you still have weapons. When they are gone, you are a slave. One day you will remember my words."[51] Millions of Germans were never seen again and some were released each year even into the 1960s.

It had truly been a war to the bitter end. The great question though is, Why did the Allies fight such a terribly expensive war and completely ignore the idea of aiding the internal opposition to Hitler? Certainly the cheapest way to win a war is by internal revolution in the camp of your adversary and then creating a new government that conforms to your desires; this, basically, is why one should be fighting a war in the first place. "The importance of the political aim -- revolution within the Reich -- was ignored."[52] Throughout Hitler's long climb to power, there was always opposition to the "little

Corporal." He was not a great popular figure who
had been elected to power; he was a dictator who had
to treat his opposition harshly to stay in power.
One group that strongly resisted the Nazi line was
the German Army.

Fuller thought that the Allies should have divided the Germans into pro- and anti-Hitlerite political groups and have offered the former the worst of
terms and the latter the best. By allying with all
Germans opposed to Hitler, and by helping them with
every means in their power, the Allies could have
attacked Hitlerism internally and overthrown it by
revolution.[53] The Allies, incensed at having been
brought into the war, became victims of their own
propaganda, which tried to establish that all Germans are the same. Our blind haste in joining with
the Communists to eradicate the Nazis did not sim-
plify matters any. The Western Allies refused to
recognize any latent conflict of interests with Soviet Russia. Their reaction to earlier appeals by
the German opposition, which had made much of the
danger of bolshevization, was completely negative.
During the war, the British and Americans should have
established contact with the German opposition and
tried to conquer Germany without destroying her, instead of extending the war to the point at which annihilation of the vanquished made a collision between the Allies inevitable. To spare the enemy
when one is unsure of one's ally has long been the
teaching of an honorable Machiavellian wisdom.

It is interesting to contrast Stalin's approach
with that of the West. Though Stalin had to mouth
Unconditional Surrender once in a while to satisfy
his allies, it was not really his policy. He maintained a Free Germany Committee in Moscow that was
very active in disseminating propaganda. In July
1943, with Stalin's agreement, the committee called
for the formation of a new German government and for
it to enter into peace negotiations. It was a completely different line from that of Casablanca. After the attempt on Hitler's life in July 1944, this
committee called for the Germans to follow these
people against Hitler.[54] The comments from London
and Washington were of a completely different vein.
Churchill suggested that it was merely a case of dog
eat dog, and Roosevelt could only expand on Unconditional Surrender.

But an opposition did exist. From 1933 to 1938,
some 500,000 to 600,000 Germans were confined to
concentration camps for political reasons, that is,
for anti-Nazi beliefs or activities. Approximately

183

12,000 persons were executed for political crimes,
and Gestapo files listed more than 2,000,000 Germans
as politically unreliable.[55] The Nazi Party was an
elite, not to exceed about 10 percent of the population; therefore, the majority of government posts
had to be filled by non-Nazis and even silent anti-
Nazis. In 1939, of 1.5 million German civil ser-
vants fewer than thirty percent were members of the
party.[56]

Throughout the war, our propaganda told us how
the German army officers were the real seat of Nazi
power. A bigger lie could hardly be imagined. Hitler had nothing but disdain for his officers. Raymond Cartier wrote how Hitler particularly hated the
generals. He mistreated, injured, hazed, and destroyed them. He probably hit, manually struck! one
of the most important of them, a marshall![57] They
were always under the eye of Himmler. Hitler felt
that the generals considered him the old corporal
from World War I, according to Keitel. Their refusal to adopt the ideology of National-Socialism,
their disdain for the party and its chiefs generated
a furious resentment in Hitler.[58] He ridiculed the
top generals with, "These ideas are too high for you;
they are not at your level but don't forget that I
wish to be obeyed."[59] His hate was particularly
aimed at the Army, and he treated them "like dogs."[60]
Shirer reported that Hitler felt his victory over
the Prussian officer corps was complete when he was
head of state, Minister of War, Supreme Commander of
the Armed Forces and Commander in Chief of the Army.
The generals were now his postmen to carry out his
orders.[61]

Hitler made all the decisions. Goering tried
to slow Hitler up in March 1939 about Czechoslovakia,
advising that if he violated the Munich agreement it
would probably topple Chamberlain and bring Churchill
to power. Hitler would not listen to him, his own
designated number-two man. When Hitler decided to
invade Russia, a momentous decision in German history, he called Goering and said: "I have decided
to go to war with Russia." No one had anything to
say about it.[62] "The conduct of total war is the
Führer's business."[63] Liddell Hart put it rather
succinctly. "The German generals had little effect
on the start of the Second World War - except as an
ineffectual brake."[64] Goering stated: "No general
was ever asked if he approved such and such a policy."[65]

Another great propaganda myth was that the
really dangerous part of the Nazi government was the

German General Staff. It was repeatedly attacked in
the West. Beveridge, in his footnote on ambitions
of rulers as a cause of war, added: "... it would
probably be fair to add the name of an organization
-- the German General Staff, masters of war, artists
waiting their chance to demonstrate their artist-
ry."[66] There was a strong tradition of noninterfer-
ence in political matters in the German Army. Contrary to the myth prevalent in America and elsewhere
that the General Staff was the real directing force
of German policy, the German Army and its General
Staff had never formulated German policy, and had
even less governmental influence under Hitler. The
Army, as a whole, remained non-Nazi despite efforts
by the Party to dominate the officer corps. Party
activities were not permitted among the troops and
recruits were not given ideological indoctrination.[67]
The chief of this staff, General Keitel, stated: "As
Chief of Staff I had no authority whatever -- no
command function -- nothing. All I could do was to
transmit his orders to the Staff and see that they
were carried out. I had no idea of his general
plan."[68] General Bobo Zimmermann, writing after the
war, noted: "It is a matter of irony that Eisenhower, the servant of the great democracies, was
given full powers of command over an armed force
consisting of all three services. With us, living
under a dictatorship where unity of command might
have been taken for granted, each of the services
fought its own battle."[69] General Gavin was more
blunt in his statement that, "the fact is that in
the last two world wars Germany did not have a German general staff."[70]

This considerable body of opposition to Hitler
tried on numerous occasions to remove him. With absolutely no support from the Allies and operating
under very difficult circumstances in a dictatorship,
they were never successful. One needs only to stop
and think about the different way world problems
might have developed differently to consider that it
was a tragic mistake on the part of the Allies not
to have given them at least some encouragement.
Shirer devoted many pages of a very long book to the
various conspiracies against Hitler.[71] On the eve
of Munich certain generals had decided to overthrow
the Führer rather than precipitate general war.
There were many attempts on his life, seven in 1943,
one failing because a bomb in his plane did not go
off.[72] The officers' putsch of 1944 was their own
way of seeking peace. With the success of the Allied landing in Normandy, Rommel realized that all

185

was over and saw that Hitler was the obstacle; he
openly said the only thing was to do away with him.
This was a remarkable change of attitude in Hitler's
favorite general, and it cost Rommel his life, but
it was too late to save Germany.[73]

The rigid Casablanca formula once again took
its toll. Some members of the anti-Nazi resistance
movement insisted that the proclamation disrupted
their organization overnight.[74] Kennan stressed
that these people were much closer to us ideologi-
cally than to either Hitler or Stalin. Yet, they
received no encouragement from the Allied side. Unconditional Surrender, implying that Germany would
be treated with equal severity whether or not Hitler
was overthrown, completely cut the ground out from
under any moderate German opposition.[75] Fuller
claimed that a revolt against Hitler was nearest to
success after the terrible defeat at Stalingrad.
Most of the field marshals as well as Generals Beck
and Zeitzler were involved, but without any assurance of British and American support they could offer nothing to the large middle group of officers
who wavered. Casablanca came at this time and their
attempts to talk to the Allies were ignored. "At
this climax in the war, what staggers one is the political blindness of British and American statesmen.
They completely failed to realize the politico-
strategical situation with which they were faced."[76]
This obstacle persisted, and thereafter many, especially key officers, refused to cooperate in plans
to overthrow Hitler unless Germany would be spared
the destruction they believed to be inherent in Unconditional Surrender.[77] Jodl and Guderian both
supposedly refused to take part because of the formula.[78]

There was one other result of this policy that
almost proved even more serious. There were some
among the oppositionists who, because of the Western
inflexibility, felt their only chance was to turn to
the East.[79] The Soviets missed no opportunity to
exploit the anti-Nazi resistance in their effort to
destroy Nazi Germany and to bring Communism to Central Europe. Only the fundamental opposition to any
form of totalitarianism by the resistance workers
prevented an agreement which might have proved disastrous to the Anglo-Americans.[80]

One of the unexplained mysteries of the war is
why President Roosevelt continually suppressed all
mention or even thought of a German resistance movement. His refusal dates back to 1939. Dr. Heinrich
Brüning, the former Centrist Chancellor of Germany,

visited Roosevelt in late 1939 requesting aid for
anti-Nazi forces in Germany. Brüning felt that the
President was sympathetic at first but later "he
changed his view and discouraged further contact
with any anti-Nazi representatives, 'apparently on
the advice of men close to him.'"[81] The shocking
part of Roosevelt's action is that he did not just
ignore it, he suppressed it. He said it did not
exist and no one was permitted to <u>think</u> otherwise.

> The existence of a widespread anti-Nazi resis-
> tance movement was denied, the profound politi-
> cal and spiritual implications of the movement
> were ignored, and reports concerning it were
> suppressed. Allied admission during the war of
> the existence of a large-scale anti-Nazi move-
> ment within Germany might have threatened the
> moral basis of Total War pursued to the achieve-
> ment of Unconditional Surrender. It could have
> invalidated punitive peace plans based on the
> assumption of the total guilt of the German
> people for the acts of the program of the Nazi
> party. For these and other reasons, the extent
> and even the existence of the resistance was
> denied, both during the war and in the immed-
> iate postwar years.[82]

Louis P. Lochner, former chief of the Berlin
office of the Associated Press, was in Paris in late
1944 as a war correspondent. He discovered that
some anti-Nazi Germans in Paris were maintaining
contact with their group in Germany and that they
often sent agents into Germany. He thought this was
good for a story, but it was censored. He went to
see the chief censor of SHAEF who told him there was
"a special regulation, 'a personal one from the
President of the United States in his capacity of
Commander in Chief, forbidding all mention of any
German resistance.'" Lochner commented that any
stories of a resistance movement did not fit into
the concept of Unconditional Surrender. "My belief
that President Roosevelt was determined to establish
the guilt of the entire German people, and not only
the Nazi regime, for bringing on World War II had
already received confirmation in the summer of
1942."[83] Anne Armstrong continued her strong indictment of Roosevelt with, "Official American policy denied the existence of a genuinely anti-Nazi
German resistance movement and, despite the flow of
reports of American intelligence agents to the contrary, American propaganda described the German

opposition forces, when they were referred to at all, as a small clique of reactionaries and militarists." This sounds extremely familiar in these days of continuous Communist propaganda (for good reason as we will soon see). Throughout the war and immediately afterward, the German anti-Nazi movement was a taboo subject in American political thinking. President Roosevelt refused any official dealing with the movement and did not want to hear about it. It is perhaps significant that American propaganda vis-à-vis Germany emanated from the German section of the Office of War Information which was headed by <u>Gerhard Eisler, a Communist Party member who later defected to East Germany.</u>[84] Both Eisler's employment and FDR's policy are certainly a blot on Roosevelt's record and the foreign policy of the United States.

A policy of Unconditional Surrender growing out of unabated hate can cause leaders to make irrational estimates and carry their countries along a path that is not really in their own best interest. The capitulation of German is probably the closest example in modern history of a true Unconditional Surrender. Yet it is not a model that one would want to copy. Now all eyes turned toward Japan. The bullheaded formula continued, but the Japanese would never accept it.

4.   Japan's Struggle To Terminate the War

The Japanese had been fighting for many years before Pearl Harbor and were a nation weary of the ordeal of war. However, the military faction that had carried them into war would not let them out. Though Japan was quite thoroughly defeated, the rigid formula of Unconditional Surrender represented an obstacle before which they agreed as one never to yield without some definite assurances for the future of the Emperor. The West ridicules the attitude of saving "face" in the Orient, but they did not bother to try to understand it well enough to see its importance at such a critical time in world history.

Although we harped on the formula until the very end, and even deluded ourselves into thinking the Japanese submitted to an unconditional surrender, it was actually more a conditional surrender. Former Secretary of State Hull wrote that Japan surrendered "when she perceived that the principle of unconditional surrender could be applied condition-

ally."[85] Though Japan had no force left to secure
victory, she did still have a large armed force
coupled with tremendous fanaticism, that could have
taken many people down with her. In the end, Japan
was able to trade the surrender of her residual
force for the key political concession, the sparing
of the monarchy.

The Japanese surrender is a perfect example of
the fact that it is much easier to start a war than
to end one. There was a peace party in Japan, but
it was faced with two great obstacles; first, the
Japanese military who had a tight grip on the country; and even if the military could be overcome, it
had to deal with the rigidity of Allied insistence
on Unconditional Surrender. Some Japanese favored
a compromise peace from early 1943. The Emperor
himself was ready to support this approach. General
Tojo, the Prime Minister, assured the new Foreign
Minister, Shigemitsu, that he had the same feelings,
but the military and navy high commands decided to
fight to the "last drop of blood." They exercised
strict control over all activities in the country,
including keeping the ministers themselves under
surveillance.[86] The Japanese Army did not know how
to stop. There is a Chinese proverb: One who rides
a tiger cannot alight. The Japanese Army was riding
an angry tiger.[87] This, combined with the demand
for Unconditional Surrender which Japan did not intend to meet, resulted in rigid positions on both
sides, reducing to a minimum the chances of the
peace group.

However, there were some naval officers who
were doubtful as to the outcome of the war. Rear
Admiral Sokichi Takagi was summoned to Tokyo to the
Naval Ministry in the summer of 1943 to survey the
war situation. By early 1944 he had reached the
solid conclusion that Japan could not possibly win
and that she should seek a compromise peace. Afraid
to circulate his findings in writing lest he be accused of treason, he spoke individually to top officials. In the fall of the same year, the Swedish
Minister to Japan, Widar Baggë, was approached on
behalf of a group that wanted peace. They saw continuation of the war as futile and providing victory
only to the Communists. They asked him to contact
the British about a compromise peace, underlining
that the big obstacle was Unconditional Surrender.[89]
Prince Konoye reported to Emperor Hirohito in February 1945:

In the last few months, the slogan "Hundred

189

Million Die Together" has become increasingly louder, seemingly among the right-wing people, but has its real basis in the activities of the Communists.

Under such circumstances, the longer we continue the war, the greater will be the danger of revolution. We should therefore stop the war as soon as possible.

The greatest obstacle to ending the war is the existence of the military group which has been "propelling" the country into the present state ever since the Manchurian Incident -- the group which, having already lost all hope of successfully concluding the war, nevertheless insists on its continuation in order to save face.[90]

Admiral Baron Kantaro Suzuki became Premier on 8 April 1945. He stated that when he assumed office, "'... it was the Emperor's desire to make every effort to bring the war to a conclusion as quickly as possible, and that was my purpose.'" All peace efforts necessarily had to be kept secret from the military. Unfortunately, the peace group turned to the Russians for help and the Russians stalled them. On 12 July the Emperor called in Konoye and secretly instructed him to accept any terms he could get and to wire the terms directly to the Emperor.[92] In early June, as Marquis Kido saw it, "Japan's outstanding requirement would be a 'peace with honor,' but he realized that this high-sounding phrase might merely signify a termination of the war on a basis only very slightly removed from unconditional surrender."[93] In this view, he had the support of the Emperor and the Cabinet. On 18 June 1945, the Supreme War Council agreed,

> Although we have no choice but to continue the war so long as the enemy insists upon unconditional surrender, we deem it advisable, while we still possess considerable power of resistance, to propose peace through neutral powers, especially the Soviet Union, and to obtain terms which will at least ensure the preservation of our monarchy.[94]

The hierarchy was facing reality. By August 1944, Japan was clearly facing defeat;[95] by 1945, Japan was being squeezed to death. Japan, with only one-half the American population, 10 percent of the industrial capacity, and only 3 percent of the arable land, could never have expected to win. Japan was well placed to overrun British and American possession in the Far East, but was powerless to strike at their homelands. The most she could hope for was a limited victory and the only real hope was in advantageous negotiations. She had shown this inclination before in her wars with China in 1894 and Russia in 1904. The Japanese recognized the inadequacy of their economy for a long war, but a prolonged war was not part of their plans.[96] According to the Bombing Survey, "Japan had no specific plan other than negotiation for ending the war she began."[97] The Japanese have good cause to reconsider what they were after that had any chance of being Victory for them in the war.

The problem existed on the other side too, for in order to win at the highest profit, and to avoid complications, it was essential that the United States should win the war with Japan single-handed. Had this been understood, the Americans would have appreciated that, since Russia was the only power that could complicate the issue, it was highly desirable for the United States to bring the war with Japan to an end before or immediately after Germany collapsed -- that is, before Russia was ready to shift her attention to Japan. Was this possible? General Fuller's answer was an unqualified "yes," provided the strategic and political aspects of the problem were kept firmly in mind. Unfortunately, Japan's political center eluded the President and his advisers. It lay in the person of the Emperor, or Tenno (the "Heavenly King"), and since he was the godhead of the armed forces, and a divinity in the eyes of his people, he was the supreme symbol of Japanese life and thought. Yet the one thing he could not do was to order his people to surrender unconditionally, thereby acquiescing in his becoming a war criminal, to be placed on trial or shot on sight.[98] The peace advocates could not entertain the thought of Unconditional Surrender so long as they did not know what was in store for the nation. All agreed it would be better to fight to the bitter end than to subject the Emperor to insult and the national pride to humiliation.[99] Unfortunately, propaganda-fed hatred prevented some high people from seeing the problem clearly, but this is not true of all of them. There were some high government officials who advocated a more sensible line, but they were not heeded.

Some urged that the Emperor should be removed;

191

others stated that the war could be ended more cheaply if Unconditional Surrender were modified so that the Japanese could keep the Emperor as a constitutional monarch if they wished. This view was skillfully urged by Joseph C. Grew, the Under Secretary of State, a man with long experience with the Japanese. For their efforts, Grew and others who agreed with him were roundly abused as appeasers.[100] It was a hard question. The War and Navy Departments had asked the State Department for its views in early 1944. State answered in a memorandum 9 May 1944 that it would probably be wise to keep the Emperor and to continue some of his functions though under an Allied commander.[101] President Truman wrote that,

> Acting Secretary of State Grew had spoken to me in late May about issuing a proclamation that would urge the Japanese to surrender but would assure them that we would permit the Emperor to remain as head of the state. Grew backed this with arguments taken from his ten years' experience as our Ambassador in Japan, and I told him that I had already given thought to this matter myself and that it seemed to me a sound idea.[102]

To some it seemed that Admiral Leahy (Chief of Staff to the President) alone opposed the invasion of Japan.[103] The Admiral himself felt that acceptable terms could be arranged, even though, as he recognized, this was counter to the principle of Unconditional Surrender. He stated that the Casablanca policy was an agreement about Europe and had not been agreed to in regard to Japan.[104]

The day of reckoning was fast approaching for the Japanese; their naval losses were terrific; and the heavy bombing was growing in ferocity. After the fall of the Koiso government, former President Hoover told FDR that everything seemed to indicate an appropriate time to launch a trial balloon offering the Japanese the options of retaining their Emperor, and in the future, a free choice by the people of a liberal government, if Japan surrendered immediately without other conditions.[105] This excellent advice came to nothing as the President suddenly died. Shortly thereafter on 16 June 1945, Grew wrote in a letter, "I think it will be a matter of plain common sense to give the Japanese a clearer idea of what we mean by unconditional surrender."[106] On 2 July, Secretary of War Stimson sent a memoran-

dum to President Truman saying that he thought we
could get the equivalent of Unconditional Surrender
from the Japanese if we called upon them to capitulate, including possible retention of the Emperor.[107]
Truman wrote that Secretary Stimson had always expressed the opinion that it would be to our advantage
to retain the Emperor, thereby keeping the only symbol of authority which all Japanese acknowledged.[108]
Still no explanation of Unconditional Surrender was
forthcoming.

The Japanese and Americans were not really as
far apart as one might imagine. Actually they were
almost arguing over technicalities. Since between
the surrender desired by the Americans and the negotiated surrender proposed by the Japanese, there was
only a psychological difference. Viewing it from
the other side, Toshikazu said the position had become clear. "The United States and Great Britain
insisted upon the formula of unconditional surrender
but intended to accord us in substance modified
treatment. We in turn were prepared to accept unconditional surrender in substance but were anxious
to obtain the formula, or appearance, of a negotiated
peace."[109] In sum, Washington could not decide about
the Emperor or whether they wanted Russia in the
Japanese war or not. They continued the "fiction
that a conditional surrender was unconditional," and
also pressed to get Russia into the war. Tokyo was
ready to accept Unconditional Surrender if they could
keep the Emperor. They wanted to keep Russia out of
the war so they offered the Soviet Union concessions
on the mainland. In Moscow, Stalin was straining to
commit his forces in the Far East before events in
Washington or Tokyo made that impossible. The United
States was offering gifts for the Soviet Union to
enter the war; Japan was offering gifts to get them
to remain neutral and eventually mediate.[110]

In early July, the new president was preparing
to attend the Potsdam Conference. The Japanese were
trying to get the Russians to mediate for them.
Since, as we have already seen, the United States was
able to intercept Japanese messages, the American
Government was well informed of the Japanese desires.
In mid-July, Togo cabled Sato in Moscow:

> See Molotov before his departure for Potsdam....
> Convey His Majesty's strong desire to secure a
> termination of the war.... Unconditional surren-
> der is the only obstacle to peace.

Sato answered that Japan was defeated and they should

act accordingly and also that Russia would not help them. Togo replied:

> In spite of your views, you are to carry out your instructions. ... Endeavor to obtain the good offices of the Soviet Union in ending the war short of unconditional surrender.[111]

Secretary of State Byrnes noted in his book that the Japanese advised their representative in Moscow on 21 July:

> We cannot consent to unconditional surrender under any circumstances. Even if the war drags on and more blood must be shed, so long as the enemy demands unconditional surrender, we will fight as one man against the enemy in accordance with the Emperor's command.[112]

Stalin informed Truman and Attlee at the Conference of the Japanese request to send Prince Konoye to Moscow to try to reach terms.[113] Nevertheless, the Potsdam Proclamation still made no mention of the disposition to be made of the Emperor. Paragraph 5 showed the Allies to be as rigid as ever.

> 5. The following are our terms. We shall not deviate from them. There are no alternatives. We shall brook no delay.[114]

In the draft proclamation that was prepared by the Department of State in May 1945, there appeared an important sentence:

> (12)... This may include a constitutional monarchy under the present dynasty if the peace-loving nations can be convinced of the genuine determination of such a government to follow policies of peace which will render impossible the future development of aggressive militarism in Japan.[115]

This sentence was omitted from the Potsdam Declaration. This one sentence caused months of arguing, continued fighting, the entry of Russia into the war, and the obliteration of two cities by atomic bombs.

When the Japanese received the Potsdam Proclamation, Shunichi Matsumoto, Vice-Minister of Foreign Affairs, presented what subsequently became the Foreign Office point of view. He felt that the proclamation was a statement of the conditions of the Unconditional Surrender formula.[116] In the deliberations on the Allied statement, there were no objections in the Inner Cabinet to ending the war. Suzuki, Togo, and Yonai felt that the declaration contained the final terms of peace and had to be accepted at once whether they liked it or not. However, the War Minister and the chiefs of staff felt that the terms were "too dishonorable."[117] There was considerable discussion back and forth. Meanwhile there were the two A-bombs, the Russian declaration of war, and finally the Emperor's acceptance of the surrender. The bloody invasion of Japan was averted when the Emperor went on the radio, a momentous occasion because few had ever heard the Emperor's voice, and declared the termination of the war. The Allies had finally regained their senses at the end and kept this god-figure who proved so helpful in ending the war without further loss.

The arguments over the use of the atomic bombs have been many and furious and will, no doubt, continue for years into the future. Suffice it here to quote the Bombing Survey. "The Hiroshima and Nagasaki atomic bombs did not defeat Japan, nor by the testimony of the enemy leaders who ended the war did they persuade Japan to accept unconditional surrender." They made it possible for the Emperor to take part overtly in the decision to accept the Potsdam declaration so "they did foreshorten the war and expedite the peace.[118]

Once again the idealistic rigidity of Unconditional Surrender had made us pay an unnecessarily high price for the termination of hostilities and this delay may have been crucial in later events. Raymond Aron felt that if we had renounced Unconditional Surrender or, at least, replied sooner to the repeated approaches by the Emperor over several months, "the war could have been ended without the atom bomb and without the Soviet intervention that mortgaged the victory."[119] The problem was not whether and how Japan could be defeated but how to arrange a capitulation without an invasion battle. The United States failed to distinguish between defeating an enemy and inducing him to surrender. We acted as if defeating Japan was the problem when, in fact, the problem was to avoid unnecessary fighting after Japan's defeat. Kecskemeti felt that even if we had given concessions to the Japanese, the war would have continued until Soviet entry because he felt the Japanese would have continued seeking better terms as long as the illusory Moscow channel was open. Yet, on the American side, confidential talks with the enemy in search of a possible basis for surrender were ruled out on principle.[120]

This is not to imply that all the mistakes were made on the Allied side. The Japanese were caught by an extremely rigid element in their government too. Kato hit the military leadership hard. "Japan's failure to understand fully that warfare is political as well as military was one of the most serious of the blunders made by her military leadership. The high command could conceive of war in no other terms than to fight on to military victory or military defeat."[121] Though their only real chance to consolidate their gains was by means of negotiations, they would have nothing to do with a compromise peace and, thereby, lost everything they had fought for during so many years. The Japanese contempt for the stamina and fortitude of the Americans was a gross error. They believed that America would be willing to barter "losing face" for a short war, when they themselves were willing to risk their very existence in a long war rather than "lose face" by withdrawing from China.

And so on the decks of the battleship Missouri, the great war that had ravaged a major part of the world was finally brought to an end. In his address after the signing of the surrender in Tokyo Bay, General Douglas MacArthur said: "We must go forward to preserve in peace what we won in war.... Men since the beginning of time have sought peace.... We have had our last chance."[122] But what was to be done with the enemy now? The great cry was "bring the boys home."[123] It was difficult to talk of occupation armies and the necessary work in the countries of the defeated Axis.

5.   Political Vacuum and the Morgenthau Plan

The policy of Unconditional Surrender and the accompanying desire to try War Criminals were bound to create a situation in any country that submitted whereby there would be no central government. Unconditional Surrender would result in a political vacuum; this would have to be filled from someplace, either from within the country or by some foreign government.

On 23 May, the Allies arrested Admiral Doenitz and the members of his cabinet. Germany no longer

196

had a government. The demands for the Unconditional Surrender of Germany were fully satisfied; the future of Germany was in the conquerors' hands. On 5 June 1945, the Allies declared, "There is no central Government or authority in Germany capable of accepting responsibility for the maintenance of order, the administration of the country and compliance with the requirements of the victorious Powers."[124] The Allied Powers assumed supreme authority. A political vacuum was formed and the Allies rushed in to fill it, separately, unfortunately, rather than jointly. The Allied aim was to introduce democratic reforms in the countries liberated from totalitarian rule, but the Allies believed this could be done only by first creating a political vacuum in each of these countries.

In 1949, British Foreign Minister Ernest Bevin complained,

> Unconditional Surrender left us with a Germany without law, without a constitution, without a single person with whom we could deal, without a single organization to grapple with the situation. We have had to build absolutely from the bottom with nothing at all.[125]

General Marshall, who became Secretary of State after the war, encountered many frustrations at the conference table which he attributed to this problem.

> There is another and I think even more fundamental reason for the frustration we have encountered in our endeavor to reach a realistic agreement for a peace settlement. In the war struggle Europe was in a large measure shattered. As a result a political vacuum was created, and until this vacuum has been filled by the restoration of a healthy European community, it does not appear possible that paper agreements can assure a lasting peace. Agreements between sovereign states are generally the reflection and not the cause of genuine settlements.[126]

The policy of Unconditional Surrender, by creating the political vacuum, particularly in Germany, which was to be filled by not one but four different nations (though the three Western Allies eventually combined their occupation zones), led directly to the division of Germany. Having discouraged all opposition to the Nazis, a total occupation was required, with each national army laying claim to a specific area of German territory. It logically followed that each occupying nation would remold its area of occupation in its own image with the result that unilateral policies left Germany a divided and dismembered nation. Thus Unconditional Surrender was a cause of the divided Germany and Berlin problems of today. If we had dealt with Germany as an entity rather than creating a vacuum and dividing the country, there might very well be no East Germany today. It is unwise to treat an enemy nation as if it were insignificant. Yet this is the questionable premise of leaders who impose a political vacuum on the defeated enemy. Physical nature like political nature, however, abhors a vacuum, and disappointment is bound to result. In Austria, where no vacuum was imposed, the Communists did not seize power, not even in the Soviet-occupied part of the country. A project that required this vacuum for its implementation was the vengeful Morgenthau Plan.

Henry Morgenthau was President Roosevelt's Secretary of the Treasury and an influential member of his cabinet. The Treasury Department had been operating on something of an emergency basis well before American entry into the war because of aid to the Allies. Talks of this subject often led the Treasury Department into the realm of what would normally have been the work of the War or State Departments. So, with this prestige behind them, the Treasury Department came up with a plan for what was to be done with Germany after the war. It would not be fair to say that the drastic terms of the plan did not also reflect the expressed feelings of Roosevelt, although he later disclaimed the plan. Secretary Byrnes wrote that there was confusion in the country, and even in the Cabinet, on the policy of the United States toward Germany. He recorded a meeting in August 1944, when President Roosevelt discussed the kind of peace he proposed for Germany. "The German people should be taught their responsibility for the war and for a long time should have only soup for breakfast, soup for lunch, and soup for dinner. It did not sound like President Roosevelt. He was angry."[127] Forrestal noted this incident in his diary for 25 August 1944. FDR said that "the Germans should have simply a subsistence level of food -- as he put it, soup kitchens would be ample to sustain life -- that otherwise they should be stripped clean and should not have a level of subsistence above the lowest level of the people they had conquered."[128] Roosevelt's feeling that all

Germans were guilty was even more clearly stated in
a letter he wrote to Secretary Stimson about an Army
handbook on military government.

> Too many people here and in England hold to the
> view that the German people as a whole are not
> responsible for what has taken place -- that
> only a few Nazi leaders are responsible. That
> unfortunately is not based on fact. The German
> people as a whole must have it driven home to
> them that the whole nation has been engaged in
> a lawless conspiracy against the decencies of
> modern civilization.[129]

FDR established a Cabinet committee of Morgenthau, Hull, and Stimson to study the German problem.
After the first meeting, Stimson noted in his diary
for 4 September 1944 that Morgenthau was, not un-
naturally, very bitter.[130] The three were unable to
agree and sent separate memorandums to the President.
Stimson recorded on 5 September that they were ir-
reconcilably divided.[131] Without deciding on any of
these papers, Roosevelt departed for Quebec. At
Quebec, on 15 September, an Agreement on Germany was
initialed by Roosevelt and Churchill (see page 200).
Morgenthau had his momentary victory. The section
headings and most of the key points of the actual
plan are listed on pages 201-202. Morgenthau himself described his plan in a book he wrote in 1945.
"My own program for ending the menace of German aggression consists, in its simplest terms, of depriv-
ing Germany of all heavy industries."[132]
Stimson wrote still another memorandum to the
President even though FDR had approved the Morgenthau
Plan at Quebec. This time he appealed on a higher
level, "'crime against civilization'" and ended up
with "'The sum total of the drastic political and
economic steps proposed by the Treasury is an open
confession of the bankruptcy of hope for a reasonable economic and political settlement of the causes
of war.'"[135] Cordell Hull wrote:

> It was obvious on its face that this plan was
> drastic.... Essentially, this was a plan of
> blind vengeance. It was blind because it
> failed to see that in striking at Germany, it
> was striking at all of Europe. By completely
> wrecking German industry it could not but part-
> ly wreck Europe's economy, which had depended
> for generations on certain raw materials that
> Germany produced.[136]

QUEBEC AGREEMENT ON GERMANY

At a conference between the President and the Prime Minister upon the best measures to prevent renewed rearmament by Germany, it was felt that an essential feature was the future disposition of the Ruhr and the Saar.

The ease with which the metallurgical, chemical, and electric industries in Germany can be converted from peace to war has already been impressed upon us by bitter experience. It must also be remembered that the Germans have devastated a large portion of the industries of Russia and of other neighboring Allies, and it is only in accordance with justice that these injured countries should be entitled to remove the machinery they require in order to repair the losses they have suffered. The industries referred to in the Ruhr and in the Saar would therefore be necessarily put out of action and closed down. It was felt that the two districts should be put under some body under the world organization which would supervise the dismantling of these industries and make sure they were not started up again by some subterfuge.

This programme for eliminating the war-making industries in the Ruhr and in the Saar is looking forward to converting Germany into a country primarily agricultural and pastoral in its character.

The Prime Minister and the President were in agreement upon this programme.

        O.K.
           F.D.R.

       W.S.C.
         15 9.

September 16, 1944[133]

"Program to Prevent Germany from starting
a World War III." better known as the
Morgenthau Plan

1. Demilitarization of Germany.

It should be the aim of the Allied Forces
to accomplish the complete demilitarization of Germany in the shortest possible period of time after
surrender. This means completely disarming the German Army and people (including the removal or destruction of all war material), the total destruction of the whole German armament industry, and the
removal or destruction of other key industries which
are basic to military strength.

2. New Boundaries of Germany.   ***

3. Partitioning of New Germany.   ***

4. The Ruhr Area.

This area should not only be stripped of
all presently existing industries but so weakened
and controlled that it cannot in the foreseeable
future become an industrial area....

5. Restitution and Reparation.   ***

... shall be effected by the transfer of
existing German resources and territories...

***

(d) ... by forced German labor outside
Germany.

6. Education and Propaganda.   ***

7. Political Decentralization.   ***

8. Responsibility of Military for Local Ger-
    man Economy.   ***

... The Allied Military Government shall
not ... take any measures designed to maintain or
strengthen the German economy, except those which
are essential to military operations. The responsibility for sustaining the German economy and people

rests with the German people with such facilities as may be available under the circumstances.

9. <u>Controls over Development of German Economy</u>.

(for 20 years) ***

10. <u>Agrarian Program</u>. ***

11. <u>Punishment of War Crimes and Treatment of Special Groups</u>. ***

12. <u>Uniforms and Parades</u>. ***

13. <u>Aircraft</u>.

All aircraft (including gliders), whether military or commercial, will be confiscated for later disposition. No German shall be permitted to operate or to help operate any aircraft, including those owned by foreign interests.

14. <u>United States Responsibility</u>.

(To the effect that we should take part but the continental neighbors of Germany should take over, then we could withdraw our troops quickly.)[134]

Secretary Hull hoped that Churchill would persuade the President that Morgenthau's views were wrong, and that a starving and bankrupt Germany would not be in British or any European interests.[137] Upon his return from Quebec, Morgenthau described Churchill's reaction to Hull.

> He said that Mr. Churchill had at first been violently opposed to the Morgenthau policy toward Germany. The Prime Minister had bluntly inquired whether he had been brought over to Quebec to discuss a scheme that would mean "England's being chained to a dead body."[138]

The Morgenthau Plan was certainly not a brilliant political document. Its major weakness was its narrow outlook. It would have substituted an economic vacuum for a productive Germany, meaning that a devastated Europe would not obtain the industrial and consumer goods that a functioning German industry could provide.

The Morgenthau Plan provided Goebbels and the constrolled Nazi press with even more ammunition than had Unconditional Surrender. They had a field day and twisted the two together expertly to incite the German people to fight harder. "'Morgenthau surpasses Clemenceau: forty million too many Germans! Roosevelt and Churchill agree at Quebec to the Jewish Murder Plan,' and 'Details of the Devilish Plan of Destruction: Morgenthau the Spokesman of World Judaism.' This, Goebbels said, was the answer: this was the ultimate meaning of Unconditional Surrender."[139] Goebbels found strong arguments in questions such as: Will they put into effect the Morgenthau Plan which would make Germany strictly an agricultural state? "A potato field and a sheep pasture." Secretary Byrnes described how he heard the Berlin broadcasts in Paris.

> In October 1944, while the war was still in progress, I was in Paris. At the Guest House, where I lived, there was a sergeant who spoke German. Each night he would interpret for me the Berlin broadcasts: these invariably included an appeal to the people of Germany not to consider the proposals of the Allies to surrender. Surrender, they warned, meant enforcement of the "Morgenthau Plan" which would destroy all industry and turn Germany into an agricultural state. The plan was greatly exaggerated to inspire the Germans to fight and

die rather than surrender.[140]

Word of the cabinet dispute over the Plan reached the press, and columnist Drew Pearson unleashed a verbal blast at both FDR and Morgenthau. Roosevelt shortly thereafter wiggled out of support of the plan and it drifted into oblivion. FDR told Stimson, "'Henry Morgenthau pulled a boner' or an equivalent expression."[141] Stimson informed Hull that the President was "frankly staggered" at hearing the sentences about turning Germany into an agricultural country and, "said that he had no idea how he could have initialed the memorandum, and that he had evidently done so without much thought."[142] Sherwood wrote that "Roosevelt admitted that he had yielded to the importunities of an old and loyal friend when he affixed his initials to this document".[143] When Truman was preparing to go to Potsdam, Morgenthau told him he had to go with him. Truman wrote:

> He replied that it was necessary for him to go and that if he could not he would have to quit.
>
> "All right," I replied, "if that is the way you feel, I'll accept your resignation right now." And I did. That was the end of the conversation and the end of the Morgenthau Plan.[144]

The Morgenthau Plan was dead but much of its spirit lived on in the directive that was issued under the title Joint Chiefs of Staff 1067. It still required that no steps be taken to aid the economic rehabilitation of Germany -- "rereading this order two years later, Stimson found it a painfully negative document."[145] Yet it was an improvement over the Morgenthau Plan.
"From the outset, war-making capitalism has proved to be full of contradictions as to destruction and preservation in and by war. The alliance of the capitalist Powers with Bolshevism came close to producing the self-destruction of the former. In the United States, the most destructive postwar plans, plans that could only serve the purposes of Communism, were hatched and propagated by the Treasury Department, the one department that ought to have looked most closely to the preservation of capitalistic concepts."[146] In view of Vagts' comments that these plans could only be in the Communist interest, it is particularly interesting that the Morgenthau Plan was largely the "work of Harry Dexter

White, Morgenthau's assistant secretary, who, in August 14, 1951, was cited before the Senate security sub-committee, and was found to be a Soviet agent."[147] So ring down the curtain on one of the low points of American diplomatic thought. The Morgenthau Plan was another example of hate run wild in war, the dominance of emotions over the clear logic of which the human mind is capable and which we expect from our political leaders. The quest for Total Victory leads to irrational acts which one may regret when tempers cool.

6. The Political-Military Problem

The Western Allies, particularly the United States, had great difficulty determining just what the purpose of the war was. Fighting in an excited emotional state, these completely unmilitary countries became entirely militaristic in their strategical conduct of the war. In knight-like fashion in search for their holy grail, Total Victory, they subordinated their political interests to what they thought were military requirements. These were not military men who took over the conduct of government, but the elected and appointed civilian leaders who thrust the military approach into all dealings about the war at the expense of normal diplomatic and political operations. This lack of balance between political and military operations I choose to call the political-military problem.

We have already seen how the American military had become politically sterile between the two wars to the point where they were almost afraid to mention the word "political." This was to cost us when some of these men became high-ranking generals and had to make certain decisions that were more political than military. This would not have been serious had there been good political leadership; but, unfortunately, the political leaders joined the military leaders in looking at the war only through military-tinted glasses. The resultant phase of obsession for victory, win the war, smash the enemy, gained full support, but there was no one keeping his eyes on the big picture and determining where the ship of state should sail after the victory. It seems rarely to have crossed anyone's mind that the actions taken to secure that opiate Total Victory might have some influence in postwar affairs, both in relationships among the Allies and their former

205

enemies.

Much of the responsibility for this outlook must be laid at the doorstep of President Roosevelt. "In American war-time policy-making the civilian militarism of the President, with the 'unconditional surrender' formula as its final expression, over-ruled the timid claims of diplomacy."[148] Policy trailed behind strategy, and destruction of the enemy seemed to be the sole aim of strategy. Unconditional Surrender was both a reflection and a symptom of Anglo-American thinking on the conduct of war and the wartime role of policy. The Casablanca Conference illustrated the priority given to military planning. Policy, when considered at all, "was a by-product and an afterthought."[149] Even though there were latent conflicts of interest between Russia and the Western Powers, both sides were anxious to continue their struggle against Germany. This was facilitated by the Allied habit of viewing the war from an exclusively military point of view that allowed nothing to interfere with the goal of defeating the enemy.

President Roosevelt even excluded his Secretary of State from most important meetings. Before Pearl Harbor, Hull had been on the War Council. Hull wrote in his Memoirs that,

> After Pearl Harbor I did not sit in on meetings concerned with military matters. This was because the President did not invite me to such meetings. I raised the question with him several times. It seemed manifest to me that, in numerous important instances, the Secretary of State should sit in on the President's war councils, particularly on those of a combined military and diplomatic nature, for it was obvious that scarcely any large-scale military operations could be undertaken that would not have diplomatic aspects. I feel that it is a serious mistake for a Secretary of State not to be present at important military meetings. I often had occasion to point out to the President that some development of a military character, which undoubtedly had been decided at one of these meetings, also had a strong foreign affairs angle of which I should have been informed at the time.

It was often difficult for Hull to be fully informed.

The President did not take me with him to the
Casablanca, Cairo, or Teheran conferences,
which were predominantly military meetings nor
did I take part in his military discussions
with Prime Minister Churchill in Washington,
some of which had widespread diplomatic repercussions.[150]

Forrestal concluded that American wartime diplomatic planning did not match the quality of planning for the conduct of the war, and that relatively
little thought was given to the political conditions
that would emerge from the destruction of Germany
and Japan. Forrestal felt that the inauspicious developments in Europe could have left no thoughtful
person pleased with the results of Unconditional
Surrender.[151] The diplomacy of the Allies unfortunately failed to match their great military achievements. The Italian negotiations and surrender
caught the Allies unprepared politically and the results reflected it. The handling of the German and
Japanese surrenders was not much better. The war
continued on its destructive path as if it were the
end itself, rather than just a means.
The military found themselves thrust more and
more into the political arena, sometimes by default
and sometimes due to the increased importance of
their positions. Butcher noted early in his career
with General Eisenhower, that the "harassed Ike,"
with his troubles as Allied Commander dealing with
America and Britain, plus the land, sea, and air
services of each and the variety of high political
problems with Spain and France, had always to consider not only purely military matters, but international politics and personalities as well.[152]
During the "Breakthrough" it was planned to withdraw from Strasbourg. Normally this is a very
simple military decision for a commander. But Ike
soon found that this was a near catastrophe for
France and threatened to topple de Gaulle's government. This was no longer a simple military problem
but an important political problem, and the military
plans were changed to conform with the new estimate.[153] The lesson is clear. The political leadership must provide the military with the objective
desired. On the other hand, the military should be
called upon to advise the political leadership on
the feasibility of the plans they are considering.
Senator Goldwater, later a presidential candidate,
pointed this out after the abortive Cuban invasion
in 1961.

Certainly the major lesson is that the Commander-in-Chief, the President, should consult
with military people before making military decisions and not solely with people who not only
are incompetent in their appointed roles but
completely unequipped to serve as military advisers. One would have thought that the dread-
ful results of Roosevelt's military ineptness --
his catastrophic demand for "unconditional surrender" and his equally ill-advised decision
concerning Berlin -- would have served as warnings forever for any of our Presidents faced
with the necessity of making decisions of war.
Obviously the lesson was not well learned.[154]

Roosevelt was not alone in this political-military
problem. Churchill said,

So long as the whole of Western civilization was
threatened by the Nazi menace, we could not afford to let our attention be diverted from the
immediate issue by considerations of long-term
policy.... Politics must be a secondary consideration.[155]

Churchill and the British had pressed for an
invasion through the Balkans. The Americans could
only see special interests in this and blocked it at
every turn.* Hanson Baldwin stated that "many of
our great military figures of the war now admit
freely that the British were right and we were wrong.
For we forgot that all wars have objectives and all
victories conditions; we forgot that winning the
peace is equally as important as winning the war; we
forgot that politico-military is a compound word."[156]
General Eisenhower, particularly when he was in
London, often was on the receiving end of the Churchill exhortations for an invasion of the Balkans.
Ike appreciated "his concern as a political leader
for the future of the Balkans. For this concern I
had great sympathy, but as a soldier I was particularly careful to exclude such considerations from my
own recommendations."[157]
While discussing the proposed Balkan invasion,
Roosevelt said the problem would be settled "purely
upon its military aspects"; Fuller's comment was
that "a war without a political aim is military

---

*Brigadier General G.A. Lincoln, who was the Army
Planner, told the author that the Balkans route was
unsupportable logistically.

nonsense."[158] President Roosevelt was aware of
Churchill's motives as shown by this conversation
with his son Elliott at Teheran:

> "Whenever the P.M. argued for our invasion
> through the Balkans, it was quite obvious to
> everyone in the room what he really meant.
> That he was above all else anxious to knife up
> into central Europe, in order to keep the Red
> Army out of Austria and Rumania, even Hungary,
> if possible. Stalin knew it, I knew it, every-
> body knew it....

> "But he never said it?

> "Certainly not. And Uncle Joe, when he argued
> the military advantages of invasion from the
> west, and the inadvisability of splitting our
> forces into two parts -- he was always con-
> scious of the political implications, too, I'm
> sure....

> "Trouble is, the P.M. is thinking too much of
> the postwar, and where England will be. He's
> scared of letting the Russians get too
> strong."[159]

In criticizing American support for an invasion
of southern France instead of through the Balkans,
Fuller felt that we failed to understand that a decisive point had to be politically profitable as
well as strategically attainable, and that to attack
in southern France in order eventually to storm the
winter sports resorts of the Black Forest would not
be decisive. On the contrary, an attack toward
Vienna "would bring the Americans and British into
central Europe, and only in central Europe could the
war be won politically."[160] General Mark Clark favored a trans-Adriatic invasion from Italy into
Yugoslavia and from there pressing on toward Vienna,
Budapest, and Prague. He wrote that Roosevelt initially expressed interest in the idea but was dis-
suaded by Harry Hopkins. General Ira Eaker, Allied
air commander in the Mediterranean who also advocated the trans-Adriatic invasion, was rebuffed by
General Marshall with the comment, "You've been too
damned long with the British." The U.S. Army's Intelligence Division warned in a memorandum of the
dangers of Soviet predominance in the Balkans. The
authors were informed by their superiors that they
were in error, that "the Russians have no political

objectives in the Balkans; they are there for military reasons only." In general, the attitude of American military planners seemed to have been that "strategy is designed to achieve one purpose, the destruction of the armed power of the enemy, that strategy has no connection with political ends."[161] The Army Intelligence Division was right again when they prepared a study opposing Soviet entry into the war in Asia. (See Appendix 2.)[162]

Unless the State Department and War Department were not talking to each other, which is quite possible, Stettinius would make someone out to be a liar. He wrote that as "early as 1941 some of the Russian demands in the Balkans and elsewhere were known to us." Speaking of June 1941, "even though the Russian armies were in retreat, Stalin indicated that he was less interested in military assistance than in political alliance and in a territorial settlement affecting Russia's borders." However, our attitude in the Atlantic Charter remained that we "would continue to discuss in general terms problems of a territorial nature, but we would delay any commitments as to specific terms until the end of the war."[163] There is no denying that this region interested the Russians greatly. Therefore, as Kennan put it, whether you were acting in agreement with them or not, "this meant that sooner or later you would end on some sort of a line in eastern or Central Europe, probably more central than eastern".[164]

Walter Lippmann wrote very prophetically during the war that when the war ended, the Russians would almost certainly have an overwhelming preponderance of military force in Central Europe, and it was inconceivable that the Red Army, if it liberated those peoples from the Nazi conquerors, would permit governments operating from London and Washington to organize anti-Russian states on the Russian border. The attempt to do this, even the suspicion of an attempt, was bound to revive bitter memories of the Allied intervention in the Russian Civil War. "Then the question will not be how firmly we can guarantee the independence of these states, but whether Russia will permit them to exist at all as independent states."[165] Lippmann observed that we must admit that nations are not always enlightened enough to know their real interests and to do what their real interests dictate. "If in this region the effort to settle territorial boundaries and to decide what governments shall be recognized discloses deep and insoluble conflicts between Russia's conception of

210

her vital interests and that of the Western Allies, then every nation will know that it must be ready and must choose sides in the eventual but unavoidable next war."[166] This is important because there were very few people who were saying anything against our great Russian "ally" in 1943.

One man, who was right in the middle of much of the terminal phase of the war, President Truman, pointed out part of the dilemma. Though he appeared clearly to recognize the problem, it was probably hindsight, for he did not act in accordance with these views in the crucial last days of the war. He stated that warfare, regardless of the weapons used, is a means to an end, and if that end can be achieved by negotiated settlements of conditional surrender, there is no need for war. He believed this to be true even in the case of ruthless powers ambitious for world conquest. Truman recognized that a major difficulty with a formula like Unconditional Surrender is that "it cuts across the line which should divide political from military decisions." Accepting Clausewitz's dictum that "war is a continuation of policy by other means," Truman observed that "many of our generals, as well as a large proportion of the public, conclude from this that, once war has begun, all decisions become military in nature." He said that Clausewitz, however, wrote a great deal more than just that easily remembered sentence. Both diplomacy and war are merely means to an end and that end is a matter for political determination. Truman recounted:

> My meetings with the Chiefs of Staff were always highly informative and productive. Many complex problems were resolved during these sessions. But the one question never fully answered was whether political considerations took priority over military considerations in the midst of war operations. It is a fact, of course, that the policy of the government determines the policy of the military. The military is always subordinate to the government. But in a situation where the military commanders are convinced that a certain political proposal is militarily too risky or costly or not practical, then the government is bound to take into account the position taken by the military.[167]

In sum, the Unconditional Surrender formula was symptomatic of an attitude toward war which tended

211

to divide strategy from political goals. American long-range goals in World War II played a secondary role. Strategy took precedence over diplomacy at the major conferences of the war, at least until the last year. Major decisions of great political importance were made primarily, even solely, on the basis of military considerations: for example, invasion routes or which ally would take Berlin. American planners were dedicated to a final goal in the war, but they perceived that goal to be Total Victory, the total destruction of enemy military power.[168] It should certainly be evident that Unconditional Surrender was an extremely important pronouncement and that its spirit or effects permeated almost every aspect of Allied policy for the remainder of the war. That the war could have been handled in a more efficient manner seems certain.

NOTES

1. Marshall, Men Against Fire, p. 32.
2. Hankey, Politics, Trials and Errors, p. 45.
3. Fuller, The Second World War, p. 275.
4. Kecskemeti, Strategic Surrender, p. 228. See also p. 207 for a discussion of the "siege" versus the "boxing match" analogy. The strong besieger initiates contacts with the besieged to get him to surrender to avoid the necessity of storming the fortress. The boxer fights for the "knockout."
5. Armstrong, Unconditional Surrender, p. 253.
6. Quoted in ibid., p. 150.
7. Ibid., p. 152. The slogan was good for unlimited defiance but it induced in the Germans "the despairing fury of the cornered rat."
8. Ibid., p. 158.
9. Ibid., pp. 133-34. See also Freidin, The Fatal Decisions, p. 269. General Westphal said, "even those who were fully informed concerning the true situation saw no alternative to fighting on until the bitter end."
10. B. H. Liddell Hart, The Other Side of the Hill, Germany's Generals, Their Rise and Fall, with their Own Account of Military Events, 1935-45 (London: Cassell, 1948), p. 304. See also Armstrong, Unconditional Surrender, p. 138. Since the Allied propaganda never said anything positive about the peace conditions, they considered that this silence tended to confirm what the Nazi propaganda said was in store for them if they surrendered.
11. Example given by Richard H. S. Crossman,

212

Deputy Director of PWD, SHAEF, quoted in Daugherty and Janowitz, Psychological Warfare, pp. 277-278. The proposed announcement in October 1944, "contained nothing more than the Military Government regulations which would be enforced immediately after the area was occupied."

12. R.J.C. Butow, Japan's Decision to Surrender (Stanford: Stanford University Press, 1954), p. 231.

13. Sir E. Llewellyn Woodward, British Foreign Policy in the Second World War, p. 570; see also pp. 569-572 about Japan.

14. Fuller, A Military History of the Western World, Vol. III, p. 627. See also The Conduct of War, p. 303.

15. Armstrong, Unconditional Surrender, p. 159. "General Eisenhower had in fact reported on November 20 /1944/ that one of the factors prolonging German resistance was the success of Nazi propaganda that unconditional surrender meant the destruction of Germany." Woodward, British Foreign Policy, p. 483. See Wilmot, The Struggle for Europe, p. 123, relative to Goebbels and his propaganda to strengthen resistance. See also Shirer, The Rise and Fall of the Third Reich, p. 1341 fn. where he said that Goebbels' success regarding Unconditional Surrender "has been grossly exaggerated by a surprisingly large number of Western writers."

16. L. C. Green, International Law Through the Cases (London: Stevens & Sons, Ltd., 1959), p. 678. See statements by FDR 21 August and 7 October 1942, Goodrich, Documents on American Foreign Relations, Vol. V, pp. 177-178. See Churchill, Triumph and Tragedy, p. 631, about the effect of the policy of putting defeated leaders to death.

17. R. Ernest Dupuy, Men of West Point (New York: William Sloane Associates, 1951), p. 324.

18. Fuller, The Second World War, p. 31.

19. From an unpublished memorandum, dated 31 July 1943, quoted in Armstrong, Unconditional Surrender, p. 155.

20. Woodward, British Foreign Policy, p. L. He then referred to Churchill's comments that it was less alarming than the actual terms. Also, after the failure of the '44 coup against Hitler, he figured no other coup was possible until after Nazi control was broken by military defeat.

21. John Gunther, Roosevelt in Retrospect; A Profile in History, p. 362.

22. Kecskemeti, Strategic Surrender, p. 226, italics in original.

23. Mourin, Le drame des états satellites de

l'Axe, p. 17. Mussolini resigned 24 July; the surrender was not until 3 September.

24. Maréchal Pietro Badoglio, L'Italie dans la
guerre mondiale, transl. from Italian (Paris: SFELT,
1947), p. 101. "The actual explanation for Badoglio's failure to sue for peace was simply that he
was unable to solve the technical problem of estab-
lishing contact with the Allies." Kecskemeti,
Strategic Surrender, p. 83; see also pp. 71-85.

25. It is interesting to recall that Churchill
had originally asked the War Cabinet to exclude
Italy from Unconditional Surrender to cause a break,
but the Cabinet was against it.

26. Sherwood, Roosevelt and Hopkins, p. 742.
Hull and FDR felt, in 1942, that Italy could be hur-
ried out of the war if the Allies had a different
attitude toward them than that toward Germany and
Japan, Hull, Memoirs, Vol. II, p. 1548. This feeling disappeared at Casablanca though.

27. George Glasgow, "Foreign Affairs - Italy
and the Settlement," The Contemporary Review, 164,
(October, 1943), p. 244.

28. Hull, Memoirs, Vol. II, p. 1571.

29. Eisenhower, Crusade in Europe, p. 184.

30. Ibid., p. 186.

31. Butcher, My Three Years With Eisenhower,
p. 372.

32. Churchill, Closing the Ring, Vol. V of The
Second World War, p. 102.

33. Butcher, My Three Years With Eisenhower,
p. 386.

34. Ibid., p. 390.

35. Churchill, Closing the Ring, p. 106. See
also Woodward, British Foreign Policy, pp. 225-238
and Kecskemeti, Strategic Surrender, pp. 85-89.
General Walter Bedell Smith was General Eisenhower's
Chief of Staff and was chief negotiator at Lisbon.

36. Badoglio, L'Italie dans la guerre, p. 135.

37. Butcher, My Three Years With Eisenhower,
p. 405.

38. Hankey, Politics, Trials and Errors, p. 44.
He considered the Allied action "dishonourable on
the part of victors whom the defeated nation was now
assisting", p. 43.

39. Badoglio, L'Italie dans la guerre, p. 153,
my translation. He could not have the first document back unless he signed the second, p. 157.

40. Ibid., p. 158, entire letter, pp. 158-160,
my translation.

41. See Ibid., p. 196 for his problems with the
Control Commission.

42. Armstrong, Unconditional Surrender, p. 86.
43. Jean Cuny, La capitulation sans conditions de l'Allemagne, p. 37, my translation. Jodl spoke in German.
44. Churchill, Triumph and Tragedy, p. 441.
45. Woodward, British Foreign Policy, p. 479.
46. Eisenhower, Report by the Supreme Commander, pp. 118-120.
47. Lüdde-Neurath, Les derniers jours du troisième Reich, p. 169.
48. See Eisenhower, Operations in Europe, pp. 118-120.
49. Ibid., pp. 119-120, the surrender was finally signed to be effective after a delay of forty-eight hours.
50. Admiral Doenitz wrote that they could not surrender in the winter of 1944-45 because there were 3½ million German soldiers on the Eastern front - still a long way from the Anglo-American front - who would have fallen into Russian hands. Memoirs. Ten Years and Twenty Days, transl. R. H. Stevens (London: Weidenfeld and Nicolson, 1959, p. 431.
51. Mourin, Le drame des états satellites de l'Axe, p. 37, my translation.
52. Fuller, A Military History of the Western World, Vol. III, p. 479, see also p. 478.
53. Ibid., Vol. III, p. 378. He felt Hitler could have been overthrown -- referred to The German General Staff, Walter Gorlitz (1953); The Critical Years, Gen. Baron Geyr von Schweppenburg (1952); Revolt Against Hitler, Fabian von Schlabrendorff (1948); The von Hassell Diaries, Ulrich von Hassell (1948); The German Opposition to Hitler, Hans Rothfels (1948); and Germany's Underground, Allen Welsh Dulles (1947).
54. See Armstrong, Unconditional Surrender, p. 56, about Stalin trying to split the German people from the Nazis.
55. Ibid., p. 173.
56. Ibid., p. 182.
57. Cartier, Les Secrets de la guerre, pp. 27-28. See also Goebbels, Diaries, p. 368.
58. Ibid., pp. 28, 30-31.
59. Ibid., p. 31.
60. Ibid.
61. Shirer, Rise and Fall of the Third Reich, pp. 1134-1135. He also had the law of absolute power of life and death over every German. He used it too. Many generals were executed. See Guderian, Souvenirs d'un soldat, p. 337.

62. Cartier, Les secrets de la guerre, p. 22.
See also General George C. Marshall, The Winning of
the War in Europe and the Pacific, p. 3.
63. Ibid., p. 80.
64. Liddel Hart, The Other Side of the Hill,
p. 11.
65. Cartier, Les secrets de la guerre, p. 23.
See also pp. 23-24 how Hitler kept different minis-
tries in the dark and all control in his hands.
66. Beveridge, The Price of Peace, p. 37.
"There can be no doubt that there is little love
lost between the Nazi Party and the majority of the
senior generals of the Reichswehr." Einzig, Can We
Win the Peace?, p. 33. Why then all the misunder-
standing about the influence of the German General
Staff?
67. Armstrong, Unconditional Surrender, pp.
184-185.
68. G. M. Gilbert, Nuremberg Diary (New York:
Farrar, Strauss and Company, 1947), p. 26. Though
he may well have been trying to escape responsibility at the trial, there had to be some truth in it.
69. Freidin and Richardson, ed., The Fatal
Decisions, p. 220.
70. Lieutenant General James M. Gavin, War and
Peace in the Space Age, p. 263.
71. Shirer, Rise and Fall of the Third Reich,
pp. 856-863, 863-867, 912-916, 1180-1187, 1316-1345,
1352-1405.
72. Roger Manvell and Heinrich Fraenkel, Dr.
Goebbels, His Life and Death (London: Heinemann,
1960), p. 226.
73. Liddell Hart, The Other Side of the Hill,
p. 261. See pp. 269-282 for a description of the
anti-Hitler plot as seen from headquarters in the
West; pp. 225 and 260 for von Rundstedt's and von
Kluge's pleas to end the war. See Armstrong, Unconditional Surrender, pp. 131-157 for what German generals would have considered as reasonable peace
terms.
74. Armstrong, Unconditional Surrender, p. 119.
75. Kennan, Russia and the West under Lenin and
Stalin, p. 367.
76. Fuller, A Military History of the Western
World, Vol. III, pp. 538-539.
77. Armstrong, Unconditional Surrender, p. 132.
Admiral Doenitz wrote that because of the Allied
"crusade," the senior Germans could not offer to
surrender. They could not tell Hitler that continuing the war was useless; they could offer no alternative. Memoirs, pp. 308-309. In early 1945,

the Germans obtained a copy of the British Operation
Order Eclipse - the plans for Germany after Unconditional Surrender. The harshness of the plan increased the German political objection to an immediate end of the war by Unconditional Surrender.
p. 430.

78. Armstrong, Unconditional Surrender, p. 188.
At Nuremberg, Jodl felt betrayed by Hitler, see Gilbert, Nuremberg Diary, p. 58. Guderian was visited
by Dr. Goerdeler in early 1943 but refused to join
him and asked him to renounce his intentions, Guderian, Souvenirs du'un soldat, pp. 287-288.

79. Armstrong, Unconditional Surrender, p. 221.
One proponent was the former Ambassador to Moscow,
Count Werner von der Schulenburg.

80. Ibid., p. 209.

81. Ibid., p. 200.

82. Ibid., pp. 170-171.

83. Ibid., p. 211. In November 1941, Lochner
had attended a meeting in Berlin of the Beck-
Goerdeler group's steering committee. He met a number of the key figures and their ideas were explained to him. They requested that he approach
Roosevelt to determine what type of anti-Nazi government would be acceptable to the United States. Upon
returning to the United States in June 1942, he
tried five times to see the President. Finally he
put his request in writing. He received an answer
informing him that the subject was "most embarrassing" and would he drop the matter, pp. 210-211. Anne
Armstrong noted that she confirmed this with Lochner
in an interview in April, 1958.

84. Ibid., p. 210.

85. Hull, Memoirs, Vol. II, p. 1582.

86. Mourin, Le drame des états satellites de
l'Axe, pp. 37-38. The Cairo declaration was also a
block, declaring that all Japanese territorial ac-
quisitions since 1895 were pure "theft."

87. Kase Toshikazu, Journey to the Missouri
(New Haven: Yale University Press, 1950), p. 175.
On 14 October 1941, "Tojo insisted that there had
been too much sacrifice to permit the withdrawal of
the troops in China." Gould, International Law,
p. 112.

88. United States Strategic Bombing Survey,
Japan's Struggle to End the War, p. 2. See also
Kecskemeti, Strategic Surrender, p. 155, R.J.C.
Butow, Japan's Decision to Surrender, pp. 39-41,
and William Craig, The Fall of Japan (New York: The
Dial Press, 1967), p. xiii.

89. Mourin, Le drame des états satellites de

217

l'Axe, p. 40. See also Butow, Japan's Decision to Surrender, pp. 54-57.

90. From a memorandum of conversation, USSBS, Japan's Struggle to End the War, p. 22.

91. Ibid., p. 6. For background of Suzuki coming in as Premier, getting Togo in as Foreign Minister and subsequent events, see Butow, Japan's Decision to Surrender, pp. 61-75. In a note on p. 226, Butow said according to Zacharias (Secret Missions, p. 335) an intelligence report in December 1944 said the next premier would be Suzuki who would be trying for peace, with a modification of Unconditional Surrender, and upon agreement to terms, Suzuki would resign and Imperial Prince Higashi-Kuni would take over to effect the surrender. This was amazingly accurate and just what took place. Evidently no one wanted to read it.

92. Ibid., p. 7.

93. Butow, Japan's Decision to Surrender, p.114, italics in the original.

94. Toshikazu, Journey to the Missouri, p. 184. See USSBS, Japan's Struggle, p. 11, about using their remaining power to gain a tactical victory in hopes of gaining better terms than Unconditional Surrender. This remaining power consisted of "2½ million combat-equipped troops and 9,000 Kamikaze airplanes in the home island." USSBS, p. 1. See the Transcript of hearings before Senate Armed Services and Foreign Relations Committees, U.S. News, 11 May 1951, p. 77, for General MacArthur's testimony about this residual force, why Japan went to war, and their certainty of defeat once we applied the blockade.

95. S. W. Kirby, The War against Japan, Military History of World War II Series (London: H. M. Stationery Office, 1957), Vol. III, p. 451. See also p. 452.

96. United States Federal Civil Defense Administration (USFCDA), Impact of Air Attack in World War II, Division II, Vol. 2, p. 11.

97. USSBS, Japan's Struggle, p. 5. The Japanese were convinced they were fighting for their national existence and life, whereas they believed the United States was pressing for economic advantages and a set of principles and not for vital security. See also p. 2.

98. Fuller, A Military History of the Western World, Vol. III, pp. 620-622.

99. Butow, Japan's Decision to Surrender, p. 41. See also his note 59 on p. 131.

100. Henry L. Stimson and McGeorge Bundy, On Active Service in Peace and War (New York: Harper &

Brothers, 1948), p. 626.

101. Hull, Memoirs, Vol. II, pp. 1591-1593.
102. Truman, Year of Decisions, p. 416.
103. Kecskemeti, Strategic Surrender, p. 161.
104. Leahy, I Was There, p. 385, during June 1945. However, FDR's statement at Casablanca included Japan.
105. Mourin, Le drame des états satellites de l'Axe, p. 43.
106. J. C. Grew, Turbulent Era, Vol. II, p.1435. See Chapter XXXVI "The Emperor of Japan and Japan's Surrender," pp. 1406-1442. Grew was against propaganda attacks on the Emperor or bombing the palace since he saw the Emperor as the only one who could order surrender, p. 1406. See also Walter Millis and E. S. Duffield, The Forrestal Diaries, eds. (New York: Viking Press, 1951), pp. 66 and 68-74, how on 19 June, Grew, supported by Stimson, vigorously pushed for explanation to the Japanese.
107. Stimson and Bundy, On Active Service, pp. 620-624.
108. Truman, Year of Decisions, p. 428.
109. Toshikazu, Journey to the Missouri, p. 203.
110. Butow, Japan's Decision to Surrender, p. 132. He called this a spectacle: "Washington sacrificing what it did not own but should have claimed for itself or China and of Tokyo dispensing what it had once held but no longer could maintain." On pp. 132-133, he added that it was not too hard then "for Stalin to foment plans whereby both the victors and vanquished would later have cause to regret their common folly."
111. Ibid., p. 130. See pp. 121-123 for the Hirota-Malik talks in Tokyo. See also p. 90 about Japanese problem in trying to barter with the Soviets not knowing they had already agreed to attack Japan 2-3 months after V-E Day. Forrestal mentioned the Japanese soundings, Millis, The Forrestal Diaries, pp. 74-77. See Mourin, Le drame des états satellites de l'Axe, p. 48 for the way the Japanese ambassador was stalled and told he would have to wait for Molotov to return from Potsdam.
112. James F. Byrnes, Speaking Frankly (New York: Harper & Brothers, 1947), p. 211.
113. Truman, Year of Decisions, p. 396.
114. Churchill, Triumph and Tragedy, p. 643. See also U. S. Department of State, A Decade of American Foreign Policy (1941-49), p. 50.
115. Grew, Turbulent Era, Vol. II, p. 1433. Secretary Byrnes called former Secretary Hull before leaving for Potsdam and mentioned that the President

had a draft statement for Potsdam including that the institution of the Emperor would be preserved. Hull was against this statement in that form and recommended they not release it. Hull, Memoirs, Vol. II, pp. 1593-1594. It is interesting that Hull blocked this key point in the Japanese surrender. It was really momentous and he had already retired because of poor health. See also Butow, Japan's Decision to Surrender, p. 140, who said Hull thought this was appeasement and that Byrnes accepted his recommendation and wrote that there would be no commitment about the throne.

116. Butow, Japan's Decision to Surrender, p. 142.

117. USSBS, Japan's Struggle to End the War, p. 8. For details of the Japanese surrender, see Butow, Japan's Decision to Surrender, pp. 129-141; Craig, The Fall of Japan; James, The Rise and Fall of the Japanese Empire, pp. 342-349; and Fuller, The Conduct of War, pp. 297-303. For details of the uprisings against the Emperor's decree to surrender, see Toshikazu, Journey to the Missouri, pp. 258-265.

118. Ibid., p. 12. See also Daugherty and Janowitz, Psychological Warfare, p. 511 and Aron, Century of Total War, p. 155. Truman made one of the most astonishing statements about the bombs and the surrender. "This second demonstration of the power of the atomic bomb apparently threw Tokyo into a panic, for the next morning brought the first indication that the Japanese Empire was ready to surrender." Year of Decisions, p. 426, my italics. This was a most unusual statement since they had been trying to surrender for quite some time.

119. Aron, Century of Total War, p. 155. He made the following interesting statement about the USA. "By a logic that is paradoxical only in appearance, the country least warlike in its taste and philosophy has thus played a decisive part in the advent of unlimited war."

120. Kecskemeti, Strategic Surrender, p. 206. "A channel for sounding out the Japanese was available: Allen Dulles' group in Switzerland had been in contact with the Japanese military attaché at Berne, General Okamoto, and a representative of the Japanese navy, Commander Fukimura." p. 187. See p. 211 for his discussion of the importance of communications during the phase before surrender.

121. Masuo Kato, The Lost War, p. 149. This criticism could also be levelled at the United States with the difference that it was the civilian leaders who did not perceive that war is political. The

military leaders did not either but they were not in
control of the government. See Whitney, MacArthur,
p. 115, for General MacArthur's report to Washington
that the Japanese were weak in leadership. He said
the military hierarchy was failing the nation. "It
has neither the imagination nor the foresighted
ability to organize Japanese resources for a total
war."

122. Whitney, MacArthur, p. 223.

123. See Kecskemeti, Strategic Surrender, pp.
164-167 for an example of those who thought the final terms to Japan were "soft" yet were not anxious
to have American soldiers stay overseas in an occupation army. Kecskemeti called this "a basic postulate of the doctrine of unconditional surrender:
that there is a causal connection between maximum
destructiveness in war and the perpetual peace that
is to succeed it."

124. U. S. Department of State, A Decade of
American Foreign Policy (1941-1949), p. 506. This
was almost a month after the surrender and almost
two weeks after the arrest of Admiral Doenitz.

125. The New York Times, 21 July 1949. The essentially negative aspect of Unconditional Surrender
handicapped the development of a positive program
for Germany. The victors had not foreseen the extensive breakdown of the German economy. Technically competent leaders were required for reconstruction, many of whom were former members of the
Nazi Party. See Ranshofen-Wertheimer, Victory is
Not Enough, p. 220 for one of the few people who
said perhaps total disarmament of Germany was not
the answer, but "it might paradoxically be prefer-
able to retain a nucleus of her army for certain
services ... to maintain internal order in Germany."

126. U. S. State Department, Decade of American
Policy, p. 110, on 19 December 1947 after the meeting of the Council of Foreign Ministers in London 25
November-16 December. He played a major role in
filling this vacuum by helping to rebuild the European economy.

See Gould, International Law, pp. 661-663
for his comparison of Unconditional Surrender with
Armistice. He recognized that under Unconditional
Surrender, the victor may entirely suppress the
government and, therefore, it is more a subjugation
than a simple cessation of hostilities. In Germany,
their sovereignty had been suspended, but it was obvious that German authority was to be returned. He
called this then a "temporary subjugation."

127. Byrnes, Speaking Frankly, pp. 181-182.

221

128. Millis, The Forrestal Diaries, p. 10.

129. Hull, Memoirs, Vol. II, p. 1603. Hull quoted FDR on let the Germans eat soup on this same page.

130. Stimson and Bundy, On Active Service, p. 569.

131. Ibid., p. 570.

132. Henry Morgenthau, Jr., Germany is Our Problem (New York: Harper & Brothers, 1945), p. 16. See Chap. VII, pp. 89-101, "Germany as an Anti Russian Smoke Screen" in which he was against all advocates of a buildup of Germany against Russia. See Chap. XV, pp. 190-200, "Bring the Men Home" in which he envisioned the soldiers getting good treatment from the Germans and forgetting all the bad things. The only suitable comment seems to be that everybody should have stayed in Washington and really learned to hate!

Einzig, Can We Win the Peace?, pp. 94-96, was just as strong though. He advocated reduction of German heavy industry with all war plants being either dismantled or demolished. He wanted the machine tool industry "dismantled to the extreme limit of possibility." and "transferred to Allied countries." So Morgenthau was not one lone voice, he reflected the feelings of many.

133. Stimson and Bundy, On Active Service, pp. 576-577. See also Neumann, Making the Peace, pp. 72-74, text is on p. 73.

134. Morgenthau, Germany is Our Problem, at the front of the book. The underlining is in the typed original and does not represent italics. Regarding forced German labor outside Germany, "In a Memorandum issued in January 1942, M. Molotov actually stated that the restoration of devastated districts of the Soviet Union by Germany was one of the Soviet Russia's war aims." Einzig, Can We Win the Peace?, p. 118.

135. Stimson and Bundy, On Active Service, pp. 578-579.

136. Hull, Memoirs, Vol. II, pp. 1605-1606. The State Department was against the partition of Germany; they favored federation (so did General Eisenhower).

137. Woodward, British Foreign Policy, p. 471.

138. Hull, Memoirs, Vol. II, p. 1615. However, an impending large American loan evidently changed his mind.

139. Armstrong, Unconditional Surrender, p. 76.

140. Byrnes, Speaking Frankly, p. 181. Woodward, British Foreign Policy, p. li, stated that the

222

Plan did not prolong German resistance. He noted
that with American elections close, FDR could not
appear lenient on Germany and did not repudiate it,
but he did say the Allies were not planning to enslave the German people.

141. Stimson and Bundy, On Active Service,
p. 581.
142. Hull, Memoirs, Vol. II, p. 1621.
143. Sherwood, Roosevelt and Hopkins, p. 832.
144. Truman, Year of Decisions, p. 327.
145. Stimson and Bundy, On Active Service,
p. 582.
146. Alfred Vagts, Defense and Diplomacy, p.467.
Vagts was hard on Hull and Stimson and this does not
appear to agree with other sources.
147. Fuller, A Military History of the Western
World, Vol. III, p. 582.
148. Vagts, Defense and Diplomacy, p. 448. See
Wilmot, The Struggle for Europe, pp. 714-715, for a
good analysis of the American attitude towards war
and its effects. He stated that everything must be
subordinated to military reasons and "Her aim should
be Victory, nothing else."
149. Armstrong, Unconditional Surrender, p. 6.
Evidently this lesson has still not been learned.
William L. Langer, "Political Problems of a Coalition," Foreign Affairs, October 1947, p. 73, still
insisted that "political decisions must be subordinated to the requirements of strategy."
150. Hull, Memoirs, Vol. II, pp. 1109-1110. By
contrast Eden took part in all war councils. Hull
appeared to have had FDR's support for FDR recommended him for the Nobel Peace Prize several times
before the war. However, he did tend to use Harry
Hopkins as Secretary of State. Admiral Leahy stuck
up for his old boss by saying that FDR made no military decisions "with any thought of his own personal
political fortunes." Leahy, I Was There, p. 345,
italics in original.
151. Armstrong, Unconditional Surrender, pp.260-
261. See Woodward, British Foreign Policy, p. li,
for FDR directing the State Department to cease
planning for the future of Germany; this was just
after the repudiation of the Morgenthau Plan.
152. London, 25 August 1942, Butcher, My Three
Years With Eisenhower, p. 73.
153. See Eisenhower, Operations In Europe, p.80.
154. Barry M. Goldwater, Why Not Victory. A
Fresh Look at American Foreign Policy (New York:
McGraw-Hill Book Co., 1962), p. 86. General Joseph
W. Stillwell wrote of the President, "Besides being

a rank amateur in all military matters, F.D.R. is apt to act on sudden impulses. On top of that he has been completely hypnotized by the British, who have sold him a bill of goods." The Stilwell Papers, ed. Theodore H. White (New York: MacFadden Book, 1962), p. 25.

155. Quoted in Fuller, The Conduct of War, p. 289.

156. Baldwin, Great Mistakes of the War, p. 45.

157. Eisenhower, Crusade in Europe, p. 194.

158. Fuller, A Military History of the Western World, Vol. III, p. 545. See Possony, A Century of Conflict, pp. 245-246, for lack of foresight of the American leadership and the lack of appreciation of political and social aspects of modern conflict.

159. Roosevelt, As He Saw It, pp. 184-185. Stimson did not agree with those who said Churchill's desire to attack through the Mediterranean was to block Russia. He said this never came up in long discussions. See Stimson and Bundy, On Active Service, p. 447.

See also John A. Lukacs, A History of the Cold War (Garden City, N.Y.: Doubleday, 1961), pp. 50-51 for how the United States foiled the two ways to limit Russia: militarily, precede the Russians in Central Europe, the United States blocked southern invasion attempts; diplomatically, get concrete commitments before the end of the war, the United States refused to even discuss political particulars until the war was over.

160. Fuller, A Military History of the Western World, Vol. III, p. 576. Regarding Ike's support of the Rhône attack, Fuller said, "he still failed to realize that war is a political instrument."

Possony wrote that the Soviets were so determined to prevent Allied conquest of the Balkans that they ordered Tito to join with the Nazis in opposing an Allied Balkan invasion. A Century of Conflict, p. 267 fn.

161. Armstrong, Unconditional Surrender, p. 49. General Mark Clark commanded the U. S. Fifth Army in Italy.

Fuller noted, "as the American official historian points out, that the Joint Chiefs of Staff developed 'a purely military perspective that considered political implications chiefly with an eye to avoiding them.'" A Military History of the Western World, Vol. III, p. 553, quoted from United States Army in World War II (American Official History), "Cross-Channel Attack," Gordon A. Harrison (1951), p. 92.

224

Marshal Bulganin wrote a book in 1948 in which he claimed bourgeois military leaders over-stress the strictly military aspects of war. See Possony, A Century of Conflict, p. 353.

162. General MacArthur, in a meeting with Secretary of the Navy Forrestal, took issue with the Navy view that it would be eighteen months after the end of the war in Germany before Japan would be defeated. MacArthur said the end would be sudden and possibly within six months. (It actually came in less than six months.) Also between January and March, the 8th U. S. Army staff prepared a detailed plan for peaceful entry into Japan based on no resistance whatsoever. Whitney, MacArthur, pp. 198-199. This shows there could have been a closer understanding between those in Washington and those in the field. Truman might have acted differently at Potsdam with some of this advice.

163. Edward R. Stettinius, Jr., Roosevelt and the Russians. The Yalta Conference (Garden City, N.Y.: Doubleday, 1949), p. 9. He was Secretary of State after Hull. See also Hull, Memoirs, Vol. II, p. 1165.

FDR evidently did not accept this idea. General Stilwell noted that in a conference on policy in China, FDR, rambling on different subjects, said "Stalin doesn't want any more ground. He's got enough." The Stilwell Papers, pp. 201-204.

164. Kennan, American Diplomacy, pp. 87-88.

165. Lippmann, U. S. Foreign Policy, p. 150. The coming of the Red Army was no liberation as in the West. Warsaw was a notorious example. See Possony, A Century of Conflict, p. 272. "This was a strategy of almost unparalleled ruthlessness; the elements which could have opposed Red domination were wiped out - by the nazis for the bolsheviks. The soviets did not hesitate to sacrifice, in addition, the Poles fighting as allies of Russia and as members of the Russian army." The Russians had called for the Poles to revolt, then let the Germans slaughter over 250,000 of them while they held back. 350,000 more were forcibly evacuated. The only thing the Russians did was to push the Polish Division into the fight to its suicide - they crossed the Vistula, then the Communists cut off their artillery support.

See also Possony, p. 268, for his discussions of how the Russians took much of Czechoslovakia by one radio message. Antonov, Stalin's Chief of Staff, radioed Ike asking him to hold behind the line Karlsbad-Pilsen-Budweis, because there might be some mix-ups between the two armies, even though the Russian army was still far away. We agreed. "An entire country was secured by one radio message." This kept us out of Prague and they also got the largest uranium mine in Europe as a result.

The British went to war because of Poland. It is interesting that they did not declare war on Russia when the Russians invaded eastern Poland and the Baltic states; see Armstrong, Unconditional Surrender, pp. 51-52; also Gould, International Law, p. 587; also Churchill, Closing the Ring, pp. 361-362, for his discussion at Teheran with Stalin about moving the Poles to the west behind the Curzon Line without their being asked and also giving the Poles some German territory.

166. Ibid., pp. 147-148. He figured that since the United States and Great Britain were air and sea powers, they could not really support governments in Eastern Europe. The only hope he saw was for neutrality for those countries, from Poland to Rumania.

167. Truman, Year of Decisions, p. 210. Possony, A Century of Conflict, p. 127, saw no great division between the two. "Political and military strategy are twin brothers and are subject to the same rules of behavior."

168. Armstrong, Unconditional Surrender, p. 249. Churchill wanted to push as far east as possible at least to have something to bargain with, but Ike went slow on Berlin and withdrew from Czechoslovakia when the Russians requested it, Lukacs, History of the Cold War, p. 59.

Truman wrote that Ike "objected to the Churchill plan on the grounds that such a procedure would inject political considerations into military operations." Year of Decisions, p. 212. Ike cabled President Truman on 23 April 1945, "'I do not quite understand... why the Prime Minister has been so determined to intermingle political and military considerations in attempting to establish a procedure for the conduct of our own and Russian troops when a meeting takes place.'" p. 215.

8
The Results

> We may, therefore, conclude
> that in Germany the Allied
> Powers achieved the uncon-
> ditional surrender as pro-
> claimed, thereby gaining
> the possibility of remodel-
> ing the country without be-
> ing bound by any previously
> agreed terms. [1]
>
>   -- K. F. Zemanek
>
> Unconditional surrender was
> not enough; German economy
> was to be utterly destroyed,
> and much of the Morgenthau
> Plan carried into the
> peace. [2]
>
>   -- J. F. C. Fuller

1. A Big Mistake

There have been very few writers who have reached
any other conclusion than that the policy of Unconditional Surrender was a big political mistake. As
noted at the beginning of Part II, Hanson Baldwin
felt that "This was perhaps the biggest political
mistake of the war." He referred to it as "a policy
of political bankruptcy," felt it delayed our military objective - Victory, and considered it as confirmation that we had no reasonable program for
peace. A high price was paid in lives and time, and
its basically negative concept handicapped the development of a positive peace program. [3]
Lord Hankey, commenting on what a pity it was

to use this policy to enliven an otherwise colorless
press conference at Casablanca, pondered how much
trouble, how many lives, how much destruction, and
what misery would have been saved if it had been
kept a secret or, better yet, if it had never been
accepted as a war aim. He deplored the results and
felt that "a snap-decision on such a far-reaching
subject was one of the gravest errors of the war."[4]
We have already seen how Secretary of State Hull was
not consulted about and very often not even present
for important decisions. He wrote that he was a-
gainst the policy for two reasons: first, he felt
it would stiffen resistance; second, the principle
logically required the victorious nations to take
over every phase of the national and local governments of the conquered countries, and to operate all
governmental activities and properties. "We and our
Allies were in no way prepared to undertake this
vast obligation."[5]

Field Marshal Bernard Montgomery called the
policy "a very great mistake" and commented on the
difficulties of the Allied Control Council which was
supposed to dictate to a central German government
how to run the country; only there was no German
government.[6] Regardless of the advantages of the
policy permitting the Allies to do as they wished,
its early announcement was a tactical mistake that
left the Allies no room for maneuver and the enemy
peoples no motive for ridding themselves of their
governments.[7]

Chester Wilmot felt that it was both illogical
and dangerous to use the same formula against countries so different as the Axis states, and also that
the Allies seemed to have overlooked the effect upon
postwar Europe of a fight to the finish.[8] He concluded that Unconditional Surrender was both unnecessary and unwise. Even though Hitler intended to
keep fighting, as he once said, "until five past
midnight," insistence on Unconditional Surrender -
combined with the Morgenthau Plan and indiscriminate
bombing of cities - guaranteed that the Wehrmacht
and the German people would fight on with him. The
policy of Unconditional Surrender, "though the
President's brain-child," (Wilmot believed Roosevelt
had noble and unselfish political aims) was a natural result of the American decision to pursue the
war to Total Victory regardless of the political consequences.[9]

President Truman wrote an interesting critique
of the policy. He felt that the Allies wanted to be
sure there would be no doubt left in the German mind

as to the reason for and the completeness of their military defeat. He was not certain, however, that things always work that way. It seemed to him that national pride outlives military defeat and it is a delusion to think otherwise. Truman thought it a mistake to insist on Unconditional Surrender for moral or educational purposes. "Any surrender is at the will of the victor, whether the surrender terms be conditional or unconditional." The only reason he saw for Unconditional Surrender was the practical matter of taking over a defeated country and making it easier to control. He reasoned that a good time for the Germans to have surrendered was after the Russians had driven them from Stalingrad and the Western Allies had landed in Italy and France. A surrender then would have meant a quicker recovery for all of Europe, especially for Germany.[10]

From the propaganda viewpoint, the policy played into the hands of Goebbels. Branding all Germans as equally responsible and demanding a total surrender that could hardly appear honorable, were bound to have an effect on the enemy's resistance. Goebbels noted in his diary even before Casablanca:

> The more radical the English are in prophesying a disgraceful peace for Germany, the more easily I succeed in toughening and hardening German resistance. We'd be in a dangerous fix now if British propaganda from the beginning of the war to this hour had respected the German will to live and the German conception of honor. That's how Chamberlain began on the first day of the war. Thank God, the English did not continue along that line. Even though we would always try to discredit them by citing 1918 as an example, they would nevertheless find foolish adherents here and there, especially since the domestic situation always becomes more strained the longer the war lasts.

The editor noted: "The historian of the future will probably have to re-evaluate the wisdom of the Allied insistence upon unconditional surrender which was predicated on the assumption that all Germans were alike. Goebbels, after all, knew something about propaganda and the psychology of the German people.[11]

Many propaganda experts - not necessarily opposed to the principle of total defeat - considered it a disastrous mistake for the President to have announced the policy publicly.[12] General Fuller, in his colorful style, gave his view about Stalin and the policy: "As to Uncle Joe, though he never had any intention other than the unconditional surrender of Germany, he was not such a simpleton as to inform his enemy of it."[13] With the benefit of hindsight, it is clear that the Anglo-American propagandists were placed at a serious strategic disadvantage, first by the lack of a clear, well-defined policy of what we expected of the enemy nations, and second, by the absence of any "hope clause" in our policy once defined and publicized. Unconditional Surrender was perhaps well conceived for bolstering home-front morale and for stiffening inter-Allied determination to fight the war to a decisive end, but it increased the burden of the propagandists responsible for convincing the enemy to capitulate.[14]

It is only natural that some of the German generals have also been critical of the policy. They wanted peace but they did not want Germany destroyed or Europe overrun by Communism. General Heinz Guderian felt the Casablanca demand certainly contributed to the death of every hope for a reasonable peace by the generals, the Wehrmacht, as well as the German people. Guderian maintained that the soft wartime Allied policy - especially the American - policy toward the Soviet Union was disastrous. He described Roosevelt, the father of Unconditional Surrender, as "the gravedigger not only of Germany but also of Europe" and asserted that the entire civilized world, not just Germany had to pay for Roosevelt's naive wartime policy. General Hasso Von Manteuffel met regularly in the postwar years with a group of former comrades to discuss mistakes of the war, on both sides. They unquestionably considered Unconditional Surrender as one of the mistakes, a boomerang which resulted in entirely unnecessary losses during the final months of the war because, with the breakthrough at Avranches in July 1944, Germany had decisively lost the war.[15]

The Allies, in their emotional rage, forgot Lord Hankey's simple sentence: "Wars usually begin and end in politics."[16] There must an objective in war or else it is sheer folly. To continue to fight urged on only by hate, particularly when one is winning and could be master of the situation, seems to leave the much-sought-after Victory standing like an empty shell, like one of the bombed-out buildings that accompany it. But in this Pyrrhic victory there was one winner - the Communists.

2. The Results - Victory for Communism

The long war was over, or so it seemed. A great relief spread across the world, people danced in the streets, and it was not long before the cry was "Bring the boys home." In less than a year, the great military colossus that had taken the Allies years to build was reduced to a shell. This unilateral disarmament before the threat of a determined enemy is unparalleled in history and was to cost us dearly. What then were the results of our Casablanca formula that finally yielded the great Total Victory in a Total War?

The demand for Unconditional Surrender doubtlessly sparked the imagination and perhaps even fired the resolve of many people in the Allied camp. What is questionable, however, is the value of the concept as an instrument of policy toward the enemy. The policy embittered the war, made a fight to the finish inevitable, precluded any possibility of either side offering terms or opening up negotiations, buoyed the Germans and Japanese with the courage of despair, enhanced the enemy leadership as their country's "only hope," aided enemy propaganda, rendered inevitable the Normandy invasion and the subsequent costly advance across northern Europe, and added further cost due to delaying the termination of the war in Asia. Over two years after the Casablanca pronouncement, our leaders were still trying to decide what it meant and what they had undertaken. Had they paused, in Miksche's view, and looked a little more deeply into the matter before making their declaration, they would have realized, as history will show, that the interests of the West run closer to Germany than to Russia and "their failure to realize this soon enough lies at the root of the greatest tragedy of our time and provides the germs of a third world war." It has not been clearly recognized that Stalingrad was a defeat for all of Europe. At that historical moment "Beelzebub Stalin" became more dangerous than "devil Hitler." Allied policy unwittingly helped the Soviets, who had no interest in seeing Europe's affairs settled too rapidly. On the contrary, the Communists knew very well that their revolutionary doctrine could find fruitful ground only in a disorganized world.[17]

Those two fateful words - Unconditional Surrender - implied, first, that the war must be fought to the point of annihilation, taking on a religious character, and becoming for the Axis powers a question

231

of salvation or damnation. Secondly, that once victory had been won, the balance of power in Europe would be smashed. Russia would be left as the greatest military power, and therefore dominant, in Europe. Hence the peace predicted by those words was "the replacement of Nazi tyranny by an even more barbaric despotism."[18] The results of Communist expansion were impressive. Stalin, who kept his strategy in step with his policy, had imposed his rule upon Estonia, Latvia, Lithuania, part of Finland, Poland, eastern and central Germany, a third of Austria, Czechoslavakia, Yugoslavia, Hungary, Rumania, and Bulgaria. Vienna, Prague, and Berlin, the vertebrae of Europe, were his, and except for Athens, so was every capital city in Eastern Europe. Russia's western frontier had been advanced from the Pripet Marshes to the Thuringerwald, a distance of 750 miles, and, as in the days of Charlemagne, the Slavs stood on the Elbe and the Böhmerwald. A thousand years of European history had been undone. "Such were the fruits of the battle of Normandy, fructified by inept strategy and a policy of pure destruction."[19]

In late 1944, Hitler told his army commanders: "If Germany loses, it will have proved itself biologically inferior and will have forfeited its future existence. It is the West that forces us to fight to the last. However, it will transpire that the winner will not be the West, but the East."[20] Thus, it came about that the "only nation that gained any advantage from the Unconditional Surrender policy was Russia," which, due to the lengthening of the war, was able to overrun Eastern Europe and impose her own political system. This was facilitated in that the Soviets "had the wisdom to avoid the imposition on those countries of Unconditional Surrender."[21]

On 4 December 1941 when the Germans had penetrated the outskirts of Moscow, Stalin gave a big dinner for General Sikorski, the Polish Prime Minister. After the dinner, Stalin said, "'Now we will talk about the frontiers between Poland and Russia.'" Wilmot commented: "Thus, in defeat as in victory, Stalin kept his post-war political objectives steadily in view." His tactics varied with his fortunes, but his final objective stayed the same. From the very first, he had decided to exploit the situation created by the war to satisfy Russian imperialistic ambitions. "What had changed by this time was not Anglo-American policy or Russian aims, but the nature and scope of Stalin's opportunity."[22]

Like any other form of unrest, war is a hotbed
of activity which the Communists do their utmost to
exploit. Raymond Aron, as well as many others, has
pointed up the importance of the Second World War,
and not Communism, as the direct cause of Russia's
rise to world power.[23] Total War, particularly
strategic bombing and Unconditional Surrender, involved high political costs. The elimination of a
major power inevitably enhances other powers, particularly its rivals. Only one of Germany's neighbors was in a position to exploit this aggrandize-
ment. Great Britain was beset by economic problems
and France by political problems and stagnation.
The result was inevitable; a Czarist or a Communist
Russia would expand its influence in Europe, particularly in those areas occupied by the Red Army.
Malenkov, while celebrating the thirty-second anni-
versary of the Communist Revolution, claimed that
World War II led to the establishment of peoples'
democratic regimes in a number of countries of central and southeast Europe and led to the Chinese
victory. "Can there be any doubt whatever,...[that]
a third world war... will be the grave not only for
individual capitalist states, but for the whole
world capitalism?"[24] One needs only to review the
effects of the wars of this century to see how the
Communists try to exploit them, relying on war to
create their opportunity to seize decadent states.
This approach has returned them excellent dividends
in the past, and they are still using the technique.

The two most serious mistakes of the war according to Chester Wilmot both concerned the Soviet
Union: Hitler's underestimation of Russian military
force and Roosevelt's misjudgment of Soviet political ambitions. A third error could be fatal for
Western civilization.[25] General Fuller blasted
Roosevelt's "Great Design" as a reversion to the
Wilsonian policy of the nations of the world united
in a great peace organization after the war, without
the 14 Points, and declared it "may be compared with
a pot of political ale - all froth." The Great Design, however, would require Russia. That would be
no problem because Harry Hopkins "had told him
[Roosevelt]" after visiting Stalin "that it was ridiculous to think of Stalin as a communist; he was
nothing of the sort, he was a great Russian nationalist and patriot.... Whatever his views might be
about the future of Europe, he must be won over. Although the President did not then realize it, appeasement of Russia was to become the linchpin in
allied policy."[26]

While the Americans poured out aid to both
their Allies and their former enemies, and the other
Western Allies were in dire straits, the Communists
alone reaped the whirlwind by extending their power
over millions of additional poor souls. The war,
begun to preserve the independence of Poland and
Czechoslovakia, ended with Soviet domination of
Eastern and Central Europe. Politically it represented failure for the West. Unconditional Surrender yielded political victory for the Soviet Union;
therefore, the war unfortunately ended up stimula-
ting and expanding Communism. Once again the Allies
had accomplished the very thing they dreaded most;
they had won the war and lost the peace.

3. Win the War, Lose the Peace

The military victory was complete. Those who
had seen Victory as the goal of the war were satisfied that their wishes had come true. But disillusionment came quickly as they surveyed the mess
they had made of the world, and it did not take long
for them to start wondering if they had really won
the war or not, for it was soon evident that they
had not won the peace. This situation did not suddenly appear at the end of the war, but its roots
were planted early in the conflict. The leaders
looked upon war as a "lethal game" rather than an
instrument of policy and, therefore, battles began
to lose their political value. During the latter
half of the war, their results were often neutral-
ized by political decisions. Thus, it came about
that major conferences, such as Casablanca, Teheran,
and Yalta, were not only more decisive than any
battle fought, but they annulled the decisions the
latter achieved.
Churchill himself gave a partial explanation of
what happened. He explained to the Parliament on 27
February 1945 two principles he was following.
"'While the war is on, we give help to anyone who
can kill a Hun; when the war is over we look to the
solution of a free, unfettered democratic election.'"
For the British and Americans to believe that those
who claimed to have killed the most "Huns" would not
also look to their own solutions was a major delusion.[27] World War II obviously failed to achieve
the hopes and aspirations of Roosevelt and Churchill.
Roosevelt tried to better the record of President
Wilson, but he also was unable to find a working

solution to the problem of international peace.[18]
The Unconditional Surrender of Germany upset the
balance of power in Europe, and that of Japan had
similar results in Asia. In each case, the might of
our former enemies was destroyed, but their hegemony
was replaced by still more dangerous Russian imperialism; therefore, not only Germany and Japan but the
whole of Western civilization lost the war.[29]

It appears that the Western Allies did not always put as much planning into the preparations for
the big conferences as they did for large military
operations, and the conferences proved to be more
important and would cast long shadows upon history.
General Deane, who spent most of the war trying to
cooperate with the Russians, wrote of the Teheran
Conference: "President Roosevelt was thinking of
winning the war; the others were thinking of their
relative positions when the war was won."[30] It is
particularly interesting to know FDR's frame of mind
when he went to Teheran.

> When William C. Bullitt, former United States
> Ambassador in Moscow, protested that his Rus-
> sian policy would fail because Stalin could not
> be trusted, the President replied: "Bill... I
> don't dispute the logic of your reasoning. I
> just have a hunch that Stalin is not that kind
> of man. Harry says he's not, and that he
> doesn't want anything but security for his
> country. And I think that if I give him any-
> thing I can and ask nothing from him in return,
> noblesse oblige, he won't try to annex anything
> and will work with me for a world of peace and
> democracy."[31]

And so in this altruistic spirit President Roosevelt
went to meet Stalin at Teheran. It was becoming
evident, even before Teheran, that Unconditional Surrender would inevitably leave Russia the dominant
power in Eastern Europe. The Russian influence in
Central Europe and the Balkans, however, was not inevitable. After Teheran though, this became almost
a certainty too.

The conference that has received the most criticism and will, no doubt, be longest remembered in
history was the Yalta Conference in February 1945.
This meeting, called "that kangaroo court of history" by one author,[32] has brought forth many cries of
"give-away" and "sell-out" to the Communists. Various statements have been made about Roosevelt's
health, as he died only two months later. Being

just before the end of the war, the conference naturally dealt with important questions regarding both Germany and Japan. Before the Yalta meeting, although it was only three months before the end of the war, there was still no agreement on what was to be done with Germany once she had been defeated. The overall judgment as one author described it was that "the consequences of Yalta were unfortunate on almost every account" and it "represented a rather sad closing chapter to a war which, on the whole, was wisely directed and gallantly fought." Of major importance was the situation that the President was willing to pay a high price for a firm agreement by Stalin to enter the war against Japan.[33] This was probably the saddest mistake of all, for to pay the Russians to come into the Asian war when they were straining every muscle to accomplish that anyway, was like paying a child to eat cake and ice cream. Before the conference assembled, FDR had decided to give Stalin a free hand in Europe as the quid pro quo. "Because of Stalin's realism and the President's idealism - he was advised by Harry Hopkins, and among others by Algar Hiss of the State Department and a Soviet underground agent - the Yalta Conference led to a super-Munich."[34]

It was only natural that Secretary of State Stettinius would defend the Yalta Conference. He wrote that it "marked the high tide of British, Russian, and American co-operation on the war and on the postwar settlement."[35] He added that this cooperation broke down shortly thereafter. Stettinius stated that some of the advisers felt that perhaps Stalin had gotten into trouble with the Politburo upon his return to Moscow, for having been "too friendly" and for having "made too many concessions" to the capitalist nations.[36] He maintained that the "Soviet Union made greater concessions at Yalta to the United States and Great Britain than were made to the Soviets."[37] It appears that the best summary is that FDR was gambling at Yalta. "His eyes were open, and he knew perfectly well the risks he was taking. What he was gambling for was permanent peace on a moral, idealistic, one-world basis. Unfortunately he lost."[38]

Potsdam was an unusual conference in that one of the main enemies had been defeated and, in the midst of it, one of the Allies changed its government. The Allies had won the war, but could not agree on what to do with their victory. Admiral Leahy noted that with the British economically prostrate, the French grappling for stability, and the

236

Chinese facing civil war, there were only two major powers remaining in the world, and there was a great chasm between their ideas and policies. "At Potsdam the only possibility of agreement would have been to accept the Russian point of view on every issue."[39] Nevertheless, many of the policies for the German occupation and the future of Germany were worked out at Potsdam.[40]

As quickly evidenced by postwar developments, the destruction of the enemies had been carried too far. This was something never considered during the war and the responsibility for it must fall upon our political leadership. The policy of Unconditional Surrender was put into practice at Yalta. "In its essence it was nothing else than a sort of unconditional surrender to Russia of the Western Powers. It meant that most, if not all, of what Stalin asked for was granted."[41] The Allied goals were not fulfilled. The great region that Hitler dreamed of putting under the control of one nation was under a single control - the Communists. "Asia for the Asiatics" had been the Japanese war aim. Curiously enough, the policy of the beaten enemy was put into effect by the Americans. Our problem was that we fought to win - period. We forgot that wars are merely an extension of politics, that wars have objectives, that attainable objectives are dependent upon the willingness of the vanquished state to accept them, and that the general objective of war is a more stable peace. In other words, we had no peace aims. We had only the vaguest idea, expressed in vague principles such as the Atlantic Charter and the United Nations, of the postwar world we desired.[42] By the time the illusions of propaganda were dissipated, it was too late, the rewards of the victory had been lost.

It was manifest that American diplomatic planning for the peace was far below the quality of the planning that went into the conduct of the war. It was not the first time we had won the war and lost the peace. Once again Americans had fought a war in distant lands and once again we had won on the field of battle. But, as we had done before, we lost those gains across the conference table. This was not quite so strange as it might seem though for the Allies had permitted themselves to become so ridiculously weak militarily in the late 1930s that when the war came, they were forced into the absurd position of having to ally with a dictatorship to win.

4. Alliance with a Dictatorship

War, even on a small scale, is not a simple
matter, but when it involves many different nations
of the world, it becomes quite difficult to visualize it as a two-sided contest. Various nations
group together for diverse reasons to conduct hostilities; however, wartime alliances against a common enemy are proverbially ephemeral for, once the
enemy is defeated, the alliance's bond weakens. The
Second World War was a coalition war, conducted by
dissimilar powers with conflicting interests and,
sometimes, no more in common than their interest in
stopping German expansion.[43]
    In line with this, then, any evaluation of the
failure of World War II to achieve a lasting peace
must first measure what was achieved against what
was achievable. There were three basic ideologies
(or forces) in powerful positions in the world: Democracy, National Socialism, and Communism. The important point was that two of the three were dictatorships. These antagonistic forces led to three
different outlooks on war: Democracies either wanted to free captive peoples or to prevent their capture; National Socialists wanted to expand the Reich
racially and territorially; and Soviet Russia wanted
to foster world revolution through extension of the
class struggle. For the Democracies, peace was an
end in itself - the cessation of war; for the National Socialists, it was a time to prepare for war;
and for the Communists, it was but another form of
war. Since all three of these are based on strong
ideas, the only way to remove one would be by replacing it with another strong idea. With the German attack on Russia, the Democracies were confronted with the problem of allying with a dictatorship
and the war became much more complicated, becoming
in reality a four-sided war.
    The war was poorly understood by the peoples
and leaders who fought it on the Democratic side because it was not fully winnable. There were four
world military power centers: the Democracies
(basically Great Britain and the United States), Germany, Russia, and Japan. Considering that Japan was
effectively limited to the Pacific, and could be defeated by the Democracies alone, then the Democracies were faced with Germany and Russia who, together, would be almost overwhelming. To defeat either
one of them, the Democracies needed the help of the

238

other. But such collaboration, if carried to Total Victory, would mean the relative strengthening of the collaborating power and its eventual appearance as a demanding and implacable claimant at the peace table.

There was some debate as to whether it was ever practical for the Democracies to hope that the Germans and Russians would fight it out between themselves. Since the West finally went to war with Germany over Poland, one group felt there was no prospect for victory over Germany without Soviet help. Such help was bound to affect the military consequences of the war for the West and to result in Soviet demands in the postwar power structure.

There were others who favored letting the dictators fight it out. Hanson Baldwin wrote: "There is no doubt whatsoever that it would have been to the interest of Britain, the United States, and the world to have allowed - and indeed, to have encouraged - the world's two great dictatorships to fight each other to a frazzle."[44] Fuller joined him with a similar comment, that since the Nazis and the Communists were on a collision course in Eastern Europe, "there can be no doubt whatsoever that in 1939 the best policy for France and Great Britain would have been to keep out of the war, let the two great dictatorial powers cripple each other, and in the meantime have re-armed at top speed."[45] On the day after the German attack on Russia, Senator Harry Truman said: "If we see that Germany is winning the war we ought to help Russia, and if Russia is winning we ought to help Germany, and in that way let them kill as many as possible."[46]

The synthesis of these two theses is that with two rival powers threatening the existing order in Europe and with the West unwilling to let them fight it out by themselves, the time of intervention should be carefully chosen so as to save the one from being destroyed by the other. For as long as there are two such giants on the continent the whole world can breathe; but if you conduct a crusade to destroy one of them, you will build the other into a greater monster than before, and it will inevitably have to be faced. To use the devil to cast out the devil is not good politics.

When the time came to ally with a dictatorship, it was a hard decision for the Democracies. Soviet-American relations had not improved after the recognition of the Soviet Government in 1933. If anything, they had deteriorated as a result of the Soviet failure to meet their obligations. By 1940,

239

relations were quite bad and the official distrust
was exceeded only by the American public's intense
aversion to Communism. The Communist dictatorship
was disliked even more when it became allied with
Nazism. We had already established ourselves as
firmly against Hitler, so when he attacked Russia,
the West was confronted with the question of whether
or not to assist the Communists against this invasion. We have already seen Churchill's reply. The
American Government and people answered in favor of
sending all possible assistance. The United States
actually supplied about 10 percent of the Russian
requirements in equipment and munitions, including
crucial items which prevented a Soviet collapse. In
effect, the West considered the Communist dictatorship the lesser of two evils. We were victims of
our own propaganda. Russian aims were suddenly good
and noble; the Communist tiger had changed its
stripes.[47]
     This alliance was certainly a shotgun marriage
for expediency, for the only thing these two governments had in common was a desire to defeat Hitler.
The Soviets did not choose the Western powers as allies; in fact, they had done their best to avoid
that situation and prior to the German attack had
been openly hostile to the Western governments and
peoples. This started the agonizing period of attempted cooperation with a completely untrustworthy
government whose announced aim was world domination.
     Stalin sent Churchill a message on 8 November
1941 stating "there is no definite understanding between our two countries concerning war aims and
plans for the post-war organization of peace."[48]
Stalin received a reply on 22 November.

> Naturally the first object will be to prevent
> Germany, and particularly Prussia, from break-
> ing out upon us for a third time. The fact
> that Russia is a Communist State and that Bri-
> tain and the U.S.A. are not and do not intend
> to be is not any obstacle to our making a good
> plan for our mutual safety and rightful in-
> terests.[49]

Problems were not long in coming. Hull wrote: "One
of the greatest preoccupations of the President and
me during the first half of 1942 was Russia's suddenly revealed territorial aims in Europe, coupled
with her determination to induce the Western Allies
to guarantee them in advance."[50]
     Some people, sensing the danger of the alliance

with Russia, became almost afraid of victory fearing
that it might bring Socialism or even Communism to
the West.[51] That this was one of the most troubled
alliances in history was clearly shown in the many
memoirs from the period. Hull reported one part of
the exasperating problem. In 1943, Russia, a complete sphinx to all other nations of the world, represented to the Allies "the most puzzling problem in
international relations." How would she act in the
postwar world? Would she cooperate with the West
and with China? Would she join the United Nations
to maintain the peace? Would she seek territorial
expansion at the expense of her smaller neighbors or
would she go to the other extreme, give up all ambitions and retire to strict isolation within her
old borders? Interest in Russia "was rapidly developing" in every important Foreign Office. Allied
statesmen were anxious to ascertain the intentions
of the Soviet Union to know how to plan for the
world that would exist after the peace.[52] As the
tide turned, particularly after Stalingrad, conditions got even worse. Thereafter, the British and
Americans were in a "perpetual quandary," and almost
all political decisions of the later part of the war
"hinged more or less directly on considerations of
the Russian problems."[53]
     These were hard people to deal with for their
word was valueless. As General Deane observed, "an
'approval in principle' by the Soviet Government
means exactly nothing."[54] The Overstreets, who have
written so much about the Communists, wrote, "The
Soviet empire rests on broken promises."[55] They
also recorded how successful this type of international double-dealing was. Stalin was able to get
away with breaking every agreement he made with respect to the East European countries, and as a result he brought another hundred million people under
Communist control.[56]
     It would not be fair to say that the Western
leaders were not aware of this problem. Their headache was what to do about it. In his State of the
Union message of January 1945, President Roosevelt
recognized: "The nearer we come to vanquishing our
enemies the more we inevitably become conscious of
differences among the victors." Averell Harriman
was aware that the "outwardly friendly relations of
our wartime alliance" would not survive the peace.
He reported to the President, the Secretary of State,
and other members of the Cabinet that "the outward
thrust of Communism was not dead and that we might
well have to face an ideological war against an

241

antagonist just as vigorous and dangerous as Nazism or Fascism."[57] Though these views on the Communist threat "were not popular at the time," he stuck by his statement that "We are going to have trouble with the Soviet Union for the rest of our lives - even if we live to be a hundred."[58] Byrnes admitted that in light of the Soviet actions in East Germany and their violations of the Yalta agreements he would have been happy if the Russians had not entered the Japanese war.[59] Truman wrote that "Force is the only thing the Russians understand. And while I was hopeful that Russia might someday be persuaded to work in co operation for peace, I knew that the Russians should not be allowed to get into any control of Japan."[60] President Truman thereafter had many opportunities to deal with the Russians before he left office.

Walter Lippmann wrote during the war that the Big Three must ally to ensure the peace. If they failed to, it would be because they were potential antagonists. Once that potential antagonism is recognized by their dissolving the wartime alliance, "one or all of the three victors will inevitably move toward arrangements with the defeated powers."[61] This had happened in 1919. It was also not long after the war before the three main members of the Axis - Germany, Japan, and Italy - were allied with the Western Democracies against the Communists. This sort of thing makes one wonder about World War II and creates questions as to whether we were always fighting with the right people and for the right reasons. This forced alliance with a dictatorship certainly dominated the results achievable from the war. The war proved to be the greatest boost Communism ever achieved, and Russia emerged from the struggle at the top of a Communist camp that effectively divided the world in two. One is reminded of Napoleon's comment to Caulaincourt on the road back from Moscow.

> "The Russians should be viewed by everyone as
> scourge. The war against Russia is a war which
> is wholly in the interests - if those interests
> are rightly judged - of the older Europe and of
> civilization.... The reverses that France has
> just suffered will put an end to all jealousies
> and quiet all the anxieties that may have
> sprung from her power or influence. Europe
> should think of only one enemy. And that ene-
> my is the colossus of Russia."[62]

Two sides of the four-sided war had been crushed,
but the other two sides remained as the world entered the postwar period.

5. The Postwar Period

With the surrenders of Germany and Japan in
1945, the terrible bloody warfare was over. There
was to be no peace though. The great fighting force
of the Western Allies was dismantled,[63] but this was
not the case with the Russians who saw that the real
fruits of the war were just now coming ripe. So the
warfare shifted from the battlefield to the conference table and from between the Allies and the Axis
to just between the Allies. The Western Allies did
not foresee the complete disruption and dislocation
of organized life which resulted from the German defeat. Feeding the Germans became an urgent task,
and the victors, in addition to caring for the vanquished, had to assume the enormous and rising costs
of occupation, with little return (at least in the
case of the Western powers) in the form of reparations. The bill from Unconditional Surrender was
not yet paid and would not be for many years to
come.

The United States and Soviet Russia emerged
from the war as the two great powers in the world.
General Eisenhower wrote: "This fact affected every
detail of American official routine in conquered
Germany, for any prolonged struggle between the two
powers would hopelessly complicate our local problems and might even nullify our costly victory."[64]
A proclamation, published on 5 June 1945, established the commander-in-chief in each zone as the
supreme authority subject only to the four com-
manders-in-chief acting in unanimous agreement in
matters pertaining to Germany as a whole. This was
the basis for the "veto" used by the French and the
Soviets to block all efforts to achieve unity in the
control council. Thus, the "new war" had started.
In the future it was to become known by the nebulous
term "Cold War" but it had not yet gained such recognition.

There were numerous meetings of the Council of
Foreign Ministers in 1945, 46, and 47, all with uniformly negative results. Secretary of State Byrnes
reported, "The first session of the Council of Foreign Ministers closed in a stalemate."[65] One of the
first arguments with the Russians was over repara-

tions from Italy. The Russians, who had very little
to do with Italy in the war in the first place, were
insisting on outrageous payments from Italy. Since
the United States was contributing hundreds of millions of dollars to Italian relief, it was ridiculous to have the Italians turn around and give this
American money to Russia.[66] Byrnes reported on the
first part of the second meeting, "The progress made
towards peace at the Paris meeting of the Council of
Foreign Ministers was disappointingly small".[67] The
problems, as was becoming a habit, were with Russia.
The Russians were still screaming for reparations
from Italy even though the United States had already advanced $900 million to Italy. They wanted
some of the Italian Navy, not to be counted as reparations; they wanted some of the Italian colonies;
they wanted certain regions around Trieste turned
over to Yugoslavia. This was truly the hungry bear
at the peace table and it made it difficult to obtain Byrnes' idea of peace - "not a peace founded
upon vengeance or greed, but a just peace, the only
peace that can endure."[68] Unfortunately the Americans gave in to the Russians at the second meeting
and reluctantly agreed that the Soviets could receive reparations up to $100,000,000.[69] Byrnes
mused, "But I sometimes think our Soviet friends
fear we would think them weak and soft if they a-
greed without a struggle on anything we wanted, even
though they wanted it too." Byrnes did not believe
that the Soviets realized the "doubts and suspicions" which they raised in countries who wanted to
be their friends by the "aloofness, coolness, and
hostility" with which they received the twenty-five-
year plan for Germany and "America's offer to guarantee jointly the continued disarmament of Germany."[70] That the occupation of Germany was not
progressing smoothly was also evident. It was no
secret that the four-power control of Germany on a
zonal basis was not working well from the point of
view of any of the four powers. The price was going
up too. Our zone was costing our taxpayers
$200,000,000 a year.[71]

The tension continued to mount. At the Paris
Peace Conference, the Russians "vigorously opposed"
the proposal for free navigation of the great international rivers of Europe.[72] Byrnes reported, on 18
October, "The thing which disturbs me is not the
lettered provisions of the treaties under discussion
but the continued if not increased tension between
us and the Soviet Union." The talks were evidently
getting rougher as he went so far as to say that

states "must not launch false and misleading propaganda against one another."[73]   One year after the end of World War II, people were talking of war again. "War is inevitable only if states fail to tolerate and respect the rights of other states to ways of life they cannot and do not share."[74]

The Americans, who had tried for so long to be friends with the Russians, were getting exasperated. The Soviet Union "charged that the United States had enriched itself during the war," and was now "seeking to enslave Europe economically." This was real gratitude from a country to which we had "advanced more than 10 billion dollars of lend-lease during the war"[75] and for which we had received only snide remarks, dastardly propaganda charges, and the great clank of the Iron Curtain slammed shut in our faces. Secretary of State Marshall encountered the same Soviet obstinacy. He described the results of the fifth meeting of the Council of Foreign Ministers as "disappointing."[76] Reparations were still a problem as he reported. Reparations from current production could be made only if those countries then supplying Germany - mainly the United States - footed the bill. "We put in and the Russians take out."[77] The Soviet Union had put a real stranglehold on East Germany, completely disrupting trade between industrial West Germany and agricultural East Germany, and absolutely refused to give out any information as to what reparations they had taken out of that country or what the situation was there. "In effect we were to tell them what has occurred in the western zones, which we had already done, and they tell us nothing." Marshall gave up on a united Germany for the time. "It finally became clear that we could made no progress at this time.... So I suggested that we adjourn."[78]

What really complicated dealings with the Soviets in addition to their just plain obnoxious manner was that they had broken almost every agreement they had ever made. This was so bad that the State Department prepared a document for the Senate in 1948 on Soviet violations of agreements.[79] The United States Ambassador to the United Nations, Warren R. Austin, described on 14 November 1949 how his hometown newspaper referred to Soviet treaty breaking with the headline: "The Sound of Breaking Treaties Familiar as Street Noises."[80] By this time the Berlin blockade had shattered all remaining dreams, if there still were any, of cooperation with the Russians. The Cold War had come into bloom, and the next year was to heat up considerably with the

Communist invasion of South Korea.

Up to now, we have been referring primarily to the problems in Europe. It is valuable to review the actions in the Far East also, particularly for their contrasts, since the surrender of Japan was not unconditional and, also, because the Red Army did not manage to get into those islands. The first difference is immediately clear in the Directive to the Supreme Commander for the Allied Powers for the Occupation and Control of Japan, 1 November 1945.

> It is contemplated, however, that unless you deem it necessary or are instructed to the contrary you will not establish direct military government, but will exercise your powers so far as compatible with the accomplishment of your mission through the Emperor of Japan or the Japanese Government.... You will occupy the Imperial capital of Tokyo, and the capitals of such prefectures as you deem necessary in order to facilitate your control over the Japanese Government. You will also occupy such strategic places as you may deem necessary. Otherwise you should not occupy any part of Japan unless it becomes essential to impose direct military government therein.[81]

This is certainly a far cry from the divided control of Germany under four different commanders working with no German government. This alone is a good indictment of Unconditional Surrender for Japan was rebuilt as a nation whereas the Germany of 1939 no longer exists.

It was no bed of roses in Japan between the pressures of the Allies and some of the not too subtle attempts from Washington to wreak vengeance. Even though the Russians declared war on Japan only a week before the surrender, and Russian fighting in the Pacific was confined to Manchuria and Korea, the Soviets requested that a Soviet general be appointed Joint Commander-in-Chief with MacArthur in Tokyo. This request was rejected, but the Soviets were granted full coequal status with the other Allies as conquerors of Japan. That was a great prize won at a very low cost.[82] At the Moscow Conference in December 1945, Secretary Byrnes surrendered our unilateral authority over Japan to an international authority of eleven nations to be seated in Washington with an advisory body in Tokyo comprised of the United States, Great Britain, China, and the Soviet Union. It quickly became an organ of Russian propaganda, so MacArthur acted in accordance with the Moscow Agreement that stated that the Supreme Commander was the "sole executive authority." "Not one constructive idea to help with the reorientation and reconstruction of Japan had been offered by either the Far Eastern Commission or the Allied Council."[83] Harassment, however, came from all sides. Policymakers at the highest governmental levels urged another Morgenthau Plan to apply the coup de grâce to Japan. British and Soviet officials insisted upon the partition of Japan into spheres of Allied responsibility, as had been so disastrously permitted in Germany. The British demanded trial of the Emperor as a war criminal. The Russians supported that request and wanted all Japanese prisoners of war to be slave laborers. MacArthur did not yield to these pressures. He was observing the problems of divided authority in Germany, and he intended to learn from that example even if others would not.[84]

General MacArthur, a very experienced old soldier, had seen military occupation after the first war, in the Rhine, and was aware of its fundamental weaknesses. He often expressed his doubts about military occupations in principle, and felt that "they frequently laid the basis for future wars."[85] When MacArthur first arrived in Japan, the 11th Airborne Division attempted to find some food for the General. They were able to find only one egg! This indication of the complete exhaustion of Japanese food resources was quickly confirmed, and he issued an order forbidding the occupation forces to consume local food, an order which remained in effect throughout the occupation.[86] The public health program instituted by the military "saved 2,100,000 Japanese lives in the first two years" and other programs such as free hot lunches for school children not only had immediate results in terms of better health, but also brought a warm response from the Japanese people. They could see that the Americans were in Japan to build and not to destroy.[87]

MacArthur's protection of the Emperor reaped great benefits. The Japanese people recognized this and, thereafter, looked upon MacArthur as a symbol of protection against those who were seeking revenge. This resulted in closer cooperation with the occupation authorities, but, more importantly, "the Emperor from the start became MacArthur's chief ally in the spiritual regeneration of Japan."[88]

MacArthur's magnanimous approach was "far indeed from the then prevailing plan of brute force, largely conceived in hate and dedicated to vengeance."

Though popular with the masses, it met with a "chilly reaction in London and the State Department in Washington."[89] President Roosevelt had his problems with the State Department and the British too. He told his son how people in the State Department had tried to conceal messages to him or delay them. He mentioned that they should be working for the British, and then added, "As a matter of fact, a lot of the time, they are." He felt that many of them thought our foreign policy should consist of finding out what the British were doing and copy that.[90] MacArthur showed his concern for American commercial interests in the Far East by resisting "British efforts to bring that unhappy land within the orbit of the Sterling Bloc."[91] Secretary Byrnes said, after the December 1945 Moscow meeting, that the British had really been more insistent upon greater participation than had the Soviets. "In Tokyo, MacArthur found constant British efforts to exploit the Japanese people one of the principal obstacles to his program for restoring Japan's shattered economy." The primary aim of the British was "to reduce Japan's competitive position in Asia. The British, however, did not give up easily and not many months before MacArthur was recalled from Japan in 1951, a senior British representative informally told him that the British Government was exerting every possible pressure upon Washington for his removal from Asia.[92] This does not speak very well for our British "friends" or for those senior American officials who permitted this form of pressure to be exerted on the United States Government.

The occupation had appeared successful enough to MacArthur so that he was able only eighteen months after the surrender, to announce that the Japanese were entitled to the restoration of full sovereign powers.[93] In contrast, this was a period of complete headache in Germany. France and Italy were fighting internally to keep from going Communist.[94] Great Britain was in dire economic straits, Eastern Europe was sinking further under the Communist heel and China was foundering in the midst of her war with the Communists. The postwar period was characterized by less bloodshed, but there was still much misery around the world. General Wedemeyer reported in 1947, that it gradually became apparent that the World War II objectives for which we and others made tremendous sacrifices were not being fully attained, and that there remained in the world a force presenting even greater dangers to world peace than did the Nazi militarists and the Japanese jingoists.[95]

The emotionally inspired drive for Total Victory and its chief manifestation, Unconditional Surrender, had resulted in an abortive war from the Allied view, and the cost of that war was unbelievable.

6. The Cost

As we have already seen in trying to determine the cost of World War I, this is a nebulous problem and varies greatly with sources of statistics and some basic assumptions made. Though there may be discrepancies in figures, there usually is general agreement on the order of magnitude of the various numbers arrived at. A good overall figure for the total deaths resulting from that carnage known as World War II is 40,000,000, approximately the population of France or Italy.[96] Regardless of how you view it, this is a staggering number of people to have been removed from the face of the earth at the hands of one's fellow man. Equally incomprehensible is when one tries to place a monetary figure on the cost of the war. The military expenditures reached astronomical figures, exceeding a trillion dollars. This war was seven times as destructive as the First World War, and the total of the direct and indirect costs was about four trillion dollars - four thou-sand thousand milion dollars.[97] These figures are certainly difficult to visualize. With the world population of 3 billion, that is enough money for over $1300 for each person in the world or almost $20,000 for each American. (These are wartime dol-lars and not adjusted for the rampant inflation since then.) If this cost were put into quarters (25¢ coins), there would be 66 stacks piled from earth to the moon, or with 32 stacks from earth to the moon, there would be enough left over for almost 21 stacks, each 10 feet high ($10,000), for every man, woman, and child in the United States.

The figures vary, particularly when it is at-tempted to determine the indirect costs. Paul Hoff-man stated that the "ultimate cost of World War II, before the last pension is paid, will be approxi-mately one trillion, three hundred billion dollars ($1,300,000,000,000).[98] The American share of the direct war cost was "roughly $335,000,000,000" or "approximately equal to the pre-war value of the en-tire national wealth in the United States."[99] This figure seems to be fairly well accepted. Another author listed the American war cost as $350,000,000,000

(including $50,000,000,000 for lend-lease against
which we received nearly $8,000,000,000 in "reverse
lend-lease" from the British and others). An unprecedented 40 percent of American wartime expenditures
were covered by taxes.[100] Much of the rest of it
went into the enormous public debt for which we pay
billions in interest each year.

About 80 million persons served in the armed
forces of the various nations. Approximately 15
million of them were killed. Millions of civilians
also perished in air raids, in concentration camps,
and from famine and disease.[101] We tend to forget
the terrible price paid in the civilian world in total war. It appears that more than two-thirds of
the deaths fell on civilians rather than soldiers on
the battlefield. A new term arose in this type of
war - genocide. It was only after Hitler revealed
his intention to destroy Poland as a nation "by killing off all natural leaders and intelligentsia"
that the Gestapo and other organizations began to
organize themselves for what was later to become
known as "genocide (until then it had been called
mass murder)."[102] The Nazi terror extended from executing hostages to exterminating Jews. They executed 29,660 French hostages during the war.[103] At
Nuremberg, the figure of 5,700,000 was given as the
number of Jews liquidated.[104]

Raymond Aron developed some casualty figures:
17 million for the Soviet Union (7 million military
and 10 million civilian) or about 10 percent of the
population; 4 to 5 million for Poland, about 15 percent of the population; 1.5 million in Yugoslavia or
10 percent; 3 million in Germany or 5 percent plus
the German prisoners lost in Russia and the loss in
births,[105] totaling some 27 million. Renouvin was
essentially in agreement with this estimate giving
the loss of human lives as exceeding 25 million.[106]
Fortunately, due to the lack of the stupid frontal
attacks of the first war, the second war was less
murderous than the first for the Western countries.
All of these figures here are without considering
the losses in China and Japan. Therefore, allowing
for errors and war-related losses, the figure of
40,000,000 dead is probably a good estimate.

The fighting to the end in the Axis countries
devastated those nations. Upon arriving in Japan,
the Americans found a nation on its economic death-
bed. Bare chimneys stood where commercial plants
had once operated. A very large percentage of Japan's industry was destroyed, and surrender came
when the country was geared entirely for war.

Consequently, Japanese plants which had escaped serious damage still were not prepared for peacetime operation. The vital textile industry was in chaos. Most of the merchant fleet was under the sea, and there was almost no food.[107] For an island nation that lived from the sea, this was catastrophic. The virtually complete destruction of Japan's merchant marine made difficult the restoration of her once great export trade.[108] During the war, the Germans milked the dominated countries for billions in "occupation costs."[109] Retribution was swift though, as the "scourge from the East" swept into Germany. There was no accurate record of the confiscated goods, but the West German Government estimated the worth of the dismantled and expropriated items as approximately $12 billion. The Soviets also profited from German patents and from the knowledge and labor of German scientists and technicians.[110] The heavy bombardment of cities in Japan left them as piles of rubble and over 20 percent of all housing throughout Germany was totally destroyed and another 20 percent was so badly damaged as to be uninhabitable.[111] All this destruction left millions homeless in both Germany and Japan. Germany, which normally produced 85 percent of her food consumption, was producing only 25 percent by 1947. The deficit, to the extent of preventing starvation, was made up by imports from the United States.[112] The denazification trials involving over a million people, most of whom were detained in prison, added to the burden and deprived the country of key individuals. This proved to be a real loss and a great waste of effort. By 1948, 85 percent of those who had been removed from office in Bavaria under the denazification program had been reinstated.[113]

The United States as the "arsenal of Democracy" provided an enormous amount of material to many different countries as well as building and transporting a large armed force of its own. One of the major sections of this aid was that given to the Soviet Union, which totaled over eleven billion dollars.[114] Not all of it was material that could only be used in the war. Great amounts of it had long-range value in strengthening the Soviet economy. Examples: a million and a half kilowatt capacity of electric power generating equipment, four huge aviation gasoline refineries, a 10-million dollar tire plant, thousands of machine tools, 50 million dollars worth of construction machinery, nearly 2000 locomotives, and 427,000 trucks - approximately half as many trucks as the Soviet Union had produced

251

in its entire history before the Nazi invasion.[115]
We cannot determine whether this aid was decisive,
but it certainly was significant.

One of the most drastic results of the war was
the "historical upheaval" particularly in Europe.
The great European loss was in its diminution of
prestige and reduced importance in the world more
than its dead and material losses. Western and Central Europe had long dominated the economic and political life of the world. The shock of World War I
brought a period of decline; little by little Europe regained some of her former influence. But, in
1945, not only were the results of this recuperation
wiped out, European interests in the general life of
the world were much more seriously damaged than they
had been twenty-five years before.[116] Great Britain,
which had been the great creditor nation, was now a
debtor nation, and she was dangerously low in foreign exchange. The government had to resort to ra-
tioning more drastic than during the war, and it was
an ironic and sad fact that the British, three years
after victory, were worse fed than the defeated Germans. The real irony of Great Britain's plight was
her losing in victory that which she had entered the
war to protect, namely her empire. It required a
massive effort to help the countries of Europe to
get back on their feet. China, one of the original
Allies was fated to lose her influence too. With
the defeat of Japan, Manchuria was returned to China.
The Russian surge into Manchuria, resulting in additional arms for the Chinese Communists, was followed
by intensification of the civil war that soon yielded the Communists the upper hand and the opportunity
to organize and launch the offensive that won control of China. The confused American support of
China did not help any.

Fortunately, the results were better in Europe
through the assistance brought to those countries by
the Marshall Plan. In the past it had been custom-
ary for victorious powers to take, not to give, and
there had been no departure from this evil custom in
the policy of the Soviet Union. "The Marshall Plan
set a new standard for which there was no comparable
historical precedent. It might be said that this
generous policy was in America's own interests, on a
long and enlightened view; but good deeds are not
the less good for being, at the same time, wise."[117]
This aid was not cheap and in the years since 1945,
the United States ended up giving money in some form
of foreign aid to almost every free or semi-free
(not completely Communist - and some of them have

received it, too) country in the world. This foreign aid grew to the astronomical figure of 150 billion dollars since World War II.[118]

It is possible to count the dead and roughly to
determine the value of destroyed buildings and
property, but there are so many intangibles that it
is really impossible to determine the cost of a war.
There are so many babies who were never born, historical and art treasures stolen and destroyed, morale and morals crushed, misery of the homeless and
countryless while they search for a new life, the
productivity that was not used and the path of history that may be forever turned to a new direction.
Nations of once proud and happy people disappear,
new nations are created, freedom may come to some
and it may be lost to others, peoples who one year
were abusing each other with the vilest sort of invective become closely allied in the face of another
threat, the marks on the minds of men and on the
souls of nations cannot be marked down on a piece of
paper. Total war and the desire to smash the enemy
into Unconditional Surrender are certainly expensive. The Casablanca formula added its weight to
that cost.

After the war, Ernest Bevin had pangs of conscience. The cost of rebuilding Europe and Japan
caused the victors to ask whether their demand for
Unconditional Surrender had been worth the price.
Billions of American dollars were spent rebuilding a
Germany that fought to total collapse rather than
accept surrender without conditions. "Now the armed
forces are debating whether to fight future wars the
same way or to plan for war and postwar problems together."[119] This last sentence, uttered four years
after the war, is one of the most fantastic ever
printed. If we could not learn from the mess we
made of World War II, we never will. As long as
there are people who see war as an end in itself
rather than only a means to an end, then that ridiculous question will continue to haunt us and cast a
long shadow across the future of man.

NOTES

1. Zemanek, "Unconditional Surrender and International Law," pp. 36-37.
2. Fuller, The Conduct of War, p. 305.
3. Baldwin, Great Mistakes of the War, p. 24.
4. Hankey, Politics, Trials and Errors, pp. 29-
31.

5. Hull, Memoirs, Vol. II, p. 1570. See also Mourin, Le drame des états satellites de l'Axe, p. 20.
6. Montgomery, The Memoirs of Field Marshal Montgomery (Glasgow: Collins Sons, 1961), pp. 364-365.
7. Woodward, British Foreign Policy, p. xlix.
8. Wilmot, The Struggle for Europe, pp. 122-123.
9. Ibid., pp. 713-714.
10. Truman, Year of Decisions, p. 209.
11. Goebbels, Diaries, pp. 144-145, entry of 26 March 1942. Unfortunately, over two months (21 December 1942-1 March 1943) of Goebbels' diaries are missing so we have no record of his comments on the Casablanca meetings or press conference.
12. Sherwood, Roosevelt and Hopkins, p. 695.
13. Fuller, A Military History of the Western World, Vol. III, p. 507.
14. Daugherty and Janowitz, Psychological Warfare, p. 273.
15. Armstrong, Unconditional Surrender, pp. 141-143. See also Guderian, Souvenirs d'un soldat, pp. 270-271.
16. Hankey, Politics, Trials and Errors, p. vii.
17. Miksche, Unconditional Surrender, p. 254, italics added.
18. Fuller, The Second World War, p. 259.
19. Fuller, A Military History of the Western World, Vol. III, p. 589.
20. Armstrong, Unconditional Surrender, p. 217. See Renouvin, Histoire des relations internationales, Vol. VIII, pp. 346-347 for Goebbels' fear of the Communization of Europe, and von Ribbentrop's idea of sending a threat to London and Washington threatening to stop the war and deliver Germany to the Communists.
21. Hankey, Politics, Trials and Errors, p. 52. See also p. 32 for how Stalin became reconciled to the policy of Unconditional Surrender which was to be so helpful to his plans for Eastern Europe.
22. Wilmot, The Struggle for Europe, pp. 708-709. See Lukacs, A History of the Cold War, p. 48, for the Allied aims. Britain was, after survival, looking for an European balance of power. Russia wanted to control Eastern Europe. American survival was not threatened so official United States aims became involved in a future world organization.
See Possony, A Century of Conflict, p. 207, for Stalin's prewar shifts. In the mid-1930s, the Soviet Union was too weak for war, so he reduced the pressure of the French Communist Party and accommo-

dated with "the United States, in line with Stalin's
alleged opinion that Victory will be won by the side
which is allied to the United States." Though Possony had no use for Stalin, he called him "one of
the great military captains of history," p. 248.
    23. Aron, The Century of Total War, p. 110.
See also Leahy, I Was There, p. 426.
    24. New York Times, 7 November 1948, p. 15.
    25. Wilmot, The Struggle for Europe, p. 716.
    26. Fuller, A Military History of the Western
World, Vol. III, pp. 458-459. On p. 450, he said
Roosevelt "obsessed by the collection of votes sedu-
lously cultivated the Communists and their fellow
travellers, who held the balance of power in New
York State.... It was the work of these agents which
deluded the President and thereby helped to shape
his war policy toward Russia."
    FDR recognized the Communist dictatorship
for what it was even if he seemed to forget it sometimes. The American Youth Congress met in Washington in February 1940. He was booed when he said,
"The Soviet Union, as everybody who has the courage
to face the facts knows, is run by a dictatorship as
absolute as any other dictatorship in the world."
Sherwood, Roosevelt and Hopkins, p. 138.
    See also Gunther, Roosevelt in Retrospect,
p. 366 for how the Russians let him down, and p. 386
for FDR's desire to get the Russians into a lasting
peace, and p. 387, "'Stalin? - I can handle the old
buzzard!' he told one intimate." FDR was in a hurry
to get things done before tempers cooled at home after the war - Stalin knew this and had no such problem.
    See also White, Majesty and Mischief, p. 46
for Roosevelt's love of power, p. 98 for his falli-
bility, and p. 118 for either-or: either he was the
"greatest man" ever or "the worst scoundrel ever
sent to the White House by a bemused and misbegotten
electorate."
    27. Neumann, Making the Peace, p. 101. See
Ivanyi, Route to Potsdam, p. 50, for the importance
of Russian views on the peace and how they were enhanced by every mile gained by the Red Army. See
also William Miller, A New History of the United
States (New York: George Braziller, Inc., 1958),
pp. 418-419. Even though Churchill was well aware
of the "menace of a victorious Stalin" he had "no
prescription for the peace to come except a return
to balance of power diplomacy." Fuller, A Military
History of the Western World, Vol. III, p. 631, recognizing that Churchill and Roosevelt "are to be

255

reckoned among the most prominent of the presidents and prime ministers of the United States and Great Britain," felt the only explanation for their fatal policy was "blind hatred! Their hearts ran away with their heads and their emotions befogged their reason."

28. See U. S. Department of State, Making the Peace Treaties, 1941-47, p. 3, for the Allied basic points of peacemaking: included the Atlantic Charter, United Nations Declaration which included complete victory and no separate peace, disarmament, denazification, unconditional surrender, and no punitive peace.

29. Miksche, Unconditional Surrender, p. 17. Fuller, The Second World War, pp. 24-25, pointed out that Britain is always for a balance of power on the continent, while France, protecting her eastern frontier, strives to keep Germany divided. These two policies are antagonistic. Wilmot, The Struggle for Europe, p. 717, felt that the military and political mistakes made by the Americans had to be so that they would learn for themselves that victory is not enough.

30. Major General John R. Deane, The Strange Alliance. The Story of Our Efforts at Wartime Cooperation with Russia (New York: The Viking Press, 1950), p. 43.

31. "Harry" is Harry Hopkins. Fuller, A Military History of the Western World, Vol. III, p. 548. In The Conduct of War, p. 275, he wrote, "This 'hunch' was the linch-pin in the President's pro-Russian policy, and it was to render abortive every victory won by the two great Western Allies, bring the Slavs to the Elbe, and replace Hitler by Stalin."

32. Admiral Ellis M. Zacharias, Behind Closed Doors. The Secret History of the Cold War (New York: G. P. Putnam's Sons, 1950) with Ladislas Farago, p. 53.

33. Langer, "Political Problems of a Coalition," Foreign Affairs, October 1947, pp. 86-88. See U. S. Department of State, Decade of American Foreign Policy, pp. 32-33, for Protocol on German Reparations. They were to be exacted by removals, annual deliveries, and by use of German labor. The basic "talking" figure was $20 billion with 50 percent to go to Russia. Churchill made a good observation about a starving Germany. "If you wished a horse to pull a wagon, he concluded, you would at least have to give it fodder." Stettinius, Roosevelt and the Russians, p. 132.

D. F. Fleming claimed that "East Europe was

given away not at Yalta but at Munich." The Cold
War and Its Origins (Garden City, N.Y.: Doubleday
& Co., Inc., 1961), p. 1041.
  See Zacharias, Behind Closed Doors, p. 56,
about the blunder by the Joint Chiefs. Of the two
Intelligence estimates, only the pessimistic one was
allowed to go forward to FDR. Also, on p. 58, the
explanation from Stalin by Bulganin to the Lublin
Poles, that "'The Yalta declaration is a scrap of
paper. It was necessary to satisfy Roosevelt and
Churchill - but we will not abide by it.'"
  See Stettinius, Roosevelt and the Russians,
p. 96, for "Military considerations of the highest
order dictated the President's signing of the Far
Eastern agreement. The military insisted that the
Soviet Union had to be brought into the Japanese
war." This insistence continued through the Potsdam
Conference and the first atomic bomb, p. 98.
  See U. S. Department of State, Decade of
American Foreign Policy, pp. 33-34, for the Agree-
ment Regarding Japan, whereby in exchange for Russian entry, they were to receive the status quo in
Outer Mongolia, southern Sakhalin and adjacent islands, the Kurile islands, a lease on Port Arthur,
Dairen to be internationalized, plus joint control
with China over some key railroads. FDR was to get
Chiang Kai-shek's concurrence since he had not been
a party thereto.
  34. Fuller, The Conduct of War, p. 294 or A
Military History of the Western World, Vol. III,
p. 584. See Whitney, MacArthur, for MacArthur's
shock at the concessions given, pp. 202-203.
  See Palmer and Perkins, International Relations, p. 857, for their explanation of this appeasement. The continued fear that the Russians might
make a separate peace "may have been a major element
in" the willingness of Roosevelt and Churchill to
grant concessions to forestall such an event. However, Langer, "Political Problems of a Coalition",
p. 89, felt this fear was "exaggerated" and that
there was no need to appease Russia.
  35. Stettinius, Roosevelt and the Russians, p.4.
He stated that FDR was under no illusions about the
Russians, pp. 25-26.
  36. Ibid., p. 309. Interesting that possibly
both Stalin and FDR were criticized for "concessions."
  37. Ibid., p. 295. Russian concessions listed
pp. 295-302. He added "What, too, with the possible
exception of the Kuriles, did the Soviet Union receive at Yalta which she might not have taken without
any agreement?" p. 304. For more on this same idea,

see Kennan, <u>American Diplomacy</u>, p. 85.

38. Gunther, <u>Roosevelt in Retrospect</u>, p. 388.

39. Leahy, <u>I Was There</u>, p. 426.

40. See U. S. Department of State, <u>Decade of American Foreign Policy</u>, pp. 36-38.

41. Miksche, <u>Unconditional Surrender</u>, p. 38.

42. Leahy, <u>I Was There</u>, p. 156, wrote, "There were times when I felt that if I could find anybody except Roosevelt who knew what America wanted, it would be an astonishing discovery."

See Fuller, <u>The Conduct of War</u>, pp. 308-309 for the views of Yale professor Nicholas J. Spykman about what aims should have been. He urged predominance in the New World and a balance of power in the Old. This did not require annihilation of Germany and Japan as Russian mastery of the areas would be no improvement over German or Japanese.

43. Neumann, <u>Making the Peace</u>, p. 100. He called the hopes of the Four Freedoms and the Atlantic Charter a "childish dream." "Those who sponsored this dream could not have been sincere in their hopes, and if millions believed, their faith is only a testimony to the power of propaganda."

44. Baldwin, <u>Great Mistakes of the War</u>, p. 10. He felt that we should barely have supported Russia and tried not to hurt Germany too much.

45. Fuller, <u>The Conduct of War</u>, p. 264. It is interesting that the Axis countries were more aware of the Communist menace than the West. On 6 November 1937, Italy joined the Anti-Comintern Pact with Germany and Japan. Von Ribbentrop even told the Duce that he considered asking England to join the anti-Communist countries, but that in England, the Communist peril was neither recognized nor understood. See Ciano, <u>Archives secrètes</u>, p. 123.

Sir Norman Angell, <u>The Great Illusion, Now</u>, p. 25, wrote in 1938 that "we are deeply divided as to whether a German or a Bolshevist Europe is the greater danger."

46. <u>The New York Times</u>, 24 July 1941.

47. Baldwin, <u>Great Mistakes of the War</u>, p. 9. For example of Stalin's propaganda, see Goodrich, <u>Documents on American Foreign Relations</u>, Vol. IV, pp. 615-616, for his speech before Supreme Soviet, 6 November 1941 - waging a "just" war of liberation, no conquests, "No interference of any kind with the domestic affairs of other nations!" See Averell Harriman, <u>Peace with Russia?</u>, pp. 10-11, for how "Stalin was well aware that to rally patriotism of the Soviet people he must proclaim the conflict as the "Fatherland War.'" "'We are under no illusions

that they are fighting for us,' he said, meaning the
Communist Party. 'They are fighting for Mother Russia.'"

48. Russia. Ministry of Foreign Affairs of the
U.S.S.R., Stalin's Correspondence with Churchill,
Attlee, Roosevelt and Truman, 1941-45 (Moscow: Foreign Languages Publishing House, 1957; New York:
Dutton & Co., 1958), p. 33. The theme throughout
this book starting with the first message from Stalin, was "open the second front" and send more supplies (planes, tanks, trucks, explosives, etc.).

49. Ibid., p. 35. Fuller, The Conduct of War,
p. 289, quoted Churchill as saying "We were as loyal
to our Soviet Allies as we hoped they were to us."

50. Hull, Memoirs, Vol. II, p. 1165. See Neumann, Making the Peace, p. 33, for division in American opinion on how to deal with the USSR.

51. See Einzig, Can We Win the Peace?, p. 13.
See also Fuller, A Military History of the Western
World, Vol. III, p. 547, about the futility of con-
tinuing the war since the political aim was lost.

52. Hull, Memoirs, Vol. II, p. 1247. See Goodrich, Documents on American Foreign Relations, Vol.
V., p. 55, for an address by Assistant Secretary of
State Berle, 4 April 1943, about Russia after the
war. "She will not, in our judgment, become the
victim of any urge to seize great additions to her
already huge empire." On p. 523 there is the record
of a press conference on 8 March 1943 by Admiral
William H. Standley, US Ambassador to Moscow, to the
effect that "news of important American aid was being kept from the Russian people and he suggested
that Russian authorities sought to give the impression that Russia was fighting the war entirely alone."

There was an interesting exchange between
Franco and Sir Samuel Hoare in February 1943. See
Guderian, Souvenirs d'un soldat, pp. 271-272. Franco
warned that the Russians would move into Germany and
would take over all of Eastern Europe. Hoare answered, "I cannot accept the theory that Russia will
be a threat to Europe after the war." (my translation). He stated that Russia would be too busy with
reconstruction and predicted that Britain would be
the strongest country on the continent.

See Woodward, British Foreign Policy, p.
290, for British policy on cooperation with Russia
after the war. They were willing "to go a very long
way in conceding Soviet demands" even though they
could not be sure of Russian good will.

53. Langer, "Political Problems of a Coalition,"
p. 83.

54. Deane, The Strange Alliance, p. 20.
55. Harry and Bonaro Overstreet, What We Must Know About Communism, p. 287.
56. Harry and Bonaro Overstreet, The War Called Peace. Khrushchev's Communism (New York: W. W. Norton & Co., Inc., 1961) p. 175.
  Harriman, Peace with Russia?, p. 12, wrote of Stalin, "His establishment of Communist regimes in Eastern Europe was designed not only to spread the faith but also to prevent anti-Soviet regimes from once more springing up on his western frontier. 'I will not tolerate a new cordon sanitaire...'".
57. Harriman, Peace with Russia?, pp. 3-4. Harriman was visiting Washington from his post as Ambassador in Moscow, where he had been, off and on, since 1941.
  At Yalta, Stalin agreed to a French zone of occupation but it was clear that he agreed only because it was to come out of the American and British zones; see Byrnes, Speaking Frankly, pp. 24-25.
58. Ibid., p. 5.
59. Byrnes, Speaking Frankly, p. 208, but we had asked them at Yalta.
60. Truman, Year of Decisions, p. 412. This proved all-important to Japan's recovery.
61. Lippmann, US Foreign Policy, p. 118.
62. Fuller, A Military History of the Western World, Vol. II, p. 449.
63. See Whitney, MacArthur, pp. 500-501, for MacArthur's views on our dissipation of military power and our disposition of our great stores of war materiel.
64. Eisenhower, Crusade in Europe, p. 457.
65. Met 11 September-2 October 1945 in London. Report on 5 October in U.S. Department of State, Decade of American Foreign Policy, p. 51.
66. See Ibid., p. 53.
67. Ibid., p. 73. The second meeting was held in two parts: 25 April-16 May 1946, report on 20 May; and 15 June-12 July with report on 15 July.
68. Ibid., p. 79. For the problems with Russia, see p. 73 ff.
69. Ibid., p. 82.
70. Ibid., p. 83.
71. Ibid., p. 84. By 1947 the combined American and British costs were up to $700 million a year, p. 109.
72. Ibid., p. 88. Conference was held 29 July-15 October 1946, with his report on 18 October.
73. Ibid., p. 89.
74. Ibid., p. 90.

75. Ibid., p. 91.
76. Ibid., p. 106. Meeting was held at London,
25 November-16 December 1947, Marshall report on 19
December.
77. Ibid., p. 109.
78. Ibid.
79. Ibid., pp. 920-933. Prepared for the Foreign Relations Committee 2 June 1948. Examples:
Germany (10 specific items), Austria (7), Poland,
Hungary (3), Bulgaria (6), Rumania (3), Korea (4),
Manchuria (3). The Russians have a reputation for
this sort of thing. Walter Kirchner, A History of
Russia (New York: Barnes & Noble, Inc., 1961), p. 20,
said "Breaches of treaties, fraticidal wars, and
civil disruptions mark the political history of Russia from the eleventh to the thirteenth century."
80. Ibid., p. 943, italics in original.
81. Ibid., pp. 634-635.
82. Whitney, MacArthur, p. 302.
83. Ibid., p. 297-299
84. Ibid., p. 297.
85. Ibid., p. 214. See also the Transcript of
the hearings before the Senate Armed Services and
Foreign Relations Committees, U.S. News, 18 May 1951,
p. 97. He felt Caesar's occupations were probably
the most successful in history.
86. Ibid., p. 216.
87. Ibid., p. 278.
88. Ibid., p. 284.
89. Ibid., p. 225. After MacArthur was relieved, the House of Representatives of the National
Diet passed a resolution of tribute and thanks of
the nation. "This tribute by the conquered to the
conqueror established for the guidance of historians
the contemporary judgment of the Japanese people and
their leaders upon MacArthur's role in the history
of Japan." p. 475.
90. Elliott Roosevelt, As He Saw It, pp. 204-
205. See pp. 35-39 for how FDR needled Churchill
about free trade after the war; pp. 121-122 for how
the British have carefully chosen their allies in
history. FDR did not intend to aid them just to perpetuate their Empire ideas. FDR mentioned, on p.163,
that the Chinese made us promise not to show the
British our air-maps before we were allowed to make
them. The Chinese were worried for British postwar
commercial reasons.
91. Whitney, MacArthur, p. 119.
92. Ibid., pp. 301-302. The British were experienced at this as they had also worked for Stilwell's relief in China. See The Stilwell Papers,

pp. 186 and 193.

93. Ibid., p. 294. On a per capita basis, the financial aid to Japan was one fourth of that extended to Germany - not counting the Berlin Airlift, p. 268.

94. Maurice Thorez, who had deserted France in 1939 and made his way to Moscow, had become Vice-Premier of the French government. "He had been amnestied by General de Gaulle who showed less leniency to many patriotic Frenchmen convicted by kangaroo courts of the resistance movement." Possony, A Century of Conflict, footnote p. 289.

95. Report of Fact-Finding Mission to China by Ambassador Wedemeyer, 19 September 1947. U.S. Department of State, Decade of American Foreign Policy, p. 705.

96. Palmer and Perkins, International Relations, p. 274. They credit this estimate to C. Hartley Grattan.

97. Ibid., p. 275, also from Grattan.

98. Paul G. Hoffman, Peace Can Be Won (Garden City, N.Y.: Doubleday & Co., Inc., 1951), pp. 160-161.

99. Statement by W.L. Thorp, 11 September 1946, in U.S. Department of State, Decade of American Foreign Policy, pp. 969-970.

100. Miller, A New History of the U.S., p. 396.

101. The 1962 World Almanac, Hansen, editor, p. 736, listed battle deaths as: Allies, 11,370,707; Axis, 5,328,494; for a total of 16,699,201. T. Dodson Stamps and Vincent J. Esposito, eds., A Military History of World War II (West Point: United States Military Academy, 1950), Vol. I, p. 669, gave a total of 15,304,500 for battle deaths and missing. They gave the Russian military losses as about 7,500,000, p. 281. Others gave total Russian losses between 15,000,000 and 20,000,000. Anne Armstrong, Unconditional Surrender, p. 158, listed the total German dead as 4 million. Westphal, in Freidin, The Fatal Decisions, p. 270, hoping for peace at the close of the book, feeling then that the Germans who died will not have died in vain, gave the figure 6 million for German dead. Toshikazu, Journey to the Missouri, p. 268, claimed the Japanese suffered 5,000,000 casualties.

102. Edward Crankshaw, Gestapo (New York: Pyramid Books, 1957), p. 114. On pp. 136-137, he gave examples of the massacres of the Jews. "Between June and October three hundred and fifty thousand were killed directly" by being herded out to mass graves, forced to strip, get on to the pile of bodies and were then shot. In two days 33,771 were

slaughtered on the outskirts of Kiev in the Babi Yar ravine.

103. Shirer, The Rise and Fall of the Third Reich, p. 1247.

104. Ibid., p. 1273, this was the so-called "final solution." See pp. 1259-1269 for his description of the extermination camps. See pp. 1274-1288 for his descriptions of the medical experiments conducted using human beings.

105. Aron, Century of Total War, p. 77. There is a misprint regarding Yugoslavia, giving the deaths as 15 million that should have been 1.5 million.

106. Renouvin, Histoire des relations internationales, Vol. VIII, p. 358.

107. Robert L. Eichelberger, Our Jungle Road to Tokyo (New York: The Viking Press, 1950), p. 269.

108. Ibid., p. 283. USSBS, Japan's Struggle to End the War, p. 11, "Eighty-eight percent of Japan's total merchant shipping available during the war was sunk." Submarines accounted for 55 percent. They started the war with 6,000,000 tons. According to Toshikazu, Journey to the Missouri, p. 268, they "lost 549 warships, approximately 2,500 merchant ships of over 500 gross tons each, and about 50,000 airplanes." There were terrible losses in the Atlantic also. Miller, A New History of the United States, p. 399, stated that "In 1940 and 1941, British, Allied and friendly neutral merchant marines lost eight and a half million tons of shipping to marauding U-boats - more than our entire output of merchant vessels in 1942."

109. Shirer, Rise and Fall of the Third Reich, p. 1230. He initially gave the figure 60 billion marks ($15 billion), of which about one half, 31.5 billion marks came from the French. He then referred to the USSBS and said Germany got from all conquered countries 104 billion marks ($26 billion).

110. Armstrong, Unconditional Surrender, pp. 241-242. We were operating under the ridiculous policy of trying to rebuild Germany at the same time we were dismantling her. This was finally stopped in 1951. On p. 234 she quotes from Germany reports, p. 203. "This report gives the following statistics for the total percentages of 1945 plant facilities which were dismantled between 1945 and 1951:

in the Soviet Zone........45
in East Berlin............33
in West Berlin............67
in the 3 western Zones..... 8."

A major American gain was from the rocket specialists

who went to the United States to work.

    111. Ibid., p. 230.
    112. Ibid., p. 236.
    113. Ibid., p. 237.
    114. Palmer and Perkins, International Relations, p. 856. Miller, A New History of the United States, p. 393, quoting from S.E. Morison and Henry S. Commager, "One year after Pearl Harbor the United States was producing more war material than all the Axis nations combined."
    115. U.S. Department of State, Decade of American Foreign Policy, p. 946. See Deane, Strange Alliance, pp. 93-95, for figures. 15,234,791 long tons arrived in Russia including over one billion dollars worth of machinery and industrial equipment.
    116. Renouvin, Histoire des relations internationales, Vol. VIII, p. 394.
    117. Arnold J. Toynbee, A Study of History, Vol. II, p. 330.
    118. U.S. News and World Report, 15 November 1971, p. 21.
    119. Ibid., 5 August 1949, p. 26, my italics. For this high cost, paid largely by the United States, "Mr. Bevin blames the 'unconditional surrender' policy and the subsequent ideas resulting from the Morgenthau plan." p. 28.

Part 3
Victory in the Nuclear Age

9
Spectrum of Conflict

> Regular warfare is the
> principal and guerrilla
> warfare the supplementary
> form.[1]
>
>   -- Mao Tse-tung
>
> If you wish for peace,
> understand war.[2]
>
>   -- B. H. Liddell Hart

By early 1945, the destructive power of war had reached a new high due particularly to the perfection of strategic bombing but due, also, to the general improvement of almost all phases of military destructiveness. With the entry of nuclear weapons into the deadly game of war, the issues became extremely complicated. Many military and political leaders have not yet been able to satisfactorily determine the role of this vast destructive power in future wars. The potential to destroy entire cities, and perhaps entire countries, has cast doubt on the concept of victory. Would it be "victory" if your country and the aggressor's were reduced to great piles of rubble with hundreds of millions of people left dead? This question is by no means settled and shows no evidence of any prospective settlement in the near future as we now anguish over parity, superiority, city-busting, improved accuracy, ABM, and SALT.

The world passed through a period of American monoply of nuclear devices, then a period of rising Soviet capability to approximate parity that is often referred to as the "balance of terror," and now a period of possible Soviet superiority in a five-

nuclear-power world. If the United States had been
so inclined, she could have displayed imperialist
tendencies with great success during the period of
nuclear monopoly. It is significant that she did
not, but, instead, drastically reduced her armed
forces and then helped to rebuild both her allies
and the defeated nations. One has only to ponder
the difference if the Soviet Union had had a monopoly on nuclear weapons during this period instead of
the United States. Even without them, this was the
greatest expansion period in the history of Communism.

Though the world has not found peace since the
Second World War, and has drifted into a new form of
conflict called a "Cold War," there has been no "big
war" between the Russians and the Americans. This
has quite possibly been due to the presence of nuclear weapons, although it is always difficult to
prove why something did not happen. Although the
rivalry between these two opposing systems of government and, more importantly, these two rival phi-
losophies of life, has not abated, war remains but
one form of antagonism throughout a broad spectrum of
possible conflict. The deadly conflict between Communism and anti-Communism is fought with all types
of weapons and techniques, with actual combat being
only the most extreme manifestation of this hostility. The rather easily defined bipolar postwar world
evolved into a more complicated power structure with
polycentric Communism, Europe, Japan, and other power centers in a world that grew from fewer than
fifty nations in 1945 to 150.

This spectrum of conflict runs the gamut from
peaceful competition (or peaceful coexistence),
through the many forms of tension (including economic, psychological and political), and strife (including rioting, border incidents) and extending all
the way to guerrilla warfare, to the various forms
of war (from limited to nuclear), and ending on the
other extreme in the possibility of mutual annihilation resulting from a thermonuclear holocaust. The
clear-cut titles are misleading as the true conflict
does not fit so neatly into word titles, but is usually a combination of two or more of these categories or a gradation thereof. Peaceful competition
goes on all the time without precluding the almost
ever-present forms of tension, and all of these may
be operating at the same time that a guerrilla war
is raging. The important point in the spectrum of
conflict is that there is neither war nor peace between the Free World and the Communists. It is all

a political conflict -- thought of in war terms.
Every act or omission made by the Communists, even
when the various Communist states do not act in harmony, is planned to play its role in the ever-present
drive to weaken or destroy the non-Communist world.
Unfortunately, there are still many who do not appreciate the seriousness of this conflict, thus
greatly complicating the ability of the Free World
to meet this threat to its existence.

The very expression "peaceful competition" (or
"coexistence") is itself a psychological warfare expression intentionally meant to deceive the peoples
of the Free World. The Communists intend it to be
neither peaceful nor, for the two camps, coexistent.
They are conducting a competition for the highest
stakes -- complete domination of the world and the
end of our freedom. Andrei Gromyko, Foreign Minister of the Soviet Union, speaking at the 24th Congress of the Communist Party of the Soviet Union,
6 April 1971, reminded us that peaceful coexistence
does not mean conciliation of ideologies. He implied continuation of the struggle for the triumph
of Communist ideas.

> Our party draws a distinct line of demarcation
> between the ideological struggle, which is in
> full blast and in which there can be neither
> peace nor truce, and our international rela-
> tions with the capitalist states, relations
> that are built on the Leninist principles of
> peaceful coexistence. The Soviet Union and its
> allies propose settling all international dis-
> putes by peaceful means through negotiations.[3]

When Khrushchev said, "We say to the leaders of
the capitalist states: Let us try out in practice
whose system is better, let us compete without
war."[4] he was facing reality. The prospect of thermonuclear rubble looks unpleasant to a Communist as
well as to us. As they have so well demonstrated in
the past, there are other ways to obtain power than
solely by the direct application of the force of
arms. But this competition in no way reduces the
basic goals of the conflict; it is merely a different means to the same end. To gamble the destruction of the Soviet Empire, or even some other Communist center, when perhaps the same results could
be gained in another way albeit more slowly, would
not be in the best interest of the Communists.

This competition extends to almost all domains
of modern life. International trade, cultural ex-

changes, scientific advancements, foreign aid, scholarships to students from other countries, and peace
drives are all carefully planned to secure an advantage for the Communists. Scientific competition has
been intense since the days of the drive to get a-
tomic weapons with the assistance of traitors such
as Fuchs and others; it reached a level of enormous
propaganda value at the time of the first Sputnik
and continued to grow with the space race. The
elaborate and well-financed Communist exhibits at
trade fairs reflect the value placed on this medium
by the Communists. The competition in Africa, Asia,
and Latin America is intense.

The Communists have extended thousands of scholarships to young people from the newly independent
countries or any place where they hope to stir up
unrest. They sometimes suffer setbacks, as shown by
incidents of racial discrimination against African
students in Moscow and the satellites, but they try
to gloss them over quickly and continue on their way.

Since Communism has not changed any of its
goals, there was serious anguish among some world
leaders in the 1950s and 1960s concerning dealing
with the Communists since they still professed intent to destroy us. One school of thought stressed
that as long as the Communists held that world revolution is preordained by history, then all conferences should be avoided. One of the leading advocates of this position was President de Gaulle of
France; however, he reversed his position with his
concept of a Europe to the Urals. The Americans
maintained the position that it never hurts to talk
and so have continued to try to bargain honestly
with the Communists. This is difficult though,
since they do not intend to give anything away and
are intent only on adding to their Empire and their
power. However, we have negotiated several treaties
including the nuclear non-proliferation and test
ban; arms limitation talks are in progress with the
Soviets, talks were held in Paris with the North
Vietnamese with regrettable final results, and President Nixon travelled to Peking and Moscow.

The Free World, wanting so hard to believe the
words "peaceful coexistence," permitted itself to be
lulled into a false sense of security. Still thinking in the old black or white terms of war or peace,
it did not keep its eye on the colors in modern
world politics. The countless combinations in this
spectrum add up to one and the same result -- war.
Although the Communists now operate with more finesse in some parts of the world -- however difficult

it may be to think of Czechoslovakia in terms of finesse -- it should be recognized that peaceful coexistence is war with no holds barred. This is a modern version of imperialist war -- a struggle as calculated to extend dominion as if territory were at stake.[5] This conflict is so relentless that even a language textbook is a weapon showing that the Communists want peace and the capitalists struggle for war; and little children in China were taught bayonet drill against a target on which is a picture of the American President. The "class struggle" continues and the only peace the Communists foresee as durable is the "proletarian peace" in the wake of the total victory of Communism.

1. Tension

Proceeding across the spectrum, after peaceful competition, we begin to encounter the first signs of friction between (and sometimes within) the two worlds. This restricted conflict we can refer to as Tension.

Tension heightens the senses of alertness and awareness as this story relates about the role of tension in life.

Every evening for six summers now Old Nosey, the raccoon, has been coming to our terrace toward sunset to receive the dog biscuits she relishes. She asks for her biscuits with dignified assurance, and likes to take them delicately from the donor's hand. But she is always apprehensive, always alert to run at any unfamiliar sound or threatening motion. And this is well. Like every form of dole, that which she gets from us is unreliable. When the house is occupied she can be sure of a meal which fills her small stomach to its highly elastic capacity. But occasionally this Bureau of Social Security is closed, and Old Nosey must and does fend for herself until reopening. If she were not so nervous I would not expect to see her again when I come back.

Anxiety, in short, is a function of freedom. Only the fully domesticated animal, only the enslaved human being, can or should expect a life devoid of continuous tension. From tension, indeed, all human progress springs.[6]

271

One of the arenas for tension between the two
worlds is international economics. World trade is
of vital importance to most nations both for the
sale of their products and to obtain international
exchange permitting them to buy the things they need
from other countries. Competition for markets can
bring nations to each other's throats. This is not
something new; several centuries ago, men-of-war and
merchant ships, naval captains and merchant captains
were interchangeable as war and commerce intermin-
gled.

When the economic policies of a nation are used
as another weapon in the arsenal of international
conflict, then we have economic warfare. Economic
warfare is defined as "all actions other than military taken to weaken or disrupt, the ability of an
enemy or potential enemy to provide economic support
for his national policy." Economic warfare is not
limited to periods of general war but can be employed in limited war or cold war and includes economic, political, and psychological actions.[7] Communist economic warfare aims for a bridgehead in the
transportation and communications industries and the
promotion of paralysis throughout the entire economic system.[8] In the 1970s, we have seen the effective use of oil as a political weapon. Communist
infiltration, and sometimes domination, of internal
organizations in free countries, particularly the
labor unions but often extending even into the government itself, presents a serious threat to the
Free World. Strikes called by Communist-dominated
labor unions are a powerful weapon in economic warfare and have more than once been the fuze that
marked the downfall of a free government.

The economic plight of the nations of Europe
after World War II and the threat of Communism pick-
ing up their pieces resulted in the Marshall Plan
for European recovery. Though it was also offered
to the Communists, they could not partake of a plan
that would potentially reduce their plans for expansion. "Zhdanov's statement of October, 1947,
that the Soviet Union would 'bend every effort in
order that this plan be doomed to failure' was in a
sense an open declaration of war."[9]

The great rivalry in the world manifested itself in the mid-twentieth century by trying to get
the underdeveloped or newly evolving nations to line
up with one of the two blocs (neither of which is
homogeneous). This resulted in much aid to those
nations but also much political pressure to draw
their governments into one of the camps. The

Communists promised them everything but were notably slow in delivering in most cases. The impatience of these countries in wanting immediately that which the older nations spent decades or centuries in developing only complicates the problem and often leads to disillusionment.

That economic warfare is an important part of the Communist plan of conquest has been pointed out by many authors but not always with much success. The arbitrary distinction between strategic and non-strategic goods seems naive in the total political context of Communist operations.[10]

Economic warfare has vast potential due to the economic weakness of so many of the countries of the Third World. In Latin America, where the military sometimes represents the largest educated body from which national leadership may be drawn, economic problems are legend. It is interesting to see that one country directed that senior military officers study economics, no doubt in hopes that with their influence they might be able to install some needed reforms.[11]

Conflict by use of economic means can pay high dividends to the Communists and may even yield them bonuses for their economy. Their "dumping" of aluminum in 1957 scared the leading aluminum-producing nations with a disruption of the market. The Communists made thrusts with other commodities such as platinum, tin, zinc, oil, and pulp. Relations with other nations are war to the Communists with international economic relations being only another battleground.

We have already reviewed psychological warfare above, under total war. Psychological activity and propaganda are an important part of all Communist actions across the full spectrum. They are a complementary weapon to all the other forms of conflict. Napoleon is credited with having said: "There are but two powers in the world, the sword and the mind. In the long run the sword is always beaten by the mind."[12] There can be little doubt that we are engaged in a long-term ideological war.

Propaganda is the big gun in the ideological arsenal of the Communist party in its quest for world domination. By means of "doublespeak," Communist propaganda attempts to destroy the very language of an opposing ideology. It becomes almost impossible to communicate since such words as democratic, liberal, peace, and justice have totally different meanings.[13]

There is a military maxim that calls for the

273

concentration of force at the decisive point. King-Hall carried this maxim beyond the battlefield: "We declare that in Total War this decisive point is to be found in the brains of the enemy."[14] The "object of war" is to make the "enemy change his mind." For propaganda to be effective in this effort, it should follow four golden rules: Truth -- Simplicity -- Practicability -- Necessity (it must satisfy a need.[15]

Though propaganda may substitute for force, to be credible it must have some evidence of supporting military power. If a very little country tried to put out threats, who would consider them? If, however, the same threats were made by the Soviet Union or the United States, then they would most likely be considered in world capitals. When Hitler was strong, Nazi propaganda was effective; today it is ludicrous.[16]

Both Lenin and Hitler were great advocates of war; however, they were also interested students of the war for men's minds and sought to win the psychological battle if possible. Lenin wrote: "The soundest strategy in war is to postpone operations until the moral disintegration of the enemy renders the delivery of the mortal blow both possible and easy." Hitler mused: "How to achieve the moral breakdown of the enemy before the war has started, that is the problem that interests me."[17] King-Hall asked the pertinent question: "Is the victory any less satisfactory because there are no human casualties?"[18] The Communist victories in Eastern Europe were in no way less important because the Red Army had fired no shots. On the contrary, it would seem that those victories should be considered among the greatest conquests of the Soviet Empire. Perhaps the lesson here is that one should not become obsessed with shooting wars and should remember that war is only one form of international conflict and not always the most decisive.

When we think of propaganda, many of us think of Goebbels, the little mouthpiece of Hitler, as one of the great masters. Paul Hoffman's evaluation of Goebbels in comparison with the Communists is then of some interest. "In comparison with the sleight-of-hand practitioners of Communist propaganda who confuse and warp men's minds, Goebbels was a neophyte and Machiavellian amateur."[19]

Though the Free World has generally maintained that Truth is the basis of good propaganda, this has not been so with the Communists. They have placed great emphasis on the Lie, a special-purpose weapon of propaganda. Hitler did not invent the "Great Lie." Lenin knew how to tell an effective lie and early recognized deceit as a useful tool of revolution.[20]

Admiral C. Turner Joy, who was the United Nations negotiator in Korea and had first-hand experience with the Communists, made some very interesting observations of how the Communists deal with the truth.

> Communists have two techniques with which to deal with truth. One: they deny it. Two: they distort it.

> The distortion of truth as practiced by the Communists is a science.[21]

> The simple fact is that with all respect to the military power of the free world, Truth is Communism's most dangerous enemy. Communism knows this, and therefore has become expert at fencing with Truth.[22]

> Americans find it difficult to visualize a breed of men who fight Truth at every turn, not just occasionally but always and repeatedly. Yet, the Communists are such a breed.

> By whatever means are most effective, they assault Truth. Indeed, dedicated as they are to the ascendancy of the greatest lie of history, they can do no other.[23]

The effective conduct of psychological warfare has never been one of the strong points of the Free World. President Eisenhower admitted this in a press conference in 1954 when he referred to propaganda as a field in which we do not seem to be as skillful as the other fellow.[24] This probably stems from our outlook on the rest of the world not being conspiratorial or officially missionary. Nevertheless, there are many opportunities for successful Free World propaganda. The whole world does not dance to a Communist tune. The Communists have their propaganda defeats and their uncomfortable moments. A good example was during the prisoner-exchange talks in the Korean War, when Communist prisoners refused to return to the "Communist paradise."[25] A similar incident occurred in 1971 when North Vietnamese soldiers refused to return to North Viet-Nam.[26] The Berlin Wall and the invasion of

275

Czechoslovakia no doubt had the Communist propagandists working overtime to refurbish their image. The wide news coverage of the various incidents with the African students should have been quite embarrassing to the Communists, particularly since discrimination is one of their favorite attacks against the United States. Such incidents should make deep impressions on the Africans and Asians and should open some eyes.

It is true that we try to reach the imprisoned peoples in the Communist orbit and the other peoples of the world by the Voice of America, BBC, and Radio Free Europe. Our effort is usually quite small in comparison with that of the Communists. The other problem is these programs are often jammed. The Communists cannot permit their people to hear the truth or other views. The Truth is what the Communist masters say it is and they cannot permit contradiction.

The question is whether there is enough emphasis on the Free World side for this important form of the conflict. We still have advocates for no American role in the "ungentlemanly game" of psychological warfare. During the war, King-Hall argued for equal importance for propaganda with military operations and the formation of a Ministry of Political Warfare with cabinet rank to take charge of all activities on the battlefield of the brains.[27] This should be all the more important now in a war that is many times more dangerous to our freedom than the second war ever was.

The Communists could be called the most complete politicians of all history for everything they do is first weighed for its political effects on their world plan. To refuse to accept this premise is to handicap oneself dangerously in this the greatest war of the history of mankind. The system that has as its very base the overthrow of our government never hesitates to employ its political weapons: the threat of rockets at the time of Suez or of Cuba, the refusal to deliver coal to France when her miners were on strike, the open threats to any country that supports the Western alliances, the support of imperialism such as Sukarno's (but in the name of anticolonialism), the support of rebellion, insurrection or revolution in any country against the incumbent government, plus a myriad of other examples too numerous to list. In a reversal of Clausewitz, politics to Communists can be called the continuation of war by other means.

True political warfare is not merely rivalry or

276

competition but a form of war whose objective is
power. And that power as it is realized may be at
the expense of our freedom. We, therefore, have the
most vital interest in the outcome of this great political war.

2.   Strife

As we progress farther toward the hot end of
the spectrum of conflict, we begin to encounter
clashes. One of the most basic forms of this strife
is rioting. We are all quite familiar with the
riots that have taken place in Venezuela, Paris, and
many other places in the world. There is rarely a
large riot in the world today that is not controlled,
manipulated, supported, or influenced by the Communists. This is not to imply that they involve a
large number of Communists; on the contrary, there
are often only a handful of them, but they often
play the key roles of leaders or instigators.

The Communists have openly stated that they
support revolution in other countries, or so-called
wars of national liberation. Khrushchev, in his 6
January 1961 speech, saw these wars as particularly
desirable from the Russian position and stated: "The
Communists fully support such just wars and march in
the front rank with peoples waging liberation struggles." This position has been reiterated on several
occasions by Communist leaders. More importantly,
they have actually supported revolutions throughout
the world, from Algeria to Laos, from Cuba to South
Viet-Nam.

This strife may take the form of insurrections
or sabotage, subversion or other forms of indirect
aggression. Stalin wrote in <u>Foundations of Leninism</u>:

> Never <u>play</u> with insurrection, but when begin-
> ning it firmly realize that you must <u>go to the</u>
> <u>end</u>. You must concentrate a <u>great superiority</u>
> <u>of forces</u> at the decisive point, at the decis-
> ive moment, otherwise the enemy, who has the
> advantage of better preparation and organiza-
> tion, will destroy the insurgents. Once the
> insurrection has begun, you must act with the
> greatest <u>determination</u>, and by all means, with-
> out fail, take the <u>offensive</u>. "The defensive is
> the death of every <u>armed rising</u>." You must try
> to take the enemy by surprise and seize the mo-
> ment when his forces are scattered. You must

277

strive for daily successes, even if small (one might say hourly, if it is the case of one town), and at all costs retain "moral ascendancy." (Lenin, Collected Works, Vol. XXI, Russian edition, pp. 319-320)"[28]

All of us are familiar with sabotage even if only through motion pictures; however, most of us are unaware that it has been occurring. Bernard Fall wrote that forty percent of equipment deliveries in the French war in Indochina had evidence of sabotage.[29] Sabotage has appeared throughout the world even in relative peacetime: there have been pylon bombings in the Tyrol, similar acts in France in the dying gasps of the Algerian War, oil fields and pipelines are favorite targets, and bombings even became a militant, juvenile sport in America.

Subversion plays a large role in the Communist plan of conquest. It is usually centered in the Communist embassies which are often abnormally large in comparison with those of other countries. Whether they are supporting the peoples of a small nation that is trying to gain its independence or whether they are trying to overthrow some other government, it is all a part of their plan to increase their influence. Subversion and indirect aggression have been developed by the Communists to a high level of art. These are their primary weapons of conquest while they keep their conventional and nuclear power in reserve as a threat to any country that resists.

Another form of strife is border incidents of which there have been many since the end of World War II. Almost every country with a border on the Communist World has experienced some form of border incident, and some have seen many repeat performances. There have been large numbers of such occurrences in the demilitarized zones in Korea and Viet-Nam. The two major Communist powers have even clashed over their own long border, particularly along the Amur River. The Chinese invasion of India in 1962, supposedly over border disputes, had the interesting twist of finding the Russians supporting the Indians against the Communist Chinese.

These border incidents often evolve into more active combat, such as the limited war that followed in Korea after the incidents of early 1950. They may also grow into guerrilla warfare. It is a paradox that since the advent of nuclear weapons, guerrilla wars, one of the oldest forms of warfare, have become the most common form of conflict. Raymond Aron wrote that "In Asia, guerrilla warfare is so changing the course of the world that the atomic age will perhaps also be called the guerrilla age."[30] He could have also included Africa and Latin America.

Guerrilla warfare can be conducted either in conjunction with conventional war or independently, as we have seen in recent years. It should not be underrated. Napoleon found the guerrillas quite disruptive in Spain, and the Grand Armée was the great fighting force of its day. Rear-area troops in areas with partisan activity are on continuous, nerve-racking alert, and such watchful waiting becomes very tiresome. As Cavour once remarked: "You can do anything with bayonets except sit on them."[31] Guerrilla activity put an edge on Sheridan's operations in the Shenandoah Valley of Virginia during the Civil War. Some of them were Colonel Mosby's, and others answered to nobody but themselves.[32]

When the Germans invaded Russia in 1941, they had a rude awakening. In the first war, the troops of the Czar were docile prisoners when cut off from their units, often marching to the rear with few or no German guards. However, from the very first day, the Germans had trouble with both Russian soldiers who were cut off and continued to fight and with civilians who joined in against the Germans. A German general, General Westphal, has described the effect of their activities:

> ... the Second World War saw another new development in warfare. This was the activities of the Partisans, which were on a scale far surpassing what had hitherto been associated with guerrillas. Particularly in the Eastern territories and in the Balkans, Partisans, often in very large formations, kept the German Army occupied for years on end. In the vast expanses of Russia the Partisans at times controlled whole districts...[33]

> The military significance of Partisan warfare can best be demonstrated by the fact that in Yugoslavia and Greece alone several Italian armies and a German army group of approximately twenty divisions were not only tied down by these irregular forces but even had, on occasion, the greatest difficulty in keeping their vital lanes of communications open.[34]

The Soviet partisans did not represent a popular uprising; the mass of the people took no part. Mainly it was the continued resistance of bypassed Red Army

279

groups, some scattered sabotage by personnel para-
chuted or infiltrated into the German rear, and the
operations of rapidly formed units of Communist
Party members and officials of the Peoples' Commis-
sariat of Internal Affairs (MKVD) to maintain some
degree of political control over the people or to
complete the destruction under the "scorched earth"
policy initiated by the Red Army.[35] The eastern
campaign was not lost in the rear areas -- partisans
do not usually win wars; but they can help prevent
others from winning them.[36] More recently, guerrillas won such as Castro and the Algerians.

This partisan concept is not dead. The French
have studied it thoroughly and the Yugoslavs base
their strategy on it. After the Soviet invasion of
Czechoslovakia and the proclamation of the Brezhnev
Doctrine, the Yugoslavs, in February 1969, implemented a defense strategy based on their World War
II partisan experience against the Germans. They
plan on instant mobilization of the territorial forces to support their army. Of particular interest
for defense programs of other countries, the Yugoslavs determined that they could arm half a million
territorial fighters for the cost of equipping one
conventional tank regiment.

It was in the mountains of Greece that the
world first became aware of the real conflict underway between the Communist and Free Worlds. This
little war had significant results in that it aroused
the United States to act after the British could no
longer cope with the problem. The stiffened position of the United States cured many people of some
of their dreams of American-Soviet cooperation. The
aid as directed by President Truman was instrumental
in defeating those guerrillas and maintaining the
freedom of Greece. Field Marshal Papagos pointed
out that the intention of the Greek ELAS partisan
force during World War II was not to assist the Allies in the war but to help Moscow after the war,
with the long-range objective of Soviet domination
in the Mediterranean.[37] This is similar to the situation in China during the war when the Nationalist
and Communist forces were more concerned with each
other than with the defeat of the Japanese invaders.
Mao Tse-tung is recognized by many as one of the
leading world authorities on guerrilla warfare for
his conduct of the civil war against Chiang Kai-shek
and for his guerrilla campaigns against the Japanese.

Mao pointed out that mobile warfare was the
primary form and that guerrilla warfare was to be

secondary against the Japanese. Although secondary, the guerrilla war was still extremely important. He added: "In the course of the prolonged, ruthless war, guerrilla warfare should not remain its old self but must develop into mobile warfare."[38] He demonstrated that a large force could conduct both mobile and guerrilla warfare. "The directive of the Eighth Route Army is: 'Basically guerrilla warfare, but lose no chance for mobile warfare under favourable conditions.'"[39] He handled this so well that it resulted in the defeat of Chiang Kai-shek and the emergence of Red China.

One of Mao's disciples, General Vo Nguyen Giap of North Viet-Nam, has shown how Mao's ideas of the protracted conflict and the use of guerrilla warfare were used in Indochina and resulted in the French defeat at Dien Bien Phu in 1954.[40] The Communists under Ho Chi Minh conducted guerrilla warfare against the French and, toward the end, expanded into large-scale operations with a regular army.

We place guerrilla warfare in a category somewhat different from war as we usually think of it because of its somewhat different political relationships. Guerrillas must have the support, voluntary or imposed, of the mass of the people. To assure this support they need some cause that is sympathetic to the people. The most common examples are a united effort against a foreign nation, land reform or other social change. Bernard Fall, later killed in Viet-Nam, stressed: "Guerrilla warfare, particularly against Communists, is as much a socioeconomic problem as a purely military problem; as long as this is not recognized, the West can expect a long losing streak of guerrilla wars, from Laos to the Congo or to Cuba."[41]

Guerrilla warfare or unconventional warfare or several other popular titles for it became the center of much attention in the 1960s, particularly due to the recognition given to the problem by President Kennedy. Conventional combat between regular armies aims at defeating the enemy in the field in order to gain control or change the policy of a state. Unconventional warfare is profoundly different in that its strategy is to win control of the population first in order to gain control of the state. The Communists have been successful because they thoroughly approached the population control requirement through positive use of political doctrine and a brutal, negative use of terrorism against those who did not voluntarily follow their leadership. Having mastered guerrilla warfare, they attacked countries

contiguous to the Communist World thus providing a
haven for training, rest, and the clandestine introduction of supplies. Also, they have effectively
exploited pent-up anti-colonial hatreds and frustrations with slow economic improvement. This has
generally been an unbeatable combination.[42]

The concept of "sanctuary" is the most frustrating problem in the current style of guerrilla warfare as conducted in the Communist war. It was even
a problem in the limited war in Korea; it was a continuous problem in Thailand, Laos, and South Viet-
Nam. The 1970 operations into Cambodia and Laos
were a major change in policy and came after years
of frustration. It has even appeared in Africa
where, due to the wildness of the area or sympathy
of neighboring governments, sanctuary appeared in
the strife in Algeria, Angola, Sudan, and the Congo
as examples. The war in Greece withered after Yugoslavia closed its border with Greece. Communist
terrorism in Malaya began to fade only when Thailand
finally policed its border more effectively and permitted the Malayan-British forces the right of hot
pursuit in a fairly deep zone along the Thai-Malayan
border. The problem of the active sanctuary must be
solved politically as well as militarily if the West
is to cope successfully with "brushfire wars." Guerrilla forces are by no means invincible; however,
considerable rethinking of the strategic premises of
Western military concepts might be required.[43] This
was initiated using as the base the idea of "Flexible Response" of General Maxwell Taylor. Unfortunately, the war in Viet-Nam badly soured many Americans and will probably stultify tactical and strategic development in this crucial area.

Counterguerrilla operations are basically political more than military; they must have a solid
political base or their military efforts will be
futile. The first step in mobilizing a civilian
population against Communist subversion and guerrilla attack is to establish political goals that the
average person can understand. Communist guerrilla
forces were suppressed and ultimately defeated in
Malaya and the Philippines, for example, when the
strategy consisted of aggressive operations in the
guerrilla areas to maintain the initiative and to
apply pressure, in conjunction with major political
programs, to win back and protect the population.[44]
There is one important fact about these two campaigns; neither Malaya nor the Philippines borders
on a Communist country, thereby excluding active
sanctuary. The Thai border did aid the Malayan

Communists but to nowhere near the extent of the aid received in Laos and South Viet-Nam from the north. Fighting in the face of active sanctuary is somewhat like trying to sweep out your house during a sandstorm while leaving the back door open.

During the long years of the war in Indochina, many French officers were captured by the Communists particularly at Dien Bien Phu. Their treatment in the prison camps and their observations of Communist Chinese techniques drove many of them to the conclusion that this brand of warfare could be defeated only by adopting similar techniques. This was the basis for the idea which swept through the French Army like wildfire -- la guerre révolutionnaire -- or Revolutionary Warfare: the new form of limited war combining political indoctrination and propaganda with new techniques of orthodox military tactics. Some French officers, with experience in Indochina and Algeria, felt that, since nuclear weapons can easily be stalemated, Revolutionary Warfare was the wave of the future to win for the West vast areas of Africa, Asia, and Latin America, areas largely unamenable to other types of war. [45]

One French author described it as a "combination of modern propaganda methods and of the political cadre systems developed by the Communist parties" consisting of three principal traits: "parallel hierarchies," "brainwashing," and "subversion." These are the weapons used by the Soviet Union in the third world war, which had already started (these French officers said). This "subversion" threatens to destroy the Western World from within; therefore, they feel that these same weapons needed to be used but with an opposing doctrine, since one cannot fight the methods of Revolutionary Warfare except by the same methods. [46] The method has yet to be proved or disproved as the French Algerian situation ended by granting independence.

That strife is an important segment of the continuous war being waged by the Communists is quite evident when one reviews the history of conflict of the years since World War II. There have been over 400 conflicts since 1945 (incidentally none with a declaration of war). [47] The fighting in Southeast Asia, the Middle East, South Asia, and Africa and the chronic troubles in Latin America indicate that the problem will remain with us for the foreseeable future. This "indirect aggression" works to the Communist advantage better than direct aggression. They learned from Korea that direct military attack even when carried out by a proxy awakens the Free

World and makes it fight. However, the Free World
has not found a formula to combat indirect aggression where Communist military equipment, advisors,
technicians, and if necessary "volunteers" or even
regular troops as long as they are not acknowledged
are fed in to a local Communist-run insurgency. This
technique has worked well for the Communists as they
can vary the pressure as they want, keep it going
indefinitely, and most importantly keep the initiative.[48]

3. War

The spectrum now opens into the more accepted
form of conflict -- war. War, though, is no longer a
simple matter of opposing armies meeting on a battlefield; it is a very complicated relationship with
varying degrees of intensity. The first of these is
something that we have heard and read much of in recent years -- limited war. Henry Kissinger wrote:

> In the history of warfare, limited wars between
> major powers have been a frequent occurrence.
> For a long time, however, they remained limited
> less by conscious choice than by considerations
> of domestic policy. In the seventeeth century
> Louis XIV employed almost his entire army for a
> period of close to twenty-five years. Still
> his military establishment utilized only a
> small proportion of the national resources be-
> cause of a domestic structure which prevented
> him from conscripting his subjects, levying in-
> come taxes, or confiscating property. His mil-
> itary establishment was therefore limited by
> the availability of resources and so were the
> wars he fought.[49]

Limiting wars is particularly important for nuclear powers. For them it is armed conflict involving their interests with some commitment of their
prestige, but with voluntary restraints upon the employment of armed force. Such war is limited because the participants want to limit it and because
they are successful in limiting it. Therefore any
war involving a great nuclear power will be limited
in spite of the fantastic capabilities even though
the war may well seem (and in fact actually be)
quite unlimited from the points of view of other
participants.

These limited or non-world or little wars have
been with us throughout the course of history. They
are just as frequent and at least as important as
before. They pose almost the same problems of tactics, strategy, and policy as half a century ago.
We find ourselves face to face with a paradox: an
enormous discontinuity of experience in the conduct
of large wars which nobody wants to fight and striking continuity of experience in the conduct of little
wars which half the world is fighting.[50] We have
lived under a continuous threat of both limited and
total war since 1945. The Communists have managed
this threat in a skillful manner to their advantage.
Limited war is an important aspect of Communist
strategy calling for limited war -- at least until
the decision is made for total war -- and meanwhile
a continuous threat of total war.[51] On the other
hand United States policy toward the role of limited
war has been inconsistent and confused. Referring
to limited wars in general, General James M. Gavin
wrote that Secretary of Defense Charles E. Wilson
said: "We can't afford to fight limited wars. We
can only afford to fight a big war, and if there is
one that is the kind it will be." Gavin felt that
if we cannot afford to fight limited wars then we
cannot afford to survive, for that is the kind we
will face and the only kind we can afford to fight.[52]

The Korean War, which will be treated in a separate chapter, had an important impact on American
thinking concerning limited wars. It resulted in a
distinct American aversion to limited wars. (An important lesson is that public memory rarely exceeds
ten years; we were soon involved in Viet-Nam and
then disillusioned again.) With the coming of the
policy of Massive Retaliation, we renounced the local war method which had been used to stop the aggression in Korea. The United States wanted no more
local wars. This left us in the uncomfortable position of having to choose between the unpleasant
prospect of a general war or conceding limited objectives to the Communists. By keeping the limited
objectives small enough so that we did not value
them highly enough for general war, the Communists
continued to make progress in their drive for world
domination even in the face of overwhelming nuclear
superiority which we were and are reluctant to use.
Herman Kahn wrote:

> ... we must be willing to fight wars on a local
> and limited basis. A myth has grown up in the
> United States that Korea is an example of a

285

U.S. "defeat." From many standpoints, this is
not so. We gained a great deal from our Korean
experience. We built on our Preattack Mobilization Base; we displayed military firmness;
and we provided an example of how to fight a
"limited" war. Conflicting estimations of the
success of our efforts in Korea are due to the
fact that Americans never accepted their necessity, perhaps because of a weakness in explanation -- or possibly more fundamental reasons.
As a result, there was a tremendous animosity
aroused against those responsible for waging
the war. I do not know if it is possible to
explain to a democratic public the rationality
and necessity for being willing to fight limited
wars. If it is not possible, I predict a very
dim future for democracy in our troubled era.[53]

Kissinger has written extensively about limited
war:

It is therefore misleading to reject a strategy
of limited war on the ground that it does not
offer a military solution to our strategic
problem. Its merit is precisely that it may
open the way to a political solution. Had we
defeated the Chinese Army in Korea in 1951, the
U.S.S.R. would have faced the problem of whether the risk of expanding the war was worth
keeping China from suffering a limited defeat.
Had we followed up our victory with a concilia-
tory political proposal to Peiping, we could
have caused it to reconsider the wisdom of being too closely tied to the U.S.S.R. Even if
we had failed in our primary task of dividing
the U.S.S.R. and China, we would have greatly
improved our position toward our allies and
even more toward the uncommitted nations in
Asia. The best counterargument to the charge
of colonialism is political moderation after a
military victory.[54]

Limited war is something that is with us and
has been with us for a long time. We can expect
more of it in the future whether it is in the fuzzy
area of guerrilla operations that may evolve into
more open operations such as happened in Indochina or
whether it comes as local wars in Africa, Asia, or
Latin America. Regardless of where it comes, it
will involve the interests of the Free World because
the Communists thrive on strife and confusion and

286

will try to turn any war to their advantage. The motely conglomeration of units called states in Africa has suffered growing pains as new combinations or divisions are tried or forced to find a viable system for government. The unrest in Latin America continues. The Arab-Israeli feud in the Middle East, the problem of Bangladesh, the continued war in Southeast Asia, and the Soviet moves into the Middle East and the Indian Ocean all show that Asia will remain unsettled for some time to come.

Although there are "hot" lines, visits, and negotiations, there is still an enormous gulf between the two worlds and they clash on almost every point in world relationships. If one side is tempted to use force on a small scale and if the only counter the other side has is to commit suicide by starting a thermonuclear war, that side is not likely to act. "Therefore, one needs Limited War capabilities to meet limited provocations."[55]

Kissinger discussed at length a possible doctrine of limited war.[56] Such a doctrine must be faced without illusions; it is not a cheaper substitute for massive retaliation; and, in this nuclear age of plenty, it is no longer possible to impose unconditional surrender at an acceptable cost. The purpose of limited war is to make the cost to the enemy out of proportion to his objectives. Such a strategy cannot depend upon military considerations alone but must reflect harmony between political and military objectives. A nuclear exchange may result if one side tries to force the other to surrender. "Limited war and the diplomacy appropriate to it provide a means to escape from the sterility of the quest for absolute peace which paralyzes by the vagueness of its hopes, and of the search for absolute victory which paralyzes by the vastness of its consequences."[57]

Being prepared to meet the many possibilities that exist across the spectrum of conflict requires a considerable military force in being. As Raymond Aron observed: "The world is living in a limited war. A semi-war requires semi-mobilization." He added that, "The United States is learning that great powers must maintain their army, navy, and air force, and not disband them immediately following victory."[58]

Man is a complicated and generally unpredictable quantity. It is impossible to say that future wars will be fought with nuclear weapons. In the First World War, chemical gases were introduced with good military results, yet the entire Second World

287

War was fought without their use even though much more efficient and deadly gases had been developed and were available at all times. Who can say that the same will not happen to nuclear weapons? Regardless, the planning must go forward with the assumption that the enemy will use them, otherwise a country would leave itself so vulnerable as to tempt the enemy to use them even if he had not planned to. Considering the destructive potential of these weapons, a country cannot afford this risk.

Korea was a limited war, yet to the Chinese it might well have been a general war as it was an all-out effort on their part. The large standing armies of the Communist World are a constant reminder of the possibility of a large war without the use of nuclear weapons. This requirement to be prepared to face such a spectrum of war obviously complicates national security policy.

The advance of technology since 1945 has resulted in a vast array of nuclear weapons from sub-kiloton yields to the monster megaton weapons. This permits limited wars fought with "tactical" nuclear weapons or even a large war fought with smaller yield weapons. Thus war grows ever more complicated. The resort to nuclear weapons in limited war would sacrifice the one unambiguous boundary marker between levels of violence although there is no certainty that this boundary holds that much importance. The problem of escalation -- from smaller to larger and larger yields until finally there is all-out war -- will have to be weighed by each government concerned in the same manner that they weigh any other large political-military problem in time of war. They must weigh the results to be gained against the price to be paid.

Although two atomic weapons were used against Japan, there has not yet been a nuclear war so the policymakers are still floating in a sea of theory. From the hundreds of nuclear tests conducted, there has come a great mass of information but there are still many blanks in the picture, particularly concerning new developments since the test ban. We have a fairly good idea of the effects on cities but the effects of fallout are less well known. The possibility of killing hundreds of millions of people in a nuclear war is now accepted but it is not clear how many might continue to be lost from residual effects.

Some people contend that our possession of nuclear weapons prevented a world war; although there are others quick to point out that it cannot be

288

proved one way or the other. Lukacs wrote: "these weapons have served as a defense of freedom but also as a restriction of freedom; they were (and still are) instruments of utmost potency as well as of historic impotence." As he noted, "an atomic war, for the sake of Hungary, was politically unthinkable."[59] Events have shown the same general feeling prevailed regarding Cuba, Viet-Nam, and Czechoslovakia.

There are nuclear weapons on station nearly all over the world, in ballistic missiles in underground silos, bombs, air-to-air missiles, mines, depth charges, artillery, and many forms of short-range ground-to-ground missiles. There are air-to-ground missiles to help bombers penetrate defenses, ground-to-air missiles to attack bombers, anti-ballistic missile missiles, and the Polaris and Poseidon missiles launched from under the sea. This plethora of destruction and deterrence has become complicated with MIRV (multiple independently-targeted reentry vehicles) warheads, LOBS (limited orbit ballistic system) coming from space even though there is a treaty precluding nuclear weapons in space, and ULMS (undersea launched missile system) which is expected to have a 6,000 mile range. One of the largest concentrations of these warheads is in Europe where the NATO forces are on constant alert in the face of the Red Army. Some in the West believe that the use of any nuclear weapons in a war involving NATO would mean the opening of the Third World War -- there are indications that the Soviet leaders agree.

This inflexibility is complicated by advocates of a war of only a few hours. They hold that after the great exchange of missile and bombs the war will be settled. The Communists, however, have remained true to their theory of protracted war and realize that there will be much more to any war than just a simple exchange of devastating weapons, and contend only that success in the nuclear phase could lead to eventual victory.[60]

The range of intensity of nuclear war could be rather wide reaching from restricted use of small or "tactical" weapons through the free use of a great variety of kiloton and megaton warheads to the all-out use of the monster or Doomsday bombs. The first part could be similar to war as we have known it and the latter could be pointed toward what some people fear as annihilation.

Herman Kahn and his colleagues researched the subject of annihilation quite thoroughly and concluded that at present any picture of total world

289

annihilation appears to be wrong.[61] There is no
doubt that an enormous amount of damage can be
caused and hundreds of millions of people killed,
but that is still not annihilation, so the popular
expression "mutual annihilation" is more figurative
than literal. Technology may bring this ridiculous
ability to man in the future but it has not yet arrived.

In this great Communist War of the twentieth
century, we find man faced with a spectrum of conflict the likes of which man has never before seen.
Every act of the Communists -- whether it be a
cultural exchange or infiltration into a foreign labor union or government, whether it be inciting foreign students to riot against their government or
the support of foreign guerrillas -- is all a part
of their world plan. This spectrum of conflict is
really the epitome of total war for it represents
the whole nation at war. The only difference on the
Free World side is that there are still some people
who prefer not to admit that there is any war in
progress; they are still waiting for the formal declaration of war. They cannot see that it was made
by Karl Marx in the last century and that it has
been reiterated in large type by every Communist
leader since.

Victory in this form of struggle is the greatest challenge of the history of mankind. "In the
kilomegaton world it becomes more difficult to win,
but it is still very easy to lose."[62]

NOTES

1. Mao Tse-tung, Selected Works (New York: International Publishers, 1954), Vol. II, p. 278.
2. B. H. Liddell Hart, Strategy (New York:
Frederick A. Praeger, Publishers, Second Revised
Edition, 1967), p. 373.
3. Gromyko, Vital Speeches of the Day, Vol.
XXXVII, No. 14, 1 May 1971, p. 429.
4. "On Peaceful Coexistence," Foreign Affairs,
October 1959, p. 4.
5. See The Overstreets, What We Must Know About
Communism, p. 276.
6. Felix Morley in Nation's Business, reprinted
in Reader's Digest (July 1961), pp. 151-152
7. George A. Lincoln, Economics of National
Security (New York: Prentice-Hall, Inc., 1954),
p. 522.
8. Kintner, The Front is Everywhere; Militant

Communism in Action (Norman: University of Oklahoma Press, 1950), p. 207.

9. Palmer and Perkins, International Relations, p. 616.

10. Karl H. Cerny wrote: "...the Soviets hope to undermine the trade embargo imposed by the West, to divide the western allies, and to secure a more 'friendly' attitude toward the Communist orbit. In view of these multiple objectives, it is at the very least questionable whether the western distinction between strategic and nonstrategic goods may not run the danger of ignoring that, to the Communists, trade and the offer of trade in all types of goods play a strategic role in their world wide campaign of unconventional war." Cerny,"The Popular Front: Its Politics, Sociology, and Economics," US Congress (84th), House Committee on Un-American Activities, Soviet Total War, p. 435, italics in original. Salvador de Madariaga wrote of East-West trade: "This business nearly always consists in capital goods, industrial equipment, whole factories. How wise is it to equip your adversary?"..." it arouses in the Western nations commercial rivalries that divide them; and it helps to soften the embargo on the trade in strategic goods. One of the British businessmen who went to Moscow for business, during a reception at the Soviet Ministry of Foreign Trade, unable to resist the fumes, not of Crimean champagne, but of Soviet contracts, drank to the abolition of the embargo on strategic goods.... British Labour Government exported two Nene aviation engines to the Soviet Union, which enabled the Soviet Air Force to develop the M.I.G.'s, and everyone knows how successful the M.I.G.'s were in Korea. East-West trade, therefore, often represented as a purely economic affair, is always political. Indeed, everything in the realm of relations with the Soviet Union is political; and sooner or later will be used as a political weapon in the cold war." The Blowing Up of the Parthenon; or How to Lose the Cold War, pp. 35-36.

11. "Some Peruvians expressed the hope that the senior officers of the Peruvian Army, all of whom are required to take advanced studies in Peru's social and economic problems, may make a start on reforms which previous Governments could not get through Congress." U.S. News & World Report, 13 August 1962, p. 61.

12. Quoted in King-Hall, Total Victory, p. 28.

13. Kintner, The Front is Everywhere, pp. 202-203.

14. King-Hall, _Total Victory_, p. 35, italics in original.

15. Ibid., p. 37. These are good rules and are encountered in other texts in many variations.

16. Paul W. Blackstock wrote: "As an instrument of controlled revolution, totalitarian propaganda aimed abroad is likewise a substitute for violence and, like its domestic counterpart, is only taken seriously to the extent that it is backed up by the threat of armed force in the background. For example, in his early beer-hall days, no one paid much attention to Hitler. But when his armies were posed for attack in 1939, the _triste fou de Berchtesgaden_ (as certain French circles described him) had to be taken seriously." "Indirect Aggression," _U.S._ Congress, _Soviet Total War_, p. 35, italics in original.

17. Quoted in King-Hall, _Total Victory_, p. 104.

18. Ibid., p. 204.

19. Hoffman, _Peace Can Be Won_ (Garden City, N.Y.: Doubleday, 1951), p. 134.

20. Kintner, _The Front is Everywhere_, p. 204.

21. Joy, _How Communists Negotiate_ (New York: Macmillan, 1955), p. 102.

22. Ibid., p. 103.

23. Ibid., p. 118.

24. _U.S. News & World Report_, 20 August 1954, p. 81.

25. "The revelation that about seventy thousand Chinese and North Korean POWs would fight to block any move to send them to Communist homelands was a serious propaganda blow to the Reds. In particular the Communists were hurt by the fact that fifteen thousand of the twenty thousand Chinese we held prisoner had declared they would rather die than return to communism. These were fifteen thousand of the Chinese the Reds claimed were 'volunteers,' who left their homeland of their own volition because they were filled with zeal to fight the 'American aggressors' in Korea." General Mark W. Clark, _From the Danube to the Yalu_ (New York: Harper, 1954) p. 37.

26. Saigon announced, 31 May 1971, that only 13 of 660 prisoners screened by the International Red Cross wished to go north. North Viet-Nam refused to accept them. _Facts on File_, 3-9 June 1971, p. 418.

27. King-Hall, _Total Victory_, p. 208.

28. In Ebenstein, _Great Political Thinkers_, p. 715, italics in original.

29. "According to a French parliamentary inquiry, about _forty_ percent of the equipment delivered to Indochina arrives with evidence of sabotage: sugar in gasoline tanks, emery oil in transmission

gears, torn or broken electrical wiring. Even e-
quipment delivered directly from the United States
to Indochina is often sabotaged." Street Without
Joy: Indochina at War, 1946-54 (Harrisburg, Pa.:
Stackpole, 1961), p. 237, italics in original. This
is not too surprising when one recalls the Communist
influence in the longshoremen's unions around the
world. That is exactly the reason why the Communists have spent years building their position in
these unions. We tend to ignore this sort of thing
but, in the future, American soldiers may die overseas due to such actions.

30. Aron, The Century of Total War, p. 158.
31. Charles A. Willoughby, Maneuver in War
(Harrisburg, Pa.: Military Service, 1939), p. 219.
32. Catton, A Stillness at Appomattox, p. 282.
33. Freidin and Richardson, The Fatal Decisions,
p. 223.
34. Ibid., p. 224.
35. Howell, The Soviet Partisan Movement, p. 42.
It is interesting to note that the Russians had organized "Proletarian Rifle Divisions" as guerrillas
as early as 1937 to be left behind against the Germans. See Joseph E. Davies, Mission to Moscow, pp.
477-478.
36. Howell, The Soviet Partisan Movement, p. 98.
37. Atkinson, "Communist Unconventional Warfare," U.S. Congress, Soviet Total War, p. 23.
38. Mao Tse-tung, Selected Works, Vol. II, p.
224, see also pp. 119-153 and 277-280.
39. Ibid., p. 225.
40. General Vo Nguyen Giap, People's War People's Army (Hanoi, Foreign Languages Publishing
House, 1961), p. 30 for the change from guerrilla to
mobible warfare, p. 48 for how guerrilla warfare is
suitable for an economically backward country to
fight a modern country, pp. 98-112 for the "long-
term resistance war" and guerrilla warfare and
eventually advancing into mobile warfare, and pp.
151-217 for his comments on Dien Bien Phu and the
actions thereafter.
41. Fall, Street Without Joy, pp. 308-309.
42. See Lindsay, "Unconventional Warfare,"
Foreign Affairs, January 1962, pp. 264-265.
43. Fall, Street Without Joy, pp. 294-296.
44. Lindsay, "Unconventional Warfare", pp. 268-
269. The end of the Huk campaign in the Philippines
brought a big surprise to the Philippine president.
"Each member of the Politburo was arrested. To
Magsaysay the greatest surprise was Jose Lava, the
head of the Politburo. He was a quiet university

professor with whom Magsaysay had innocently been having lunch every week or so. It was this unobtrusive professor who had planned Magsaysay's death." Douglas, North from Malaya, p. 112.

45. See Fall, Street Without Joy, p. 279. One author has described the use of nuclear weapons against guerrillas as: "A nuclear weapon has no more hold on a guerrilla than a cannon on a fly." Gaston Bouthoul, Sauver la guerre, p. 117.

46. Maurice Duverger, La Cinquième République (Paris: Presses Universitaires de France, 1960), p. 260.

47. Jesse Orlansky, The State of Research on Internal War (Arlington, Va.: Institute for Defense Analyses, Research Paper P-565, August 1970), p. 9.

48. See Finletter, Power and Policy, p. 101.

49. Kissinger, Nuclear Weapons and Foreign Policy, p. 138.

50. William K. Hancock, Four Studies of War and Peace in this Century, p. 17.

51. Lincoln, Economics of National Security, p. 380.

52. Gavin, War and Peace in the Space Age, p. 124.

53. Kahn, On Thermonuclear War, p. 529.

54. Kissinger, Nuclear Weapons and Foreign Policy, pp. 148-149.

55. Kahn, On Thermonuclear War, p. 12.

56. Kissinger, Nuclear Weapons and Foreign Policy, p. 145.

57. Ibid., p. 233. He has a chapter, "The Problems of Limited War," pp. 132-173, which is good; also a chapter, "The Problems of Limited Nuclear War," p. 174.

For a very good study of the problems of limited war both historically and in relation to strategy, see Robert E. Osgood, Limited War: the Challenge to American Strategy (Chicago: University of Chicago Press, 1957).

58. Aron, The Century of Total War, pp. 207-208.

59. Lukacs, A History of the Cold War, pp. 136-137.

60. See Dinerstein, War and the Soviet Union, p. 11.

61. Kahn, "Alternative National Strategies," Asilomar Proceedings, p. Kahn-19.

62. Hadley, The Nation's Safety and Arms Control, p. 36.

10
Stalemate in Korea

> The hand of the aggressor
> is stayed by strength --
> and strength alone![1]
>
> -- Dwight D. Eisenhower
>
> There is no substitute for
> victory.
>
> -- Douglas MacArthur
>
> There was the spectacle of
> Korea, where, with the vic-
> tory in our hands, we chose
> instead the bitterness of
> stalemate.[2]
>
> -- Barry Goldwater

1. United Nations Intervention

Korea was another problem left over from World War II. At the conclusion of the war, it had been divided along the 38th Parallel to facilitate acceptance of the Japanese surrender, the Russians accepting the surrender to the north and the Americans to the south. As we had seen in Europe, the Communists never tolerated free elections or reunification. That this was a trouble area between the Communists and the Allies was quickly evident to Secretary of State Byrnes before the end of 1945.[3]
In a period of wide United States military involvement in occupations, Korea was a special case in that it was under the supervision of the State Department and not any military commander and was seemingly jealously guarded as a private preserve.

The State Department seemed to ignore MacArthur who was nearby and, of course, interested in his flank, and came up with some unusual solutions, particularly to military problems. The unilateral decision to limit the South Korean military to light weapons and to organize them along constabulary lines was supposedly necessary to prevent the South Koreans from attacking North Korea. This handicap probably tempted North Korea and left South Korea vulnerable when the attack came. MacArthur and his staff were highly critical of the competence of the State Department personnel in Korea and felt that certain errors were inescapable when diplomats attempt to exercise professional military judgment.[4]

The rapid demobilization after the Japanese surrender had reduced our forces, particularly in the Far East, to a shell. Additional economies were implemented in the late 1940s so that, by June 1950, American forces in Japan were quite limited and at reduced strength. By June the occupation forces had only four divisions. Each division still had three regiments, but most regiments were short a battalion and most battalions were short a company. Even MacArthur's corps headquarters had been abolished. General Whitney, who was in MacArthur's headquarters, wrote: "Had these two Washington agencies, the State Department and the Defense Department, coordinated on carefully laid plans to put the U.S. in a militarily impossible position in Asia, they could not have done better."[5]

The United Nations General Assembly adopted a resolution in November 1947 calling for elections in both zones. This resulted in the election of the Rhee government in South Korea, verified by the UN Temporary Commission on Korea. The Communists refused entry to the Commission into North Korea and a puppet government was established there. In December 1949, the General Assembly recognized the South Korean government as the only "legal" government in Korea. Tension continued to run high between North and South Korea, the protégés of the Soviet Union and the UN. There were frequent clashes during 1949 including the 4 August invasion of the Ongjin Peninsula which juts below the 38th Parallel which was repulsed only after heavy fighting.[6]

On 12 January 1950, Secretary of State Acheson supposedly wiped Formosa and South Korea off the American map implying they were outside "our defensive perimeter." This statement was interpreted by some as meaning the United States was no longer interested in these areas[7] and served as an open invitation to the Communists to move in. Acheson strongly rebutted this accusation in his memoirs.[8]

This then was the situation when the North Koreans rolled across the 38th Parallel on 25 June 1950. Jarred from our complacency, the United States was faced with a momentous decision. Fortunately, John Foster Dulles (then a consultant to the Secretary of State) and John Allison (then Deputy Director of Far Eastern Affairs) were in Tokyo and could relay their first-hand views to Washington to aid in this decision. They cabled Secretary Acheson:

> "We believe that if it appears the South Koreans cannot themselves contain or repulse the attack, U.S. forces should be used, even though this risks Russian countermoves. To sit by while Korea is overrun by unprovoked armed attack would start a World War."[9]

MacArthur realized that Communism had challenged the Free World to war and that it was the time for decision. "Now was the time to recognize what the history of the world has taught from the beginning of time: that timidity breeds conflict, and courage often prevents it."[10] Whitney added: "It counseled leading from strength. It correctly emphasized that a failure to fight would be more likely to precipitate another world war than a decision to fight."[11]

With rare speed the UN Security Council sprang into action. At Lake Success on 25 June, with a report already in from the Commission on Korea, it passed a resolution stating that a "breach of the peace" had occurred. It called for the withdrawal of the North Koreans which was ignored. On 27 June, the Security Council called on member states to aid the Republic of Korea. Only late the night before, President Truman had already made his crucial decision to go to the assistance of South Korea.[12] On 7 July, the Council established a combined command in Korea to operate under the United Nations flag and the United States was asked to provide a commander. President Truman named General of the Army Douglas MacArthur to this position.

This decisive action by the Security Council was possible due to unique circumstances. The Russians had walked out in January over the issue of recognition of Red China; therefore, they were not present to veto the proposals. The UN Commission on Korea was in Korea and able to report the facts about aggression immediately. Finally, the presence of American forces in Japan permitted the rapid commitment of forces before the whole of South Korea was overrun. Thus the UN found a new unity and was supported by significant military force to back up its resolutions. Truman's resoluteness electrified the Free World and gave it confidence. "Like Churchill's in June 1940 in the Second World War, June 1950 was America's finest hour in the cold war."[13]

A very important fact that must be kept ever in mind is that during this period, the United States still had a virtual monopoly on nuclear weapons. The nuclear deterrent had not had the expected effect. "The deterrent failed to prevent war. (To claim it didn't fail is to argue Korea wasn't a war.)"[14] Nevertheless, the possible American employment of nuclear weapons was a fact any enemy had to consider.

Weak American units from Japan were quickly thrown into the line to try to stop the Communist penetration that was driving rapidly toward the south. These understrength units fought one of the bravest rearguard actions in history, culminating in the holding of the Pusan perimeter. Up to this point in history, when American boys were dying on a field of battle, nothing had been too good for them and there had been nothing that their government would not have done for them. But the Korean was a new type of war; our first experience with limited war was bound to have its rough edges.

We wanted to stop the North Korean aggression but we were very reluctant to provide the commander with the means to accomplish this mission. On 7 July, MacArthur called for reinforcements: 4-4½ infantry divisions, an airborne regimental combat team, three tank battalions, artillery, etc. He was turned down by Washington.

> The reasons given were that: (1) no increase in any part of the armed services had been authorized; (2) a suitable United States military posture in other parts of the world had to be maintained; and (3) there was a shortage of shipping. What all this amounted to actually was the old faulty principle of "priorities," under which the Far East was placed near the bottom, if not at the bottom, of the list.[15]

This was the old "Europe-first" principle even though we were not fighting there. He asked again on 10 July; he was refused again. He was also turned down twice in his requests for the 1st Marine Division in in mid-July.[16] The contingents from other members of the United Nations performed commendably but were for the most part token forces and not immediately available. It was primarily an American fight and Washington kept a tight rein on the available resources to conduct the war. A paradox developed wherein the high echelons in Washington continually displayed nervous apprehension whereas the high echelons in Japan and Korea, who were under the gun, continually displayed cool efficiency and confidence in their ability to do the job if only Washington would permit them and support them a little.

When MacArthur planned his brilliant Inchon invasion during the summer while the situation was still very gloomy, Washington did everything possible to talk him out of it. The Army Chief of Staff, General Collins, and the Chief of Naval Operations, Admiral Sherman, went to Tokyo to dissuade MacArthur from the Inchon operation.[17] But MacArthur had a better view of the "big picture" than did those in Washington. He told them:

> The prestige of the Western world hands in the balance. Oriental millions are watching the outcome. It is plainly apparent that here in Asia is where the Communist conspirators have elected to make their play for global conquest. The test is not in Berlin or Vienna, in London, Paris or Washington. It is here and now -- it is along the Naktong River in South Korea. We have joined the issue on the battlefield. Actually, we here fight Europe's war with arms, while there it is still confined to words. If we lost the war to Communism in Asia, the fate of Europe will be gravely jeopardized. Win it and Europe will probably be saved from war and stay free. Make the wrong decision here -- the fatal decision of inertia -- and we will be done. I can almost hear the ticking of the second hand of destiny. We must act now or we will die.[18]

The Inchon Landing, coupled with the breakout from the Pusan perimeter, threw the North Korean Army into rout. There followed the controversial decision to send the UN Forces into North Korea. This was not a local military decision but was directed from the highest level -- the General Assembly resolution of 7 October 1950 which authorized its military forces to achieve the establishment of a unified and independent government in all Korea (essentially as proposed by the General Assembly in 1947). Trygve Lie had clearly stated that, "'The aim of the United Nations is and must be a united and independent Korea.'"[19]

The decision to push on to the Yalu has come under fire from many sides in the years since. D. F. Fleming is one of the opponents. He has written, "The decision to conquer North Korea was the cardinal error in our foreign policy to date."[20] He admitted that, "From the standpoint of the great power struggle, the grounds for defending South Korea were strong."[21] But, in his words, "The UN was in Korea to repel aggression, not to commit it."[22] By this interpretation, all fighting then takes place on the land of the invaded, thereby, combined with the policy of "sanctuary," further reducing the margin of gamble by an aggressor. Fleming takes the somewhat astounding position that, "North Korea was one of the most sensitive and strategic areas in the world. It was of the utmost importance to both Russia and China that it not be in hostile hands."[23] -- yet the peninsula had an extremely low American priority before the attack.

Thomas K. Finletter, who was Secretary of the Air Force during the Korean War, wrote:

> ... the idea that we were after "victory" in Korea is incorrect, if by "victory" we mean the total defeat of the Chinese and their unconditional surrender. We were in Korea to stop the aggression where it started, at the 38th Parallel, which is what we did. It is no part of collective security to take territory away from the aggressor by force. On the contrary, the purpose of collective security is to stop nations from taking away territory by force.[24]

Finletter's premises are weak on several points. First of all, he has a very specialized definition of victory. He should have used nothing less than the expression "total victory" because he describes the most extreme form of victory; the only thing he omitted was the unconditional surrender of Russia too. When the majority of writers spoke of victory in Korea, they were referring to something less than the unconditional surrender of China.

Also, it would be rather difficult to defend the position that collective security is only to repel aggression and never to take away territory. By his definition, World Wars I and II were not collective security even though they did involve a large

300

number of nations acting together since, after each
war, the aggressor nations were stripped of their
possessions and frontiers were changed. He also
rather pointedly ignores the word "liberation." It
is surprising that he did not want to liberate North
Korea or any other part of the Communist empire of
satellite states. By default, he was agreeing with
the Communist policy that everything they take in
the Communist War is irrevocable, and the Communists
can continue to try to take the rest. This is a
most unsatisfactory national policy and is incompatible with our heritage of freedom. During World War
II, we made a great point of emphasizing the "liberation" of conquered nations, yet in the great Communist War, this word had become taboo.

While the UN Command waited for orders to cross
the 38th Parallel, South Korean President Syngman
Rhee ordered his ROK troops to go north regardless
of what the Americans did, even though his troops
were under American command. When the United States
did move across, the ROK troops "had already gone
north days before."[25] Peking was, of course, seriously concerned about Korea. In October 1950, Peking
made it known that if the United Nations or United
States crossed the 38th Parallel, she would aid
North Korea. However, if only South Korean troops
crossed, China would take no action.[26] Evidently
we did not believe them.

The immediate objective was to stop the North
Korean aggression and preserve the Republic of Korea.
The hope of uniting Korea was more in the nature of
an aspiration and one for which the nations were not
willing to pay as high a price. Therefore, the
United Nations found themselves in a limited war in
which they continually had to balance how much they
were willing to pay against the results to be obtained and the risks to be encountered.

2. Limited War -- By Tacit Agreement

The Korean War was unusual from the start.
There were those who refused to admit that it was a
war, preferring to call it a "police action" or an
"incident." It does meet the definition of a limited war given in the previous chapter as there were
some very definite limiting features imposed on the
war and the interests and prestige of the great powers were at stake. It was marked by actual combat
between American and Communist troops. The American

301

participation was overt and conducted under the banner of the United Nations; the Communist Chinese and Russian participation was covert. The Chinese Communists claimed that their field armies fighting in Korea were actually "volunteers." Although Russians flew combat missions against the Americans and were present on the ground as advisors,[27] they never admitted to even being in the area.

There were some very important limitations. The major restraint of the entire Korean War was that the Soviet Union did not openly intervene. This greatly limited the war's prestige and other commitments to its outcome, and was significant because North Korea was a Russian, not a Red Chinese, satellite. The continuation of this Communist restraint was indicated when the Chinese intervention was camouflaged as an independent action by "volunteers." Although many Americans were outraged by this subterfuge, it was probably a welcome indication to the US Government that the Sino-Soviet treaty would not be invoked and that the Russians did not intend to intervene directly. Other major restraints were no use of nuclear weapons, no use of air power outside the Korean peninsula, negligible use of Communist air power in South Korea, no use of American naval power outside Korean waters, and negligible Communist naval activity.[28]

Warring nations in history have been accustomed to recognizing neutral nations and thereby agreeing not to violate their territory. However, in the Korean War, something new was added - "sanctuary." The concept was not really new, but it was given a new twist in areas outside of Korea proper in which overt activities were conducted as part of the war. Although all of the supply and support for the Chinese Communists (and a great deal for the North Koreans) came in through northern China and Manchuria, Red China and Russia were left untouched as privileged areas. In Manchuria, enormous Soviet supply installations could be seen just beyond the Yalu River. Russian MIG fighters that ventured south to fight returned to bases on the north side of the river where they could operate in perfect calm, even with light at night, under no fear of attack.[29]

After the Chinese Communist intervention, General MacArthur ordered his B-29s to bomb the Yalu bridges to cut this easy link over which Chinese armies were swarming. He informed the Joint Chiefs of Staff of his order. An immediate message from Secretary Marshall countermanded his order and

302

directed him "'to postpone all bombing of targets within five miles of the Manchurian border.'" The astonished MacArthur violently protested to Washington, but all he received was permission to bomb the "'Korean end of the Yalu bridges.'"[30] General Whitney described the situation:

> At the same time MacArthur was cautioned to exercise extreme care to avoid violation of the Manchurian border and air space -- that is, the sanctuary that had been granted to the enemy -- because of the "necessity for maintaining the optimum position with regard to the United Nations policies and directives, and because it was vital to the national interests to localize the fighting in Korea."

> Thus it was openly admitted by Washington that, so far at least, even this surreptitious attack by the Chinese Communists was not to be punished except by meek half-measures.[31]

An unusual twist of the sanctuary policy developed when certain targets in North Korea were placed in the sanctuary category. On 22 October, the State Department asked MacArthur to issue a statement that he would not change the status quo of the Siniho Hydroelectric Power Plant near Sinuiju, North Korea, which served both Manchuria and Siberia. The hydroelectric plants along the Yalu were not to be bombed. This policy was then broadened to include every plant in North Korea capable of furnishing power to Manchuria and Siberia. There was to be no bombing of the important supply center at Racin -- in North Korea -- "a depot to which the Soviet Union forwarded supplies from Vladivostok for the North Korean Army." This policy, combined with the denial of "hot pursuit" of Communist aircraft across the Yalu by UN aircraft,[32] a generally recognized right in international law, made the Korean War very difficult for the military commanders.

The most damning testimony on the entire war is the repeated appearance of statements that the Chinese Communists were informed of the sanctuary policy ahead of time -- otherwise, they would never have attacked the UN forces. Referring to the time when the UN forces were already well into North Korea, having taken Pyongyang, General Whitney wrote:

> Thus the war in Korea had reached a crucial point in much more than a military sense. This

303

was the time, MacArthur firmly believed, when
some government in the United Nations, or at
least a so-called "neutral" government with
representatives in or connections with the
United Nations, assured the Chinese Communists
that many of the U.N. government leaders -- and
possibly some officials in the United States as
well -- would see to it that the Chinese could
attack in Korea without fear of any powerful
retaliation.[33]

General Van Fleet was of the same opinion, testifying before the Senate Interior Security Subcommittee on 29 September 1954 that the enemy "'would
not have entered Korea if he did not feel safe from
attack in North China and Manchuria.... My own conviction is there must have been information to the
enemy that we would not attack his home bases.'"[34]
General Almond, who was MacArthur's Chief of Staff
and subsequently commanded the Tenth Corps in Korea,
testified: "'that the things as they happened looked
very strange in so far as the assurance with which
the enemy appeared to operate.'" He considered it
would have been "'a very hazardous thing for the
Chinese to enter North Korea'" in strength if they
had thought their bases would be subject to attack.[35]
General Whitney expressed the sense of futility
that must have repeatedly gripped those closely involved: "Small wonder the question was asked time
and time again: 'On which side are Washington and
Lake Success?'"

> Small wonder, too, that MacArthur expostulated
> to members of his staff: "For the first time in
> military history, a commander has been denied
> the use of his military power to safeguard the
> lives of his soldiers and safety of his army.
> To me it clearly foreshadows a future tragic
> situation in the Far East and leaves me with a
> sense of inexpressible shock. It will cost the
> lives of thousands of American soldiers and
> place in jeopardy the entire army. By some
> means the enemy commander must have known of
> this decision to protect his lines of communi-
> cation into North Korea, or he never would have
> dared to cross those bridges in force."[36]

"The Chinese commander-in-chief of the forces that
entered North Korea is reported to have stated he
had definite advance information that MacArthur's
hands would be tied by this 'sanctuary' doctrine.

Otherwise, he is reported to have said, 'I would not
have dared risk almost certain destruction by cross-
ing the Yalu in force. No competent commander,' he
added, 'would have been such a fool.'"37

There was much criticism of the policy that allowed the Communist forces sanctuary in Manchuria.
However, there was little recognition that United
Nations forces enjoyed equally privileged sanctuary,
not only in Japan, Guam, and Okinawa, but also in
South Korea, where the three fighter fields and two
ports were not attacked. This matching of sanctuaries continued throughout the Korean War. "Sanctuaries" have become standard in limited wars, with
the homelands of the great nuclear powers as the ultimate sanctuaries.

The actions of various nations at Lake Success
did not reflect well on their sense of justice.
Even though the United Nations had courageously acted
after the invasion by the North Koreans and eventually did condemn the Red Chinese as aggressors, there
were some members that quickly became frightened and
looked for a more appeasing line toward Red China
and Russia. These countries kept up a continual
barrage at the UN and put great pressure on the
United States. Some governments, pledged under the
Charter of the United Nations to uphold law and justice and to resist aggression, abandoned principle
to expediency. This willingness to repudiate the
whole population of South Korea was an admission
that the crime of aggression can pay.

After the Chinese intervention, there was another long UN retreat with a second invasion from
the north. There followed a series of battles which
finally resulted in a form of equilibrium near the
38th Parallel. The Chinese masses were beginning to
wilt even though the American forces were not conducting the all-out effort of which they were capable. So, in consonance with the normal Communist
doctrine that when the situation is bad, stop and
talk about it, the Communists asked for a truce.
Jacob A. Malik, Soviet delegate to the United Nations, in a New York radio address on 23 June 1951,
presented a proposal for cease-fire discussions.
The Red Chinese government broadcast an unofficial
endorsement on 25 June. The opposing commanders
agreed on 4 July for liaison officers to meet on 8
July for preliminary discussion. Thus started a
long series of negotiations that progressed in normal Communist style until mid-1953. Although the
intensity of the war was shifted from the battlefield
to the conference table, limited-objective attacks

and heavy patrolling continued. The Communists tried on several occasions to make major military efforts to influence the talks; but the Americans showed that, if they wished, they could continue to push the Chinese farther north.

This bargaining with the Communists at a conference table while we had combat troops in contact was something new for the Americans and, therefore, we failed to make the most of the situation. The leaders in Washington continually changed their objectives, putting our negotiators in impossible positions; they failed to realize the relationship between the military pressure applied on the ground to the results obtained at the conference table. When pressure was put on the Chinese armies, the results were quickly evident at the table, when we let up on the ground, their recalcitrance quickly returned. Unfortunately, Washington missed this point and the negotiations dragged on for two years. Kissinger wrote of both sides jockeying for bargaining position:

> The fluctuation of our objectives demonstrated that it is impossible to conduct limited wars on the basis of purely military considerations.... The attempt by both sides to achieve a position of strength prior to negotiation resulted in a vicious circle of gradually expanding commitments which was brought to a halt only because an equilibrium was gradually established between the physical inability of Communist China to invest more resources in the conflict and our psychological unwillingness to do so.[38]

It was this exasperating two-year negotiating phase, during which we permitted ourselves to be deluded at the conference table, while continuing our fight in a limited way, that soured so many people on limited war. We suffered as many casualties during the talking phase as during the first year of heavy fighting. It appears that we could have continued fighting at our heavy rate for a shorter time and achieved greater results with fewer casualties. We were slow to realize the old maxim, never let the pressure up to negotiate. When you do, you only give the enemy a breathing spell, time to regroup and, with the Communists, the opportunity for maximum utilization of their propaganda techniques. If there is any one lesson from Korea, it is probably this one: Never stop to talk. Talks progress remarkably rapidly when the military campaign continues as before.

Our first experience at limited war ended on a sour note and, with the relief of General MacArthur, a great debate swept the country.

3.   The Great Debate

The United States involvement in the Korean War brought on a public review of American foreign policy that became popularly known as the Great Debate. Actually, there were two great debates.   The first, started by former President Herbert Hoover in December 1950, was centered on our foreign policy relative to Europe and lasted until the passing of the Troops-for-Europe Resolution in early April 1951. The second arose one week later when the President relieved General MacArthur from all his commands in the Far East; it centered on Far Eastern policy. The President's action officially acknowledged that the American people faced unresolved issues in American Far Eastern policy which was, of course, inseparable from American global policy.   What ought to be done and what could be done had not been determined.   The action of the President precipitated a national and an international debate unrivalled in modern times for its significance, scope, and confusion.[39]

As General Whitney wrote, "No one has questioned the right of Mr. Truman, as President, to remove MacArthur, although millions have questioned his judgment.   But the form his action took established a new and incredible low in military precedent and procedure."[40]   When General MacArthur returned to the United States for the first time in fourteen years, he received a hero's welcome rather than one for a deposed commander.   This outpouring demonstrated to Whitney that "MacArthur was right and Truman wrong."[41]   The great debate was on.

President Truman delivered an address on 11 April 1951:   "In the simplest terms, what we are doing in Korea is this: We are trying to prevent a third world war."   Referring to the peace-loving nations, he continued:

> If they had followed the right policies in the 1930's - if the free countries had acted together, to crush the aggression of the dictators, and if they had acted in the beginning,

when the aggression was small - there probably
would have been no World War II.

Why don't we bomb Manchuria and China itself:
Why don't we assist Chinese Nationalist troops
to land on the mainland of China?

If we were to do these things we would be run-
ing a very grave risk of starting a general war.
If that were to happen, we would have brought
about the exact situation we are trying to prevent.[42]

Senator Taft attacked the President's position
in a speech the following day.

The President's position is completely inconsistent. He justified an active move against
Korean aggression as a means of preventing
World War III. In the second half of his speech
he claims World War III is prevented by a timid
war against Communist China, and maintaining a
Maginot line defense against an aggressor who
has already accomplished half his purpose. He
justifies two completely inconsistent courses
as means of preventing World War III. I don't
suppose there has ever been a more ridiculously inconsistent justification for vital moves
in foreign policy.[43]

The advice of certain advisers and, perhaps
more importantly, the positions of certain foreign
governments had taken a toll on the original firm
stand that the President took when the North Koreans
invaded:

... the courageous decision of Harry Truman to
meet aggression with force in Korea was apparently giving way to timidity and cynicism.
Truman was evidently listening to a little
group of advisers, under whose beguiling influence he found himself in the anomalous position of openly expressing his fears over calculated risks that he had willingly taken only a
few months before.[44]

General MacArthur was given a special honor in
that he was asked to address a joint session of the
Congress. In one of the most dramatic speeches of
the century, he pointed up the major points in the
great debate: "The issues are global and so inter-

locked that to consider the problems of one sector, oblivious to those of another, is but to court disaster for the whole." Referring to the rise of China, he continued: "This was further and more successfully developed under the leadership of Chiang Kai-shek but has been brought to its greatest fruition under the present regime to the point that it has now taken on the character of a united nationalism, of increasingly dominant aggressive tendencies." In reference to the Chinese intervention, he stated:

> This created a new war and an entirely new situation, a situation not contemplated when our forces were committed against the North Korean invaders, a situation which called for new decisions in the diplomatic sphere to permit the realistic adjustment of military strategy.

> Such decisions have not been forthcoming.

> While no man in his right mind would advocate sending our ground forces into continental China, and such was never given a thought, the new situation did urgently demand a drastic revision of strategic planning if our political aim was to defeat this new enemy as we had defeated the old.

> I called for reinforcements, but was informed that reinforcements were not available. I made it clear that, if not permitted to destroy the enemy build up bases north of the Yalu, if not permitted to utilize the friendly Chinese forces of some 600,000 men on Formosa, if not permitted to blockade the China coast to prevent the Chinese Reds from getting succor from without, and if there were to be no hope of major reinforcements, the position of the command from the military standpoint forbade victory.

> I know war as few other men now living know it, and nothing, to me, is more revolting. I have long advocated its complete abolition, as its very destructiveness on both friend and foe has rendered it useless as a means of settling international disputes.

> But once war is forced upon us, there is no other alternative than to apply every available

309

means to bring it to a swift end. War's very
object is victory, not prolonged indecision.

In war there is no substitute for victory.
There are some who, for varying reasons, would
appease Red China. They are blind to history's
clear lesson, for history teaches, with unmis-
takable emphasis, that appeasement but begets
new and bloodier war. It points to no single
instance where this end has justified that
means, where appeasement has led to more than a
sham peace.[45]

Almost every American wanted what MacArthur
wanted -- the advantages of total victory over the
Chinese Communists without the disadvantages of total war. MacArthur advocated a course of action involving great risk in the hope of great gain, calling for a limited extension of the war beyond Korea
to force Communist China to abandon the Korean adventure.[46] Regardless of how many Chinese might be
killed in Korea, MacArthur saw no end to Red Chinese
aggression "so long as her power to make war remained inviolate."[47]
These hearings started in May and continued for
some seven weeks resulting in over 2,000,000 words
of testimony from thirteen distinguished witnesse,[48]
covering almost every possible facet of United States
foreign policy in the Far East. General MacArthur
listed three alternatives for Korean policy:

"You have various potentials:

First is that you can go and complete this war
in the normal way and bring about a just and
honorable peace at the soonest time possible
and with the least loss of life by utilizing
all of your potential.

The second is that you bring this thing to an
end in Korea by yielding to the enemy's terms
and on his terms.

The third is that you go on indecisively, fighting, with no mission for the troops except to
resist and fight in this accordion fashion up
and down - which means that your cumulative
losses are going to be staggering. It isn't
just dust that is settling in Korea, Senator;
it is American blood."[49]

The fact that MacArthur wanted to attack the
Chinese Communists north of the Yalu was well known
but the extent of his proposed operations is less
well known. Many writers have tried to picture him
as favoring only Total Victory and the unconditional
surrender of the Communist Chinese. This does not
appear to be substantiated in the many pieces of
public testimony available.

General MacArthur: "I believe that against the
modern scientific methods of the United Nations,
the potential of the United Nations, of the
United States, if you would have it so, is sufficient to force the Chinese to stop their aggression in Korea."

"I believe that then you hit her base potential
that way she would be forced to stop her aggression in Korea. I believe under those conditions she would take a reasonable ceasefire
procedure."[50]

General MacArthur: "I do not believe that any
bombing effort we might make in Manchuria would
alter the fact that Russia knows just as well
as we know that we haven't got an iota of imperialistic design against Manchuria or any
other part of China, that it would merely be in
an effort to make the Red Chinese withdraw
their predatory attacks in North Korea."[51]

We suffered an additional 80,000 American casualties during the truce phase. General MacArthur
"estimated that he could have won the war with Red
China with less than half this loss had his advice
been accepted."[52] Considering the low casualty
rates he had throughout his brilliant Pacific campaigns, it is difficult to disagree with him.
Finletter, the Secretary of the Air Force at
the time, felt that anyone advocating extended bombing was seeking Total Victory. He could see only
limited war precisely within the borders of Korea or
total war; he could visualize no middle ground.

The argument for extended bombing though was
not military in nature. It was based on a fundamental political objection to the course the
US government was following in the Korean War.
The US government intended to limit the war to
Korea if it possibly could; it saw Korea as a
war to stop aggression and to restore the

311

status quo ante, as all wars to enforce collective security are supposed to be. The proponents of extended bombing wanted total victory over the Chinese; they wanted to use the opportunity to roll back the Communist power.[53]

President Truman initially wanted operations restricted to below the 38th Parallel except for destroying military supplies.[54] As the possibility of pursuing into North Korea developed, he authorized planning for the occupation of North Korea. "However, no ground operations were to take place north of the 38th Parallel in the event of Soviet or Chinese Communist entry."[55] Any suggested expansion of operations was weighed against Soviet and Chinese reactions, consultations with friendly United Nations members, and the risk of general war.

The biggest, and still unanswerable, question is whether the Chinese and Russians would have moved into general war if the Manchurian bases had been bombed. Truman clearly feared that Russia and Communist China would have moved into full-scale war.[56] The President, who had risked a general war in June 1950 by committing American troops to stop the North Koreans, summed up the differences nicely: "I was left with just one simple conclusion: General MacArthur was ready to risk general war. I was not."[57]

There is another aspect of the question that is worth considering. Both Russia and Red China were already mobilized, therefore our attacking them could not have changed too much. Yet if they had attacked Japan or Formosa, there would have been drastic changes. Japan would have had to reconsider her constitution banning war, and would have most likely remobilized -- this would have had significant impact on Europe. Also, the Chinese Nationalist Army would have come into the war greatly increasing the size of the United Nations forces. It appears logical then that we could have pushed limited war much farther before the Russians or Chinese Communists would have openly attacked in Korea or extended the conflict -- they had much more to lose!

The deep schism in opinion regarding the conduct of the Korean War was not a case of the military against the civilian political leaders. General Marshall, as Secretary of Defense, and the JCS, under the chairmanship of General Omar Bradley, supported the President. It is more accurate to state that the top generals in the Far East supported General MacArthur against the Washington generals and the Europe-First elements.[58]

A large part of the dispute centered on the
Europe-First policy that had made its debut early in
World War II. Even though we were attacked by the
Japanese, thus bringing us into the war, the decision was made to defeat the Nazis first and then
deal with the Japanese. This emphasis on Europe
carried over after the war. As the fighting was
raging in Korea, General Eisenhower was recalled to
duty to go to Europe to organize the NATO forces and
we were sending troops to Europe to be "ready" at
the same time we were sending troops to Korea to
fight. General Almond pointed out some of these
differences of opinion in testimony before Congress:

> General Almond: "I say General Bradley's analy-
> sis of the world situation was oriented towards
> Europe, he says so himself, and nothing could
> budge him from it. He could not visualize the
> effect on Russia or China in the logical sup-
> position that we might win."

> "The opportunity to deal a death blow to ex-
> panding Communism presented itself in Korea.
> But I don't believe General Bradley ever could
> see it.

> He could never see that victory in our grasp in
> Korea would be the one beacon to anti-Communism
> throughout the world. We are exactly where we
> started in 1950, on the 38th parallel."[59]

Bradley felt our original mission was to repel
the aggression and that something less than renuni-
fication of Korea could have been considered a victory. General Hoyt Vandenberg, Chief of Staff of
the Air Force, saw our objective as a negotiated
peace, not as driving the Communists out of Korea.
He agreed that we wanted a unified, free Korea; however, he did not think it was a war aim.[60] This
does little to clarify our operations in North Korea.
As the hearings brought out, the United States aims
were not at all clear.

Bradley's unfortunate slogan came out in the
MacArthur hearings: "'Frankly, in the opinion of the
Joint Chiefs of Staff, this strategy would involve
us in the wrong war, at the wrong place, at the wrong
time, and with the wrong enemy.'" Kissinger explained:

> The literalness of our notion of power is well

313

expressed in our certainty that a war <u>against</u>
the U.S.S.R. must necessarily take the form of
a battle <u>with</u> the U.S.S.R., probably over Europe. This was the real bone of contention between MacArthur and his opponents, and it was
also reflected in their disputes over the nature of preparedness. "You have got a war on
your hands," MacArthur maintained, "and you
can't just say, 'Let that war go on indefini-
nitely while I prepare for some other war.'...
Does your global plan for defense of this United States ... consist of permitting war indefinitely to go on in the Pacific?... If you
are not going to bring the war to a decisive
conclusion, what does preparedness mean?"[61]

Top military officers, including the admiral
who conducted the frustrating peace talks with the
Communists, felt that the war could have been satisfactorily won without encountering the great war
feared in Washington and Allied capitals. Admiral
C. Turner Joy felt that military victory was not impossible or even particularly difficult to achieve.
He thought it was the considered judgment of senior
military commanders of the United Nations Command
that, with removal of the restraints imposed on
American forces and an effective blockade of Red
China, a military victory probably would have resulted in less time than was involved in truce talks.
In his view the United Nations should have gone to
war with Red China. He knew no senior military commander in the Far East who believed the Soviet Union
would have entered the war with the United States
because of any action we might have taken regarding
Red China. As he saw it, if the Soviets had entered a Sino-American war on the Chinese side, Soviet aims in Asia would have been wrecked in the resulting conflict and a position of unassailable
strength established for the Free World.[62]
General Carl Spaatz, the retired Chief of Staff
of the Air Force, took exception with General Bradley's unfortunate slogan feeling it could have been
the right war in the right place. He focused the
blame on the political limitations placed on the
United Nations objectives rather than on the original decision to fight.[63] General James Van Fleet
joined this opposition to Bradley's simple slogan
and disagreed with those who believed American intervention in Korea had been a mistake from the
start. He felt that the Communists had lost the war
stragegically in Korea and if we had to have a war

with the Communists anywhere - which was their
choice - Korea was for us the right war in the right
place at the right time.[64]

The Red Chinese could have been completely defeated on several different occasions according to
General Van Fleet. In May 1951, the United Nations
forces repulsed another offensive, then counterattacked. As the Chinese retreated in disorder, Van
Fleet saw total victory within his grasp; then he
was ordered not to advance any farther.[65] Opportunities presented themselves repeatedly where he
was fully aware of his chance to defeat the enemy
once and for all and was restrained only by high
policy. The mistake we made in Korea and in Washington, he said, was to overestimate the strength of
the Red Chinese armies, which attack with far more
fury than staying power. This misjudgment created a
state of mind which plagued us throughout the war
and in the peace discussions[66] and probably continues as part of the myth of "don't get sucked into
Asia."

The Senate Internal Security Subcommittee, after having questioned many witnesses, issued some
conclusions and recommendations:

(1) The senior military commanders in the Korean war theater who appeared before the
Internal Security Subcommittee of the Senate Committee on the Judiciary believe that
victory in Korea was possible and desirable.

(2) ...Believe that the action required to
achieve victory would not have resulted in
World War III.

(3) ...Believe that political considerations
were permitted to overrule military neces-
sities.

(4) ...Expressed grave concern over the conduct
of this first U.N. "police action," and
hoped we could never again hazard our
troops under similar circumstances.

(5) ...Believe that possible subversion, wishful thinking, European orientation and Allied pressure denied them victory.

(6) ...Believe that failure to win in Korea has
jeopardized our position in the Far East.

315

(7) ...Supplied some clues to possible subversion in Government departments, but were
unable to make specific charges.

(8) ...Expressed the hope that the investiga-
tion would be continued and would encompass
the source from which their orders were received - the Pentagon, State Department,
our allies, certain ambassadors.

(9) ...Hoped that the subject of direction of a
U.N. war would be satisfactorily clarified
before the United States again commits its
forces, its prestige, and its vital interests in another U.N. military engagement.

Recommendations

(3) ...Recommend that the proper sphere for political decisions in the conduct of war
should be outlined and the area of military
operations to be conducted by professionals should be defined.

(4) ...Recommend that methods should be explored to eliminate political interference
in the conduct of hostilities and the negotiation of a military armistice.[67]

President Truman's Administration had quite obviously rejected the ideas of General MacArthur, but
this reduced popularity in the country to a new low
and in the presidential elections of 1952, the electorate did not return the Democrats to power. The
handling of the Korean War probably played a significant role in this defeat. One of the weakest points
in the Korean policy was the inability to determine
exactly what would be "victory" in the war. The
Chiefs of Staff in Washington, the State Department,
and some political leaders came to reject the idea
of victory in Korea either because it seemed unobtainable or because it was not even considered desirable.

By spring 1951, there were those in Washington
who questioned "there is no substitute for victory."
While we had all-out victory in World War II, the
result had not been entirely satisfactory. The idea
of Unconditional Surrender needed re-examination and
the idea of Total Victory was shelved in the Korean
settlement provided aggressors would still be taught
that aggression would not be permitted to succeed.

316

To Senator Fulbright, this was "a new kind of objective" and not as glamorous as old-fashioned victory.[68]

Kissinger has shown how we rationalized our decision not to win in Korea by the strangest type of logic. "The postulate that an all-out war had to be avoided short of an overt attack by the U.S.S.R. on us or on Europe was the reverse side of our inability to conceive goals of war other than the total defeat of the enemy." This is why MacArthur's opponents tried to label him as the advocate of total victory as that was the thing they feared would cause Russia to start a world war. Or, as Kissinger summed up this weird logic, "In short, we thought we could not afford to win in Korea, despite our strategic superiority, because Russia could not afford to lose."[69] A doctrine of this sort seems bound to result in a timid, vacillating, nebulous foreign policy.

General MacArthur's views on the purpose of victory in war are best shown in relation to the Inchon landing. This brilliant stroke turned defeat into victory and virtually recaptured South Korea.

> And so, his military mission accomplished, MacArthur eagerly awaited the diplomatic action that would exploit it. But he waited in vain; nothing was done. He was astonished to see Allied diplomacy fail so completely to capitalize on this moment of triumph. The object of victory in battle is to pave the way for diplomacy to achieve peace. MacArthur expressed his surprise to General Walker. "The whole purpose of combat and war," he said, 'is to create a situation in which victory on the battlefield can be promptly translated into a politically advantageous peace. Success in war involved political exploitation as well as military victory. The sacrifices leading to a military victory would be pointless if not translated promptly into the political advantages of peace.

> "The golden moment to liquidate this war which has already been won militarily now presents itself.... but I am beginning to fear a tremendous political failure to grasp the glittering possibilities of ending the war and moving decisively toward a more enduring peace in the Pacific."[70]

In an April 1953 letter to Senator Byrd, MacArthur

again referred to this political failure to exploit a military victory and added, "The overriding deficiency incident to our conduct of the war in Korea was not in the shortage of ammunition or other materiel, but in the lack of the will for victory."[71]

As the great debate pointed out, there was much unfinished business in the Far East and we had no policy for handling it. When General Whitney informed General MacArthur of the signing of the Korean Armistice, "he exclaimed: 'This is the death warrant for Indochina.'"[72] With the pressure off the Chinese Communists in Korea, they were able to shift their support to Indochina. It only took about a year before Viet-Nam was divided and a new Communist regime was installed in North Viet-Nam. The great debate was still unresolved, though, as now it was the Republicans, despite pouring billions of dollars into Indochina to support the French, who could not find the answer to the same old questions, how much to commit ourselves and what would be "victory"? Unable to adequately meet the problem, we accepted a defeat, the Communist empire expanded still farther, the problems of the area are still with us, and we are even more heavily committed in the area now, having fought the longest war in our history there at even greater expense than Korea. It is obvious that the Communists did not feel that they could not win because we could not afford to lose!

The Alsop brothers wrote an interesting column about MacArthur and Indochina:

> "One of the things the Indo-Chinese crisis is doing is to vindicate the judgment of General Douglas MacArthur," the Alsops wrote in their syndicated column of June 13, 1954. "The free world would not now be menaced with a catastrophe in Asia if MacArthur had won his fight against the artificial limits on the Korean War."

> "MacArthur was in fact right in three different ways and on three different levels. He was right, first, in proclaiming that there was no 'substitute for victory'... MacArthur was right, second, in his view that the Korean war was a crucial test which it was necessary to win at all costs and risks. Indo-China is the proof.

> "The danger in Indo-China is the direct result of the failure in Korea."

318

"Third and finally, MacArthur was right in feeling as he obviously did that the time of the Chinese intervention in Korea was the right time for a showdown in the world struggle between the Soviet and the free halves of the world."[73]

The Communist Chinese threat in the Far East, which we refused to recognize during World War II and which was underestimated by Marshall on his mission to China after the war, continued to dominate all policy in that part of the world. General MacArthur continually placed more emphasis on the Red Chinese than on the Russians in the Far East. In a statement that is just as valid today, if not more so, he stressed this imperialistic nature of Communist Chinese policy.

"I have from the beginning believed that the Chinese Communists' support of the North Koreans was the dominant one. Their interests at present are parallel to those of the Soviet but I believe that the aggressiveness now displayed, not only in Korea but in Indo-China, and Tibet and pointing toward the south, reflects predominantly the same lust for the expansion of power which has animated every would-be conqueror since the beginning of time."[74]

Although Kissinger also labeled General MacArthur as an advocate of Total Victory only, he did succinctly sum up the dilemma of the lack of flexibility in our strategic thinking as it was demonstrated during the Korean War.

By thus posing absolute alternatives as our only choices, by denying the existence of any middle ground between stalemate and total victory, both MacArthur and his opponents inhibited a consideration of strategic transformations which would be compatible with a policy of limited objectives. It was perhaps true that the U.S.S.R. would not permit an unambiguous defeat of China in an all-out war leading to the overthrow of the Communist regime. But it did not follow that the U.S.S.R. would risk everything in order to forestall any transformation in our favor, all the more so as our nuclear superiority was still very pronounced. Had we pushed back the Chinese armies even to the narrow neck of the Korean peninsula, we

would have administered a setback to Communist
power in its first trial at arms with the free
world. This might have caused China to question the value of its Soviet alliance while the
U.S.S.R. would have been confronted with the
dilemma of whether it was "worth" an all-out
war to prevent a limited defeat of its ally. A
limited war is inconsistent with an attempt to
impose unconditional surrender. But the impossibility of imposing unconditional surrender
should not be confused with the inevitability
of a return to the status quo ante.[75]

The debate continued for years. With the publication of the Truman memoirs, many old wounds were
reopened. Noting that many other distinguished figures had challenged the integrity of the work, General MacArthur felt that it was necessary to answer
some of the statements made by the former President.
There was little new information added except that
the Maclean-Burgess defection had taken place by
then.[76]
    The confusion in our Far Eastern policy con-
tinued. Although the "old soldier" faded away, the
controversy that surrounded him never died. However, on 16 August 1962, General MacArthur went to
Washington and on the steps of the Capitol received
a resolution expressing the "thanks and appreciation" of the Senate and the House of Representatives
for his service in three wars. Although most of the
original principal characters of the debate have now
also "faded away," our problems in South Viet-Nam,
Laos, Cambodia, and throughout the Far East show
that the Great Debate was never resolved.

4.   Stalemate

    The importance of the Korean War is not that it
was a limited war but that our government was willing to settle it by long, drawn-out negotiations
after permitting it to degenerate into what one author called "one of the strangest military actions
in all history"[77] even though we still had great
power which was not employed. It was this lack of a
desire for victory and the resulting foggy notion of
what we were fighting for in Korea that soured the
American people on limited wars. This feeling was
expressed by Whitney: "Not by the wildest stretch of
his imagination could MacArthur have conceived that

his superiors would break with American tradition. That tradition has always been that, once American troops are committed to battle, the full power and means of their nation are mobilized and dedicated to fight for victory - and not for stalemate or compromise."[78]

The courageous commitment to defend South Korea in 1950 was widely applauded but, as Senator Barry Goldwater put it, "we allowed the fear-mongers among us to whittle that initial commitment to victory down to an acceptance of a humiliating stalemate."[79] The decisive reaction to open Communist aggression quickly gave way to worry about Europe instead of Asia and over-concern for Communist Russia. This feeling was reflected by the Joint Chiefs of Staff in a message to the Far East stating their belief that Korea was not the place to fight a major war.[80] From this statement, General MacArthur perceived that "the administration had completely lost the 'will to win' in Korea." and that the Joint Chiefs were willing "to give up without a hard fight."[81]

With the refusal of the administration to permit the commanders to use all of their potential power, the war continued for over two more years. Herman Kahn observed that, "In all probability the immediate slackening of our 'victorious' offensive as soon as the Chinese offered to negotiate, and our subsequent unwillingness to use serious military operations to put pressure on the Chinese, not only caused the negotiations to be drawn out, but may have easily resulted in larger over-all casualties, despite lower daily rates. In addition, partly because we did not understand the rationale of wars (which being limited could only end by negotiation and not by total victory), the war left a very bad taste with most Americans. It is believed by some that an important factor in the loss of the 1952 election by the Democrats was their involvement of the country in this very unpopular war. It is quite clear that if there is another unpopular Limited War followed by the loss of the ensuing national election by the party in power, the ability of the United States to fight Limited Wars will be sadly impaired."[82] This stalemated period resulted in many additional casualties and was characterized by some fierce fighting for certain pieces of terrain in addition to intensive patrol activity. Key hills changed hands several times and some, such as Porkchop Hill, have gained a permanent place in our history.

This stalemate and the concept that "we would

simply stay there, resisting aggression"[83] as General MacArthur referred to it, since we did not intend to pursue the hostilities to some form of military victory, was bound to result in eventual negotiations with the Communists for some form of end to the war. The Communist spring offensive had been brought to a halt by 22 May with high casualties and great loss of materiel. It was now clear that the Communists did not have the power to defeat the Eighth Army, much less to drive it into the sea. The United Nations forces under General Van Fleet had counterattacked and were driving the Reds north behind the 38th Parallel again. However, as we have seen, he was not permitted to make too much progress. As Admiral Joy observed: "Here, then, was a Communist army on the verge of crushing military defeat, seeking a respite from our military pressure - an armistice."[84]

The Communists handled their propaganda adroitly, though, striving to make it appear that the United Nations forces were begging for an armistice, even though the initiative had come from the Russians in New York. Their major gain in this ploy was when we naively agreed to meet at Kaesong and later at Panmunjon. These towns were in South Korea but they were under the control of the Communists making the United Nations negotiators go into Communist areas to meet with the Communists. "Obviously, the Communists wished to make it appear that the United Nations Command was in need of a cessation of hostilities and therefore came hat in hand to a Communist citadel to ask a truce."[85] Admiral Joy continued: "As their renegade British reporter Alan Winnington told Western newsmen: 'this is the first time Oriental Communists have ever sat down at a conference table on terms of equality with Americans, and they intend to make the most of it.' After all, what nation but Red China in all the world today can boast of fighting the United States and her allies to a stalemate?"[86]

Any form of armistice talks was certain to help the Reds in several ways. First, it reduced the heavy military pressure of the United Nations Command on the Chinese and North Korean forces that were in bad shape and needed a respite. This would give them time to reorganize and to build strong defenses. Talks would permit reduction of Communist Chinese expenditures which were no doubt placing a heavy strain on their economy. This also could apply to the Russian expenditures which were the basic support of the Communist forces. As one article

noted: "Russia may prefer to go no further than a
cease-fire, to keep talking peace without reaching
peace. Crack U.S. and Western troops thus would be
kept in Korea facing Chinese and Korean Communist
forces. But Russia could cut down military aid to
Communists in Korea and move Russian troops on guard
duty in Siberia to the frontiers of Iran, Yugoslavia
or elsewhere."[87] Shrewd propaganda could possibly
even give them a semblance of victory that they were
impotent to win on the field of battle. To keep
from being defeated by the United Nations could, in
itself, be a prestige victory for them in the Far
East; if they could openly attack the American and
Allied forces and not be defeated by them, then the
other nations of the Orient would have to take note
of this.

The negotiations started and immediately took
on the air characteristic of all such dealings with
the Communists. Each minute point of order was
fought over at length with the Communists always
jockeying for the advantage and never showing any
sincere desire to come to any fair agreements. The
United States was hampered from the first by not being able to determine what it wanted. Despite the
conscientious efforts of the United Nations Negotiators under Admiral Joy, Washington never developed a consistent position. As the Admiral wrote:
"It seemed to us that the United States Government
did not know exactly what its political objectives
in Korea were or should be."[88] This continually
changing nature of American objectives wreaked havoc
with the negotiators and greatly hampered their efforts.[89]

The Communist system of stalling and arguing
pays off in eventual concessions when their adversaries grow weary and yield in an effort to get the
talks moving. This technique worked perfectly in
Korea with the Communists gaining concessions of the
utmost importance when Washington yielded in spite
of the strong objections of their negotiators on the
scene. The most damaging of these unfortunate decisions was the Washington order to agree to a truce
line across Korea. This completely pulled the rug
out from under the United Nations negotiators and
destroyed our position at the bargaining table.[90]
As has been repeatedly shown over the years, "Communists regard any concession made by their opponents
as a sign of weakness."[91]

During the negotiations, when the Communists
offered the USSR as a "neutral" country for aiding
in the peace settlement, our delegation was not

permitted to attack Russia as the main force behind the Korean War. Our delegation was told to disallow Russia on the weak basis of their common border with North Korea.[92] The Communists must have laughed at this gutless lack of resolve on our part.

The concessions continued as we successfully gave in on the point of constructing airfields, which countered the basis principle we had started the talks on, and then gave in on aerial reconnaissance for verifying the peace, a situation which the Admiral compared to having a "sightless floor detective in a department store."[93] Admiral Joy noted, that even though the Communist position was weak, by sticking to it unyieldingly, we usually conceded. In the Admiral's opinion, all our problems went back to our failure to take decisive action against the Communist Chinese from the start which also cast doubt on our resolve in Asia.[94]

The Communists, not being able to win the war they had started, wanted to have it end where it had started, on the 38th Parallel. That way they would suffer no loss of territory. We, unfortunately, tended to listen to their story even though it followed no particular logic.[95] As we have seen though, this policy had many advocates among our high officials - particularly Mr. Finletter who could not visualize the moving back of the enemy in the name of collective security.

Throughout the negotiations and, in general, in our dealings with the Communists, we have failed to take advantage of the close relationship between force and results obtained. "Nothing is so persuasive to Communists as force."[96] Admiral Joy emphasized that "armistice conferences should be brief"[97] with a very definite time limit. We have seen in history an example of a general who would not quit attacking to talk over evasive plans. Marshal Foch refused to delay his plans for attack in November 1918. "Immediately thereafter, November 9th, Kaiser William abdicated and fled to Holland."[98]

If one were to put on graph paper the pressure applied to the Communists on the battlefield and the progress obtained at the conference table along a time scale, there would probably be a very close correlation between the two curves. Admiral Joy wrote: "Sitting in my tent at Munsan after a day of unprecedented progress at Panmunjon, and cocking an ear at the sound of our shells and bombs crunching against Communist positions, our Colonel Kinney remarked to me, 'Those (the explosions) are your most effective arguments.' I am convinced beyond any doubt that had our powerful offensive during the autumn of 1951 been continued, we would have had an armistice in Korea a year earlier than we did."[99] General Mark Clark noted the same thing in his experiences with the Communists from Vienna to Korea.[100] We have tended to forget that to the Communists the conference table is not a place for sincere negotiations as we think of them. Mark Clark related how "Marshal Konev in Vienna was laughing and telling me that, if I accepted all of his preposterous demands one day, he would have ten new ones to hit me with the next."[101] The Communists consider negotiations as only another battlefield. Where we are willing to compromise they yield only when forced to. They, therefore, regard us with contempt when we yield on a point when there was not sufficient force backing their side to justify it. By constantly playing on our impatience and our desire to get a quick and definite solution, they stall and delay as much as possible so that we will concede important points in hopes of making some overall progress. We usually have the power to back up the demands we could make; our difficulty has been in our failure to use this power. Admiral Joy described it neatly: "We must negotiate not merely from strength, but with strength."[102]

The "incident" is a part of Communist conference table technique just like quibbling over every small point. After the 22 August 1951 "incident" of United Nations bombing of Kaesong, the Communists broke off negotiations when we refused responsibility showing they were lying. They wanted to attack to push the line back down to the 38th Parallel. They sustained very heavy losses though and the United Nations Command ultimately pushed them farther north; so they returned to negotiating again. Also they made much propaganda mileage out of various incidents during the interim.[103] "One thing is certain: future negotiations with the Communists will be marked by more incidents. The 'incident' is one of their tested techniques."[104] The more important point, though, is that when the military situation turns against them, they cry for talks. That is the time to step up the pressure and real results might appear at the conference table.

Korea was a hard infantry war which proceeded generally oblivious to the nuclear age. However, tactical nuclear weapons had been developed and the 280mm atomic cannon was shipped to the Far East. Nuclear projectiles were shipped, not to Korea, but to nearby storage areas and "word of this shipment was allowed to fall into Communist hands." This could have spelled doom for massed Communist armies. Then Stalin died on 5 March 1953. At the same time a "pervasive rumor" was in the air "that the United States would not accept a stalemate beyond the end of summer."[105] The pressure was on the Chinese.

The frustrating negotiations finally ended in July 1953 after the long, drawn-out problem of no forceful repatriation of prisoners and some changes on the world scene. Eisenhower was now President, and Stalin had died leaving Russia in the grips of an internal struggle for power. The supposedly "neutral" Commission soon showed that it was being hampered by its Czechoslovakian and Polish members. With no effective enforcement apparatus, the Communists immediately violated the armistice and have continued to do so ever since. We should not forget "An agreement has no special validity of its own, no matter how solemnly ratified. An agreement is binding on Communists only if it operates to the advantage of their purposes."[106] "Never trust a Communist promise, however given: trust only Communist deeds."[107]

Thus, the war that started out to stop Communist aggression became bogged down in a tangled web of Allied diplomacy and turned to stalemate resulting in the most unpopular war in American history until that time. With the decision not to pursue the war to a military victory, it fell into two years of negotiations that greatly confused the American people. However, as the Overstreets pointed out, "The tedious, repetitive effort to negotiate with the USSR has done more, perhaps, than any other one thing to convince the community of free nations that cold war is not peace."[108]

5. Who Won?

When the Korean War finally came to an end, it was quite difficult to answer the question: Who won? It was certain, though, that neither the United Nations forces nor the Communists could claim total victory. After three years of fighting and talking, a truce was not an armistice dictated after victory but a truce negotiated in a stalemate. The compromised end to the fighting was sought by both sides and did not generate a disgruntled loser seeking revenge even though the issues of the war remained as unsettled as ever.

The Communists did not win in the sense of their immediate objective of seizing South Korea. It can be said that the United Nations forces won in the sense that aggression was repelled. For a war that ended approximately where it started, it had certainly been expensive. The Chinese and North Koreans were estimated to have lost over 1,500,000 casualties. The United Nations Command suffered more than 500,000 casualties with over 94,000 dead in a war that cost the United States over 83 billion dollars.[109] However, with the policies of sanctuary and "no-win," the biggest loser was South Korea, where the heaviest fighting took place, with three million civilian dead or wounded, millions homeless, and great property damage to industry.[110]

There were certain pluses registered on the Communist side even though they did not get South Korea. In MacArthur's words: "Its disastrous consequences were reflected through Asia. Red China was accepted as the military colossus of the East. Korea was left ravished and divided. Indo-China was partitioned by the sword. Tibet was taken almost on demand. Other Asian nations began to tremble toward neutralism."[111] Probably the most important plus was the prestige the United States lost in the Far East by failing to defeat a minor power. This is a nebulous quantity to measure, but it is manifested by diplomatic difficulty and drifting away from the Western nations towards a position of neutrality or nonalignment. The Great Debate possibly weakened our position also by casting doubt among other nations of the Free World on the American capability to lead the tough struggle against Communist imperialism. However, some of these same concerned United Nations members did not give us wholehearted support. Throughout the war, great pressure was exerted by certain members to settle with the Communists on almost any terms. The enthusiasm of some members to admit Red China into the United Nations, give her Formosa, or agree to almost anything to get the war stopped surprised American diplomats.

The failure of the Free World to gain victory in Korea "strengthened the Communist enemy by giving him increased confidence in his second-team armies" and cast doubts in the minds of some of the smaller and weaker non-Communist nations "about the ability and determination of the free world to protect them against Red aggression."[112] When the United Nations, and particularly the United States, stood up to Communist aggression, all Asia applauded. However, when, little by little, the resolve of the

United Nations and America evaporated, "Asian admiration turned to shocked disillusionment."[113] The abrupt removal of General MacArthur when he was advocating a strong policy in the Orient gave further support to the Communist belief that we had no steel in our policy, that we were, in the still current appellation used by Communist China toward the United States - a "paper tiger" - even though Khrushchev later took exception with this view.[114]

The United States, at the same time, lost an opportunity to restore a friendly regime in China. It is often said it takes a generation to forget. Almost two decades passed before the first steps were taken by President Nixon, in 1971, to start normalizing relations with the People's Republic of China.

The war provided a testing ground for equipment and techniques for some of the Communist armies, much as the Spanish Civil War did for Nazi Germany. Of particular value to the Soviet Union was the chance to try out the MIG-15 jet fighter which proved no match for American pilots. No doubt the improvements put into the MIG-19s and MIG-21s were based on the lessons learned in Korea.

At the same time that the United States lost prestige in the Orient, the Red Chinese gained. By holding America to a stalemate in a war, they thrust themselves on the world scene as a nation to be reckoned with, at least in the eyes of the nations in the Far East. Having committed aggression against the largest of the Free World nations and gotten away with it, no nation in Asia was safe now from Chinese imperialistic pressures. They played their propaganda to the hilt, claiming that they won the war. This was bound to have an effect on the other nations in Asia and was why General Van Fleet kept calling for a victory to deflate this Chinese balloon. He felt that signing an armistice or anything less than military victory over the Communists in Korea would be a defeat.[115]

The newly found power of the Red Chinese led to the fall of Indochina and the continuous unrest in Southeast Asia thereafter. The end of the Korean War increased Chinese influence and aided further aggression to the south by releasing Communist war materiel and technical assistance from Korea to be employed against the French in the battle developing at Dien Bien Phu.[116]

Although it was certainly no victory as we have known them in our history, the Korean War did have certain results that should be listed on the plus

side for the Free World.[117] Even though the outcome was somewhat humiliating, perhaps due to an
overly timid approach to both the Communists and our
Allies, South Korea did not fall into the Communist
camp. The significance of this became apparent in
recent years when we saw a thriving South Korean
economy and a Korean Army that was strong enough to
send a two-plus division force to help in South
Viet-Nam.

It would appear that the most important gain
from the war was the awakening of the Free World to
the Communist threat. We should have awakened with
the Berlin airlift in 1948-1949 but there were still
many people, particularly Americans, who would not
take even the Soviet threat seriously. We were fortunate the Communists clearly showed their colors so
that even the most complacent could see. This resulted in increased military strength in America and
no effort to disband the armed forces, which had
been stripped to mere skeletons after World War II.
There was increased aid for augmenting the military
capability of our allies and increased assistance to
rebuild or help build the economies of our allies
and friends in the Free World. NATO grew from the
Korean War, as did many other alliances all around
the world specifically directed at containing the
spread of world Communism and protecting the nations
of the Free World. This reaction to the Communist
aggression provided a longrange potential of greatly strengthening the Free World in the Communist
War.[118]

The United States also derived valuable experience in the problems of fighting a limited war.
Military planning was complicated by the lack of
clear military objectives.[119] A liberal rotation
policy for the soldiers became necessary for morale
(seen again with the one year tour in Viet-Nam).
The delay in setting up ammunition production showed
that it was difficult for the administration to convince manufacturers to convert to war production;
therefore, there was again demonstrated the need for
a war production base sustained in peacetime by regular orders and ready for immediate expansion. There
was little mobilization of our industrial potential
and the civilian economy was hardly disturbed by the
guns and butter policy.[120]

The unification of Korea was not achieved, but
that was more in the nature of a hope than a military objective. Coyle, in his book on the United
Nations, stated that the world body does not contemplate military action to liberate peoples even though

329

their conditions may be deplored. As he put it, "It was not a defeat in Korea when the UN armies stopped fighting before liberating North Korea."[121]

As we know, the UN action was possible only because the USSR was absent from the Security Council meetings and, therefore, could not veto the proposals. As soon as they returned, in August, the Security Council returned to its ineffective status. To overcome this obstacle and to permit continuance of the already started UN operation, a small revolution took place in the procedures of the United Nations. This consisted of the Uniting for Peace Resolution which shifted the importance from the Security Council to the General Assembly where there is no veto. This greatly enhanced the UN ability to meet aggression since the Russian veto had completely stymied the apparatus as designed in 1945.

If it were necessary to name a relative winner, it would probably have to be Red China. The Communist Chinese, who had only seized full control on the mainland the year before the war, evolved as a force of increased stature on the world scene. Her's was a victory of prestige rather than of power and her gains were made at the expense of Russia more than America. The Sino-Soviet dispute erupted into the open only seven years later. However, it is possible that the Communists may prove to be the long term losers by having stirred up the Free World. They probably could have continued in their successful way if they had not been so greedy. In the sense of the Communist War, the Communists probably consider the Korean War a miscalculation. The awakening of the Free World from its complacency was one factor the Communists should have avoided. They will probably never forgive Dean Acheson for telling them we had no interest in Korea and then turning around and defending it.

The Communist losers were the Soviets because they lost control of North Korea to Chinese influence. If Stalin had tried to put a squeeze on Mao, it went to the grave with him and foundered at the 38th Parallel. The real winners were the Japanese. The Korean War made Japan extremely valuable as an American base. They quickly had a peace treaty and rejoined the world and the billions of American dollars poured into Japan during the war sparked an economic boom that propelled Japan into being the third economic power in the world.

The most far-reaching result is reflected in the ominous question General Gavin raised. Did our failure to win in Korea mark the beginning of our decline, much like the decline of the Roman Empire? "Korea was the first war that we failed to win; was it also the symptom of our decline? Did we reach the high noon of military achievement, and with Korea turn toward the long afternoon shadows of a deteriorating republic?"[121] To find the answer to this momentous question, we must await the verdict of history. But if the Free World loses the Communist War, then the failure to win in Korea will have been shown as the turning point of history.

NOTES

1. Palmer and Perkins, International Relations, p. 268.
2. Goldwater, Why Not Victory? A Fresh Look at American Foreign Policy (New York: McGraw-Hill, 1962), p. 45.
3. See U.S. Department of State, A Decade of American Foreign Policy, p. 70, Byrnes' report on 30 December 1945 on Moscow Meeting.
4. See MacArthur, Reminiscences, pp. 329-330 and Whitney, MacArthur, His Rendezvous with History, pp. 318-320. General Whitney served as secretary and was very close to MacArthur. Whitney stated that MacArthur's headquarters informed Washington of the growing danger of a North Korean attack with more than 1500(!) warnings between June 1949 and June 1950, one even suggesting June 1950 as a likely time.
5. Whitney, MacArthur, p. 318.
6. See Palmer and Perkins, International Relations, pp. 1128-1129.
7. See Frazier Hunt,"Untold story of General MacArthur," US News, 15 October 1954, p. 135.
8. See Acheson, Present at the Creation: My Years in the State Department (New York: Signet, 1969), pp. 467, 476, 534, 880-881, and 970-972. See Ridgway, The Korean War (Garden City, New York: Doubleday, 1967), p. 10 for how we did not want to become involved there.
    Harrison Salisbury felt that Stalin ordered the Korean attack to put pressure on Mao Tse-tung, War Between Russia and China (New York: Norton, 1969), pp. 91-98.
9. Ibid., p. 322. MacArthur, Reminiscences, p. 328.
10. MacArthur, Reminiscences, p. 330. Also Whitney, MacArthur.
11. Whitney, MacArthur.

12. See Glenn D. Paige, The Korean Decision (June 24-30, 1950) (New York: Free Press, 1968), pp. 178-180.

13. Lukacs, A History of the Cold War (Garden City, New York: Doubleday, 1961), p. 91

14. Hadley, The Nation's Safety and Arms Control (New York: Viking, 1961), p. 13.

15. MacArthur, Reminiscences, p. 337. Also Whitney, MacArthur, p. 337.

16. Whitney, MacArthur, p. 343.

17. MacArthur, Reminiscences, p. 347.

18. Ibid., p. 350. MacArthur's complete presentation is included. He ended by staking his professional reputation on the operation and stating that it would save 100,000 lives -- powerful arguments for younger officers to oppose.

19. Fleming, The Cold War and its Origins (Garden City, New York: Doubleday, 1961), p. 615, quoted from the New York Times, 9 September 1950.

20. Ibid., p. 655. Fleming seems to take the Russian side on almost every point.

21. Ibid., p. 603.

22. Ibid., p. 614, italics in original. The author tries to stir up the idea that South Korea invaded North Korea. See pp. 597-601. He also contends that the invasion was not directed by Moscow but by North Korea, pp. 604-608.

23. Ibid., p. 614. By this logic, Finland, Norway, Europe, Greece, Turkey, Iran, Afghanistan, Pakistan, Burma, Thailand, Laos, Viet-Nam, any country touching the Communist empire, should not be permitted to be in hostile hands. This says the Communists should expand to the water frontiers -- then what about the islands? This form of logic soon leads to the explanation that the Communists must have the world.

24. Finletter, Power and Policy: U.S. Foreign Policy and Military Power in the Hydrogen Age (New York: Harcourt, Brace, 1954), pp. 115-116.

25. T. R. Fehrenbach, This Kind of War: A Study of Unpreparedness (New York: Pocket Books, 1963), p. 288.

26. Ibid., p. 295.

27. See, for example, Clark, From the Danube to the Yalu, pp. 206-207 and Ridgway, The Korean War, "each NKPA division had assigned to it approximately fifteen Soviet Army advisers." p. 10.

28. See James E. King, Jr., "The Nature and Characteristics of Limited and Local Wars," Asilomar Proceedings, pp. King--12-13.

29. See, for example, G.E. Stratemeyer, "We

weren't permitted to win in Korea," excerpts from
hearing before Senate Internal Security Subcommittee,
U.S. News, 3 September 1954, p. 84, and Mark Clark,
"You can't win a war if diplomats interfere," transcript of testimony before Senate subcommittee, U.S.
News, 20 August 1954, p. 78.
    30. MacArthur, Reminiscences, pp. 368-369.
MacArthur wanted to be relieved of his command but
relented. He said Eisenhower stated in the press
several years later that he would have ignored such
an order, pp. 369-370. See also Transcript of hearings before Senate Armed Services and Foreign Relations Committees, Douglas MacArthur, U.S. News, 11
May 1951, pp. 58-59.
    31. Whitney, MacArthur, pp. 406-407.
    32. MacArthur, Reminiscences, pp. 365, 368-370
and Whitney, MacArthur, p. 402. MacArthur's air
chief, General Stratemeyer, said of bombing the Korean end of the bridges with anti-aircraft installations on the north side: "It cannot be done --
Washington must have known, it cannot be done." and
it was not either. The explanation by General Em-
met O'Donnel, Jr., then head of Far East Bomber Command, to the Senate hearings in 1951 makes one appreciate the vexing frustrations of the military.
See Whitney, pp. 407-408.
    33. Whitney, MacArthur, p. 401.
    34. Quoted in ibid., p. 455.
    35. "Orders from Washington kept US from win-
ning Korea War," excerpts from testimony before Internal Security Subcommittee by General E. M. Almond,
U.S. News & World Report, 10 December 1954, p. 89.
    36. "There can be no doubt in any reasonable
mind that Red China was informed that if it entered
the war it need not fear the conventional counterstroke by our forces. MacArthur thought they had
the benefit of such prior knowledge, as evidenced by
the statement in his letter to Senator Byrd of April
10, 1953: 'By one process or another it was conjec-
tured by, or conveyed to, the Red Chinese that even
though they entered the fray in large force it would
be under the sanctuary of being relieved from any
destructive action of our military forces within
their own area.'" Whitney, p. 455. The author
noted the Washington Post loudly cried that this
could not have been so.
    37. "MacArthur agrees and holds to the firm be-
lief that had the Communist strategists not been
given assurance that they could continue to enjoy
the sanctuary of Manchuria, the Red Chinese armies
would not have entered the Korean war." Whitney,

p. 394. "The Maclean-Burgess defection has shown how he could have known." MacArthur, "Mr. Truman yielded to counsels of fear," U.S. News, 17 February 1956, pp. 48-52.

38. Kissinger, Nuclear Weapons and Foreign Policy, p. 50, italics in original. He was to become intimately familiar with this problem later in Viet-Nam.

39. Clyde, The Far East, p. 827.

40. Whitney, MacArthur, p. 473.

41. Ibid., p. 432.

42. Truman, "Preventing a new world war," U.S. Department of State Bulletin, 16 April 1951, pp. 603-604. He emphasized keeping Korea limited and ended the talk of unification.

43. Taft, "Korean War and the MacArthur dismissal," Vital Speeches, 1 May 1951, p. 421.

44. Whitney, MacArthur, pp. 396-397. The President called the war "a police action;" the JCS called it "the Korean incident" - Whitney called this "group self-deception" which underestimated the entire nature of the conflict to which the government had committed American fighting men. He added: "In this display of deliberate wishful thinking the President and his clique of advisers were listening to the blandishments of some of the more timid politicians from other U.N. members."

45. MacArthur, Address to Congress, 19 April 1951, U.S. News, 27 April 1951, pp. 71-72, italics added. Also in MacArthur, Reminiscences, pp. 400-405.

46. Clyde, The Far East, p. 828.

47. See Whitney, MacArthur, p. 462.

48. See Palmer and Perkins, International Relations, pp. 975-979.

49. Transcript, Far East Hearings, U.S. News, 11 May 1951, p. 63.

50. Ibid., p. 72. Note that he mentions a possible Chinese ceasefire and not Total Victory. See Ridgway, The Korean War, pp. 144-150 for a long discussion of MacArthur's idea of victory. Washington considered it carefully and disagreed. Ridgway felt MacArthur sought the global defeat of Communism by use of armed force.

51. Ibid., U.S. News, 18 May 1951, p. 75.

52. Whitney, MacArthur, pp. 508-509. President Truman disagreed. See Years of Trial and Hope, Chapter 24 for the development of his loss of confidence in MacArthur.

53. Finletter, Power and Policy, p. 115, italics in original. He makes no mention of the UN aim

to reunify Korea.

54. Truman, _Years of Trial and Hope_, p. 341, (June 1950).

55. Ibid., p. 359, National Security Council policy statement, 11 September 1950.

56. Ibid., p. 383. Kissinger (_Nuclear Weapons_, p. 137) felt "the Chinese probably made the maximum military effort of which they were capable." Mac-Arthur also felt they were in all-out war with us (Transcript, Far East Hearings, _U.S. News_, 18 May 1951, p. 59): "I believe that they are using every ounce of power to achieve victory in Korea, and that their aim in Korea is the complete destruction of the United Nations forces there, and that they intend to occupy and administer and govern, if they are successful, every inch of Korean territory."

However, Lukacs (_Cold War_, p. 151) supported Truman: "Truman, and not MacArthur, was proved right in 1951, as he understood that an eventual war between China and America in the Far East might, after all, have served the ends of Stalin's Russia, which might have profitably stayed largely outside such a conflict."

57. Truman, ibid., p. 416.

58. The controversy over muzzling of the military that came out in the early 1960s was nothing new. General MacArthur had his problems in this field too. The 4 December 1950 directive to all commanders, later admitted by Marshall to have been directed at MacArthur, stated: "'until further notification, no speech, press release, or other public statement concerning foreign policy or military policy will be released without clearance from the Department of the Army. Overseas army commanders will exercise caution in public statements, ...and will refrain from direct communication on foreign or military policy with newspapers, magazines or other publicity media in the United States.'" Quoted in Whitney, _MacArthur_, p. 450.

59. "Senator Welker: 'Had you been permitted to win the war in Korea, in that event you would have saved Indo-China also? Is that a correct assumption?'"

"General Almond: 'I think so, sir, decidedly.'"

"General Almond: 'It is bad enough to have to fight the enemy; it is terrible to fight both the enemy and those that you are supposed to have support from.'" Almond, _U.S. News_ 10 December 1954, pp. 89, 90, 92, and 94. In comparing Bradley with MacArthur regarding strategy, one must lean toward

MacArthur. Bradley had risen to Army Group Commander in Europe but he was always under Eisenhower in a military rather than a political position. Collins had been a Division and Corps Commander. The only strategist against MacArthur was Marshall, who was Europe-First, had operated in a political-military vacuum under FDR and was not noticeably successful in his handling of China after the war.

60. See Fleming, Cold War, p. 642.

61. Kissinger, Nuclear Weapons, p. 45, italics in the original.

62. Joy, How Communists Negotiate (New York: Macmillan, 1955), p. 176. On p. 177, he stated that total war would have come only if it "had already been decided upon by the Soviets." (his italics) See Stratemeyer, U.S. News 3 September 1954, p. 84, for his view that the Russians were afraid to enter the Korean War and how neither MacArthur nor any of the top generals feared the Russians.

63. See Whitney, MacArthur, p. 510.

64. Van Fleet, "Truth about Korea: from a man now free to speak," Time, 11 May 1953, p. 125, excerpts from his article in Life of the same date and the following week.

65. Ibid., p. 25.

66. Ibid., p. 125.

67. "Korea victory was denied," concluding sections of Senate Internal Subcommittee report, U.S. News, 4 February 1955, p. 44.

68. Vagts, Defense and Diplomacy, p. 486. However, Vagts pictures MacArthur as an advocate of unconditional surrender.

69. Kissinger, Nuclear Weapons, pp. 47-48.

70. Whitney, MacArthur, p. 400, italics added.

71. MacArthur, "What went wrong in Korea," Letter to Senator Byrd, U.S. News, 1 May 1953, p. 28. MacArthur himself noted: "'I have always been able to take care of the enemy in my front - but I have never been able to protect myself from sniping in the rear.'" (Whitney, MacArthur, p. 440) A good example is the blast by Harold Ickes in the New Republic, 17 July 1950, p. 17. He hit MacArthur for not being ready in Korea (not under his command), said it was his fault Korea was poorly armed (State Department policy) and then proceeded to attack him regarding operations in the Philippines in World War II - all of this right at a crucial moment of our commitment in Korea and Ickes generally spoke for Democratic circles.

72. Whitney, MacArthur, p. 509.

73. Ibid., pp. 511-512, particularly in view of

our nuclear advantage at that time.

74. Ibid., pp. 410-411.

75. Kissinger, Nuclear Weapons, p. 49, italics in original.

76. See Douglas MacArthur, "Mr. Truman yielded to counsels of fear," U.S. News, 17 February 1956, pp. 48-52. He added: "But what may well have triggered my removal was my recommendation, made in January shortly before my relief, that a treason trial be initiated to break up a spy ring responsible for the purloining of my top-secret reports to Washington." ... But the obstinacy which dictated the failure of President Truman to recognize the damage that could be done by Red infiltrators and his 'red herring' characterization of all efforts to unmask them are among the astounding features of an astounding epoch."

77. Littlefield, History of Europe Since 1815, p. 284.

78. Whitney, MacArthur, p. 333. Raymond Aron considered Korea a "war waged always as a function of politics and never with a view to military victory alone." Peace and War, p. 28. Fehrenbach has a good discussion of Korea as a political war and not a crusade, This Kind of War, pp. 91-93.

79. Goldwater, Why Not Victory?, p. 159.

80. See Whitney, MacArthur, p. 430.

81. Ibid., pp. 430-431. Another author has described this loss of the will for victory and the resulting difficulty in determining what our policy was: "In Korea, for example, it became quite clear that the stalemate was produced by a paralysis of will' on the political level. Lieutenant Colonel Melvin B. Voorhees reports the following from an interview with General James Van Fleet. 'Reporter: "General, what is our goal?" Van Fleet: "I don't know. The answer must come from higher authority." Reporter: "How may we know, General, when and if we achieve victory?" Van Fleet: "I don't know, except that somebody higher up will have to tell us."'" C. Wright Mills, The Power Elite, pp. 184-185. The quote is from Voorhees' book and was cited in Time, 3 August 1953, p. 9.

82. Kahn, On Thermonuclear War, p. 418, italics in original, very prophetic in light of President Johnson and the 1968 election.

83. See Transcript, Far East Hearings, U.S. News, 11 May 1951, p. 70.

84. Joy, How Communists Negotiate, p. 24.

85. Ibid., p. 2.

86. Ibid., p. 4.

87. "Problems in ending a war," U.S. News, 6 July 1951, p. 17.

88. Joy, How Communists Negotiate, pp. 173-174.

89. "All personnel in the United Nations Command delegation were aware of the chameleon-like character of American political objectives in Korea. United States forces entered Korea, in accord with political objectives, to prevent an impending collapse of the South Korean Government and to help repel aggression against South Korea. When the North Korean aggressor was thrown back north of the 38th Parallel from whence he came, these two political objectives had been secured. The United States policy shifted to the intent to unify Korea.... When the Red Chinese plunged into the fray, the controlling political objective of the United States became a desire to avoid all-out war with China. When the Soviets suggested an armistice, the political objective in Korea became an honorable cease fire. During the armistice negotiations, we took on a political objective of gaining a propaganda victory over Communism in respect to prisoners of war.... delegation... never knew when a new directive would emanate from Washington to alter our basic objective of obtaining an honorable and stable armistice agreement." Ibid., p.173.

90. "At this point the United Nations Command delegation, over our and General Ridgway's strenuous objections, received instructions from Washington directing us to agree to immediate delineation of a truce line across Korea.... In effect, this decision gave the Communists what they had been seeking - a 'de facto' cease fire for thirty days which enabled them to dig in and stabilize their battle line. This concession to the Communists was the turning point of the armistice conference.... Our delegation no longer had a strong lever to use against Communist intransigence. Thereafter we were confronted with Communist stalling and delaying tactics at every turn. It is my considered judgment that this error in offering a concession to gain nothing more than apparent (and illusory) progress in the negotiations cost the United States a full year of war in Korea and armistice terms far more disadvantageous than otherwise could have been obtained." Ibid., p. 129, italics in original.

91. Ibid., p. 119.

92. See ibid., pp. 90-93.

93. Ibid., p. 88. "...the Communists flatly refused agreement to refrain from building airfields. Weak as was their argument regarding 'interference

in internal affairs,' the Communists clung to it until higher authorities in Washington finally directed the United Nations Command delegation to concede
the issue to the Communists. This concession utterly departed from the basic principle on which the
United Nations Command delegation had been trying to
arrange the armistice - the principle of freezing
the military capabilities of both sides so that neither could add substantially to its strength during
the period of truce." (p. 72).

"Later on, Washington required the United
Nations Command delegation to concede the question
of aerial reconnaissance to the Communists.... Without aerial reconnaissance, armistice supervision becomes blind." (p. 88).

94. Ibid., pp. 163-164. "Failure to take immediate punitive action against Red China /when they
invaded in 1950/ was at the root of most of the difficulties encountered in the Korean armistice negotiations. Our seemingly weak and fearful withdrawal
in the face of an unprovoked attack on our forces in
the Far East gave the Communists good reason to believe that the United States would not stand firm on
any aspect of the continental Asian problem."

95. Admiral Joy compared this approach with
World War II: "Their chief point was that since the
war began on the 38th Parallel, it should end there.
Such a policy applied to our war with Japan would
have resulted in our surrendering every area of the
Pacific we had won in battle back to Pearl Harbor,
since it was at Pearl Harbor that the war began."
Ibid., p. 138.

96. Ibid., p. 29. Admiral Joy has given us the
benefit of his frustrating experience with the Communists at the conference table.

"Let no one think that in negotiating with
the Communists we should reject the threat of force.
On the contrary it is only through the imminent
threat of application of our military power that the
Communists can be compelled to negotiate seriously
for the alleviation of the basic issues between
their world and ours. We must be prepared to accept
the risk of war if we hope to avoid war.

"They will not be bluffed, however."

"We must be prepared to carry through that
threat or it cannot succeed in its peaceful purpose.
We must accept whatever risk of world war may attend such a procedure, knowing that should the Communist world choose war, war was coming in any e-
vent." (p. 175, italics in original).

"The armistice effort in Korea taught this:

Never weaken your pressure when the enemy sues for
armistice. Increase it."
  "Force is a decisive factor, the only logic
the Communists truly understand."
  "The lesson is: Do not stop fighting until
hostilities have ended, not if you want an armistice
with the Communists on acceptable terms within a
reasonable period of time." (p. 166).

  97. Ibid., p. 166.
  98. Horne, Source Records of the Great War,
Vol. VI, p. xxxix.
  99. Joy, How Communists Negotiate, pp. 139-140.
  100. "... I found the Communists to be the same
breed of bandits. They are ruthless in their exploitation of weakness; they stop, look and listen
only when confronted by force." Clark, From the
Danube to the Yalu, p. 4.
  101. Ibid., p. 13.
  102. Joy, How Communists Negotiate, p. 178,
italics in original.
  103. See Walter G. Hermes, Truce Tent and
Fighting Front, pp. 42-51.
  104. Joy, How Communists Negotiate, p. 38.
  105. Fehrenbach, This Kind of War, pp. 685-686.
  106. Joy, How Communists Negotiate, p. 134.
  107. Ibid., p. 136.
  108. The Overstreets, What We Must Know About
Communism, p. 291.
  109. Hermes, Truce Tent and Fighting Front,
p. 501.
  110. "Who won the war?" U.S. News, 13 July
1951, pp. 14-15.
  111. MacArthur, "Mr. Truman yielded to counsels
of fear," U.S. News, 17 February 1956, pp. 48-52.
  112. Clark, From the Danube to the Yalu, p. 83.
  113. Whitney, MacArthur, p. 368.
  114. Joy, How Communists Negotiate, p. 165.
  115. "Van Fleet tells story of Korea; answers
to questions by House and Senate Armed Services Committees," U.S. News, 13 March 1953, p. 101. "Now
the whole sentiment out in the Far Pacific is along
the lines of the Communist propaganda - they say
they are the victors, that we are defeated, that we
are the imperialist invaders to destroy liberty in
China; that they have stopped us by defending their
homeland. That is the Communist line of propaganda,
and it keeps discrediting us. And the fact that we
are stopped is somewhat of an admission that we cannot do any better, so that our allies wonder about
this American might and prestige, and can they count
on us - that they are tottering, and what we need to

re-establish American might and prestige, not only in the Pacific but throughout the world, is a military victory to show that we are supreme and that the Communist arms are nothing.

That is why I say we need a victory for prestige, for honor and for influence and for our own good feeling." (p. 103).

116. See Joy, How Communists Negotiate, p. 177.

117. Some thought it was a victory. General Ridgway felt that we missed Total Victory there, if ever possible, but "we did deliver to international Communism its first resounding defeat." The Korean War, p. 240.

118. "The response of the United States was to take the leadership in United Nations actions to deal with the aggression, to commit the bulk of her regular armed forces to the operation, to undertake a major defense effort which called for substantial increases in her armed forces and the production of more and better weapons, to coordinate her many programs of foreign aid and military assistance into a single Mutual Security Program in which the accent was heavily on military aid, to enter into security pacts with Japan, the Philippines, Australia, and New Zealand, to take the initiative in the preparation of a Japanese peace treaty (signed on September 8, 1951, by representatives of 48 nations), and in many other ways to strengthen herself and to assume the leadership of the growing alliance of free nations against Communist imperialism." Palmer and Perkins, International Relations, p. 972.

119. By 1949, our strategy was that the next war would be global and Korea was of minor importance, anyway it was "indefensible." "The concept of 'limited warfare' never entered our councils." Ridgway, The Korean War, p. 11.

120. See Hermes, Truce Tent and Fighting Front, pp. 501-502.

121. Coyle, The United Nations and How it Works, pp. 111-112.

122. Gavin, War and Peace in the Space Age, p. 157.

341

11
Cold War

> Freedom is still expensive.
> It still costs money. It
> still costs blood.[1]
>
>   -- Harry S. Truman
>
> The Western military ex-
> perts are not sufficiently
> freed from traditional con-
> ceptions, and keep wonder-
> ing whether war will come,
> when it is raging all the
> time. [2]
>
>   -- Raymond Aron

1. Freedom versus Force

The international conflict that has been raging
for years known by the popular name of "Cold War"
does not fit any of our old definitions of war. This
is the reason that the term Cold War has become
widely used even though it is not accurate with the
two words being contradictory and the whole term inaccurate as the Communist War, to use a different
term, has often been "hot."
This, the greatest war in the history of mankind, is total war in the sense that it is all-en-
compassing in that every facet of human life and
thought is exploited, from business to ballet, from
missiles to music, from tourists to terror, and from
war to writing, as the Communists try to impose
their ideology on the world. It is difficult to
visualize their society being more completely regi-
mented under war supervision since their industry is
already completely state-controlled and their every

energy is weighed in terms of their world conflict, from the construction of arms, to the dumping of oil, to the control of the arts where music and poetry must conform since they are ideological weapons. All of this massive energy is directed relentlessly against the Free World.

Yet, this is also a limited war in that many limited wars have been and are being fought throughout the world. It is not the stakes that are limited but "the means employed by the belligerents."[3] In military perspective, the Cold War appeared, according to Raymond Aron, as "a race for bases, allies, raw material, and prestige."[4] Although the Soviets and Americans have generally tried to avoid direct conflict between themselves, this has not prevented war by remote control, through satellites, subversive organizations, guerrillas, or many other forms in the Communist repertoire. In reality, this conflict encompassed the entire spectrum of conflict.

The long hoped-for peace after World War II never came. The Communist War was extremely expensive and precluded a return to normalcy. "A conflict which has cost us more than five hundred billion dollars in the last ten years is hardly a normal condition of world affairs."[5] No clearcut line between war and peace existed in the Cold War period. Miksche wrote: "War or Peace - these are the alternatives with which we are faced to-day and, paradoxically, there is practically no difference between them."[6]

It could be said that the Cold War dates from the days of Marx and Engels; however, it could not pose much of a world threat before the Russian Revolution since it had no state power. However, even though there has been continuous trouble with the Russians since the Communists came to power, the popular expression, Cold War, refers generally to the period of tension since World War II, although the Cold War actually started before the war was over.

Admiral Zacharias wrote: "From the Russian viewpoint, the cold war started in the winter of early 1945, when it became evident to Stalin that the wartime co-operation of the Allies would not continue after the war."[7] ... "If anyone with a keen sense of history desires to fix the exact date of the outbreak of the cold war, he may regard January 5, 1945, as that day."[8] That was the date the Soviets recognized the Lublin Committee as the Government of Poland.

The Overstreets date the beginning of the Cold

War as a few months later. In the May 1945 issue of
Les Cahiers du Communisme, the theoretical monthly
of the French Communist Party, there appeared an
article by Jacques Duclos attacking Earl Browder
(CPUSA) who was advocating that American Communists
might work through normal political means. "We can
say, then, with good reason, that the cold war dates
from the publication of this article - while the
Soviet Union was still ostensibly allied with the
West."9

     Admiral Leahy dated the opening of the conflict
at Potsdam.10 Gould emphasized that an electoral
campaign speech by Stalin on 9 February 1946 "was to
all practical purposes, the formal announcement of
the end of the wartime East-West cooperation"11 and
resulted in Communist stress on the division of the
world into two blocs.

     Regardless of what one takes as the date of the
beginning of the Cold War, it is evident that the
tension which had existed since 1917, in spite of
the efforts of Roosevelt to get along with Stalin,
quickly surfaced again before World War II was over.
The end of the second war, and particularly the way
we ended it, left us face to face with expanding
Communism. Our war alliance with the Soviets successfully thwarted the world designs of the Nazis.
"That was a victory beyond price, but, says Toynbee,
we 'could not have put down Hitler without consequently producing the situation with which all of us
now find ourselves confronted.'"12 Salvador de
Madariaga described World War II as "a triangular
fight. The West against Nazism-Fascism and Communism; Nazism-Fascism against Communism and the West;
and Communism against the West and Nazism-Fascism."
With the end of the war, the third point of the triangle vanished, and the struggle was again two-sided,
"the present cold war between Communism and the West,
a permanent feature of our world since Lenin became
master of Russia." As he points out, "the cold war
is not some obscure aftermath of the second world-
war, due to an unfortunate worsening of the relations between Moscow and the West."13

     Elliott Roosevelt recorded how his father
dreaded what actually came about. "'The only thing
that could upset the apple-cart, after the war, is
if the world is divided again, Russia against England and us.'"14 D. F. Fleming, in his apologetic
manner, made the astounding comment: "Yet it is altogether probable that if Roosevelt had been able
to finish his fourth term in the White House there
would have been no Cold War."15 This is extremely

hard to believe, particularly since FDR toward the
end had a most brutal exchange of messages with
Stalin, which some even claim hastened his death.

Communist Russia, which proved to be an impossible ally in war, quickly increased its uncoopera-
tive policy in the early postwar years. To briefly
summarize some of these conflicts, here are some excerpts from a statement by Ambassador Warren R.
Austin at the United Nations on 14 November 1949 in
reply to a Soviet table thumping outburst. "This
talk of peace sounds more like war."

> The principle of unanimity of the five perma-
> nent members of the Security Council is based
> on the assumption that they will cooperate to-
> wards a common goal of peace. But the Soviet
> Union has twisted that principle into a weapon
> of obstruction and sabotage of world peace.

> At Yalta, at Potsdam, in the Allied Control
> Council, in the Council of Foreign Ministers,
> and in the long negotiations for peace treaties,
> the unanimity principle has been used by the
> Soviet Union, not to promote agreement but to
> delay settlements and to force concessions.
> And in the Security Council, a long list of ve-
> toes provides evidence that Soviet cooperation
> is available only on Soviet terms and only for
> Soviet purposes.

> Confidence in Soviet pledges has been under-
> mined by the experience of the past few years.
> To find cause for concern, it is not necessary
> to recall the Friendship Pact with Nazi Germany,
> or the Soviet nonaggression pacts with Finland,
> Latvia, Estonia, and Lithuania. We need only
> look at the long, unhappy list of broken Soviet
> pledges that has grown since we have been en-
> gaged in the common effort to create the United
> Nations.

> You will recall the promises that free elec-
> tions would be held in Poland, in Bulgaria,
> Hungary, and Rumania. (Soviet UN representa-
> tive had delivered the ultimatum in Bucharest
> for a hand-picked pro-Soviet government to be
> put in in 2 hours and 5 minutes.)

> A Soviet agreement to withdraw troops from Iran
> at the end of the war was only fulfilled be-
> cause the non-Soviet members of the Security

Council stood together in demanding that the
pledge be honored.

> The depredation of Manchuria, the forced parti-
> tion of Korea, guerrilla warfare waged against
> Greece, the threats to Turkey, the obliteration
> of freedom in Czechoslovakia, the relentless
> destruction of all democratic opposition in
> Bulgaria, Hungary, and Rumania, and now, the
> subjugation of Poland to the point where a Mar-
> shal of the Red Army has been installed as that
> partitioned country's Minister of Defense - all
> these are power-grabbing actions by the Soviet
> Union that peaceful words cannot hide.[16]

The list of tension spots between the Communists and
the Free World has grown so that it now includes
practically every spot in the world and every aspect
of international (and often internal) relations.

Winston Churchill, in a speech at Boston on 31
March 1949, asked the interesting question: Why have
the Russians deliberately acted so as to unite the
Free World against them? His answer reflects the
familiar position of dictators in history.

> It is because they fear the friendship of the
> West more than its hostility. They cannot,
> they cannot afford to allow free and friendly
> intercourse to grow up between the vast areas
> they control and the civilization of the West.
> The Russian people must not see what is going
> on outside, and the world must not see what
> goes on inside the Soviet domain. Thirteen
> men in the Kremlin, holding down hundreds of
> millions of people and aiming at the rule of
> the world, feel that at all costs they must
> keep up the barriers. Self-preservation, not
> for Russia but for themselves, lies at the
> root and is the explanation of their sinister
> and malignant policy.[17]

The Communists, with their intent to seize control of the globe, are the self-appointed enemy of
the world. They stir up a cacophony of noise about
capitalism and imperialism and other words that they
sling about loosely with their own warped definitions; but, in the final analysis, they wish to take
over the world and are using every means available
to them without becoming involved in a war that
would wipe them off the face of the earth. It should

be remembered that our enemy in the Cold War is not
Russia or China but the Communist Parties. "If the
Communist Party did not exist, there would be no
cold war to-day."[18] The great struggle, "they blare
out through their loudspeakers, is one between communism and capitalism. This, of course, is nonsense.
The two 'isms' in question are as old-fashioned as
the beards of Engels and of Marx. Socialism has
penetrated all free life so that every party is
tainted by it; while capitalism at its worst is rampant in all the countries exploited by Russia."[19]
Referring to Eastern Europe, Madariaga continued:
"It is indeed an impressive witness to the monumental gullibility of western masses that Soviet leaders dare speak of American imperialism from behind
a barrier of chained slave-nations." He summed it
up, that in the Cold War between the Communists and
all the other nations of the world, the true issue
is "freedom versus force."[20]

2.   Ideological War

     The great struggle in the world today is be-
tween one group of nations that believes in freedom
of the individual and the liberty to govern and
live as one chooses and a pagan ideology that counts
the individual for nought but to serve the state as
the omnipotent masters command. These differences
are irreconcilable. Nevertheless, there would be
no cause for conflict between them if each remained
in its own sphere. The Free World, trying to enjoy
its way of life, is not waging a war of liberation
of the Communist World, but is trying to keep the
non-Communist world free. The impetus for the conflict comes from Communist imperialism. Not satisfied to remain in their area, they are intent on
trying to convert the world to their system, by
force if necessary.
     The major battleground in this war in the minds
of men. Striving to control man to deprive him of
his right to think for himself, the Communists follow an archaic doctrine that was already out-of-
date before they ever came to power. They operate
in the name of the people to create their utopian,
classless society which could never come for that
would remove the Communists themselves who have created a class more rigid, exploiting and dictatorial
than that which they overthrew. Never has the world
seen such an egotistical breed of plotters; they

348

have an explanation for everything, the truth notwithstanding; no other explanation is tolerated;
their holy word is law; their fanatical ideas must
be accepted by everyone as they are the self-appointed saviors of the world even if they have to force
their immoral ways on the world. This group of dictatorial prophets wants to reduce all of us to their
simple utilitarian status excluding independent
thought and action.

The Communists are at war with everyone, including their own people. They want to destroy democratic governments, and the free system cannot survive unless Communism evolves or disappears because
Communism "cannot exist without wanting to destroy
the western system, since that is what communism
is."[21] Communism maintains its control by means of
arms, as we have seen repeatedly in Eastern Europe
and the fanatical clashes of the Cultural Revolution
in China.

The Communist War is an ideological struggle
unlike any wars of the past, even the religious wars.
Total war, particularly for a cause that must triumph at all costs, demands that all weapons be kept
under the control of the central government. If
peace is but a cold war, ideas will be no more than
abstractions since nations wage war with ideas as
well as with explosives. If enemies are unwilling
to give up their material weapons, "it is useless to
expect them to abandon ideological weapons." Victory is considered too important to surrender any
weapon: nuclear bomb or idea. The ideological arm
must be muted by means of censorship, jamming, and
other techniques. "For it is a principle of contemporary warfare, cold as well as hot, that it is more
essential that an ideology survive and prosper than
that men should."[22]

For the Communists to control the minds of
their captives, they must have absolute control of
all communications media and strictly regulate travel. The result is the closed society. As the Berlin Wall so vividly demonstrated, the Iron and Bamboo Curtains are not to keep foreigners out but to
keep the people in. The mere fact that so many
people wanted to leave their native land was indictment enough of Communism. It is often hard for
Americans to understand why the Russian people, for
example, tolerate certain things. They forget that
the Russian people do not have access to the other
side of the story, which quite often is the truth.
They read what the government permits to be printed;
they hear and see what the government permits to be

349

broadcasted; there is no criticism of anything unless the government directs it. When this is endured throughout a lifetime, it is difficult to comprehend anything other than what they are told to
believe.

The question is often posed, why don't the people rise up against this sort of dictatorship? In
the all-pervading police state, as developed by the
Communists, this is much easier said than done. The
Communists have perfected the techniques of inform-
ers, dummy anti-Communist organizations, and loyalty
tests where the subversive contact must be turned in
to the police or the citizen will be arrested for
failing to if the contact is a secret police agent.[23]
This highly developed program of terror and repression has created a significant degree of thought
control. Victor Zorza, the English Kremlinologist,
studied the use of computers in the Soviet Union as
a tool for thought control by the political police.
The Russians had started a crash program which was
to triple their computer "population" in the next
five years for an economic control system with con-
comitant "social" aspects.[24] George Orwell may yet
be the prophet.

In a closed society, the people live in a sea
of propaganda for the government is always trying to
control the feelings, knowledge, and reactions of
the people. The other side of this same coin is the
psychological warfare that these same governments
conduct against all the rest of the world. This
warfare appears in an infinite number of variations:
the world forums are one scene; the United Nations,
summit meetings when they can get Western leaders
to meet with them, disarmament and various other
conferences. The Communists conducted several peace
campaigns that had some far-reaching results. Peace
campaigns so conditioned the Free World that the
leaders could not do anything without incurring the
disapprobation of the press. Yet Khrushchev issued
ultimatums, Brezhnev proclaimed that the Soviet Union had the right to change governments in Eastern
Europe, Chou En-lai or Mao Tse-tung could order
bombardments and invasions, Kim Il Sun invaded
South Korea, Ho Chi Minh invaded the other countries
of Indochina, but not the West.[25] Another important element is the Communist parties within each
country which provide a full time Fifth Column that
is busy trying to spread the gospel and to bring
down the government.

An extremely important phase of this war was
the call for "peaceful coexistence." This was well

designed so that the Westerner looked upon it as honest competition and a reduced threat of war. However, for the Communists, it was merely a continuation of the conflict with a reduced emphasis on overt military operations. "Coexistence then, for the East, is a way of buying time for the inevitable settlement of accounts between capitalism and communism."[26] Peaceful coexistence has been the source of great confusion in the West. Finletter saw coexistence as "the development of the world situation in such a way that the two Communist empires will not try to expand their respective areas by war."[27] This brings us back to the Western differentiation between war and peace that is so unclear in the Communist War. This was not Khrushchev's definition as he openly declared that he supported wars of liberation and this Communist policy has not changed.

Peaceful coexistence developed in the West a fear of its own strength, which remained considerable. The timid reactions of the West to some of the periodic crises created by the Communists convinced them that they had an upper hand. Dinerstein wrote in 1959: "The Soviet leaders now believe that the world military balance of power has changed decisively in their favor. They believe the new Soviet military strength makes a war not of Soviet choosing less likely."[28] In the 1970s, the Russians should be even more confident as they passed nuclear parity with the United States and pushed forward to superiority.

With the growth of the Russian nuclear capability and the ever present reluctance of the Americans to use theirs, there developed a nuclear stalemate, often referred to as the "balance of terror." In 1955, "Churchill believed that the hydrogen-bomb had made the stakes so high in a war between great powers that such a war would never break out. Malenkov evidently shared this belief; but he was rebuked by his colleagues for suggesting that a nuclear war would destroy both Communist and Capitalist civilization, and he later reverted to the orthodox view that only the latter would be destroyed."[29] Are we approaching an end to war? No, answered Fuller, "because in an ideological age the fundamental causes of war are profoundly psychological; they cannot be eliminated either by a negation, or a surplus, of physical force." One form of war has become obsolete only to be replaced by another - cold war. "It is a combination of psychological war, the weapons of which are the emotions;

of economic war aimed at destroying financial stability; of guerrilla war, the most primitive form of war; and civil war, its most brutal form."[30]

After the fighting of World War II, Russia expanded her influence over all of Eastern Europe without firing a shot. Since then, the Soviets have waged this form of conflict by "propaganda, sabotage and subversion in every non-Communist country in the world; for all countries which have not accepted Soviet Communism are held to be active enemies of Russia."[31]

The Cold War is a struggle of predominantly moral forces while hot war is a struggle of predominantly physical forces. Western powers place considerably more faith in physical than in moral forces. "In this way, they are making every day more certain of their victory in a hot war which the H-bomb makes less and less likely, while making every day more likely their defeat in a cold war which is actually swallowing us all in its turmoil."[32] The probability of World War III was greatly reduced, perhaps even near zero; but the Cold War was likely to continue indefinitely between the two great power blocs. The conclusion was that things might not get any worse, but they would probably not get much better.[33] The tempo of the Cold War varied from the seemingly harmless shipment of thousands of tons of Communist propaganda throughout the world to threats over Berlin to fighting in Viet-Nam. Although there were peaks and troughs of action, the great ocean of activity flowed along spewing forth into every corner of the world.

Politics is still the basis of relationships between nations. Wars may appear but they should be thoroughly steeped in political motives and activities. Those who had hoped that unconditional surrender would end the second war better than a negotiated surrender were soon disappointed by the dawning of the Cold War. This highlights the grave problem of keeping politics dominant - a problem we failed to master during World War II. In an ideological conflict approaching the ferocity of a religious war, it becomes increasingly difficult to maintain the primacy of politics - in cold war or hot war.[34]

Should we try to compromise with the Communists or agree to talks? We believe in compromise; they do not. We talk in hope of solving problems; they talk in hope of gaining an advantage in their drive to bury us. Stalin was of the opinion that "sincere diplomacy is no more possible than dry water or wooden iron." This is a dilemma for us: "while our adversaries are absolute and dogmatic, we are relative and empirical. Such is one of the reasons why we are ever ready to parley (as a matter of strategy) while our adversaries only talk of parleying (as a matter of tactics)."[35] We tend toward the position that it never hurts to talk, but this is not always true. John Kennedy popularized the slogan "Never negotiate from fear; but never fear to negotiate." We are engaged in a psychological war with experts and they can turn almost any circumstance to their profit. When we go to them, it is made to appear that we are weak; when we do not agree to their preposterous demands, they portray us as blocking the road to peace; when we tire of talking to them for years on the same subject with no progress, they accuse us of not being sincere. This goes on and on as we have seen in the trying years since World War II.

A major aspect during most of the years of the Cold War was that there really was nothing to negotiate. It takes two parties to negotiate; so when one party is not prepared to make any concessions, there is no basis for meaningful talks. With the changed circumstances in the 1970s, particularly the evolution of Red China as Russia's major concern, there may be some areas for legitimate accommodations; however, the West must proceed cautiously and defend its interests.

One of the few factors that seemed to be clear about the Cold War was that there was small likelihood of winning it by doing nothing. The great problem for the West was what to do. The general United States policy since 1945 had been "reaction" or "inaction." By reacting to each individual crisis as if it were not related to the whole Cold War, or by completely failing to act, hoping that the problem would go away (Castro in Cuba in 1959), we conducted the Cold War in a most unsatisfactory manner. It has been difficult to come up with a positive policy.

Cold war may well be "the only possible war that remains between big powers."[36] Yet there was no positive policy to carry the conflict to the Communists, who to some were weak in many aspects and we could have tried to weaken them further. "The cold war must be fought eastward with at least as much energy as it is westward. The Communist regime is frail. No effort, no attempt is made to drive wedges into the splits."[37] David Sarnoff wrote: "Whether we freeze to death or burn to death,

our civilization would be equally finished."38   For
him, our duty was clear - go for victory: "Our duty
and our best chance for salvation, in the final
analysis, is to prosecute the cold war - to the
point of victory.   To survive in freedom we must
win."39

The Cold War is the true "protracted conflict"
and will not be solved by looking away and hoping
that the problem will not be there when we look
again.   The Free World has a great ideological heritage, but we accept it and do not make a fetish of
it trying to jam it down people's throats.   We live
with it and cherish it but we do not talk much about
it.   We do not think of it as a propaganda piece
that should be held up and waved all the time like a
campaign slogan and we have not set out with missionary zeal to spread our enlightenment to others.
This proved to be a handicap; for, though we have a
strong ideological basis to our culture, we do not
preach it.   To those who do not have our benefits,
there is a tendency to think that we are merely ma-
terialistic and do not really have anything of value.   This reluctance to "sell" our way of life put
us at a great disadvantage in the Communist War.

3.   Peace Is War!

In this age of quasi-peace, it is very easy to
let our desire for peace blind us to the true state
of affairs.   It is easy to lose ourselves in enjoyment of our affluent society or the concern for our
domestic problems and ignore the harsh realities of
the deadly war that is being waged against us.   It
is easier to think of these complicated problems of
the modern world as being far away and not concerning us rather than to face the stark fact that if we
lose this war, we will lose everything we hold dear:
our freedom, our culture, our heritage, our complete
way of life.   This threat is being steadfastly conducted against us in the name of peace.
In the Cold War, then, peace is a very deadly
state of affairs; it is waged much like war but in
a more subtle and insidious manner.   To the Communists, peace is synonomous with war.   This, then, is
the challenge of the century: the Free World, which
can get its hate up in time of war but cruises along
in blithe complacency in so-called peacetime, must
strive to prevent its destruction in time of peace.
The Communists start from a premise that results

354

from only the weirdest logic: to the effect that
what's mine is mine; what's yours is negotiable.
This means that the Communist World is holy; no
frontier of it can be pushed back; yet all the rest
of the world is up for grabs by the Communists. This
means we cannot liberate Hungary but they can take
Cuba; we cannot liberate North Korea but they can
take North Viet-Nam and then, of course, proceed to
"liberate" South Viet-Nam. (It is interesting to
note that there is a strong school of thought that
believes the Soviet Union would not tolerate a liberation of Cuba.) The world can go forward to Communist tyranny but it cannot go back to freedom.
Since they regard the Communist domination of the
world as their historic mission, all the areas that
have not already been "liberated" are merely future
Communist conquests. Or, as the Overstreets put it:
"The orbit where the Party holds power is endowed
with the same sacrosanct impenetrability that Lenin
bestowed upon the Party. But the rest of the world
is regarded as rightly open to penetration - because
it is future Communist territory."[40] The acceptance
of this premise, even tacitly, guarantees the eventual victory of Communism and our ignominious defeat.

As we have already seen, this war involved every imaginable aspect of potential conflict: economic, emotional, and social. Bernard Fall noted the
comments of a mobile group commander in Indochina:
"'This is not a military war in the old sense. It
is not even a political war. What we're facing here
is a social war, a class war.'"[41] The ever-present
threat of nuclear war has been important in the
change of emphasis on the diverse forms of war. The
Damocles sword of mass destruction has not wiped out
armaments and military conflict; however, it has intensified other methods of conflict - the economic,
political, and psychological - once considered secondary.

The Communist cause was aided by the nebulous
nature of this unclear form of warfare. The name
"Cold War" itself helped them by prolonging the idea
that it was not a shooting war, thereby leading us
to underestimate its importance. Colonel William R.
Kintner gave it another name - termite warfare - the
eating away of governmental power both from within
and from without and including the use of violence.[42]

The Cold War has been characterized as a period
of intense anti-colonialism and fiery nationalism.
Though the Communists have effectively used both of
these trends against us, they may one day come back
to haunt them. Soviet Russia is now the largest

355

colonial power in the world and the same nationalist
fever that the Communists support in other parts of
the world is ruthlessly suppressed in the Soviet Union and in the Soviet orbit. This powder keg may
one day blow them apart. There have been riots in
the Soviet Union, and the revolts in Eastern Europe
had to be ruthlessly smashed by the Red Army to keep
those countries under Soviet control. Beyond the
Soviet empire, the political map of the world changed
almost monthly in the 1960s. Africa was the scene
of the greatest changes but future adjustments may
be all over the world. The day of the older sover-
eignties may be growing to its end. The nations of
men unite and frontiers fall - and this is not only
a gospel for Europe.

The machinations of the Soviet empire on the
world scene since the late 1930s have presented examples of world power politics incomparable with any
others in history. Their cold-blooded system of alliances and non-aggression pacts, the advantages
they gained from their allies in World War II, the
great coups that delivered Eastern Europe into the
Red empire, the rise of Red China and turmoil in
Asia, their pressure throughout Asia, Africa, and
Latin America, plus countless other examples point
up the high pressure game they have been playing.
Berlin is an example of a pawn on the great chess-
board of power politics that they have moved all
over the board to achieve varying degrees of tension
as if it were controlled by a faucet.

Cuba, 1962, is another example and one of the
watersheds of the Cold War. Walter Lippmann, whose
name is closely linked with the expression "Cold
War," felt that, after the Soviet missiles were
shown to be in Cuba, President Kennedy sought a limited objective and obtained it. "This was possible
because he sought a negotiated settlement which did
not call for and does not mean an unconditional surrender.... But the results could not have been
achieved simply and peaceably if the President had
made his objective not the dismantling of the bases
but unconditional surrender - that is to say the
dismantling of Castro's Communist regime.... As in
all good settlements, neither party is a loser and
both are the gainers."[43] Not all opinion felt that
the President came off quite so well. A report from
Mexico gave the feeling that the President won the
military showdown but lost the peace; Khrushchev
lost face but turned defeat into political victory.[44]
This festering sore on our southern flank continued
to spread its poison throughout Latin America (and

356

more recently into Africa) and remained a key crisis point in the Cold War, such as whether Cienfuegos was a Soviet nuclear submarine base.

Although the Cold War encompassed all forms of conflict, it was often quite "hot" in various forms of armed conflict from guerrilla warfare to the limited (but large) wars in Korea and Viet-Nam. The list of these small wars is quite long - over 400 conflicts since World War II[45] - but it is significant to remember, as we review a few of them, that not all represent Communist victories or even gains.

The first clear-cut instance was the guerrilla warfare that broke out in Greece. This resulted in American assistance and, after the Yugoslavs discontinued their support, the guerrillas were defeated. Although the Communist-Nationalist fight for China predated the war, it blew forth with great fury and a great defeat for the Free World when the Chinese Communists took control of the mainland.[46] In the meantime, several guerrilla wars broke out in Asia and then the invasion of South Korea came in 1950. The Huks were finally defeated in the Philippines and, after a much longer campaign, the British defeated the Communist terrorists in Malaya.

Indonesia went through a period of civil war, various uprisings, increased flirting with the Soviets, formation of the Djakarta-Hanoi-Peking Axis, confrontation with Malaysia, the Communist purge, and rebuilding the bankrupt shambles Sukarno left. The problems in Indochina had appeared during the war and continued after the defeat of the Japanese in 1945. Indochina must be considered as at least a partial defeat, if not major, since it resulted in the loss of what was called North Viet-Nam to the Communists. This was an expensive[47] war that, combined with Algeria, had longrange effects on the French Army and people. It was a confused war as regards Allied policy in that when the Americans considered intervening, the British were against it and the French unenthusiastic.[48] These same two countries had dragged their feet on the Korean War. too. The problem, as General Ridgway wrote in his memoirs, was that if we were to commit our forces to Indochina, we would have had to be willing to pay the price to win.[49]

With the pressure off the Chinese as a result of the settlement in Korea in 1953, it was not long before the Communists had made significant gains in Indochina, resulting in the French defeat at Dien Bien Phu and the Geneva settlement in 1954. "The cease-fire negotiated at Geneva on July 20, 1954, all pios cries of 'sell-out' notwithstanding, was, like that of Panmunjon one year earlier, the best obtainable under the circumstances."[50]

The area of old Indochina had been divided up but the problems continued in Viet-Nam, Laos, and Cambodia which we will review in more detail in the next chapter. The guerrilla war was renewed there and, in the early 1960s, the Americans became more heavily committed with military advisors, helicopters, and other air support. In late 1964, the North Vietnamese committed regular army units to the south and in 1965 the United States sent in combat troops to keep the country from being divided across the highlands. The commitment of over half a million American troops in the longest war in United States history turned sour with appalling results across America. President Johnson did not stand for reelection; President Nixon "Vietnamized" the war and reduced the American role. After long negotiations in Paris, an agreement was signed, and immediately violated by North Viet-Nam. South Viet-Nam fell in 1975 as did Laos and Cambodia. Soon Viet-Nam and Kampuchea (the paranoid Cambodia) were fighting as well as Viet-Nam and China. The third Indochina War was underway.

Korea remained tense through the years with repeated incidents along the DMZ and along the coasts, such as the seizure of the Pueblo. An insurgency developed in Thailand and the same old one continued in Burma. India and Pakistan went to war over East Pakistan which became Bangladesh and still faced each other over Kashmir with more ferocity than toward their common enemy, Communist China, which invaded India in 1962 and may well do so again in the vast mountain areas along their long border. Pakistan was friendly with Communist China and India signed a 20-year friendship treaty with the Soviet Union. Even Sri Lanka experienced bloody rioting. Afghanistan suffered coups and moved closer to Russia. Asia has continued as a paradise for Communist meddling.

Not all the upheaval was in Asia; Africa had its share and will probably have more in the future as the old colonies in Africa became independent, thus facing sometimes insurmountable problems in a hard, unfamiliar world. There was fighting in Algeria, Angola, Kenya, Sudan, and the confusion in the Congo, Nigeria suffered a bitter civil war over Biafra. There was a plethora of coups and some counter coups. There is still fighting in Rhodesia, Ethiopia, Somalia, and Mozambique. The Arab states

358

remained embroiled in the feud with Israel which,
due to increased Soviet presence, kept the feud
critical lest there be a Soviet-American confrontation.

There were repeated crises in Syria, Iran, Jordan, Lebanon, Yemen, and Iraq. The 1958 confusion
in Lebanon resulted in an American force landing
there for a short time with a peaceful outcome. Now
Lebanon has been almost destroyed by a fratricidal
civil war. The Palestinian guerrillas added their
weight to the welter of confusion and terrorism, and
there was an unsuccessful insurgency in Oman on the
Arabian peninsula (supported for a time by the Red
Chinese). Libya, with its new oil wealth and a dynamic young ruler delighted in stirring up the region. Malta threw a NATO headquarters out; there is
a large Russian fleet in the Mediterranean; Algeria
is socialistic with close contacts with Russia; and
Morocco was unstable and fighting an insurgency
(backed by Algeria) in the former Spanish Sahara.

Communism reached the Americas in Guatemala
where it was finally removed, reached its zenith in
Cuba, and then Chile. Our policy of "wait and see"
toward Cuba was unsuccessful. Then with a new administration in power, Cuba was invaded at the Bay
of Pigs, but the operation was turned over to civilians in the intelligence field and it failed miser-
ably. After the humiliation of ransoming the prisoners from the abortive invasion, we were still
faced with a Cuba that became a Soviet arsenal with
Soviet troops there, exporter of revolution and vile
propaganda throughout Latin America, and Soviet
proxy by providing combat troops in Africa. The
Cold War grew hot with the guerrilla fighting in
Venezuela, Bolivia, the Dominican Republic, and with
the urban guerrilla fighting such as evidenced by
the Tupamaros. The social problems and political
instability of Latin America continue to provide
fertile soil for Communist exploitation.

The fighting in Europe was on the Communist
side of the Iron Curtain where the satellites peri-
odically revolted against the paradise imposed on
them by the Russians. Except for the recurring harassment of Berlin over the years and the terrorism
of the Red Brigades, Europe has remained heavily
armed and tense but relatively quiet. However, the
stability of the division of Europe is deceptive.
The Europeans do not like it; it is based on the
stability of the dividing powers, and there is no
ideological consensus. Each side denies "the legitimacy of existing European arrangements."[51]

The list of "hot" spots in the Cold War is rather long and, therefore, it is unrealistic to think that war does not exist anymore. It may not be present in the forms that some people expected, but it is, nevertheless, quite prevalent in our contemporary world and shows every indication of remaining with us for a long time to come.

Closely allied with the concept that the Communist march toward conquest can go only forward and never backward, is the belief that the Soviet Union will never accept a defeat - either for itself or a satellite. This is a terribly un-American, defeatist attitude that leaves us in a fatalistic position; they can expand to take over the world but we cannot do anything about it. This is a patently ridiculous concept which accepts their propaganda but, unfortunately, it has many adherents in the West. This concept is completely contrary to basic Communist doctrine in that they will do anything to preserve themselves. They like our doctrine, no doubt, since they can push so hard with it. But as with the Berlin Wall in 1961, when the Communist guards had no ammunition; and in Cuba, where they pulled out their missiles; they bluff us - if we call their hand they quickly change direction and make up a suitable "explanation." If we are to survive, we must push them. In an overseas war, which should prove unpopular at home since they would not be protecting Mother Russia, they would not be as strong as we paint them. We have become timid in a world where only strength will survive.

Over the years we have often heard the Communists claim that time is on their side. Part of their explanation for this is that democracies have difficulty in fighting a protracted quasi-war. Americans are impatient people who like to get things over with quickly with nice, neat, complete solutions. It is for just this reason that it is to the Communist advantage never to take the Cold War to the point of hot war, which might result in a complete solution - the destruction of Communism. This Communist patience is in marked contrast with the democratic yearning for normalcy.[52]

What, then, are the chances for victory in the Cold War? First there are some, such as Fleming, who feel that our confidence that we can do whatever we want is so strong it almost precludes realization that cold wars are "self-defeating in their very nature" and cannot be won. He sees the conclusion as unavoidable. "The objective of a cold war is to isolate enemies and win friends, but the very act of

waging it repels friends and makes more enemies.
Waging a cold war and winning a cold war are thus
mutually exclusive."[53] Cold war involves an infinite variety of forms any conflict might take. But
the heavy cloud hanging menacingly overhead at all
times is the threat of a general nuclear war, "a war
which neither side can hope to win (the word victory
has long since lost such rational content as it still
possessed in 1945)."[54] Intercontinental missiles, as
Henry Kissinger pointed out, "will make it almost
impossible for either side to achieve total victory
through all-out war."[55]

The prospect of tremendous destruction including damage to the economic base serves as a strong
deterrent to nuclear war as the price for victory
would be exorbitant. Total victory, in the political sense, cannot be reasonably expected in any
meaningful sense in total war. Only a relatively
modest gain can be reasonably expected by the winner
and that gain will come in limited war.[56] General
Fuller sorted wars into two categories: "those with
limited and those with unlimited political aims, and
it is the first and not the second which have been
profitable to the victor."[57]

This threat of nuclear war created so much confusion that many Cold War issues were deemphasized
in fear of this great impending holocaust that might
come but yet was not expected to come. It was repeatedly preached to us that nuclear war would be
completely different from conventional warfare. But
since these spokesmen were speaking on the basis of
no experience with those weapons, it would seem prudent to question their claim. Is the line really so
clear between nuclear and conventional war? Would
the use of sub-kiloton weapons against truly military targets justify or result in the use of megaton
weapons against cities? This is a tremendous step.
A small nuclear weapon might do less damage than a
large artillery concentration or a heavy air strike.
We do not desire nuclear war but we must not sacrifice flexibility in our planning by closing options
before they have been thoroughly tested.

The confusion carried over into the field of
policy. The Free World, generally refusing to recognize that it was involved in a war for its survival, was unable to present a united front and a positive policy. John Foster Dulles, the man who
brought brinkmanship into the vocabulary, was roundly criticized at home and abroad for his hard attitude toward the Communists. However, in an article
in Life, he showed his insight into the importance

of going to the brink to stand up to the Communists: "'You have to take chances for peace, just as you must take chances in war. Some say that we were brought to the verge of war. Of course we were brought to the verge of war. The ability to get to the verge without getting into war is the necessary art. If you cannot master it, you inevitably get into war.'"[58] Our few successes in the Cold War point up conclusively that "a show of strength on our part does not bring on a crisis... Rather, it is what prevents crisis...".[59] This is a bigtime gambling game that is going on and the stakes are the highest imaginable; this is no place for the timid and weak of heart.

There were many criticisms of our lack of a policy for handling the crises of the Cold War. The year 1956 was a big year: there were riots in Soviet Georgia in March, in Poland in June, riots in Hungary in October, and also the Suez crisis. That October has been called "the most crucial month of the most crucial year, the most dramatic time in the entire history of the cold war." Lukacs lamented, "It is hardly understandable why they were caught without a policy...".[60]

The important requirement is to look at the big picture rather than to be continuously looking at only a small facet each time it flashes on the world scene. One Communist agent once remarked to a prominent Communist from South America that the Spanish Civil War was just a skirmish not a war. He emphasized that one can afford to lose one or a hundred skirmishes, as long as one wins the war.[61] To keep these skirmishes in perspective, we must never take our eyes off the war. We do not intend to surrender our wonderful way of life to amoral Communism and the problem does not seem likely to disappear on its own. As Francis Walter said, "either we prevent the achievement of Communism's 'historic mission' - or we perish."[62] We have a magnificent heritage in America and it is our duty to preserve it.

In recent years, there were recurrent cries that our government was following a "no-win" policy - that is, they acted if forced to but there was little initiative displayed on our side and no real program for winning the Cold War. Dean Rusk, who was active in the Korea decision and who served as Secretary of State for eight years during the Kennedy and Johnson Administrations, answered these claims: "'That is simply not so. Of course we intend to win. And we are going to win. Our objective is a victory for all mankind.... The global

struggle for freedom and against Communist imperialism is our main business in the State Department.'
To win this struggle, he stated, the U. S. and its
friends must achieve 'a world free of aggression...
a world of independent nations... a world which
yields continuing progress in economic and social
justice for all peoples.' Mr. Rusk said the Kennedy
Administration hoped for victory without a devastating war, but he added, 'We shall defend our vital
interests and those of the free world by whatever
means may be necessary.'"[63] The courageous decisions to stand in Korea and Viet-Nam turned to political disasters both abroad and at home.

The future is not at all clear and the prospects for no drastic changes in the world are perhaps dim. Miksche stated that there are only two
choices - but to him there was no question of the
choice: "Communism or Americanism are the alternatives confronting us; the first is essentially Asiatic, and foreign to us.... Communists in France and
other free parts of Europe should not imagine that
their regime would be different from that of Moscow.... America, on the other hand, constitutes a
part of our own civilization, and if a choice has to
be made it should not be a difficult one."[64]

General Mark Clark finished a book calling for
courage and victory in our war against Communism.
"But peace will be granted us only if we are strong,
if the Russians and their followers know we are
strong and if they are convinced we have the determination and courage to use that strength to achieve
a military victory the next time we are called to
war against communism."[65] To this should be added
the desire to meet Communism on all the various
battlefields of the war, cold or hot, and show it
for what it is, the greatest fraud ever designed to
perpetuate a dictatorship.

The Cold War, an euphemism for one of the most
total wars of all times, was prosecuted across almost the entire spectrum of conflict (with the more
violent end being used mainly as a threat) and was
worldwide in scope, even reaching into outer space.
Faced with the announced threat of an oppressive,
totalitarian ideology to bury us, our greatest weakness was in the refusal of vast segments of the Free
World to face up to this challenge to our future.

At the time of a possible Berlin settlement and
talks about arms limitations and force reductions,
there were many who claimed the Cold War was over.
In recent years, a complete revisionist school of
history appeared that tried to blame the Cold War

and all the world's ills on the United States. It
will be difficult to determine the true end of the
Cold War until honest historians can make a clear
and complete analysis years after the facts. However, there was sincere doubt that the Cold War was
over,[66] new era or not, when one considered the Soviet drive for superiority, not parity, in strategic
weapons; their increased defense spending; the extensive expansion of their navy and its moves into
the Mediterranean, the Indian Ocean, the Caribbean,
and the Gulf of Mexico; and their continued support
of North Viet-Nam. The expulsion of 105 Soviet diplomats and trade delegation members from Britain on
spy charges in September 1971 put a chill back into
the Cold War and reminded many of the harsh face of
the Soviet bear.

It is clear that, nuclear and thermonuclear
weapons notwithstanding, war is still an important
element in contemporary international relations.
The problem appears in divergent or nonexistent concepts of victory. To ever win the Cold War, the
Free World must determine what Victory would be.
However, before reviewing the concepts of victory,
we must consider the impact of the longest and most
difficult war in our history.

NOTES

1. Palmer and Perkins, International Relations,
p. 268.
2. Aron, The Century of Total War, p. 233.
3. Ibid., p. 171.
4. Ibid., p. 173.
5. Goldwater, Why Not Victory?, p. 27. The
figure is probably well over a trillion dollars.
6. Miksche, Unconditional Surrender, p. 281.
7. Admiral Ellis M. Zacharias, Behind Closed
Doors: the Secret History of the Cold War, p. 51.
8. Ibid., p. 53, italics in original.
9. The Overstreets, What We Must Know About
Communism, p. 99, italics in original.
10. Leahy, I Was There, p. 429. Woodward wrote
of Potsdam: "A meeting between Mr. Churchill and
Stalin on the second evening of the Conference
showed the 'offensive-defensive' line which the Russians intended to take. Stalin... thought that the
sending of observers to Greece during the elections
would show a lack of confidence in the honesty of
the Greek people. He maintained that Russian policy
in the countries liberated by the Red Army was

directed towards the establishment of strong, independent, sovereign States. He did not want to
'Sovietize' these countries, and would allow free
elections in which all except fascist parties would
take part. He protested against Mr. Churchill's
complaints that instead of the agreed '50-50' arrangement, the Russians had a 99 per cent control of
Yugoslavia. He said that he had been 'hurt' by the
American demand for a change of government in Rou-
mania and Bulgaria, where 'everything was peaceful.'" British Foreign Policy in the Second World
War, p. 542.
   11. Gould, An Introduction to International
Law, p. 90.
   12. Fleming, The Cold War and Its Origins,
p. 1042. The Toynbee quote is from an article in
The New York Times Magazine, 1 May 1955.
   13. Madariaga, The Blowing Up of the Parthenon,
p. 19.
        Lukacs (A History of the Cold War, p. 17),
however, put more emphasis on the second war: "We
must not forget that the cold war has been a direct
consequence of the Second World War, even more than
the Second World War was the direct consequence of
the First."
        Raymond Aron (Peace and War, p. 28) felt
that FDR mistook Russia as an occasional ally when,
in fact, it was more of a permanent enemy.
   14. Roosevelt, As He Saw It, pp. 206-207.
   15. Fleming, Cold War, p. 213.
   16. Quoted in U.S. Department of State, A Decade of American Foreign Policy (1941-1949), pp.
942-943. The Russians had cast over 100 vetoes
while the other four permanent members together had
cast only a handful. The first U.S. veto was not
cast until 17 March 1970 on the Rhodesia question.
   17. Quoted in Harold F. Harding, Ed., The Age
of Danger. Major Speeches on American Problems (New
York: Random House, 1952), p. 12.
   18. Madariaga, The Blowing Up of the Parthenon,
p. 20.
   19. Ibid., p. 29.
   20. Ibid., p. 30, italics in original.
   21. Ibid., p. 77.
   22. Gould, An Introduction to International
Law, p. 506.
   23. "The organization of clandestine activities
in a Communist state faces extraordinary obstacles.
It is, for example, common practice for the Communists to undertake provocative activities designed
to test the loyalty of each individual in the regime.

A person may at any time be contacted by someone
purporting to represent a clandestine organization.
Even though the sympathies of the person approached
may be strongly anti-Communist and his fondest hopes
that the Communists be overthrown, he must assume
that this is not a genuine resistance movement but
rather one conducted under the control of, and at
the direction of, the secret police. To prove his
loyalty he must not only refuse to join the purport-
ed clandestine organization, but must also inform
the police. If he does not, he will have failed to
demonstrate his positive loyalty to the regime and
will be subject to reprisals and imprisonment. Thus
a clandestinely organized resistance within a consolidated Communist regime is not likely to get very
far before someone has, out of fear, reported its
existence to the police."
          "A second device used by the Communists is
to form a clandestine anti-Communist organization
under their own secret control, to encourage its
growth by recruiting unwitting members, and to permit them to conduct actual operations against the
regime until finally, having attracted a large number of the most aggressive anti-Communists, its entire membership is arrested." Franklin A. Lindsay,
"Unconventional Warfare," Foreign Affairs, January
1962, p. 272.
          24. Zorza, "Kremlin Prepares for a Computer-
ized 1984," The Washington Post, Outlook, 25 July
1971.
          25. See Madariaga, The Blowing Up of the
Parthenon, p. 84.
          26. Ibid., p. 58, italics in original.
          27. Finletter, Foreign Policy, p. 64.
          28. Dinerstein, War and the Soviet Union, pp.
1-2.
          29. Woodhouse, British Foreign Policy Since the
Second World War, p. 85.
          30. Fuller, A Military History of the Western
World, Vol. III, p. 634.
          31. Ibid., p. 635.
          32. Madariaga, The Blowing Up of the Parthenon,
p. 63, italics in original.
          33. See Woodhouse, British Foreign Policy Since
the Second World War, p. 73.
          34. Vagts, Defense and Diplomacy, pp. 448-449.
"Anglo-American policy had invited this warfare as
much as Russo-Communist ideology had incited it, for
Roosevelt and his captive, Churchill, had neglected
- for the sake of smooth coalition, complete victory and utopian peace - precautions usually en-

entrusted to the care of diplomacy. They were put
aside, almost contemptuously by Roosevelt, who had
always vaguely hoped that it would be possible to
come to an understanding with Stalin."
     35. Madariaga, The Blowing Up of the Parthenon,
p. 33, italics in original. "And, therefore, every
time that, in the name of this or that 'peace' or
'relaxation of tensions' or any other empty slogan,
we consent to talk with those who are oppressing
freedom, we are not only misguided; we are downright
foolish, because we lose our moral authority not to
gain anything, albeit hard and material, such as
'peace,' or 'relaxation of tensions;' but on the
contrary to increase the tensions, and the war that
is bound ever to go on beyond the Iron Curtain between communism and freedom." (p. 91).
     36. Ibid., p. 33.
     37. Ibid., pp. 67-68.
     38. Sarnoff, "Program for a Political Offensive
against World Communism," U.S. Congress, Soviet Total War, p. 257, italics in original.
     39. Ibid., p. 259, italics in original. He ad-
ded, "If the weapon is our message, one of its basic
elements is propaganda." p. 264.
     40. The Overstreets, The War Called Peace,
p. 22, italics in original.
     41. Fall, Street Without Joy, p. 236, italics
in original. A good analysis of the problem in
Viet-Nam follows this passage.
     42. "Various names have been given to the pre-
liminary war of Communism. The term 'cold war' has
been popularized, but this is inaccurate for it implies the absence of violence. And the revolutionary offensives of 1947, which Lippmann labeled 'cold
war,' included active military fighting on many
fronts. 'Termite warfare' is a more accurate desig-
nation.... Termite warfare presents every non-Communist state with two enemies - one without and the
other within. The enemy without is the U.S.S.R., of
whose rivalry with the capitalist world Stalin remarked, 'One or the other must conquer.' The enemy
within is the Communist fifth column and its friends,
sympathizers, and followers. Through termite warfare Communists incite the territory of potential
enemies movements that they never tolerate in their
own. Stalin maintains an elaborate secret police
system to prevent just that type of subversive infiltration which his agents promote in the states of
his more loosely organized opponents.
     "The divisions of termite warfare include
psychological warfare, political warfare, diplomatic

warfare, scientific warfare, and economic warfare.
Termite warfare does not preclude the use of violence. Violence, however, is used less conspicuous-
ly than in open war, and the maker of violence often
finds it advantageous to conceal his identity. Bit
by bit is the strategy of termite warfare."
  "Termite warfare tactics have one cardinal
purpose: the incapacitation of the government,
brought about by the deliberate cultivation of social dislocations, moral breakdowns, ideological
bankruptcy, leadership failures, economic paralysis,
and social hatred. This last factor, the undermining of good feeling between segments of the people,
is especially valuable to the Communist campaign. A
part of this campaign is devoted to driving a wedge
between the mass of the people and their civil, financial, and military leaders." Kintner, The Front
is Everywhere, pp. 169-172.
  43. New York Herald Tribune, European Edition,
30 October 1962.
  44. U.S. News & World Report, 12 November 1962,
p. 44. It is interesting that Fleming (Cold War,
p. 965), quoting the New York Times, could not see
Castro as a Communist.
  45. Jesse Orlansky, The State of Research on
Internal War, p. 1, and without a declaration of war
among them!
  46. General Marshall had recommended the military embargo by which the Chinese received almost no
U.S. aid from August 1946 until early 1948. See
Possony, A Century of Conflict, p. 333.
  47. "Vincent Auriol said on October 25, 1952,
that France had spent twice as much on the Indo-China
war as she had received in Marshall Plan aid. Since
it had amounted to $2,285,000,000, this meant that
France had spent nearly five billion dollars on the
war, a sum probably footed entirely by American taxpayers, since direct American aid for the war was
running about a billion a year." Fleming, Cold War,
p. 676.
  48. "Published accounts of the allied consultations in March and April 1954 show that by then the
U.S. Government was contemplating the extension of
the Indo-China war by a major intervention, possibly
including the use of nuclear weapons. The British
Government resisted this policy, and the French
viewed it without enthusiasm." Woodhouse, British
Foreign Policy Since the Second World War, p. 129.
  49. "If we did go into Indo-China, we would
have to win.... We could not again afford to accept
anything short of decisive military victory.... We

368

could have won, if we had been willing to pay the tremendous cost in men and money that such intervention would have required." Ridgway, Soldier, p. 277.

50. Fall, Street Without Joy, p. 293. Fleming came to some conclusions on Southeast Asia (Cold War, pp. 705-706):

"1. The day of the white man as master in Asia is over.

2. Our support of colonialism has promoted communism.

3. We cannot permanently control the fringes of Asia.

4. We must accept neutralism in Asia and avoid an American imperialism."

51. Zbigniew Brzezinski, "America and Europe," Foreign Affairs, October 1970, pp. 12-13.

52. "There is no particle of reason to suppose that the present rulers of Russia want immediate war. Patient men, they have not got the neurotic urgency of Hitler or his conviction that, if a war was to come, it had better come before he was fifty or died of cancer. The Soviet leaders can bide their time. There lies the danger, greater than from the paranoiac urgency of Hitler, for well-meaning, comfortable and indolent democracies, which thrive on 'normalcy.'" George Catlin, What Does the West Want?, p. 34.

53. Fleming, Cold War, p. 1071, italics in original. He continued: "Our urge to limit Russia's gains in Europe became so strong that it frightened the West Europeans we were intent upon saving until they feared that our overwhelming urge to destroy communism everywhere would lead us into a war which would destroy them in the process. They even thought that many Americans would be willing to see Europe destroyed if Russia fell in the process."

54. Hancock, Four Studies of War and Peace in this Century, p. 29.

55. Kissinger, Nuclear Weapons and Foreign Policy, p. 123.

56. See Kecskemeti, Strategic Surrender, p. 249.

57. Fuller, The Conduct of War, p. 13.

58. Quoted in Fleming, Cold War, p. 772.

59. The Overstreets, What We Must Know About Communism, p. 292.

60. Lukacs, Cold War, p. 124. General MacArthur, in his many speeches around the nation after his relief in Korea, tried to point out that "far from having a foreign policy that was right or wrong, the United States seemed in fact to have no foreign policy at all." Whitney, MacArthur, p. 497.

61. See Atkinson, "Communist Unconventional Warfare," in U.S. Congress, Soviet Total War, p. 26.
62. In the Foreword by Chairman Walter, U.S.
Congress, Soviet Total War, p. IX.
63. Speech at VFW Convention at Minneapolis,
reported in U.S. News & World Report, 27 August 1962,
p. 14.
64. Miksche, Unconditional Surrender, pp. 34-
35. Fuller ended one of his books with a similar
unknown future: "Is the future to see a Pax Ameri-
cana or Pax Tartarica? We hazard to suggest that
the answer will be found, not in the contending military strengths of the United States and the Soviet
Union, but in their antagonistic political, social,
economic and cultural systems. Which of the two is
the more fitted to solve the crucial problem set to
mankind by the Industrial Revolution - the status of
man, his government and way of life in a fully mechanized world?" Fuller, A Military History of the
Western World, Vol. III, p. 636, italics in original.
65. Clark, From the Danube to the Yalu, p. 330,
italics in original. This was not to be in Viet-Nam
either.
66. Some of the White House Fellows made a trip
to Russia in June 1971 (not too surprisingly the
Fellows who were military officers were barred from
going 30 minutes before take-off from Eastern Europe). One of the staff members, a young man, made
some significant observations. He was convinced we
must take seriously their goal to dominate the
world. For our youth, he said they should see a
"closed" society to appreciate our "open" society.
"Their plan for the world... is non-negotiable." "A
Look Inside Russia," U.S. News & World Report, 2
August 1971, pp. 64-67, particularly p. 67.

12
Viet-Nam: Indochina II

> The answer lies not in pour-
> ing more troops into the
> jungle but in the hearts
> and minds of the people.
>
> -- General Templer
> Malaya, 1952
>
> The trouble with you Ameri-
> cans is that whenever you
> double the effort you some-
> how manage to square the
> error.[1]
>
> -- Robert Thompson

The tragedy of Viet-Nam was a long struggle
spanning more than a generation. In the days of
Asian fighting before the beginning of World War II,
the Viet Nam Doc Lap Dong Minh Hoi - or Viet Minh -
the League for Vietnamese Independence, was sponsored by the Chinese Nationalists in 1941 to harass
the Japanese forces in Indochina. By 1945 the Communists had complete control of the Viet Minh movement under Nguyen Tat Thanh, who achieved fame among
his own people as Nguyen Ai Quoc but who attracted
worldwide attention as Ho Chi Minh.
President Roosevelt strongly felt that the
French had not done well by their colonial rule in
Indochina and he did not want them to return after
the war. This led to some embarassing orders late
in the war when aid was refused to the French in
Indochina who were trying to fight the Japanese.[2]
However, there were larger problems to occupy the
new American President, Truman, resulting in a sort
of no policy in spite of OSS contacts and a limited
United States presence in Indochina. In the chaos
of the aftermath of the war, Ho Chi Minh seized

power in Hanoi and, on 2 September 1945, proclaimed
the Democratic Republic of Viet-Nam (DRVN). A new
struggle began as the French, after the humiliation
of defeat, tried to reestablish their colonial empire and only half-heartedly negotiated with Ho Chi
Minh's government at Dalat and at Fontainebleau. Ho
tried to improve the image by "dissolving" the Indochinese Communist Party, but it all came to nought
and the war with the French broke out on 19 December
1946. The war flags of the new drama had been un-
furled and remain so even to this day in what is now
probably Indochina III. There is one consistent,
unifying theme of this drama: "the unrelenting struggle of the Vietnamese Communist Party to acquire
political control over all of Viet Nam."[3]

1.   Indochina I - End of French Colonialism

There was strong nationalistic fervor in Indochina to eject the French and be independent. Various nationalist organizations had arisen; but the
Viet Minh, often in league with the French, smashed
all of them and completely usurped the independence
movement. As we saw repeatedly in the decolonizing
process, nationalist organizations were unified in
their objective of independence but soon fell to
squabbling among themselves about how to run their
country after gaining their independence. It was
different with the Viet Minh (and any Communist Party); they were able to ride to victory by stressing
the theme of independence, but they had a more complete plan for victory. Their program included the
revolutionary reorganization of the country in accordance with their ideology. Thus, a harsh new
phase was entered in the "40-year campaign which the
leadership of the Indochinese Communist Party has
waged to acquire complete political control over all
of Viet Nam, hegemony over Laos and some form of
suzerainty over Cambodia."[4]
One of the problems throughout the fighting in
Indochina since 1946 has been the overemphasis we
have placed on Chinese and Soviet influence. This
reappeared in 1965, when we claimed we were acting
to stop China. A characteristic of Asian Communism
has been the emphasis on self-reliance, repeatedly
stressed in Chinese writings. The Indochinese Communist Party received only modest support from other
Communist parties. The European Communists did
little; Stalin was Europe oriented. The USSR did

not even recognize the DRVN until January 1950, after the Chinese Communist takeover in 1949, when
there was a "new Soviet awareness of the importance
of the Asian Communists."[5] More importantly, the
Chinese Communists were fully occupied with their
own fight and could offer Ho little help until after
they gained full control of China in 1949, at which
time they started providing assistance and advisors
which were critical to the outcome.
     The question often arises, sincerely, as to
whether the world would have been better if Ho had
been permitted to take control; the thesis being
that he would have been another Tito. This is not
the place for a long discussion of this theory but,
from private discussion, the consensus of the few
scholars we have who are truly knowledgeable on both
Yugoslavia and North Viet-Nam is that it was most
unlikely. Tito was thrown out of the Cominform in
hopes of dethroning him; he pleaded for a reversal
of the decision as he had been a loyal servant of
the Soviet Union. There was no Communist country to
help him so he turned to the United States to bail
him out. The situation was totally different in
Hanoi. The DRVN is the most internationalist of the
Communist states. Ho was a charter member of the
French Communist Party; he went back to Asia as an
agent of the Comintern; he rejected Tito; he wanted
all Communist countries working together in harmony;
he could not tolerate Khrushchev because of the disruption of de-Stalinization but quickly made up with
Moscow when Khrushchev was ousted; he was appalled
at the activities in Eastern Europe; he refused to
permit mention of the Chinese Cultural Revolution in
North Viet-Nam because it was so disorganized and
potentially disruptive to the DRVN; he cheered the
Russian invasion of Czechoslovakia; Ho could not
tolerate disorganization. There would have been no
reason for the Communist states to disown Hanoi so
he would have been able to receive assistance from
them.
     Victory, to the French, would have meant a re-
newal of their prestige if they could preserve at
least some of the trappings of their empire. Their
weak efforts to reach an accommodation and near desire to fight with Ho are understandable in light of
so much humiliation they had suffered.[6] It is easy
to criticize them with the benefit of hindsight, but
the wave of decolonization was not yet apparent in
1946 and they could not see that they were bucking a
world wide whirlwind. Ho certainly would have made
some agreements but they would have been tactical

measures as his longrange objectives never varied.
Professor Paul Mus, a Vietnamese scholar, then a
paratroop captain, met with Ho early in the war, May
1947, at Pont des Rapides, north of Hanoi inside the
Viet Minh area. He was permitted considerable latitude for negotiating, but the French Army adamantly
demanded that Ho surrender to the French all the
foreign specialists who were helping him. (They
were critical to his operations.) Ho had champagne
and ice in a cooler, no mean logistical task, obviously expecting to sign an agreement. Ho discussed this point at length with Mus, finally said
I would be a coward to agree, there is no place in
the French Union for cowards, shook hands, and went
back into the jungle for seven more years of war
which he won.[7]

The world was facing, also in China at the same
time, what was being called a "people's war." General Vo Nguyen Giap, Ho's military chief, defined it
as "essentially a peasant's war under the leadership
of the working class."[8] He appropriately recognized
their weaknesses and realized that it would be a
protracted war and pressed for "long-term resistance" not "speedy victory" and called for Viet Minh
victory by accumulating "thousands of small victories."[9] The corollary to people's war is the political role of the people's army -- which contains important lessons. Giap wrote: "The People's Army is
the instrument of the Party and of the revolutionary
State for the accomplishment, in armed form, of the
tasks of the revolution.... Therefore, the political
work in its ranks is of the first importance. It is
the soul of the army."[10] We saw the role of armed
propaganda teams in later years in South Viet-Nam.
Giap clearly preached that political action was more
important than military action and that fighting was
less important than propaganda.[11]

How did the United States become involved? From
the beginning, America found itself in a dilemma.
As the champion of self-determination and nationalism, we did not want to see the French reestablish
their colonial rule, but the French were our ally.
As the leader of the Free World, we were against
Communist expansion particularly since we realized
that most nationalists really desired freedom, even
though they expressed it in terms of independence,
and Communism would cost them their freedom. When
the Communists captured the nationalist movement, we
were faced with a hard choice and took the lesser
evil of supporting France and urging reforms. The
United States provided major assistance in rebuild-

ing France under the Marshal Plan after the Second War. On 8 May 1950 (before the Korean War), the United States advanced $10 million to France to help in Indochina.[12] With the increased anti-Communist feeling of the Cold War and the Korean War, our support of the French grew rapidly and became part of a larger whole. Unfortunately, the nationalist side of the war won out. General Navarre, in a secret report to his government in 1953, stated that the war could not be won militarily.[13] An international conference was scheduled for Geneva in the spring of 1954. As it approached, the terrible battle of Dien Bien Phu flooded toward its climactic end just as the conference was convening. There had been great pressure on President Eisenhower to intervene in Indochina, particularly to save Dien Bien Phu. American troops actually loaded out of Japan but the Army Chief of Staff, General Ridgway, convinced the President that the cost would be equal to or greater than Korea, so we desisted.[14]

The cost to France was enormous: twice what the United States pumped into France during this period and ten times the value of all French investments in Indochina.[15] The lack of political support at home and the terrible price paid by the French Army were not measurable in financial terms. Bernard Fall placed the American costs at approximately one billion dollars and the French costs at close to $11 billion.[16] The cost on the North Vietnamese side must be measured as the price they paid for Ho coming to power. In addition to the heavy casualties of eight years of fighting, the Land Reform Campaign resulted in the execution of 100,000 or more North Vietnamese with a half million suffering dire hardship, many in forced labor camps. Out of a population of 18 million, this would be comparable to executing one million Americans. The party followed as a principle: better to kill 10 innocent people than to let one enemy escape.[17] Even more than that, the North Vietnamese lost their freedom as one of the strictest Communist governments installed its regime.

The French were still militarily strong after Dien Bien Phu; and the Viet Minh, who had bled themselves terribly to get that great psychological victory, would have found it difficult to finish the job. However, the French were finished at home and were ready to settle at Geneva. When Pierre Mendes-France took over the French government on 20 June 1954 and promised an agreement in a month or he would resign, the die was cast. The clock had to be

stopped at midnight on 20 July for him, due to some
late problems with Cambodia, but by dawn the Geneva
Accords were agreed upon. The North Vietnamese may
have thought they were high pressured by their Chinese and Russian comrades but they learned a lesson
in world politics. The Russian interest in 1954 was
to block the proposed European Defense Community
(EDC) and a possible French-German Army, which was
anathema to the Russians. Therefore, they helped
the French at Geneva and the French later recipro-
cated by vetoing the EDC. Some in Hanoi felt that
they were cheated of the full fruits of their victory, "but on the whole the Communists had no reason to be dissatisfied with the results."18 The
representative of the Government of Viet-Nam (GVN),
or South Viet-Nam, refused to sign the accords and
so did the Americans, although they announced their
support for them. The firing temporarily ceased;
the French prepared to depart; one million people
voted against the DRVN with their feet by going
south; and there was an interlude in Indochina.

2. Indochina II - Ho Tries Again

President Eisenhower was unwilling to pay the
high price required to save Indochina but he saved
"most" of it. There was probably a consensus at
Geneva that the rest of Viet-Nam, and perhaps Laos
and Cambodia, would fall to Ho Chi Minh in 1956, if
not earlier, barring a miracle. That miracle took
the form of an unknown face on the scene, Ngo Dinh
Diem. He felt the talks in Geneva were a disgrace
and would not permit his government to be associated with the accords. An ardent nationalist, he
set out to rebuild South Viet-Nam, with no intention of permitting it to fall under DRVN domination.
He surprised everyone. He took on and beat the
Binh Xuyen underworld and then the Hoa Hao and Cao
Dai religious sects in spite of French support of
those dissident elements. Forebodings of future
difficulties in dealing with him were evidenced
early as Ambassador J. Lawton Collins turned completely against him. There were many precarious
moments19 but by 1956, there was no liklihood that
Diem was going to turn his country over to Ho Chi
Minh, particularly by rigged elections.
About the only voice crying out that everything
was not rosy in South Viet-Nam was Bernard Fall20
and he was not receiving much audience. Fall dated

the beginning of public discontent with Diem -- the
textbook requirement for an insurgency -- in 1956,
not the early 1960s.[21] Having smashed the non-Communist opposition, Diem proceeded to attack the old
Viet Minh structure. He was so successful that the
Viet Minh cadres had to turn to guerrilla warfare to
prevent being wiped out.[22] It had been only a very
brief interlude for the Vietnamese people as guerrilla warfare started anew in 1957.[23] These years
attracted little attention in the United States but
the record shows that the Viet Cong (Vietnamese Communist or VC) terrorists had been quite active, killing large numbers of local officials each year. A
new expression was slowly coming into the lexicon,
but we were slow to grasp the significance of "wars
of national liberation." We were still not fully
alerted when Khrushchev announced Soviet support in
his January 1961 address. Referring specifically
to Viet-Nam and Algeria, he stated that wars of national liberation are revolutionary wars and are inevitable. "The Communists fully support such just
wars and march in the front rank with the peoples
waging liberation struggles." Bernard Fall complained at Christmas, 1961, of how he had been trying to alert officials in "Washington for almost
four years about the subversive threat to South
Vietnam, due in large part as much to our mistakes
as to the Communists' cleverness (say: 60-40)."[24]
    The role of Hanoi in the actions in South Viet-
Nam is critical to the intense debate of some years
later. The Communists apparently learned well their
lesson of what happens when there is overt aggression across a boundary such as Korea in June 1950.
This mistake was not repeated in South Viet-Nam.
Viet Minh cadres were deliberately left behind in
1954, either to quickly effect the takeover after
hopefully winning the elections or to be ready to
come out of hibernation on order of Hanoi. Hanoi
was not satisfied with the progress of the Viet
Cong, so, in late 1958, Le Duan (who took over as
Party Secretary General from Ho in September 1961)
himself undertook an extensive inspection trip in
the South, returning early in 1959. The Lao Dong
Committee adopted his recommendations, referred to
by the Viet Cong as "Resolution 15," which outlined
the future course of insurgency in the South, "including the establishment of a National Liberation
Front to be controlled by the Central Committee of
the South Vietnamese branch of the Lao Dong Party"
supported by a liberation army. In a May 1959 meeting, the Central Committee decided to "smash" the

GVN and, thereafter, infiltrators began moving down the Ho Chi Minh Trail network.[25]

Hanoi's hand in these events was imperfectly concealed. "In August 1958 Hanoi Radio, billing itself as 'the voice of the Liberation Front,' broadcast instructions to the Viet Cong." Similar broadcasts followed. In September 1960, Le Duan made public the Lao Dong decision on the national front, which was made official as of 20 December 1960 as the National Front for the Liberation of South Viet-Nam (NLF).[26] At the Geneva Conference of 1962, a North Vietnamese delegate inadvertently admitted that the Lao Dong Central Committee roster was incomplete because of some secret members who were directing operations in South Viet-Nam.[27]

Additional supervisory guidance, yet not obvious DRVN control, was required and after a meeting in the South late in December 1961, the People's Revolutionary Party (PRP) was officially established as of 1 January 1962. That it was only a change in name of the control apparatus was revealed by a captured Party directive.

> The reasons for the change in the Party's name must be kept strictly secret. According to the instructions of the Central Committee, one must not tell the people or the party sympathizers that the People's Revolutionary Party and the Lao Dong Party of Vietnam are one. One must not say that it is only a tactic because it would not be good for the enemy to know.[28]

The field control of all aspects of all phases of the insurgency was placed under the Central Office for South Viet-Nam (COSVN) or later referred to as the PRP's Central Committee. In the Lao Dong hierarchy, COSVN reported to the Party's Reunification Department, which was under the Lao Dong Politburo. General Nguyen Chi Thanh, a member of the NVN Politburo and National Defense Council, was Commander-in-Chief of the Viet Cong forces and Chief of the Military Affairs Section of COSVN;[29] he was reportedly killed in action in the South. In 1967, there were reportedly eight North Vietnamese Generals in the South who were either full or alternate members of the Lao Dong Party Central Committee.[30]

The COSVN Resolution of March 1966 expressed agreement with the Lao Dong 12th Resolution and provided guidance for execution of the Hanoi directive. The document referred to "the Southern branch of the Party" and frankly showed Hanoi leadership since the

"Southern branch is closely led by the Party Central Committee"[31]... "headed by Chairman Ho."[32] It is interesting that the National Front for the Liberation of South Viet-Nam was barely mentioned in this resolution devoted to the Viet Cong war and political efforts. This resolution stressed that, at a certain time, they would fight and negotiate at the same time to attain decisive victory[33] and that their revolution was "part of the world revolution" and that it is "related to the movements of national liberation".[34]

To most close students of the area, it was obvious that South Viet-Nam was in the midst of a war "waged by a Communist-controlled insurgent movement supported and directed from Hanoi."[35] Not all agreed, however. Bernard Fall took issue with Carver that the NLF was completely directed from Hanoi.[36] He particularly mentioned that the DRVN sent two notes to Diem, 7 March and 22 December 1958, conceding temporary division of the country and offering programs involving interzonal trade, travel, and nonaggression. There was no reply from Saigon.[37] The crux of the later debate was expressed by Arthur Schleisinger: "few scholars believe that the growing resistance was at the start organized or directed by Hanoi."[38] It was not clear whether this was semantics or "wish-hope."

Another shibboleth that must be mentioned is the controversial Domino Theory set forth by President Eisenhower. Although most people went to some length to disclaim this concept, many important people believed in it to some degree. Clark Clifford, who later turned against the war, wrote how the President's Foreign Intelligence Advisory Board supported, in 1961, the assessment of the Eisenhower Administration that withdrawal in the cases of Viet-Nam and Thailand could result in the collapse of the whole area. Also, in 1962, President Kennedy did not withdraw from Viet-Nam because the result would have been the collapse of Southeast Asia.[39] Sir Robert Thompson felt that the Domino Theory was real to Southeast Asian leaders "in the sense that the loss of South Vietnam would compel them to make drastic realignments of policy"[40] -- "certainly" in Southeast Asia, "probably" in Africa and "possibly" even in Latin America. In his view, everything Western would be significantly downgraded.[41] The effects of United States policy in Viet-Nam on other areas were critical to arguments concerning appropriate American policy.

Viet-Nam was not exactly on the front burner

379

yet. There were other problems: Laos had started in 1959,[42] Berlin, and Cuba. Bernard Fall wrote pessimistically: "Between wishful thinking, lousy intelligence and a psychological block against seeing the grim facts as they are (and they'll get grimmer for a long time to come, out here...); we're not in a terribly good position to lick this thing."[43] President Kennedy increased the number of advisors and the amount of assistance, including American helicopters. As the tide of the insurgency grew, so also grew our difficulties with Diem, culminating in his ouster and death on 1 November 1963, followed in three weeks by the assassination of President Kennedy. President Johnson, in retrospect, felt that the threat to withhold support from Diem was a "serious blunder" because it launched two years of deep political confusion.[44] This period was filled with repeated coups which greatly facilitated Viet Cong operations. They were truly "gifts from heaven" for the NLF.[45]

New decisions were made in the North, no doubt scenting the kill, and in late 1964, members of the North Vietnamese Army were identified in the South.[46] By early 1965, having completed the arduous infiltration, the 325th North Vietnamese Army Division, consisting of the 95th, 32nd, and 101st Regiments, was inside South Viet-Nam.[47] By the time of the 7 February attack on Pleiku, the situation in South Viet-Nam had grown critical. The retaliatory strike against the North was launched and the first American troops were brought into Danang shortly thereafter. Premier Kosygin was in Hanoi when the first strikes were made; the question is still open as to whether Kosygin was in Hanoi to persuade the North Vietnamese to make peace[48] - or to help with the coup de grâce.

The question of aggression from the North was another crucial argument about this war. The State Department published a White Paper[49] in February 1965, and the study written in Saigon mentioned earlier[50] detailed the preparation, infiltration, and introduction of regular units of the North Vietnamese Army into South Viet-Nam. Giap contended that North Viet-Nam was an independent, sovereign country, and a component of the socialist camp.[51] Some countries granted the DRVN diplomatic recognition and many more recognized the GVN. If the DRVN was sovereign, then the GVN had to be and the commitment of North Vietnamese troops into the South was clearly aggression. In fact, the DRVN regularly referred to "liberating" the South and reunifying the country.[52]

In the typical Communist technique of charging the
opponent with the same crime of which they stand accused, Ho Chi Minh repeatedly referred to American
aggression in his letter to President Johnson.[53]
Ambassador Robert Komer succinctly described it as a
war that "began as an externally supported revolution in the south" and which became "essentially an
internally supported invasion from the north."[54]
    This was not the first American military excur-
sion in Viet-Nam. The USS Constitution, commanded
by Captain "Mad Jack" Percival, was in Asian waters
showing the flag when he learned the French bishop
in Hue was about to be executed. Percival put into
Danang on 10 May 1845; marched some Marines ashore;
captured some high Vietnamese officials (who probably had never heard of America); and held them hos-
tage until Hue gave assurance that the bishop would
not be harmed. It seems unlikely that any of the
Marines who went into Danang in 1965 had any inkling
that it was a return engagement.[55]
    The bombing of the North, which soon started in
earnest, was another highly controversial aspect of
a very controversial war. Strategic bombing has already been discussed in considerable detail. About
two million tons of air ordnance were dropped by the
United States in World War II and about one million
tons in the Korean War. In Indochina, the total was
nearly eight million tons.[56] The bombing of the
North was "the most accurate and the most restrained
in modern warfare."[57] General Giap felt that it was
"obvious that the independent activities of an air
force - even if it is the modern air force of the
U.S. imperialists - cannot have the effect of deciding victory on the battlefield."[58] If he was right,
and there were many who agreed with him, then it was
significant for two reasons: first, we should already have learned this from World War II and Korea,
and second, the ramifications this held for the Nixon Doctrine which was so dependent on air and naval
power.
    The introduction of North Vietnamese troops
into the war was met by sending American troops and
bombing. Escalation went back and forth until, in a
short time, a large war was underway. As it grew
longer and more costly, the American homefront began
to waver. Although the credibility of big government came under attack, McGeorge Bundy summed up an
important point. What was most important about the
twenty years or so after World War II was that "most
of the great decisions were right."[59] Not all were
ready to write off Viet-Nam as inconsequential. Sir

381

Robert Thompson wrote that the "outcome of the war
will be of vital consequence to the future of the
world... and that it may well prove to be as decisive as any war in this century."[60]   As the grumblings
intensified, the foreboding comment by Diem years
earlier appeared even more ominous: "'This war can
only be lost by the American press'."[61]

3. Disillusionment - Negotiations - End of LBJ

The war in Viet-Nam never was a popular war
since there was no crusade to fire up the people to
save the world or some other stirring cause.   This
was a purely political war and the Americans still
had not learned to face such tests of national power.
As the years went by and it became the longest war
in American history and soon one of the most costly,
the dissent increased from normal grumblings to a
deafening roar that drove a president from office
without seeking reelection and demanded an end to
the war.
As Robert Scalapino wrote, "It would be tragic
if this bloody war were needlessly prolonged because
of Communist miscalculation regarding American resolve."[62]   There is no doubt that the psychological
aspect of the Communist strategy was of the utmost
importance; they had learned that lesson in the Indochinese War, for it was won in Paris.   They expected
to win this war in Washington and they did.   Time
will have to pass to permit historians to sort it
out but there seemed to be little doubt that years
were added to this war by the open debate in America.
The United States had not previously succumbed
to the path of some Latin countries, where the universities became deeply involved in the political
arena.   But the rebellion was on at the college campuses and, for the first time, we heard of "teach-
ins."   Most Americans were shocked when a college
professor, proudly a Marxist and socialist, professed "I do not fear or regret the impending Viet
Cong victory in Viet Nam.   I welcome it."[63]   The
radical acts and talk on the campuses angered many
people but the television cameras kept them in the
public eye.   Another Great Debate swept the land.
Some of the more pragmatic hardliners, such as Senator Richard Russell, took another tack, "We should
go in and win - or else get out."[64]   It was a new experience to have a Mary McCarthy write: "The worst
thing that could happen to our country would be to

win this war."[65] Ramsey Clark essentially agreed
with her but argued for our complete withdrawal from
a higher plane: "Violence as a way of solving problems must be relegated to the past. It is no longer
tolerable. It can no longer succeed. The once ro-
mantic ideal of peace has become essential realism."[66] Senator Fulbright, one of those at the eye
of this tornado, saw the central issue as "whether
the sacrifices imposed on the present generation of
young Americans are justified by the stakes of the
war".[67] The real argument for those few who discussed the situation in that depth was over the United States national interest. Everyone can talk about
the national interest but only the President, in the
final analysis, can actually determine it.
    Pessimism countered by occasional optimism from
Secretary of Defense Robert McNamara or Secretary of
State Dean Rusk widened the "credibility gap" between the people and their government. Arguments
tended to become extremely simplistic and emotional.
Views ranged from sincere concern to absolute anti-
Americanism, from the view that the war could be
settled only between the Vietnamese and that the
ideological orientation of Vietnamese politics did
not affect American vital interests[68] to the view
that American action was "counterrevolutionary" by
blocking a "war of independence," an indigenous revolutionary movement, and whether it was Communistic
or not was irrelevant.[69] Some viewed the war as immoral with an open-ended commitment resulting from
our limited objective, but which required frustration of the North's aim, leading to wanton destruction.[70] Senator George McGovern decried that we had
sent "almost three million young men into the
jungles in pursuit of an impossible and immoral victory." The Editor of Army magazine took strong exception with him stating that "It may even turn out
to be one of the most moral wars in history...".[71]
The Senator's denunciations of the war were unending
-- "I regard this war as the most barbaric and inhumane act that our country has ever committed."[72]
    Senator Fulbright admitted that the acrimonious
debate in the Senate could be misunderstood abroad.
"It seems reasonable to suppose that the debate has
given the Viet Cong, the North Vietnamese, and the
Chinese a distorted impression of internal divisions
within the United States."[73] Fulbright did not like
to be told that his statments were "irresponsible"
or that they gave "aid and comfort" to our enemies,[24]
but the vitriolic debate strained the cohesive fiber
of our nation and severely weakened the Government's

capability to prosecute the war to a conclusion.

The opponents of the war realized that without American support, South Viet-Nam would probably be controlled by the Communists and they accepted this. Fulbright's rationale was that United States interests "are better served by supporting nationalism than by opposing communism," and that if both are encountered, "it is in our interest to accept a communist government rather than to undertake the cruel and all but impossible task of suppressing a genuinely national movement."[75] He felt, then, that we should not have helped the French or Diem and not have sent advisors or troops. All he wanted was "a peace short of victory."[76] For those who would agree to let it all go Communist, their basic assumption was that we could not win the war by Vietnamization or other means. They saw, at best, a Communist-leaning government in the South with a high likelihood of a Communist reunification of Viet-Nam. This would be "regrettable" but "inescapable." A partition of Laos similar to the present de facto partition would be acceptable and Sihanouk should be returned to Cambodia.[77] With such a clamor at home, it is understandable why there was no progress at Paris. This plum appeared ripe.

The Tet offensive of 1968 was the watershed of the American effort. It took Tet to break the official optimism.[78] The enemy suffered a crushing military defeat. The enemy units went into the cities under the impression that the South Vietnamese would rise up and join them and that the war was about over. Many of the Viet Cong cadre surfaced at this time and were wiped out. The true weaknesses of the Viet Cong were shown as the South Vietnamese were appalled at the violation of the truce of a great holiday and rallied behind their government.[79] It was only after Tet 1968 that South Viet-Nam finally mobilized for this war. This victory in Viet-Nam turned into a great psychological defeat in the United States.

This defeat was created by American journalists who had rarely served the country well in their coverage of this controversial war. Peter Braestrup, The Washington Post's bureau chief in Saigon in 1968 wrote an exhaustive seven-year, 1500 page study, Big Story: How the American Press and Television Reported and Interpreted the Crisis of Tet 1968 in Vietnam and Washington. He assessed the majority performance as journalism of distortion. The Communist successes in the early days of the Tet offensive were exaggerated and the word was circulated that it was a great defeat for American forces.

As the weeks passed, evidence mounted that the
early assessments of the Tet offensive were
absolutely backward, the reverse of reality.
It became clear that American forces had not
suffered a defeat but had in fact inflicted a
crushing defeat on the Communist forces. Some
sensed that Tet would prove to be a watershed.
But a critical negative decision was taken by
the press: Despite more accurate knowledge, the
press as a whole refused to correct itself.
Robert Northfield, an NBC executive, was approached by NBC reporter Jack Fern, who suggested that a special broadcast should be
mounted to set the record straight that Tet was
an American victory. Northfield, whose agency
had helped to spread the distortion and miscon-
ception, refused, saying, "The public perceived
it as a defeat, and therefore it was a defeat."
But the public's perception had been in large
part created by the press in the first place![80]

As Herman Kahn expressed it, we handed it to
them.[81] On 31 March President Johnson removed himself from the election race, partially halted the
bombing, and put his hopes in negotiations at Paris.
Clark Clifford, who replaced McNamara as Secretary
of Defense for the last year of the Johnson Administration, came in as a hawk and went out as a dove
and played a major role in the turnabout by the
President. He agreed that United States intentions
in going into Viet-Nam to help a small nation resist
subjugation from without were exemplary and that the
decisions that brought us there were "based on a
reasonable reading of the past three decades." What
had transformed his thinking was his conclusion that
the world situation had dramatically changed and
that American involvement had to change with it.[82]
Talks started in Paris but not much negotiating. The
first drought set in while the participants waited
to see who would be the new American President.
Sir Robert Thompson posed the thesis that if
the war had been kept defensive in the South, then
the dissenters would have had no rational arguments
that defense was immoral. This idea was destroyed
by the bombing of the North. Therefore, in his view,
it was the bombing and not Hanoi which brought the
United States to the conference table "ready to
settle for less than victory." The intransigence of
North and South Viet-Nam showed that they well

understood that less than victory means defeat because concessions eventually lead to collapse of the
will to resist. But the "plaintive offers to negotiate" from the United States "showed the main contestants that she lacked the determination to win."[83]
As one analyst put it, Hanoi did not go to Paris to
give up South Viet-Nam. The tactic of fighting and
negotiating which was mentioned in the COSVN Resolution of March 1966 could have the practical purposes
of driving a wedge between Washington and Saigon and
to force the United States out by troop withdrawals.[84]

When a country is fighting for its very existence, there is usually nothing to negotiate. Our
offer to negotiate "positively implied that the future of South Vietnam was negotiable" and that even
if Hanoi did not get all she wanted she could at
least get something at the conference table. The
United States said, in effect, that "she did not intend to win the war" and that she was prepared to
"settle for less at South Vietnam's expense." Hanoi
got the message and the result was her four points
which were tantamount to total victory.[85]

For those who were confused by the hassle over
the shape of the table and wonder how over four
years were spent at Paris with no results, Henry
Kissinger's article provided some insights. He noted that "the way negotiations are carried out is almost as important as what is negotiated." There are
no "easy" issues; each is symbolic; each prejudges
the final settlement.[86] Just because the United
States is ready to negotiate does not guarantee that
the U.S. Government has a negotiating position or
that it has articulated its objectives. Kissinger
has an interesting discussion of the role of bureaucrats in blocking the development of a negotiating
position thereby weakening the American position at
the conference table.[87]

Senator Robert Kennedy felt that military victory in Viet-Nam might be unattainable since it required the crushing of both the enemy's strength and
his will to fight. Kennedy realized that negotiations might not be possible in this war because "our
political aims are irreconcilable" in which case the
war would continue, but he thought there was a middle way possible, to "admit them to a share of power
and responsibility."[88] The history of coalition
governments is not good and there are few who were
optimistic about such a course and, naturally, the
South Vietnamese found it anathema. Kissinger's
view was no brighter. "It is beyond imagination

386

that parties that have been murdering and betraying each other for 25 years could work together as a team giving joint instructions to the entire country."[89]

The prospects for a ceasefire were equally gloomy. If the Saigon forces were permitted unhampered movement, it would amount to victory for the South. However, if Saigon were limited in movement, it would actually be partition and, as we have seen in Laos, would tend to become permanent.[90] Although a tacit ceasefire might be attainable, in this type of war a ceasefire "is almost a practical impossibility."[91]

The talks droned on; there were those who felt that Washington was less than sincere in some of its offers;[92] withdrawal was fading as an issue as President Nixon's plans removed the Americans from most of the fighting; and the only issue remaining was the return of the American prisoners. It was learned that Henry Kissinger, President Nixon's Special Assistant for National Security Affairs, had met secretly in Paris with the North Vietnamese representatives on numerous occasions with no progress. In late March 1972, the United States discontinued attending the fruitless Thursday meetings in Paris. On 30 March, the North Vietnamese invaded the South with a spearhead of tanks and supported by heavy, Russian artillery. President Nixon ordered the bombing of the North again and the mining of the harbors. The South Vietnamese held on and the President went to the Moscow summit meeting.

4. Vietnamization - American Withdrawal

Tet 1968 was the key for the GVN: the Vietnamese Army fought well; the time was finally ripe for mobilization; and, most important, the people did not join the Viet Cong. As an example, the majority of the students in a high school in Hoi An, Quang Nam Province, rallied to the Government, requested arms, and helped capture most of the VC cadres moving in to set up their administration.[93] When the dust had settled and President Nixon was in office, it became clear that Vietnamization was the major trend and that American withdrawal was underway. However, in this war of emotions on the American scene, even to turn the war over to the Vietnamese, to provide them the capability to defend themselves, was suspect. According to Ramsey Clark, "Vietnami-

zation of the war is ignoble as an end in itself.[94]
According to another author, Nixon, like LBJ, wanted
to "win" the war in the "sense that he wants to
leave behind a non-communist government in Saigon
able to withstand any communist threat." In his
perspective, "the Vietnamization strategy is clearly
a strategy for winning the war."[95] It seems odd
that a President would be criticized for attempting
what the previous three presidents had committed
American prestige, blood, and gold to accomplish.

Clark Clifford had left the Pentagon on 20 January 1969 feeling there was nothing more to achieve
with our military force and that it was time to dis-
engage.[96] This approach was implemented by President Nixon and from a high of almost 550,000 American personnel, American troops were fully withdrawn
shortly after the Agreement was signed in Paris on
27 January 1973. This was not accomplished at the
expense of the South Vietnamese because Vietnamization was working and there was more security in 1971
than in any recent year. The North Vietnamese invasion in the Spring of 1972, however, subjected
Vietnamization to its severest test.

For those who felt we had lost the war, there
were defects in the Vietnamization policy. There
was no provision for political accommodation between
Communist and non-Communist forces in South Viet-
Nam -- that is, the central issue was unresolved.
There was (before 1973) no assured basis for total
withdrawal of American forces. The President had
successfully refused to name a date for all forces
to be out of Viet-Nam, which would have totally destroyed any negotiating position he might have had.
There was no new international machinery to be responsible for Viet-Nam. Judging by the meager results of international supervision in history, that
was idle speculation. The policy did not deal with
the problems of Laos and Cambodia.[97] President
Nixon was moving forcefully on both of them as we
will discuss below, but part of the United States
Congress was intent on preventing him from having
any policy in those two countries. With a seriously
divided nation and agonizing economic problems,
President Nixon successfully defused the Viet-Nam issue in 1971 only to have it come alive again in 1972.

Sir Robert Thompson, back in Saigon late in
1971, saw the ground war almost completely in South
Vietnamese hands and the situation satisfactory to

permit accelerated American withdrawals in 1972. He saw no end to protracted war but recommended what he called "stable war" as the answer. In it, the South Vietnamese had to be able to contain the North Vietnamese Army indefinitely, keeping it away from the main parts of the country, while they developed their security and prosperity.[98] This was consistent with his views of 3½ years earlier when he called for a change of strategy to the indirect approach emphasizing nation building, pacification, and merely containing the military threat. As he stressed, attacking the enemy main force units is strategically defensive and the strategic offense is nation building and pacification. The major military task was to keep the enemy main force units at a distance.[99]

In late 1971, Joseph Alsop reported from Viet-Nam the great improvement of the South Vietnamese Army. Vietnamization, which had been impossible before the terrible Viet Cong losses of the Tet offensive, was working; and security was greatly increased, thereby accelerating pacification.[100] He quoted from a very pessimistic, secret, "burn on reading," Viet Cong assessment that had been circulated only to relatively high officials of the VC hierarchy. It pointed out how the attacks on the infrastructure since 1969 had been quite successful.[101] The war in Viet-Nam was certainly not over, but it had clearly entered a new phase.

A new offensive had been expected for months in early 1972, but the ferocity with which it hit when it finally was unleashed surprised most observers. North Vietnamese divisions with tanks and heavy artillery attacked across the DMZ and seized Quang Tri in the north and threatened the old imperial capital of Hue, as well as Kontum in the highlands, and An Loc north of Saigon. The offensive was so intense that President Nixon finally ordered the bombing of targets in the North again and the mining of the ports of North Viet-Nam. This reaction was interwoven with the aftermath of the President's trip to Peking and his trip to Moscow in the midst of the offensive.

President Nixon offered complete American withdrawal within four months after the return of our prisoners and an internationally supervised ceasefire. The North Vietnamese seemed to be more intent on total victory.

5. Cambodia - Laos

In the spring of 1970, President Nixon made one
of the major decisions of the Vietnamese War. With
the confusion in Cambodia after the ouster of Sihanouk and the requirement for security of American
troops as Vietnamization progressed, he elected to
put an end to sanctuary in Cambodia and Laos. As we
have already seen, sanctuary is a nightmare to counterinsurgent forces. The reaction inside the United
States was violent but the results on the ground
were significant. Not too surprisingly, these operations kindled the reappearance of the term "Indochina War."102
The operation into Cambodia was a combined
American-Vietnamese move to prevent a North Vietnamese takeover of the weak Lon Nol government in
Phnom Penh. Sihanouk had masterfully kept Cambodia
out of war since 1954 by walking a tightrope between
the camps. In the later 1960s, he sensed a Communist victory and hopped on the bandwagon. The North
Vietnamese were using eastern Cambodia, whether he
liked it or not, as an extension of the Ho Chi Minh
Trail network and as sanctuaries for units from South
Viet-Nam. Soon Sihanoukville was a major port of entry for supplies destined for southern Viet-Nam. Due
to the proximity to Saigon and the excellent conceal-
ment in the Angel's Wing area, Cambodian sanctuary
was immensely important to the Viet Cong. Jean
Lacouture typically thought the operation was "suici-
dal" and a gift to Giap.103 There were several major
gains from the operation. The Viet Cong lost their
privileged sanctuary along the South Vietnamese border. South Viet-Nam controlled the Parrot's Beak and
firepower or ground thrusts could strike any border
build-ups as was seen in 1971. Crucial to logistical support for the Delta and the Saigon area, no
more supply shipments would be coming through the
Cambodian coast.104 Sihanouk, living in Peking,
could only "hope for the total victory of the revolution," in which he would have no place.105
Additional time was bought to permit Cambodia
to consolidate its position. Its little army was
hastily expanded; military assistance was provided
by the United States and other Free World nations;
and training was provided in South Viet-Nam. A small
Military Equipment Delivery Team was set up in Phnom
Penh, with no American advisors, particularly due to
significant opposition in the U.S. Congress. The

Cambodian Army occupied large numbers of North Vietnamese Army troops which helped Vietnamization. The future of Cambodia was unclear but its strength was growing rapidly.

Lam Son 719, the operation into Laos, was a Vietnamese show with only American support, no ground troops. It was a tremendous gamble because the South Vietnamese moved into the North Vietnamese Army's area, where they had large stocks of supplies, artillery, tanks, and dense antiaircraft deployments. The two armies fought nose to nose for the first time in large unit engagements with no quarter given.[106] Fighting on almost even terms in completely unfamiliar terrain, the South Vietnamese Army came out much better than expected and showed that it could go it alone. (U.S. advisors did not accompany the Vietnamese into Laos.) The operation disrupted operations on the Ho Chi Minh Trail system sufficiently to delay any major attack in 1971, and destroyed the sanctuary since the South Vietnamese could return when they chose.

Laos, the forgotten war, where people had been dying quietly since 1959 when most people did not even know where Laos was, had long been the running sore of Southeast Asia. It was a pawn in the Cold War, not only between the Communist and Free Worlds but also among the Communist trio of Hanoi, Peking, and Moscow. Laos, a nation only in the weakest sense, suffered partition for many years. The northern provinces of Sam Neua and Phong Saly were kept under Communist control after the 1954 Accords. With only a minimum of cooperation among the three factions - rightist, neutralist, and Pathet Lao, with approximately 40,000 North Vietnamese soldiers "permanently entrenched in a zone which covers almost half the country,"[107] with the Chinese building a road from Yunnan to Nam Tha near the Thai frontier, with the Ho Chi Minh Trail network expanding farther westward, and with continued fighting on the Plaine des Jarres, Laos continued as a hot spot and an indicator of Communist intentions. The long negotiations that led to the 1962 Geneva agreements and which were never adhered to by the North Vietnamese, gave us a good indication of our prospects for successful negotiations in Paris and our expectations for compliance.[108]

In 1971, Laos continued in the spotlight as Congress investigated American involvement[109] and as part of the overall Nixon Doctrine which was reducing United States deployments throughout the world but particularly in Asia. Complicating the situation was the continuing political ascendency of the

Pathet Lao[110] which was gradually expanding, approaching control of almost two-thirds of the country. General Vang Pao, the guerrilla leader of the Meo tribesmen, was restive and threatened to "lead his army and the Meo people out of the war and perhaps out of Laos."[111] This would have been the death blow for Laos. With the slow encroachment toward the Thai border, the Thais had taken a larger role in helping the Lao Army and increased numbers of Thai troops had joined the fighting, particularly as Thai troops had been withdrawn from South Viet-Nam.[112] The operations in Cambodia and Laos served to remind us that Indochina is basically one area, as the Communists have always considered it. Cambodia and Laos were important to North Viet-Nam in its longrange plans for control but critical in its shortrange logistical requirements to support the war in South Viet-Nam.

6. Victory?

The American troop withdrawals had proceeded through 1972 and the negotiations, after four years, were nearly completed and peace was at hand. Then the North Vietnamese became recalcitrant and President Nixon sent the B-52s over Hanoi in December. On 27 January 1973 the Agreement on Ending the War and Restoring Peace in Vietnam was signed in Paris. The U.S. Government proclaimed peace with honor had been obtained. America's largest war was over but the question of victory in this long and unfortunate war was not agreed upon or settled.

It had only slowly become clear to us that "purely military victory neither necessarily wins nor loses the broader war." Victory will be determined by the political, economic, and socio-psychological outcomes.[113] The key is that "counterinsurgency is a matter of restoring law and order."[114] This is quite true however the whole dispute is about "whose laws" and "who" will control the order. It is probably true that there are no final solutions in international relations short of a Carthaginian peace, that even unconditional surrenders yield results impossible to predict, and that the final solution in Viet-Nam will probably not be our idea of victory.[115] However, evidently not all the protagonists subscribe to this view lest we have Clausewitz's "senseless thing without an object." The use of terror, "the violent act for psychological rather than military reasons," has shown that in revolutionary war control of the population separates victory from defeat.[116] Henry Kissinger called the "consolidation of governmental authority," the only meaningful definition of "victory" in a guerrilla war.[117] The struggle is for control of that government.

Although the war in Viet-Nam was not a world war, it had world participation or support. The Communist World supported the insurgency although not all for the same reasons perhaps. Without the continuing supplies and arms from Russia and Red China, there would have been no significant insurgency in South Viet-Nam. The United States was not alone in supporting the South; 31 other Free World nations helped, compared to only 21 in Korea. With three groups of Vietnamese who wanted to rule in the South (GVN, DRVN, and VC), two sides in Cambodia, three factions in Laos, Americans and anti-war Americans, Chinese and Russians with their own feud going, interested Southeast Asian neighbors, and French who never could stomach the prospect of the Americans succeeding where they failed, there were obviously some diverse views on victory.

With the supposedly numerous aims and objectives, Americans had their normal difficulties in maintaining the political and military aspects of the war in perspective. In fact, in many ways, there were different wars being fought - the Communists view war as between classes while we view war as between nations - and everyone thought he was winning.[118] De Gaulle saw that France could win militarily in Algeria but lose politically, so he settled.[119] Bernard Fall made it an equation whereby revolutionary warfare equals guerrilla warfare plus political action.[120] Neglect of the political factors of insurgency, and concentration on the military, encourages the "crusade" aspect with no quarter given, and no other considerations but the total elimination of the guerrilla threat. This extends the Unconditional Surrender concept to revolutionary war.[121] Proper use of the military as one of the political weapons is not always easy and we have been unable sometimes to subordinate that military power to political objectives.[122] "We fought a military war; our opponents fought a political one." - we aimed for attrition; they sought our psychological exhaustion. This resulted in our declared political objectives and our military operations not always being closely related.[123] "The American forces fought a separate war which ignored its politi-

cal and other aspects, and were not on a collision
course with the Vietcong and North Vietnamese, who
therefore had a free run in the real war. It was
just as if the Americans, having been frustrated in
the chess game, thought that they could win by going off and playing poker instead."[124]
     Less was heard in this war of our Total Victory
concept of once the diplomats have failed and the
country is at war, then turn it over to the military.[125] Even though anti-military fervor was rampant, it was very clear that the war, correctly, was
conducted by civilians. George Ball wrote in News-
week that the Pentagon Papers showed plainly "that
the military did not push us into Vietnam half so
much as the civilian theoreticians with theses to
prove - doctrines of counterinsurgency and guerrilla
tactics."[126] For counterinsurgency operations, the
indirect approach requires primarily a civilian effort. Thompson felt that civilian control was imperative; however, he accepted a general in a civilian post - it might even be better.[127] All were
tried in Viet-Nam: General Maxwell Taylor was Ambassador for a time and John Vann (a former officer)
became the senior United States official in Military
Region 2 in 1971 (unfortunately killed during the
1972 offensive). The basic point is still quite
valid, however, as it stresses the political importance over the military, regardless of the background of the individual.
     What were the aims of the insurgents? Because
of the several Communist elements involved, there
was more to it than merely the drive to take over
South Viet-Nam. For Hanoi and its southern associates, the objective of the war was more than simply winning military victory in a nationalist cause.
It was a desire to completely transform South Vietnamese society and its economy, based on the Communist concept of a successful "national democratic"
revolution led, of course, by the Communist Party
with its experience in the North.[128] As the war es-
calated, it became a full fraternal commitment to
the Communist World, as well as an issue between
the Chinese concept of revolutionary war and the
Soviet concept of coexistence as to which was the
correct path to the inevitable triumph of world Communism.[129] In the fall of 1971, instead of the
Vietnamese going hat-in-hand to Moscow for their annual assistance package, Soviet President Podgorny
joined his peripatetic associates, Brezhnev and
Kosygin, in capital-hopping to enhance the Soviets
over the Chinese prior to President Nixon's trip to

Peking, and personally went to Hanoi to boost Soviet
influence there. He pledged "all-sided assistance"
in the struggle for the "consolidation" of the Democratic Republic of Viet-Nam.[130] The Soviets
stressed that they provided $500 million of military
assistance annually or 65 percent of the foreign aid
with China providing about 25 percent.[131]

The interests of China and North Viet-Nam, although they overlapped at times, have never been
identical because China viewed Viet-Nam in light of
its worldwide competition with the United States and
the Soviet Union. The Chinese, no doubt, had mixed
feelings about the prospects of a reunified Viet-Nam
under Ho; they consistently used the war as a means
to weaken the United States in order to reduce American influence in Asia, to embarrass the Russians,
and to slow any Soviet-American detente. China
sought to avoid both negotiations and extension of
the war to China itself, instead promoting a protracted war.[132] In this light, those who interpreted Lin Piao's 1965 article as aggressive may have
overlooked one aspect. At the end of the section on
"self-reliance," he stressed that there is no victory if it is not won independently even if aid
comes from "socialist countries."[133] The Chinese
have repeatedly stressed this self-reliance, realis-
tically of course when there was little they could
do to help. The North Vietnamese must always remain
leery of the Chinese because, after 1000 years of
Chinese domination and another 1000 years fighting
to keep it from happening again, they are suspicious
of their northern neighbors, for once in they were
hard to get out.

There were several non-military paths to victory for Hanoi. Robert Thompson listed four: if
American resolution failed; if Vietnamese resolution
failed; if the South Vietnamese and Americans failed
to adopt the correct strategy against the enemy; and
if the South Vietnamese, with American help, failed
to build a stable and viable GVN. If one or more of
those paths were open, Hanoi would win its "minimum
aim of reunification if not its maximum aim of inflicting a humiliating defeat on the United
States."[134] The Communist strategy was to impose on
the South Vietnamese and Americans a cost which they
could not accept indefinitely at a cost which the
North Vietnamese and Viet Cong could accept indefi-
initely. At that point, the Communists must be
winning.[135] The key to this approach was resolve.

During the guerrilla phase of an insurgency,
prior to embarking on the mobile phase, the political

objective is control of the population, destroying
the government's authority, and prestige. Neutra-
lizing the armed forces so they cannot save the
country is the military objective.[136] Hanoi was in
a very favorable position with little to lose and
everything to gain by direct involvement in the
South. She could always fall back on the status
quo, to the situation in the late 1950s. Having
started with nothing, anything the NLF/DRVN acquired
in the South would be a net gain. For Hanoi this
was a "no-lose policy." The problem encountered in
determining resolve in Hanoi was that Western eval-
uations of the people's war are in the political and
economic terms of a Western, industrialized, democratic society. The cost to the Communists is low
and, if they keep the initiative, acceptable. Put
very bluntly, all that was required of the North
Vietnamese from 1965 to 1968 "was to exist and
breed. The United States Air Force could not in-
terrupt either of these activities."[137]
     The advantages are with the insurgent: he can
destroy; he need not build; he can kill; he need not
heal; he can disrupt; he need not govern; he is totally irresponsible. That is what makes the counterinsurgent's role so difficult, because he is responsible and must continue to be responsible while
he provides security for his people and defeats the
insurgent - effective government is crucial. The
insurgent fights a total war and, therefore, will
not let scruples get in his way; while the government fights only a limited war and cannot be un-
scrupulous.[138] It is supposedly one of the maxims
of guerrilla warfare: "the guerrilla wins if he
does not lose"[139] because there cannot be two governments over the same land and people.
     American aims in Southeast Asia, in spite of
being maligned as numerous, nebulous, and confusing,
were in fact quite simple and, despite occasional
frills and philosophizing, remarkably consistent.
The United States objectives in Southeast Asia included the development of free and independent
countries according to their own views and that the
nations of the area should not threaten each other.
The major challenge was the Communist strategy of
"wars of national liberation" and it was to be disproved. Specifically, the aim was the continued
independence of South Viet-Nam and its freedom from
attack.
     In the letter from President Eisenhower to
President Diem of 1 October 1954, there were repeated reaffirmations of American support for

Saigon.[140] Our actions backed up our words as we sent first assistance, then advisors, and finally our own troops to help. American political leaders made it quite clear that we had answered the call for help from South Viet-Nam and that we intended to stand by that commitment.

It was alleged that in the spring of 1961, Roswell Gilpatric, Deputy Secretary of Defense, "was told victory was the goal, and it was his assignment to draw up plans to ensure that victory." The objective of that victory was to prevent Communist domination of South Viet-Nam.[141] General Maxwell Taylor - advisor to President Kennedy, Chairman of the Joint Chiefs of Staff, and then Ambassador to Saigon - gave his definition of victory in Viet-Nam. He saw it as the attainment of our basic objective: a South Viet-Nam free from aggression with the people permitted to choose their own government and their own way of life.[142]

Perhaps the most damaging aspect of our expressed aims was the occasional use of the negative approach: to prevent, to block, to stop, etc. Robert Thompson was one of those who stressed that an aim should be positive and constructive and should represent the final objective of the war. He has expressed his version of this aim in several places and has made it his first principle of counterinsurgency: "to establish and maintain a free, independent and united country which is politically and economically stable and viable."[143] This negative side of the objective misled some people into thinking that the United States was pursuing a no-win policy because there was no call for a smashing military victory which would have been tangible. This objective was really only an improvement on the status quo ante and, therefore, was rather mundane and undramatic.

One other major subject that repeatedly arose as a possible aim was the containment of China. Dean Rusk was one who frequently made reference to China in this vein, much to the consternation of some of his Viet-Nam specialists. Senator Fulbright was one who felt the "central issue is the contest between Chinese and American power" in Southeast Asia and he wanted a general accommodation.[144] Robert Thompson also thought the containment of China was a basic issue at stake in Viet-Nam. However, he lumped it together with "Asian communism and the whole concept of revolutionary war as an instrument of expansion" which brings it closer to Administration pronouncements concerning the test case of "wars of national

liberation." His point was that various crises had
led to a general understanding with the Soviet Union
where not to push and that "no such understanding
had been established with China" and the 17th Parallel seemed like a suitable line.[145] It was difficult
to assess the significance of the Sino-Soviet dispute in the early years; therefore, in retrospect,
Chinese influence was probably overestimated, yet
the proximity of China and its continued support of
the DRVN were crucial.

In discussion of the possible alternatives,
General Maxwell Taylor concluded that no alternative
appeared more promising than the course followed.[146]
Or as Leslie Gelb stated it: "No one seemed to have
a better solution."[147] Gelb's paper is important
because he stressed throughout that the Presidents
were not seeking total victory over the Vietnamese
Communists,[148] were not even seeking military victory, and were not deluded but led the United States
into Viet-Nam "with their eyes open,"[149] with one
consistent objective, "to deny the Communists control
over all Vietnam."[150] A political settlement was
their longer term goal,[151] and their strategy "always was to persevere."[152] President Kennedy, after
all the tribulations leading up to, and culminating
in, the Diem coup, determined that we would stay.
President Johnson agonized over Viet-Nam and did not
want to be the President who let Indochina go like
China had gone. "Lady Bird Johnson quoted him as
saying: 'I can't finish it with what I have got. So
what the Hell can I do?'" As Gelb put it: he "per-
severed and handed the war on to his successor."[153]
American leaders felt that they could not permit the
loss of Viet-Nam to Communism and in that they had
been successful so far. It is significant, in view
of our earlier discussion of victory and cost, that
"the importance of the objective was evaluated in
terms of cost, and the perceived costs of disengage-
ment outweighed the cost of further engagement."[154]
Those who made our policy still believe they were
right and "lament only the domestic repercussions of
their actions."[155]

The strategy and tactics of Viet-Nam will provide the grist for arguments, no doubt, for years to
come. One of Robert Thompson's insights early in
the war was: "If we plan for a long haul, we may get
quick results. But if we go for quick results, we
may at best get a long haul."[156] One of the most
important conditions for the insurgents is to maintain the initiative; therefore, a major aim of government forces must be to force the insurgents on to

the defensive.[157] Our strategy followed the doctrine that victory would result from "control of territory" and "attrition of the opponent." Victory would result from inflicting substantial casualties on the North until they became "unacceptable" while suffering less ourselves. This of course foundered on resolve and the determination of what was "unacceptable." Our military strategy produced an unfortunate feature of the war: "military success that could not be translated into permanent political advantage." Henry Kissinger ended his strategic review with the observation that "American 'victories' were empty unless they laid the basis for an eventual withdrawal."[158] For, although our aim was to keep South Viet-Nam free, that meant the direct American aim was to create conditions such that no further American presence was required. Those of us who went out there in the early years heard this as "work yourself out of a job." Unfortunately, most of us went back for a second try! Tactically, the military dilemma was where to place the primary military effort - in the more aggressive "search-and-destroy" operations or the more passive "secure-and-hold" tactics? However, the most difficult dilemmas of counterinsurgency proved to be the ancient political dilemma: "how to marry idealism to state-craft"[159] - how to translate our noble intentions into tangible results at an acceptable cost.

One of the lessons from Viet-Nam in an age of deterrence, was that "American power is more limited than many people have assumed." Since it is very difficult, after committed, to cut our losses, strong pressure developed in the country to try to preclude interventions.[160] However, our minimum objective had been achieved in that "Hanoi is unable to gain a military victory."[161] and had negotiated trying to gain something at the table that she could not win on the ground.

As Henry Kissinger expressed it: "the commitment of 500,000 Americans has settled the issue of the importance of Viet Nam. For what is involved now is confidence in American promises. However fashionable it is to ridicule the terms 'credibility' or 'prestige,' they are not empty phrases".[162] The defeat of the United States would drastically affect our role as a global power[163] and possibly increase "the risk of a third world war".

In addition to the drastic accommodations the countries of Southeast Asia would have to make, India, Japan, and Australia would have to consider going nuclear.[164] On 12 December 1967, fourteen

399

renowned members of the academic community issued a
long statement on our Asian policy and problems. In
it they stated:

> To accept a Communist victory in Vietnam would
> serve as a major encouragement to those forces
> in the world opposing peaceful coexistence, to
> those elements committed to the thesis that
> violence is the best means of effecting change.
> It would gravely jeopardize the possibilities
> of a political equilibrium in Asia, seriously
> damage our credibility, deeply affect the
> morale -- and the policies -- of our Asian al-
> lies and the neutrals. These are not develop-
> ments conducive to a long-range peace. They
> are more likely to prove precursors to larger,
> more costly wars.[165]

The aim of Laos continued to be survival, which
was dependent upon American help. As one high Lao
official said: "We chose to put our fate in the hands
of the United States." The problem was "four divisions of North Vietnamese regulars" and the "questioned credibility of the Nixon doctrine in protecting small Asian states from Communist aggression."[166]
Although not of quite the same critical proportions,
the problem was similar in Cambodia primarily because of the very concerted effort by some members
in the U.S. Congress to pass legislation blocking
all American actions in those countries.
    The aim of Thailand, with its own insurgency to
surmount, was to keep war at a distance - as already
noted, the commitment of troops to support Laos in
addition to their troop support in South Viet-Nam -
and to make minimum accommodations as necessary. For
the other Free World nations, success or failure of
American aims was important to their perception of
the future of Asia. The American presence had shown
that Communism was not necessarily the wave of the
future in Asia. This was vital to the turn-around
in Indonesia in 1965. The United States action had
"bought vitally needed time for governments that
were weak or unstable or leaning toward Peking as a
hedge against the future." Mr. Nixon continued,
Asian leaders from India to Japan knew why we were
in Viet-Nam and, "privately, if not publicly, they
urge us to see it through to a satisfactory conclusion."[167]
    Samuel Huntington concluded that we had pro-
duced a tremendous social revolution in South Viet-
Nam - the shift of population to cities - where

400

40 percent of the total, 6,800,000 of 17,200,000
lived in cities of 20,000 or more. "By this standard
South Viet Nam is now more urban than Sweden, Canada,
the Soviet Union, Poland, Austria, Switzerland and
Italy.... Apart from Singapore, it is easily the most
urban country in Southeast Asia."[168] The Saigon
metropolitan area grew to approximately 4,000,000 -
almost one-fourth of the country. This urbanization
was instrumental in the striking percentage increase
of the people living under Government control. "The
Maoist-inspired rural revolution is undercut by the
American-sponsored urban revolution."[169] The United
States may well have "stumbled upon" an answer to
"wars of national liberation" in an "absent-minded
way." It was neither the "quest for conventional
military victory" nor the "esoteric doctrines and
gimmicks of counter-insurgency warfare" but instead
"forced-draft urbanization and modernization" rapidly bringing the country out of the conditions in
which a rural revolutionary movement could hope to
amass adequate strength to seize power. In that
type of revolution, time would be on the side of the
Government.[170] At least we were finally on the
right subject. The issues were political not military and, therefore, required political solutions.
    The "peace without victory" was accepted with a
sigh of relief and only a few grumbles in America.
The prisoners were welcomed home from Hanoi but there
was general indifference to the continued violations
of the Agreement by the North. The indifference
turned to surprise as the Vietnamese Army which had
fought so hard for so long collapsed in the new offensive in early 1975. The U.S. Congress refused
further assistance and, on 30 April 1975 with the
Unconditional Surrender in Saigon, the "peace without victory" turned into defeat.

7. Defeat

    Even though American troops had been gone from
Viet-Nam since March 1973, it was difficult to dis-
connect the United States from the defeat. Some,
such as Nguyen Cao Ky, former Premier and Vice President, tried to assuage our feelings. Ky said the
United States was not to blame for the fall of South
Viet-Nam, the Americans had done much, even too
much, for them.[171] In a very complex war, the Americans had won all their battles but lost the war.
    The Tet offensive of 1968 was a crushing defeat

for the Communists; there was no local uprising to
support the VC; but we permitted it to be turned into a psychological defeat for ourselves. By 1971,
the insurgency had been defeated. Giap was left
with no alternative but a conventional invasion. He
violated all the rules of revolutionary warfare when
he attacked in the Spring of 1972 in an effort to regain the initiative. The invasion (eventually 14
divisions) was defeated by June 1972 and Hanoi had
to negotiate.[172] As we have seen earlier, Communists only negotiate when the pressure is on. They
had gained a considerable respite by foot-dragging
at Paris; the December 1972 bombings of Hanoi brought
more serious responses from the North Vietnamese.

Robert Thompson felt that at that point "the
United States could have won the war and established
a real peace."[173] However, the attacks that had
been generated in America had taken their toll and
any Presidential initiative was implausible. Instead, we accepted the "face-saving" Paris "Agreement on Ending the War and Restoring Peace in Viet-
nam" of 27 January 1973.

But there was no peace. The Agreement was meant,
from Hanoi's side, to restore security to Hanoi's
rear areas. Not one of the major provisions of the
Agreement -- except returning the prisoners and U.S.
troop withdrawal -- was implemented. North Viet-Nam,
Laos, and Cambodia were safe again and the full brunt
of the war returned to South Viet-Nam. The "peace"
after January 1973 was bloody and expensive as the
level of fighting increased. Of 27 years of war,
only 1972 was bloodier than 1974 for the South. They
lost nearly 19,000 dead and estimated 62,000 dead
among the North Vietnamese and Viet Cong.[174] The
United States allocated over $8 billion after the
Paris Agreement to support the "ceasefire."

America was rapidly trying to forget Viet-Nam
but the budget requirements would not permit it.
Thus the anti-war sentiment that had driven the United States out of Viet-Nam then focused on the U.S.
Congress to obtain drastic cuts in American military
and economic aid to South Viet-Nam in order to break
its will to resist. Soon the incoming supplies were
less than the expenditures and the enemy knew it.
South Viet-Nam was set up for the taking.

The North Vietnamese were surprised at their
good fortune but took full advantage of it. They
launched their major effort -- a 5-corps, 17 division conventional attack. The Vietnamese Army had
been fighting hard and well, but we had trained them
for counter-guerrilla operations! The end came

surprisingly fast. There were mistakes and then
panic in the Highlands and withdrawal turned into
rout. Then the northern area fell and the die was
cast. President Thieu fled and General Duong Van
"Big" Minh announced the Unconditional Surrender of
South Viet-Nam on 30 April 1975.

Secretary of State Henry Kissinger said that
Watergate and Congress enabled Hanoi to win. Watergate had diminished presidential power and the Congress had passed the War Powers Act, which prohibited enforcement of the Paris Agreement. Kissinger
also noted that as the erosion of morale in the
South became evident, they tried hard to get negotiations going. However, once the North Vietnamese
sensed the kill, they refused to negotiate and opted
for the military solution.[175]

Of course, there were those who were pleased
with the defeat. There was a parade at Berkley near
the University of California campus to hail the Communist takeover.[176] But many others were sobered by
what was referred to as America's first defeat. The
Washington Post (30 April 1975) had an article entitled "The Dominoes Are in Fact Falling" referring
to the controversial Domino Theory of the impact on
the rest of Southeast Asia.

The effect on American credibility was a major
concern. Robert Thompson lashed out at the U.S.
Congress. Referring to the Congressional cuts in
aid to South Viet-Nam he wrote, "... there can be
only one real lesson to be learnt from the Vietnam
war -- do not rely on the United States as an
ally."[177] Shortly before the end he wrote that, "The
Administration can no longer conduct a credible foreign policy. But, do not worry, a new foreign policy line has already been laid down by Congress: If
you surrender, the killing will stop. It is a clean
message, to the world, of the abject surrender of
the United States."[178] President Ford and his Administration called for emphasis on future goals
rather than past failures as this chapter closed in
the American experience.[179]

But there were scars on the body politic as well
as on the gallant men who fought. It had divided
American politics sharply for a decade, driven one
President from seeking reelection and tarnished
others, upset the economy, generated a controvery
over war powers, brought back isolationist sentiment
and antimilitarism, endangered the alliance system,
and cast a shadow over American credibility.

This was our first "television war" and it may
well be that it is impossible for a free country to

fight even a limited war in the world of modern communications.[180] The American public had watched the horrors of the war during supper for too many years. Television evolved as a most powerful force.

Was there anything positive about our sacrifices? We went into Viet-Nam with the loftiest of ideals -- to protect the freedom of our fellow men. We wanted nothing in return. In fact, we at least delayed the day of reckoning by 21 years, for Ho Chi Minh felt that he should have received all of Viet-Nam in 1954. Those two decades gave neighboring countries time to make adjustments if desired. That time also provided world focus on Southeast Asia which accentuated the roles of the United States, the Soviet Union, and Communist China.

This was the victory that Ho Chi Minh spent his life working for even though he had died in 1969. In his honor, the Provisional Revolutionary Government of South Viet-Nam renamed Saigon, Ho Chi Minh City. The Paris of the Orient was gone and so was the fiction of a civil war!

What was the cost of this tragic war? The conflict was the longest in American history and it has only been surpassed by World War II as the most costly. American military costs were over $150 billion (plus $60 billion or more for veterans' benefits in the future); $3.5 billion in economic aid to Viet-Nam, Cambodia, and Laos. American casualties numbered over 46,000 killed, over 300,000 wounded, and 10,000 nonhostile deaths. Allied casualties included over 240,000 South Vietnamese killed and over 300,000 wounded, plus other Free World losses of 4,000 killed and 10,000 wounded. There were more than one million combined North Vietnamese and Viet Cong combat deaths. Civilian casualties were estimated at well over one million including 325,000 killed, millions of refugees (figures varying from 5 to 11 million) in Viet-Nam and 300,000 to 600,000 in Laos (varying with sources), plus 25,000 killed by Communist terrorists and 40,000 kidnapped by the VC.[181] The casualties in Cambodia were estimated at 600,000 war dead plus another 600,000 injured. On the first anniversary of the end of the war, Kampuchea authorities declared there had been 800,000 war dead and 240,000 disabled.[182] There were 15,000 to 35,000 killed in Laos.[183] For some degree of perspective, while those 46,000 men were being killed in Viet-Nam, over 100,000 Americans between the ages of 15 and 24 were killed in traffic accidents. Even

404

during the worst year, 1968, traffic killed 2,000 more than the war.[184]

The figures on the other side are skimpy, but it appears that the Soviets and Chinese provided support that amounted to nearly $1 billion yearly. The Russians provided the North with more than adequate equipment, including tanks and artillery. The Soviets were afforded an opportunity to test their surface-to-air missile (SAM) system and make necessary improvements. The SAM coverage around Hanoi was the densest ever seen. One aspect that has been difficult for Westerners to comprehend was the inclination of the Communists to spend manpower the way we spend dollars. The DRVN had a pool of 250,000 young men who reached 17 each year and Robert Thompson estimated that Hanoi could spend "roughly 100,000 a year and not feel it politically or economically."[185] Only a totalitarian government could cope with the morale problem since of those who went South, very few ever returned.[186] The frightful cost continued as man tried to dominate his fellow man.

There was really only one basic issue in Viet-Nam -- either the North was going to get the South or it was not.[187] Revolutionary wars must end in a decision -- victory for one side or the other. Either South Viet-Nam would be an independent state or be absorbed by Hanoi, even if after a period of delay.[188] Kissinger concluded, "However we got into Viet Nam, whatever the judgment of our actions, ending the war honorably is essential for the peace of the world. Any other solution may unloose forces that would complicate prospects of international order."[189] What sounded good in 1973 left a bitter taste in 1975.

North Viet-Nam paid a high price to obtain a Total Victory in Viet-Nam, but they did not have to push their costs too high -- we gave it to them relatively cheap.

This was America's introduction to protracted war and wars of national liberation. It was a long, expensive, gruelling, discouraging experience for the United States and we did not evidence the tenacity to stay the long haul. The real effects are not yet known, but, as a hot war within the Cold War, it may prove to be the most important war in American history. But for Indochina, which has not known peace since World War II, it was only another turning point in its tragic history.

405

8. Indochina III

The Communists soon learned that it was easier
to liberate a country than to absorb it. Hanoi was
not only still having trouble three years later in
bringing South Viet-Nam into the fold, it was fighting with its onetime friends, the Communists in Cambodia, and even against the Chinese.

Political unification of the two Viet-Nams was
almost complete; however, the South was far from being socialized and there had been almost no economic
integration.[190] There was passive resistance in the
South and even some armed resistance. There were
problems with the Hoa Hao, the Montagnards, former
soldiers, and even disaffected Southern Communists.
Except for the Montagnards in the Highlands, most of
the activity was in the Delta and Ho Chi Minh City
area, but there was no unified command.

One group was the "Phuc Quoc Quan" or "National
Restoration Front." The PQQ supposedly had "popular
support" and, often wearing black pajamas, assassinated North Vietnamese officials.[191] Other groups
ambushed Communist patrols, attacked isolated out-
posts, and conducted raids to get arms and ammunition.[192] The outlook for these resistance groups
was dim as they were not receiving outside support.

There evidently was no blood bath in the South
but an estimated 100,000 higher level military and
civilian officials were still in political reeducation camps. A similar number was in limbo, not permitted to hold responsible jobs.[193] Even the Southern Communists were being purged, which is not surprising in Communist history. Hanoi had always been
suspicious of Southern parochialism.[194]

The Vietnamese who escaped by boat facing terrible odds and extreme hardship showed by their action that all was not rosy in the "Communist paradise."

The most bizarre case was Cambodia, renamed
Kampuchea when the Khmer Rouge came out of the jungle
and took over Phnom Penh on 17 April 1975. They implemented a revolution unlike any seen before. On
that very day, they ordered the evacuation of Phnom
Penh, a city of 2.5 million people, telling the people that the Americans were going to bomb the city.
Water and electricity were cut off to enforce their
order. The exodus began, including patients from
hospitals limping along or even being pushed in
their beds.[195] Towns and villages were also

evacuated in this mass migration.

Yugoslav journalists were the first foreign press group admitted. They reported a dead Phnom Penh with a population of about 20,000, no cars, no money, no mail system, only a handful of embassies (all on one street with no telephones), no television, and a newspaper, The Revolution, that was issued three times per month.[196] Diplomats earlier had called Phnom Penh a "ghost city" with useless currency lying in the streets after the National Bank had been blown up and with side streets closed off with vegetables growing in them.[197]

Mass executions started immediately to eliminate the military and civilian members of the former government who did not flee and the educated and professional class. Officers in Battambang, for example, were told to put on their best uniforms because they were going to Phnom Penh to greet Prince Sihanouk; 14 truckloads were taken outside of town and executed. The non-commissioned officers met a similar fate.[198] This was the pattern throughout the country where orders for executions were immediate and at the lowest level.

These fanatical, paranoid Khmer Rouge were against anything that was "imperialist" or modern. They slashed bolts of cloth in shops, broke every bottle and vial in drugstores[199] and were totally without compassion. They followed the Empty Basket theory. The population is a basket. Rather than removing the bad apples, empty the basket and keep what you want.[200] It was a reign of terror; the only punishment and the only law were death. Kill. "Nothing to gain by keeping them alive, nothing to lose by doing away with them." These young animals enjoyed killing.[201]

Everything was done in the name of the Angkar -- like "divinity" but which means "organization."[202] This organization turned back the clock in Cambodia, taking the people back to the land, supposedly from which a new race would be born. It appeared, at a minimum, that the old Cambodia had been destroyed. No one knew how many had died but it appeared that 1 to 1½ million people had been killed in this genocide.[203] Some estimates were two million.

The tide of refugees trying to cross the heavily patrolled border with Thailand had increased, to include even Khmer Rouge. Evidently there were three different "purification" programs. The first in 1975-76 concentrated on intellectuals and former officials. The second in 1977 aimed at seditious regional commanders who had supported or sympathized

with the Vietnamese, then fighting Cambodia. The
third appeared to be more diverse, directed at peasants, minor civilian officials, professionals who
had successfully hidden their identities and a few
Khmer Rouge regional commanders.[204]

The Third Indochina War seemed to be under way.
Border incidents between Viet-Nam and Cambodia grew
into major military operations. The Chinese living
in Viet-Nam came under intense pressure from the
Vietnamese and many were expelled. China withdrew
its advisers from Viet-Nam.[205] There was general
agreement that Cambodia was the aggressor in most
incidents and that Viet-Nam had become fed up with
their insolence and arrogance.[206] There was fighting between Viet-Nam and China on their border. On
3 November 1978 the Soviet Union and Viet-Nam signed
a 25-year peace and cooperation treaty.[207] The Soviets were strongly supporting Viet-Nam again. Communist China was supporting Cambodia. Some saw it
as a "war by proxy" between Russia and China.[208]

Viet-Nam was attacking in the Fall of 1978 but
the Khmer Rouge were acting like Viet Cong while the
Vietnamese were attacking with MIGs and captured
American F-5 aircraft.[209] Hanoi now had its own
"Viet-Nam"! There was little expectation that it
would end soon.[210]

The peoples of Indochina have known war for
thousands of years. The rivalries within the area
are enough to keep it unstable. The addition of outside powers only complicates an already complex international relationship. Whether Hanoi was striving for hegemony of the area remained to be seen.
What was clear was that although Hanoi had won victory over South Viet-Nam, there still was no peace
in Indochina.

NOTES

1. Thompson, "Squaring the Error," Foreign Affairs, April 1968, p. 442.
2. See Bernard Fall, Last Reflections on a War,
pp. 130-134.
3. George A. Carver, Jr., "The Faceless Viet
Cong," Foreign Affairs, April 1966, p. 347.
4. George A. Carver, Jr., "The Real Revolution
in South Viet Nam," Foreign Affairs, April 1965.
p. 404.
5. Donald S. Zagoria, Vietnam Triangle, p. 39.
6. Robert Shaplen, The Lost Revolution, particularly the first two chapters, is excellent

for the background of French-Viet Minh relations in 1945-1946.

7. Fall, Last Reflections, pp. 87-88.

8. Giap, People's War People's Army, p. 27, italics in original. The term "people's war" is not really new. Clausewitz devoted a chapter to it, On War, p. 457.

9. Ibid., p. 28.

10. Ibid., p. 55, italics in original.

11. Ibid., p. 79.

12. Harrison E. Salisbury, "Image and Reality in Indochina," Foreign Affairs, April 1971, p. 385. Salisbury's article is an interesting study of perceptions, particularly errors concerning monolithic Communism such as relations between Mao and Stalin. The world situation might have evolved quite differently if we had recognized Peking early, which evidently we almost did.

13. Fall, The Two Viet-Nams, p. 122.

14. Fall, Last Reflections, p. 139.

15. Fall, The Two Viet-Nams, p. 223.

16. Ibid., fn p. 281.

17. Fall, ibid., pp. 155-156, gives the figure 50,000 as a best-educated guess. He was no supporter of most of U.S. policy; therefore, his figure is rock bottom and probably low. Carver, "The Faceless Viet Cong," Foreign Affairs, April 1966, pp. 354-355, estimates 100,000. Other estimates go as high as 500,000.

18. Carver, "The Faceless Viet Cong." Foreign Affairs, April 1966, p. 356.

19. See Shaplen, The Lost Revolution, pp. 100-139.

20. See, for example, his article "South Viet-Nam's Internal Problems," in Pacific Affairs, September 1958.

21. Fall, Last Reflections, pp. 197-198.

22. See ibid., p. 201.

23. Fall, The Two Viet-Nams, p. 114.

24. Letter to author, 25 December 1961, from Cambodia. He had a similar comment on the "Laos mess."

25. Carver, "The Faceless Viet Cong," Foreign Affairs, April 1966, pp. 359-360.

26. Ibid., pp. 360-361. Wilfred Burchett, the Australian Communist, wrote of talks with Nguyen Huu Tho, head of the NLF, that although the NLF was officially set up in 1960, it had existed as an idea since 1954. Vietnam: Inside Story of the Guerrilla War, p. 178.

27. Carver, ibid., p. 364.

28. This quote is on p. 7 of a 21-page study prepared by the U.S. Embassy in Saigon, "Hanoi's Direction and Support of the Communist Effort in South Vietnam," sent as Enclosure #1 to State Message A-63 from Saigon to the State Department, 28 July 1967. This is an excellent study based on intelligence sources.

29. Ibid., p. 9.

30. Page 3 of State Message A-73 from our Embassy in Saigon to the State Department, Subject: "Release to Press of Captured Enemy Documents," 29 July 1967. The enclosure to this message was the VC Top Secret 60-page document "Resolution of COSVN of March 1966" covering the "program of the Hanoi-COSVN hierarchy on every aspect of the Viet Nam conflict". The 4-page message and excerpts from the document may be found in Hobbs, Focus on Southeast Asia, pp. 204-208.

31. Resolution, p. 20 and Saigon's A-73, p. 2.

32. Resolution, p. 60 and Saigon's A-73, p. 2.

33. Resolution, p. 16 and Saigon's A-73, p. 3.

34. Resolution, p. 31, italics in message.

35. Carver, "The Real Revolution in South Viet Nam," Foreign Affairs, April 1965, p. 387. He said the South was, less obviously, also in the midst of a social revolution. Robert Scalapino wrote: "In my opinion, the facts demonstrate conclusively that the NLF, although it has sought to use local grievances and nationalist appeals to win a broad popular base, is and always has been an instrument of the Communist Party of North Vietnam." Vietnam Perspectives, February 1966, p. 4.

36. Fall, "Viet Nam in the Balance," Foreign Affairs, October 1966, pp. 14-15.

37. Ibid., p. 16.

38. Schleisinger, The Bitter Heritage, p. 17.

39. Clifford, "A Viet Nam Reappraisal," Foreign Affairs, July 1969, p. 605.

40. Thompson, No Exit From Vietnam, p. 114. He said "ask the dominoes." See his discussion of views of various Southeast Asian leaders. Revolutionary War in World Strategy, p. 154.

41. Thompson, No Exit From Vietnam, p. 196. See General Maxwell Taylor, Responsibility and Response, pp. 21-22 for his views on the effects of U.S. relations around the world. See also McGeorge Bundy, "The End of Either/Or," Foreign Affairs, January 1967, p. 195, who felt there would be effects elsewhere, "but victory for Ho would not mean automatic communization of all Asia."

42. This was the author's introduction to Asia,

except for attending the British Jungle School in
Malaya in 1958, having spent six weeks in Japan on
standby in case of commitment into Laos in the fall
of 1959.

43. Letter to author, 25 December 1961.

44. From his book, The Vantage Point, in The
Evening Star, Washington, D.C., 18 October 1971,
p. A-6.

45. Burchett, Inside Story, p. 216, in conversation with Nguyen Huu Tho. See Shaplen, The Lost
Revolution, for details of coups.

46. See, for example, Taylor, Responsibility
and Response, p. 24.

47. See Saigon's A-63, p. 15. Also Lieutenant
General Richard G. Stilwell, "Evolution in Tactics -
The Vietnam Experience," Army, February 1970, pp.
13-17. I recall a briefing at the Vietnamese 42d
Regiment on 1 April 1965 in which they stated that
they had encountered dug-in enemy that they thought
were the 101st Regiment and that two other regiments
were in country under control of the 325th Division -
not bad intelligence!

48. See Zagoria, Vietnam Triangle, p. 46.

49. Department of State, Aggression From the
North, The Record of North Viet-Nam's Campaign to
Conquer South Viet-Nam.

50. Saigon's A-63, particularly pp. 15-20.

51. Giap, Big Victory, Great Task, p. 28. It
is interesting that the USSR proposed simultaneous
admission of the two Viet-Nams to the UN in 1957.
See Zagoria, Vietnam Triangle, p. 102.

52. Giap, ibid., and in the captured COSVN Resolution for example, Saigon's A-73. This wording
appears regularly in North Vietnamese documents and
publications.

53. Reply of 15 February 1967 to letter from
President Johnson 10 February 1967.

54. Komer, "Clear, Hold and Rebuild," Army,
May 1970, p. 24.

55. Fall, Last Reflections, pp. 44-45.

56. The Washington Post, 15 August 1973, p. 1.
The Boston Globe, p. 16.

57. McGeorge Bundy, "The End of Either/Or,"
Foreign Affairs, January 1967, p. 197. I have discussed these attacks with pilots who flew them and
their restrictions and problems were horrendous.
Harrison E. Salisbury, Behind the Lines - Hanoi, pp.
65-66, stated that the diplomats in Hanoi felt that
the civilian damage was due to the pressure on the
pilots of the heavy antiaircraft fire. Even one of
Bertrand Russell's commission, which was preparing

411

a mock trial of LBJ for war crimes, was not sure it was intentional.

58. Giap, Big Victory, Great Task, p. 81. One dissenter was retired Admiral U.S. Grant Sharp who felt that air power could have won the war if it had not been so restricted by Washington. He concluded that US forces should never be committed unless it is decided to use our available nonnuclear power to win in the shortest possible time. Air Force Magazine, September 1971, pp. 82-83.

59. Bundy, "The End of Either/Or," p. 191. Bundy felt the South would have fallen in 1961 and 1965 without US aid and he felt the decisions were right in the Vietnamese and U.S. interests and for peace and progress in the Pacific. p. 195.

60. "Squaring the Error," Foreign Affairs, April 1968, p. 442. For discussions of the tactics of the war, see Stilwell, "Evolution in Tactics"; Lieutenant Colonel Richard A. McMahon, "Indirect Approach," Army, August 1969, pp. 57-63; Robert W. Komer, "Clear, Hold and Rebuild," Army, May 1970, pp. 16-24 and June 1970, pp. 20-29; Col. John J. McCuen, "Can We Win Revolutionary Wars?," Army, December 1969, pp. 16-22; and a rebuttal by George Fielding Eliot, "Next Time We'll Have to Get There Faster," Army, April 1970, pp. 32-36.

61. Thompson, Defeating Communist Insurgency, p. 100, in a conversation with President Diem at the end of 1962, long before the Buddhist troubles.

62. Scalapino, Vietnam Perspectives, February 1966, p. 4.

63. Professor Eugene D. Genovese of Rutgers University at a "Teach-in" on 23 April 1965.

64. U.S. News and World Report, 2 May 1966, p. 56.

65. McCarthy, Vietnam, p. 33.

66. Clark, "On Violence, Peace and Law," Foreign Affairs, October 1970, p. 32. "Military victory would have been far more disastrous than military failure for the United States. The apparent lesson of victory would have been that force and violence were still possible as solutions of international problems. Force and violence would be relied on again." p. 37.

67. Fulbright, The Arrogance of Power, p. 37. He pondered "whether the diversion of hundreds of thousands of our young men from their homes and jobs and families will yield rewards of freedom and security commensurate with their sacrifices." The arrogant implication seemed to be: For a bunch of Asians?

68. See Townsend Hoopes, "Legacy of the Cold War in Indochina," Foreign Affairs, July 1970, p. 612.

69. David Schoenbrun in Introduction to Giap, Big Victory, Great Task, pp. vi-vii. Hoopes, "Legacy", "As a nation we had little perception that we might be frustrating a widely supported national independence movement by lending our aid and our prestige to what were at best colonial puppets, who suffered an innate incapacity to win over any sizeable segment of the Vietnamese people to their side" (p. 605) and could not govern without large U.S. presence. (p. 606). He also mentions our "delusion" of nation building. (p. 608).

70. Hoopes, "Legacy", p. 610.

71. L. James Binder, "Front and Center," Army, July 1971, p. 7.

72. The New York Times, 22 February 1971, p. 12. He also gave short shrift to the idea of self-determination.

73. Fulbright, Arrogance of Power, p. 55. But can't impressions be more important than facts in international relations?

74. Ibid., p. 61. The Communists regularly quoted him. This is the same man who had the military muzzled in June 1961 (pp. 58-59). He can speak out but not the military!

75. Ibid., p. 78. Were there no nationalists in the GVN?

76. Ibid., pp. 181-182. Fulbright pointedly never visited Viet-Nam thereby facilitating his detached perspective.

77. See Robert H. Johnson, "Vietnamization: Can It Work?" Foreign Affairs, July 1970, pp. 646-647. It is interesting that, even though Viet-Nam may have been almost ungovernable, it was still one of the most democratic and constitutional nations in Southeast Asia -- even under stress of war. The anti-government demonstrations, plethora of newspapers, and general freedom did not reflect a dictatorship.

78. Hoopes, "Legacy", p. 611. He refers to LBJ's "visceral preference for victory." It is interesting that Townsend Hoopes is the culprit suggested in Lloyd Norman, "The '206,000 Plan' - The Inside Story," Army (April 1971, pp. 30-35), on p. 35, who may have leaked the plan for increased troops to Viet-Nam to the press. The request for more troops was part of a detailed study made for the President and not a panicked plea for massive reinforcements.

79. The massacre in Hue, where the VC rounded up people on their lists and executed them, was a harbinger of what would happen if the Communists won control of South Viet-Nam.

80. Dr. Anthony Wermuth's review of Big Story in Parameters, Journal of the U.S. Army War College, Vol. VII, No. 4, p. 83, italics in original.

81. See Kahn, "If Negotiations Fail," Foreign Affairs, July 1968, p. 634. For more on military victory but political defeat, see Henry A. Kissinger, "The Viet Nam Negotiations," Foreign Affairs, January 1969, p. 215.

Hanson Baldwin, writing in late 1967, before Tet, predicted that the impending VC offensive would be aimed at the U.S. public, The New York Times, 26, 27, and 28 December 1967.

82. Clifford, "A Viet Nam Reappraisal," Foreign Affairs, July 1969, pp. 602-603. A military operation as large as Tet requires a long planning time. It appears that the Viet Cong were thinking of it in the COSVN Resolution of March 1966. There was repeated mention of decisive victory in "a relatively short period of time." Stressing that the armed struggle must be closely coordinated with the political struggle, it added: "We have the capability of coordinating our armed struggle with the popular uprising to liberate the cities and towns, and of coordinating our offensive with the mass revolt in preparation for a general attack and uprising which will take place when the opportunity avails itself and the situation ripens." Enclosure to Saigon's A-73, p. 17, italics in message.

83. Thompson, No Exit From Vietnam, p. 178.

84. Lloyd Norman, "What Does Hanoi Want?" Army, April 1969, p. 38.

85. Thompson, No Exit From Vietnam, pp. 176-177.

86. Kissinger, "Viet Nam Negotiations," p. 218, italics in original.

87. Ibid., p. 221. "Pragmatism and bureaucracy thus combine to produce a diplomatic style marked by rigidity in advance of formal negotiations and excessive reliance on tactical considerations once negotiations start.... In the process, we deprive ourselves of criteria by which to judge progress." No doubt this was one of his main target areas for improvement after he was in an influential position to change it.

88. U.S. News & World Report, 7 March 1966, p. 104.

89. Kissinger, "Viet Nam Negotiations," p. 228.

90. Ibid., p. 226. Thompson wrote that cease-

fire and partition were only of interest to those
who would not do it to themselves. "No Democratic
contender for the Presidency offered a seat in his
cabinet to the 'Black Power' movement and no American politician has yet suggested a standstill in the
ghetto with 'Black Power' as a separate authority in
legal control." Revolutionary War in World Strategy,
p. 157.

91. Thompson, No Exit From Vietnam, p. 182.
92. See, for example, Mission to Hanoi (A
Chronicle of Double-Dealing in High Places) by Harry
S. Ashmore and William C. Baggs.
93. Samuel P. Huntington, "The Bases of Accommodation," Foreign Affairs, July 1968, p. 652.
94. Clark, "On Violence, Peace and Law," Foreign Affairs, October 1970, p. 37.
95. Robert H. Johnson, "Vietnamization: Can It
Work?" Foreign Affairs, July 1970, p. 642.
96. Clifford, "Viet Nam Reappraisal," p. 617.
97. Johnson, "Vietnamization," p. 643.
98. U.S. News & World Report, 1 November 1971,
pp. 64-65.
99. Thompson, "Squaring the Error," pp. 450-451.
100. The Washington Post, 15 October 1971,
p. A-23.
101. Army Times, 27 October 1971, p. 13.
102. There was a "brotherly" meeting of "old
Indochina hands" in a little village in southern
China on 24 April 1970. Nguyen Huu Tho of the NLF,
Souphanouvong of the Pathet Lao, Pham Van Dong of
the DRVN, and Sihanouk of Cambodia interestingly
enough communicated in French. They stressed the
"solidarity" of the four, the original nature of
each movement, and "neutralist" themes. Jean
Lacouture, "From the Vietnam War to an Indochina
War," Foreign Affairs, July 1970, p. 627.
103. Ibid. This article was written too close
to April 1970 to have any perspective.
104. William Beecher, "Vietnamization: A Few
Loose Ends," Army, November 1970, p. 15.
105. Prince Norodom Sihanouk, "The Future of
Cambodia," Foreign Affairs, October 1970, p. 10.
106. A South Vietnamese airborne brigade commander and some battalion commanders were captured
after a hard fight. The North Vietnamese Radio announced that they were all executed on the spot as
"war criminals."
107. Lacouture, "Vietnam War to an Indochina
War," p. 622. Even Lacouture admitted they were in
Laos!
108. For a good review of the early years, see

Col. Edwin F. Black, "Laos: A Case Study," Military Review, December 1964, pp. 49-59. Early Communist optimism over Laos was expressed by Khrushchev to Ambassador Llewellyn Thompson: "Why take risks over Laos? It will fall into our laps like a ripe apple." Roger Hilsman, To Move A Nation, p. 130.

109. Congressional Record, 3 August 1971, pp. S12930-S12966, particularly the staff report starting on p. S12960.

110. See Lacouture, "Vietnam War to an Indochina War", p. 623 and Eric Pace, "Laos: Continuing Crisis," Foreign Affairs, October 1964, p. 71, about how the Pathet Lao had established a functioning state.

111. Robert Novak, The Washington Post, 23 September 1971, p. A-19.

112. The Evening Star, Washington, D.C., 23 September 1971, p. A-Back Page, about 12,000 Thais were to be available in early 1972.

113. Brigadier Richard L. Clutterbuck, The Long, Long War, p. ix.

114. Ibid., p. 178.

115. Hamilton Fish Armstrong, "Power In a Sieve," Foreign Affairs, April 1968, p. 467.

116. Fall, The Two Viet-Nams, p. 138.

117. Kissinger, "Viet Nam Negotiations," p. 216.

118. This phenomenon was brought home to me in 1965 when I was directing the North Vietnamese side of a five-sided war game in the Pentagon conducted by experts in government and all sides thought they were winning. Interestingly enough, we, as the DRVN, thought there was nothing that could keep us from hanging on until the 1968 elections!

119. Fall, Last Reflections, p. 221.

120. Ibid., p. 210. He felt that a country being subverted was being outadministered not being outfought. p. 220. Fall saw Ho in 1962, who told him since it took 8 years to defeat France, the "stronger Americans could in all likelihood be defeated in 10 years." p. 231.

121. Fall, The Two Viet-Nams, p. 390.

122. Zagoria, Vietnam Triangle, p. 135.

123. Kissinger, "Viet Nam Negotiations," p. 214.

124. Thompson, No Exit From Vietnam, p. 144. He disagreed with the view that there were three wars: the shooting war, pacification, and nation building - there was only one war. p. 145.

125. It came out at least once though. See U.S. News & World Report, 30 May 1966, p. 19. Admiral U.S.G. Sharp raised the subject in Strategy for Defeat (San Rafael, California: Presidio Press, 1978).

416

126. Ball, "In Defense of the Military," Army,
August 1971, pp. 8-9. He added a very important
point: "we may well drive our most gifted and competent officers out of our armed forces - men we shall
desperately need when the going again gets rough."
127. Thompson, "Squaring the Error," p. 452.
128. Justus M. van der Kroef, "The War Seen
From Hanoi," Vietnam Perspectives, February 1966,
p. 25.
129. Thompson, No Exit From Vietnam, p. 16.
130. The Evening Star, Washington, D.C., 4 October 1971, p. A-2.
131. The Washington Post, 12 September 1971,
p. A-25. Of interest, 4,000 Soviet specialists
worked in the DRVN since 1965, 7,000 Vietnamese were
trained by the Soviets and 10,000 were at that time
training in the Soviet Union.
132. Zagoria, Vietnam Triangle, pp. 28-29.
133. Lin Piao, "Long Live the Victory of People's War!" originally published in the People's
Daily on 3 September 1965, pamphlet, Foreign Language Press, Peking, pp. 41-42.
134. Thompson, No Exit From Vietnam, p. 63.
135. Ibid., p. 62.
136. Thompson, Defeating Communist Insurgency,
pp. 29-30.
137. Thompson, No Exit From Vietnam, p. 60.
138. Thompson, Revolutionary War in World Strategy, p. 21.
139. "The conventional army loses if it does
not win." Kissinger, "Viet Nam Negotiations," p. 214.
140. For a good, brief history of the U.S. involvement, see William P. Bundy, "The Path to Viet-
Nam: A Lesson in Involvement," Department of State
Bulletin, 4 September 1967, p. 275, also in Hobbs,
Focus on Southeast Asia, p. 8.
An invaluable collection of documents was
first assembled in 1965 and revised annually thereafter, Background Information Relating to Southeast
Asia and Vietnam, Committee on Foreign Relations,
United States Senate. A broad selection is also in
Focus on Southeast Asia, The statements by Kennedy,
Johnson, Rusk, McNamara, and other Government officials are all there for review, plus chronologies
and listings of commitments.
141. Claude Witze, Air Force Magazine, September 1971, p. 17.
142. Taylor, Responsibility and Response, p. 22.
143. Thompson, Defeating Communist Insurgency,
pp. 50-51. The wording is very similar specifically
for Viet-Nam in "Squaring the Error," p. 448. It is

417

also in No Exit From Vietnam, p. 116, appearing again on p. 197 but with a slight modification - "at a cost acceptable to the United States."

A staff writer for The Sunday Star, Washington, D.C., wrote "Stability is still a basic U.S. goal in South Vietnam." 5 September 1971, p. H-11.

144. Fulbright, The Arrogance of Power, p. 186.

145. Thompson, No Exit From Vietnam, p. 114.

146. Taylor, Responsibility and Response, pp. 37-41.

147. Gelb, "Vietnam: The System Worked," Foreign Policy, Summer 1971, p. 145. This is an extremely important analysis of US involvement in Viet-Nam. Gelb gained fame as the editor of the McNamara study which Daniel Ellsberg made famous as the Pentagon Papers.

"The question of whether our leaders would have started down the road if they knew this would mean over half a million men in Vietnam, over 40,000 U.S. deaths, and the expenditure of well over $100 billion is historically irrelevant. Only Presidents Kennedy and Johnson had to confront the possibility of these large costs. The point is that each administration was prepared to pay the costs it could foresee for itself."

148. Ibid., p. 147.

149. Ibid., p. 141. In response to those who tried to label it a Presidential war, Senator Goldwater, in a speech in the Senate, stated that Congress knew what was going on from the start and gave "its approval in advance to almost everything that has occurred there." U.S. News & World Report, 16 August 1971, p. 88.

150. Ibid., p. 145.

151. Ibid., p. 150.

152. Ibid., p. 152.

153. Ibid., p. 165.

154. Ibid., p. 145.

155. Ibid., p. 166.

156. Thompson, "Squaring the Error," p. 453. He raised the question of a no-win strategy because "in a People's Revolutionary War, if you are not winning you are losing, because the enemy can always sit out a stalemate without making any concessions." No Exit from Vietnam, p. 144.

157. Thompson, Defeating Communist Insurgency, p. 116.

158. Kissinger, "Viet Nam Negotiations," pp. 212-214.

159. George K. Tanham and Dennis J. Duncanson, "Some Dilemmas of Counterinsurgency," Foreign

418

<u>Affairs</u>, October 1969, pp. 114 and 122.
      Similar to the Chinese philosophy, it can-
not all be done by foreign assistance. "Hearts and
minds cannot be won by bribery alone." Thompson,
<u>Revolutionary War in World Strategy</u>, p. 69. General
Lansdale felt the main thing we needed to give the
Vietnamese was a "cause" - a unifying feeling that
the population would support against the VC. Major
General Edward G. Lansdale, "Viet Nam: Do We Understand Revolution?" <u>Foreign Affairs</u>, October 1964,
p. 82. In this light, "The great majority of the
Vietnamese peasants are not committed to the Viet
Cong, and if they could be given real security, they
would refuse to cooperate with it." Robert A.
Scalapino, "Vietnam and World Peace," <u>Vietnam Per-
spectives</u>, February 1966, p. 7.
      Indicators of progress came under consid-
erable scrutiny in this statistical war; however, as
security improves, two of the best guides of progress are "an improvement in intelligence voluntarily given by the population and a decrease in the
insurgents' recruiting rate." "Confidence is the
most precious ingredient for success," and three indispensable qualities in counterinsurgency are
"patience," determination," and an "offensive spirit." Thompson, <u>Defeating Communist Insurgency</u>, pp.
170-171.
      See also Hobbs, "All the Answers Are Not
in the Statistics," <u>Army</u>, March 1968, pp. 77-78.
      160. Graham Allison, Ernest May, and Adam Yar-
molinsky, "Limits to Intervention," <u>Foreign Affairs</u>,
January 1970, p. 251.
      161. Kissinger, "Viet Nam Negotiations," p. 230.
      162. Ibid., pp. 218-219.
      163. Thompson in <u>Revolutionary War in World
Strategy</u>, p. 137, felt "the United States would
cease to be a global power and would in the end be
compelled to become instead a very super nuclear
power."
      164. Therefore, Thompson thought it vital for
the U.S. to stand by Viet-Nam. <u>No Exit From Vietnam</u>,
pp. 196-197.
      165. A. Doak Barnett, Leo Cherne, Harry D.
Gideonse, Oscar Handlin, William W. Lockwood, Richard L. Park, Guy J. Pauker, Lucian Pye, Edwin O.
Reischauer, I. Milton Sacks, Robert A. Scalapino,
Paul Seabury, Fred von de Mehden, and Robert E. Ward.
      166. Robert Novak, <u>The Washington Post</u>, 27 Sep-
tember 1971, p. A-21.
      167. Richard M. Nixon, "Asia after Viet Nam,"
<u>Foreign Affairs</u>, October 1967, pp. 111-112. Robert

Shaplen wrote in the same issue about an awareness of Asian leaders "that the United States has bought time in Viet Nam for the rest of Southeast Asia to get together and avoid another Viet Nam." "Viet Nam: Crisis of Indecision," p. 110.

168. Huntington, "Bases of Accommodation," p. 648.

169. Ibid., p. 650.

170. Ibid., pp. 652-653.

171. The New York Times, 5 May 1975, p. 1.

172. See Robert Thompson, "Military Victory: Political Defeat - the Failure of US Strategy in Vietnam," International Defense Review, #6 (December 1974).

173. Ibid.

174. U.S. News & World Report, 13 January 1975, p. 50.

175. The Baltimore Sun, 5 May 1975, p. 2.

176. The Washington Post, 1 May 1975, p. 10.

177. Thompson, "Military Victory."

178. Thompson, "Retreat," Philadelphia Enquirer, 3 April 1975.

179. See The Wall Street Journal, 30 April 1975, p. 2.

180. See James Reston, "The End of the Tunnel," The New York Times, 30 April 1975.

181 U.S. News & World Report, 26 July 1971, p. 17, The Evening Star, Washington, D.C., 14 October 1971, p. 1 and 23 May 1972, p. A-9, and The New York Times, 1 May 1975, p. 20.

182. François Ponchaud, Cambodia: Year Zero, translated by Nancy Amphoux (New York: Holt, Rinehart and Winston, 1977), p. 71.

183. See Roland A. Paul, "Laos: Anatomy of An American Involvement," Foreign Affairs, April 1971, p. 539.

184. See U.S. News & World Report, 13 September 1971, p. 57.

185. Thompson, "Squaring the Error," pp. 445-446. The readiness to accept heavy casualties is a major difference between People's Revolutionary War and guerrilla war. Guerrillas cannot afford heavy losses. "Hanoi knew quite well that there was only one asset in the North which was vital to the war and that was the human material i.e. the manpower." No Exit From Vietnam, pp. 58-59.

186. See The Evening Star, 28 October 1971, p. A-13.

187. Thompson, "Squaring the Error," p. 447.

188. Thompson, Revolutionary War in World Strategy, p. 156.

189. Kissinger, "The Viet Nam Negotiations,"
p. 234.

190. U.S. News & World Report, 23 January 1978,
p. 39.

191. Army Times, 14 November 1977, p. 40.

192. The Washington Star, 30 January 1978,
p. A-10.

193. U.S. News & World Report, 23 January 1978,
p. 40.

194. See John P. Roche, "The Vietnamese brand
of genocide," The Washington Star, 7 October 1978.
p. A-11.

195. Ponchaud, Cambodia: Year Zero, pp. 6-7.
This book is a good reference for this unbelievable
episode in Cambodia.

196. The Washington Star, 21 March 1978, p. A-4.

197. The Boston Globe, 23 January 1978, p. 2.

198. Ponchaud, Cambodia: Year Zero, pp. 41-44.

199. Ibid., p. 32.

200. Ibid., pp. 50-51.

201. Ibid., pp. 64-66.

202. Ibid., p. 88. See also Time, 21 November
1977, p. 42.

203. Ibid., p. 71.

204. The Washington Star, 1 October 1978, p.
B-12.

205. The Washington Star, 25 May 1978, p. A-4.

206. The Los Angeles Times, 5 January 1978,
pp. 1 and 12.

207. The Washington Star, 5 November 1978,
p. A-7.

208. U.S. News & World Report, 23 January 1978,
p. 39.

209. The Washington Star, 20 October 1978,
p. A-10.

210. U.S. News & World Report, 10 July 1978,
pp. 27-28. See also Tai Sung An, "Turmoil in Indochina: The Vietnam-Cambodia Conflict," Asian Affairs
(Mar-Apr 78), p. 256.

13
Concepts of Victory

The basic aim of world Communism is world domination.[1]

-- William R. Kintner

The West is not animated by
any crusade or desire to
conquer. [2]

-- Raymond Aron

The various contestants of the Cold War, with
their divergent ideologies, view the world conflict
with different ideas as to what would be victory.
The Communist World, operating on the offensive, is
marching toward a specific goal, while the Free
World, always operating on the defensive, suffers
from the lack of any longrange, dynamic objective.
There is a theory often heard that the Russians
and the Free World are drifting toward each other
and may one day join forces against the Chinese or
else live together peacefully. The Western nations
have been moving away from private enterprise toward
state enterprise, while the Communists have moved
away from state control to a somewhat freer social
order. One of the best studies on the subject concluded that convergence is not too likely and, more
importantly that, even if the two super states were
more similar, there is no basis to assume that they
would be more peaceful.[3] Although there will certainly be changes in the governments in the future,
Communism would have to change its ideology completely to be compatible with democracy.
All states long for world organization, world
economic stability, and peace. But the various concepts and methods for accomplishing them are quite
different: they are not the same organization, the
same economy, or the same peace. Since the ideolo-

423

gies are incompatible, international morals and
methods of practicing cooperation are not the same.
The quest for peace is nothing new; St. Augustine
wrote centuries ago that peace is the object of war:

> Whoever gives even moderate attention to human
> affairs and to our common nature, will recog-
> nize that if there is no man who does not wish
> to be joyful, neither is there any one who does
> not wish to have peace. For even they who make
> war desire nothing but victory - desire, that
> is to say, to attain to peace with glory. For
> what else is victory than the conquest of those
> who resist us? and when this is done there is
> peace. It is therefore with the desire for
> peace that wars are waged, even by those who
> take pleasure in exercising their warlike na-
> ture in command and battle. And hence it is
> obvious that peace is the end sought for by
> war. For every man seeks peace by waging war,
> but no man seeks war by making peace. For even
> they who intentionally interrupt the peace in
> which they are living have no hatred of peace,
> but only wish it changed into a peace that
> suits them better.

> He, then, who prefers what is right to what is
> wrong, and what is well-ordered to what is per-
> verted, sees that the peace of unjust men is
> not worthy to be called peace in comparison
> with the peace of the just.[4]

Peace is more than merely the absence of war.
We could have that sort of peace quite quickly if
all of the Free World would simply surrender to the
Communists. There would be no further threat of nuclear war as there would be no one capable of resisting them. (However, as we see, they might well
be threatening each other.) But would this be peace
to what was once the Free World? Salvador de
Madariaga wrote an open letter to left wing intellectuals, particularly of the British Labor Party,
in January 1960 in which he defined peace for them
and reprimanded them for their lack of comprehension
of the value of American armaments: "You cannot be
unaware of the true nature of peace. Peace is not
mere quiescence. It is the active enjoyment of liberty and order combined by and under reason. How
can you seek peace with those who condemn reason as
an 'objective deviation,' and liberty as bourgeois
prepossession? Real peace is the outcome of a free

agreement among free parties."[5]

The essential objective of war is to require the enemy to change his policy, or as Kecskemeti pointed out, where the victor is striving for "a monopoly of strength that can be used to dictate terms."[6] The complicating factor, however, is the vastly increased destructive power now available to belligerents which has a deterrent effect on their chances of dominating an opponent without having to pay too high a price. The question of victory in a thermonuclear war has not yet been resolved. It has been made quite clear that the United States wishes to avoid a nuclear war, and our actions over the years support this. Khrushchev clearly recognized that a nuclear war would destroy Russian Communism as well as capitalism and was not an acceptable means for expanding Communism. The threat of a Russia in ruins next to a relatively undamaged China of 800,000,000 people certainly aided his perception. Even though the Soviets probably accept a higher risk of war than the Americans, they desire to avoid nuclear war, as their withdrawal of the missiles from Cuba indicated.

Under these conditions, then, the powers must "accustom themselves to thinking in terms of relatively small political payoffs."[7] This has not been difficult for the Communists who regard revolution, subversion, and intrigue as basic tools in their foreign policy. However, the Free World has been slow to adapt to this problem and has not yet developed a policy. There have been too many people who felt that since total victory was not possible, then we were in a stalemate; they refused to accept any other alternative. Henry Kissinger pointed out that there is still a broad middle ground between these two extremes:

> Nevertheless, a strategic doctrine which renounces the imposition of unconditional surrender should not be confused with the acceptance of a stalemate. The notion that there is no middle ground between unconditional surrender and the status quo ante is much too mechanical. To be sure, a restoration of the status quo ante is often the simplest solution, but it is not the only possible one. The argument that neither side will accept a defeat, however limited, without utilizing every weapon in its arsenal is contradicted by both psychology and by experience. There would seem to be no sense in seeking to escape a limited defeat through

425

bringing on the cataclysm of an all-out war,
particularly if all-out war threatens a calam-
ity far transcending the penalties of losing a
limited war. It simply does not follow that
because one side stands to lose from a limited
war, it could gain from an all-out war. On the
contrary, both sides face the same dilemma:
that the power of modern weapons has made all-
out war useless as an instrument of policy, except for acts of desperation.[8]

Over the years, both sides have accepted limited defeats without reverting to their heavy weapons.
    As we review the concepts of victory, we should
keep in mind three major characteristics of the Communist threat:
    1. It is worldwide. Non-Communist areas are
devoured one by one and their strengths added to
that of the Communist World.
    2. It is total. Every form of human endeavor
is affected. Armed forces may attack across frontiers or, since they learned a major lesson in Korea,
attack may take the form of internal subversion.
Economic and psychological warfare, political infiltration, sabotage, subversion, and attack are interchangeable and mutually supporting aggressive weapons.
    3. It is of indefinite duration. A permanent
accommodation based on mutual advantage, considered
normal as the foundation of arrangements between
great nations, is unlikely. Reductions in Communist
pressure are temporary expedients forced by adverse
power elements or a tactical move to establish a
more favorable situation.[9]

                1. Victory to the Communist World

    It appears that, from innumerable sources, we
can safely say that the Communists have world domination as their one objective of ultimate victory.
This is made abundantly clear throughout Communist
literature and has remained extraordinarily consistent for over a hundred years. We are all quite familiar with Khrushchev's quaint pronouncement, "We
will bury you."[10] Many people acted quite startled
when it was published, but the metaphor was not even
new. A Comintern resolution of 1922 stated: "It
is the historical mission of the Communist International to be the gravedigger of bourgeois society."[11]

426

The Western World deludes itself terribly when it thinks that the Communist enmity toward us is ephemeral, having arisen only as a part of the Cold War. This enmity is the basis of the Communist ideology; without it they would have no ideology. Lenin said in 1920: "As long as capitalism and socialism exist, we cannot live in peace: in the end one or the other will triumph - a funeral dirge will be sung either over the Soviet Republic or over world capitalism."[12] Stalin stated in an interview in 1927: "In the course of the further development of the international revolution two world centres will form themselves: the Socialist centre, attracting to itself those countries tending towards Socialism, and the Capitalist centre, attracting to itself those countries tending towards Capitalism. The struggle of these two centres for the mastery of the world economy will decide the fate of Capitalism and Communism throughout the world. For the final defeat of world Capitalism is the victory of Socialism in the arena of world economy."[13] One can go back to that most sacred document in Communist ideology, The Communist Manifesto of Marx and Engels: "In short, the Communists everywhere support every revolutionary movement against the existing social and political order of things."

> The Communists disdain to conceal their views and aims. They openly declare that their ends can be attained only by the forcible overthrow of all existing social conditions. Let the ruling classes tremble at a Communist revolution. The proletarians have nothing to lose but their chains. They have a world to win.[14]

The Communists, from Marx and Engels through Lenin, Stalin, Khrushchev, and Brezhnev have repeatedly told us that their aim is to take over the world in the name of Communism. It is certainly no credit to the intelligence of the people of the Free World that they have generally ignored this open threat and many times ridiculed anyone who tried to arouse the people against this avowed intent to destroy us and our way of life.[15] Communists tolerate no other form of government or concept of life. It is an all-inclusive "religion" that has its answer for every aspect of life, from birth to the grave, directed from one center (even though polycentrism has created an ideological argument over the location of that center). "The Communists' ideological goal is to make the whole world one unit, operated from one center. This type of ultimate 'monolithic unity' represents the ideal. Until it has been achieved, the 'historic process' is incomplete; and, until then, there can be on earth only a tactical sort of 'peaceful coexistence' - not genuine peace."[16]

Peace to the Communists is not the continual preoccupation that it is with the Western World. For, as Raymond Aron has pointed out, "the Kremlin's ultimate objective is world empire, not peace."[17] The Communists focus their aims on the United States as their chief target and use "peace" to aid them. For them peace is war and war is peace. The United States and the Soviet Union "stand for two antithetical concepts of the nature of man." We believe in truth, justice, and honor and the dignity and liberty of the individual. "The Russian doctrine is dedicated, in the words of Stalin, 'to the destruction of all capitalist society.... The individual is of no importance except as he serves the state.... The end is justifiable by any means. The individual has no rights. The individual is only a cipher. Let me tell you the democratic concept of man holds that each man is a sovereign being. This is the illusion, dream, and postulate of Christianity.'" Communist strategy and tactics are directed at removing the United States, the major barrier to their objective of world domination.[18]

This difference in the meanings of words is one of the most effective weapons in the Communist arsenal. It restrains many people from acting to stop the Communist march. Dr. Frederick Schwarz, testifying before the Committee on Un-American Activities on 29 May 1957, gave an idea of what "peace" means to a Communist.[19] The Overstreets described this Communist "doublespeak." "When Khrushchev speaks, we hear what he says; and we think he is saying what his words mean to us. Instead he is saying what they mean to him; and knowing that we misunderstand, he does nothing to set us straight, because he intends us to misunderstand."[20] Even though he deliberately deceives us, "he is not, in the ordinary sense, lying. He is speaking with Communist sincerity." This "double-talk" repeatedly evoked "from the non-Communist world a response to fit his own purposes."[21]

Since "peace" means the victory of world Communism, then there will, necessarily, always be war until their "peace" is achieved. War, then, is the normal course of events to the Communists as they proceed toward their victory. It is thereby some-

what easier to comprehend how the Communists can
view all forms of international relations as "war."
This is why Communism is such a militant doctrine.
In this view, international relations will always be
"war" since once they win, there will be no more international relations as there will be no independent
nations only areas within the Communist empire which
will receive their orders from Moscow (or Peking) and
will have no need to deal freely with other areas.
(Of course, polycentrism and Communist nationalism
have greatly complicated this ideal.) Rather than
peace being the normal state of man and war being
the unfortunate exception, they view war as the normal state with what they call peace as their goal.[22]
     The point that the Free World has ignored is
that the word "war" to the Communists is not restricted to merely armed conflict. We tend to associate war solely with shooting; if there is no
shooting, there is peace. This is not the Communist
view. Everything is war, from Khrushchev visiting
the United States, to Russian farmers walking through
Iowa cornfields; from foreign students receiving
scholarships to study in Russia, to shipping propaganda all over the world; from dumping oil on the
world market; to supporting nationalism and revolution in underdeveloped countries; from supporting a
Communist Party in almost every country in the world,
to rattling rockets, setting off 100-megaton bombs,
sending men into orbit, and maintaining the largest
standing army in the world. If there is ever to be
a total war more all-inclusive than that which the
Communists are conducting, then it is inconceivable
within the present limitations of man's intelligence.
     The Communists are not stupid; they understand
the tremendous power unleashed by modern weapons.
They do not want to see the fruits of over half a
century of Communism go up in smoke. Similarly, they
do not intend to abandon their goal of world domination. Although a great war was once considered inevitable, that was before the nuclear age. It is
only wise to wish to avert a nuclear war; however,
this does not mean they have to abandon other forms
of war. If they can still win the world without a
terribly expensive war, then that is only smart politics. As John Gunther wrote, "The Russians want
peace," that is, they do not want to be destroyed,
"but they are still gambling for the world."[33] A
report prepared for the U.S. Senate in 1960 by Harvard listed several relevant major tenets of Communist ideology among which was:

429

The ultimate victory of Communism.
(1) Confidence in this seems to have grown recently to the point where military conflict between Communism and capitalism may no longer be
deemed necessary, because the balance will instead be turned by:
    (a) The struggle for economic growth in
        newer nations.
    (b) The industrial growth of the Communist
        nations.
(2) This view would undoubtedly change if it
were calculated that military victory were possible without impossible losses.[24]

    Stalin once told our Ambassador, General Walter
B. Smith, that, "'We do not want war any more than
the West does, but we are less interested in peace
than the West, and therein lies the strength of our
position.'"[25] Being obsessed with peace, the West
often compromised itself to maintain it. However,
the Communists, viewing this same period as war instead of peace, conducted it as a campaign with
their goal always clearly in mind rather than looking upon each sharp turn in international affairs as
a crisis. Catlin observed, "It would seem then that
the Soviet Union is not so much in the position of
being obligated to avoid war, as in the position of
finding that it may still attain its ends in victory
by other means of politics, economics and propaganda."[26]
    It is important to point out that the Commu-
nists do not necessarily agree on all aspects of
their world plot. This is the basis of the feud between Communist China and the Soviet Union which
grew such that their harshest blasts were often
aimed at each other. Although much policy for the
world movement continued to come from Moscow, the
monolith had dissolved into polycentrism. Tito and
Castro and Albania, North Korea, and North Viet-Nam
showed their independence and even maneuvered between the Communist giants. Nationalism had exacted
its toll in the Communist World too. They agreed on
the final victory of Communism but not on the means
of attaining it. The center of their dispute was
over the inevitability of war: "... the Soviets hope
to reap the fruits of war, if possible, without war.
The Chinese line is much harder: War against the
'imperialists' is not only possible, but even probable in spite of nuclear weapons."[27]
    The Chinese asserted that armed struggle is
necessary and indispensable, that "victory must be

won by force," not by compromise. They have several
reasons for their position. A revolutionary war is
part of the global war against capitalism and imperialism; therefore, a local victory is "a victory
against the global enemy and contributes to his ultimate defeat." The insurgents' authority is absolute after victory in armed struggle, greatly facilitating the implementation of the Communist postwar
program. Through armed struggle, the Party gains
experience, finds its best leaders, and wins by its
own efforts. If they are installed by means of outside intervention, the Party will be plagued for
years by its internal weakness. Finally, they will
have come to power with a tested military establishment, which will protect the Party in the political
transformation to follow.[28]

In 1960, Communist leaders met in Moscow for a
three-week world congress at which the argument between the Soviets and the Chinese over the inevitability of war was a main issue. The manifesto issued 6 December 1960 showed that the Soviets kept
the upper hand. Referring to Communist progress, it
stated: "'In these conditions a real possibility will
have arisen to exclude world war from the life of
society even before socialism achieves complete victory on earth, with capitalism still existing in a
part of the world. The victory of socialism all
over the world will completely remove the social and
national causes of war.'" The following was interpreted by American observers as a concession to the
Chinese: "'Peaceful coexistence of countries with
different social systems does not mean conciliation
of the socialist and bourgeois ideologies. On the
contrary, it implies intensification of the struggle
of the working class, of all the Communist parties,
for the triumph of socialist ideas.'" Being true
to their form, they could not put out anything without threatening to destroy someone: "'But should the
imperialist maniacs start war, the peoples will
sweep capitalism out of existence and bury it.'"[29]

Although the Chinese and Russians have a great
mutuality of interests in the Communist War, they
also have a long history of controversy.[30] Many of
the Soviet missiles are now aimed toward China and
over 40 Soviet divisions are deployed along the Sino-
Russian border. Their border clashes of recent
years have grown bloody and the vituperation directed at each other has become as scathing as that normally reserved for the capitalist enemy. "Controversy though there may be, communist ideological arguments are, nevertheless, over means, not ends - a

431

discussion between gravediggers over which shovel to
use in burying us."[31] Their real struggle is over
leadership. They agree on doing away with all freedom; they differ on whether this new world should be
dictated to from Moscow or Peking. Neither is ever
likely to be our friend against the other. However,
we might one day find it wise to support both in a
Sino-Russian War to reduce the world Communist threat.
     Population is always a main consideration to
the Chinese. The joke that has made the rounds about
the Chinese view of a nuclear war points this up.
Mao Tse-tung is supposed to have said that a great
nuclear war would not be so bad - even if each side
lost 200 million people. 200 million Americans -
that wipes them out; 200 million Europeans - that
about wipes them out; 200 million Russians - only a
handful left; 200 million Chinese - that leaves
500 million or more and we would be masters of the
world. In reality, the loss of 200 million Chinese
would be a blessing because of the pressure of such
a large population on a weak economy. The idea of
China growing as an industrial and nuclear power
must certainly give Soviet leaders nightmares.[32]
     The Russians have not renounced nuclear war;
they merely treat the subject with respect. Realizing the vast losses that could be dealt them, they
have put emphasis on the measures necessary to save
that proportion of their population they believe to
be compatible with "victory." This works best for
them if they attack first. To accept the first blow
might be fatal; so, if they thought the West were
going to attack, they would strongly consider a preemptive attack.[33] The most significant aspect of
this policy is the Soviet effort on Civil Defense.
We, on the other hand, have continued to scoff at
any shelter program and have done almost nothing in
the way of a sane program to protect our population
and resources in case of nuclear war. (Of course,
this can be read as a signal that we have no intentions of attacking but it leaves our population as
hostages.) In various discussion with Westerners
after the secret Kissinger trip to Peking, Chou En-
lai repeatedly emphasized the trenches built in Chinese cities to protect the population. Nuclear attack does not appear likely but the capability certainly increases tension and could well lead to nuclear blackmail. A Soviet "surgical" nuclear attack
to destroy the Chinese nuclear capability remains
possible.
     The Communists have never put a time schedule
on their plans for victory. They prefer to retain

432

flexibility to move with the situation. This is
probably a hard thing for a Communist dictator to
do, particularly as he grows old. Khrushchev showed
a slight weakness in this direction before his ouster, although he always stood by the party line of
inevitability but no time schedule. "But by the
Summer of 1960, during his visit to Austria, he was
ready to be at least half serious in saying, 'Life
is short, and I want to see the Red flag fly over
the whole world in my lifetime.'"[34] Techniques may
vary from time to time, but as Averell Harriman
said, "Though their methods have changed since Stalin's time, their aim remains the same."[35]

     One of the most dangerous theories that was
popular contended that we cannot push the Communists
too hard or they will start a nuclear war. The adherents of this theory take as their premise that
the Communists will not retreat on any issue. This
is the height of pessimism and surrenders all initiative to the enemy. Most important of all, it is
in absolute contradiction with Communist ideology
and with the experience of history. John Gunther
listed what he considered were some basic Soviet
principles: "Soviet foreign policy has three permanent, overriding principles. First, perpetuation of
the regime. Second, the closest wariness and vigi-
lance to forestall, dissipate, or counteract any
consolidation of force against the regime and its
satellites, and to attack by all indirect means such
consolidations that already exist, like NATO. Third,
as to the rest of the world, pick up pieces where
they fall."[36] His first principle is historically
correct, the second is basically only a continuation
of the first, and the third is opportunistic.

     To claim the Communists will not change their
course, particularly under pressure, is to ignore
the basic concept of ebb and flow in Communist history. Stalin wrote many years ago:

     To carry on a war for the overthrow of the in-
     ternational bourgeoisie (says Lenin), a war
     which is a hundred times more difficult, pro-
     tracted and complicated than the most stubborn
     of ordinary wars between states, and to refuse
     beforehand to maneuver, to utilize the conflict
     of interests (even though temporary) among
     one's enemies, to refuse to temporize and com-
     promise with possible (even though transient,
     unstable, vacillating and conditional) allies -
     is not this ridiculous in the extreme? Is it
     not the same as if in the difficult ascent of

433

an unexplored and heretofore inaccessible mountain we were to renounce beforehand the idea
that at times we might have to go in zigzags,
sometimes retracing our steps, sometimes giving
up the course once selected and trying various
others?[37]

The taking of unnecessary risks - those risks that
far exceed possible gains - is considered "adventur-
ism" and is taboo according to Communist doctrine.
Tactical retreat has been seen in Communist history
from the Brest Litovsk Treaty to the withdrawal of
missiles from Cuba. The Communists do not like to
accept a challenge at the time and place chosen by
the enemy as this deprives them of their most prized
possession - the initiative. Settlements by concession instead of war are even more likely when the
demands of the stronger power are piecemeal and permit face-saving devices.[38]
    The Communist World is more vulnerable than the
broad-based popular governments of the Free World.
The Communists can never be sure that the people
would support them in time of external war; the satellites have shown more than once their dislike for
their colonial status; and the non-committed areas
of the world are not quick to support the Communists.
The Communists must maintain their power or they
would become an ideology without a country - a valueless myth on the world scene. They talk a good game
but fundamentally they have more at stake than we
have. Their strength has been in that they have
played a more daring form of power politics and have
gotten the less courageous Free World to yield on
many points in the face of Communist threats.
    The historical process of Communist expansion
has been one-way and has kept all "crises" in the
area of the Western nations and involving questions
outside of the Communist World.[39] This policy of
what is ours is inviolable and what is yours is negotiable has been one of the hallmarks of the Communist "crisis strategy." All of the negotiable issues that the Communists have tolerated have involved threats to the interests and territory of the
West. This is an ideal "heads I win, tails you
lose" policy because any Western compromise results
in a net gain for the Communists. By this method,
no Communist territory or any of their internal issues are ever even "talked about" by the diplomats.[40]
This is a downhill trend that cannot be tolerated
indefinitely as it provides no future for the free
nations.

434

In this fashion, all of the Free World is the "war zone" in which the Communists are completely free to operate and in which all issues should be handled by East-West diplomacy. On the other side of the coin, the Communist World is the "peace zone" in which the Western powers must not meddle, even diplomatically, under pain of Soviet retaliation.[41] This ridiculous set of "rules" established by the other side, and which we blindly follow, is intolerable for the future of the Free World. The only way to stop this farce is for the Free World to seize the initiative and make the Communist World face some of these difficult decisions. The more hard decisions they are faced with in their own area, the less trouble they can generate in our area.

With the Communist "divine mission" to take over the world, anything that gets in their way stems from the "devil." Averell Harriman wrote: "An essential element of the world's status today, as Khrushchev sees it, is the Communist march toward world domination. Anything that opposes Communism on the march he considers is altering the status quo and is therefore an act of aggression."[42] A Harvard-Columbia research group at the Russian Institute at Columbia University published a report in February 1960 in which they listed a number of Soviet operating assumptions. One of these was, "In the conduct of Soviet international relations, 'peace' becomes a symbol to connote nonresistance to Soviet aims." They also pointed out what the Soviet "status quo" connotes:

   a. Western recognition of Soviet right to control territories won during or since World War II.
   b. Western agreement not to interfere with revolutionary change occurring outside the Soviet bloc.
   c. Joint U.S.-Soviet agreement prohibiting change of frontiers by military force.
      (1) This specifically excludes "internal" problems.
      (2) "Internal" problems include Chinese claims on Formosa, Communist moves on border territories such as North Vietnam.

Along with these, they stated that this could be done without war.

The desired political changes abroad can and should be obtained without resort to war because:

435

(1) Soviet military power is being increased,
and a balance favorable to the Soviets already
exists.
(2) Absence of war best serves Soviet internal
goals for economic development and consolidation of satellite countries.43

Over the years we have tried to develop the
principle that crime does not pay. We have tried to
apply the same idea to war. Judging by the magnitude of organized crime as it is sometimes exposed,
that campaign has not been too successful. Similarly, the history of the world has not shown the principle to be valid in relation to war either. Possony wrote of the Communist view on this question
and how it can prove to be to their advantage. "Yet,
communists do not think that war must necessarily be
a deficit proposition. While there is always a
price to pay, war may be profitable. The communists
reason that successful revolution from without will
prevent further suffering from 'oppression' and, on
balance, will pay for itself." In a more mundane
and fundamental analysis, "war increases the power
of the victorious belligerent. War should be used
in such a fashion that the fighting forces taken as
a whole are not being weakened but strengthened.
War, in other words, is an effective method of accumulating both capital and power."44 It is for
this reason that "The communists, although they fav-
or revolution by political warfare, place their
trust on military force as the ultimate means to political ends."45 Although they may not use them,
they keep large standing armies on hand to back up
their policies if their other means fail or if they
go too far and are finally attacked by the Free
World. This applies both externally and internally:
for example, the suppression of the Hungarian uprising in 1956 and the "Brezhnev Doctrine" of 1968
with the invasion of Czechoslovakia.
    The fundamental point, then, is that Communism
is a universal doctrine and their aim is the communization of the whole world. This Communist imperialism conducted in the false name of the international proletariat does not aim to give the newly
"liberated" nations equality in the Communist World.
Instead they are to become Communist colonies like
the long line of countries before them. The Soviets,
who condemn colonialism so vehemently in the world
forums, maintain the largest and most oppressive
colonial empire in the world.
    Khrushchev, on 28 January 1959, spelled out the

standard Communist position against colonialism:
"'There are no people more steadfast and devoted to
the cause of the struggle against colonialists than
communists.'" In October 1960 Khrushchev, at the
United Nations, called for the end of all colonialism. Australian Prime Minister Robert G. Menzies,
on 5 October 1960 in the General Assembly, called
Khrushchev a hypocrite: "'I venture to say it is an
act of complete hypocrisy for a Communist leader to
denounce colonialism as if it were an evil characteristic of the western powers, when the facts are
that the greatest colonial power now existing is the
Soviet Union itself.'"[46] This resulted in the famous desk-pounding display by the rotund little Russian.

When a pig squeals, there is usually a reason
for it. In this case, the reason was that the Communists cannot tolerate the truth being spread about
the Communist colonial empire. By his desk-thumping,
Khrushchev unwittingly told the world that, while
the Soviet Union exploits the propaganda value of
Western colonialism, it is vulnerable and needs to
conceal Soviet colonialism. This is also what was
"said" by "his shouting fury against the Philippine
representative's reference to Soviet colonialism as
among the kinds that should be eliminated."[47] The
Soviets rule "over forty-nine colonial and semi-
colonial territories: lands and peoples that are not
free to choose their own political forms or to establish their own economic system."[48] John Gunther
depicted the USSR as a conglomeration: "The Soviet
Union is not a country, but a patchwork," containing "no fewer than sixty different nationalities,
who may be further subdivided into 169 distinct
groups." Most of these are quite small. "Between
20 and 25 per cent of the total population is non-
Slav, and 22 per cent is considered to be 'non-
white.'" - mostly Mongols or Mongoloid.[49]

The way the Communists plundered the satellites
and East Germany has been quite well documented.
Whole factories, as well as anything else that would
help the Soviet economy, were shipped to Russia. Exploitation was continued in that the economies of
these colonies and satellites were closely controlled
by Moscow. Efforts were made to adapt their economies to support the overall Soviet plan, with less
success in the satellites. Many items go almost exclusively to the metropolitan area.[50]

The significance in terms of colonialism is
that, within the USSR, Russia exploits the "rim
countries - which are kept by force - in precisely

the manner she accused the Western countries of exploiting backward nations - those same nations for
which Russia demanded immediate freedom. Taking
Turkestan as an example, the Overstreets pointed out
that, "By collectivizing the peasants, the government has forced them to abandon their traditional
crops and to concentrate on raising cotton. Today,
the role assigned to the inhabitants of the region
is simply that of producing the raw materials that
go to supply the Soviet economic machine."[51] One is
reminded of the definition of Communism, attributed
to Lenin, as being "Soviet rule plus electrifica-
tion."

Self-determination is strictly a Cold War term
to the Communists. They have no intention of permitting it to be applied to their colonies; and,
their high-powered propaganda notwithstanding, they
would not tolerate it in any other part of the
world if they ever get control of it. "The subjugated nationalities, in short, in spite of their
manifest wish for independence, remained subjugated.
Their destiny, formerly in control of the Tsar, was
now shifted to the control of the Communist Party.
And 'self-determination' was redefined to mean
'struggling for socialism.'"[52] John Gunther recorded that the Western "imperialists" have released
from colonial status about 600,000,000 people since
1945, about the same number that Communism has put
under their much stricter form of colonialism.[53] As
the Overstreets observed, "It was a queer moment in
history, but perhaps a prophetic one, when the Hungarian freedom fighters, giving a new twist to an
old Marxian phrase, begged the workers of the world
to unite - against Communism."[54]

Without their colonial empire, the Soviets
would be masters of only a small eastern European
country that would not stir much notice on the
world scene. It is no wonder, then, why the charge
of colonialism is so touchy to them and why they
try to keep it quiet. As a West German document
stated: "'Moscow cannot give up its colonies since,
without them, it would no longer be a factor loom-
ing large in world politics and the world economy.'"[55] It is for just this reason, then, that we
should attack Communist colonialism, or in their
euphemism, "proletarian internationalism," as a major psychological warfare target. Their captive
empire is the basis of their strength and yet it is
so vulnerable that it could be the basis of their
ruin. "Yet with all this long opportunity to tap
not only the discontents and mutual antagonisms of

men and nations, but also their hopes, idealisms, and unsuspicious decencies, the Communists have never won a country by free election. Theirs is the triumph of bringing under their control, by subversion and naked force, one-third of the earth's people and one-fourth of the earth's surface; and theirs is the most colossal failure in all history."[56]

Victory to the Communist World, then, consists of the destruction of the Free World, its concepts of freedom and its recognition of the liberty of the individual. They wish to dominate the world, purely and simply, and we must not forget it. Peace, a respite for another war as Lenin saw it,[57] can exist only in a completely Communist world. We, therefore, can have "peace" anytime we want it if we would only stop resisting them and their "wave of the future." "The free world, in short, by surrendering without a struggle, can put an end to the 'permanent revolution;' otherwise, it goes on."[58] Their great future wave, though, is based theoretically in the last century and is completely out of step with the modern world. A mad religious system that will not provide adequately for its enslaved people in a time of general plenty in the Free World does not deserve to be called the new destiny. But, as with all totalitarian empires that have appeared in history, they must be squarely met and defeated or they will bring their dream to reality. It is with no sense of friendship or competition that they say "We will bury you." It is their goal in life. We must face the reality and act to dispatch them down the road of history where they can be forgotten as another sad epoch in the long history of man.

2. Victory to the Third World

For many purposes, we consider the world divided into two blocs: the Free World and the Communist World. These never were homogeneous blocs, but convenient social and political labels, and became less so after the overt Sino-Soviet split in the 1960s. In spite of the polycentric Communist World, not completely unlike the mutual independence of the Free World, it is still often convenient and appropriate to refer to the collection of Communist states. However, before discussing the concepts of victory to the Free World, it is valuable to consider the aspirations and problems of one part of the Free

439

World: those in-between countries and regions that
are less developed or under-developed and which have
become an important battleground of the Cold War.

   This Third World includes many nations that are
very old but "Many of the newer ones are nations by
international courtesy rather than by ethnic or cultural unity."[59] Thus many of the countries - 150
now in the United Nations - with which we must deal
are not nation-states in the usual sense of the term.
"Though in the United Nations they may speak in
tones of aggressive nationalism, domestically the
government may have only titular control of large
areas."[60] In most of the new nations, there are internal tensions usually being increased by population pressure. This has the unfortunate result
that, with few exceptions, the newly independent
countries of Asia and Africa are economically weak
and politically unstable. To compound their problems, these new states sometimes became pawns in the
Cold War. However, even without the Cold War, there
would be great problems in the Third World. As The
President's Committee to Study the United States
Military Assistance Program concluded in 1959: "Entirely aside from the threat of communist aggression,
the United States and other free nations face the
challenge of the revolutionary insistence on progress by the hundreds of millions of people in the
less-developed areas.'"[61]

   For many years now, a great effort has been
made to reduce deaths in the world; but, due to certain religious objections and other reasons, little
effort has been put into birth control. The world
is facing a potential population explosion that is
complicating all other world problems at a terrific
pace. The population of the world reached one billion in 1830; it took a century to double to two
billion in 1930, 30 years for the third billion,
only about 15 years for the fourth billion, and perhaps only 10 years for the fifth. If the population
growth is not arrested, there may be six or seven
billion people on this planet by the end of this
century. The population of the industrialized countries will increase slowly to perhaps one billion
this decade, which is a supportable growth. However,
the less developed countries will bound from a
little over two billions to almost three billions.
The 19 richest countries in the world have about 70
percent of the world revenue although they account
for only about 15 percent of the global population.
The 15 poorest countries, where more than half the
human race lives, have only about 10 percent of the

world revenue. Life expectancy, which ranges from 60 to over 70 in the technically advanced countries, does not reach 30 in India. Approximately 80 percent of the global population is undernourished as compared with 40 percent before World War II.[62] A stagnant and impoverished country has great difficulty upholding democratic institutions - it is fertile soil for anarchy and dictatorship.

The Third World presents enormous social and economic problems. For instance, illiteracy in Africa runs at approximately 80 percent complicated by some 300 languages in sub-Saharan Africa.[63] The prospects of satisfying the wants of a billion people in a hurry are remote. There is a danger of giving these people promises for progress that is impossible to accomplish in the near future. It is impossible to close in a few years the gap, between their standard of living and ours, which has opened over two centuries. To develop viable economies presents some overwhelming problems. "In some areas, especially in Africa, the concept of ownership hardly exists. The formulation of rules for the definition and protection of property is an important prerequisite of a modern, free economy."[64]

The economic requirements just to stand still are fantastic. One report stated: "With 1% annual population growth, an investment of from 3 to 4% of national income yields static rates of per capita output, i.e., no growth at all."[65] However, populations are growing at over 2 percent per year in many of the poorer countries. Consequently, 5 to 12 percent of national income will have to be invested just to maintain present standards of living in many countries. As an example, population is increasing in India approximately 10,000,000 a year; it has been estimated that over two billion dollars of new capital will be needed annually to maintain the present standard of living. However, incomes are near subsistence levels in these same countries so capital formation is dishearteningly slow.

It is terribly clear that population control is imperative in certain parts of the world. Rush hour congestion should remind us daily of our own growing problem in this area. Only some millions of dollars are annually spent on birth control, while billions are spent on death control. The sad part is that the gap between the more advanced countries and the less developed areas is widening and 2/3 of the world's population lives in the latter.[66]

What then is the concept of victory in this Third World? First of all, most of these countries

441

do not consider the Cold War as their war. The war, for them, is the struggle to find enough to eat for their growing populations, the struggle to raise their standard of living and, finally, a search for a stable form of government. The great majority of these peoples still know little of the industrialized world. However, the young leaders who have had some contact with the Western or Communist World know that there are better things to be had and they are impatient to have them in their countries. The fact that it may have taken those countries centuries to develop their modern lives means nothing to these people. They want these things now even though in many cases they do not even know what they are asking for. Some expressed the feeling that the world owed this to them and they quickly learned the trick of the Cold War; demand it of the Western nations and if they balk, threaten to go Communist. Maurice Couve de Murville, when he was Foreign Minister of France, said: "The weak who know how to play on their weakness are strong. This is the secret of women, and of the developing nations."

About the only thing common among the many less developed countries, except their massive problems, is a fiery nationalism. This form of nationalism, often bordering on xenophobia, though it may inspire a new nation, delivers little in the way of positive results. The Harvard Report included the following:

> Nationalism seldom yields positive doctrine beyond the demand for a sovereign state, independent of alien overlords.
> a. It tends to be "anti" in character.
> b. While based on mass support, it is not necessarily democratic and frequently leads to autocratic government.
> c. In foreign affairs, nationalist ideology:
>   (1) Prescribes no clear politics.
>   (2) Can inhibit useful international contact because of distrust and fear of alien intrusion.
> d. Economically, it tends to be restricted to the quest for economic development.
>   (1) It provides no guidelines for economic programs.
>   (2) Paradoxically, it may lead to policies against the best interests of a country (e.g., restrictions against foreign investment).
> Nationalism does, however, have much to contribute to the development of new countries, by:

442

     a. Providing a sense of social and politi-
        cal solidarity.
     b. Injecting dynamism and political acti-
        vism into the society.[67]

This nationalism is so strong that it is recognized
that we can not even get some of these countries to
cooperate regionally.[68]

The Communists have taken maximum advantage of
this rabid nationalism and have turned it to their
advantage, often linking it polemically with anti-
colonialism and anti-imperialism. This technique of
identifying Communism with the aspirations of the
under privileged has been unfortunately effective
with successes even in NATO - witness the disturb-
ingly high Communist vote in some of the NATO countries. We realize this technique is a cruel fraud,
designed not to help but to enslave, but that is not
always the perception of those on the spot with many
long memories or short perspective. The only good
in it is that it stimulates the West to see that
there are a few injustices within Western society to
provide ammunition for the Communists. We may be
able to beat them in our own Western society but it
will be difficult in the rest of the world.[69] To be
"anti-establishment" is effective politics internationally as well as domestically!

The Communists have no use for nationalism within their own sphere for they repress it at every opportunity. The stark truth that the naive young
leaders of the Third World refuse to accept (although
many of them have been awakened in recent years) is
that "Communism is the antithesis of nationalism."[70]
The Soviets portrayed themselves as internationalists
until 1931. They changed their course when nationalism started appearing as a significant force on the
international scene, although running counter to
Communism. Thereafter, they manipulated this tremendous nationalistic sentiment to support the Communist movement. After World War II, they portrayed
themselves as the champions of small nations and of
all nationalistic aspirations. This Communist super-
nationalism has been an effective weapon in their
battle against American "imperialism."[71] The Communists have found that nationalism can be a two-edged
sword, as Nasser and others taught them by accepting
Communist aid but by keeping the indigenous Communists in jail. Such treatment has taught the Communists, and particularly the Soviets, to be much more
pragmatic in their dealings with the Third World.
Nationalism is on the march throughout the less

developed countries and is playing a key role in the
Cold War, often expressing itself as non-alignment
hoping to maintain independence, stay out of the
Cold War, and, when countries are working together,
to apply leverage on the great powers.

The ability of the less developed countries to
withstand Communism in the long run depends on their
political, economic, and social - rather than military - strength. Although the threat of military
aggression is continually evident, it appears that
subversion and other forms of indirect aggression
present the most serious threat to the independence
of the less developed countries. The Communist
threat varies from terrorism as shown in Malaya and
South Viet-Nam to the soft sell as shown in this example by Averell Harriman:

> Every year thousands of visitors from Southeast
> Asia pour through the big international airport
> of Tashkent and are taken on tours of the gi-
> gantic model collective farms, malaria-free
> villages, and big factories producing everything
> from shoes to heavy agricultural machinery, to
> say nothing of the schools, universities, hos-
> pitals and open houses. These developments
> provide telling ammunition to the Communist
> parties of Southeast Asia, who point them out
> to those who are impatient to develop their
> countries. To people with little understanding
> of the values of free institutions they provide
> a tempting alternative to the slower procedure
> of democracy.[72]

All is not rosy with the Communist propaganda
drive, as evidenced by countries that accept Communist aid and then ban the Communist Party and by the
troubles with African and Near Eastern students in
the Soviet Union. In 1961, Everest Mulekezi, a
young African from Uganda who had gone to Russia to
study, wrote an article called, "I Was a 'Student'
at Moscow State." His eyes were opened on many
counts. "On our arrival in Moscow we were puzzled
to find that we were segregated from the main student body.... We Africans at the university were
simply stooges." They were used for propaganda,
pictures, tapes, statements, resolutions, etc., but
were told: "We could not behave in the same fashion
as we might in capitalist countries where students
were paying their own expenses. With the Soviet Un-

ion financing our education, we would be expected to do and think what we were told.... New and dangerous forms of colonialism and discrimination are being fostered by the communists and are a grave threat to the future of Africa."[73]

The great condemnation of Communism comes when one compares their promises with their performance. They promised "land to the peasants" yet they took all the land. They promised "perpetual peace" and give only war, against both their own people and the rest of the world. They promised production for the people and used production for expanding power. They promised plenty and gave scarcity. The state was to "wither away" but now they have a total state. They promised freedom and now there is no freedom. They promised the "worker's paradise" and they live behind prison walls. They cried for "national self-determination" and "anti-imperialism" but they have become the most imperialist, colonial government in history.[74]

The inhuman approach of the Communists may yet help mankind if it stirs us to meet our international responsibilities.[75] This may prove of longrange benefit to the Third World. There is an interesting fear among some of the less developed nations, particularly those who try to play one bloc off against the other to get benefits from both. "A Communist member of India's Parliament commented: 'The thing we are most worried about is an agreement between America and Russia. If an agreement were reached, aid from both sides would stop and we would have a very difficult time.'"[76]

The role of the United States in the emergence of the Third World has not always been easy. For the most part, they look to us as an example because of the success of our revolution which they wished to emulate. We have been somewhat tainted, sometimes, because of our close associations with the colonial powers which are our close allies. A basic problem of American foreign policy has been to sympathize with nationalistic aspirations throughout the world and yet not antagonize the European colonial powers whose goodwill has been essential in the Communist War.

With many diverse problems and varying resources in these different areas, some of which do not represent, in their present boundaries, viable national structures, American policy must be tailored to fit the individual case. We must tread between

445

supporting a Balkanization of Africa, Asia, and the Middle East with its resultant strife, and supporting leaders setting up new empires at the expense of the present peoples and their countries.[77] We are faced with the "paradox of the billions." One billion people are undernourished while we have a billion dollars' worth of surplus food rotting in our warehouses.[78] However, providing aid without any longrange goal only facilitates Communist penetration.[79] The moral of self-reliance in the old proverb is still valid: give a man a fish and he will have one meal; teach him to fish and he will never be hungry.

Most of the Third World has long been connected with the West and not all colonialism was bad; many good links were also forged. Therefore, at present, the Third World, with its basic desire for peace and freedom of choice, fits into the Free World system better than into the Communist World. The American image should be strengthened by emphasizing not only our material prosperity but our dynamic society which has brought so much to the common man, our creativity, and our desire for peace and human progress everywhere.[80]

The Third World must be kept aware that the strong desire for national sovereignty will be of no value if the Communists win and turn them into satellites. The West has done an enormous amount for the Third World. By contrast, the Communist contribution, always with great fanfare, "has been miniscule, cunningly contrived and always laced with ulterior motives."[81] The struggle of the Third World is a side issue of the Cold War and one of longrange worth. Overstress on it tends to keep our eyes off the main issues with the Communist World. "Although we might lose the protracted conflict in the underdeveloped areas, we cannot win it there."[82]

Victory to the Third World, then, is whatever will help them to leap into the twentieth century, for they see no war. They see only powerful nations that could overwhelm them but that have the capital and the technology they must have for progress. Few of the less developed countries are concerned with ideology; their war is survival. Victory to them is new capital, favorable trade, enough food, economic take-off, sustained growth, education, and effective government. Victory to the Third World is sustained progress before the revolution of rising expectations brings the structure crashing down into anarchy and chaos.

3. Victory to the Free World

The term "Free World" is a convenient label but it is not an organized entity. At best, it is defined negatively as states that are not Communist. There are many states included in the Free World but the centers of power are the United States, Western Europe, and Japan. The Free World has no world objective, as such, other than the basic desire for continuation of the independent nation-state system with free international political, economic, and social relations under some degree of international law. With only a strong desire for peace and improvement of life, not having a messianic or imperialistic world goal places the Free World at a disadvantage in any competition with the missionaries of Communism.

The end of the Cold War and the age of danger that had existed since the end of the Second War was a paramount desire of the Free World. Peaceful coexistence was not peace for the Free World. A prime complicating factor was that most of the Free World did not consider itself at war; thus, there was no major effort mounted, but a continuation of business as usual. This included trading with Red China while Chinese were killing Free World troops in Korea. This was seen again with the trade with Hanoi during the Vietnamese War. There was trade and other intercourse with Russia throughout the period and rarely was it mentioned that one was dealing with an enemy. The Free World was a reluctant protagonist in the Cold War and, unless forced to the wall, tried to ignore it and continue as if it did not exist.

When the only desire was for peace, and with the Free World not considering itself at war, there was little consideration of winning;[83] and, therefore, any concept of Victory was nebulous and idealistic. Peace is a stirring but dangerous objective if one yields more basic interests for its attainment. Henry Kissinger stressed this when he wrote: "Whenever peace - conceived as the avoidance of war - has become the primary objective of a power or group of powers, international relations have been at the mercy of the state willing to forego peace." Therefore, peace should not be sought directly as "it is the expression of certain conditions and power relationships."[84] American leadership generally recognized this for as Finletter wrote: "United

States foreign policy falls into two grand lines:
one, the Struggle against Communist Imperialism; the
other, the Search for Peace. Unfortunately, the
first line occupies nearly all our attention. The
second line is more of a hope, an aspiration, than
an active precept vigorously pushed in the day-to-
day work of government."[85] Success in the first
line was required prior to realization of the second.

The world did not evolve according to our
wishes after World War II, particularly in Eastern
Europe and North Korea and later in China and North
Viet-Nam. The Communists were willing to fight to
expand, but we were not willing to go to war to roll
back the Iron or Bamboo Curtains. It was an aspiration of the Free World that the satellites be liberated, and even the people of Russia and China themselves, but not by means of military force. The
West accepted coexistence in the sense that it would
not fight to liberate the areas dominated by Communism, however the West did not accept as permanent
the extension of Communist influence.[86]

Along with the Cold War came the most dangerous
arms race in the history of man. Nuclear weapons
overshadowed all the destructive force of previous
history and a divided world was extremely unstable.
Efforts at arms reductions were fruitless. Although
Khrushchev called for total disarmament, it was
merely a propaganda play since the Soviets needed
arms to exploit opportunities as they might arise in
the world; they would have quickly lost their satellite empire without arms to keep them in line.[87]
The world edged to the brink of nuclear war in the
Cuban Missile Crisis of 1962. The Soviets evidently decided never to be humiliated like that again
and started a major build-up, resulting in increased
numbers of missiles, nuclear submarines, and new emphasis on the Soviet Navy with the dispatch of
fleets into the Mediterranean and the Indian Ocean.
In the late 1960s, the United States stopped the expansion of its strategic forces and, by attrition,
actually started a reduction. By the early 1970s,
the Soviets had attained rough parity with the United States, but the Russians continued their build-up
evidently striving for superiority. The Soviets had
earlier deployed an anti-ballistic missile (ABM)
system. The Americans procrastinated and only half-
heartedly started a deployment. With the growing
threat of Chinese nuclear power, the Soviets became
more amenable and the strategic arms limitation
talks (SALT) and discussions on mutual and balanced

force reductions (MBFR) began. The stumbling block
in all previous talks with the Soviets was always
the question of inspections. Until this was resolved, there was little hope of success. Advances
in satellite surveillance were such that SALT I was
signed. However, Goldwater was probably right when
he wrote: "The only real disarmament will come when
the cause for arms is removed. In our case that
cause is communism. In the Soviets' case, that
cause is the free world."[88] Of course, Communist
China complicated that dichotomy for both sides.

The threat of nuclear war and the disillusionment of the policies of Unconditional Surrender and
Total Victory in total war placed a new emphasis on
limited war. Kissinger wrote that: "The prerequisite for a policy of limited war is to reintroduce
the political element into our concept of warfare
and to discard the notion that policy ends when war
begins or that war can have goals distinct from
those of national policy."[89] Of course, this was
pure Clausewitz and we were overdue for a return to
Clausewitz, whose "outstanding contribution to military theory" was his "insistence on the relationship
of war and policy."[90] He stated that the aim in war
is the "overthrow of the enemy"[91] and listed three
elements of a concept of victory that would be
"something more than mere slaughter.... 1. The
greater loss of the enemy in physical forces. 2. The
greater loss of the enemy in moral forces. 3. His
open admission of this by his renunciation of his
intention."[92] A major problem is that we have no
words for expressing different degrees of victory.[93]

Counterinsurgency became an active form of limited war as a result of the Communist encouragement
of revolutionary wars. David Galula, in stressing
the primacy of the use of political over military
power, wrote the stake is "the country's political
regime, and to defend it is a political affair" and
that the requirement was for about 20 percent military action and 80 percent political.[94] Victory in
counterinsurgency warfare is not just the destruction of the insurgent's forces and political organization in a certain area but "that plus the permanent isolation of the insurgent from the population,
isolation not enforced upon the population but maintained by and with the population."[95]

Clausewitz set the pattern when he wrote: "No
war is begun, or at least, no war should be begun,
if poeple acted wisely, without first finding an answer to the question: what is to be attained by and
in war? The first is the final object; the other is

449

the intermediate aim."[96] For him, tactically, "The
end is victory." However, "For strategy, the victory, that is the tactical success, is primarily
only a means, and the things which should lead directly to peace are its ultimate object."[97]

The Allies did not always keep their eyes on
peace but pursued emotional aims in the prosecution
of war in the twentieth century with disappointing
results. Being non-conspiratorial, that is with no
master plan or grand design, then in an idealistic
way, it was easy to equate war with evil. If war
were evil, then the only way to fight it would be
with religious zeal as good versus evil. And so the
crusade syndrome was typical of Democracy at war in
the first half of the twentieth century. It was
difficult to appreciate the limitations on war as a
vehicle for achieving the objectives of a democracy
where it is dependent on the resolution of the people to support and fight it. Our notion of "aggression as an unambiguous act and our concept of war as
inevitably an all-out struggle"[98] made it difficult
for us to deal effectively with the power politics
we faced. It was difficult because the time had
come "to turn away from the concept of total war and
the nation in arms for total victory"[99] which had
been basic since the Napoleonic wars. This meant
the revision of some of our traditional attitudes,
"such as our rejection of compromise and our faith
in extreme, ideal solutions when the chips are
down."[100] The dangerous, nuclear world demanded a
pragmatic approach including significant military
forces in-being and a tough-minded but genuine view
of bargaining.[101]

The simplistic days were gone. No longer could
the statesman abdicate his responsibility for the
conduct of war to the soldier. Similarly, the necessity for the soldier to be intimately familiar
with state policy was never clearer. It took us a
long time to learn but the conduct of war and policy
at the higher levels coincides.[102] Learning to manipulate votes, handle press campaigns, control pa-
tronage, influence Congress, etc. are important for
progress in American politics; however, they do not
prepare one for the conduct of world strategy.
Statesmen should be students of history - particularly of war - to be prepared to lead.[103]

The term balance of power may not have been in
vogue for some years but the realities of power
politics have not changed. The Communists, knowing
that the West wanted to avoid war, expected the West
to "capitulate or retreat."[104] However, as Raymond

450

Aron saw it, "The object of the West is and must be
to win the limited war in order not to have to wage
the total one."[105] One cannot afford to find final
victory or defeat in every round of a long and difficult contest. There were bound to be gains and
setbacks; some developments needed to be tolerated
and others offered an advantage.[106] In spite of the
potential for destruction, it was never questioned
that "deterrence was to be achieved by strategic
striking power and that victory depended on inflicting maximum destruction on the aggressor".[107] It
was clear that throughout the period we had doctrine
to meet aggression, but we were unable to transform
this doctrine into a strategy for positive action.[108]

Although the West had the aspiration or hope
for the demise of Communism, it had no desire to
fight and its strategy was defensive. However, it
is important to determine what would be a victory
over Communism; what would be a satisfactory governmental arrangement if the Communist regimes were
removed? If the Communists were deposed now, there
is no basis for anything approaching Democracy in
those countries. Any traces there ever may have
been have been erased by years of totalitarian rule.
It does not appear that we would be willing to go in
and occupy those countries; however, they would need
a great amount of assistance. Without outside imposition of a form of government, there would probably be a long, slow evolution to their own style of
government and it is difficult to predict the form
that might take.

We must realize that our enemy is not a nation
or nations but a political movement or now the wings
of a political movement.[109] Our objective must not
be the punishment of peoples but the removal of certain forms of government and their replacement by
some more representative and free form. Police-
state rule has proved so efficient in controlling
people that there appears little likelihood that the
Communists can be overthrown from within.[110] However, George Kennan felt there was a possibility
that Soviet power "bears within it the seeds of its
own decay"[111] and might fall of its own weight.
Therefore, although war is not particularly desired
on either side, it remains a possibility. War has
come closest when we wavered in our resolve; the
Communists have backed down when we stood firm.[112]

The United States has had the bad habit of
thinking of military victory as the end. A war a-
gainst Communist power which we might evaluate as at
least relatively successful militarily would, of

451

itself, provide no assurance of the emergence of the kind of state we would prefer to see. War, in itself, will not bring about such a Russia or China. "Indeed it would be most unlikely to lead in that direction unless accompanied by many wise and strenuous efforts besides the military one."[113] If war comes, what can we do to promote the emergence of a more desirable state? First, we should know what we want - the image of the kind of state we would like to see evolve. Second, we should insure that our military operations facilitate, rather than impede, the coming into being of what we want. We could avoid, this time, "the tyranny of slogans" toward the captive peoples trying not to given them the impression that we are their enemies.[114] We should be realistic in our expectations. There is no national understanding in the Communist states which would permit early establishment of anything resembling the private enterprise system as we know it. Many features of the Communist system will remain since everything else has been destroyed which might have served as an alternative.[115] We would not want to occupy a former Communist country - the vast majority of the people are not Communists - but they probably would require considerable assistance and guidance to establish any sort of free government after so many years of dictatorship.[116]

The Sino-Soviet animosity complicates this discussion.[117] It seems unlikely that the Communist government in one could fall without attracting the intervention of the other. The destruction of the military might of China would create a power vacuum. We would have to go in with large numbers of men to fill that vacuum, thereby facing the Russians along a seven-thousand-mile frontier. If we did not go in, then Russia would and our security would be further endangered.[118] The prospect of prying to occupy China and reorganize 800 million people into a free society with some form of free government is overwhelming. However, we know there is a wellspring of Chinese organizational ability and dynamism that would make it succeed.

Are the concepts of victory of other Free World countries different from those of America? The disparities in power were so pronounced that the other Free World states could leave many Cold War issues to the United States to handle and pursue their own interests confident of their security under the American nuclear umbrella. This often left the United States carrying the burden with minimal support from the others and exacerbated American

balance of payments problems and internal dissatisfaction. The French, under de Gaulle, lost faith in
the alliance system, withdrew their forces from NATO,
and developed their force de frappe which was supposedly aimed in all directions. Japan followed basic-
cally an economic policy under the American shadow.
Britain tried to continue its world-power status
but finally joined the Common Market, followed by
others, which may well result in a new Europe being
one of the great powers of the world. The Free
World countries other than the United States tended
to be more pragmatic in their concepts of victory
without responsibility for formulation or implementation of many of the thornier aspects of great power politics.

The younger generation, however, evidenced
changing concepts. Relatively few were absolute
pacifists; but, the nuclear age had given them the
impression that traditional collective security was
obsolete. "They see no country for whose security
they would fight." Few under thirty now worry about
countries "going Communist." "The old kind of American idealism is gone - and with it the sense of
world mission. Youth does not think America is the
showcase of democracy." - many even viewing America
as a repressive, intolerant society. "The traditional 'victory' over the enemy in war lies outside
the frame of reference of Second-World-War babies.
Growing up in a compromise atmosphere - balance of
terror, of fear, of power - they find the alternatives to winning not only acceptable but imperative."[119] No doubt, as these young people move into
positions of responsibility, some of their views will
change; but their views have already had a significant impact on American foreign policy.

Nuclear war presented the dilemma to the com-
batants that none would probably win; it was even
difficult to imagine what Victory might mean in a
nuclear war. Yet this threat of mass destruction did
not remove war from the political arsenal as wars
were rampant around the world. What it did stress
was that the return to Clausewitz was mandatory in
that war, if it could not be banned from international relations, had to be solely conducted as a function of policy and not permitted to fly off on emotional tangents. The world was perilous but still
better, and as one write put it: "who would revert
to the days of our poverty and isolation in order to
escape the cares that now concern us?"[120]

NOTES

1. Kintner, The Front is Everywhere, p. 155.
2. Aron, The Century of Total War, p. 227.
3. Brzezinski and Huntington, Political Power: USA/USSR, pp. 419-429. The common political structure has not prevented the bitter hostility in the Communist World and most of the great European wars were fought between states with similar political and social systems.
4. From The City of God in William Ebenstein, Great Political Thinkers, pp. 179-181.
5. Madariaga, The Blowing Up of the Parthenon, pp. 11-14. He continued: "As for war, why it is on! A war is not merely a string of battles. It is a conflict of wills. To-day there is a war between the communist will and the liberal democratic will."
"... you ask what the use of American armaments can be? You complain that 'no one has yet tried to put any sense' in these armaments. Let me try. To begin with, they keep you alive..."
"Finally, American armaments are indispensable to place the West in a position to talk to Moscow at all. For Moscow understands no language but that of force. Once the West is strong, it can insist on a settlement with a reasonable chance of getting it. And of getting it without a war. For the only danger of war in the West comes from the West's own weakness; and one of the elements of this is the division of opinion caused by the intellectual and moral chaos you are contributing to create."
6. Kecskemeti, Stragegic Surrender, p. 23.
7. Ibid., p. 257.
8. Kissinger, Nuclear Weapons and Foreign Policy, p. 146, italics in original.
9. Lincoln, Economics of National Security, p. 25.
10. Uttered at a reception at the Polish Embassy 17 November 1956 in honor of Wladyslaw Gomulka's visit to Moscow, reported in the New York Herald Tribune on 19 November.
11. See Kennan, Russia and the West, p. 185.
12. Lenin, Works, Vol. 25, p. 512, 3d Russian edition, 1935. Quoted in Madariaga, The Blowing Up of the Parthenon, p. 22.
13. Stalin, Interview with the First American Labour Delegation in Russia, 1927, Works, Vol. X, pp. 122-123, Moscow, 1949. Quoted in Madariaga, Parthenon, p. 27.
14. Quoted in Ebenstein, Great Political

Thinkers, p. 687.

15. The House Study on Communism ended with:
"In the midst of all superficial changes of the ideology, the basic intent of Communism remains what it
always has been: the destruction of all societies
not ruled by the Party and the re-making of men into
the Communist image." U.S. Congress, House Committee
on Un-American Activities, Facts on Communism, Vol.
I, The Communist Ideology, December 1959, p. 137.

16. The Overstreets, The War Called Peace, p.
232.

17. Aron, The Century of Total War, p. 188.

18. Goldwater, Why Not Victory?, p. 26.

19. "Dr. SCHWARZ: You have to understand that
their basic concept is that class war is a fact of
being and that peace is the historical synthesis
when communism defeats the remainder of the world
and establishes world Communist dictatorship, which
is peace. If you ask a true Communist to take a lie
detector test and ask him if he wants peace, he
would pass it with ease. He would look at you with
a light in his eye and say he longs for peace....
Every act that contributes to the Communist conquest
is a peaceful act. If they take a gun, they take a
peaceful gun, containing a peaceful bullet, and kill
you peacefully and put you in a peaceful grave.
When the Chinese Communists murder millions, it is
an act of peace. When the Russian tanks rolled into
Budapest to butcher and destroy, it was glorious
peace. Peace is wonderful and within their frame-
work of ideology whatever helps their conquest is
peaceful, good and true." Quoted in Gavin, War and
Peace in the Space Age, p. 183.

20. The Overstreets, The War Called Peace, p.
156, italics added.

21. Ibid., pp. 156-157, italics in original.
They have an excellent chapter on language, pp. 156-
173.

Kautsky wrote in his Social Democracy versus Communism that the Communists "defend democracy
only where they are in the opposition. They anni-
hilate it and practice the most cruel subjugation of
any form of popular freedom where they are in power." Quoted in Ebenstein, Great Political Thinkers,
p. 747.

22. "The Comminists view their war as something
more than just the temporary destruction of a rival
nation's power. Theirs is a war aimed at the social,
economic, political, and military fiber of all non-
Communist societies as such. And they do not regard
this war as an abnormal break in peaceful relations,

455

a temporary pursuit aimed at a temporary objective. They believe that all human society is split into warring elements, that this warfare will continue indefinitely, and that it can be used by them to further the destruction of freedom wherever it exists. To them 'peace' has only one value - as a useful strategem for lulling anti-Communist societies until such time as the Communists wish to return to other devices such as terror, intimidation, aggression, and infiltration." Goldwater, Why Not Victory?, p. 167. For a similar view, see Fuller, The Conduct of War, p. 213.

23. John Gunther, Inside Russia Today, p. 475.

24. Jay H. Cerf and Walter Pozen, Strategy for the 60's, p. 123. They added, "Acquiring and consolidating power is a central preoccupation of Communist ideology."

25. Time, 13 June 1949, p. 25.

26. George Catlin, What Does the West Want?, p. 40, italics in original.

27. Robert Strausz-Hupé, William R. Kintner and Stefan T. Possony, A Forward Strategy for America, p. 153.

28. David Galula, Counterinsurgency Warfare, pp. 48-49.

29. Hansen, ed., The 1962 World Almanac and Book of Facts (New York: New York World-Telegram, 1962), p. 85.

30. See Strausz-Hupé, et al., Forward Strategy, p. 24.

31. Ibid., p. 23.

32. See Fuller, The Conduct of War, pp. 332-333 and Finletter, Foreign Policy, p. 12.

33. See Dinerstein, War and the Soviet Union, p. 24. Malenkov and company did not believe in the possibility of surviving a nuclear war. For this they were called complacent and defeatist. Khrushchev said they would suffer great destruction but they would win the war (p. 23). It is interesting that, having reached nuclear parity in the 1970s, Brezhnev and company were pushing on for superiority.

34. The Overstreets, The War Called Peace, p. 18. On p. 78, they made the interesting statement that if Khrushchev did not do it, the chances are against any future Communist dictator doing it.

35. Harriman, Peace with Russia?, p. 18. Harriman in 1971 called for a settlement with the Soviet Union, The Washington Post, 10 August 1971, p. A-8.

36. Gunther, Inside Russia Today, p. 447, italics added.

456

37. Stalin, Foundations of Leninism, Selected Works, Vol. X, p. 111, quoted in Ebenstein, Great Political Thinkers, p. 717.

38. See Strausz-Hupé, et al., Forward Strategy, pp. 30-31 for a good discussion of this point.

39. As the Overstreets wrote: "Marx's 'fated' historical process is a one-way process. It calls for a progressive expansion of the Communist domain, but never for a contraction of it. Capitalism, in short, must always and everywhere be on the way out; never on the way in. This has come to mean in practice that all Communist grabs are for keeps; and they are no less for keeps simply because they have been made under cover of a treaty that proclaimed them to be temporary. For Stalin to have encouraged - or tolerated - the reunification of Germany, by free election, along non-Communist lines would have amounted to his countenancing a reversal of the 'historic process.'" The War Called Peace, p. 181, italics in original. See Harriman, Peace With Russia?, p. 165, for Khrushchev's comment that he would tolerate no reunification of Germany that did not provide for the Communist system. See also Raymond Aron, The Century of Total War, p. 184, for the Russian aim to prevent any new strong German force similar to the one that almost won the last war, even with American industry against it.

40. See Strausz-Hupé, et al., Forward Strategy, pp. 211-212 for a good discussion.

41. See ibid., pp. 224 and 256.

42. Harriman, Peace with Russia?, p. 167.

43. Cerf and Pozen, Strategy for the 60s, pp. 135-136. That such agreements are not impossible is shown by the fact that in 1942, the U.S. Communists got a pledge from the State Department that the United States would not oppose the Chinese Communists or support Chiang in the civil war. This was in writing from Under Secretary of State Welles to Earl Browder, General Secretary of CPUSA and was published in the Daily Worker. See Possony, A Century of Conflict, pp. 317-318.

44. Possony, A Century of Conflict, p. 388.

45. Strausz-Hupé, et al., Forward Strategy, p. 106.

46. The Overstreets, The War Called Peace, p. 220. One big difference is that Russia absorbed her colonies because they were neighbors while Western countries ruled distant lands.

47. Ibid., p. 239.

48. Ibid., p. 229. "The colonial territories included in the USSR are as follows:

457

Colonial areas	Colonies within these areas
Central Asia (Turkestan)	Kazakhstan, Kirghizstan, Uzbekistan, Tadzhikistan, Turkministan
Caucasus	Armenia, Azerbaijan, Georgia, Dagestan, the lands of the Chetchens, Ingush, Ossets, Kabardines, Cherkessks, et cetera
Southwest portion of the European part of the Soviet Union	Moldava, Ukraine
Miscellaneous	The Baltic States - Latvia, Lithuania, and Estonia; Komi; Yakutsk; the areas inhabited by the Mongol tribes; and other areas to the east and north

All these belong in the category of 'rim' countries - the 'Republics' - that appear on the map as integral parts of the USSR."

"To these must be added the semi-colonial countries which, although they remain at present outside the geographical boundaries of the USSR, are politically and economically dominated by that power through the machinery of puppet regimes: Poland, Hungary, Czechoslovakia, Rumania, Bulgaria, Albania /broke away and is supported by China/, the Soviet-occupied zone of Germany, and the Asian satellite, Mongolia." The Overstreets, The War Called Peace, pp. 229-230. "These countries are said to be 'fraternally related' to the Soviet Union. But they have been exploited as colonies." (p. 234).

49. Gunther, Inside Russia Today, p. 4.

50. The total production percentages of coal, oil, iron ore, manganese ore, nonferrous and rare metals, uranium ore, gold, diamonds, wool, cotton, silk, sugar as a finished product, tea, wine, southern fruit, Indian corn, wheat, vegetable oil, and pelts "which are sent to Metropolitan Russia from Central Asia, the Caucasus, and the 'rim' countries of the southwestern European part of the Soviet Union range from 58 percent to 100 percent. In fact, the metropolitan area absorbs the entire or almost

458

the entire production of such vital items as oil,
manganese ore, nonferrous and rare metals, gold,
cotton, silk, sugar, India corn, vegetable oil, and
pelts." The Overstreets, The War Called Peace, pp.
230-231.

51. Ibid., p. 228. Gunther wrote that in 1954
the USSR probably drew $5 billion a year from the
satellites but by 1957 was putting out $1 billion a
year. This does not change the situation as most of
the Western nations ended up pouring money into
their colonies. Inside Russia Today, p. 483.

52. Overstreets, The War Called Peace, p. 224.
The constitution of the USSR (as amended by Supreme
Soviet 25 February 1947), Chap. II The State Structure, sounds good: Art. 13 says that it is a voluntary federation of equal republics. Art. 17 says
they can freely secede, and Art. 18 says their territory may not be altered without their consent (yet
this was done in cental Asia). Beukema, et al.,
Contemporary Foreign Governments, p. 566.

53. Gunther, Inside Russia Today, p. 484.

54. Overstreets, What We Must Know About Communism, p. 123.

55. Quoted in the Overstreets, The War Called
Peace, p. 231.

56. Ibid., p. 80, italics in original. The e-
lection in Chile that brought Allende to power with
a minority stirred violent reaction in Chile resulting in Allende's death and a military government.

57. The Overstreets, What We Must Know About
Communism, p. 88.

58. Ibid., p. 90.

59. Strausz-Hupé, et al., Forward Strategy,
p. 47.

60. Henry M. Wriston, "Thoughts for Tomorrow,"
Foreign Affairs, April 1962, p. 381.

61. "The Time Has Come to Face the Facts," a
summary of the four reports of The President's Committee, p. 17.

62. See, for example, Pierre Gerbet, Les Organizations Internationales, p. 29.

63. Cerf and Pozen, Strategy for the '60s, p. 65.

64. Strausz-Hupé, et al., Forward Strategy,
p. 197fn.

65. Report on economic problems prepared by
Corporation for Economic and Industrial Research,
Inc., Cerf and Pozen, Stragegy for the '60s, p. 35.
The report also pointed up the importance of free
trade: "Protectionist policies in U.S. and Western
Europe inhibit growth in underdeveloped areas."
     The problem is close to home since Latin

America has the highest rate of population growth in the world (2.7 percent average - Costa Rica high with 4.3 percent).

66. Ibid., p. 45. India has an extensive birth control program. This is important because India has 40 percent of the population of the Third World (p. 145), but must deal with extremely large numbers to make any dent in a population of over 600 million. To feed these people is the great problem as food production is lagging behind population growth. Great strides must be made in places like Africa where about 75 percent of Africans are engaged in subsistence agriculture (p. 64).

67. Ibid., p. 122.

68. Ibid., p. 6. On p. 8, it was recommended that this nationalism merits U.S. sympathy even when it conflicts with the policy of our allies. One report recommended that we "Firmly support nationalism as an avowed U.S. policy." p.83.

69. Finletter, Power and Policy, p. 88.

70. Strausz-Hupé, et al., Forward Strategy, p. 274.

71. Kintner, The Front is Everywhere, p. 160.

72. Harriman, Peace With Russia?, p. 34.

73. Reader's Digest, July 1961, pp. 100-104.

74. See Strausz-Hupé, et al., Forward Strategy, pp. 276-277. See also "Communist Vulnerabilities," by Bertram D. Wolfe, in Hahn and Neff, editors, American Strategy for the Nuclear Age, pp. 89-102, particularly p. 100.

75. Ibid., p. 100.

76. U.S. News & World Report, 29 October 1962, p. 28.

77. Strausz-Hupé, et al., Forward Strategy, p. 48. They pointed out the danger of civil wars in the present world. Although we fought ours with little outside intervention, civil war now invites great power intervention and thus threatens total war, p. 56.

78. Ibid., p. 201.

79. Ibid., p. 57. On p. 206, they point out that unilateral aid shipments do not help wean them away from the USSR.

80. U.S. Congress, 86th, Conlon Associates, United States Foreign Policy - Asia, p. 25. Also Cerf and Pozen, Strategy for the '60s, p. 74.

81. Strausz-Hupé, et al., Forward Strategy, pp. 51-52.

82. Ibid., p. 204.

83. Senator Barry Goldwater was representative of those who believed this was a no-win policy. He

wrote in Why Not Victory? that our "repeated defeats" since 1950 were "because we have failed to
recognize the stark reality of the existence of Communist aggression." (pp. 33-34). Referring to
peaceful coexistence, he wrote: "Now we are told
that this is the only feasible approach; that we
can't hope for victory; that we can't risk a war;
that we couldn't cope with victory if we won it. I
say this is the most dangerous kind of sheer nonsense." (p. 153). He felt that "the failure to proclaim victory as our aim in the Communist War is not
just an oversight but a calculated policy of influential men." (p. 150). His principal target was
Senator Fulbright - "He was excessively bemused with
one of my phrases - 'total victory.' He seemed to
think there was something funny about it. He referred to total victory as a 'stirring term with a ro-
mantic ring.' He ridiculed it as something that
'quickens the blood like a clarion call to arms.'
The Senator from Arkansas says he does not know what
victory would mean - as he puts it - 'in this age of
ideological conflict and nuclear weapons.'" (p. 152).
      84. Kissinger, Nuclear Weapons and Foreign Pol-
icy, pp. 428-429. Goldwater stressed "freedom, not
peace, because peace without freedom is unacceptable
to the American people." Why Not Victory?, p. 129.
      85. Finletter, Power and Policy, p. 83.
      86. See ibid., pp. 106-107, 109, and 122 and
Finletter, Foreign Policy, pp. 64-65.
      87. See the Overstreets, The War Called Peace,
p. 327.
      88. Goldwater, Why Not Victory, p. 170.
      89. Kissinger, Nuclear Weapons and Foreign Pol-
icy, p. 141.
      90. Fuller, The Conduct of War, p. 63. See
Clausewitz, On War, pp. 596-601, for his section on
war as an instrument of policy.
      91. Clausewitz, On War, p. 511.
      92. Ibid., p. 182.
      93. Ibid., p. 184.
      94. Galula, Counterinsurgency Warfare, p. 89.
      95. Ibid., p. 77. Galula felt "No greater
crime can be committed by the counterinsurgent than
accepting, or resigning himself to, the protraction
of the war. He would do as well to give up early."
      96. Clausewitz, On War, p. 569.
      97. Ibid., pp. 77-78. It is interesting that
General J.F.C. Fuller felt that one of Clausewitz's
worst "blind shots" was that "he never grasped that
the true aim of war is peace and not victory" and
commented that "the word 'peace' barely occurs half

a dozen times in On War." The Conduct of War, p. 76.

98. Kissinger, Nuclear Weapons and Foreign Policy, p. 10.

99. Brigadier General W. J. Thompson, "Muzzle on the Military Mind," Army, February 1962, p. 37.

100. Paul Kecskemeti, Strategic Surrender, p. 258.

101. See Herman Kahn, On Thermonuclear War, p. 525.

102. Fuller, The Conduct of War, p. 67.

103. Referring to the civilian assistant secretaries of Defense, Kintner wrote in Forging a New Sword, "'In our conflict with the Soviet Union, Soviet professionals are stacked up against United States amateurs at the decision-making level.'" Quoted in Gavin, War and Peace in the Space Age, p. 259.

104. Aron, The Century of Total War, p. 198.

105. Ibid., p. 367.

106. Henry L. Roberts, Russia and America: Dangers and Prospects, pp. 250-251. It was Napoleon who said: "'Take advantage of all your opportunities. Fortune is a woman; if you let her slip one day, you must not expect to find her again the next.'" Wartenburg, Napoleon as a General, Vol. I, p. 84. Some great moments of history have been partially bluff and partially geared for the lack of resolve expected on the opposing side such as when "The Wehrmacht contingents that occupied the demilitarized zone in March 1936 had orders to retire if the French Army crossed the frontiers of the Reich." Aron, The Century of Total War, p. 46. When the Berlin Wall went up in 1961, the Communist troops had no ammunition in their weapons.

It was interesting that the NATO countries lived in fear for years of a Soviet bloc that had about half the population density available for war if need be. See Arthur T. Hadley, The Nation's Safety and Arms Control, p. 70.

107. Kissinger, Nuclear Weapons and Foreign Policy, p. 31. Herman Kahn asked the unthinkable question: "What price would we be willing to pay?" His answer was that many American, after considerable discussion, gave as estimates of the population as a price "between 10 and 60 million, clustering toward the upper number.... in other words somewhat less than half." On Thermonuclear War, pp. 29-30.

108. Kissinger, ibid., p. 13.

109. Goldwater, Why Not Victory?, p. 169. Goldwater felt that we should announce to the world that "defeat is unacceptable" and that our national

462

objective should be "victory over communism" (pp. 34-35) but that "armed conflict may not be necessary to defeat communism." (p. 31).

110. See Harriman, Peace With Russia?, p. 21. See Fuller, The Conduct of War, p. 75, discussing Clausewitz on Russia and that it cannot be conquered by force but only from within.

111. Kennan, American Diplomacy 1900-1950, p. 125.

112. See Goldwater, Why Not Victory?, p. 154 and p. 161 - "The rulers of the Kremlin would sooner reduce their territory to the ancient state of Muscovy than to die fighting for their ideology."

113. Kennan, American Diplomacy, p. 129.

114. Ibid., pp. 130 and 145.

115. Ibid., pp. 133 and 135.

116. See Goldwater, Why Not Victory?, p. 160.

117. See Harrison E. Salisbury, War Between Russia and China, for the history of the dispute and the prospects.

118. General Matthew B. Ridgway, Soldier, p. 279. It was interesting to reread in 1971 what Justice William O. Douglas wrote in 1953, North From Malaya, p. 331. "The long-range strategy must be to pry China loose from the Soviets.... A strong China is Russia's great menace. A strong China, like a strong United States, makes Russia's dream of world conquest uneasy."

119. James A. Johnson, "The New Generation of Isolationists," Foreign Affairs, October 1970, pp. 130, 140, 143-145.

120. Henry M. Wriston, "Thoughts for Tomorrow," Foreign Affairs, April 1962, p. 380.

Part 4
War and Victory

14
Is War the Solution?

> Political power grows out
> of the barrel of a gun.[1]
>
> -- Mao Tse-tung

> Peoples make war, but never
> do they aspire so passion-
> ately to peace.[2]
>
> -- Raymond Aron

1. Is Peace Normal?

We draw a sharp distinction between war and
peace in our language and tend to consider peace as
the normal state of international relations with war
as an aberration. Thomas Hobbes wrote in his famous
Leviathan that when men live in anarchy or, in his
colorful words, "without a common power to keep them
all in awe, they are in that condition which is
called war". He continued: "For war consists not in
battle only, or the act of fighting, but in a tract
of time, wherein the will to contend by battle is
sufficiently known... All other time is peace."[3]
With the international anarchy that exists as a
world order, there is not much prospect for peace by
that definition. Since men do not always get along
too well, and since nations are groups of men, we
should not be too surprised that nations quarrel. As
General Fuller wrote, "war is endemic in civilization"[4] and "Coexistence of incompatibles is the father of war."[5] Throughout history, war has been the
final means of resolving disputes between nations.
As one French author described it in a modern context, "history without war is like a car without a
motor."[6]
Some analyses of the history of mankind show

467

that from the fifteenth century before Christ until
the present, almost thirty-five hundred years, there
have been less than two hundred and thirty-five
years of peace - roughly fifteen years of war for
every year of peace.[7] War throughout history has
been not only universal but also almost continuous
in some part of the world. "The world has never
been long without war; and human nature does not
really change."[8] Yet human nature is quite flexible
and war has always been based on calculation, not
madness. It is perhaps debatable whether war is
necessary for the evolution of mankind; however,
throughout recorded history, it seems to have been
his dominant preoccupation. With no period in human history totally free from war, and rarely a generation without a major conflict, great wars have
ebbed and flowed across history almost as regularly
as tides.[9] Machiavelli wrote in The Prince (p. 65),
"there are two methods of fighting, the one by law,
the other by force: the first method is that of man,
the second of beasts; but as the first method is
often insufficient, one must have recourse to the
second."

There is no indication that there will ever be
a time when states will renounce war and deal with
each other only peacefully. The lessons of history
are against it. There have always been men and nations willing to use arms to defend their interests
and to advance their own policies. After two great
wars to end wars in the first half of this century,
there have been over 400 wars since the end of World
War II. It appears, then, unfortunately inaccurate
to say that peace is the normal state of affairs.
It certainly has not been so for the Communists; so
far, they have always been at war.

According to Lenin: "Peace is the time to ac-
cumulate one's forces. History proves that Peace is
only a truce between two wars and that war is a
fight for a better peace."[10] With such a theory,
conquest becomes a necessity. This Communist War
has been waged around the world since 1918 with the
twin purposes of winning the world for Communism
without the use of arms, if possible, and of improv-
ing the Communist military power position if arms
become necessary. Armed insurrection is regarded by
the Communists as the "supreme political act" in internal affairs and war itself as the "supreme political act" in international affairs. Communist revolutionary strategy ultimately depends on war. "Communist theory regards war, any war, as favorable to
the extension of Communist power, and disadvanta-

468

geous to capitalism."[11] The Communist strategic objective of weakening the West psychologically, politically, and economically so that battle will be
unnecessary is not only wise but also prudent in the
nuclear age.

Western confusion in dealing with the Communists
arises from the fact that we have not declared war
on them; however, they have declared war on us -
more precisely, Marx declared war for them. The
acute state of tension in the world is abnormal to
us. "They think of it as normal - because a war is in
progress."[12] This is not a struggle that can be
negotiated because it cannot end in peace according
to Marxist-Leninist theory before the liquidation of
the capitalist class.[13] Thus the conference table
is simply one more location for war; because, although we approach negotiations to achieve significant agreements, they view negotiations as only one
of many forms of wartime strategy. It is not the
West that provokes the Communist World. Rather it
is the Communist World that is in permanent conflict
with all countries that rebel against their divine
message.

It is important to remember that war - brutal
and destructive as it is - itself can achieve no
positive aims. Military victory makes possible, but
by no means assures, some further and more positive
achievements.[14] The war aim of strategy is to
clinch a political argument by force instead of
words. This is normally accomplished by battle, the
true object of which is not physical destruction,
but the mental submission of the enemy. International anarchy is not the cause of war but it permits war to occur by providing the soil in which the
causes or seeds of war can take root. Until the
soil is removed, the purpose of war will continue to
be to eliminate or modify those seeds, or the causes,
of the war. Belligerent states strive to break each
other's will to prosecute war. The seat of that
will varies according to the make-up of governments
and may reside in an individual or with a whole community. In the past, war was waged to change the
enemy's policy, to change the government's mind, but
not to change his government. However, total war,
and particularly ideological war, aims to overthrow
the government even though that would leave no organized body with which to make peace. That was a
complication for us and a goal for the Communists.
The objective must be to make sure that the postwar
situation is such as to further one's longrange objectives.

It is generally agreed that the behavior of men and nations in conflict is more complex than the normal behavior of man in peaceful groupings and that the processes of war are essentially sociological phenomena. When the earliest man invented tools, he quickly used them to kill his fellow man. When the Peking Man learned to preserve fire, he "used it to roast his brothers."[15] This could not go on unchecked or soon the tribe or other social grouping would be destroyed so there developed responsible mcrality which prohibited killing within the group even though it continued against other groups. Freud felt that civilization owed its existence to the possibility of "sublimating love for one's family into the wider friendship and loyalty for the group, society, and lastly, the state." Yet this transformation "creates tensions and frustrations that strengthen the aggressive impulses in man." Progress in civilization is, therefore, a "constant struggle between the cooperative and aggressive impulses in man, whose frustrations and conflicts turn into aggressive attitudes toward himself or others."[16] It is this collective aggressiveness that makes war a social epidemic.[17]

Naturally, common people do not want war; but, it is their chiefs who make policy and, as Goering observed at Nuremberg, it is easy to indoctrinate people, in a dictatorship or a democracy.[18] We should not forget that Hitler was a popular leader, that the Japanese were as one behind their Emperor, and in December 1941 Americans rushed to join the Army with the ring of "Remember Pearl Harbor." The pugnacity of man seems to play some role in his impulsion toward war.

Hegel saw one nation dominant in each epoch, with victory in war indicating where the world spirit was taking up residence; the nation losing in war thereby proving that the world spirit was no longer in harmony with it.[19] Heinrich von Treitschke stated in a lecture in the winter of 1891-92: "We have now agreed that war is just and moral, and that the ideal of eternal peace is both unjust and immoral, and impossible.... So long as human nature, with its passions and its sins, remains what it is, the sword shall not depart from the earth.... Again and again it must be repeated that war, the violent form of the quarrels of the nations, is the direct outcome of the very nature of the State. The mere fact that there are many States proves, of itself, that war is necessary."[20] Albert Einstein, in an exchange of letters with Sigmund Freud, felt that

the only road to international security and an end
to anarchy was through the "unconditional surrender
by every nation" of its liberty of action or sovereignty.[21] War may have been rampant through the an-
nals of history, and it may still be epidemic in the
world, but the Free World still likes to consider
peace as something normal in spite of the Communist
War around us. The strength of Western freedom will
be reinforced if it outlasts the Communists, thus
proving a morality in the Western view.

2.   The Plus and Minus of War

It is not an impartial judgment to indict war
as having no positive value. War, Jomini's terrible
and passionate drama, is not all evil. "It is a
true tragedy, which must have nobleness and triumph
in it as well as disaster."[22] The great changes in
history have generally been preceded by armed conflict of a vast scale. Quincy Wright wrote that war
has been the "method actually used both for achieving the major political changes of the modern world
and for maintaining stability in that world."[23] All
the great nations have risen from the field of battle; the great cultures, modern civilizations, discoveries, and mighty progress in technology have
resulted from war; the achievement of liberty, the
building of democracy, and their security are based
on war. War has contributed to unanticipated historical results, some good and others bad. War,
then, in history cannot be judged unequivocally as
"wholly destructive or wholly constructive."[24]
The question of whether there is nothing worth
fighting for is basic in the arguments between pacifists and patriots. These arguments may become
overly simplistic sometimes: appeasement or war,
suicide or surrender, humiliation or holocaust, to
be either Red or dead; for there is usually more
latitude in our choices than either/or. Our own
history is replete with cases in which we determined
the issues were worth fighting for. We would have
no country without this concept! A variation of
this theme came about in the Second War in the Philippines. A Filipino doctor was trying to get a
Filipino Governor to collaborate with the Japanese.
The Governor replied:

"You may not agree with me but the truth is
that the present war is a blessing in disguise

471

to our people and that the burden it imposes and the hardships it has brought upon us are a test of our character to determine the sincerity of our convictions and the integrity of our souls. In other words, this war has placed us in the crucible to assay the metal in our being. For as a people, we have been living during the last 40 years under a regime of justice and liberty regulated only by universally accepted principles of constitutional government. We have come to enjoy personal privileges and civil liberties without much struggle, without undergoing any pain to attain them. They were practically a gift from a generous and magnanimous people - the people of the United States of America.

"Now that Japan is attempting to destroy those liberties, should we not exert any effort to defend them? Should we not be willing to suffer for their defense?"[25]

Mao Tse-tung probably had similar feelings toward his Party bureaucrats and the younger generation in Communist China. They had not been on the Long March and had not fought the Japanese and the Nationalists; they had not experienced the Revolution. To give them such an experience, he sent them into the Cultural Revolution, one of the most unimaginable rampages in the history of modern man.

The rise and fall of empires, cultures, and ideologies, changes in the frontiers of the states of the world, migrations and movements of populations have been the result of war. Homer Lea wrote: "All kingdoms, empires, and nations that have existed on this earth have been born out of the womb of war and the delivery of them has occurred in the pain and labor of battle," So, too, have they perished on similar fields.[26] Sigmund Freud, in a reply to Albert Einstein, wrote: "Thus the Roman conquests brought that boon, the pax romana to the Mediterranean lands. The French kings' lust for aggrandisement created a new France, flourishing in peace and unity. Paradoxical as it sounds, we must admit that warfare well might serve to pave the way to that unbroken peace we so desire, for it is war that brings vast empires into being, within whose frontiers all warfare is proscribed by a strong central power."[27] The changes of frontiers in history represent a study of the geography of war. Forcible annexation, although condemned by international morality, "is not forbidden by international law."[28] Up to the most recent wars, we have seen the shifting of frontiers, annexations, and the division, creation, or dissolution of states. Likewise, we have seen the major shifts of populations, such as in eastern Poland and Tibet. Migration has taken the form of invasion, conquest, colonization, and immigration. The millions of refugees created in wars usually result in permanent changes in population distributions.

Many of the great scientific discoveries and inventions have been spurred by the pressure of war. A spokesman of the Du Pont company stated in 1942: "'The war is compressing into the space of months scientific developments which, without the spur of necessity, might have taken half a century to realize. As a result, industry will emerge from the war with a capacity for making scores of chemical and other raw materials on a scale that, only two years ago, was beyond comprehension.'"[29] This was before the atomic bomb and all the advances that have resulted from the Manhattan Project. Not only were these inventions and ideas often crucial to wars - such as the atomic bomb and the development of radar, which permitted victory in the Battle of Britain and the clearing of U-boats in the Battle of the Atlantic[30] - but from them came new products that improved the kitchen, the home, or some other aspect of life. Electronic advances also yielded the transistor radio, which has reached every corner of the world and has played a major role in the revolution of rising expectations.

War has served, to some degree, as a brake on population growth through history. Arnold Toynbee saw the traditional cure for over-population as "famine, pestilence, civil disorder, and war" to return peoples to their traditional low standard of living.[31] The bubonic plague epidemics of the mid-1300s "wiped out a third of the people of western Europe. A hundred years of almost continuous warfare then cut down the flower of the surviving families."[32] War deaths are still large even in this century - 40 million in World War II, 2 million in Korea, 2.5 million in Viet-Nam (Laos, and Cambodia), even "a million dead" in Bangladesh (with 9 million refugees fled to India)[33] - but populations are so large now, that these losses hardly slow the growth. However, as Raymond Aron observed, war is "remarkably inefficient" as a method of reducing excess population. Also, it produces reverse selection in that "it spares the old and the malingerers, and

eliminates the young and courageous."[34] Nevertheless, the fears produced by Malthusian theory continue and will grow stronger as our population explosion continues as we multiply ourselves toward
six billion on earth before the end of this century.
The modern world does have a population problem and
one in which force may well play a role.

Nothing is gained from war without paying a
price. We have already looked at the costs of some
of the wars in the past. However, the cost of a total war in the future is difficult to comprehend.
Herman Kahn tabulated the economic recuperation
times for "Tragic but Distinguishable Postwar States"
for varying numbers of dead: e.g. 2,000,000 - 1 year,
10,000,000 - 5 years, 80,000,000 - 50 years, and
160,000,000 - 100 years. "Will the survivors envy
the dead?" Kahn predicted that the majority of the
survivors and their descendants could live normal
and happy lives.[35] We tend to forget that man is
still a resilient beast. Again we need perspective.
More people are injured on our highways every year
than the total casualties suffered in any war in our
history. For so long, we have taken for granted the
blessings of liberty and the vast freedom we possess,
do we really want to pay the price of indifference
to limited and revolutionary wars? Many things do
not seem precious until they are lost.

Even though "war has tended to increase in
costs and to decline in value", it has shown itself
to be still useful to despotisms.[36] As long as
there are nations, or more precisely, political leaders, who judge that some gain can be achieved through
war, it will remain with us as a part of world politics. In spite of the hazards of war, until there
is no likelihood of victory, it is not likely to be
abolished. Such an abolition appears no where on
the world horizon. War continues as a means of politics and the last resort for opposing tyranny. It
must not be forgotten that peace is desirable and is
our goal, but it is not the most important condition
in the world.

3.   Do Victors Win?

Few wars have been waged at low cost, but from
the dust and blood of battle rose those empires
which built the foundations of civilization as we
know it. It is important to recall those decisive
battles of history; we cannot afford to be selfish

474

or overly egotistical for, to have a true perspective of history, we must remember that a few men at a particular spot did change history. The Battle of Marathon broke Persian invincibility and permitted the gradual ascendancy of the principles of European civilization. The Athenian defeat at Syracuse determined that Latin rather than Greek would be the basis of languages in Europe and that Roman law would predominate rather than the law of Athens. The Battle of Tours determined why we are not under the civil and religious edicts of the Koran instead of Christendom. The defeat of a 3,500-man expeditionary force at Saratoga assured the birth of the United States of America and the world power that it has become.[37]

From the empires and revolutions, new orders grew, new ideas, new systems of government. In great wars, tyranny was blocked or destroyed. In our Civil War, the Union was preserved. It is not likely that we would be the same world power if the Confederate States of America existed. Allied efforts may have been inefficient, but Hitler and his philosophy were stopped.

France, bled white in World War I draining its emotional stamina for World War II, and Great Britain were winners in the Second War, but the cost was so high for them that they have never regained their former stature. Germany and Japan were smashed to rubble yet they have rebuilt and are major powers in the world again. The United States won but had to help rebuild both sides and has been paying the bills for the world since. Nearly $150 billion have been dispensed in foreign aid and the United States has paid almost one-half of the costs of the United Nations over the years. World War II, fought inefficiently as a crusade, enjoyed full popular support in America. However, in Korea and Viet-Nam, where the government attempted to fight war in a more restrained, political manner, a terrible domestic price was paid. In spite of the very high cost, the Soviets consider World War II to have been terribly valuable, because it provided the setting for Communist expansion into Eastern Europe, China, Korea, and eventually Indochina. All the major Communist gains have resulted from war: World War I gave birth to the Soviet Union, the World War II results were just noted, the Indochina War produced the Democratic Republic of Viet-Nam, and even Cuba resulted from a shoestring guerrilla war against Batista.

What are the prospects for Victory in the

future? Initially, we must remember that we are dealing with an entire spectrum of conflict as already discussed. Victory then can take as one end of the spectrum, the "bloodless victory" where a whole campaign is conducted without engagement.[38] This obviously is the most efficient and desirable. Clausewitz felt that "For the victor the engagement can never be decided too quickly, for the vanquished it can never last too long. The speedy victory is a higher degree of victory; a late decision is, on the side of the defeated, some compensation for the loss."[39] Quick victory in the Six-Day War was important to the Israelis because, as a small country, a war of attrition works against them and because they are vastly outnumbered. However, it still did not end the conflict which exploded again and will again if there is no agreement. An example of a limited victory would be the Chinese attack on India in 1962. The Chinese hit hard and then withdrew. Their objectives were accomplished: some frontier area was regained, the Russians were embarrassed, and the Indians, particularly Mr. Nehru, were driven from the neutralist ranks. Much was accomplished at little cost and, in fact, with few people understanding what had happened.

Indochina is a little more complicated in that, on the Communist side, it is a protracted war but in search of Total Victory - that is, the complete reorientation of the governing system and full control of the people. However, on the defending side, it is a fight for a more limited victory since the fight is more for the status quo, maintenance of freedom, with no designs on North Viet-Nam.

The future for limited victory appears to be at least good. The Frederick the Great style of a hard attack followed by generous terms would appear to continue to be feasible. However, the quest for a more absolute victory is considerably more dangerous and much less sure. The Communists learned well their lesson from Korea, that obvious aggression begets Western reaction. Therefore, so long as aggression can be clouded or confused, as in Viet-Nam, the lethargic Western response leaves a door open for exploitation. If the Communists feel they must move overtly, as they did in Czechoslovakia, then they move as rapidly as possible and put a quick end to their action.

Even before the advent of nuclear weapons, there was serious doubt as to the utility of large-scale war as an instrument of policy. Part of the problem was the still lingering doubt as to what is victory.

"It is very difficult to determine whether a war has
been fundamentally successful, partly because there
is no universally accepted criterion as to what constitutes success in a war." The other lingering
doubt concerned the appropriate price to pay for victory. "It is entirely possible to pay too much in
the way of war for too little in return. This last
fact has raised the question as to whether any modern full-sized war, waged at enormous cost in men,
money and resources, can be successful in the wider
sense, even for the technically winning side. It is
now commonly conceded that both sides of any large
scale modern war must lose in the larger and more
fundamental sense."[40] With the addition of nuclear
weapons, war has attained a deadliness and a character which, always terrible and long since evident as
a poor instrument of policy, seems conceivable only
as a last and desperate resort. "After the First
World War, Winston Churchill wrote: 'Victory was to
be bought so dear as to be almost indistinguishable
from defeat. It was not to give security even to
the victors.' His judgment was seconded by Aristide
Briand who said, 'In modern war there is no victor.
Defeat reaches out its heavy hand to the uttermost
corners of the earth, and lays its burdens on victor
and vanquished alike.'"[41]
    Judging by the weaknesses of strategic bombing
in three wars now, it is not certain that a country
can be blasted into subservience even with nuclear
weapons, unless perhaps the country were laid a
wasteland - but then why bother to attack in the
first place? A nuclear exchange might bring a war
to an end quickly, but as "the victor would be
scarcely less mangled than his opponent, and indeed
hard to identify as the victor, this line of strategy has little to recommend it."[42] Unless one of
the nuclear opponents desired a Carthaginian peace,
which seems totally infeasible in a highly dependent, multi-polar world, then, as Walter Millis wrote,
"The war of nuclear mass destruction is unusable for
any positive end." In this suspicious, frenetic
world, nuclear weapons are needed for their deterrent
effect. Yet the real objective of the Cold War is
the change of the form of government on the opposing
sides, not the destruction of nations. Therefore,
the nuclear exchange itself is of "no value to anyone as an instrument of positive policy."[43] However,
the possession of nuclear weapons does provide significant power and leaves the way open for nuclear
blackmail, still an undeveloped art which may well
come into its own in the last third of the twentieth

century.

The question of preventive war is sometimes raised. Preemptive war can be launched as a surgical operation to reduce the slaughtering effect of a war, such as the Israeli Six-Day War; however, preventive war is logical nonsense. "War cannot be fought to prevent war." However, war can and occasionally must be fought to prevent disaster. "Only one thing is worse than nuclear war: Defeat in such a war."[44]

Disarmament has already been discussed, and arms limitations are a major subject of talks in the 1970s with, hopefully, some prospects for success. There may be arms limitations, arms controls, and even arms reductions, but disarmament is not realistic. As Herman Kahn wrote: "It has probably always been impractical to imagine a completely disarmed world, and the introduction of the thermonuclear bomb has added a special dimension to this impracticality."[45] Nuclear weapons are no longer a novelty. A vast reservoir of knowledge has been amassed in the detonation of nearly 800 nuclear devices since 1945[46] even with a test ban treaty for a decade. Given the large nuclear stockpiles in the Soviet Union, the United States, the British Isles, France, Communist China, and who knows what in Israel and India, "it would be child's play for one of these nations to hide completely hundreds of these bombs."[47] Disarming nations of their capability to make war is impossible prior to the establishment of one world government. We will be extremely fortunate if our statesmen are able to reduce even some of the strategic weapons on a world scale.

All of us yearn for the abolition of war as an instrument of national policy, no one more than those who have fought in war. Those who talk of the glory of war must not have seen much of the misery of war. The man who described war as long periods of boredom interrupted by short periods of sheer horror had seen war. General Douglas MacArthur, one of the most experienced military men in history, strongly appealed for the abolition of war. He saw the cost of victory rising possibly as high as the victor's own total destruction, a mutual suicide. The great masses of the world's population oppose war - on this all sides can agree he felt - only the leaders persist in using it as a means of policy. It was MacArthur who pressed for the abolition of war as a sovereign right of the nation in the Japanese constitution. (It was never objected to in any form by the Japanese. He saw this proscription against war as a vital step forward toward war's final abolition. MacArthur was perturbed by limited war, sanctuary, prisoners rotting in Communist jails, and never reconciled these with his strong feeling for "There is no substitute for victory." for which he has been greatly criticized. MacArthur was a total warrior in our worst tradition of the first half of the twentieth century. However, this great man had a keen feel for the major issues and he felt that the fate of the world would never be settled by force of arms.[48]

The problem is that all the world leaders, or aspiring leaders, have not yet received the message that war is useless as a means of advancing policy. Limited war, in particular, has yet to be disproved. Guerrilla war is still relatively cheap and "safe" as an indirect or proxy form of war. Limited war is not necessarily small war. Parts of the war in Viet-Nam were quite large involving large bodies of troops in pitched battle. The Communist invasion of Czechoslovakia involved approximately one-half million troops, yet with a limited objective - to reorient an uncomradely Communist government. The West Pakistani operations in East Pakistan (which became Bangladesh) caused over a million dead as we have already seen and the short war between India and Pakistan was across long frontiers and on a large scale. If total war comes again, it will come only as a failure. It would be a last resort on the part of the West; and, on the aggressor's side, it would be stupid as they have managed quite well with indirect war.

The Romans had a maxim, "If you want peace, prepare for war." Liddell Hart, even before World War II, altered it to, "If you want peace, understand war." In more recent years, he expanded it to, "If you want peace, understand war - particularly the guerrilla and subversive forms of war."[49] The major asset that a national leader can possess is an understanding of power politics and the use therein of military power. Preparation for war communicates resolve. Understanding war insures that the military instrument will be properly used within the overall context of national policy. Homer Lea wrote, back near the turn of the century, "Whenever a nation's attitude toward war is evasive, its conduct indecisive and its preparations an indifferent, orderless assembling of forces, it prepares for defeat."[50] T. R. Fehrenbach, writing after the Korean War, wrote: "A nation that does not prepare for all forms of war should then renounce the use of war in national policy. A people that does not prepare to fight should then be morally prepared to surrender."[51]

No, war is not the solution. But that does not yet mean that war - that "mad kind of burglary - the plundering of one's own house"[52] - is obsolete as an instrument of politics. As long as there is some chance of gaining desired objectives through its use, there will be national leaders who will take that chance. On the other side, as long as there are leaders who would try to take away the freedom of others, there will be some, even though the price may be extremely high, for whom freedom is more important than peace, and they will fight, as a last resort, to preserve their way of life.

NOTES

1. Mao Tse-tung, Selected Works, Vol. II. p.272.
2. Aron, The Century of Total War, p. 97.
3. Ebenstein, Great Political Thinkers, p. 346, italics in original.
4. Fuller, A Military History of the Western World, Vol. I, p. 3.
5. Ibid., Vol. III, p. 635.
6. Gaston Bouthoul, Sauver la guerre, p. 225, my translation.
7. See Homer Lea, The Valor of Ignorance, p. 11, who must have had some acquaintance with the sources used by L. L. Bernard, War and Its Causes, p. 11. Bernard quoted from Jacques Novicow, the Russian-French sociologist, quoting from the Moscow Gazette, for the figures up to 1861, adding "'Within the last three centuries there have been 286 wars in Europe.' Quoting the French writer, M. Volbert, he adds, 'From the year 1500 B.C. to 1860 A.D. more than 8,000 treaties of peace meant to remain in force forever were concluded. The average time they remained in force is ten years.'" from J. Novicow, War and Its Alleged Benefits (New York: Henry Holt and Co., 1911), p. 14.
8. Lukacs, A History of the Cold War, p. 165.
9. Fuller, A Military History of the Western World, Vol. I, p. xi. Toynbee, A Study of History, Vol. II, p. 272, has a table of cycles of Wars in Modern Western History with four cycles roughly a century apart - Spanish Armada, Louis XIV, Napoleon, and Germany - with mid-cycle smaller wars.
10. Miksche, Unconditional Surrender, p. 345, italics in original. In a speech to the Soviet

Congress, 21 December 1920, Lenin discussed granting certain concessions to capitalists. He stressed that it was not a peaceful agreement with capitalists, but an "agreement concerning war." Quoted in The Overstreets, What We Must Know About Communism, p. 282.

11. Kintner, The Front is Everywhere, pp. 162, 163, and 168. "The Communist leaders can take no chances on the basic Marxian dogma's being wrong, for their very lives depend upon its being correct. Hence, they must prove the historical necessity of Communism, if necessary, by force. That is why Communist aggression is inescapable." p. 14.

12. The Overstreets, What We Must Know About Communism, p. 94, italics in original.

13. Ibid., p. 281.

14. Kennan, American Diplomacy, p. 144.

15. Konrad Lorenz, On Aggression (New York: Harcourt, Brace & World, Inc., 1966), p. 239.

16. Ebenstein, Great Political Thinkers, p.788.

17. Bouthoul, Sauver la guerre, p. 135.

18. Gilbert, Le journal de Nuremberg, pp. 281-282.

19. Ebenstein, Great Political Thinkers, p. 572.

20. Brooke, ed., War Aims and Peace Ideals, p. 5.

21. Ebenstein, Great Political Thinkers, p. 803.

22. Sir Gilbert Murray, "How Can War Ever Be Right?" (September 1914) in Brooke, War Aims and Peace Ideals, p. 100.

23. Wright, A Study of War, p. 77. See also Palmer and Perkins, International Relations, pp. 281-289, on the functions of war. See particularly pp. 284-285 where they quote from Professor James T. Shotwell's War as an Instrument of National Policy, and from Professor Quincy Wright.

24. Wright, A Study of War, p. 86.

25. Whitney, MacArthur, pp. 136-137.

26. Lea, The Valor of Ignorance, pp. 10-11. See also Phillips, Roots of Stragegy, p. 7.

27. Ebenstein, Great Political Thinkers, p. 806. This end had not been attained because the fruits of victory had been short-lived. He continued: "our hope that these two factors - man's cultural disposition and a well-founded dread of the form that future wars will take - may serve to put an end to war in the near future, is not chimerical.... Meanwhile we may rest on the assurance that whatever makes for cultural development is working

also against war." p. 810.

28. Coleman Phillipson, Termination of War and Treaties of Peace (London: T. F. Unwin, Ltd., 1916), p. 31.

29. Quoted in Fuller, The Second World War, p. 409.

30. See Miller, A New History of the United States, p. 392.

31. Toynbee, A Study of History, Vol. II. p. 166.

32. Miller, A New History of the United States, p. 4.

33. Time, 25 October 1971, p. 37.

34. Aron, The Century of Total War, pp. 75-76.

35. Kahn, On Thermonuclear War, pp. 20-21.

36. Quincy Wright, A Study of War, pp. 83-84.

37. See Creasy, Fifteen Decisive Battles of the World, pp. 1, 35, 159, and 351.

38. Clausewitz, On War, pp. 26-27.

39. Ibid., p. 187.

40. Bernard, War and Its Causes, p. 41.

41. Wriston, "Thoughts for Tomorrow," Foreign Affairs, April 1962, p. 379.

42. Dickens, Bombing and Strategy, pp. 82-83.

43. Millis, Arms and Men, pp. 309-310.

44. Ferreus, "Fourteen Fundamental Facts of the Nuclear Age," U.S. Congress, House Committee on Un-American Activities, Soviet Total War, p. 217, italics in original.

45. Kahn, On Thermonuclear War, p. 5.

46. The Sunday Star, Washington, D.C., 7 November 1971, p. A-8.

47. Kahn, ibid.

48. See for example, Whitney, MacArthur, pp. 258, 260, 541, 543-546.

49. Liddell Hart, Strategy, (2nd Revised Edition) p. 373.

50. Lea, The Valor of Ignorance, p. 240.

51. Fehrenbach, This Kind of War, pp. 701-702.

52. Fuller, The Conduct of War, p. 129.

15
Total Victory

> Victory can be a reality;
> it can also be a mirage.[1]
>
> -- Stephen King-Hall
>
> There are ways of conquer-
> ing that quickly transform
> victory into defeat.[2]
>
> -- Raymond Aron

1. Total Victory - Is It Worth It?

In the summer of 1945, the great Total War was
over with a victory probably as total as any in recorded history. The enemies had been reduced to
dislocated, hungry peoples whose countries were, in
many areas, piles of rubble. President Truman wrote
of the period.

> We had won the war. It was my hope now that
> the people of Germany and Japan could be reha-
> bilitated under the occupation. The United
> States, as I had stated at Berlin, wanted no
> territory, no reparations. Peace and happiness
> for all countries were the goals toward which
> we would work and for which we had fought. No
> nation in the history of the world had taken
> such a position in complete victory. No nation
> with the military power of the United States of
> America had been so generous to its enemies and
> so helpful to its friends. Maybe the teachings
> of the Sermon on the Mount could be put into
> effect.[3]

However, the problem of the postwar years was
as Raymond Aron described it. "We are trying to

efface the consequences of a too complete victory, and to get back to a victory compatible with the resurrection of the vanquished."[4] This desire for Total Victory had been present from the beginning; it was incorporated immediately after American entry into the war as part of the United Nations Pact of 1 January 1942 - "Being convinced that complete victory over their enemies is essential to defend life, liberty, independence, and religious freedom, and to preserve human rights and justice...".[5]

"The demand for total victory," as Aron saw it, "was not so much the expression of a political philosophy as a reflex reaction to total war."[6] He felt it was in the Western interest to weaken Germany but not to destroy her and that, therefore, "their actions were completely unreasonable." That we forced the Germans to continue a hopeless struggle, he attributed to the "irresistible momentum of total war."[7] Vagts wrote, "Total victory seems the logical outcome of total war to pseudo-logicians, and unconditional surrender its seal."[8]

King-Hall, in his very interesting book, called for a difference between war aims and peace aims - "in total war, Peace Aims and War Aims should be integrated into a single AIM - the achievement of Total Victory." He recommended that "War Aims should be renamed Military Aims and Peace Aims should be renamed Political Aims."[9] With this differentiation in aims, he saw a difference between a military victory and victory in war - "the achievement of a military victory cannot of itself guarantee VICTORY in the fullest sense of the word. Military victory is not necessarily Total Victory."[10] His definition of Total Victory was not the same as came to be used by the Allied leadership in their desire to smash the enemy as a viable force and to compel them to surrender unconditionally, thereby throwing themselves at the mercy of the Allies and turning their countries and people over to Allied supervision. He wrote: "The final object of war is Total Victory. Such a victory is achieved when the enemy has changed his mind to our way of thinking about the settlement of the issue in dispute. Therefore the purpose of warlike operations (military and political) is to bring about this change of mind."[11] Unfortunately, our leaders did not see the problem quite that clearly; they wanted to change the enemy's mind by force and by occupation of his country rather than by just enough force to coerce him to change his mind himself. The difference was between a negotiated peace and Unconditional Surrender, between military destruction and the terrible civilian destruction, between war as an instrument of policy and cataclysmic, ideological, emotional Total War.

Walter Lippmann wrote of how we drifted into World War II obsessed by the ideal of peace which diverted our attention from national security. Also, "The ideal of disarmament caused us to be inadequately armed."[12] This caused him to question "whether peace, as so many say, is the supreme end of foreign policy." At that time, in the midst of the war (1943), it was obvious "that the survival of the nation in its independence and its security is a greater end than peace." To him it then became apparent that "If the logic of peace as the supreme national ideal leads to absurdity, then it must be a grave error to think and to say that peace is the supreme end."[13] It might be worth considering the reverse of Churchill's phrase of 1918 - "no peace till victory."[14] - is there really a victory until there is peace? But peace is such an elusive and nebulous thing. Has the world ever really known it? What really is peace? Its definition varies with different people and different governments. Certainly the Communist and Democratic definitions, at present, are not compatible. Peace is a simple matter to the Communists; if the rest of the world would quit resisting them, then they could take over the world and there would be "peace." However, we define that state of world affairs as slavery not "peace." It is not always good to be too obsessed with the ideal of peace. "The generation which most sincerely and elaborately declared that peace is the supreme end of foreign policy got not peace, but a most devastating war."[15] It is better to keep an eye on the stark reality of world politics and to operate within its limitations. This does not preclude our ideal of peace; it only keeps us acting logically and not acting irrationally in search of the elusive specter which may not be immediately obtainable.

As one of our statesmen wrote, "War, at best, is a futile method of solving disputes."[16] Our problem has been that "The United States has fought wars differently from other peoples. We have fought for the immediate victory, not for the ultimate peace."[17] In this light, Fuller called it the "black day in Europe's history" when the United States became involved in the first war, which produced the "dictated" Peace of Versailles resulting in the second war, which led to no peace at all. He frankly stated that the Americans did not covet any

485

of Europe's land. The reason was "their failure to
understand that war is an instrument of policy. They
did not know how to wage war, and in consequence
they did not know how to make peace. They looked
upon war as a lethal game in which the trophy was
victory."[18]
The main mistakes that Hanson Baldwin pointed
out were: "the attempt to find total victory, to inflict absolute destruction, to use unlimited means,
and to mistake military victory for political victory."[19] Kecskemeti professed that "the war would
have been shorter if the Allies' basic war aim had
not been total victory". A negotiated conclusion to
the war would have shortened the conflict and provided a better political situation after the war.
"But few critics maintain that this would have been
the correct policy. Most critics, rather, take the
objective of total victory for granted and argue that
it would have been attained more quickly and more
easily if a more positive formula than unconditional
surrender had been used."[20] The problem is to try
and understand if there really is a difference between Unconditional Surrender and Total Victory. The
two may not be exactly synonumous but they are
closely related and flow from the same concept of
how to conduct a war.
Henry Kissinger felt that the "renunciation of
total victory is repugnant to our military thought
with its emphasis on breaking the enemy's will to
resist and its reliance on the decisive role of industrial potential." Victory has been identified by
the enemy's physical impotence since war was thought
of more in moral than in strategic terms. The physical contest is decided by military strength, but
the price to be paid and the intensity of the struggle are determined by political goals.[21] We were
willing to pay the price for Unconditional Surrender
to gain Total Victory in the war; however, the price
has gone up now and it may be prohibitive in the e-
vent of another war.
Fuller also explored this problem of conceiving
war in moral terms.

> The lesson is this: Should you, when waging war,
> lack a politically sane and strategically pos-
> sible aim, you are likely to be thrown back on
> an insane moral one, such as attempting to
> eliminate ideas with bullets or political be-
> liefs with bombs. Hitler's aim was sane and

possible and Japan's sane and impossible, though
both were monstrously unjust, but not more so
than the imperialistic aims of other heads of
state and of other nations in the past. Though
the means adopted in gaining sane aims are
sometimes atrocious, in the case of insane aims
they are always so. It is for this reason that
crusades and civil wars are so destructive of
moral values, as well as of life and property,
and the Second World War was both a crusade and
a European civil war.[22]

To complicate the moralistic approach to the war, we
became lost in our emotions and our enthusiasm. Anne
Armstrong gave two reasons why no alternative to Unconditional Surrender was even considered: "first,
that the major decisions regarding aims of policy
were made by the President and by his personal advisers as more or less an afterthought to strategic
decisions and, second, because the emotions and en-
thusiasms engendered by the war seem to have blurred
the realism of the planners' analysis of German and
of Russian history."[23]
George Kennan disagreed with the concept that
"in war there can be no substitute for victory" - a
tactical "victory" in battle, perhaps; but, in war
he saw "only the achievement or nonachievement of
your objectives." Success would be a measure of how
close military operations brought you to your objectives. "But where your objectives are moral and
ideological ones and run to changing the attitudes
and traditions of an entire people or the personal-
ity of a regime, then victory is probably something
not to be achieved entirely by military means or indeed in any short space of time at all; and perhaps
that is the source of our confusion." Kennan frankly concluded: "there is no more dangerous delusion,
none that has done us a greater disservice in the
past or that threatens to do us a greater disservice
in the future, than the concept of total victory."[24]
The shock of the Cold War created a realism that
was not present during World War II. Many of our
attitudes are quite different now from those of 1945.
"This American renversement diplomatique has, in a
sense, been a repudiation of both the theory and the
content of Unconditional Surrender. It has been an
acknowledgment de facto of the realities of the balance of power, and an implicit acknowledgment that
perhaps the moral basis of the doctrine of total vic-

tory was neither historically nor philosophically sound."[25] As Cicero said long ago, "An army is of little value in the field unless there are wise counsels at home."[26]

Our military forces fought valiantly and brought home the Total Victory that the politicians requested. Was it worth it? Was the terrible price paid in the intense struggle of World War II worth the political results obtained? There were millions of dead and maimed on all sides; physical destruction had been wreaked on an unprecedented scale; and the world balance of power was drastically altered with the decline of Europe, the rise of the United States, and the invasion of the Russian Empire deep into Central Europe. The war brought Communism to a new prominence and gave the world a threat much more serious than those it had fought so hard to eliminate. For those searching only for peace, it left nothing but disillusionment, for there has been no peace, only a new, "cold" war which has seen little wars flaring continuously since 1945. Those who fought for the freedom of countries in the East found those countries under a new, more terrible dictatorship. Those who fought to defend their empires soon found they no longer had empires. Those who fought so that they could rest quietly behind their oceans found themselves supporting military forces in many corners of the globe and spending as much money as they did during the war. Those who smashed the enemy found themselves rebuilding those same countries only a short time later. Those who were our hated enemies one year were now our allies; one who was our ally and to whom we gave so much assistance now wished to "bury" us. The rebuilding was an enormous undertaking and was completely out of proportion with what had been gained. As General MacArthur said, "The last two wars have shown it. The victor had to carry the defeated on his back."[27]

By whatever criteria one chooses to judge the results, it seems difficult to find anything that justifies the incalculable cost of our fanatical drive to Total Victory. As Benjamin Franklin said: "in my opinion, there never was a good war or a bad peace. What vast additions to the conveniences and comforts of living might mankind have acquired, if the money spent in wars had been employed in works of public utility!"[28] Senator Fulbright, decrying our crusading spirit and our unwise doctrine of Unconditional Surrender, observed: "The West has won two 'total victories' in this century and it has barely survived them."[29]

2. Total Victory in the Nuclear Age

Two brilliant flashes of light that rivalled the sun in intensity and the sudden obliteration of two cities in August 1945 unfolded unto the world a new era. Man, that ingenious technician, had unleashed the tremendous power of the atom. Man, who has never learned to live with himself, now had a tool of destruction that made the invention of gunpowder and the still evident strategic bombing look like toys. Having just terminated a war in which the policy of Total Victory had proved to be a great delusion, what were the prospects of Total Victory in the nuclear age?

After the first atomic bomb fell on Japan, the following appeared in the Vatican City newspaper: "'Humanity did not think like da Vinci. Humanity behaved as he feared it would. It gave precedence to hatred and invented instruments of hatred. There was ever more frightful destructive competition on land, in the water, and in the air, summoning for this purpose all the spiritual and material gifts granted by God. This war provides a catastrophic conclusion. Incredibly this destructive weapon remains as a temptation for posterity, which, we know by bitter experience, learns so little from history.'"[30] Since 1945, an armaments race has brought so many nuclear weapons into being that their explosive capability is now almost beyond comprehension. To top this off, the world is divided into two camps in the strongest ideological contest since the crusades. Arthur T. Hadley summed it up:

> This is at a moment when the weapons in the United States stockpile have an explosive power roughtly equivalent to 35 kilomegatons (35 billion tons of TNT). This is 1-3/4 million times as much explosive as the 20-kiloton (20 thousand tons of TNT) bomb dropped on Nagasaki, or enough bang to provide 10 tons of explosive for everyone in the world. In the form of TNT this much explosive power would fill a string of freight cars stretching from the earth to the moon and back 15 times. Since the Soviet Union is estimated to have around another 20 kilomegatons in its stockpile, we are in an explosive world.[31]

And the stockpiles continue to grow!

Who knows if all this explosive power will ever be used in war? Nevertheless, it does represent a fantastic outlay of resources which may one day be considered as conventional weapons.[32] Though parts of their launching take on the air of the oft-mentioned "push-button" war, it is becoming quite evident that push-button war is not to come; instead, there will be requirements for more rather than less manpower in future warfare.[33]

The idea of "quick victory" seems to be as much a mirage as ever. In an age of possibly unlimited air or guided missile attack upon relatively defenseless targets, the chances for quick victory have been reduced and the deadliness of war greatly increased. "Prior to World War II, the exponents of mechanized power both contended that their weapons would make war less costly in the long run, not only in lives, but in money." The war showed that they were mistaken even though their weapons performed even better than expected. They erred in that they misunderstood the nature of war and misread the history of its development.[34]

These weapons add nothing to war but more destructiveness, and not against the soldier in the foxhole so much as for the true basis of society, the cities and centers of a nation. "The true objective not only of the atomic weapon but of rockets and modern bombing fleets is the physical destruction of society, just as in limited war the true objective of short-range weapons was the annihilation of its military forces."[35] This is not likely to be changed by policy declarations or international agreements. Megaton weapons were not designed to strike limited targets.

Technical advances have permitted the development of low-yield, tactical nuclear weapons, but the great mass of explosive capability in the stockpiles remains in larger yield weapons. This is very important if one considers Western Europe as a potential nuclear battlefield. One writer stated that he knew of "no area in Western Europe where a nuclear battle could be fought without causing considerable damage to non-military targets." He then illustrated this point by a representative scenario involving just three NATO Corps. Nuclear weapons

> ...were "used" against military targets only, in an area of 10,000 square miles which contained no large towns or cities. In this "battle," lasting only a few days, it was assumed that the two sides together used a total

of between 20 and 25 megatons in not fewer than
500 and not more than 1,000 strikes. It turned
out that 3-1/2 million people would have had
their homes destroyed if the weapons were air
burst, and 1-1/2 million if ground burst. In
the former case, at least half the people concerned would have been fatally or seriously injured. In the case of ground burst weapons,
all 1-1/2 million would have been exposed to a
lethal readiological hazard and a further 5
million to serious danger from radiation.[36]

It should be kept in mind that this was a quite limited scenario. Khrushchev was proud of his 50-
megaton bomb and later brandished a 100-megaton
one[37] so this example is probably well on the con-
servative side.
  One should be aware of the effects of a fairly
large weapon on a large city. Kissinger gave an
example of a 10-megaton bomb dropped on New York
City (over 42nd Street at Fifth Avenue). The total
destruction radius for buildings and 75 percent mor-
tality rate would extend 3 miles. This would destroy "all of Manhattan south of Ninety-sixth Street,
parts of Jersey City, all of the cities on the west
bank of the Hudson up to Hudson Heights, as well as
Queens, Long Island City, Hunter's Point and Wil-
liamsburg." This would result in 3 million deaths
with the remaining 1 million people in serious condition. The 7-mile radius of heavy damage would
include parts of the Bronx, Queens and Brooklyn and
all of Jersey City, resulting in perhaps another
900,000 dead and 600,000 injured. Light damage
would reach out to a distance of 10 miles. "At the
outer edge of this circle, the heat and radiation
would be sufficient to kill or injure severely in-
dividuals caught outside of shelter and to set fire
to buildings."[38]
  It would be difficult for a Communist in any
target city after such an attack, if he were still
alive, to feel that the Soviets were "liberating"
him. This is one of the real problems of nuclear
war but it is rarely mentioned. Likewise, "It will
be indispensable, but singularly difficult, to convince the masses in the Soviet Union that the West
bears no ill will except toward their tyrants, if
atom bombs unite in death Stalinists and their opponents, women, children, and the secret police."
Raymond Aron added in a footnote, "On the level of
realistic politics, this is the strongest argument
against the use of weapons of mass destruction."[39]

491

This brings us back to the subject of chemical and biological warfare. Perhaps the neutron bomb will eventually reduce destruction but that has not yet been demonstrated.[40]

Liddell Hart wrote "A reversion to chemical weapons would at least offer a better alternative, and more hope of successful defence without suicide - if deterrence fails."[41] The progress made with the psycho-chemicals was quite good with the best example being the photographs of the now famous cat and mouse experiment.

> Their effect is most striking, and, laughably, demonstrated by putting a mouse into a box along with a cat. The cat promptly pounces on the mouse - but, after a whiff of the new gas, has its instincts reversed. Every time the mouse approached, the cat jumps back in fright - even falling over backwards in its efforts to avoid the mouse! Such a demonstration, and such a gas, provide a far more hopeful portent for peace and humanity than the multiplication of the atomic deterrent.[42]

But this is "inhumane" for modern man prefers to be blown to bits or let a lethal dose of radiation slowly sap his life away. I do not particularly espouse the use of chemical agents; I merely do not like to see men blown apart.

Herman Kahn discussed a most interesting form of attack - disguised warfare. "Certain types of bacteriological and chemical warfare might be developed, and used so subtly that the nation under attack will not know it is being attacked. The possibility of debilitating a nation over a period of years to reduce its competitive capabilities is not out of the question."[43] This form would lend itself perfectly to the Communist mind since he believes time is on his side and follows no time schedule. The impatient Democracies would find it difficult to use because they seek fast solutions and think in clear-cut terms of war and peace while this is a war weapon that would serve best in "peacetime." For these same reasons, the Democracies would be good targets for this sort of attack because they cannot ever get their "anger up" and react until there is an overt attack. With no overt attack, they could lose before they ever figured out they had been attacked.

The important point is that chemical and biological warfare offer weapons of great potential in

492

any future war and could quite possible reduce the terrible destruction. They certainly could not cause any more! Possession of chemical or biological weapons does not mean that they must be used. Significant quantities in being can produce a deterrent effect on potential adversaries. A critical point for our planning is that we not be in a position in which the only answer available to a chemical attack would be with nuclear weapons. The Russians have shown extreme interest in chemical and biological weapons in the past, so it must be hoped they will reciprocate our actions in banning these weapons.

The ever-increasing destructiveness of war has driven world war closer to being suicide, but still we are no nearer to any ban on war. As a Japanese woman so poignantly wrote of the war in Japan, "I could not associate such sporting terms as winning and losing with the terrible tragedy of a world war. I could only say more and more desperately, 'when will they stop fighting?'"[44] The idea of victory had certainly lost its glamour from the days of the knights in armor. The abolition of war had become imperative; but this was impossible until control of atomic energy could be concentrated in the hands of some single political authority which, of necessity, would have to assume the role of a World Government. The effective seat of that Government, in 1955, would have to have been either Washington or Moscow; but neither was prepared to place itself at the mercy of the other. The traditional solution was the "knock-out blow" by battle. But now "the knock-out blow might knock out not only the antagonist but also the victor, the referee, the boxing-ring, and all the spectators."[45] All-out nuclear war continues to be less and less inviting as a means of attaining political objectives.

Soviet Premier Khrushchev admitted this at East Berlin on 14 January 1963, while attending the East German Communist Party Congress, when he barred war as the method to bring about the victory of Communism over capitalism. Mr. Khrushchev said:

"I shall shout hurrah when capitalism is buried. But the burial of capitalism will be carried out by the working class in each country.

"We shall welcome this when they do it. But we shall not fight in order to establish the socialist social order in any country. That is an internal matter for them.

"But our sympathies and support will be on the side of those who bury capitalism."[46]

Two days later, while attacking the Communist Chinese war theories, he warned that Communism would not win a nuclear war.

"The United States has 40,000 atomic or nuclear warheads," he said. "What would happen if one let all those bombs come down on humanity? Seven hundred to eight hundred million people would perish. Countries would be rubbed out.

"I don't want to scare anybody through mentioning this. I only cite the facts. Would socialism win by a thermonuclear war? No. You cannot build socialism in an atomic-infested territory."

Departing from his text, Mr. Khrushchev then brandished the Soviet Union's giant nuclear bomb against the West.

"Dear Comrades, now I tell you a secret. Our scientists have developed a new 100-megaton bomb. This bomb could not be used in Western Europe because it would hit France and Germany and you too. This bomb could only be used overseas against a potential aggressor."[47]

Though decrying the terrible effects of nuclear war and the inevitable lack of victory in one breath, he could not refrain from rattling his saber and bragging about ever more monstrous bombs.

The goal of total war has become, almost invariably, the overthrow of the opposing leadership rather than changes in the actions of a government. War has not only been transformed into a variety of civil war, but the margin of superiority required to impose the victor's will has increased. After overthrowing the enemy government, the victor assumes responsibility for the civil administration of the defeated. However, an all-out thermonuclear catastrophe makes it doubtful whether any society would have the capability to undertake the administration and rehabilitation of other countries. Without physical occupation, victory may prove illusory, leaving a vacuum which could be exploited by powers whose relative position had been improved by the devastation of all-out war. "The destructiveness of modern weapons deprives victory in an all-out war of its historical

meaning."[48]
Total Victory was not a part of war in the traditional Balance of Powers system. Under that system, the total defeat of any major power was wrong since that power would be needed in the reordering of the balance.[49] For Total Victory to be meaningful at the end of any war, the victor must retain enough physical resources to impose his will. The more total the victory sought, the greater must be the margin of superiority. This contrasts with nineteenth-century warfare in which the margin could be relatively small if the peace terms offered were moderate.[50]

In the great political-emotional preoccupation of the Cold War, when the image of the Soviet leaders replaced that of Hitler in so many Western minds as the center and source of all possible evil, it was particularly desirable that we not repeat the mistake of believing that either good or evil is total. We must not condemn an entire people and wholly exculpate others. "Let us remember that the great moral issues, on which civilization is going to stand or fall, cut across all military and ideological borders, across peoples, classes, and regimes - across, in fact, the make-up of the human individual himself. No other people, as a whole, is entirely our enemy. No people at all - not even ourselves - is entirely our friend."[51] This was a real challenge to those who fought World War II in such an emotional frenzy; we can only hope they learned their lesson.

Modern nuclear war is often referred to as mutual suicide, lunacy, and unthinkable. Perhaps the world is returning to the era of small wars, such as have been raging all over the world since 1945. But it would be foolish to think that there can be no nuclear war, for these weapons are controlled by men, those simple mortals who are not always renowned for their rational behavior. Walter Lippmann, speaking in Paris, said: "Nuclear war will not be prevented by fear of nuclear war. For, however lunatic it might be to commit suicide, a great power - if it is cornered, if all the exits are barred, if it is forced to choose between suicide and unconditional surrender - is quite likely to go to war."[52] Although Total Victory is not logical, who can say it will not be tried again. Total war can no longer serve such political aims as "the dictation of terms, temporary 'pedagogic' occupation, or even outright conquest." These presuppose that something worth "dictating to, reeducating, or an-

nexing survives on the losing side." The only appropriate political objective in all-out nuclear war
is the elimination of the adversary, which carries
the risk of self-elimination. Such a risky objective is lunacy, not strategy. Unfortunately, people
sometimes act in an insane fashion and insane strategies have been applied in the past. "Where is the
guarantee that even more insane ones will not be applied in the future?"[53]
Certainly man has developed great destructive
power, but it is the height of conceit to think he,
a puny creature in a vast universe, can destroy the
world or the human race. "Never has war been so
scientifically destructive, and it is certain that
another world war would blight some centers of civilization; but it would be parochial to suppose that
no civilization anywhere would survive. Individual
lives are fragile. But man as such is a tough animal, and a very widespread one."[54] There is no assurance that some group of men will not try to win
a Total Victory in a nuclear war. The only thing
that seems to be sure is that, if they do, their
victory will be just as hollow as the Total Victories of the past.

Total Victory has failed to yield an appropriate political objective for the Democracies and
they have had to pay a prohibitively high price for
what they received. So far, then, in history, Total
Victory has proved to be a great delusion.

NOTES

1. King-Hall, Total Victory, p. 3.
2. Aron, The Century of Total War, p. 158.
3. Truman, Year of Decisions, p. 437.
4. Aron, The Century of Total War, p. 194.
5. The UN Pact is printed in full as Appendix
IV, in Fuller, The Conduct of War, p. 340.
6. Aron, The Century of Total War, p. 28.
7. Ibid., p. 53.
8. Vagts, Defense and Diplomacy, p. 448. He
strongly condemned Total Victory and Unconditional
Surrender as causing the self-destruction of the
Western world, contributing toward making the war
total and following the war aim of annihilation of
the enemy which was not like older diplomacy.
9. King-Hall, Total Victory, p. 113. He made a
point of including economic aims under political
aims. Italics and capitals in original.
10. Ibid., p.4, italics and capitals in original.

11. Ibid., p. 12. See p. 11 also. He said Total Victory would be when the "ex-enemy regards acceptance of the peace settlement... as a permanent
factor in his foreign policy." This is quite different from Unconditional Surrender and Total Victory as actually applied during the war.

He also stated that when this Total Victory
is achieved, "we shall have progressed far along the
road to our final goal, which must be the world-wide
acceptance of the principles of the free life," p.
161. This overlooked the problem of having Russia
as an ally. Their definition of free life was not
the same as ours.

12. Lippmann, U.S. Foreign Policy: Shield of
the Republic, p. 47.

13. Ibid., p. 50.

14. Brooke, War Aims and Peace Ideals, p. 138.

15. Lippmann, U.S. Foreign Policy, p. 54.

16. Joseph C. Grew, Turbulent Era, Vol. II,
p. 1371.

17. Baldwin, Great Mistakes of the War, p. 1.
He said "we lost the peace" at Yalta and on D-Day.

18. Fuller, The Conduct of War, p. 308.

19. Baldwin, Great Mistakes of the War, pp. 107-
108. He also pointed out that these mistakes have
in the past been characteristic of totalitarian
states or dictatorships.

20. Kecskemeti, Strategic Surrender, p. 224.

21. Kissinger, Nuclear Weapons and Foreign
Policy, pp. 86-87.

22. Fuller, The Second World War, p. 402.

23. Armstrong, Unconditional Surrender, p. 261.

24. Kennan, American Diplomacy 1900-1950, p.
102.

25. Armstrong, Unconditional Surrender, italics in original.

26. From De officiis, quoted in King-Hall,
Total Victory, p. 55.

27. Transcript of hearings before Senate Armed
Services and Foreign Relations Committees, U.S. News,
11 May 1951, p. 111.

28. Quoted in Alice Hubbard, ed., An American
Bible, p. 64.

29. Fulbright, The Arrogance of Power, p. 254.

30. Osservator Romano, 7 August 1945. Quoted
in Fuller, The Second World War, p. 397. Leonardo
da Vinci was supposed to have thought of the idea of
the submarine but he banished the thought when he
realized the uses to which it could be put.

31. Hadley, The Nation's Safety and Arms Control, p. 3. His figures date from 1961 and many

more weapons have been added to the inventories, but even these low figures emphasize the inconceivable explosiveness in the world.

32. See Gavin, War and Peace in the Space Age, p. 265. He said "Nuclear weapons will become conventional for several reasons, among them cost, effectiveness against enemy weapons, and ease of handling."

33. See ibid., p. 139, for "more rather than less manpower would be required to fight a nuclear war successfully." Also p. 229, "And more men rather than fewer will be required in the missile-space age than in the past."

In Airborne Warfare, p. 170, he wrote, "The nation or group of nations that control the air will control the peace. This means being able to deliver these troops, trained and equipped, and capable of imposing their will on any potential or actual belligerent."

34. Marshall, Men Against Fire, p. 30.

35. Ibid., p. 31.

36. Sir Solly Zuckerman, "Judgment and Control in Modern Warfare," Foreign Affairs, January 1962, p. 201.

37. At the East German Communist party conference, quoted in the New York Herald Tribune, European Edition, 17 January 1963.

38. Kissinger, Nuclear Weapons and Foreign Policy, pp. 68-69.

39. Aron, The Century of Total War, p. 157.

40. See Hadley, The Nation's Safety, p. 57. "The neutron bomb, if developed, according to some experts, would be a slow-exploding fusion weapon. It would hang over a city, taking maybe half an hour to go off fully. People would be killed by neutron bombardment rather than by heat and shock as in current atomic and thermonuclear weapons." This bomb does not offer the possibility of removing people from action without killing them that certain chemical and biological agents can do, even though it might reduce physical destruction.

41. Liddell Hart, Deterrent or Defense, pp. 87-88.

42. Ibid., p. 88.

43. Kahn, On Thermonuclear War, p. 500.

44. Sumie Seo Mishima, The Broader Way, A Woman's Life in the New Japan, p. 9.

45. Toynbee, A Study of History, Vol. II, p. 326.

46. Reported in the New York Herald Tribune, European Edition, 15 January 1963.

47. Ibid., 17 January 1963. The 19-20 January issue of the newspaper had a small article saying perhaps Khrushchev underrated American nuclear power because a "recently published United States study estimates the American stockpile as perhaps 50,000" warheads.

48. Kissinger, Nuclear Weapons and Foreign Policy, p. 90.

49. Padelford and Lincoln, The Dynamics of International Politics, First Edition, p. 11.

50. Kissinger, Nuclear Weapons and Foreign Policy, p. 89.

51. Kennan, Russia and the West, p. 369.

52. Address before the Anglo-American Press Association in Paris 29 November 1962. New York Herald Tribune, European Edition, 30 November 1962.

53. Kecskemeti, Strategic Surrender, p. 246, italics added.

54. Palmer, A History of the Modern World, p. 821.

16
Victory in War

> Only fools could cling to
> the idea of victory in a
> nuclear war.[1]
>
> -- John F. Kennedy

> It is not the purpose of
> war to annihilate those
> who provoked it, but to
> cause them to mend their
> ways.[2]
>
> -- Polybius, 125 B.C.

Clausewitz rather clearly pointed out that war
is strictly an instrument of policy.[3] Wars are not
determined by the military; they derive from the interplay of policy among nations. This interplay is
not normally the realm of the military but the field
of the diplomats and the political leadership of the
nations. When a certain objective of foreign policy
cannot be met by normal diplomatic channels, there
is often recourse to more stringent means. However,
the policymakers are usually well aware of the price
they are willing to pay for the political objective
desired. This is much like shopping for a car, if
the price is too high, then perhaps the wisest thing
to do is to change the policy or reduce your demands.
Wise policymakers do not become obsessed with
war itself for they look ahead to the postwar conditions that they are trying to create. War is only a
means and not the end in itself. Unfortunately, we
have seen examples in history of the political leadership that became so deeply engrossed in the war
itself that the goals to be achieved were completely
ignored. This results in the surrender of the political guidance of the state to the military operations of the minute. Clausewitz warned against this:

Accordingly, war can never be separated from political intercourse, and if, in the consideration of the matter, this occurs anywhere, all the threads of the different relations are, in a certain sense, broken, and we have before us a senseless thing without an object.[4]

What is ultimately important is the political impact of military actions.

In past wars, the political objective was rarely Total Victory. The glaring exceptions are the Religious Wars with their fanatical, moral overtones. World War I, with its complicated alliances, became bogged down both in the trenches and in the minds of the political leadership. The armistice-surrender of 1918, an armistice the likes of which the world had never seen and will probably never see again, was not a solution to the problem. It was only a postponement. The enormous price paid was not commensurate with the political objectives obtained. The great legacy of the First World War was the Russian Revolution. The inept handling of that crisis by the Allies faced the world with the greatest challenge yet encountered in the history of man.

Following the Industrial Revolution and the other great scientific advances of man, the Twentieth Century brought the era of Total War. Psychological warfare, economic warfare, and strategic bombing became commonplace. Strategic bombing was probably the most terrible addition made to the conduct of war. The obliteration of cities drastically changed the relationship of desired political objective and appropriate price to be paid. Although the techniques of strategic bombing came from military or pseudo-military people, it should be remembered that strategic bombing is a political decision. It can never be done without direction from the policy-making body of the government. This form of warfare is still much with us and has become more complicated due to the addition of nuclear weapons and intercontinental missiles. The complication is that these new weapons are so expensive and so devastating that they have little value against any target smaller than a city. They are in the category of nation-versus-nation weapons rather than the more normal army-versus-army weapons. It is difficult to find an army target appropriate for a megaton weapon.

UNCONDITIONAL SURRENDER

The policy of Unconditional Surrender certainly

502

played an important role in World War II. Unconditional Surrender means giving up a country with all its people, resources, history, government, and way of life to a foreign government with no assurance of what they will do with it in return. Is it any wonder that people have fought so hard against Unconditional Surrender? Would we surrender unconditionally to Communist Russia with their tyrannous form of government? I think not; we would rather fight to the bitter end. And they probably feel the same way.

The demand for Unconditional Surrender is basically emotional, displaying a moral approach to war. It is certainly not political where one is trying to continually balance the price required to be paid against the objective to be gained. It is in this type of war that we see the importance of propaganda; atrocity stories are fed to the people to keep their hate aroused, the enemy is characterized as the embodiment of all that is evil, and our own actions are cloaked with the mantle of goodness. This mass-produced hate has great power. Unfortunately, we came to believe our own propaganda in the Second War and made some important decisions based on propaganda rather than the facts of the world situation.

We prejudged all the peoples of the Axis as guilty; therefore, we set out on our holy mission to punish them and reconstruct their countries in our image. This moral basis was expressed in our demand for Unconditional Surrender and was the reason for our goal of Total Victory. American leadership suffered from a misinterpretation of Clausewitz to the effect that, upon the commencement of hostilities, the demands of politics should be subordinated to the military demands of the war. This abdication of political leadership mortgaged the peace and left the war without an objective. Clausewitz recognized this turnabout in the case of a war of pure hatred.

> That the political point of view should end completely when war begins would only be conceivable if wars were struggles of life or death, from pure hatred. As wars are in reality, they are, as we said before, only the manifestation of policy itself. The subordination of the political point of view to the military would be unreasonable, for policy has created the war; policy is the intelligent faculty, war only the instrument, and not the reverse. The subordination of the military point of view to

the political is, therefore, the only thing
which is possible.[5]

The refusal to modify the policy or to negotiate with the enemy showed the inflexibility of the
Casablanca formula. President Roosevelt saw World
War II as a civil war as evidenced by his continual
defense of his policy by referring to Grant and Lee
at Appomattox, even though he was mistaken in his
historical facts. A civil war is generally considered as a rebellious uprising against legal authority, whereas an international war is thought of as a
conflict between sovereign states. This difference
is important as the Allies tended to consider all
the Axis leaders as renegades rather than as leaders
of sovereign states.
Perhaps the major conclusion to be drawn is
that the leaders of the Western Allies, and particularly the United States, failed to understand that
war is an instrument of policy. They fought the war
valiantly but in a crusading spirit as if the war
itself was the important issue, and left many of the
important decisions to the military or until after
the war. The seizure of Berlin was more a political
question than military, but it was left to the military. The invasion route into Europe was the most
important political decision for the postwar world
yet it too was left to the military. Our great interests did not lie in France but rather in posi-
tioning ourselves so that the Red Army could not become dominant in Eastern and Central Europe. The
Western political leadership proved to be inadequate.
It is a basic tenet of leadership to know one's self
- and that should include one's allies - and then to
know one's adversaries. The leadership proved deficient in both.
The alliance with a dictatorship put a heavy
mortgage on the war long before it was over. This
basically destroyed the moral justification of the
war but it was glossed over and never admitted.
Roosevelt did everything he could to make the alliance with the Communists work. Also, he tolerated
no mention of any German opposition as that would
have disproved his theory that all Germans were
guilty, thereby destroying the moral basis of the
demand for Unconditional Surrender and Total Victory.
Unconditional Surrender caused the problems of
today's divided Germany and Berlin. If we had dealt
with Germany as an entity, rather than creating a
vacuum and dividing the country, there would be no

East Germany or East Berlin. The differences in the
handling of the occupations of Japan and Germany
point up the futility of reducing an enemy country
to a non-entity when there is not accord among allies. And since there is rarely full accord among
allies, the implementation of a policy of Unconditional Surrender by more than one nation is of doubtful wisdom.

It seems certain beyond doubt that the policy
of Unconditional Surrender and the quest for Total
Victory prolonged the war and resulted in stiffened
Axis resistance. As the Peace of 1919 brought only
a 20-year respite in hostilities, Unconditional Surrender brought an even shorter respite when the Free
and Communist Worlds quickly evidenced their incom-
patibilities in almost all fields. The three main
Axis powers are all presently very closely linked
with the Western nations, tending to prove that the
aim of smashing them was not in our best interests,
particularly since we had to pay to rebuild them.
Since we only wanted to reorient their governments
rather than assimilate their countries, it seems it
could have been done much more efficiently. This is
somewhat like not liking the color of paint on a
neighbor's house. So you burn his house to the
ground, then rebuild it, refurnish it, and put the
color of paint on it you like. Perhaps it would
have been cheaper to have given him a few cans of
paint.

The communications difficulties between Premier
Khrushchev and President Kennedy during the Cuban
crisis of October 1962 pointed up the importance of
keeping open the channels of communications between
belligerents or potential belligerents. Since war
is a policy of trying to force another nation to
change its policy, it appears ridiculous to try to
change someone's mind and then refuse to talk to him
to see if he is willing to comply. Washington and
Moscow acknowledged this important lesson with the
installation of their "hot line." Hopefully we will
soon have such a line to Peking. Perhaps the major
lesson learned from recent wars is the requirement
for open communications between belligerents. It
would seem to be the height of folly for nations to
break diplomatic relations because times of crisis
are when direct communications are most needed.
Open communications, combined with intelligence information, are necessary to understand the true
situation. The perceptions that are the basis of
determining enemy intentions and friendly interests
are the key to what Victory can be!

505

The great winner of both world wars was world
Communism. World War I permitted the birth of the
first Communist state. World War II permitted the
great expansion of this new form of totalitarianism.
It is no wonder, then, that Communist leaders claim
that a third world war could not help but give them
more influence in the world, since Communism thrives
on unrest and turmoil. The only fear that complicates their reasoning now is the possible use of
nuclear weapons. They could cause ruinous damage to
the homeland and it has long been a basic Communist
tenet not to gamble the homeland when trying to expand.

VICTORY NOW

The advent of nuclear weapons has had no direct
influence on most wars. The effect of these weapons
has been on the role of the nuclear powers themselves if they were not in agreement. Thus they
have been able to deter each other in certain crises.
The Soviets deterred the West from intervening in
Eastern Europe. Fear of direct confrontation led
the Soviets to restrain their direct participation
in Korea and to be extremely careful of their roles
in Southeast Asia and the Middle East. For, as the
note on the State Department briefing room wall said
during the Cuban Missile Crisis, "In a Nuclear Age,
nations must make war as porcupines make love - very
carefully."
The crusade syndrome whereby Democracy fights
only a righteous crusade has not been characteristic
of the Cold War. In both Korea and Viet-Nam, American political leadership returned to Clausewitz and
applied the military instrument as a subordinate
part of political policy. However, Clausewitz was
never faced with the problems of a democracy fighting a limited war. The results were disastrous in
terms of domestic politics for the party in power.
In each case the incumbent President did not stand
for reelection and his party subsequently lost the
election. This leads to the disturbing proposition:
Can Democracy fight a political war or is it doomed
to fight only crusades? To overcome the crusade
syndrome will require a major improvement in the political maturity of a Democracy, a change that does
not appear to be on the horizon. For, as Hans
Morgenthau wrote, "We still think about foreign policy in demonological terms and allow our actions to
be influenced by them."[6]
There has been ample recognition of the problem.

Raymond Aron wrote: "If the cold war should unfortunately develop into open and general war, let us hope that this time statesmen will not let themselves be carried away by the blind fury of combat, but will remember that the object is not to crush the enemy but to attain certain political ends after the war. There are ways of conquering that quickly transform victory into defeat."[7] This was officially noted in the U.S. Army over a century ago. War Department General Order No. 100, April 1863, stated: "Modern wars are not internecine wars in which the killing of the enemy is the object. The destruction of the enemy in modern war, and, indeed modern war itself, are means to obtain that object of the belligerent which lies beyond the war." In the nuclear context, General Gavin wrote that it is no longer true "that something shining and definite called 'victory' can be achieved by destroying enough people and property."[8] The victories that are acceptable come through quiet diplomacy, which Dean Rusk believed were victories without triumphs. The deterrence of war, particularly nuclear war, has become a major objective. Therefore, "Deterrence of war and the attainment of political objectives must be recognized as 'victory,' at even the lowest tactical level."[9]

This more pragmatic doctrine of war, particularly required for the conduct of limited war in the nuclear era, is what Morris Janowitz has termed the "constabulary concept." Constabulary forces are continuously prepared to act, committed to the minimum use of force, and to seek viable international relations rather than victory.[10] Adding to the complexity of modern warfare is the difficult requirement for integration of military operations with political, economic, psychological, and sociological measures.

As much as we might hope for a peaceful world, the Cold War, unfortunately, continues. The Russians continue their support of the North Vietnamese as well as the radical Arabs in the volatile Middle East. The Red Chinese have entered the United Nations but, in their opening speech, they hurled invective at the United States (and some at the Soviets too plus a later scathing attack on the Russians) and claimed that the world was ready for revolution. The Soviet desires for the 1970s may well be as Sir Robert Thompson expressed them: "managed instability within the illusion of a detente."[11] They appear to have been quite successful.

The implementation of the Nixon Doctrine

drastically reduced American involvement around the world. President Nixon referred to his era of negotiations as he prepared to visit China and the Soviet Union as the "end of ideology." The Congress joined him by voting an end to Foreign Aid, partially as a result of the United Nations vote that expelled Taiwan and more as a manifestation of the American weariness of paying more than everyone else for so long.

In spite of protests to the contrary, a spirit of neo-isolationism evolved in the 1970s, not as in 1939, when Americans felt that world problems did not concern them, but through an indifference in which Americans did not care about world problems. Of course, this was a ridiculous development since nearly one-half of all world overseas investments were American. This same feeling drove America to voluntary armed forces, which may well become so reduced in conventional capability that it could easily return the United States to a massive retaliation strategy.

THE FUTURE

Where does the world go now? The great antagonism continues to smoulder in the world between two opposing ideologies. "Marxism must surely stand in our time as the spectacular flop of history as prophecy."[12] Yet such a distinguished historian as Arnold Toynbee regretfully concluded that Lenin's career might be the "wave of the future." Toynbee saw a certain legitimacy in dictatorship because it "has often been accepted as a lesser evil than anarchy in times of very revolutionary change" since the characteristics of democracy are "spiritual luxuries" of tranquil and secure times. For Toynbee, "the conditions of the world today are pretty like the condition of Russia in Lenin's lifetime. We have worldwide anarchy today - nationalism, racialism, inflation, sabotage of all kinds, the generation-war, the revolt of the under-dog, the pollution of the natural environment by technology. Any one of those things is enough to hoist a dictator into power, and we have them all." He, therefore, felt the world was ripe for a coming world dictatorship.[13]

In earlier times, these opposing ideologies would already have clashed in war. However, the nuclear stalemate has complicated the problem; there is less interest in a big war, yet it always looms menacingly in the background. A nuclear war could destroy or reduce the belligerent nations with a resultant elevation of other, unaffected, powers.

Victory can be had perhaps between lesser nations or between one of the giants and a smaller state (if it is not directly supported by the other giant). However, victory, in the larger sense, appears impracticable at this time between the giants while they possess the capacity to cripple each other. President Kennedy said that agreement could be reached on major issues between the two blocs but the Communists moved extremely slowly to resolve them as they continued to push for world domination. Mr. Kennedy said:

> "For we seek not the world-wide victory of one nation or system but a world-wide victory of man. The modern globe is too small, its weapons too destructive, and its disorders too contagious to permit any other kind of victory."[14]

Though the big war could come at any time, it appears to be stalemated. However, this has not stopped the small wars that have raged unceasingly since 1945. As Liddell Hart pointed out: "It is essential to realize that while the H-bomb has become a check on the deliberate launching of an all-out attack, it has not reduced the possibilities of limited war to the same extent, and may even increase them."[15]

It has been said that the best way to win a war is to prevent it from occurring. Our best efforts are and should be devoted to the prevention of war. The United States has been a major force for peace; and war, when necessary, is waged not to win a war, but to win a peace. But peace, as such, is not the prime politcal goal, for it may mean peace for one side and not the other. It can mean an imperial peace or a Communist peace, most convenient to those in power but perhaps slavery to others. There are other goals such as Freedom or Justice or Human Dignity or a Higher Standard of Living that could reasonably claim a higher priority. There are many kinds of freedom. The objective, then, is not just peace, but a just peace, qualified by respect for human life, civil liberties, and social justice even though we realize there can be debate about the definition of these rights.[16]

Victory has long been a siren drawing men onto the rocks of war and it appears likely to continue to do so in the future. For, as long as international anarchy, known as the nation-state system, persists, there will be conflicts between nations that will not be settled peacefully. Victory in war

509

is relative. It is a function of the political objective attained and the price paid. To some extent,
Victory may be psychological; thus, face-saving devices can play a significant role in separating defeat from victory. Through patient and sincere efforts, there can be peace without victory. As a
rule though, with the emotional bluster so characteristic of man, there is more apt to be victory
without peace.

Victory in nuclear war is a chimera. Gone are
the days of the fight for glory or a place in the
sun; yet war is a continuing part of life for man.
However, the use of military power is supposed to
accomplish ends other than victory; indeed, victory,
however defined, is not an end in itself, but simply
a means to other ends of policy. Rational victory
in war, then, is the attainment of specific political objectives at appropriate price or the creation
of conditions which enhance the probability of the
attainment of political goals. As long as man tries
to impose his will on his fellow man, there will be
war. As long as there is war, there will be a quest
for victory.

War is an ugly thing, but not the
ugliest. The decayed and degraded
state of moral and patriotic feeling
which thinks nothing is worth a war
is worse. A man who has nothing
which he cares about more than his
personal safety is a miserable creature and has no chance of being free,
unless made and kept so by the
exertions of better men than himself.

-- John Stuart Mill

NOTES

1. Arthur M. Schleisinger, Jr., A Thousand Days, p. 391.
2. Quoted in General Maxwell D. Taylor, Responsibility and Response, pp. 32-33.
3. Clausewitz, On War, pp. 594-601.
4. Ibid., p. 596.
5. Ibid., p. 598.
6. Hans J. Morgenthau, "Changes and Chances in American-Soviet Relations," Foreign Affairs, April 1971, p. 433.
7. Aron, The Century of Total War, p. 158.
8. James M. Gavin, with Arthur T. Hadley, Crisis Now (New York: Random House, 1968) p. 12.
9. Robert G. Gard, Jr., "The Military and American Society," Foreign Affairs, July 1971, p. 704.
10. Janowitz, The Professional Soldier (New York: The Free Press, 1960), p. 418.
11. Thompson, Revolutionary War in World Strategy, p. 147.
12. Arthur M. Schleisinger, Jr., The Bitter Heritage (Boston: Houghton Mifflin Co., 1967) p. 87.
13. Toynbee, "A Centenary View of Lenin," International Affairs, July 1970, pp. 496-497.
14. New York Herald Tribune, European Edition, 15 January 1963.
15. Liddell Hart, Deterrent or Defense, p. 62.
16. See Catlin, What Does the West Want, pp. 17-19.

Appendixes

Appendix 1. Positions of Selected American Officials

James F. Byrnes

U.S. Senator 1930-1941
Associate Justice of Supreme Court
1941-1942
Director of Economic Stabiliza-
tion 1942-1943
Director of War Mobilization
1943-1945
Secretary of State 1945-1947

General of the Army
Dwight D. Eisenhower

Supreme Commander Allied Expedi-
tionary Forces 1942-1945
Chief of Staff, U.S. Army 1945-48
Supreme Commander NATO 1950-52
President of the U.S. 1953-1961

James V. Forrestal

Under Secretary of Navy 1940-44
Secretary of Navy 1944-1947
The first Secretary of Defense
1947-1949

Joseph C. Grew

Ambassador to Japan 1931-1941
State Department 1942-1944
Under Secretary of State 1944-45

Averell Harriman

Chief Administrator Lend-Lease
(Europe) 1941
Ambassador to Soviet Union 1943-46
Ambassador to England 1946
Secretary of Commerce 1946-1948
Ambassador-at-large in command of
European Recovery Program 1948
Head of Mutual Assistance Program
1952

Harry Hopkins

Secretary of Commerce 1938-1940
In charge of Lend-Lease admini-
stration 1941
Special Assistant to President
Roosevelt 1942-1945

Cordell Hull

Secretary of State 1933-1944
Nobel Peace Price 1945

George F. Kennan

Career diplomat, served in Europe
Ambassador to Soviet Union 1952-53
Ambassador to Yugoslavia 1961-63

515

Fleet Admiral William D. Leahy	Chief of Naval Operations 1937-39 Ambassador to Vichy France 1940-42 Chief of Staff to Presidents Roosevelt and Truman 1942-1949

General of the Army
Douglas MacArthur
	Chief of Staff, U.S. Army 1930-35
	Assisted Philippine Army 1937-41
	Supreme Commander Allied Forces
	  Southwest Pacific 1942-1945
	Supreme Allied Commander Japan
	  1945-1951
	Supreme Commander UN Forces Korea
	  1950-1951

General of the Army George C. Marshall	Chief of Staff, U.S. Army 1939-45 Ambassador to China 1945 Secretary of State 1947-1949 (Marshall Plan) Secretary of Defense 1950-1951
Henry Morgenthau	Secretary of Treasury 1934-1945
Franklin D. Roosevelt	President of the U.S. 1933-1945
Edward R. Stettinius, Jr.	Under Secretary of State 1940 Lend-Lease Administratory 1943 Secretary of State 1944-1945 (attended Yalta Conference) Delegate to UN 1945-1946
Henry L. Stimson	Secretary of War 1911-13, 1940-45 Secretary of State 1929-1933
Harry S. Truman	U.S. Senator 1935-1945 Vice President of U.S. 1945 President of the U.S. 1945-1953
Henry Wallace	Vice President of U.S. 1941-1945
Sumner Welles	Assistant Secretary of State 1933-1937 Under Secretary of State 1937-43

Appendix 2. Army Intelligence Division Study Opposing
Soviet Entry in Pacific War

"The conflict reached a decisive head on April 12
when a group of senior officers of the War Department's
intelligence service presented to Marshall a strongly
phrased study opposing the Soviet entry and, because of his
well-known view that Japan was facing imminent collapse,
urging that MacArthur be brought back to discuss the matter
directly before the President.

'1. The entry of Soviet Russia into the Asiatic War
would be a political event of world-shaking importance,
the ill effect of which would be felt for decades to come,'
the report stated. Then it went on: 'Its military significance at this stage of the war would be relatively
unimportant.

'2. Many military experts believe that the United
States and Great Britain, without further help, possess the
power to force unconditional surrender upon Japan or to occupy the island and mainland possessions.

'3. It may be expected that Soviet Russia will enter
the Asiatic War, but at her own good time and probably
only when the hard fighting stage is over. [It is interesting to note that we deplored considering this between Russia and Germany.]

'4. The entry of Soviet Russia into the Asiatic War
at so late a moment would shorten hostilities but little,
and effect only a slight saving of American lives.

'5. It is not believed any diplomatic action we can
take or fail to take, or any concession we make now or in
the forseeable future, will influence Soviet Russia to
speed up or retard entry into the Asiatic War. [It took
the atomic bombs and the impending surrender to get them
to hurry in before it was over.]

'6. Strong enough to crush Japan ourselves, the
United States should make no political or economic concession to Soviet Russia to bring about or prevent an action
which she is determined to take anyway.

'7. The entry of Soviet Russia into the Asiatic War
would destroy America's position in Asia quite as effectively as our position is now destroyed in Europe east of
the Elbe and beyond the Adriatic.

517

'8. If Russia enters the Asiatic War, China will certainly lose her independence to become the Poland of Asia; Korea, the Asiatic Romania; Manchukuo, the Soviet Bulgaria. Whether more than a nominal China will exist after the impact of the Russian armies is felt very doubtful. Chiang may well have to depart and a Chinese government may be installed in Nanking which we would have to recognize.

'9. To take a line of action which would save a few lives now, and only a little time - and simultaneously destroy our ally China, would be an act of treachery that would make the Atlantic Charter and our hopes for world peace a tragic farce.

'10. Under no circumstances should we pay the Soviet Union to destroy China. This would certainly injure the material and moral position of the United States in Asia.

'11. It should be reiterated that the United States Army is by no means united in believing it wise to encourage the Soviet Union to enter the Asiatic War.

'12. The President of the United States would be well advised, before he made any commitments to Russia in Asia which would clearly have dire political and moral consequences for the United States, to consult that particular American field commander who is steeped in every phase of the Asiatic War and in the political background of that struggle.'

"After reciting these courageous and prophetic conclusions, the officers' group then recommended to Marshall: 'General MacArthur should be summoned to Washington immediately. The President should consider the all-important matter of Soviet Russia's entry into the Asiatic War with General MacArthur eye to eye. All other political and military personages should be excluded from the conference.'"

General Whitney ended with, "Had their views prevailed and their recommendations been adopted, the country might have been spared one of the most tragic blunders in its history."* As we know though, Roosevelt, with General Marshall's support, had given away all of those concessions months earlier at Yalta.

This does point up though that not all military men are stupid and politically naive as it is so commonplace to hear them referred to by the civilian members of government.
*Whitney, MacArthur, pp. 200-201, my italics.

Bibliography

BIBLIOGRAPHY

GENERAL

Military Works

Angell, Sir Norman. The Great Illusion Now. Harmondsworth: Penguin Books, Limited, 1938.

Comments on his book of 1908 on the futility of war.

Aron, Raymond. The Century of Total War, Garden City, New York: Doubleday & Co., Inc., 1954.

A brilliant survey of warfare from World War I to the cold war era with a good critique of the inept handling of World War II.

Bernard, L. L. War and Its Causes. New York: Henry Holt & Co., 1943.

A sociological study of war.

Clausewitz, Karl von. On War. Translated from the German by O. J. Matthijs Jolles. New York: The Modern Library, 1943.

Still a classic work on war, particularly famous for his comments on politics and war.

Clausewitz, General Carl von. Principles of War. Translated and edited by Hans W. Gatzke. Harrisburg, Pa.: Military Service Publishing Co., 1943.

Essay he wrote for Prussian Crown Prince Frederick William.

Cline, Ray S. Washington Command Post: The Operations Division. Washington, D.C.: Office of the Chief of Military History, Department of the Army, 1951.

Daugherty, William E. and Janowitz, Morris. A Psychological Warfare Casebook. Baltimore: Johns Hopkins Press, 1958.

An excellent compilation and analysis of past psychological warfare operations and their methods, techniques, and achievements.

Doenitz, Admiral. Memoirs. Ten Years and Twenty Days. Translated by R.H. Stevens. London: Weidenfeld and Nicolson, 1959.

Dupuy, R. Ernest. *Men of West Point. The First 150 years of the United States Military Academy.* New York: William Sloane Associates, 1951.

Study of famous graduates of USMA.

Earle, Edward M., ed. *Makers of Modern Strategy: Military Thought from Machiavelli to Hitler.* New York: Atheneum, 1966, originally published by Princeton in 1941.

Fuller, Major-General J.F.C. *Armored Warfare.* Harrisburg, Pa.: Military Service Publishing Co., 1943.

Series of lectures prepared originally in 1932.

_____. *The Conduct of War 1789-1961.* New Brunswick, New Jersey: Rutgers University Press, 1961.

An excellent study of war with good critiques of World War II and the Cold War.

_____. *A Military History of the Western World.* 3 Vols. New York: Funk & Wagnalls, 1954-1956.

Excellent study of war from early times through World War II; covers many of the key political factors.

Gard, Robert G. Jr. "The Military and American Society." *Foreign Affairs* July 1971, p. 698.

Gavin, Lieutenant General James M. *War and Peace in the Space Age.* New York: Harper & Brothers, 1958.

Hancock, William Keith. *Four Studies of War and Peace in this Century.* Cambridge: University Press, 1961.

Kahn, Herman. *On Thermonuclear War.* Princeton, N. J.: Princeton University Press, 1960.

Kingston-McCloughry, Air Vice-Marshal Edgar J. *The Direction of War; A Critique of the Political Direction and High Command in War.* London: J. Cape, 1955.

Lea, Homer. *The Valor of Ignorance.* New York: Harper & Brothers, 1942.

A fabulous book originally published in 1909 by a little hunchback who predicted the U.S.-Japanese war well before World War II.

Leighton, Richard M. and Coakley, Robert W. Global Logistics and Strategy 1940-1943. Washington, D.C.: Office of the Chief of Military History, Department of the Army, 1955.

Liddell Hart, B. H. Deterrent or Defense: A Fresh Look at the West's Military Position. New York: Frederick A. Praeger, Publishers, 1960.

_____. Strategy. Second Revised Edition. New York: Frederick A. Praeger, Publishers, 1967.

MacArthur, General of the Army Douglas. Reminiscences. New York: McGraw-Hill Book Company, 1964.

Matloff, Maurice and Snell, Edwin M. Strategic Planning for Coalition Warfare 1941-42. Washington, D.C.: Office of the Chief of Military History, Department of the Army, 1953.

Matloff, Maurice. Strategic Planning for Coalition Warfare 1943-1944. Washington, D.C.: Office of the Chief of Military History, Department of the Army, 1959.

Millis, Walter. Arms and Men: A Study of American Military History. New York: A Mentor Book, 1958.

   Good study of the relationship of military forces and the developing political situation in a democracy.

Morton, Louis. Strategy and Command: The First Two Years; The War in the Pacific. Washington, D.C.: Office of the Chief of Military History, Department of the Army, 1962.

Pogue, Forrest C. The Supreme Command; The European Theater of Operations. Washington, D.C.: Office of the Chief of Military History, Department of the Army, 1954.

Ridgway, General Matthew B. Soldier: The Memoirs of Matthew B. Ridgway. New York: Harper & Brothers, 1956.

Thompson, Brigadier General William J. "Muzzle on the Military Mind." Army, February 1962, pp. 32-37.

   Shows how pre-World War II U.S. Army kept out of politics.

Vagts, Alfred. Defense and Diplomacy; The Soldier and the Conduct of Foreign Relations. New York: King's Crown Press, 1958.

   Detailed historical work; however, his presentation of MacArthur casts doubts on his unbiased over-all approach.

Wright, Philip Quincy. The Causes of War and the Conditions of Peace. London: Longmans, Green & Co., 1935.

_____. A Study of War. 2 Vols. Chicago: University of Chicago Press, 1944.

Zuckerman, Sir Solly. "Judgment and Control in Modern Warfare." Foreign Affairs, January 1962, pp. 196-212.

An article concerning employment of nuclear weapons in modern warfare.

Politics and International Relations

Aron, Raymond. Peace and War; A Theory of International Relations. Translated from the French by Richard Howard and Annette Baker Fox. New York: Frederick A. Praeger, Publishers, 1966.

Blum, Robert. The United States and China in World Affairs. New York: McGraw-Hill Book Company, 1966.

Brockway, Thomas P. Basic Documents in United States Foreign Policy. Princeton: D. Van Nostrand Co., Inc., 1957.

Brzezinski, Zbigniew and Huntington, Samuel P. Political Power: USA/USSR; Similarities and contrasts; Convergence or Evolution. New York: The Viking Press, 1963.

Catlin, George E. G. What Does the West Want? A Study of Political Goals. London: Phoenix House, 1957.

Chaumont, Charles. L'O.N.U. Paris: Presses Universitaires, 1957.

A general work on the United Nations.

Coyle, David Cushman. The United Nations and How it Works. New York: A Mentor Book, 1958.

Ebenstein, William. Great Political Thinkers. New York: Rinehart & Co., Inc., 1951.

Eisenhower, Dwight D. The White House Years. 2 Vols. Garden City, New York: Doubleday & Co., Inc.:
Mandate for Change 1953-1956   (1963),
Waging Peace 1956-1961   (1965).

Encyclopédie Française. Tome XI. La Vie Internationale. Paris: Société Nouvelle de l'Encyclopédie Française, Libraire Larousse, Dépositaire Générale, 1957.

524

Much on history but the section on strategy is particularly good.

Fauchille, Paul. Traité de Droit International Public.
Tome II. Paris: Rousseau, 1921.

Good for discussion of armistice and peace treaty.

Gerbet, Pierre. Les Organisations Internationales. Paris:
Presses Universitaires de France, 1958.

Gould, Wesley L. An Introduction to International Law. New
York: Harper & Brothers, 1957.

Green, L.C. International Law Through the Cases. London:
Stevens & Sons Limited, 1959.

Useful for the Nuremburg Judgment.

Hoffmann, Stanley. The State of War; Essays on the Theory
and Practice of International Politics. New York:
Frederick A. Praeger, Publishers, 1965.

Jacobsen, G.A. and Lipman, M.H. Political Science. New York:
Barnes & Noble, Inc., 1959.

Kennan, George F. American Diplomacy 1900-1950. Chicago:
The University of Chicago Press, 1951.

_____. Memoirs 1925-1950. Boston: Little, Brown, &
Co., 1967.

Langer, William L. "Political Problems of a Coalition."
Foreign Affairs, October 1947, pp. 73-89.

Mills, C. Wright. The Power Elite. New York: Oxford University Press, 1957.

A hard-hitting book on American political, economic, and
military leaders who he says are a clique which he calls
the power elite.

Morgenthau, Hans J. Politics Among Nations; The Struggle for
Power and Peace. 3rd ed. New York: Alfred A. Knopf, 1965.

Padelford, Norman J. and Lincoln, George A. The Dynamics of
International Politics. 2nd ed., 1967. New York: The
Macmillan Company, 1962.

Palmer, Norman D. and Perkins, Howard C. International Relations: The World Community in Transition. Boston: Houghton Mifflin Co., 1953.

Peaselee, Amos J. International Governmental Organizations.
2 Vols. The Hague: Martinus Nijhoff, 1961.

Brief explanation, constitutions, and basic documents on
international organizations (NATO, UN, SEATO, CENTO,
ANZUS, etc.).

Prélot, Marcel. Histoires des Idées Politiques. Paris:
Dalloz, 1961.

Renouvin, Pierre. Histoire des Relations Internationales.
8 Vols. Paris: Librairie Hachette, 1958.

Reuter, Paul. International Institutions. Translated from
French by J.M. Chapman. New York: Frederick A. Praeger,
Publishers, 1961.

Rostow, W. W. The United States in the World Arena; An Essay
in Recent History. New York: Harper & Row, Publishers,
1960.

Rousseau, Ch. Droit International Public Approfondi. Paris:
Dalloz, 1961.

Sabine, George H. A History of Political Theory. 3rd ed.
London: Harrap & Co., Ltd., 1959.

Last two chapters good for Communism, Nazism, and Fascism.

History

Churchill, Winston S. A History of the English Speaking
Peoples. 4 Vols. New York: Dodd, Mead & Co., 1956-1958.

Clyde, Paul Hibbert. The Far East: A History of the Impact
of the West on Eastern Asia. New York: Prentice-Hall,
Inc., 1952.

Hubbard, Alice, ed. An American Bible. East Aurora, New
York: The Roycrofters, 1918.

Excerpts of writings of Benjamin Franklin, Thomas Jeffer-
son, Thomas Paine, Abraham Lincoln, Walt Whitman, Robert
Ingersoll, Ralph Waldo Emerson, and Elbert Hubbard.

Kirchner, Walther. A History of Russia. New York: Barnes &
Noble, Inc., 1962.

Landman, J. H. and Wender, Herbert. World Since 1914. New
York: Barnes & Noble, Inc., 1959.

Littlefield, Henry W. History of Europe Since 1815. New
    York: Barnes & Noble, Inc., 1961.

Miller, William. A New History of the United States. New
    York: George Braziller, Inc., 1958.

    Interesting new history - often critical - not the glossy,
    grammar school type.

Palmer, R. R. A History of the Modern World. New York:
    Alfred A. Knopf, 1952.

    _____, ed. Atlas of World History. New York: Rand
    McNally & Co., 1957.

Tocqueville, Alexis de. Democracy in America. edited and
    abridged by Richard D. Heffner. New York: The New Ameri-
    can Library, A Mentor Book, 1956.

Toynbee, Arnold J. A Study of History. 2 Vols. New York:
    Oxford University Press, 1956-1957.

    Abridgement of original monumental ten volumes to two
    by D. C. Somervell.

Economics

Despres, Emile; Friedman, Milton; Hart, Albert G.; Samuelson,
    Paul A.; and Wallace, Donald H. "The Problem of Economic
    Instability." The American Economic Review, Vol. XL,
    September 1950, Number Four.

    Article by some top economists.

James, Clifford L. Principles of Economics. New York:
    Barnes & Noble, Inc., 1960.

Lincoln, George A. Economics of National Security. New
    York: Prentice-Hall, Inc., 1954.

Samuelson, Paul A. Economics. 2d ed. New York: McGraw-Hill
    Book Co., Inc., 1951.

PAST WARS

Catton, Bruce. A Stillness at Appomattox. Garden City, New
    York: Doubleday & Co., Inc., 1954.

    _____. This Hallowed Ground; The Story of the Union
    Side of the Civil War. Garden City, New York, Doubleday &
    Co., Inc., 1956.

527

Creasy, Sir Edward S. Fifteen Decisive Battles of the World. Edited with nine new chapters by Robert Hammond Murray. Harrisburg, Pa.: Military Service, 1943.

Department of Military Art and Engineering, USMA. Great Captains Before Napoleon. West Point, New York: USMA, 1952.

_____. Jomini, Clausewitz and Schlieffen. West Point, New York: USMA, 1951.

_____. Summaries of Selected Military Campaigns. West Point, New York: USMA, 1953.

Keller, Werner. The Bible as History: A Confirmation of the Book of Books. Translated by William Neil. New York: William Morrow & Co., 1956.

Archaeological study of the Bible and history.

Lanza, Colonel Conrad H. Napoleon and Modern War - His Military Maxims. Harrisburg, Pa.: Military Service Publishing Co., 1943.

Phillips, Major Thomas R., ec. Roots of Strategy. Harrisburg, Pa.: Military Service Publishing Co., 1940.

Works of Sun Tzu, Vegetius, Saxe, Frederick the Great, and Napoleon. Many are as pertinent today as they were hundreds of years ago or even B.C. in the case of Sun Tzu.

Randall, J.G. The Civil War and Reconstruction. Boston: D. C. Heath & Co., 1953.

Extensive study of the political aspects of the Civil War and the postwar phase.

Steele, Matthew Forney. American Campaigns. Washington, D.C.: Combat Forces Press, 1951.

Swanberg, W. A. First Blood: The Story of Fort Sumter. New York: Charles Scribner's Sons, 1957.

Wartenburg, Count Yorck von. Napoleon as a General. Seventh book of the Wolseley Series. Edited by Major Walter H. James. 2 Vols. London: Gilbert & Rivington, Ltd., n.d.

Williams, T. Harry. Lincoln and His Generals. New York: Grosset & Dunlap, 1952.

Woodham-Smith, Cecil. The Reason Why. New York: McGraw-
Hill Book Co., Inc., 1954.

History of the charge of the Light Brigade in the Crimean
War.

WORLD WAR I

Brooke, Charles F. T., ed. War Aims and Peace Ideals. New
Haven: Yale University Press, 1919.

Selections in prose and verse of aspirations of modern
world.

Carnegie Endowment for International Peace. The Cost of War.
Washington, D. C.: 1940.

Churchill, Winston S. The World Crisis 1911-1918. London:
Macmillan, 1943.

Horne, Charles F. Editor-in-Chief. Source Records of the
Great War. 7 Vols. Indianapolis: The American Legion,
1930.

Extensive compilation of parts written by people on both
sides.

Moorehead, Alan. The Russian Revolution. New York: Harper
& Brothers, 1958.

Stamps, T. Dodson and Esposito, Vincent J. eds. A Short Military History of World War I. West Point, New York: United
States Military Academy, 1950.

WORLD WAR II

Political Aspects

Baldwin, Hanson W. Great Mistakes of the War. New York:
Harper & Brothers, 1950.

Beveridge, William. The Price of Peace. London: Pilot, 1945.

Byrnes, James F. Speaking Frankly. New York: Harper &
Brothers, 1947.

Churchill, Winston S. The Second World War. 6 Vols. Boston:
Houghton Mifflin Co., 1948-1953.

_____. _Step by Step 1936-1939_. London: Macmillan, 1943.

Churchill's views as war approached - mainly calling for
the nation to get ready for it.

_____. _War Speeches '42_. Compiled by Charles Eade.
London: Cassel & Co., 1943.

Ciano, Comte, _Archives secrètes_. Paris: Plon, 1948.

Coverage of period 1936-1942 particularly Italian relations with Germany.

_____. _Journal politique_. 2 Vols. Paris: Presses
Française et Etrangère, 1946.

The diary from 1939-1942 of the Italian Foreign Minister;
good view of German-Italian difficulties.

Einzig, Paul. _Can We Win the Peace_? London: Macmillan, 1942.

Review of the Atlantic Charter. He saw need for economic disarmament and division of Germany.

Goodrich, L.M. ed. _Documents on American Foreign Relations_.
Boston: World Peace Foundation, 1942.

Grew, Joseph C. _Ten Years in Japan_. New York: Simon &
Schuster, 1944.

Good review and insight of American-Japanese relations
because Grew was Ambassador in Japan 1932-1942.

_____. _Turbulent Era; A Diplomatic Record of Forty
Years 1904-1945_. 2 Vols. Boston: Houghton Mifflin, 1952.

Particularly important for American-Japanese relations
before World War II and his role before Japan surrendered
in urging retention of the Emperor.

Gunther, John. _Roosevelt in Retrospect; A Profile in History_.
New York: Harper & Brothers, 1950.

Hull, Cordell. _The Memoirs of Cordell Hull_. 2 Vols. New York:
Macmillan Co., 1948.

International Military Tribunal for the Far East. _Record of
Proceedings_. 148 Vols. Tokyo: 1946-1948.

Ivanyi, B.G. _Route to Potsdam; The Story of the Peace Aims
1939-1945_. London: A. Wingate, 1945.

King-Hall, Stephen. Total Victory. New York: Harcourt Brace
& Co., 1942.

Leahy, Admiral William D. I Was There. New York: Whittlesey
House, 1950.

The war as viewed by the Chief of Staff to Roosevelt.

Lippmann, Walter. U.S. Foreign Policy: Shield of the Republic. Boston: Little, Brown & Co., 1943.

Review and critique of U.S. Foreign Policy in the 20th
Century - great foresight about problems of Eastern
Europe and relations with the Russians.

_____. U.S. War Aims. London: H. Hamilton, 1944.

Noted that the Atlantic Community was already leery
of the Russians.

Millis, Walter. ed. with the collaboration of E. S. Duffield,
The Forrestal Diaries. New York: Viking Press, 1951.

Morgenthau, Henry Jr. Germany is Our Problem. New York:
Harper & Brothers, 1945.

Complete text and justification for Morgenthau Plan for
destruction of German industry; a basic reference for
the Morgenthau Plan.

Neumann, William L. Making the Peace 1941-45; The Diplomacy
of the Wartime Conferences. Washington, D.C.: Foundation
for Foreign Affairs, 1950.

Post-War Peace Objectives. International Conciliation. New
York, February 1940, no. 357.

Prime Minister Chamberlain's radio speech 26 Nov 1939,
Lord Halifax's speech in the House of Lords, and a letter
from Roosevelt to the Pope. Their ideas in 1939 about
peace after the war.

Le procès de Nuremberg. 4 Vols. Paris: Office français, 1946.

Good short review of the Nuremberg Trials.

Procès des grands criminels de guerre devant le tribunal
militaire international. 42 Vols. Nuremberg: Texte officiel
en langue française, 1947.

Ranshofen-Wertheimer, Egon. Victory Is Not Enough: The Strategy for a Lasting Peace. New York: W.W. Norton, 1942.

Ideas on rehabilitation of Germany after the war.

Roosevelt, Elliott. As He Saw It. New York, Duell, Sloan & Pearce, 1946.

FDR's son accompanied the President to several of the Big Three meetings.

Russia. Ministry of Foreign Affairs of the U.S.S.R. Stalin's Correspondence with Churchill, Attlee, Roosevelt and Truman 1941-45. 2 Vols. Moscow: Foreign Languages Publishing House, 1957. Combined 1 Vol. New York: Dutton & Co., Inc., 1958.

Sherwood, Robert. Roosevelt and Hopkins. New York: Harper & Brothers, 1948.

Shirer, William L. The Rise and Fall of the Third Reich; A History of Nazi Germany. Greenwich, Conn.: Fawcett Publications, Inc., 1962.

Stettinius, Edward R. Jr. Roosevelt and the Russians: The Yalta Conference. Garden City, New York: Doubleday & Co., Inc., 1949.

Defense of Yalta Conference with important documents in appendices - Big Three statement, protocol and agreement for Russians to enter the Japanese war.

Stimson, Henry L. and Bundy, McGeorge. On Active Service in Peace and War. New York: Harper & Brothers, 1948.

Strauss, Harold. The Division and Dismemberment of Germany from the Casablanca Conference (Jan 43) to the establishment of the East German Republic (Oct 49). Ambilly: Les Presses de Savoie, 1952. Thesis, Geneva, 1951.

Toshikazu, Kase. Journey to the Missouri. New Haven: Yale University Press, 1950.

View of high level actions before and during World War II by a Japanese diplomat.

Truman, Harry S. Memoirs. 2 Vols. Garden City, New York: Doubleday & Co., Inc., 1955.
  Vol. I Year of Decisions,
  Vol. II Years of Trial and Hope 1946-1952.

U.S. Department of State. A Decade of American Foreign Policy (1941-49). Washington, D.C.: US Government Printing Office, 1950.

_____. Making the Peace Treaties, 1941-47. Washington, D.C.: 1947.

U.S. National Archives. Federal Records of World War II, 2 Vols. Washington, D.C.: 1950-51.

Lists military and civilian agencies during the war.

Welles, Sumner. The Time for Decision. New York: Harper & Brothers, 1944.

White, William S. Majesty and Mischief; A Mixed Tribute to FDR. New York: McGraw-Hill, 1961.

Winant, J.G. A Letter from Grosvenor Square. London: Hodder & Stoughton, 1948.

Early war period in England before Pearl Harbor by our Ambassador to London.

Woodward, Sir E. Llewellyn. British Foreign Policy in the Second World War. London: Her Majesty's Stationery Office, 1962.

Official British history - good.

Unconditional Surrender

Armstrong, Anne M. Unconditional Surrender; The Impact of the Casablanca Policy upon World War II. New Brunswick, New Jersey: Rutgers University Press, 1961.

Thorough study with extensive coverage of German sources.

Badoglio, Maréchal Pietro. L'Italie dans la guerre mondiale. Translated from Italian. Paris: SFELT, 1947.

Italian view, particularly good for their side of the Italian surrender.

Butow, R.J.C. Japan's Decision to Surrender. Stanford: Stanford University Press, 1954.

Excellent, detailed study of the Japanese surrender.

Craig, William. The Fall of Japan. New York: The Dial Press, 1967.

Excellent coverage of last weeks of the war.

Cuny, Jean. La capitulation sans conditions de l'Allemagne
    et ses precedents historiques. Berlin: Imprimerie
    Nationale, 1947. Law Thesis Paris 1946.

    View immediately after the war before many sources
    were available.

Glascow, George. "Foreign Affairs - Italy and the Settle-
    ment." The Contemporary Review. London, 164, October
    1943, pp. 243-249.

    Critical article on our poor handling of the Italian
    surrender.

Hankey, Lord M.P. Politics, Trials and Errors. Oxford:
    Pen-in-hand, 1950.

    Considers Unconditional Surrender and the War Crimes
    Trials as the greatest errors of the war.

Kecskemeti, Paul. Strategic Surrender: The Politics of Vic-
    tory and Defeat. Stanford: Stanford University Press,
    1958.

    Excellent study on surrender in war and the problems of
    total victory. The author theorizes that some bargaining
    power always remains on the losing side. He concludes
    our Unconditional Surrender formula was ill-conceived and
    develops this thesis in his studies of the French,
    Italian, German, and Japanese surrenders.

Miksche, Ferdinand O. Unconditional Surrender; the Roots of
    World War III. London: Faber & Faber, 1952.

    States that Unconditional Surrender is basis of present
    world problems.

Mourin, Maxime. Le drame des états satellites de l'Axe de
    1939 à 1945. Reddition sans conditions. Paris: Berger-
    Levrault, 1957.

    Excellent source with good bibliography on Unconditional
    Surrender and details of German and Japanese surrenders.

"Price of Unconditional Surrender." U.S. News 5 August 1949,
    pp. 26-28.

United States Strategic Bombing Survey. Japan's Struggle to
    End the War. Washington, D.C.: Government Printing Office,
    1946.

Very good coverage of political events leading to the
surrender.

Zemanek, Dr. K.F. "Unconditional Surrender and International
Law." Association des auditeurs et anciens auditeurs de
l'Academie de droit internationale de La Haye, _Annuaire_
26, 1956, pp. 29-37.

Development of the War

Bryant, Arthur. _The Turn of the Tide: A History of the War_
Years Based on the Diaries of Field-Marshal Lord Alan-
brooke, Chief of the Imperial General Staff. Garden City,
New York: Doubleday & Co., Inc. 1957.

Years 1939-43. There is a second volume for the remainder of the war.

Butcher, Harry. _My Three Years with Eisenhower_. New York:
Simon & Schuster, 1946.

Excellent view of General Eisenhower and British-
American relations by his naval aide.

Cartier, Raymond. _Les secrets de la guerre dévoilés par_
Nuremberg. Paris: Arthème Fayard, 1946.

Good study of Hitler.

Crankshaw, Edward. _Gestapo_. New York: Pyramid Books, 1957.

Davies, Joseph E. _Mission to Moscow_. New York: Simon &
Schuster, 1941.

By American Ambassador to Russia 1936-1938.

Deane, Major General John R. _The Strange Alliance; The Story_
of our Efforts at Wartime Co-operation with Russia. New
York: The Viking Press, 1950.

Eichelberger, Robert L., in collaboration with Milton MacKaye.
Our Jungle Road to Tokyo. New York: The Viking Press,
1950.

By a general who spent three years fighting in jungles
and three years in occupation of Japan.

Eisenhower, Dwight D. _Crusade in Europe_. Garden City, New
York: Doubleday & Co., Inc., 1948.

535

_____. Report by The Supreme Commander to the Combined Chiefs of Staff on the Operations in Europe of the Allied Expeditionary Force 6 June 1944 to 8 May 1945. Washington, D.C.: Government Printing Office, 1946.

Fleming, Peter. Operation Sea Lion: The Projected Invasion of England in 1940 - An Account of the German Preparations and the British Countermeasures. New York, Simon & Schuster, 1957.

Freidin, Seymour and Richardson, William. eds. The Fatal Decisions. Commentary by Siegfried Westphal. Translated from German by Constantine Fitzgibbon. New York: Berkley Publishing Corp., 1958.

Fuller, Major-General J.F.C. The Second World War. London: Eyre and Spottiswoode, 1948.

Gavin, Major General James M. Airborne Warfare. Washington, D.C.: Infantry Journal Press, 1947.

Gilbert, G.M. Nuremberg Diary. New York: Farar, Strauss and Company, 1947.

By a U.S. doctor who visited the top Nazis regularly in their cells and observed them during the trials.

Goebbels, J. The Goebbels Diaries. Edited, translated, and with an introduction by Louis P. Lochner. Garden City, New York: Doubleday, 1948.

Guderian, Heinz. Souvenirs d'un soldat. Translated from German by Francois Courtet with the collaboration of André Leclerc-Kohler. Paris: Plon, 1954.

Views of a senior German general, particularly good for his views on Hitler.

Howell, Edgar M. The Soviet Partisan Movement 1941-1944. Washington, D.C.: DA Pamphlet 20-244, August 1956.

Good on anti-partisan operations, particularly German mistakes.

James, David H. The Rise and Fall of the Japanese Empire. London: Allen & Unwin, 1951.

Kato, Masuo. The Lost War. New York: A.A. Knopf, 1946.

Good account written by a Japanese reporter who was in Washington on 7 Dec 1941 and then returned home.

Kernan, W.F. Defense Will Not Win the War. New York: Pocket Books, Inc., 1942.

Kirby, S. Woodburn. The War Against Japan. 3 Vols. Military History of World War II Series. London: H. M. Stationery Office, 1957.

Liddell Hart, B.H. The Other Side of the Hill: Germany's generals, their rise and fall, with their own account of military events 1939-45. London: Cassell, 1948. The American version is entitled German Generals Talk.

Lüdde-Neurath, Walter. Les derniers jours du troisième Reich; Le gouvernement de Doenitz. Translated from German by Rene Jouan. Paris: Berger-Levrault, 1950.

Story of period under Doenitz by an officer of his staff.

Manvell, Roger and Fraenkel, Heinrich. Dr: Goebbels: His Life and Death. London: Heinemann, 1960.

Marshall, General George C. The Winning of the War in Europe and the Pacific. Biennial Report of the Chief of Staff of the United States Army July 1, 1943 to June 30, 1945, to the Secretary of War. Washington, D.C.: Published for the War Department in Cooperation with the Council on Books in Wartime by Simon and Schuster, 1 September 1945.

Marshall, S.L.A. Men Against Fire. Washington, D.C.: Combat Forces Press, 1947.

Mishima, Sumie Seo. The Broader Way, A Woman's Life in the New Japan. London: Gollanez, 1954.

An interesting view of World War II and the occupation of Japan by a woman who studied in the U.S. for five years in the mid-1920s.

Montgomery, Bernard. The Memoirs of Field-Marshal Montgomery. Glasgow: Collins Sons, 1961.

Stamps, T. Dodson and Esposito, Vincent J. eds. A Military History of World War II. 2 Vols. West Point, New York: USMA, 1953.

Stilwell, General Joseph W. The Stilwell Papers. Arranged and edited by Theodore H. White. New York: MacFadden Book, 1962.

War Reports of General of the Army George C. Marshall, General of the Army H. H. Arnold and Fleet Admiral Ernest J. King.

Philadelphia: J. B. Lippincott, 1947.

Whitney, Major General Courtney. MacArthur. his Rendezvous with History. New York: A.A. Knopf, 1956.

Wilmot, Chester. The Struggle for Europe. New York: Harper Colophon Books, Harper & Row, 1963, first published in 1952.

Good coverage of the war in Europe with interesting conclusions at the end.

Strategic Bombing

Brittain, Vera. Seed of Chaos, What Mass Bombing Really Means. London: New Vision Publishing Co., 1944.

Book during the war against mass bombing with a detailed account city by city.

Dickens, Admiral Sir Gerald. Bombing and Strategy; The Fallacy of Total War. London: S. Low, Marston & Co., 1946.

A good attack on proponents of strategic bombing based on the principles of war.

Rumpf, Hans. The Bombing of Germany. Translated from the German by Edward Fitzgerald. New York: Holt, Rinehart and Winston, 1962.

Seversky, Alexander. Victory Through Air Power. London: Hutchinson, 1942.

Famous and important book early in World War II.

U.S. Federal Civil Defense Administration. Impact of Air Attack in World War II.

Exhaustive study of civil defense.

U.S. Strategic Bombing Survey. Over-all Effort (European War). Washington, D.C.: Government Printing Office, 30 September 1945.

Basic document on strategic bombing in Europe.

_____. The Effects of Strategic Bombing on the German War Economy. Washington, D.C.: Government Printing Office, 1945.

_____. *Summary Report (Pacific War)*. Washington, D.C.: Government Printing Office, 1946.

Webster, Sir Charles and Frankland, Noble. *The Strategic Air Offensive Against Germany 1939-1945*. 4 Vols. London: H. M. Stationery Office, 1961.

Detailed history of British (and American) air operations against Germany.

COMMUNISM

Barnett, A. Doak. *China After Mao; With Selected Documents*. Princeton, New Jersey: Princeton University Press, 1967.

Djilas, Milovan. *Conversations With Stalin*. Translated from the Serbo-Croat by Michael B. Petrovich. New York: Harcourt, Brace & World, Inc., 1962.

_____. *The New Class; An Analysis of the Communist System*. New York: Frederick A. Praeger, 1957.

Sharp critique of Tito's Communism by one of his former close associates, who remained a Marxist.

Gallico, Paul. *Trial by Terror*. New York: A Dell Book, 1951.

A novel based on Communist brainwashing for "confessions."

Gunther, John. *Inside Russia Today*. New York: Harper & Brothers, 1958.

Hoover, J. Edgar. *Masters of Deceit; The Story of Communism in America and How to Fight It*. New York: Henry Holt & Co., 1958.

Joy, Admiral C. Turner. *How Communists Negotiate*. New York: The Macmillan Company, 1955.

Excellent work on Communist techniques of negotiation in international relations by the chief UN negotiator in Korea. Advocates negotiation with strength.

Kennan, George F. *On Dealing With the Communist World*. New York: Harper & Row, Publishers, 1964.

_____. *Russia and the West under Lenin and Stalin*. Boston: Little, Brown and Co., 1961.

Excellent study of Soviet foreign policy.

539

Kintner, William R. The Front is Everywhere. Militant Communism in Action. Norman: University of Oklahoma Press, 1950.

Excellent. One of the basic books on militant Communism. Still one of the outstanding works dealing with the Communist conduct of unconventional and conventional warfare.

Koestler, Arthur. Darkness at Noon. Translated by Daphne Hardy. New York: The Modern Library, 1941.

A novel about the Soviet system that is more realistic than many factual studies.

Lall, Arthur. How Communist China Negotiates. New York: Columbia University Press, 1968.

Mao Tse-tung. Selected Works, Vol. 2. New York: International Publishers, 1954.

Particularly valuable for "On the Protracted War," a classic in Marxist-Leninist theory which is required reading for all students of Communist conflict management.

Orwell, George. 1984. New York: A Signet Book, 1949.

Overstreet, Harry and Bonaro. What We Must Know About Communism. New York: W.W. Norton & Co., Inc., 1958.

_____. The War Called Peace. Khrushchev's Communism. New York: W.W. Norton & Co., Inc., 1961.

Pasternak, Boris. Doctor Zhivago. Translated from Russian by Max Hayward and Manya Harari. New York: Pantheon Books, Inc., 1958.

Penkovskiy, Oleg. The Penkovskiy Papers. Translated by Peter Deriabin. New York: Avon Books, 1965.

Controversial and fascinating inside look at the Kremlin.

Possony, Stefan T. A Century of Conflict: Communist Techniques of World Revolution. Chicago: Henry Regnery Company, 1953.

Excellent study of Communist doctrine of conflict management and bolshevik "science of victory."

Salisbury, Harrison E. War Between Russia and China. New York: W. W. Norton & Co., Inc., 1969.

Schapiro, Leonard. The Government and Politics of the Soviet Union. Revised ed. New York: Vintage Books, 1967.

Strausz-Hupé, Robert; Kintner, William R.; Dougherty, James E.; and Cottrell, Alvin J. Protracted Conflict. New York: Harper & Row, 1963.

One of the best books on Communism.

United States Congress. House Committee on Un-American Activities, Facts on Communism. Vol. I. The Communist Ideology, December 1959. Washington, D.C.: U.S. Government Printing Office, 1960.

_____. House Committee on Foreign Affairs. Sino-Soviet Conflict. Washington, D.C.: U.S. Government Printing Office, 14 May 1965.

Testimony by outstanding witnesses.

_____. House Committee on Un-American Activities (84th). Soviet Total War. 2 Vols. Washington, D.C.: Government Printing Office, 1956.

An outstanding study of the new warfare of the Soviets by over 120 leading analysts.

THE COLD WAR

General

Acheson, Dean. Present at the Creation: My Years in the State Department. New York: A Signet Book, 1969.

Man at center stage during early years of the Cold War.

Fleming, D.F. The Cold War and its Origins. 2 Vols. Garden City, New York: Doubleday & Co., Inc., 1961.

Extremely detailed but so biased as to seriously detract from the work and create doubt in its validity. Takes pro-Russian and anti-American stand on almost every point.

Lukacs, John A. A History of the Cold War. Garden City, New York: Doubleday & Co., Inc., 1961.

Madariaga, Salvador de. The Blowing Up of the Parthenon; or, How to Lose the Cold War. London: Pall Mall Press, 1960.

Zacharias, Admiral Ellis M. Behind Closed Doors: The Secret History of the Cold War. New York: G. P. Putnam's Sons, 1950.

Strategy

Bouthoul, Gaston. Sauver la guerre (Lettre aux futurs survivants). Paris: Grasset, 1961.

Stated that collective aggressiveness will continue to lead to war.

Cerf, Jay H. and Pozen, Walter, eds. Strategy for the 60's. New York: Frederick A. Praeger, 1961.

A summary and analysis of studies prepared by 13 foreign policy research centers for the U.S. Senate.

Ginsburgh, Robert N. U. S. Military Strategy in the Sixties. New York: W. W. Norton Co., Inc. 1965.

Harriman, Averell. Peace with Russia? New York: Simon and Schuster, Inc., 1959.

This work by a former ambassador to Moscow, one of the authors and architects of the Marshall Plan, is a statement of the many problems that lie in the way of achieving peace with Russia.

Hoffman, Paul G. Peace Can Be Won. Garden City, New York: Doubleday & Co., Inc., 1951.

Jordan, Colonel Amos A. Jr., ed. Issues of National Security in the 1970's; Essays Presented to Colonel George A. Lincoln on His Sixtieth Birthday. New York: Frederick A. Praeger Publishers, 1967.

Kissinger, Henry A. The Troubled Partnership: A Re-appraisal of the Atlantic Alliance. New York: McGraw-Hill Book Company, 1965.

Proceedings of the Asilomar National Strategy Seminar, 25-30 April 1960, Monterey, California.

Reischauer, Edwin O. Beyond Vietnam: The United States and Asia. New York: Vintage Books, 1967.

Strausz-Hupé, Robert; Kintner, William R.; and Possony, Stefan T. A Forward Strategy for America. New York: Harper & Brothers, 1961.

542

Taylor, Maxwell D. The Uncertain Trumpet. New York: Harper
     & Brothers, 1960.

U.S. Congress. Senate Committee on Foreign Relations. U.S.
     Policy with Respect to Mainland China. Washington, D.C.:
     US Government Printing Office, 1966.

     Testimony by top China scholars in the United States.

Foreign Policy

Finletter, Thomas K. Power and Policy: U.S. Foreign Policy
     and Military Power in the Hydrogen Age. New York:
     Harcourt, Brace and Company, 1954.

     _____. Foreign Policy: The Next Phase, The 1960's.
     New York: Harper & Brothers, 1960.

Goldwater, Barry M. Why Not Victory? A Fresh Look at American
     Foreign Policy. New York: McGraw-Hill Book Company, 1962.

Hilsman, Roger. To Move a Nation: The Politics of Foreign
     Policy in the Administration of John F. Kennedy. Garden
     City, New York: Doubleday & Co., Inc., 1967.

Roberts, Henry L. Russia and America: Dangers and Prospects.
     New York: Harper & Brothers, 1956.

Rockefeller Brothers Fund Special Studies Project. America
     at Mid-Century Series. Panel I Report: The Mid-Century
     Challenge to U.S. Foreign Policy. Garden City, New York:
     Doubleday & Co., Inc., 1959.

     _____. Panel II Report, International Security. The
     Military Aspect. Garden City, New York: Doubleday & Co.,
     Inc. 1958.

Schleisinger, Arthur M. Jr. A Thousand Days: John F. Kennedy
     in the White House. Boston: Houghton Mifflin Co., 1965.

Thomas, Hugh. Suez. New York: Harper & Row, Publishers, 1966.

U.S. Congress, 86th. Conlon Associated Ltd., United States
     Foreign Policy - Asia. Studies prepared at the request
     of the Committee on Foreign Relations, United States
     Senate, No. 5. Washington, D.C.: US Government Printing
     Office, 1 November 1959.

Woodhouse, C. M. British Foreign Policy Since the Second
     World War. London: Hutchinson & Co., 1961.

Unofficial review of British foreign policy by a Con-
servative member of Parliament.

Wriston, Henry M. "Thoughts for Tomorrow." Foreign Affairs
    April 1962, pp. 374-391.

Nuclear Age

Aron, Raymond. The Great Debate: Theories of Nuclear Strategy.
    Translated from the French by Ernst Pawel. Garden City,
    New York: Doubleday & Co., Inc., 1965.

Dinerstein, Herbert S. War and the Soviet Union: Nuclear
    Weapons and the Revolution in Soviet Military and Politi-
    cal Thinking. New York: Stevens, 1959.

Garthoff, Raymond L. Soviet Strategy in the Nuclear Age. New
    York: Praeger, 1958.

Hadley, Arthur T. The Nation's Safety and Arms Control. New
    York: The Viking Press, 1961.

Hahn, Walter F. and Neff, John C., eds. American Stragegy for
    the Nuclear Age. Garden City, New York: Anchor Books,
    Doubleday & Co., Inc., 1960.

    Collection of writings by experts on the various aspects
    of the Communist War.

Halperin, Morton H. Limited War in the Nuclear Age. New York:
    John Wiley & Sons, Inc., 1963.

Kaufmann, William W. The McNamara Strategy. New York: Harper
    & Row, 1964.

Kissinger, Henry A. Nuclear Weapons and Foreign Policy. New
    York: Harper & Brothers, 1957.

    Outstanding book considering how to support political
    objectives without excessive risk of all-out war.

    _____. The Necessity for Choice; Prospects of American
    Foreign Policy. New York: Harper & Brothers, 1961.

Knorr, Klaus. On the Uses of Military Power in the Nuclear
    Age. Princeton, New Jersey: Princeton University Press,
    1966.

544

KOREA

The War

Almond, Lieutenant General E. M. "Orders from Washington kept
U.S. from winning Korean War." Excerpts from testimony
before Senate Internal Security Subcommittee. U.S. News
10 December 1954, pp. 86-90+.

Appleman, Roy E. South to the Naktong, North to the Yalu.
Washington, D.C.: Office of the Chief of Military History,
Department of the Army, 1961.

Clark, Mark W. From the Danube to the Yalu. New York: Harper,
1954.

The views of the UN Commander 1952-1953 toward period
of stalemate and the truce talks.

_____. "You can't win a war if diplomats interfere,"
from transcript of testimony before Senate subcommittee.
U.S. News 20 August 1954, pp. 75-81.

del Vayo, J. Alvarez. "Political War." Nation 22 July 1950,
pp. 75-76.

Department of Military Art and Engineering, United States
Military Academy, Operations in Korea. West Point, New
York: USMA, 1954.

Fehrenbach, T. R. This Kind of War: A Study of Unpreparedness.
New York: Pocket Books, Inc., 1963.

"At Geneva: how reds block peace for Korea: three statements"
U.S. News 4 June 1954, pp. 62-69.

Hermes, Walter G. Truce Tent and Fighting Front. Washington,
D.C.: Office of the Chief of Military History, Department
of the Army, 1966.

"Korea victory was denied," concluding sections of Senate Internal Security Subcommittee Report. U.S. News 4 February
1955, p. 44.

Lawrence, David. "Defeat that means victory." U.S. News 22
December 1950, p. 52.

Paige, Glenn D. The Korean Decision (June 24-30, 1950). New
York: The Free Press, 1968.

"Problems in ending a war." U.S. News 6 July 1951, pp. 16-17.

Ridgway, Matthew B. The Korean War. Garden City, New York:
    Doubleday, 1967.

Russ, Martin. The Last Parallel: A Marine's War Journal. New
    York: Rinehart & Co., Inc., 1957.

Stevenson, Adlai E. "Korea in Perspective." Foreign Affairs
    April 1952, pp. 349-360.

Stratemeyer, Lieutenant General G. E. "We weren't permitted
    to win in Korea" excerpts from hearing before Senate In-
    ternal Security Subcommittee. U.S. News 3 September 1954,
    pp. 81-86.

"Truce without victory: new idea for U.S." U.S. News 5 June
    1953, p. 32+.

Truman, Harry S. "Preventing a new world war," address 11
    April 1951. U.S. Department of State Bulletin 16 April
    1951, pp. 603-605.

    Speech at time MacArthur was relieved.

Van Fleet, James A. "Truth about Korea: from a man now free
    to speak." Life 11 May 1953, pp. 126-138+ and 18 May 1953,
    pp. 156-158+.

    _____. "Van Fleet tells story of Korea; answers to
    questions by House and Senate Armed Services Committee.
    U.S. News 13 March 1953, pp. 100-107.

"Who won the war?" U.S. News 13 July 1951, pp. 14-15.

"Why U.S. decided to halt in Korea." U.S. News 20 July 1951,
    pp. 18-19.

Yang, Y. C. "Republic of Korea on total victory," summary of
    address 20 November 1952. UN Bulletin 1 December 1952,
    p. 493.

MacArthur

"ABC's of the big debate: Marshall vs. MacArthur" U.S. News
    18 May 1951, pp. 19-20.

Gunther, John. The Riddle of MacArthur; Japan, Korea and the
    Far East. New York: Harper, 1951.

Hunt, Frazier. "Untold story of General MacArthur," excerpts.
    U.S. News 15 October 1954, pp. 136-155.

Lawrence, David. "Civilian Stupidity." U.S. News 11 May 1951,
    p. 131.

MacArthur, Douglas. "Address to Congress, April 19, 1951."
    U.S. News 27 April 1951, pp. 70-73.

_____. "Mr. Truman yielded to counsels of fear." U.S.
    News 17 February 1956, pp. 48-53+.

_____. "What went wrong in Korea," letter to Senator
    Byrd. U.S. News 1 May 1953, p. 26+.

"Real Story of MacArthur and the Russians" with a statement by
    MacArthur 20 October 1955. U.S. News 28 October 1955,
    pp. 31-36.

Taft, Robert A. "Korean War and the MacArthur dismissal" ad-
    dress 12 April 1951. Vital Speeches 1 May 1951, pp. 420-
    422.

Transcript of hearings before Senate Armed Services and For-
    eign Relations Committees (the Far East or MacArthur
    Hearings). U.S. News 11 May 1951, pp. 52-64+ and 18 May
    1951, pp. 52-66+.

Truman, Harry S. "MacArthur was ready to risk general war. I
    was not." U.S. News 17 February 1956, p. 54+.

VIET-NAM

Background

Bain, Chester A. Vietnam: The Roots of Conflict. Englewood
    Cliffs, New Jersey: Prentice-Hall, Inc., 1967.

Bone, Robert C. Jr. Contemporary Southeast Asia. New York:
    Random House, 1966.

Buttinger, Joseph. Vietnam: A Political History. New York:
    Frederick A. Praeger, Publishers, 1968.

Butwell, Richard. Southeast Asia Today - And Tomorrow. A
    Political Analysis. Revised edition., New York: Frederick
    A. Praeger, Publishers, 1964.

Darcourt, Pierre. De Lattre Au Viet-Nam: Une Année de Vic-
    toires. Paris: La Table Ronde, 1965.

Fall, Bernard B. Hell in a Very Small Place: The Siege of Dien
    Bien Phu. Philadelphia: J.B. Lippincott Co., 1967.

_____. Street Without Joy: Indochina at War, 1946–54.
Harrisburg, Pa.: The Stackpole Company, 1961.

_____. The Two Viet-Nams: A Political and Military
Analysis. New York: Frederick A. Praeger, Publishers, 1963.

Giap, General Vo Nguyen. People's War People's Army. Hanoi:
Foreign Languages Publishing House, 1961.

McAlister, John T. Jr., and Mus, Paul. The Vietnamese and
Their Revolution. New York: Harper & Row, 1970.

Scigliano, Robert. South Vietnam: Nation Under Stress. Boston:
Houghton Mifflin Co., 1964.

Shaplen, Robert. The Lost Revolution: The U.S. in Vietnam,
1946-1966. Revised ed. New York: Harper & Row, 1966.

U.S. Army, Area Handbook for Viet Nam. Washington, D.C.: SORO,
American University, September 1962.

_____. Area Handbook for South Vietnam. Washington,
D.C.: FAS, American University, U.S. Government Printing
Office, April 1967.

The War

Allison, Graham; May, Ernest; and Yarmolinsky, Adam. "Limits
to Intervention." Foreign Affairs January 1970, p. 245.

An, Tai Sung. "Turmoil in Indochina: The Vietnam-Cambodia
Conflict." Asian Affairs March-April 1978, pp. 245-256.

Armstrong, Hamilton Fish. "Power In a Sieve." Foreign Affairs
April 1968, p. 467.

Ashmore, Harry S. and Baggs, William C. Mission to Hanoi: A
Chronicle of Double-Dealing in High Places. New York:
G.P. Putnam's Sons, 1968.

Braestrup, Peter. Big Story: How the American Press and Television Reported and Interpreted the Crisis of Tet 1968 in
Vietnam and Washington. 2 Vols. Boulder: Westview Press,
1977.

Bundy, McGeorge. "The End of Either/Or." Foreign Affairs
January 1967, p. 189.

Burchett, Wilfred G. Vietnam: Inside Story of the Guerrilla
War. New York: International Publishers, 1965.

By an Australian Communist.

Carver, George A. Jr. "The Real Revolution in South Viet Nam."
    Foreign Affairs April 1965, p. 387.

_____. "The Faceless Viet Cong." Foreign Affairs April
    1966, p. 347.

Clifford, Clark M. "A Viet Nam Reappraisal; The Personal His-
    tory of One Man's View and How It Evolved." Foreign Af-
    fairs July 1969, p. 601.

Cooper, Chester. The Lost Crusade: America in Viet Nam. New
    York, Dodd Mead, 1970.

    Good coverage of whole war; 50 pages of chronology;
    good on various tries at negotiations.

Department of State. Aggression From the North: The Record of
    North Viet-Nam's Campaign to Conquer South Viet-Nam.
    Washington, D.C.: U.S. Government Printing Office,
    February 1965.

Department of State Message A-73 from American Embassy Saigon
    to Department of State, Subject: "Release to Press of
    Captured Enemy Documents," 29 July 1967. The enclosure
    to this message was the Viet Cong Top Secret 60-page doc-
    ument "Resolution of COSVN of March 1966."

    An invaluable document on the Hanoi-COSVN role in every
    aspect of the Viet-Nam conflict.

Fall, Bernard B. "Viet Nam in the Balance." Foreign Affairs
    October 1966, p. 1.

_____. Last Reflections on a War. Garden City, New
    York: Doubleday & Co., Inc., 1967. Compiled by his wife
    after he was killed in Viet-Nam.

Fulbright, Senator J. William. The Arrogrance of Power. New
    York: Vintage Books, 1966.

Gelb, Leslie H. "Vietnam: The System Worked." Foreign Policy
    Summer 1971, pp. 140-167.

Gettleman, Marvin E., ed. Vietnam: History, Documents, and
    Opinions on a Major World Crisis. New York: Fawcett World
    Library, 1965.

Giap, General Vo Nguyen, Big Victory Great Task: North Viet-
    Nam's Minister of Defense Assesses the Course of the War.
    New York: Frederick A. Praeger, 1968 with a terrible in-
    troduction by David Schoenbrun.

549

Goodwin, Richard N. Triumph or Tragedy: Reflections on Vietnam. New York: Vintage Books, 1966.

"Hanoi's Direction and Support of the Communist Effort in South Vietnam," prepared by the American Embassy in Saigon and sent as Enclosure #1 to Message A-63 from Saigon to the Department of State, 28 July 1967.

An excellent study based on intelligence sources.

Hobbs, LTC Richard W. "All the Answers Are Not In the Statistics." Army March 1967, pp. 77-78.

_____. ed. Focus on Southeast Asia: Readings in International Relations, Vol. III, Operation Statesman. West Point, New York: Department of Social Sciences, USMA, May 1968.

Hoopes, Townsend. "Legacy of the Cold War in Indochina." Foreign Affairs July 1970, p. 601.

Huntington, Samuel P. "The Bases of Accommodation." Foreign Affairs July 1968, p. 642.

Johnson, Robert H. "Vietnamization: Can It Work?" Foreign Affairs July 1970, p. 629.

Kahin, George and Lewis, John W. The United States in Vietnam. New York: A Delta Book, 1967.

Kahn, Herman. "If Negotiations Fail." Foreign Affairs July 1968, p. 627.

Kissinger, Henry A. "The Viet Nam Negotiations." Foreign Affairs January 1969, p. 211.

Komer, Robert W. "Clear, Hold and Rebuild." Army May 1970, pp. 16-24 and June 1970, pp. 20-29.

Important articles by former civilian deputy to military commander in Viet-Nam.

Lacouture, Jean. "From the Vietnam War to an Indochina War." Foreign Affairs July 1970, p. 617.

Written too close to April 1970 to have perspective.

_____. Vietnam: Between Two Truces. New York: Vintage Books, 1966.

_____. *Ho Chi Minh: A Political Biography*. Translated from French by Peter Wiles. New York: Random House, 1968.

Marshall, S.L.A. *Battles in the Monsoon: Campaigning in the Central Highlands, South Vietnam, Summer 1966*. New York: William Morrow and Company, Inc., 1967.

McCarthy, Mary. *Vietnam*. New York: Harcourt, Brace & World, Inc., 1967.

Message No. 10 from JUSPAO-Saigon to USIA Washington Subject: "Nguyen Van Be Campaign Report," 7 August 1967.

A recent example of the Big Lie in Communist propaganda.

Nixon, Richard M. "Asia after Viet Nam." *Foreign Affairs* October 1967, p. 111.

Norman, Lloyd. "What does Hanoi Want?" *Army* April 1969, pp. 39-40.

Pace, Eric. "Laos: Continuing Crisis." *Foreign Affairs* October 1964, p. 64.

Ponchaud, François. *Cambodia: Year Zero*. Translated from the French by Nancy Amphoux. New York: Holt, Rinehart and Winston, 1977.

Raskin, Marcus G. and Fall, Bernard B., eds. *The Viet-Nam Reader: Articles and Documents on American Foreign Policy and the Viet-Nam Crisis*. New York: Vintage Books, 1965.

Salisbury, Harrison E. *Behind the Lines - Hanoi: December 23, 1966 - January 7, 1967*. New York: Harper & Row, 1967.

Schleisinger, Arthur M. Jr. *The Bitter Heritage: Vietnam and American Democracy 1941-1966*. Boston: Houghton Mifflin Co., 1967.

Schurmann, Franz; Scott, Peter Dale; and Zelnik, Reginald. *The Politics of Escalation in Vietnam*. New York: Fawcett World Library, 1966.

Shaplen, Robert. "Viet Nam: Crisis of Indecision." *Foreign Affairs* October 1967, p. 95.

Sharp, Admiral U.S.G. *Strategy for Defeat*. San Rafael, California: Presidio Press, 1978.

Sihanouk, Prince Norodom. "The Future of Cambodia." *Foreign Affairs* October 1970, p. 1.

Stilwell, Lieutenant General Richard G. "Evolution in Tactics
- The Vietnam Experience." Army February 1970, pp. 14-23.

Taylor, General Maxwell D. Responsibility and Response. New
York: Harper and Row, 1967.

Taylor, Telford. Nuremberg and Vietnam: An American Tragedy.
Chicago: Quadrangle Books, 1970.

Thompson, Sir Robert. "Is Ground War Over for U.S. in Viet-
nam?" U.S. News & World Report 1 November 1971, pp. 64-65.

_____. "Military Victory: Political Defeat - The Fail-
ure of U.S. Strategy in Vietnam." International Defense
Review #6, December 1974.

_____. No Exit from Vietnam. New York: David McKay Co.,
Inc., 1969.

_____. "Squaring the Error." Foreign Affairs April
1968, p. 442.

U.S. Congress. Senate Committee on Foreign Relations. Background Information Relating to Southeast Asia and Viet-
nam. Washington, D.C.: US Government Printing Office,
1965 with revised edition annually thereafter.

Prime source of speeches and documents.

_____. Supplemental Foreign Assistance Fiscal Year
1966 - Vietnam. Washington, D.C.: U.S. Government Printing
Office, 1966.

Outstanding testimony and papers on expanding role in
Viet-Nam.

Walt, General Lewis W. Strange War, Strange Strategy. New
York: Funk and Wagnalls, 1970.

Zagoria, Donald S. Vietnam Triangle: Moscow, Peking, Hanoi.
New York: Pegasus, 1967.

Revolutionary War

Clutterbuck, Brigadier Richard L. The Long, Long War: Counterinsurgency in Malaya and Vietnam. New York: Frederick A.
Praeger, Publishers, 1966.

Director of Operations, Malaya. The Conduct of Anti-Terrorist
Operations in Malaya. 3rd ed. 1958.

552

Douglas, William O. North from Malaya: Adventures on Five Fronts. Garden City, New York: Doubleday & Co.,Inc., 1953.

Duverger, Maurice. La Cinquieme République. Paris: Presses Universitaires de France, 1960.

Good section on revolutionary warfare.

Galula, Davis. Counterinsurgency Warfare: Theory and Practice. New York: Frederick A. Praeger, Publishers, 1964.

Jureidini, Paul A. Case Studies in Insurgency and Revolutionary Warfare: Algeria 1954-1962. Washington, D.C.: SORO, The American University, December 1963.

Lansdale, Major General Edward G. "Viet Nam: Do We Understand Revolution?" Foreign Affairs October 1964, p. 75.

Lartéguy, Jean. The Centurions. New York: E.P. Dutton & Co., Inc. 1962.

Lederer, William J. and Burdick, Eugene. The Ugly American. Greenwich, Conn.: Fawcett Publications, Inc., 1961.

Political novel about an American in Southeast Asia.

Lindsay, Franklin A. "Unconventional Warfare." Foreign Affairs January 1962, pp. 264-274.

Molnar, Andrew R., et. al. Undergrounds in Insurgent, Revolutionary, and Resistance Warfare. Washington, D.C.: SORO, The American University, November 1963.

Orlansky, Jesse. The State of Research on Internal War. Arlington, Va.: Institute for Defense Analyses, Research Paper P-565, August 1970.

Piao, Lin. "Long Live the Victory of People's War!" pamphlet Peking: Foreign Language Press, originally published in the People's Daily on 3 September 1965.

Important Chinese Communist document on rural areas surrounding urban areas of the world.

Tanham, George K. and Duncanson, Dennis J. "Some Dilemmas of Counterinsurgency." Foreign Affairs October 1969, p. 113.

Thompson, Sir Robert. Defeating Communist Insurgency: The Lessons of Malaya and Vietnam. New York: Frederick A. Praeger, Publishers, 1966.
_____. Revolutionary War in World Strategy: 1945-69. New York: Taplinger Publishing Co., 1970.

Index

237, 256n, 258n
Chiang Kai-shek, 257n, 280,
  281, 309
China, 246, 248, 252, 261n,
  319, 336n, 516
China, Nationalist, Republic
  of, or Taiwan, 308, 309, 357,
  368n
China, Red, Communist or People's Republic of, 297, 302,
  303, 304, 305, 306, 308, 309,
  310, 311, 312, 314, 315, 318,
  319, 322, 324, 327, 328, 330,
  333n, 334n, 335n, 339n, 353,
  356, 357, 358, 393, 395, 397,
  398, 404, 405, 406, 408, 423,
  425, 430, 507
Churchill, Winston, 7, 11, 18,
  26, 29, 36, 37, 40, 45, 60,
  64, 93, 94, 113, 114, 115,
  139, 148, 149, 150, 151, 152,
  184, 207, 208, 209, 224n, 234,
  226n, 234, 240, 255n, 256n,
  257n, 261n, 347, 351, 364n,
  365n, 366n; and Morgenthau
  Plan, 199, 200, 203; on strategic bombing, 76, 77, 80, 81;
  and Unconditional Surrender,
  142, 143, 144, 145, 146, 148,
  154, 156, 158, 159, 161, 162,
  179, 181, 183, 214n; US role
  leading to World War II, 137
Clark, Mark W., 209, 244n, 325,
  363
Clausewitz, 3, 6, 7, 10, 11,
  106, 211, 276, 449, 453, 461n,
  463n, 476, 501, 503, 506
Clemenceau, Georges, 4, 38-40,
  55, 164n, 203
Clifford, Clark, 379, 385, 388
Coexistence, peaceful, 120,
  268-271, 350, 351, 394, 400,
  428, 431, 447, 448, 461n
Cold War, 44, 81, 122, 243,
  245, 268, 291n, 298, 326,
  343-370, 375, 391, 405, 423,
  427, 440, 442, 444, 446-448,
  477, 487, 488, 495, 506, 507;
  beginning, 344, 345; cost,
  344, 364n; freedom vs. force,
  343-348, 354, 355; peace is

war, 354-364; and psychological warfare, 105, 120; revi-
  sionists, 363-364; victory,
  354, 364
Column, Fifth, 106, 120, 350,
  367n
Communism, 1, 8, 9, 40, 51, 53,
  54, 60, 149, 186, 204, 230,
  233, 234, 238, 240-242, 268,
  270, 297, 329, 345, 349, 355,
  359, 362, 363, 365n, 366n,
  367n, 370n, 374, 394, 398,
  400, 409n, 423, 425, 427-430,
  435, 436, 438, 447-451, 455n,
  468, 481n, 488, 493, 494,
  506; defeats, 357; failure,
  439; peace with, 6, 429; and
  war, 7, 8, 63, 352, 369n, 436,
  455n, 456n, 468, 428-430
Communist threat, 426, 432,
  444, 488
Communist World, 9, 119, 120,
  278, 280, 282, 288, 348, 355,
  393, 394, 423, 426-439, 442,
  446, 454n, 469, 505
Communists, 183, 188-190, 230-
  242, 248, 252, 268-278, 281-
  290, 295, 301, 306, 313-315,
  322-330, 414n, 424-439, 443,
  446, 448, 450, 451, 468, 469,
  471, 476, 509; Cold War, 343,
  347-361; Viet-Nam, 371, 377,
  395, 396, 405, 406
Conflict, spectrum of, 267-294,
  344, 363, 476; strife, 277-
  284, 286; tension, 268, 271-
  277
Congress, U.S., 80, 148, 167n,
  308, 310, 315, 316, 320, 508;
  Viet-Nam, 383, 388, 390, 391,
  400-403, 418n
Counterguerrilla operations,
  282, 402
Counterinsurgency, 390, 392,
  394-397, 399, 401, 419n, 449
Credibility, 383, 399, 400,
  403
Cripps, Sir Stafford, 115,
  124n
Cuba, 280, 281, 353, 355, 359,
  380; crisis of 1962, 121, 276,

259n, 475; Italian surrender,
177, 178, 180, 181; Morgenthau Plan, 201-204, 223n; occupation, 244, 246, 248; Unconditional Surrender, 181-
188, 197-200, 227

Giap, Vo Nguyen, 281, 374, 380,
381, 390, 402

Goebbels, Joseph, 70, 73, 114-
116, 145, 154, 156, 160, 175,
203, 213n, 229, 254n, 274

Goering, Hermann, 162, 172n,
184, 470

Goldwater, Barry, 207, 295,
321, 418n, 449, 460n, 461n,
462n

Grant, U.S. "Unconditional Surrender," 144, 156

Great Britain, 30, 33, 37, 39,
41, 43-45, 52, 77, 79, 80,
136, 141, 177, 233, 239, 246,
248, 252, 256n, 475

Grew, Joseph C., 137, 192,
219n, 513

Guderian, Heinz, 186, 217n,
230

Gunther, John, 146, 176, 429,
433, 437, 438, 459n

Hankey, Lord Maurice, 5, 11,
152, 173, 227, 230

Harriman, Averell, 120, 154,
241, 433, 435, 444, 513

Himmler, Heinrich, 109, 155,
161, 184

Hiroshima, 1, 65, 195

Hiss, Algar, 236

Hitler, Adolf, 7, 53, 60, 62,
64, 66, 70, 71, 75, 97, 99,
101, 102, 105, 106, 108, 109,
113, 138, 142, 149, 150-152,
159-163, 164n, 169n, 172n,
177, 181, 184, 228, 231-233,
237, 240, 250, 256n, 345,
470, 475, 486; and bloodless
victory, 106; and German
Army, 184, 185, 215n; negotiations with, 145, 146, 147,
149, 160, 162; opposition
to, 173, 175, 175, 177, 182,
183, 185-187, 215n, 216n;

and propaganda, 113, 116, 274,
275, 292n; move into Rhineland, 136

Hobbes, Thomas, 18, 467

Ho Chi Minh, 281, 350, 371-377,
379, 381, 395, 404, 416n

Ho Chi Minh Trail, 378, 390,
391

Hoffman, Paul, 249, 274

Hoover, Herbert, 192, 307

Hopkins, Harry, 144, 151, 154,
158, 171n, 209, 223n, 233,
235, 236, 256n, 513

Hull, Cordell, 25, 116, 137,
178, 188, 199, 203, 204, 206,
214n, 219n, 220n, 222n, 223n,
228, 240, 241, 513; Unconditional Surrender, 154, 155,
157, 159, 170n

Indochina, 281, 283, 286, 318,
327, 328, 335n, 350, 355,
357, 358, 368n, 369n, 371-
421, 475, 476; sabotage 278,
292n, 293n

Indochina I, 372-376; cost,
375; victory to French, 373

Indochina II, 376-406

Indochina III, 358, 372, 406-
408

Insurgency, 377, 380, 393-396,
398, 400, 402, 431, 449

Iron Curtain, 53, 245, 349,
367n, 448

Italy, 39, 40, 177-181, 229,
242, 244, 248

Japan, 1, 20, 21, 39, 68, 71,
79, 80, 86, 89, 90, 91, 96,
138, 140, 181, 188-196, 207,
225n, 235, 236, 242, 246,
247, 253, 330, 475, 486; Army,
189; Emperor, 188-195, 219n,
220n, 246, 247, 470; Unconditional Surrender, 157-158,
175, 177, 178

Jodl, Alfred, 181, 186, 217n

Johnson, Lyndon B., 358, 362,
380, 381, 385, 388, 398

Joy, C. Turner, 275, 314, 322-
325, 339n

Kahn, Herman, 31, 82, 136, 285, 289, 321, 385, 462n, 474, 478, 492

Kampuchea, 358, 406, 407, 408; genocide, 407; See Cambodia

Kecskemeti, Paul, 177, 195, 425, 486

Kennan, George F., 142, 186, 210, 451, 487, 513

Kennedy, John F., 281, 353, 356, 362, 363, 379, 380, 394, 398, 505, 509

Keynes, John Maynard, 30, 69

Khmer Rouge, 406-408

Khrushchev, Nikita, 9, 120, 269, 277, 328, 350, 351, 356, 373, 377, 416n, 425-429, 433, 435-437, 448, 456n, 491, 493, 494, 505

King-Hall, Stephen, 274, 276, 484

Kintner, William R., 8, 11, 355, 423

Kissinger, Henry A., 10, 26, 284, 286, 287, 306, 313, 317, 319, 335n, 361, 386, 387, 393, 399, 403, 405, 417n, 425, 447, 449, 486, 491

Korea, North, 296-305, 312, 324, 327, 330, 355

Korea, South, 297, 299, 300, 305, 317, 321, 327, 329, 350, 358; force to South Viet-Nam, 329; State Department supervision, 295, 296, 336n

Korean War, 275, 278, 282, 283, 285, 286, 288, 292n, 295-341, 357, 363, 375, 475; cost, 306, 311, 321, 327; Great Debate, 307-320, 327; Inchon landing, 299, 317, 332n; lack of will for victory, 318, 320, 321, 322, 337n; lost US prestige, 327, 328, 340-1n; negotiations, 305, 306, 315, 318, 320-326, 338n, 339n, 340n; stalemate, 320-326

Laos, 281-283, 320, 358, 372, 376, 380, 384, 387, 388,

390-392, 400, 402, 404, 409n, 415n, 416n

Lea, Homer, 472, 479

League of Nations, 25, 34, 39, 55, 137

Leahy, William D., 115, 157, 192, 223n, 236, 345, 514

Le Duan, 377, 378

Lenin, 7, 8, 51-54, 105, 107, 269, 274, 275, 278, 345, 355, 427, 433, 438, 439, 481n, 508

Liddell Hart, B. H., 4, 92, 94, 174, 176, 184, 267, 479, 492, 509

Lie, Big, 112, 274, 275; Nguyen Van Be in Viet-Nam War, 112, 113

Lincoln, G. A., 208fn

Line, Maginot, 136, 308

Lin Piao, 395

Lippmann, Walter, 139, 210, 242, 356, 367n, 485, 495

Lloyd George, 39, 40, 43

Lochner, Louis P., 187, 217n

Lukacs, John A., 289, 335n, 362

MacArthur, Douglas, 7, 11, 115, 118, 121, 196, 221n, 225n, 246, 257n, 260n, 261n, 295, 478, 488, 514-516; Japan, 347-348; Korea, 296-299, 302-304, 307-322, 327, 328, 331n-337n, 369n

Madariaga, Salvador de, 345, 348, 424

Malaya, 282, 357

Malenkov, 233, 351, 456

Manchuria, 252, 302-305, 308, 311, 312, 333n, 347

Mao Tse-tung, 9, 11, 66, 267, 280, 330, 331n, 350, 409n, 432, 467, 472

Marshall, George C., 89, 138, 197, 209, 245, 302, 312, 319, 335n, 336n, 368n, 514-516

Marshall Plan, 252, 272, 368n, 375

Marx, Karl, 7, 60, 290, 344, 348, 427, 469

results, 227–264; victory for Communism, 231–234
Suzuki, Baron Kantaro, 190, 195, 218n

Taft, Robert, 308
Taylor, Maxwell, 282, 394, 397, 398
Teheran Conference, 154, 207, 209, 226n, 234, 235
Terror, 377, 392, 404, 444
Thailand, 282, 358, 379, 392, 400, 407
Third World, 273, 439–446
Thirty Years' War, 17, 23
Thompson, Robert, 371, 379, 382, 385, 388, 394, 395, 397, 398, 402, 403, 405, 418n, 419n, 420n, 507
Tocqueville, Alexis de, 8, 9, 11
Togo, 193–195, 218n
Tojo, 189, 217n
Toynbee, Arnold, 345, 473, 508
Truman, Harry, 118, 140, 211, 220n, 225n, 226n, 343, 371, 483, 514; Germany vs. Russia, 239; Greece, 280; Japan, 192–194; Korea, 297, 298; MacArthur, 307, 308, 312, 316, 320, 334n, 335n; Morgenthau Plan, 204; Russia and Japan, 242; Unconditional Surrender, 157–159, 228, 229
Tzu, Sun, 3, 176

United Nations, 25, 237, 241, 256n, 411n, 475, 507, 508; Cold War, 346, 350, 365; Korea, 296–305, 311, 312, 314–316, 322, 323, 325–330, 334n, 335n, 339n, 341n
United States, 141, 181, 188, 204, 239, 243, 246, 268, 475; ability to fight limited wars, 321, 337n; Civil War, 19, 20, 23, 24, 32, 60, 69, 279; isolationism, 137, 508; paper tiger, 328; and Japan, 137, 191, 195, 247, 248; and USSR, 230, 244, 245, 251,

259n, 280, 314, 344, 438; Viet-Nam, 374, 375, 379–381, 392–405, 419n; World War I, 29, 33, 34, 37, 40, 41, 43–45, 52; World War II, 71, 79, 80; See also America, Unconditional Surrender, and Total Victory

Vagts, Alfred, 204, 336n, 484, 496n
Van Fleet, James, 304, 314, 315, 322, 328, 337n, 340n, 341n
Versailles, Treaty of, 40, 41, 42, 44, 49–51, 135, 137, 164n, 167n, 485
Victory, 1–10, 15, 16, 25, 31, 32, 34, 39, 41, 45, 62, 76, 96, 139, 149, 191, 205, 230, 234, 267, 349, 475–477, 479, 506, 507, 509, 510; through air power, 75, 77, 78, 80, 85, 87, 95, 381; bloodless, 106, 476; to Communist World, 426–439; concepts, 423–463; to Free World, 447–453; Korea, 300, 310, 315–317, 321, 323; limited, 2, 191, 476; military, 140, 196, 227, 234, 286, 314, 317, 318, 326, 328, 340n, 341n, 363, 368n, 397, 398, 401, 412n, 430, 451, 469, 484, 486; psychological, 375, 384, 402; to Third World, 439–446
Victory, Total, 1, 2, 9, 16–18, 21, 35, 36, 39, 46, 61, 63, 72, 117, 122, 139, 205, 212, 228, 231, 239, 249, 287, 361, 425, 449, 450, 461n, 476, 483–499, 502, 503, 504, 505; Is it worth it?, 483–488; Korea, 300, 310–312, 315–317, 319, 321, 326, 341n; in the nuclear age, 489–496; US Senate, 142; Viet-Nam, 386, 389, 394, 398, 405; World War II, 141–143, 147–149, 151, 158, 159, 163, 173, 177
Vienna, Congress of, 17–19

Viet Cong (VC), 377-384, 387-
390, 394, 395, 402, 404,
408, 419n
Viet Minh, 371, 372, 374, 375,
377, 409n
Viet-Nam, North, 318, 355, 357,
358, 372, 373, 375, 378,
380, 383, 385, 387-390, 392,
394, 395, 396, 399-405, 410n,
416n, 435, 476
Viet-Nam, South, 282, 283, 285,
289, 320, 329, 355, 358, 374,
376-380, 384-406, 412n-414n,
419n, 444
Viet-Nam War, 275, 282, 292n,
352, 357, 358, 363, 371-421,
475, 479; aggression, 380,
381, 402; American aims, 396-
399, 404; bombing of North,
381, 385, 387, 389, 411n,
412n; containment of China,
397, 398; cost, 402, 404,
405, 420n; COSVN, 378, 386,
410, 414n; defeat, 401-405;
fight and negotiate, 379, 386;
National Liberation Front
(NLF), 377-380, 409n, 410n,
415n; negotiations, 385, 386,
388, 391, 392, 395, 399, 402,
403, 414n; operation into
Cambodia, 390, 391; operation
into Laos, 391, 392; press
(TV), 382, 384, 385, 403, 404;
Tet offensive, 384, 387, 389,
401, 414n; victory, 392-401,
405, 408; Vietnamization, 387-91

Wallace, Henry, 141, 514
War, 2-5, 7, 10, 15-19, 21,
24-26, 50, 267, 284-290, 344,
436, 467-471, 501, 509, 510;
abolition of, 478, 479, 493;
civil, 352, 404, 460n, 494,
504; emotional, 149-152, 450;
guerrilla, 2, 267, 268, 278-
282, 286, 293n, 352, 357, 358,
377, 393, 396, 479; ideological, 241, 269, 273, 348-354,
469; of liberation, 258n, 351;
limited, 2, 20, 268, 283-288,
298, 301-307, 311, 312, 320,

321, 329, 341n, 344, 361, 396,
404, 426, 449, 451, 479, 506,
507, 509; losses, 21-24; as
a means, 3, 68, 253, 501; of
national liberation, 277,
377, 379, 396-398, 401, 405;
nuclear, 268, 287-289, 355,
361, 424, 425, 429, 432, 433,
448, 449, 453, 456n, 478,
493-495, 501, 507, 508, 510;
objective of, 3, 4, 10, 95,
96, 106, 237, 274, 424, 425,
449, 461n, 484, 507; partisan, 279, 280, 293n; plus and
minus, 471-474; and politics,
4, 6, 20, 237, 276, 277, 486,
501, 507; preemptive, 478;
preventive, 478; protracted,
9, 281, 289, 354, 374, 388,
395, 405, 476; religious, 17,
21, 24, 61, 63, 64, 502;
revolutionary, 377, 393, 394,
397, 402, 405, 431, 449
War, Communist, 290, 301, 329-
331, 343, 344, 349, 351, 354,
431, 445, 461n, 468, 471;
cost, 344
War, Spanish Civil, 106, 328,
362
War, Total, 6, 15, 17, 24, 25,
31, 32, 35, 46, 51, 59-72,
86, 107, 109, 118, 122, 138,
148, 184, 187, 231, 233, 253,
285, 290, 310, 311, 336n,
343, 349, 361, 396, 429, 449,
450, 460n, 469, 474, 479,
483, 484, 494, 495, 502; as a
crusade, 122, 139, 151, 152,
239, 393; and propaganda,
112
Warfare, Chemical and Biological, 91, 102, 287, 288, 492,
493; casualties, 92; incapacitating chemicals, 92-95, 492;
renunciation, 93-94
Warfare, economic, 272, 273,
291n, 352, 355, 426, 502
Warfare Psychological, 105-126,
275, 350, 351, 353, 355, 426,
502; American contempt for,
111, 123n, 276; and Commu-

565

nists, 106, 107, 269,
273; definition, 106;
leaflets in France, 115; and
policy, 109-111, 116, 118,
276; problem with Unconditional Surrender, 159; and
propaganda, 106, 273; Russian
use on Germans, 115; and the
United States, 110
Warfare, Revolutionary, 283
Warfare, termite, 355, 367n,
368n
Warfare, unconventional, See
war, guerrilla
Weapons, nuclear, 94, 267, 268,
278, 283, 287-289, 294n, 298,
302, 325, 364, 368n, 430,
448, 476-478, 489-491, 502,
506
Wedemeyer, Albert C., 174,
248, 262n
Welles, Sumner, 80, 514
Westphalia, Peace of, 17, 23
White, Harry Dexter, 138, 204,
205
Whitney, Courtney, 296, 297,
303, 304, 307, 318, 320,
331, 334n
Wilmot, Chester, 143, 228,
232, 233
Wilson, Woodrow, 30, 33, 35,
36, 38-41, 55, 56, 64, 111,
152, 233, 234
World War I, 19, 20, 25,
29-54, 61, 67, 68, 140, 141,
184, 475, 502, 506; Armistice terms, 36, 37, 41; cost,
45-51, 47, 48, 52; Fourteen
Points, 39-41, 111, 160;
Peace Conference, 37, 38, 40;
reparations, 42-44; and Russia, 107
World War II, 1, 20, 23, 49,
61, 71, 139, 184, 187, 234,
238, 242, 245, 475, 488,
503, 506; aims, 139, 143,
212, 248, 254n, 258n;
chronology, 129-133; cost,
249-253, 260n, 262n, 263n;
as crusade, 139, 151, 169n,
239, 475; lend-lease, 71,

245, 250, 264n; Nuremberg,
65, 250; and psychological
warfare, 105; and rise of
Communism, 233, 242; triangular fight, 345
World War III, 283, 288, 289,
297, 307, 308, 315, 352, 399,
506
Wright, Quincy, 3, 10, 471

Yalta, 140, 161, 234-237, 242,
257n, 260n, 346

Zacharias, Ellis M., 118, 119,
158, 218n, 344; See also
Propaganda